Abraham Ibn Ezra *Latinus* on Elections and Interrogations

Études sur le Judaïsme Médiéval

Fondées par

Georges Vajda

Rédacteur en chef

Paul B. Fenton

Dirigées par

Phillip Ackerman-Lieberman, Benjamin Hary, and Katja Vehlow

TOME LXXXIII

The titles published in this series are listed at brill.com/ejm

Abraham Ibn Ezra *Latinus* on Elections and Interrogations

A Parallel Latin-English Critical Edition of *Liber Electionum*, *Liber Interrogationum*, and *Tractatus Particulares*

Abraham Ibn Ezra's Astrological Writings, Volume 7

Edited, translated, and annotated by

Shlomo Sela

BRILL

LEIDEN • BOSTON
2020

The Library of Congress Cataloging-in-Publication Data is available online at http://catalog.loc.gov
LC record available at http://lccn.loc.gov/2020014932

Typeface for the Latin, Greek, and Cyrillic scripts: "Brill". See and download: brill.com/brill-typeface.

ISSN 0169-815X
ISBN 978-90-04-43143-0 (hardback)
ISBN 978-90-04-43144-7 (e-book)

This book is printed on acid-free paper and produced in a sustainable manner.

To my beloved wife, Lea

CONTENTS

Preface xi
Abbreviations xiv

General Introduction 1
Contacts with Christian Scholars in the Twelfth Century 9
The Ibn Ezra Renaissance in the Latin West 12
Liber Electionum, *Liber Interrogationum*, and *Tractatus Particulares* 18
I. *Liber Electionum* and *Liber Interrogationum* 20
Earlier Research on *Liber Electionum* and *Liber Interrogationum* 20
Authorship, Links with Ibn Ezra's Work, and the Dates of Composition of *Liber Electionum* and *Liber Interrogationum* 22
Ibn Ezra's Approach to Elections in *Liber Electionum* 25
Ibn Ezra's Approach to Interrogations in *Liber Interrogationum* 29
The Organization and Contents of *Liber Electionum* and *Liber Interrogationum* 31
The Sources of *Liber Electionum* and *Liber Interrogationum* 33
Special Features of *Liber Electionum* and *Liber Interrogationum* 37
Linguistic Features of *Liber Electionum* and *Liber Interrogationum* 41
II. *Tractatus Particulares* 48
Earlier Research on *Tractatus Particulares* 49
Manuscripts, General Features and Transmission of Tp^{A} and Tp^{Q} 51
Structure and General Features of Tp^{A} and Tp^{Q} according to Their Incipits and Explicits 56
a. General Organization 59
b. Name 59
c. Authorship 60
d. Translator 60
e. Source Language 61
Contents and Sources of Tp^{A} and Tp^{Q} 62
I. *Liber de Occultis* 63
II. *Liber Servorum* 72
III. *De Significationibus Planetarum* 74
IV. *Dogma Universale in Iudiciis* 76
General Features of Tp^{H} 77

III. Manuscripts and Editorial Principles 81
Manuscripts for the Critical Edition of *Liber Electionum* and *Liber Interrogationum* 81
Witnesses for the Critical Edition of *Tractatus Particulares* 82
Editorial and Translation Principles 84

Part One: *Liber Electionum*: Latin Text and English Translation 91

Part Two: Notes to *Liber Electionum* 133

Part Three: *Liber Interrogationum*: Latin Text and English Translation 173

Part Four: Notes to *Liber Interrogationum* 225

Part Five: *Tractatus Particulares*: Latin Text and English Translation .. 271

Part Six: Notes to *Tractatus Particulares* 333

Part Seven: Appendices 389
1. The Debate about the Validity and the General Principles of the Doctrine of Elections 391
2. The Debate about the Validity and the General Principles of the Doctrine of Interrogations 399
3. Elections 406
4. Interrogations 431
5. Planets, Signs and Horoscopic Places 465
6. The Modena Fragments of *Mivḥarim* III and *She'elot* III 483
7. Passages of *She'elot le-Māshā'allāh* in *Tractatus Particulares* .. 497
8. A Section of *She'elot le-Talmai* and Its Counterpart in Ptolemy's *Iudicia* 505
9. *Significationes Planetarum in Domibus* Ascribed to Gergis 510
10. The Account of the Seven Planets in *Mishpeṭei ha-Mazzalot* .. 517
11. Māshā'allāh's Book on Reading Thoughts 525
12. The Section on Elections at the End of *Nativitates* 528
13. Fragments of *Epistola Argafalau ad Alexandrum* 531
14. English-Latin Glossary of Technical Terms (*Liber Electionum, Liber Interrogationum, Tractatus Particulares*) 535
15. Latin-English Index to the English-Latin Glossary 579
16. Authorities and Sources in *Liber Electionum, Liber Interrogationum* and *Tractatus Particulares* 590

17. Literal Renderings in *Liber Electionum* of Hebraisms and Hebrew Words/Expressions Employed by Abraham Ibn Ezra . 599
18. Literal Renderings in *Liber Interrogationum* of Hebraisms and Hebrew Words/Expressions Employed by Abraham Ibn Ezra 601
19. Indications of the Horoscopic Places in *Liber Electionum*, *Mivḥarim* I, *Mivḥarim* II, and *Epitome* 603
20. Indications of the Horoscopic Places in *Liber Interrogationum*, *She'elot* I, *She'elot* II, and *Epitome* 606
21. Index of Technical Terms and Biographical Notes 610

Bibliography 616
Index 625

PREFACE

The present volume is the seventh installment of a series of critical editions, with English translation and commentary, of Abraham Ibn Ezra's astrological writings, broken down according to the several branches of Greek and Arabic astrology addressed by him. The present volume is also the natural sequel to its immediate predecessor. This is clearly signaled by the first words of their titles: "Abraham Ibn Ezra *Latinus*." By choosing this leitmotif I meant that the two volumes are intended to look at the same cultural phenomenon—the Ibn Ezra renaissance in the Latin West—from two different angles: As a result of Ibn Ezra's increasing popularity after his death, collections of his Hebrew astrological treatises were translated in repeated waves into Latin and the emerging European vernaculars. Some of these texts are translations of treatises whose Hebrew originals have been lost; their study affords us a golden opportunity to shed light on a significant missing link in our knowledge of Ibn Ezra's astrological oeuvre. They also illustrate how Abraham Ibn Ezra was "reborn" in the Latin West and how his astrological lore was received there.

Because the allocation of texts to the volumes of this series was done thematically, by astrological genre, the Latin texts selected for the current volume address two branches of Greek and Arabic astrology: (1) the doctrine of elections, on choosing the most auspicious moment for performing specific actions, by selecting a convenient ascendant among several possible astral configurations and then casting and analyzing the corresponding horoscope; (2) the doctrine of interrogations, designed to allow astrologers to reply to questions related to daily life by casting and analyzing an horoscope for the time when the querent poses his question to the astrologer. That elections and interrogations were the most popular branches of Greco-Arabic astrology in the Middle Ages, including among Jews, is indicated in part by the fact that Ibn Ezra composed no fewer than three versions of *Sefer ha-Mivḥarim* (Book of Elections) and three versions of *Sefer ha-She'elot* (Book of Interrogations).

Volume Three of the current series, published in 2011, contained critical editions, with English translation and commentary, of the Hebrew originals of the first and second versions of *Sefer ha-Mivḥarim*, and of the first and second versions of *Sefer ha-She'elot*. The present volume completes the picture and restores the third versions of *Sefer ha-Mivḥarim* (henceforth

Mivḥarim III) and of *Sefer ha-She'elot* (henceforth *She'elot* III). Although these two Hebrew astrological texts are almost completely lost, their contents survive in two complete anonymous Latin translations, the *Liber electionum* (henceforth *Electiones*) and the *Liber interrogationum* (henceforth *Interrogationes*). The present volume relies on the two extant manuscripts to offer the first critical editions, with English translation and commentary, of these two Latin texts.

I say that the Hebrew source texts of *Electiones* and *Interrogationes* are *almost* completely lost because a parchment bifolium, recently discovered in the Archivio di Stato, Modena, contains a fragment of *Mivḥarim* III and another fragment of *She'elot* III. Under close scrutiny, it turns out that these two Hebrew fragments have a perfect Latin counterpart in two corresponding fragments of *Electiones* and *Interrogationes*. This demonstrates without a shadow of doubt that *Electiones* and *Interrogationes* are Latin translations of *Mivḥarim* III and *She'elot* III. On a recent visit to Modena, with the assistance of an ultraviolet lamp, I was able not only to read the flesh side of the bifolium more accurately, but also to decipher substantial parts of the hair side, particularly the fragment of *She'elot* III. The Hebrew texts of the legible parts of the two Modena fragments, accompanied by an English translation, are found in an appendix to this volume.

The most mysterious category of Latin translations of Ibn Ezra's astrological writings consists of Latin texts explicitly assigned to Ibn Ezra but that have no surviving Hebrew counterpart in Ibn Ezra's astrological corpus and whose affiliation with Ibn Ezra is unclear. One example is *Liber Abraham Iudei de nativitatibus*, which was studied, edited, and translated in the previous volume of this series. Another specimen in the third category is the *Tractatus particulares*, a four-part work assigned to Abraham Ibn Ezra, addressing various topics related to the doctrines of elections and interrogations and extant in two Latin translations. Despite the efforts of scholars from the nineteenth century to the present, the source texts behind the bulk of *Tractatus particulares* remain a *terra incognita*, and so too the reason this text was attributed to Abraham Ibn Ezra. The present volume offers the first critical edition, with English translation and commentary, of *Tractatus particulares*. In addition, a preliminary study attempts to determine, taking account of the evidence provided by all the available manuscript and print witnesses of this text, (1) all the sources on which *Tractatus particulares* drew; (2) the modus operandi of its originator; (3) why this text was attributed to Abraham Ibn Ezra; and (4) the circumstances in which the Hebrew source text behind *Tractatus particulares* originated.

I wish to express my sincere gratitude to a number of people who have contributed toward the realization of this volume. Carlos Steel carefully read the Latin texts and was very helpful regarding their edition. David Juste provided me with kind access to manuscript copies of *Tractatus particulares*. Charles Burnett made helpful suggestions about the transmission and interpretation of the Latin texts. Lenn Schramm revised the translations and the English sections of this book; he also made helpful suggestions about the translation of the Latin texts. The Israel Science Foundation (Grant No. 289/17) provided a generous grant. My warmest thanks to all of them.

Sh. S.
January 2020

App. 1, Q. 4, 393	Appendix 1 (which assembles quotations related to the debate about the validity of elections), quotation 4, on p. 393
App. 2, Q. 7, 401	Appendix 2 (which assembles quotations related to the debate about the validity of interrogations), quotation 7, on p. 401
App. 3, P. 1, Q. 1, § 1:2, 406	Appendix 3 (which assembles quotations related to elections), part 1 (which assembles quotations related to elections about taking a purgative), quotation 1, section1, sentence 2, on p. 406.
App. 4, P. 22, Q. 1, 461	Appendix 4 (which assembles quotations related to interrogations), part 22 (which assembles quotations related to interrogations about color), quotation 1, on p. 461
App. 5, Q. 47, 480	Appendix 5 (which assembles quotations related to planets, signs and horoscopic places), quotation 47, on p. 480
App. 7, P. 1, 1–4, 498	Appendix 7 (which brings passages from *She'elot le-Māshā'allāh*), passage 1, sentences 1–4, on p. 498
App. 8, *She'elot le-Talmai*, § 1:1–2, 505–506	Appendix 8 (which brings a whole section of *She'elot le-Talmai* and its counterpart in Ptolemy's *Iudicia*), *She'elot le-Talmai* (which brings the section of *She'elot le-Talmai* and its English translation), paragraph 1, sentence 1–2, on pp. 505–506
App. 8, Ptolemy's *Iudicia*, § 1:1–2, 507–508	App. 8, Ptolemy's *Iudicia*, § 1:1–2, 507–508 = Appendix 8 (which brings a whole section of *She'elot le-Talmai* and its counterpart in Ptolemy's *Iudicia*), Ptolemy's *Iudicia* (which brings the section of Ptolemy's *Iudicia* and its English translation), paragraph 1, sentence 1–2, on pp. 507–508
App. 9, Sol, § 1:1, 510	Appendix 9 (which brings the complete text

	of *De significationibus planetarum in domibus*, ascribed to Gergis), Sol, § 1:1 (which brings the first part, on the Sun), section 1, sentence 1, on p. 510
App. 10, I: The Sun, 14–15, 517–518	Appendix 10 (which brings passages of the account of the seven planets in *Mishpeṭei ha-mazzalot*), I: The Sun (which brings the brings the first part, on the Sun), sentences 14–15, on pp. 517–518
App. 11, II 1:2–5, 525	Appendix 11 (which brings the fragment of the Hebrew translation and a complete Latin translation of a lost Arabic work by Māshāʾallāh on reading thoughts), II (which brings the Latin translation), section 1, sentences 2–5, on p. 525.
App. 13, III: Mercury, 532	Appendix 13 (which brings a section of *Epistola Argafalau ad Alexandrum*), III: Mercury (which brings the third part of this section, on Mercury), on p. 532
Benedictum	*Benedictum sit nomen domini* in *Alchandreana*, ed. Juste 2007
BnF	Bibliothèque nationale de France
De nativitatibus	*Liber Abraham Iudei de nativitatibus* (assigned to Abraham Ibn Ezra)
De nativitatibus, I 7:1, 254–255	*De nativitatibus*, ed. Sela (2019), part I (introduction), section 7, sentence 1, on pp. 254–255
De nativitatibus, II i 4:2, 274–275	*De nativitatibus*, ed. Sela (2019), part II (the twelve horoscopic places), section i (addressing the first horoscopic place), section 5, sentence 2, on pp. 274–275
De rationibus tabularum	*Liber de rationibus tabularum* (assigned to Abraham Ibn Ezra)
El, I 7:3	*Electiones*, part I (introduction), section 7, sentence 3, in the current volume
El, II i 3:2	*Electiones*, part II (the twelve horoscopic places), chapter i (addressing the first horoscopic place), section 3, sentence 2, in the current volume

Electiones	*Liber Electionum* (Abraham Ibn Ezra; Latin translation of *Mivḥarim* III)
Epistola Argafalau	*Epistola Argafalau ad Alexandrum* in *Alchandreana*, ed. Juste 2007
Epitome	*Epitome totius astrologiae*
Epitome, ed. Heller (1548), 26, E2r	*Epitome*, ed. Heller (1548), *Isagoge in astrologiam*, chapter 26, sig. E2r.
Epitome, ed. Heller (1548), I:10, H2r	*Epitome*, ed. Heller (1548), *Liber primus, de gentibus, regibus, civitatibus, aeris mutatione, fame & mortalitate*, chapter 10, sig. H2r.
Epitome, ed. Heller (1548), II:2, I4v	*Epitome*, ed. Heller (1548), *Liber secundus, de nativitatibus*, chapter 2, sig. I4r
Epitome, ed. Heller (1548), III:2, Q2r	*Epitome*, ed. Heller (1548), *Liber tertius, de interrogationibus*, chapter 2, sig. Q2r
Epitome, ed. Heller (1548), IV:2, R3v	*Epitome*, ed. Heller (1548), *Liber quartus, de electionibus*, chapter 2, sig. R3v
Int, I 3:2	*Interrogationes*, part I (introduction), section 3, sentence 2, in the current volume
Int, II vii 3:2	*Interrogationes*, part II (the twelve horoscopic places), section vii (addressing the seventh horoscopic place), section 3, sentence 2, in the current volume
Interrogationes	*Liber interrogationum* (Abraham Ibn Ezra; Latin translation of *She'elot* III)
Me'orot § 25:4, 472–473	*Sefer ha-me'orot* (Abraham Ibn Ezra), ed. Sela (2011), section 25, sentence 4, pp. 472–473
Mishpeṭei ha-mazzalot § 15:1, 500–501	*Mishpeṭei ha-mazzalot* (Abraham Ibn Ezra), ed. Sela (2017), section 15, sentence 1, pp. 500–501
Mivḥarim I, § 5.4:2, 66–67	First version of *Sefer ha-mivḥarim* (Abraham Ibn Ezra), ed. Sela (2011), chapter 5, section 4, sentence 2, pp. 66–67
Mivḥarim II, § 7.1:6, 164–165	Second version of *Sefer ha-mivḥarim* (Abraham Ibn Ezra), ed. Sela (2011), chapter 7, section 1, sentence 6, pp. 164–165
Mivḥarim III, II vii 5:2, 486–487	The Modena fragment of *Mivḥarim* III, part II, chapter 7, section 5, sentence 2, on pp. 486–487 of the present volume
Moladot	*Sefer ha-moladot* (Abraham Ibn Ezra)
Moladot, I 9:4, 88–89	*Sefer ha-moladot* (Abraham Ibn Ezra), ed. Sela

	(2013), part I (preface), section 9, sentence 4, pp. 88–89
Moladot, II 7:8, 96–97	*Sefer ha-moladot* (Abraham Ibn Ezra), ed. Sela (2013), part II (introduction), section 7, sentence 8, pp. 96–97
Moladot, III vi 8:4, 152–153	*Sefer ha-moladot* (Abraham Ibn Ezra), ed. Sela (2013), part III (the twelve horoscopic places), chapter 6 (addressing the sixth horoscopic place), section 8, sentence 4, pp. 152–153
Moladot, IV 14:2, 194–195	*Sefer ha-moladot* (Abraham Ibn Ezra), ed. Sela (2013), part IV ("Revolutions of the Years"), section 14, sentence 2, pp. 194–195
Nativitas	*Liber Servi Dei de Mechlinia de Ducatu Brabantie super inquisitione et verificatione nativitatis incerte ex iudiciis ac subsequentibus nato post nativitatem* (Henry Bate)
Nativitates	*Liber nativitatum* (Abraham Ibn Ezra; Latin translation of *Moladot* II)
Nativitates, I v 1:2, 86–89	*Liber nativitatum*, ed. Sela (2019), part I (introduction), chapter v, section 1, sentence 2, on pp. 86–89
Nativitates, II vii 1:2, 138–139	*Liber nativitatum*, ed. Sela (2019), part II (the twelve horoscopic places), chapter vii (addressing the seventh horoscopic place), section 1, sentence 2, on pp. 138–139.
Neḥoshet	*Keli ha-neḥoshet* (Abraham Ibn Ezra, Book of the astrolabe)
Neḥoshet I, 148r	First version of *Keli ha-neḥoshet* (Abraham Ibn Ezra), MS Paris 1061, fol. 148r
Neḥoshet II, 188r	Second version of *Keli ha-neḥoshet* (Abraham Ibn Ezra), MS Paris 1045, fol. 188r
ʿOlam	*Sefer ha-ʿolam* (Abraham Ibn Ezra)
ʿOlam I, § 16:1, 62–63	First version of *Sefer ha-ʿolam* (Abraham Ibn Ezra), ed. Sela (2010), section 16, sentence 1, pp. 62–63
ʿOlam II, § 14:7, 164–165	Second version of *Sefer ha-ʿolam* (Abraham Ibn Ezra), ed. Sela (2010), section 14, sentence 7, pp. 164–165
Proportiones	*Proportiones competentes in astrorum industria* in *Alchandreana*, ed. Juste 2007

Reshit ḥokhmah § 8.4:1, 218–219	*Reshit ḥokhmah* (Abraham Ibn Ezra), ed. Sela (2017), chapter 8, section 4, sentence 2, pp. 218–219
Reshit ḥokhmah II 2010, 54	Second version of *Reshit ḥokhmah* (Abraham Ibn Ezra), ed. Sela (2010), on p. 54
She'elot I, § 7.3:15, 272–273	First version of *Sefer ha-she'elot* (Abraham Ibn Ezra), ed. Sela (2011), chapter 7, section 3, sentence 15, 272–273
She'elot II, § 12.8:5, 394–395	Second version of *Sefer ha-she'elot* (Abraham Ibn Ezra), ed. Sela (2011), chapter 12, section 8, sentence 5, pp. 394–395
She'elot III, II vii 3:2, 495	The Modena fragment of *She'elot* III, part II (the twelve horoscopic places), chapter 7 (addressing the seventh horoscopic place), section 3, sentence 2, on p. 495, in the current volume
Ṭe'amim	*Sefer ha-ṭe'amim* (Abraham Ibn Ezra)
Ṭe'amim I, § 2.6:2, 36–37	First version of *Sefer ha-ṭe'amim* (Abraham Ibn Ezra), ed. Sela (2007), chapter 2, section 6, sentence 2, pp. 36–37.
Ṭe'amim II, § 5.1:11, 218–219	Second version of *Sefer ha-ṭe'amim* (Abraham Ibn Ezra), ed. Sela (2007), chapter 5, section 1, sentence 11, pp. 218–219
Tequfah § 9:5, 378–379	*Sefer ha-tequfah* (Abraham Ibn Ezra), ed. Sela (2013), *Tequfah*, section 9, sentence 5, pp. 378–379
Tp	*Tractatus particulares* (assigned to Abraham Ibn Ezra)
Tp, I i 7:2	*Tractatus particulares*, part I (first part), chapter i (first chapter of the first part), section 7, sentence 2, in the current volume
Tp, I ii 4:3	*Tractatus particulares*, part I (first part), chapter ii (second chapter of the first part), section 4, sentence 3, in the current volume
Tp, I iii 3:4	*Tractatus particulares*, part I (first part), chapter iii (third chapter of the first part), section 3, sentence 4, in the current volume
Tp, I iv 5:1	*Tractatus particulares*, part I (first part), chapter iv (fourth chapter of the first part), section 5, sentence 1, in the current volume
Tp, II iii 4:1	*Tractatus particulares*, part II (second part),

	chapter iii (addressing the significations of Saturn), section 4 (addressing the fourth category of the significations of Saturn), sentence 1, in the current volume
Tp, III 7:2	*Tractatus particulares*, part III (third part), section 7 (addressing the significations of the seventh horoscopic place), sentence 2 (addressing the significations of the Sun in the seventh horoscopic place), in the current volume
Tp, IV 2:3	*Tractatus particulares*, part IV ("General doctrine of judgements"), section 2, sentence 3, in the current volume
Tp^{A}	Peter d'Abano's translation of *Tractatus particulares*
Tp^{H}	the Hebrew source text behind Tp^{A} and Tp^{Q}
Tp^{Q}	Arnoul de Quincampoix's translation of *Tractatus particulares*

GENERAL INTRODUCTION

Abraham Ibn Ezra (ca. 1089–ca. 1161) was a prolific writer and a pioneer of medieval Hebrew science. An essential feature of his huge and multifarious corpus is that almost all of it was written in Hebrew.[1] Geographically, his literary production, at least as it has come down to us, was not written in Muslim Spain, where he spent the first five decades of his life and received his Jewish and scientific education within the ambit of the Arabic language and Arabic culture. In those years he apparently made his living as a poet, traveling from one patron to another, and wrote next to nothing related to biblical exegesis and astrology, the fields in which he was to excel later.[2] Chronologically, the second stage of Ibn Ezra's career stretched from 1140—when he left his homeland at the age of 50 and began an itinerant life through Italy, France, and England—to the end of his days. That he presumably commenced his scientific activities in 1140, and that he did so in Hebrew, demonstrates that the message he sought to transmit in that language became seriously relevant only after he moved from Muslim Spain to Latin Europe.[3] This suggests that had he not left Spain and changed his linguistic vehicle from Arabic to Hebrew, in all likelihood he would have sunk into complete oblivion, instead of becoming a prolific writer on a wide variety of subjects.[4]

Abraham Ibn Ezra's fame rests in part on his outstanding biblical commentaries. Their popularity begot a new Hebrew literary genre, which flourished in the fourteenth century—supercommentaries on his fascinating but often obscure biblical commentaries[5]—and led to his subsequent inclusion in the *Miqra'ot Gedolot*.[6] The success and popularity of Ibn Ezra's

---

[1] For Ibn Ezra's approach to the creation of a new Hebrew scientific vocabulary, see Sela 2003, 93–143.

[2] For Abraham Ibn Ezra in Muslim Spain, see Schirmann 1997, 14–18.

[3] For Ibn Ezra's biography during his wanderings through Italy, France, and England, see: Fleischer 1930/2, 69–106; Fleischer 1931, 69–76, 107–111, 129–133, 160–168, 189–203; Fleischer 1932/3, 97–100, 129–131, 148–150, 169–171 (1932), 134–136, 152–155 (1933); Fleischer 1934, pp. 107–124; Friedlander 1894/5, 47–60; Golb 1976, pp. 45–66.

[4] For an assessment of Ibn Ezra's biography that views him as continuing his former mode of life as a poet-scholar, traveling from one patron to another, after his arrival in Italy in 1140, but now writing works of biblical exegesis, grammar, and science, and not just poetry, see Freudenthal 2013, 53–65.

[5] For Ibn Ezra's supercommentaries, see Simon 1993, 86–128; Schwartz 1996, 92–114.

[6] This is an exclusive compilation of the most prestigious and distinguished medieval Jewish commentaries that also became the normative Jewish biblical exegesis.

biblical commentaries may be due to some extent part to the fact that, in addition to his profound understanding of the biblical text, he incorporated material on all branches of the sciences of his age, including astrology, astronomy, chronology, calendrics, mathematics, philosophy, grammar, and logic. But Ibn Ezra also wrote religious and secular poetry and a series of religious-theological monographs and grammatical treatises. His intellectual interests extended to the sciences as well. His scientific corpus, comprising more than thirty treatises, deals with mathematics, astronomy, scientific instruments and tools, and the Jewish calendar—but especially with astrology.[7]

From the Middle Ages until the present, the development of astrology among Jews has been associated with the name of Abraham Ibn Ezra. For medieval Europe culture, *Abraham Avenezra* was mainly an intermediary and transmitter of Arabic science and astrology to the Latin West. From a Jewish perspective, Abraham Ibn Ezra's contribution was different and is important in two ways. First, by incorporating astrological notions into his influential biblical commentaries he promoted the smooth absorption of astrology into the hard core of Jewish culture.[8] In addition, he produced the first comprehensive corpus of Hebrew astrological textbooks that address the main systems of Arabic astrology and provided Hebrew readers with access to the subject. Judging by the numbers of extant manuscripts, Ibn Ezra's Hebrew astrological treatises circulated widely. His astrological achievement has never been repeated, neither in the Middle Ages nor in the Modern Era.[9] Thanks to recent discoveries, today we know of twenty treatises by him, covering the main genres of Greek and Arabic astrological literature, as follows:

- Introductions to astrology, conveying basic elements of the worldview that underlies astrology and explaining technical concepts of the various branches of astrology:

[7] For a chronological listing of Ibn Ezra's scholarly writings (biblical commentaries; books related to the Hebrew language or bearing on theology; scientific treatises), see Sela and Freudenthal 2006, 13–55. For a general evaluation of Ibn Ezra's scientific contribution, see Steinschneider 1880, 59–128; Steinschneider 1925, 327–387; Millás Vallicrosa 1949, 289–347; Baron 1958, VIII, 138–220; Levey 1971, IV, 502–503; Goldstein 1996, 9–21. Levy 2000, 60–75; Sela 2003, 17–92.

[8] Langermann 1993, 28–85; Sela, 1999; Sela 2003, 9–12, 288–323; Langermann 2014.

[9] For lists of and studies on Ibn Ezra's astrological writings, see Steinschneider 1870, 339–346; Steinschneider 1880, 124–128; Steinschneider 1897, 136–150; Levy 1927, 11–57; Smithuis 2006.

(1) The complete version of *Reshit ḥokhmah* (Book of the Beginning of Wisdom), which is extant in at least 70 manuscripts, and (2) *Mishpeṭei ha-mazzalot* (Book of the Judgments of the Zodiacal Signs), which survives in at least 25 manuscripts. These two works were edited in the fifth volume of this series.[10] This edition is used for all quotations from or references to the Hebrew text and English translation of *Reshit ḥokhmah* and *Mishpeṭei ha-mazzalot*, in the format: (i) *Reshit ḥokhmah* § 9.1:6, 234–235 = *Reshit ḥokhmah*, ed. Sela (2017), chapter 9, section 1, passage 6, on pp. 234–235; (ii) *Mishpeṭei ha-mazzalot*, § 38:7, 522–523 = *Mishpeṭei ha-mazzalot*, ed. Sela (2017), section 38, passage 7 on pp. 522–523.
(3) The lost second version of *Reshit ḥokhmah*, a fragment of which was recently discovered and has been published in a separate study and edition.[11] That edition is used for all the references to the Hebrew text of this fragment in the format: *Reshit ḥokhmah* II 2010, 54 = *Reshit ḥokhmah* II, ed. Sela (2010), on p. 54.

- Treatises explaining the astrological reasons behind the concepts employed in both versions of *Reshit ḥokhmah*:
  (4–5) The two versions of *Sefer ha-Teʿamim* (Book of Reasons; referred to as *Ṭeʿamim* I and *Ṭeʿamim* II). The first version is extant in at least 32 manuscripts and the second in at least 25 manuscripts. The critical editions of the Hebrew texts of these two commentaries, accompanied by an English translation and commentary, were published in the first volume of this series.[12] This edition is used for all quotations from or references to the Hebrew text and English translation of *Ṭeʿamim* I and *Ṭeʿamim* II, in the format: (i) *Ṭeʿamim* I, § 3.2:1, 70–71 = *Ṭeʿamim* I, ed. Sela (2007), chapter 3, section 2, passage 1 on pp. 70–71; (ii) *Ṭeʿamim* II, § 4.3:1, 208–209 = *Ṭeʿamim* II, ed. Sela (2007), chapter 4, section 3, passage 1, on pp. 208–209.
- Nativities, which posit that the destiny of the newborn is determined by the configuration of the celestial bodies at the instant of birth and may be learned from the natal horoscopic chart:
  (6) The first version of *Sefer ha-moladot* (*Book of nativities*; henceforth *Moladot*). This version is extant in at least 53 manuscripts. The critical edition of the complete extant Hebrew text of *Moladot*, accompanied by an English translation and commentary, was published in volume four of

[10] See Sela 2017; *Reshit ḥokhmah*, ed. Sela (2017); and *Mishpeṭei ha-mazzalot*, ed. Sela (2017).
[11] See *Reshit ḥokhmah* II, ed. Sela (2010).
[12] See Sela 2007, *Ṭeʿamim* I, ed. Sela (2007) and *Ṭeʿamim* II, ed. Sela (2007).

this series.[13] This edition is used for all quotations from or references to the four parts of the Hebrew text and English translation of *Moladot*, in the following formats: (i) The preface: *Moladot*, I 9: 4, 88–89 = *Moladot*, ed. Sela (2013), part I, section 9, sentence 4, on pp. 88–89; (ii) The introduction: *Moladot*, II 7:8, 96–97 = *Moladot*, ed. Sela (2013), part II (introduction) section 7, sentence 8, on pp. 96–97; (iii) The chapters on the twelve horoscopic places: *Moladot*, III vi 8:4, 152–153 = *Moladot*, ed. Sela (2013), part III (the twelve horoscopic places) chapter 6 (addressing the sixth horoscopic place), section 8, sentence 4, on pp. 152–153; (iv) The part on continuous horoscopy in nativities: *Moladot*, IV 14:2, 194–195 = *Moladot*, ed. Sela (2013), part IV ("Revolutions of the Years"), section 14, sentence 2, on pp. 194–195.

(7) The second version of *Sefer ha-moladot*, whose Hebrew original is lost but which survives in a Latin translation entitled *Liber nativitatum* (henceforth *Nativitates*). *Nativitates* is extant in two manuscripts. The critical edition of the Latin text of *Nativitates*, accompanied by an English translation and commentary, was published in volume six of this series.[14] This edition is used for all quotations from or references to the three parts of *Nativitates*, in the following formats: (i) The introduction: *Nativitates*, I v 1:2, 86–89 = *Nativitates*, ed. Sela (2019), part I (introduction), chapter v (fixed stars and rectification of the nativity), section 1, sentence 2, on pp. 86–89; (ii) The chapters on the twelve horoscopic places: *Nativitates*, II vii 1:2, 138–139 = *Nativitates*, ed. Sela (2019), part II (the twelve horoscopic places), chapter vii (addressing the seventh horoscopic place), section 1, sentence 2, on pp. 138–139; (iii) The "chapter on generalities": *Nativitates*, III i 1:2, 154–155 = *Nativitates*, ed. Sela (2019), part III, chapter 1, section 1, sentence 2.

(8) *Liber Abraham Iudei de nativitatibus* (henceforth *De nativitatibus*), a Latin treatise on nativities commonly assigned to Abraham Ibn Ezra.[15] *De nativitatibus* is extant in at least 16 manuscripts, three print editions, and one German translation. The critical edition of the Latin text of *De nativitatibus*, accompanied by an English translation and commentary, was published in volume six of this series.[16] This edition is used for all quotations from or references to the two parts of *De nativitatibus*, in the following formats: (i) The introduction: *De nativitatibus*, I 7:1, 254–255 =

13 See Sela 2013; *Moladot*, ed. Sela (2013).
14 See Sela 2019; *Nativitates*, ed. Sela (2019).
15 See below, p. 10.
16 See Sela 2019; *De nativitatibus*, ed. Sela (2019).

De nativitatibus, ed. Sela (2019), part I (introduction), section 7, sentence 1, on pp. 254–255; (ii) The chapters on the twelve horoscopic places: *De nativitatibus*, II i 4:2, 274–275 = *De nativitatibus*, ed. Sela (2019), part II (the twelve horoscopic places), section i (addressing the first horoscopic place), section 5, sentence 2, on pp. 274–275;

- Continuous horoscopy in nativities, which postulates that a new horoscopic chart should be cast on every anniversary or "revolution of the year"—when the Sun arrives at the same point in the zodiac where it was at the time of the native's birth—or even at the beginning of every month, week, day, or hour, and that this new chart should be compared with the natal chart. In addition, certain periods of life are allocated to governing planets in a fixed sequence; these period-governors in turn share their authority with other planets by granting them subperiods:
(9) The recently discovered *Sefer ha-Tequfah* (Book of the Revolution; referred to as *Tequfah*), which is extant in four manuscripts. The critical edition of the Hebrew text of *Tequfah*, accompanied by an English translation and commentary, was published in the fourth volume of this series.[17] This edition is used for all quotations from or references to the Hebrew text and English translation of *Sefer ha-Tequfah*, in the format: *Tequfah* § 9:5, 378–379 = *Tequfah*, ed. Sela (2013), section 9, sentence 5, on pp. 378–379.
In addition, the fourth part of *Moladot*, a veritable treatise within a treatise entitled *Tequfot ha-shanim* (Revolutions of the years), constitutes a separate work on continuous horoscopy in nativities that bears striking resemblances to *Tequfah*.
- Elections, on choosing the most auspicious moment for performing specific actions. This time is determined by finding or choosing a convenient ascendant among several possible astral configurations and then casting and analyzing the corresponding horoscope:
(10) The first version of *Sefer ha-Mivḥarim* (Book of Elections; referred to as *Mivḥarim* I), which is extant in at least 33 manuscripts. The critical edition of the Hebrew text, accompanied by an English translation and commentary, was published in the third volume of this series.[18] This edition is used for all quotations from or references to the two parts of *Mivḥarim* I, in the following formats: (i) The introduction: *Mivḥarim* I, § 1:2, 46–47 = *Mivḥarim* I, ed. Sela (2011), section 1, passage 2, on pp. 46–47; (ii) The chapters on the twelve horoscopic places: *Mivḥarim* I, § 5.4:2,

17 See Sela 2013; *Tequfah*, ed. Sela (2013).
18 See Sela 2011; *Mivḥarim* I, ed. Sela (2011).

pp. 66–67 = *Mivḥarim* I, ed. Sela (2011), chapter 5 (addressing the fifth horoscopic place), section 4, sentence 2, on pp. 66–67.
(11) The second version of *Sefer ha-Mivḥarim* (henceforth *Mivḥarim* II), which is extant in at least 28 manuscripts. The critical edition of the Hebrew text, accompanied by an English translation and commentary, was published in the third volume of this series.[19] This edition is used for all quotations from or references to the two parts of *Mivḥarim* II, in the following formats: (i) The introduction: *Mivḥarim* II, § 1:3, 142–143 = *Mivḥarim* II, ed. Sela (2011), section 1, passage 3, on pp. 142–143; (ii) The chapters on the twelve horoscopic places: *Mivḥarim* II, § 7.1:6, 164–165 = *Mivḥarim* II, ed. Sela (2011), chapter 7 (addressing the seventh horoscopic place), section 1, sentence 6, on pp. 164–165.
(12) The lost third version of *Sefer ha-Mivḥarim* (henceforth *Mivḥarim* III), of which a complete Latin translation, entitled *Liber electionum*, survives today. The present volume contains a critical edition, translation, and commentary on this Latin work. For the method of reference to specific parts of *Liber electionum*, see below, Editorial and Translation Principles, on p. 88.
A fragment of the Hebrew of *Mivḥarim* III survives in the parchment bifolium 368.2 in the Archivio di Stato, Modena. The text and translation of this fragment are found in this volume, in Appendix 6, pp. 484–489. This edition is used for all quotations from or references to the fragment of *Mivḥarim* III, in the format: *Mivḥarim* III, II vii 1:2, 485 = The Modena fragment of *Mivḥarim* III, part II, chapter 7 (addressing the seventh horoscopic place), section 1, sentence 2, on p. 485.

- Interrogations, designed to allow astrologers to reply to questions relating to daily life by casting and analyzing an horoscope for the time when the querent poses his question to the astrologer:
(13) The first version of *Sefer ha-She'elot* (Book of Interrogations; referred to as *She'elot* I), which is extant in at least 29 manuscripts. The critical edition of the Hebrew text, accompanied by English translation and commentary of *She'elot* I, was published in the third volume of this series.[20] This edition is used for all quotations from or references to the two parts of *She'elot* I, in the following formats: (i) The introduction: *She'elot* I, § 2:1, 240–241 = *She'elot* I, ed. Sela (2011), section 2, passage 1, on pp. 240–241; (ii) The chapters on the twelve horoscopic places: *She'elot* I,

[19] See Sela 2011; *Mivḥarim* II, ed. Sela (2011).
[20] See Sela 2011; *She'elot* I, ed. Sela (2011).

§ 5.3:2, pp. 264–265 = *She'elot* I, ed. Sela (2011), chapter 5 (addressing the fifth horoscopic place), section 3, sentence 2, on pp. 264–265.
(14) The second version of *Sefer ha-She'elot* (henceforth *She'elot* II), which is extant in at least 18 manuscripts. The critical edition of the Hebrew text, accompanied by English translation and commentary of *She'elot* II, was published in the third volume of this series.[21] This edition is used for all quotations from or references to the two parts of *She'elot* II, in the following formats: (i) The introduction: *She'elot* II, § 1:3, 348–349 = *She'elot* II, ed. Sela (2011), section 1, passage 3, on pp. 348–349; (ii) The chapters on the twelve horoscopic places: *She'elot* II, § 7.1:2, 368–369 = *She'elot* II, ed. Sela (2011), chapter 7 (addressing the seventh horoscopic place), section 1, sentence 2, on pp. 368–369.
(15) The lost third version of *Sefer ha-She'elot* (henceforth *She'elot* III), which survives in a complete Latin translation, entitled *Liber interrogationum*. The present volume contains a critical edition, translation, and commentary on this Latin work. For the method of reference to specific parts of *Liber interrogationum*, see below, Editorial and Translation Principles, on p. 88.
A fragment of the Hebrew of *She'elot* III survives in the parchment bifolium 368.2 in the Archivio di Stato, Modena. The text and translation of this fragment are found in this volume, in Appendix 6, on pp. 489–496. This edition is used for all quotations from or references to the fragment of *She'elot* III, in the format: *She'elot* III, II vii 2:7, 494–495 = The Modena fragment of *She'elot* III, part II, chapter 7 (addressing the seventh horoscopic place), section 2, sentence 7, on pp. 494–495.

- World astrology, concerned with the reconstruction, interpretation, and prognostication of political, historical, and religious events, on the one hand, and with weather forecasting, on the other, by means of a set of doctrines such as the interpretation of solar and lunar eclipses, the analysis of horoscopes cast in years of Saturn-Jupiter conjunctions, and the use of a great variety of periods, indicators, and cycles:
(16–17) The two versions of *Sefer ha-'Olam* (Book of the World; referred to as *'Olam* I and *'Olam* II). The first version is extant in at least 34 manuscripts and the second in at least 26 manuscripts. The critical editions of the Hebrew texts, accompanied by English translations and commentaries, of *'Olam* I and *'Olam* II, were published in the second volume of this series.[22] This edition is used for all the quotations from

21 See Sela 2011; *She'elot* II, ed. Sela (2011).
22 See Sela 2010; *'Olam* I, ed. Sela (2010); *'Olam* II, ed. Sela (2010).

or references to the Hebrew text of *ʿOlam* I and *ʿOlam* II, in the format: (a) *ʿOlam* I, § 45:1, 82–83 = *ʿOlam* I, ed. Sela (2010), section 45, sentence 1, on pp. 82–83; (b) *ʿOlam* II, § 28:3, 174–175 = *ʿOlam* II, ed. Sela (2010), section 2, sentence 1, on pp. 174–175.

(18) The lost third version of *Sefer ha-ʿOlam* (henceforth *Olam* III), whose existence is demonstrated by two future-tense cross-references in *El*, II vi 1:5 (see below, note on pp. 153–154) and in *Nativitates*, I i 3:29, 82–83 (see note in Sela 2019, 170–171). A hitherto unknown Latin translation of *Olam* III was recently identified in Vatican, BAV, MS Pal. lat. 1407, 14th–15th c. fols. 55r–58r. An edition of this Latin translation, accompanied by an English translation and an introductory study has been recently published.[23]

- Medical astrology, based on the Greek theory of the critical days, according to which the course of acute diseases is determined by "crises" or "critical days," when marked changes in the symptoms of a disease take place and it tends to reach a climax, whether good or bad. The Moon's position with respect to its position at the onset of the disease was thought to be connected to the time and character of these "critical days":

  (19) *Sefer ha-Meʾorot* (Book of the Luminaries, henceforth *Meʾorot*), which is extant in at least 35 manuscripts. The critical edition of the Hebrew text, accompanied by an English translation and commentary, of *Meʾorot* was published in the third volume of this series.[24] This edition is used for all quotations from or references to the Hebrew text and English translation of *Sefer ha-Meʾorot*, in the format: (a) *Meʾorot*, § 25:4, 472–473 = *Meʾorot*, ed. Sela (2011), section 25, passage 4 on pp. 472–473.

  (20) The lost second version of *Sefer ha-Meʾorot*. Two quotations from this work survive in *Ṣafenat Paʿneaḥ*, a supercommentary on Ibn Ezra's commentary on the Pentateuch composed by Joseph ben Eliezer Bonfils at the end of the fourteenth century.[25]

This list reveals the main characteristics of Ibn Ezra's astrological corpus. First, the titles of Ibn Ezra's Hebrew astrological treatises are evocative of their foundations in the well-established branches and genres of Greco-Arabic astrology: introductions to astrology, nativities and continuous horoscopy, historical and meteorological astrology, elections, interrogations, and medical astrology. Second, the individual treatises were designed to be

---

[23] See Sela et al. (2020).

[24] See Sela 2011; *Meʾorot*, ed. Sela (2011).

[25] See *Ṣafenat Paʿneaḥ*, ed. Herzog (1911), II, p. 35, lines 6–7; p. 36, lines 10–12. The two quotations are cited and translated in Sela 2011, 536.

chapters of "astrological encyclopedias" and are linked by a network of cross-references.[26] Third, Ibn Ezra usually produced at least two different versions or recensions of each individual treatise. This phenomenon is typical of his literary career. The multiple versions of many of his biblical commentaries, scientific treatises, and astrological writings are an artifact of his nomadic existence and reflect the fact that he supported himself by his pen. When he arrived in a new town he would write a new version of an old work for a new patron, and in this way continued to stimulate the attention and curiosity of readers all along his wanderings through Latin Europe. The last point highlights why this volume offers the critical edition, accompanied by an English translation and commentary, of the Latin translations of the third versions of Ibn Ezra's *Sefer ha-Mivḥarim* and *Sefer ha-She'elot*.

Contacts with Christian Scholars in the Twelfth Century

There are strong indications that Ibn Ezra's astronomical and astrological works became known to Christian scholars during his years in the Latin West and shortly after his death, either because they were then translated or elaborated for Latin readers, or because Christian scholars had direct contact with Ibn Ezra during his years among them. This is supported by codicological evidence: some Latin works ascribed to Ibn Ezra, supposed to have been written with his participation or based on material derived from his work, survive in manuscripts copied in the twelfth century. Six texts of this type survive.

Epitome totius astrologiae (henceforth *Epitome*), dated in some parts to 1142, shortly after Ibn Ezra arrived in the Latin West, has been associated to Ibn Ezra but has no Hebrew counterpart in his extant Hebrew astrological oeuvre. *Epitome* is extant in at least 63 manuscripts, the earliest dating to the thirteenth century, and one print edition, produced by Joachim Heller in Nuremberg 1548.[27] This popular astrological work consists of an introductory book, the *Ysagoge in astrologiam*, and the *Liber quadripartitus*, which addresses the four main subdivisions of Arabic astrology. The third and fourth parts of the *Epitome*, dealing respectively with the doctrines of elections and interrogations, bear striking similarities to *Liber electionum* and *Liber interrogationum*, two of the texts studied in this volume, as will be

[26] For example, *Reshit ḥokhmah*, *Ṭeʿamim* I, *Moladot*, *Mivḥarim* I, *She'elot* I, *ʿOlam* I, and *Me'orot* were composed in 1148 CE in the city of Béziers.

[27] *Epitome*, ed. Heller (1548).

shown in the notes to these texts. It was Charles Burnett who first advanced the thesis of close links between Ibn Ezra's astrological works and the *Epitome*.[28] Burnett's conjecture was fleshed out by Renate Smithuis, who found additional parallels between various parts of Ibn Ezra's astrological oeuvre and the *Epitome*.[29] I continued along this line in the previous volumes of this series.[30]

Liber Abraham Iudei de Nativitatibus (Book on nativities by Abraham the Jew; henceforth *De nativitatibus*), a Latin astrological treatise on nativities that evinces striking resemblances to Ibn Ezra's *Moladot*, employs literal Latin translations of Ibn Ezra's Hebrew neologisms, includes substantial Jewish material, and incorporates virtually identical explanations of the rationale behind astrological procedures and theories as those found in other Hebrew works by Ibn Ezra, but has no surviving Hebrew counterpart. *De nativitatibus* has been known to modern scholarship almost exclusively from the first print edition, produced in Venice in 1485. Building on the mention there of 1154 as the date of composition,[31] it has been argued that *De nativitatibus* was written in Latin by Ibn Ezra or with his active participation for a Latin readership. However, a recent study of this text, taking into account the evidence provided by virtually all the available manuscript witnesses of this text and previously unknown sources, presents a totally new picture. This study shows that *De nativitatibus*, although based on a Hebrew archetype, was composed in Latin in 1166 or slightly later, when Ibn Ezra was no longer alive, and was transmitted in four very different versions, the earliest of which dates to around 1280.[32]

The third text is a Latin treatise on the astrolabe, edited by José Maria Millás Vallicrosa, which bears striking resemblances to Ibn Ezra's Hebrew works on that instrument.[33] This treatise, which was written down *Abraham dictante* (while Abraham dictated), is extant in two manuscripts, one copied in the second half of the twelfth century and the other at the end of the twelfth or beginning of the thirteenth century.[34]

The fourth text is a treatise explaining the astronomical rationale behind astronomical tables, ascribed to Abraham Ibn Ezra and edited by Millás

28 See Burnett 2002, 75–77; Burnett 2008, 219–265; Burnett 2010 70–75.

29 Smithuis 2004, Ch. III, 169–199.

30 See, for example, Sela 2019, 27–28, 32–33, 42, 71, 168, 174, 176–177, et passim.

31 *De nativitatibus*, ed. Ratdolt (1485), sig. C2v.

32 See Sela 2018, 313–348; Sela 2019, 49–71.

33 *Astrolabio*, ed. Millás Vallicrosa (1940).

34 *Astrolabio*, ed. Millás Vallicrosa (1940), 9–29; Sela 2003, 31–36. See London, British Library, MS Cotton Vesp A II, fols. 37v–40v; Arundel 377, fols. 63r–68v.

Vallicrosa.[35] This treatise, extant in eight manuscripts, including three from the late twelfth century,[36] is known to modern scholarship as *Liber de rationibus tabularum* (Book of the reasons behind astronomical tables), although this title does not occur anywhere in its text.[37] *Liber de rationibus tabularum*, according to most of the manuscripts, begins *Dixit Abraham Iudeus* (Abraham the Jew said), and mentions a certain "Abraham" several times.[38] The author of *Liber de rationibus tabularum* says that he compiled a set of astronomical tables according to the meridian of Pisa, which he adapted from the tables of al-Ṣūfī.[39] Ibn Ezra was in fact acquainted with al-Ṣūfī[40] and in his astrological work evinces some familiarity with Pisa.[41] This city is located not far from Lucca, where Ibn Ezra lived around 1143 to 1145, and where he compiled a set of astronomical tables and its canons, now lost.[42] *Liber de rationibus tabularum* also reads: *anno 1154 ab incarnacione Domini, quo hanc edicionem fecimus* ("In the year 1154 from the incarnation of the Lord, in which I made this edition").[43] Ibn Ezra was alive in 1154, although by then he was no longer in Italy but in France. Moreover, *ab incarnacione Domini* is a formula that could not have been possibly used by a Jew.

Astronomical tables with structural features similar to the Pisan tables mentioned in *Liber de rationibus tabularum* are commented in *Ptolomeus et multi sapientum*, a text that survives in a manuscript copied in 1175 or soon thereafter.[44] *Ptolomeus et multi sapientum* does not mention *Abraham Iudeus* or *Abraham* tout court, as *Liber de rationibus tabularum* does, but

35 *De rationibus tabularum*, ed. Millás Vallicrosa (1947); Birkenmajer 1919, 147–155; Birkenmajer 1950, 237–249; Sela 2003, 22–27, Samsó 2012.

36 See the following manuscripts: Erfurt, Universitäts- und Forschungsbibliothek, MS Amplon. Q. 381, fols. 1r–28r; Cambridge, Fitzwilliam Museum, McClean 165, fols. 67r–76v; London, British Library, MS Arundel 377, fol. 56va–63ra. See also *De rationibus tabularum*, ed. Millás Vallicrosa (1947), 20–21.

37 The first to study *Liber de rationibus tabularum* was Aleksander Birkenmajer, who also created the title *Liber de rationibus tabularum*. See Birkenmajer 1919, 147–155; Birkenmajer 1950, 241. The title *Liber de rationibus tabularum* occurs also in a cross-reference to the latter work in another Latin work assigned to Abraham Ibn Ezra. See *De nativitatibus*, I 14:1, 260–261.

38 *De rationibus tabularum*, ed. Millás Vallicrosa (1947), 73, 156, 159.

39 *De rationibus tabularum*, ed. Millás Vallicrosa (1947), 87: "Tabulas medii cursus solis secundum Azofi composui … Et he tabule composite sunt secundum meridiem Pisanorum."

40 See *'Olam* I, § 17:10–11, 62–63.

41 See *'Olam* II, § 15:24, 166–167; *Nativitates*, I ii 2:7, 82–83.

42 See *Mispar*, ed. Silberberg (1895), 27, 79; Sela 2003, 22.

43 *De rationibus tabularum*, ed. Millás Vallicrosa (1947), 78; cf. ibid., 109.

44 Fitzwilliam Museum, McClean 165, fols. 67r–80v. For this text, see Nothaft 2018, 145–210, esp. pp. 153–154.

it does state that the tables were compiled in 1143,[45] a year that coincides with Ibn Ezra's residence in Lucca. However, *Ptolomeus et multi sapientum* refers to *anni domini nostri Ihesu Christi* (years of our Lord, Jesus Christ),[46] a formula that could not have been possibly used by a Jew.

Hence, neither *Liber de rationibus tabularum* nor *Ptolomeus et multi sapientum* could have been written by Abraham Ibn Ezra himself, although the Pisan tables mentioned or referred to in Latin texts of the second half of the twelfth century are an adaptation of Ibn Ezra's Hebrew astronomical tables, now lost. There are two possibilities: either Ibn Ezra was invited by Christian scholars to share with them the methods he used for his own astronomical tables composed during his stay in Lucca, or Christian scholars adapted their own astronomical tables from a Latin translation of Ibn Ezra's Hebrew astronomical tables.

The sixth text, *Sefer ha-Middot* (Book of Measurements), which has been studied and edited by Tony Levy and Charles Burnett, consists of notes on arithmetic and a systematic treatise on geometry, and survives in two versions (Hebrew and Latin). The Latin version, extant in a manuscript apparently copied in the mid-twelfth century, is a translation of the Hebrew.[47]

The Ibn Ezra Renaissance in the Latin West

The evidence offered above notwithstanding, it seems that Ibn Ezra never had more than sporadic contacts with Christian scholars. In contrast to the quick diffusion of his Hebrew astrological work among Jews,[48] and the transmission of astrological lore to Christian readers via Latin translations of Arabic astrological sources,[49] Ibn Ezra's astrological writings remained generally unknown to Latinate scholars until the last decades of the thirteenth century. This emerges from the fact that neither Ibn Ezra's name nor references to any of his works are found in the catalogue of astrological writings in the *Speculum astronomiae* (Mirror of astronomy), probably composed around the middle of the thirteenth century,[50] and in the *Liber astronomicus*, the most important astrological work of the thirteenth cen-

45 Fitzwilliam Museum, McClean 165, fol. 70v: "Tabule autem nostre, composite scilicet anno Christi 1143, habent secundum annum bissextilem."

46 Fitzwilliam Museum, McClean 165, fol. 68r.

47 Lévy and Burnett 2006, 57–238. See Oxford, Bodleian Library MS Digby 51, fols. 38v–42v.

48 Leicht 2012, 262–273; Sela 2012, 296–299; Sela 2014, 189–241.

49 Juste 2016, 173–194; Boudet 2006, 35–82.

50 *Speculum astronomiae*, ed. Caroti et al. (1992).

tury, written by Guido Bonatti around 1270.[51] Soon after, though, Ibn Ezra was "reborn" in the Latin West, thanks to almost simultaneous translation projects carried out in the last decades of the century.

In 1273, a Jewish scholar known as Hagin le Juif was commissioned by Henry Bate, a student at the University of Paris, to translate a collection of Ibn Ezra's astrological works from Hebrew into French. They include four items, preserved in two manuscripts: (1) *Li livres du commencement de sapience*, a French translation of *Reshit ḥokhmah*; (2) *Livre des jugemens des nativités*, a French translation of *Moladot*; (3) *Le livre des elections Abraham*, a French translation of *Mivḥarim* II; and (4) *Le livre des interrogations*, a French translation of *She'elot* II.[52] We have substantial bibliographical information only for the first item, from whose colophon we learn that the Hebrew original of *Li livres du commencement de sapience* was composed by Abraham Ibn Ezra, translated by Hagin from Hebrew into French, and transcribed in French by a certain Obers de Mondidier in Bate's house in Mechelen (Malines), Flanders, at the end of 1273.[53]

Hagin's French translations exerted a huge influence on later Latin translations of Ibn Ezra's astrological writings: Henry Bate, Pierre de Limoges, Pietro d'Abano, and Arnoul de Quincampoix, as well as two anonymous translators, used Hagin's French as their source texts. A recently identified charter reveals that Hagin le Juif was still alive in 1288 and resident in Mechelen, not far from Henry Bate's home, fifteen years after the latter commissioned him to translate Ibn Ezra. Given that they were neighbors, Bate could have consulted his Jewish translator whenever his astrological interests made it necessary.[54]

In 1280, Henry Bate composed an astrological autobiography, commonly known as *Nativitas*.[55] Bate incorporated many astrological texts in order to ground the astrological interpretation of his own life, including at least 130 paraphrases, translations, and quotations from twelve astrological treatises written by or attributed to Abraham Ibn Ezra. These are the earliest known references to Ibn Ezra the astrologer in the Latin West.[56]

---

51 *Liber astronomicus* (1550); Thorndike 1923–1958, vol. II, ch. 67, 825–835, esp. 826–827.

52 Paris, BnF, fonds français, MS 24276, fols. 1ra–125ra, and MS 1351, fols. 1ra–123rb.

53 BnF, français 24276, fol. 66rb: "Ci define li livres de Commencement de Sapience que fist Abraham Even Aze ou Aezera qui est interpretes maistre de aide que translata Hagins li Juis de ebrieu en romans et Obers de Mondidier escrivoit le romans et fu fait a Malines en la meson sire Henri Bate et fu fines l' en de grace 1273."

54 See Sela forthcoming (a): "The Impact of Hagin Le Juif's French Translations."

55 *Nativitas*, ed. Steel et al. (2018).

56 For a study of these references, see Sela 2017a, 163–186.

Bate produced seven Latin translations of astrological treatises by Ibn Ezra. The first, completed on September 3, 1278, was the recently discovered Latin rendering of the lost *Olam* III.[57] The second, carried out in 1281, was *De mundo vel seculo*, a Latin rendering of *Olam* I. This translation, equipped with a prologue by Henry Bate himself, had a wide diffusion: it survives in at least 33 manuscripts[58] and a print edition.[59] In 1292, eleven years after the first translation and nineteen years after Hagin's French translations, Bate, who was then living in Orvieto, produced five more Latin translations of astrological treatises by Ibn Ezra: (1) *Introductorius ad astronomiam*, a translation of *Reshit ḥokhmah*, was completed on August 22, 1292, and is extant in five manuscripts.[60] This is the only one of Bate's Latin translations of Ibn Ezra that uses one of Hagin's French translations as its source text.[61] (2) *De luminaribus seu de diebus creticis*, a translation of *Me'orot*, is extant in at least ten manuscripts and a print edition as well.[62] (3) *Liber introductionis ad iudicia astrologie*, a Latin rendering of *Mishpeṭei ha-mazzalot*, is extant in at least five manuscripts.[63] (4) *Liber causarum seu racionum super hiis que dicuntur in Introductorio Abrahe qui incipit Sapiencie timor domini* (Book of causes or reasons on what has been said in the Introduction by Abraham, which begins "the beginning of wisdom is the fear of the Lord"), a Latin translation of *Ṭeʿamim* I that concludes with an epilogue by the translator, is extant in two manuscripts.[64] (5) *Liber causarum seu racionum* (Book of causes or reasons), a Latin rendering of *Ṭeʿamim* II, is extant in two manuscripts.[65]

A second translation project was organized in the second half of the thirteenth century by Pierre de Limoges, who went to study in Paris, where he was a member of the college for students of theology and probably a master of arts. Pierre de Limoges commissioned, and perhaps himself carried out, a Latin translation of *Me'orot*, entitled *Liber Abraham de terminatione morborum* (Book by Abraham on the boundary of diseases), a Latin translation of a section of *Reshit ḥokhmah*, which is copied immediately after the translation of *Me'orot*, and a Latin translation of two separate sections of *Moladot*,

57 See Sela et al. (2020).
58 For a list of manuscripts, see Steel et al. 2018, 51.
59 See *De mundo* (Bate), ed. Liechtenstein (1507). For the prologue written by Henry Bate himself, see *De mundo* (Bate), ed. Liechtenstein (1507), sig. LXXVIr1–LXXVIIv2.
60 For a list of the manuscripts, see Steel et al. 2018, 53.
61 See Sela forthcoming (a).
62 For a list of manuscripts, see Steel et al. 2018, 52.
63 For a list of manuscripts, see Steel et al. 2018, 53.
64 For a list of manuscripts, see Steel et al. 2018, 53.
65 For a list of manuscripts, see Steel et al. 2018, 53.

entitled *Liber Abraham de iudiciis* (Book by Abraham on judgments). In the earliest of the extant manuscripts (Paris, BnF, MS lat. 7320, fols. 44r–46r), Pierre de Limoges himself set down, one after the other, the Latin translation of *Me'orot* and of a section of *Reshit ḥokhmah* in a minuscule and tight handwriting, filling all four margins around an astrological-medical treatise copied in a different hand.[66] Glosses in Pierre's hand are found in the margins of one of the two manuscripts that conserve Hagin le Juif's French translations of Ibn Ezra's astrological writings (Paris, BnF, fonds français 24276).[67] This indicates that this manuscript belonged to him and was commissioned by him or given to him for his own use.[68] Pierre de Limoges, unlike other Latin translators of his time, was acquainted not only with Ibn Ezra's astrological work but also with his biblical commentaries: He based two brief texts on ideas he borrowed from Abraham Ibn Ezra's long commentary on Exodus 20:14 and long commentary on Genesis 1:31.[69]

The most extensive and ambitious of all the translation projects, which included seven items, was carried out by Pietro d'Abano (ca. 1250–1316), the Italian philosopher, astrologer, and professor of medicine, during his years in Paris (1293–1307): (1) *Principium sapientie*, which survives in eighteen manuscripts and one print edition, is a Latin translation, without additions or omissions, of *Reshit ḥokhmah*. The explicit of *Principium sapientie* says that Pietro d'Abano was moved to restore the original sense of Ibn Ezra's *Reshit ḥokhmah* because he had found a defective, corrupt, and sometimes meaningless French translation of that work. There is solid evidence that the French translation referred to here is Hagin's *Li Livres du Commencement de Sapience*.[70] (2) *Liber de Rationibus*, extant in ten manuscripts and one print edition, is a complete Latin translation of *Ṭeʿamim* II. *Liber de Rationibus*, following the translation, brings an extensive tripartite addition, and includes two explicits: one after the end of the translation and the other after the end of the addition.[71] (3) *Liber de nativitatibus et revolutionibus earum*, extant in at least sixteen manuscripts and one print edition, is a full Latin translation, with no additions or omissions, of *Moladot*. This is the only complete Latin translation of *Moladot* produced in the Latin West. There is solid evidence that Pietro d'Abano used Hagin's French transla-

[66] For a picture, see Sela 2019 (b), 16–17.
[67] For a picture, see Sela 2019 (b), 30.
[68] See Sela 2019 (b), 9–36, and David Juste, "Bate and the University of Paris," in Steel et al. 2018, 68–80.
[69] Sela 2019 (b), 36–51.
[70] Ibid., 17–35.
[71] Ibid., 35–47.

tion of *Moladot* for his own Latin translation.[72] (4) *Liber de interrogationibus*, extant in at least twelve manuscripts and one print edition, is a full Latin translation of *She'elot* II. In the middle of the sixth chapter, *De interrogationibus* interpolates an addition of approximately 250 words that is a *verbatim* Latin translation of a passage found in the two manuscripts of Hagin's French translations of Ibn Ezra's astrological writings. This interpolation demonstrates without a shadow of doubt that Pietro d'Abano used a manuscript of Hagin's French translations of Ibn Ezra's astrological writings.[73] (5) *Liber de electionibus*, extant in at least nine manuscripts and one print edition, is a full Latin translation of *Mivḥarim* II. There is solid evidence that Pietro d'Abano used Hagin's French translation of *Mivḥarim* II for his own Latin translation.[74] (6) *Liber de luminaribus* (henceforth, *De luminaribus*), extant in at least nine manuscripts and one print edition, is a complete Latin translation of Ibn Ezra's *Me'orot*. There is evidence showing that Pietro d'Abano, Henry Bate, and Pierre de Limoges employed the same source text for their Latin translations of *Me'orot*.[75] (7) *Tractatus particulares*, a four-part work assigned to Ibn Ezra. A critical edition, English translation, and commentary on this work are included in the present volume.

Arnoul de Quincampoix (d. before 1136), the court physician to Philip IV the Fair (r. 1285–1314), was responsible for three Latin translations of works by Ibn Ezra. They are preserved in a single manuscript, Ghent, MS Univ. 5 (416), copied in the fifteenth century, which contains four items related to Ibn Ezra's astrological writings: (1) a prologue by Arnoul, in which he presents his modus operandi in his translations of Ibn Ezra's astrological writings;[76] (2) *Liber de questionibus*, Arnoul's translation of *She'elot* II;[77] (3) *Liber de electionibus*, his translation of *Mivḥarim* II;[78] and (4) *Liber de inventione occultorum*, his translation of three parts of the *Tractatus particulares*.[79] The last of these is studied in the current volume.

There are at least twelve more anonymous Latin translations of astrological treatises by Ibn Ezra, as follows:

72 Ibid., 48–57.
73 Ibid., 57–61.
74 Ibid., 61–66.
75 Ibid., 66–70.
76 Ghent, MS Univ. 5 (416), fols. 84v–85r.
77 Ibid., fols. 85r–91v.
78 Ibid., fols. 91v–96r.
79 Ibid., fols. 96v–103r.

(1) *Moladot* II: In nomine illius qui scit res futuras incipiam librum nativitatum. Dicit Abraham additor: Oportet me loqui secundum vias communes. Erfurt, UFB, Amplon. O.89, fols. 43r–68v; Vienna, ÖNB, Cod. 5442, fols. 203va–217vb. This translation, which has no Hebrew source text, appears with English translation and commentary in volume six of this series.

(2) *Mivḥarim* I: Liber electionum Abenesra Israelita. Priusquam loquar de elecionibus, dicam tibi regulam universalem (cf. *Mivḥarim* I, § 1:1, 46–47). Oxford, Bodleian, Canon. Misc. 109, fols. 160r–180v.

(3) *Mivḥarim* II (a): Incipit alius liber electionum ab Abraham Avenezre bonus. Sapientes legis sustinent quod homo habet posse faciendi bonum et malum (cf. *Mivḥarim* II, § 1:1, 142–143). Erfurt, UFB, Amplon. O.89, fols. 46v–52v; Vienna, ÖNB, Cod. 5442, fols. 198v–203v; Darmstadt, Hessische Landes- und Hochschulbibliothek, MS 739, fols. 183vb–184va.

(4) *Mivḥarim* II (b): Hic incipiunt electiones Abraham. Sapientes legis examinaverunt quod homo de libero arbitrio potest facere bonum et malum (cf. *Mivḥarim* II, § 1:1, 142–143). Oxford, Bodleian, MS Digby 212, fols. 64v–67v; Oxford, Bodleian, MS Auct. F.5.29, fols. 105v–111v; London, British Library, MS Royal 12.C.XVIII, fols. 26rb–30va.

(5) *Mivḥarim* III: Abraham additor. Incipiam librum electionum. Communes sunt semper gradatim succedentes et scientia eorum est fidelis. Erfurt, UFB, Amplon. O.89, fols. 39b–46b; Vienna, ÖNB, Cod. 5442, fols. 192b–198b. This translation, which has no Hebrew source text, appears with English translation and commentary in the present volume.

(6) *She'elot* I: Liber quaestionum Abraham Aben Esra Israelita. In nomine Dei qui facit magnalia incipiam librum quaestionum. Sapientum astronomorum diversa sententia est (cf. *She'elot* I, § 1:1, 240–241). Oxford, Bodleian, Canon. Misc. 109, fols. 110r–143v.

(7) *She'elot* II (a): Incipit liber de interrogationibus ab alio editus. Capita sapientum signorum fuerunt .2. Doroneus et Tpholomeus et ambo fuerunt reges (cf. *She'elot* II, § 1:1, 348–349). Erfurt, UFB, Amplon. O.89, fols. 30r–39v; Vienna, ÖNB, Cod. 5442, fols. 186r–192v.

(8) *She'elot* II (b): Incipit liber questionum Abraham et cetera. Et superbis et principalibus sapientibus signorum et planetarum sunt duo, unus Tholomeus et alter Duronius et ambo fuerunt reges (cf. *She'elot* II, § 1:1, 348–349). Oxford, Bodleian, MS Digby 212, fols. 67v–71v; London, British Library, MS Sloane 312, fols. 1r–8v; London, British Library, MS Sloane 332, fols. 71v–72r.

(9) *She'elot* III: In nomine illius qui scit abscondita et aperta, incipiam librum interrogationum. Et diviserunt se sapientes iudiciorum signorum in .2. societates. Erfurt, UFB, Amplon. O.89, fols. 19v–30r and Vienna, ÖNB, Cod. 5442, fols. 180r–186r. This translation, which has no Hebrew source text, appears with English translation and commentary in the present volume.
(10) *Mishpeṭei ha-mazzalot* (section): Principia domorum possunt esse quilibet punctus circuli signorum sive de die sive de nocte et partitur circulus signorum super .4. puncta (cf. *Mishpeṭei ha-mazzalot* § 12:1, 498–499). Erfurt, UFB, Amplon. O.89, fols. 5r–19v.
(11) *Me'orot*: Liber luminarium Aben Esra Israelita. Luminaria duo vis majoris sunt vi aliquid stella, eo quod sol terra propior sit (cf. *Me'orot* § 1:3, 452–453). Oxford, Bodleian, Canon. Misc. 109, fols. 144r–159r.
(12) *Tequfah*: Nunc incipit liber suus de revolutionibus. In nomine illius cuius nomine est admirabile incipiam librum revolutionum. Cum Sol revertit ad gradus et ad minutum in quibus fuerit in nativitate (*Tequfah*, § 1:1, 372–373). Erfurt, UFB, Amplon. O.89, fols. 69r–72v; Vienna, ÖNB, Cod. 5442, fols. 218ra–220vb.

Liber Electionum, *Liber Interrogationum*, and *Tractatus Particulares*

Horoscopic astrology, invented in Babylonia, was transmitted to Hellenistic Egypt in the late second or early first century BCE. Over the next few hundred years this art was systematized in Greek science and subsequently transferred to the Arabic, Hebrew, and Latin civilizations, where it was gradually elaborated and refined. The main tool used by astrologers to make predictions about human beings and nature is the horoscope, a diagram of the heavens showing the relative positions of the planets with respect to the horoscopic places, which were taken to govern the main aspects of human life. The word horoscope is derived from the Greek ὥρα, meaning "time" or "hour." It is no wonder, then, that the "time" for which the horoscope is cast is not only the first and most important thing the astrologer must know before casting the horoscope,[80] but also the fundamental parameter that distinguishes the various branches of astrology.

[80] The zodiac is the band of fixed stars through which the seven planets move and which can be seen at any given moment as a wheel constantly moving with the daily motion and rising above the eastern horizon. For horoscopic astrology, the rising degree of the zodiac at the moment the horoscope is cast plays the crucial role of the starting point from which the

In the doctrine of elections, which aims to choose the most auspicious moment for performing some action, the time is chosen because it corresponds to a specific astral configuration that the astrologer deems be propitious for beginning the undertaking in question. In the doctrine of interrogations, which deals with replying to questions addressed to the astrologer, the horoscope is cast at the time when the querent poses the question. For the doctrine of nativities, concerned with making predictions about the fate of individuals, the horoscope should be cast at the precise instant of birth. In historical astrology, the time of the horoscope corresponds to specific astronomical events, such as the moment when the Sun enters Aries, which evokes the creation of the world, or the moment of the conjunction of Saturn and Jupiter.

This volume, the seventh installment of Ibn Ezra's complete works on astrology, offers the first critical edition of three Latin texts, accompanied by an English translation, a commentary, and a preliminary study: *Liber electionum* (henceforth *Electiones*), *Liber interrogationum* (henceforth *Interrogationes*), and *Tractatus particulares*. They were selected for this volume for three main reasons. First, the allocation of works among the volumes of this series was thematic, by astrological genre, and the three works in the current volume address the doctrine of elections and the doctrine of interrogations. Second, although these three works were written by Abraham Ibn Ezra or attributed to him, no complete Hebrew counterpart of them survives, so that their study affords us a golden opportunity to shed light on a significant missing link in our knowledge of Ibn Ezra's astrological oeuvre. Third, *Interrogationes* and *Tractatus particulares* include alternative Latin translations of some parts of the lost *She'elot* III,

Despite these common features, in the present volume these three works are studied in two separate groups—*Electiones* and *Interrogationes*, on the one hand, and *Tractatus particulares*, on the other—for several reasons. *Electiones* and *Interrogationes* are undoubtedly anonymous Latin translations of Ibn Ezra's *Mivḥarim* III and *She'elot* III, they are basically similar in structure to Ibn Ezra's other works on elections and interrogations, they are preserved in the same two manuscripts, and, as will be shown, they were rendered into Latin by the same translator. On the other hand, even though the incipits and explicits of the four parts of *Tractatus particulares* repeatedly claim that it was composed by Ibn Ezra, and "Abraham" is cited

zodiac is divided into the twelve horoscopic places. These twelve were taken to govern the main aspects of human life: the first horoscopic place was taken to signify life; the second, wealth; the third, brothers; the fourth, the father; the fifth, sons; and so on.

in the body of the text as the originator of some ideas, neither the quadripartite structure nor the bulk of the text has a counterpart in Ibn Ezra's Hebrew astrological corpus. In addition, two different translations of *Tractatus particulares* survive. One of them, by Pietro d'Abano, was transmitted in seventeen manuscripts and one print edition; the other, by Arnoul de Quincampoix, is extant in only one manuscript.

Hence I begin here with a preliminary study of the main features of *Electiones* and *Interrogationes*, continue with an attempt to explain what *Tractatus particulares* is and identify the Hebrew source texts behind its four parts, and end with the presentation of the manuscripts used for the editions of the three texts as well as of the editorial and translation principles employed in this volume.

I. *LIBER ELECTIONUM* AND *LIBER INTERROGATIONUM*

Earlier Research on *Liber Electionum* and *Liber Interrogationum*

In 1944, Lynn Thorndike published a landmark article that included a list of all the Latin translations known to him of astrological treatises by *Abraham Avenezra* (the Latinized form of Abraham Ibn Ezra).[81] He accompanied the Latin translations with a list of the manuscripts of which he was aware, sorted by their incipits and explicits. Six items in Thorndike's article deal with elections.[82] One of them, assigned to an otherwise unknown *Abraham Additor*,[83] is identical with our *Electiones*, which Thorndike found in the same two manuscripts used for the edition presented in the current volume.[84] Four items in Thorndike's article are on interrogations.[85] One of them is identical with our *Interrogationes*, which Thorndike found in the same two manuscripts used for the edition presented in the current volume.[86]

---

[81] Thorndike 1944, 293–302.
[82] Ibid., 299.
[83] For the identity of *Abraham additor*, see below, p. 22.
[84] Erfurt, Universitäts- und Forschungsbibliothek, Amplon. O.89, fols. 39v–46v; Vienna, Österreichische Nationalbibliothek, Cod. 5442, fols. fols. 192v–198v. These two manuscripts are used for the edition of *Electiones* in this volume.
[85] Thorndike 1944, 298–299.
[86] Amplon. O.89, fols. 19v–30r; ÖNB, Cod. 5442, fols. 180r–186r.

A major shortcoming of Thorndike's list is his failure to take account of previous studies on Ibn Ezra's astrological work (particularly those by Moritz Steinschneider and Raphael Levy),[87] and the consequent failure to distinguish among the different versions of Ibn Ezra's astrological texts, in general, and of *Sefer ha-Mivḥarim* and *Sefer ha-She'elot*, in particular.[88] This deficiency was remedied by Renate Smithuis, who put *Electiones* and *Interrogationes* into their proper setting in Ibn Ezra's astrological corpus, in general, and vis-à-vis the other versions of *Sefer ha-Mivḥarim* and *Sefer ha-She'elot*, in particular. Smithuis also provided evidence that *Electiones* and *Interrogationes* were translated into Latin via a French intermediary.[89]

That *Electiones* and *Interrogationes* are genuine Latin translations of Hebrew treatises on elections and interrogations written by Ibn Ezra was demonstrated without a shadow of doubt by the recent discovery in the Archivio di Stato, Modena, as part of the research on the "Italian Geniza,"[90] of a parchment bifolium that contains two Hebrew fragments on elections and interrogations. Under close scrutiny, the right side of the verso and the left side of the recto of this bifolium turned out to hold a fragment of the original *Mivḥarim* III; and the left side of the verso and the right side of the recto, a fragment of the original *She'elot* III.[91] Strikingly, these two Hebrew fragments have a perfect Latin counterpart in two corresponding fragments of *Electiones* and *Interrogationes*.[92] Note that in the fragment of *She'elot* III we read, ואני אברהם ניסיתי פעמי' ("I, Abraham, have tested ⟨many⟩ times"), which has its Latin equivalent in *ego Abraham temptavi multotiens*. Moreover, the author of both fragments identifies himself as the author of several astrological treatises that were written by Abraham Ibn Ezra: the fragment of *Mivḥarim* III refers in the past tense to *Sefer Reshit ḥokhmah* and to *Sefer Mishpeṭei ha-ʿOlam*, an alternative name for *Sefer ha-ʿOlam*; the fragment of *She'elot* III refers in the past tense to *Sefer Reshit ḥokhmah* and to *Sefer ha-Me'orot*.

---

[87] For Steinschneider's lists of Ibn Ezra's astrological writings, see Steinschneider 1870, 339–346; Steinschneider 1880, 124–128; and particularly Steinschneider 1897, 136–150. See also Levy 1927, 11–57.

[88] This omission was already pointed out in Birkenmajer 1950, n. 5. Birkenmajer remarked that even Abraham Ibn Ezra's name was not mentioned in Thorndike's article.

[89] Smithuis 2004, 123–127; Smithuis 2004: 266–269.

[90] In Italy, thousands of parchment folios and bifolia from medieval Hebrew manuscripts ended up in various archives and libraries, where they were reused, especially during the sixteenth and seventeenth centuries, as book bindings or to cover archival volumes and registers. Known as the "Italian Geniza," this scattered collection has received extensive research and cataloguing attention over the last three decades.

[91] See Sela and Smithuis 2009, 225–240.

[92] See Modena fragments below, on pp. 483–496.

Authorship, Links with Ibn Ezra's Work, and the Dates of Composition of *Liber Electionum* and *Liber Interrogationum*

Abraham Ibn Ezra's authorship of the Hebrew source text behind *Electiones* and *Interrogationes* is unmistakable, for several reasons. First, in the introduction to *Electiones* we read *Ego, Abraham additor, dico* ...,[93] ("I Abraham, the author, say ..."), and *Abraham additor* is presented as the author of *Electiones* before the incipit of the two surviving manuscripts.[94] *Abraham additor* represents אברהם המחבר ("Abraham, the author"), which is one of the names Ibn Ezra uses for himself in his monographs and biblical commentaries, usually in their prefaces.[95] The same applies more strongly to *Interrogationes*. Its author introduces himself as *Ego Abraham, qui addo hunc librum*[96] ("I Abraham, who authored this book"), and as *Ego, Abraham Addens*[97] ("I Abraham, the author"). Here *addens* is an alternative form of *additor*, both meaning "author"; the translator coined the verb *addere* (i.e., authoring a book) from the participle *addens* or the noun *additor*. Further, we find *Dicit Abraham additor*[98] twice and *Dicit Abraham*, tout court, five times.[99]

Second, Abraham Ibn Ezra's authorship of the Hebrew source texts behind *Electiones* and *Interrogationes* is supported by the two fragments from the lost *Mivḥarim* III and *She'elot* III that have been recently identified in a parchment bifolium in the Archivio di Stato, Modena. Although the fragments are untitled, it is certain that they are parts of the lost *Mivḥarim* III and *She'elot* III: (1) both have perfect Latin replicas in corresponding fragments of *Electiones* and *Interrogationes*;[100] (2) both include cross-references to several items in Ibn Ezra's astrological corpus;[101] (3) in one of

[93] *El*, I 3:1. For the method of reference used in this volume to specific parts of *Electiones*, see below, "Editorial and Translation Principles," p. 88.

[94] *El*, I 1:1.

[95] See note on *El*, I 1:1.

[96] *Int*, I 3:1. For the method of reference used in this volume to specific parts of *Interrogationes*, see below, "Editorial and Translation Principles," p. 88.

[97] *Int*, II i 2:1.

[98] *Int*, II i 9:1 and II xii 2:1.

[99] *Int*, II i 5:1, II i 10:1,2; II vi 1:5; II xii 11:1.

[100] See "The Modena Fragments of *Mivḥarim* III and *She'elot* III," on pp. 483–496

[101] For cross-references from the Modena fragment of *Mivḥarim* III, see: *Mivḥarim* III, II vii 6:3, 487 (*Reshit ḥokhmah*) and *Mivḥarim* III, II vii 6:4, 487 (*Sefer ha-'Olam*); for cross-references from the Modena fragment of *She'elot* III, see: *She'elot* III, II vi 1:3, 491 (*Reshit ḥokhmah*) and *Mivḥarim* III, II vi 2:7, 492–493 (Sefer *ha-Me'orot*).

them the author refers to himself as *Abraham*;[102] and (4) they use Ibn Ezra's typical Hebrew astrological terminology.[103]

Third, Ibn Ezra's authorship of the Hebrew source text behind *Electiones* and *Interrogationes* is further confirmed by the fact that *Electiones* and *Interrogationes* (1) are replete with Hebraisms and literal renderings of Ibn Ezra's Hebrew neologisms, as shown in two lists[104] and in the notes to the translations of *Electiones* and *Interrogationes*; (b) rely on the same authorities employed by Ibn Ezra in his Hebrew work, such as Māshā'allāh, Abū Maʿshar, Ptolemy and King Ptolemy, Dorotheus and King Dorotheus, Enoch and King Enoch, Sahl, the scientists of India, and the Ancients;[105] (c) contain multiple cross-references to works by Ibn Ezra: *Electiones* contains a cross-reference to *Moladot* II,[106] three cross-references to *Sefer ha-ʿOlam*,[107] and a cross-reference to *Reshit ḥokhmah*;[108] *Interrogationes* includes two cross-references to *Moladot* II,[109] four cross-references to *Reshit ḥokhmah*,[110] and one to *Sefer ha-Me'orot*.[111]

Fourth, *Electiones* and *Interrogationes* exhibit striking terminological links with each other and with Ibn Ezra's *Mishpeṭei ha-mazzalot*, *Moladot* II, and *Tequfah*, as follow: (1) *signa veridica*, lit. "truthful signs," a calque of מזלות נאמנים, to denote the fixed signs;[112] (2) *altitudo*, lit. "highness," a calque of גבהות, to denote the astrological concept of exaltation;[113] (3) *pars gratie*, lit. "part of grace," a calque of s מנת החן, to denote the lot of Fortune;[114] and (4) *domus belli sui*, lit. "its house of war," a calque of בית מלחמתו, to denote the house of detriment.[115]

The date of composition of *Electiones* follows from its reminder to readers that they not fail to consult the chapter on elections incorporated (in the past tense) after the account of the twelve horoscopic places in a cer-

---

102 See *She'elot* III, II vi 1:5, 491.

103 For example, for the use of משרת (*lit.* "servant" but with the sense of "planet"; see note on *Int*, II i 1:5), Ibn Ezra's most distinctive neologism, see the Modena fragment, *Mivḥarim* III, II vii 5:5, 486–487, and *She'elot* III, II vi 1:7, 491.

104 See lists on pp. 597–600.

105 See list of authorities in *Electiones* and *Interrogationes*, on pp. 588–596.

106 See *El*, I 7:3 and note.

107 See *El*, II vi 1:5, II vi 2:1, II vii 6:5 and notes.

108 See *El*, II vii 6:3 and note.

109 See *Int*, II i 10:2 and II i 15:1, and notes.

110 See *Int*, I 4:2, II i 11:3, II ii 1:3, and II vi 1:3, and notes.

111 See *Int*, II vi 2:7 and note.

112 See *El*, II viii 1:5 and note, and *Int*, II i 1:3 and note.

113 See *El*, II ii 2:2 and note.

114 See *Int*, II i 9:1 and note.

115 See *Int*, II vii 2:8, and note.

tain *Liber nativitatum*.[116] There is no such chapter in *Moladot*, Ibn Ezra's only extant Hebrew treatise Ezra on nativities. But there is an entire section on elections after the chapter on the twelve horoscopic places in *Liber nativitatum*, the Latin translation of the lost *Moladot* II, which appeared in volume six of this series.[117] A scrutiny of *Liber nativitatum* reveals that it was written in 1158, the year when one of the two star lists included in it was drawn up.[118] Hence, *Electiones* was certainly written in 1158 or after.

As already noted, Abraham Ibn Ezra was first brought to the knowledge of the Latin West by Henry Bate (1246–1310). A surprising aspect of Bate's involvement with Ibn Ezra is that he assigns astrological treatises we now know to have been written by or that were attributed to Abraham Ibn Ezra to three different authors. All three are *Abraham*, but they have distinguishing cognomens.[119] One of them is *Abraham Princeps*, Abraham the Prince,[120] to whom Bate assigns three treatises.[121] Another is a reference in *Nativitas*, an astrological autobiography composed by Bate in 1280,[122] to a certain *Tractatus de electionibus*, to the *trutina Hermetis* or "balance of Hermes," a procedure used in the doctrine of nativities to determine the ascendant of the natal horoscope on the basis of the period of pregnancy when the time of birth is not known (the usual situation).[123] *Mivḥarim* I and *Mivḥarim* II have nothing to say about the *trutina Hermetis*, but *Electiones* allots the bulk of the chapter on the fifth horoscopic place to a detailed account of it (without using this name). It follows that in 1280 Bate was aware of the existence of *Mivḥarim* III, the Hebrew source text of *Electiones*, which he designated *Tractatus de electionibus*.

The date of composition of *Interrogationes*, too, can be deduced from the fact that this work includes a passage in which *Abraham* says that, according to what is written in the chapter on the sixth horoscopic place of certain *Liber nativitatum*, the tenth horoscopic place signifies the mast of a ship.[124] There is no such reference in *Moladot*, Ibn Ezra's only extant Hebrew

116 *El*, I 7:3 and note.

117 The text of this chapter on elections is found in Appendix 12, "The section on elections at the end of *Nativitates*," below, on pp. 528–530.

118 See *Nativitates*, II i 7:1, 110–111 and Sela 2019, 27, 43.

119 Sela 2017a, 163–186.

120 *Abraham Princeps*, Abraham the Prince, is a confusion with Abraham Bar Ḥiyya (ca. 1065–ca. 1136). Bar Ḥiyya, who vanished from the scene just before Abraham Ibn Ezra began his literary career, was known to medieval Jewish society as *Abraham ha-Naśi'*, Abraham the Prince.

121 One is *Mishpeṭei ha-mazzalot*, the second is the lost *Moladot* II. See Sela 2017a, 175–180.

122 In which Bate incorporated at least 130 quotations from or references to passages from twelve astrological treatises written by or attributed to Abraham Ibn Ezra.

123 See *Nativitas*, ed. Steel et al. (2018), lines 106–117.

124 See *Int*, II i 10:2, and note.

work on nativities. However, according to the chapter on the sixth horoscopic place in *Liber nativitatum*, the Latin translation of the lost *Moladot* II, if Saturn is in the tenth place there will be panic at sea because something will happen to the ship's mast.[125] Because *Liber nativitatum*, as shown above, was composed in 1158, it is certain that *Interrogationes* (like *Electiones*) was composed after that date. There is solid evidence that *Mishpeṭei ha-mazzalot* and *Tequfah*, which display striking terminological links with *Liber nativitatum*, *Electiones*, and *Interrogationes*, were also composed around or after 1158, in the last phase of Ibn Ezra's career, when he was living near Rouen or in England.[126]

Ibn Ezra's Approach to Elections in *Liber Electionum*

In contrast to the main text of his astrological writings, which were designed as textbooks to educate Hebrew readers in standard astrological knowledge, most of the introductions to these works present creative and idiosyncratic ideas. *Electiones* starts with a stunning statement disparaging the doctrine of elections: whereas astrological judgments about collectives are trustworthy, the elections of individuals are unstable and not to be relied on, because individuals are very different and exercise their will differently.[127] The contrast between astrological judgments about collectives and those about individuals, and particularly the statement that the former take precedence over the latter, is an idea that goes back to Ptolemy's *Tetrabiblos*.[128] Ibn Ezra applies it to several branches of astrology, particularly the doctrine of nativities.[129] *Electiones* is the only work in Ibn Ezra's astrological corpus where this idea is applied to the doctrine of elections.[130]

Next, by quoting suitable passages from authoritative Jewish sources, *Electiones* makes the case for a strong version of astral determinism. First *Electiones* paraphrases Psalms 148:6, to claim that "the stars cannot change

[125] See Elections in *Nativitates*, II vi 8:5, 136–137 (quoted in App. 5, Q. 28, 473).
[126] See Sela 2017, 28–29; Sela 2013, 74–75.
[127] See *El*, I 1:2 and note.
[128] See *Tetrabiblos*, ed. Robbins (1980), II:1, 117–119; quoted in App. 1, Q. 4, 393.
[129] Regarding the doctrine of nativities, see (1) the preface of *Moladot* (I 1:2; 84–85; quoted in App. 1, Q. 1, § 1:2, 391), where this principle is the leitmotif of the entire preface (*Moladot*, I 2:1–4 through I 9:1–5, 84–89); (2) Elections in *Nativitates*, I iii:1, 82–83; quoted in App. 1, Q. 2, § 1:1, 392; and (3) *Nativitates*, I vi2:1, 92–93; quoted in App. 1, Q. 2, § 2:1, 392. Regarding the astrological theory of the critical days, see *Me'orot*, § 9:2–4, 460–461; quoted in App. 1, Q. 3, 392.
[130] Cf. *Mivḥarim* I, § 1:1–4 through § 8:1–5, 46–51; *Mivḥarim* II, § 1:1–6 through § 6:1–19, 142–149.

their course or their nature, neither in their elections nor in their exercise of will."[131] Then *Electiones* quotes Ecclesiastes 3:14, according to which nothing can be added or taken from God's works, to state that these divine decrees were decreed about every person at the moment of conception and birth.[132] Finally, *Electiones* quotes the Babylonian Talmud, according to which "length of life, children, and sustenance depend not on merit but rather on *mazzal*."[133] This passage is frequently quoted in medieval Hebrew literature to highlight that even the most authoritative Jewish text endorses astrology or astral determinism. Two instances close to Ibn Ezra's times are in the fifth chapter of *Megillat ha-Megalleh* (Scroll of the Revealer), where Abraham Bar Ḥiyya (ca. 1065–ca. 1136) included a Jewish and universal astrological history,[134] and the queries on astrology sent to Maimonides in Egypt at the end of the twelfth century, which incorporate *verbatim* quotations from *Moladot*.[135]

Without a pause, as if it were the natural consequence of endorsing astral determinism, *Electiones* next reports that a group of astrologers say that "elections are false, deceiving, and worthless."[136] Such a negative attitude towards elections cannot be found in the introductions to *Mivḥarim* I and *Mivḥarim* II, although some doubts about their effectiveness are expressed there. But why should the presentation of astral determinism lead to such a harsh attack on the doctrine of elections? Ever since Antiquity, the doctrine of nativities, in which the newborn's fate is sealed at the time of birth by the movements and changes in the heavens, has been seen as the nucleus of astrology and, even more so, identified with astral determinism, more than any other branch of astrology.[137] Hence, just as the opponents of horoscopic astrology usually aimed their shafts at the doctrine of nativities, so sympathizers with astrology considered the doctrine of elections to be incompatible with the doctrine of nativities. Surely it is superfluous to

---

131 See *El*, I 1:3 and note.

132 See *El*, I 1:4–5 and note.

133 The passage is from *Mo'ed Qaṭan* 28a. See *El*, I 1:6 and note.
See *El*, I 1:4–5 and note.

134 See *Megillat ha-Megalleh*, ed. Poznanski (1924), V, 111, lines 15–20.

135 See *Queries on Astrology*, ed. Sela (2004), § 6, 104–105.

136 *El*, I 2:1.

137 One remarkable case, contemporary with the earlier stages of the development of horoscopic astrology and echoing down through the centuries in the work of both its opponents and advocates, is the attack on astrology unleashed by Cicero (106–43 BCE) in his *De divinatione*. Cicero presumes there a "hard version" of nativities, in which the fate of the newborn is totally sealed at the time of birth by the movements and changes in the heavens. See *De divinatione*, ed. Falconer (1923), XLIII:89, 470–473; for an analysis of Cicero's attack on astrology, see Long 1982, pp. 168–178.

cast an electional horoscope to choose the most auspicious moment for performing specific actions if their outcome can be or has been predicted by the natal horoscope? It is inherently irreconcilable with the core of horoscopic astrology to postulate that an electional horoscope can modify or override the predictions of a natal horoscope?

It comes as no surprise, then, that *Electiones* makes Ptolemy say that the astrologer should not make an election for someone who does not know his nativity, because the election may be incompatible with the indications of the nativity.[138] Moreover, "Abraham," the author of *Electiones*, adds a divine dimension to the decrees of the natal horoscope, namely, that elections do not have the power to significantly alter the ways of God in natural matters.[139] To press home the latter point, *Electiones* offers several examples to show that an election that fails to take account of the nativity will redound to the querent's harm[140] and proclaims that it is futile to make an election against what has been decreed by the querent's nativity.[141]

Rather unexpectedly, *Electiones* then turns to a defense of elections. Because electional astrology is focused on choosing the best time to begin an activity, it highlights the possibility that human beings can change their own destiny and thereby calls attention to the tension between free will and astral determinism. In *Yesod Mora'* (The Fundament of Awe), the last and most brilliant of his monographs, written in England in 1161, Ibn Ezra expresses the belief that human beings can exercise free will because their rational soul has the capacity to overcome the other components of the tripartite human soul (the vegetative or appetitive soul; the animal or locomotive soul; and the wise or rational soul).[142] In the opening section of the introduction to *Mivḥarim* II, Ibn Ezra cites a talmudic passage and Deuteronomy 30:15 to make the case for free will (the ability to choose between good and evil).[143] *Electiones* refers to the same biblical verse, and for the same purpose.[144]

But at this point *Electiones* continues the defense of elections by presenting a new idea: "It is right that all the decrees of the stars be according to the disposition of the receiver of astrological influence, and therefore the person who makes an election can augment or reduce what is signified

138 See *El*, I 2:4 and note.
139 See *El*, I 3:1 and note.
140 *El*, I 2:2; I 3:2; I 3:3.
141 *El*, I 2:3; I 2:5; I 3:5.
142 See *Yesod Mora'*, ed. Simon (2007), VII, 140–145.
143 See *Mivḥarim* II, § 1:1, 142–143 (quoted in App. 1, Q. 6, 1–3, 393), and notes.
144 See *El*, I 4:1–2 and note.

by the stars."[145] The idea that the "disposition of the receiver of astrological influence" makes it possible to evade the decrees of the stars, through the doctrine of elections, is not found in either of the two extant versions of *Sefer ha-Mivḥarim* or elsewhere in Ibn Ezra's astrological corpus. However, the idea that the tension between astral determinism and free will can be resolved by invoking the "disposition of the receiver of astrological influence" is frequent in his theological essays and biblical commentaries.[146] The statement here that "the person who makes an election can augment or reduce what is signified by the stars" highlights the idea that the doctrine of elections allows only a partial escape from the decrees of the stars. The same idea occurs in *Mivḥarim* I and *Mivḥarim* II, where, however, it is predicated on the notion that man has been endowed with a "supernal soul," the highest component of the tripartite soul.[147] In other parts of his astrological corpus, though, Ibn Ezra propounds total liberation from the decrees of the stars by communion of the supernal soul with God.[148]

All in all, the introductions to *Mivḥarim* I or *Mivḥarim* II, on the one hand, and to *Electiones*, on the other, are rather different. After presenting the case for free will and the need to combine elections with nativities, the bulk of the introductions to *Mivḥarim* I and *Mivḥarim* II is devoted to the presentation of two methods for elections: one assuming that the querent's nativity is known, which makes key elements of the electional horoscope depend on the natal horoscope; the other if the querent's nativity is not known, and accordingly determining the position and features of the planet that conforms to the querent's wishes or the matter asked about.[149] By

---

145 See *El*, I 4:3 and note. Note here the stark contrast between the statement that "the person who makes an election can augment or reduce what is signified by the stars," presented in the framework of a defense of elections, and Ecclesiastes 3:14, quoted at the beginning of the introduction to *Electiones* (I 1:4), in the framework of an attack on elections: "Whatever God has brought to pass will recur evermore: *Nothing can be added to it and nothing taken from it.*"

146 See the following works: (1) *Yesod Mora'*, ed. Simon (2007), VII, 140–145; quoted in App. 1, Q. 13, 393. (2) The introduction to Ibn Ezra's commentary on Ecclesiastes, the first biblical commentary written by Ibn Ezra in Rome after he left Muslim Spain; quoted in App. 1, Q. 16, 396. (3) The exegetical excursus in Ibn Ezra's long commentary on Exodus 33:21; quoted in App. 1, Q. 17, 396–397. (4) *Me'orot* § 6:2, 458–459; quoted in App. 1, Q. 18, 397.

147 See *Mivḥarim* I, § 1:1, 46–47 (quoted in App. 1, Q. 15, 1, 396); and *Mivḥarim* II, § 1:3, 142–143 (quoted in App. 1, Q. 6, 3, 393–394).

148 See *Moladot*, I 9:1–5, 88–89 (quoted in App. 1, Q. 1, § 3:4–5, 391–392); *Reshit ḥokhmah* § 1:1–2, 48–49.

149 See *Mivḥarim* I, § 1:4, 46–47 (quoted in App. 1, Q. 15, 4, 396) through *Mivḥarim* I, § 5:1–2, 48–49; and *Mivḥarim* II, § 1:6, 142–143 (quoted in App. 1, Q. 6, 6, 393–394) through *Mivḥarim* II, § 5:1–3, 146–147.

contrast, *Electiones* observes a resounding silence about these two methods and instead gives some examples bearing on the cases when the querent's natal horoscope is or is not known.[150]

IBN EZRA'S APPROACH TO INTERROGATIONS IN *LIBER INTERROGATIONUM*

As is his wont, Ibn Ezra transforms the presentation of certain topic into a debate among schools and scientists of different eras, nations, and religions.[151] A telling example is the dispute among astrologers about the validity of the doctrine of interrogations in the introductions to *Interrogationes*, *She'elot* I, and *She'elot* II. The introduction to *Interrogationes* is the shortest, because it is strictly limited to the presentation of the dispute among astrologers and Ibn Ezra's opinion about the doctrine of interrogation. All three present two groups of astrologers, one endorsing interrogations, the other rejecting them. For this approach Ibn Ezra seems to have been inspired by the introduction to the section on interrogations in Ibn abī l-Rijāl's *Kitāb al-Bāriʿ*.[152]

Interrogationes speaks of two groups of *sapientes iudiciorum signorum* ("scholars in the judgments of the signs"); in contrast to *She'elot* I and *She'elot* II, it provides long lists of names: ten astrologers in the first group, among them King Dorotheus; six astrologers in the second group, among them King Enoch and King Ptolemy. Some of these astrologers are Arabs, other are identified as Indian, Persians, and Jews; but *Interrogationes* says that all were great scholars and that their books were found written in the Arabic language.[153] In the same breath, *Interrogationes* supplies extensive lists of the astrological doctrines endorsed by each of the two groups. Most of these doctrines are not directly related to interrogations.[154] By contrast, *She'elot* II reduces the clash to an argument between two leading astrologers who are also kings: King Dorotheus and King Ptolemy.[155] Finally, *She'elot* I refers to "two great schools of thought," and mentions Dorotheus, the scientists of India, the scientists of Persia, the scientists of Egypt, and

150 See *El*, I 5:1–5 through I 7:1–2 and notes.

151 See, for example, the discussion about the value of the Sun's declination in *ʿOlam* I, § 14:1–9, 60–61, and the discussion about the length of the solar year in *Moladot*, IV 1:1–9, 182–185.

152 See *De iudiciis astrorum*, ed. Petri (1551), I:5, 16b, quoted in App 2, Q. 3, 400–401.

153 *Int*, I 1:2; I 1:7–8; I 2:1.

154 *Int*, I 1:3 and I 2:2.

155 See *She'elot* I, § 1:1, 348–349 and notes.

his astrologers contemporary with Ibn Ezra, on the one side, and Enoch, Ptolemy, and many of the Ancients, on the other.[156]

She'elot I is the only member of this group that offers a full account of the rationale behind the positions of the "two great schools of thought": Both parties concur that change in the sublunary domain is caused by the motions of the bodies in the supralunar domain, such that scrutinizing them gives an indication about mundane and individual affairs, as may be learned by means of the doctrines of historical astrology and nativities.[157] The bone of contention between them is whether the human soul is also susceptible to this influence. But why should such a question be relevant for the validity of the doctrine of interrogations? The answer is that this doctrine presupposes that astral configurations produce a question in human minds that is analogous to the celestial configuration, and that the astrologer may discover the querent's thoughts and interrogations by studying the celestial configuration.[158]

The school of Dorotheus, which approves of the doctrine of interrogations, maintains that because the stars cause the natural make-up of the body and because thoughts change in accordance with the changes in the physical nature of the body, the astrologer can determine thoughts and interrogations by knowing the motions of the stars.[159] On the other hand, Ptolemy, who does not agree that interrogations are accurate, maintains that the supernal nature of man's soul affords him a measure of protection against the influence of the stars; hence the celestial bodies give no indication about human thoughts or interrogations.[160]

Interrogationes, *She'elot* I, and *She'elot* II convey Ibn Ezra's endorsement of the doctrine of interrogations, but in different degrees. *Interrogationes* provides by far the strongest and most outspoken endorsement. Speaking in the first-person singular, and identifying himself explicitly as the author of the book (*Ego Abraham, qui addo hunc librum*), Ibn Ezra not only expresses agreement with the supporters of interrogations, but also reports that he has tried them many times and found them to be roots and tested (*radices et probate*).[161] But in *Interrogationes* Ibn Ezra is scrupulous about following the rules. His only reservation is that the interrogational horoscope be cast

156 *She'elot* I, § 1:1–2, § 2:1, 240–241 and notes.
157 See *She'elot* I, § 1:2, § 2:2, 240–231; *She'elot* II, § 1:2, 348–349, and notes.
158 *She'elot* I, § 3:4, 240–243, and notes.
159 *She'elot* I, § 2:2–3, 240–241, and notes.
160 *She'elot* I, § 1:2–6, 240–241, and notes.
161 *Int*, I 3:1–2.

exactly when the thought of the question rises in the querent's mind and that the querent be sincere in his question. But if a delay takes place, or if the querent is cheating, the astrologer will make his prediction on the basis of an erroneous celestial configuration.[162] Ibn Ezra no doubt believed that there is a close correspondence between the configuration of the stars at the moment the interrogational horoscope is cast and the querent's thoughts then, and the corresponding prediction that the astrologer can make about them. By contrast, the support in *She'elot* I is conditional and qualified: interrogations are reliable in most cases, but they are not as powerful as nativities.[163] Nowhere in *She'elot* II does Ibn Ezra explicitly support interrogations. The furthest he goes is to express admiration for Māshā'allāh, one of the main proponents of interrogations, and to say that "I too have pursued him and followed in his footsteps."[164]

The bulk of the introductions to *She'elot* I and *She'elot* II discuss how the astrologer can know what the querent is thinking and present general rules for interpreting the interrogational horoscope.[165] A special feature of *Interrogationes* is that the discussion of the general principles for casting the interrogational horoscope take up almost the entire chapter on the first horoscopic place, the longest chapter in that work,[166] while the discussion of how the astrologer can read the querent's thought and make sure that the querent is not pretending or cheating is deferred to its very end, the chapter on the twelfth horoscopic place.[167]

The Organization and Contents of *Liber Electionum* and *Liber Interrogationum*

Electiones and *Interrogationes* are not the same size—6,000 and 8,500 (Latin) words, respectively. The difference between them, though, is close to that between *Mivḥarim* I and *She'elot* I—6,000 and 8,400 (Hebrew) words, respectively; and between *Mivḥarim* II and *She'elot* II—4,500 and 6,700 (Hebrew) words, respectively. Although they deal with different branches of astrology, the organization of *Electiones* and *Interrogationes* is virtually

162 *Int*, I 3:2–4.
163 *She'elot* I, § 3:5, 242–243.
164 *She'elot* II, § 1:4, 348–349.
165 See *She'elot* I, § 4:1–4 through § 11:1–4, 242–247; *She'elot* II, § 2:1–3 through § 10:1–6, 348–357; and notes.
166 *Int*, II i 1:1–5 through II i 14:1–3, and notes.
167 *Int*, II xii 2:1–9, and notes.

identical. After a prefatory canticle or incipit, both works have an introduction on the pros and cons of elections and interrogations. The contents of these introductions were studied above.

The last sentence of each introduction prepares the reader for the next part of the work, announcing that the book is divided into twelve chapters, one for each of the twelve horoscopic places. Here Ibn Ezra seems to emulate the organization of earlier medieval Arabic treatises on elections and interrogations, such as those by Sahl Ibn Bishr al-Yahūdī and ʿAlī ibn abī-l-Rijāl on interrogations and elections, which are also divided into twelve chapters corresponding to the twelve places.[168] While *Electiones* informs about the division into twelve chapters curtly, *Interrogationes* expands on this point and says that this is done "to make it easier for students."[169] Virtually all of Ibn Ezra's works on elections, interrogations, and nativities tell readers that they are divided into twelve chapters, one for each of the twelve horoscopic places;[170] some of them highlight the pedagogical motivation for this organization.[171]

The twelve horoscopic places were taken to govern the main aspects of human life. In brief, the first horoscopic place was taken to signify life; the second, wealth; the third, short journeys; the fourth, landed property, houses, fields, and buildings; the fifth, sons; the sixth, diseases; the seventh, women and wars; the eighth, death and fear; the ninth, long journeys; the tenth, kingship and crafts; the eleventh, love; and the twelfth, captivity and riding animals. Hence, broadly speaking, the topics addressed in each of the chapters into which treatises on the doctrines of elections and interrogations are usually divided correspond to the domain of significations of each of the twelve horoscopic places. This applies, of course, to *Electiones* and *Interrogationes*.

To provide an idea of the contents of the bulk of *Electiones* and *Interrogationes*, tables at the end of this volume display the subject matter of all the elections and interrogations addressed in them.[172] The items in these table are sorted according to their order of appearance in *Electiones* and

---

[168] See Sahl Ibn Bishr's *Book of elections*, Paris, BnF, lat. 16204, 488a–500a; *Book of Interrogations*, Paris, BnF, lat. 16204, 445a–482a; Ibn Abī l-Rijāl, *Kitāb al-Bāriʿ fī aḥkām al-nujūm*, *De iudiciis astrorum*, ed. Petri (1551), 1–113 (Books 1–3, interrogations), 296–356 (Book 7, elections).

[169] *Int*, I 4:2.

[170] See *Mivḥarim* I, § 8:5, 50–51; *El*, I 7:4; *She'elot* I, § 11:4, 246–247; *She'elot* II, § 10:6, 356–357; *Moladot*, II 8:5, 98–99; *Nativitates*, I x 9:1–3, 104–105; *De nativitatibus*, I 22:1, 270–271.

[171] See *She'elot* I, § 11:4, 246–247 and *Moladot*, II 8:5, 98–99.

[172] See Appendix 19, on pp. 601–603, and Appendix 20, on pp. 604–607.

Interrogationes. To highlight the correspondences between *Electiones* and Ibn Ezra's other works on elections, each item in the first table is accompanied by a reference to *Mivḥarim* I, *Mivḥarim* II, and the fourth part of the *Epitome totius astrologiae*, which deals with elections, if any. To show the correspondences between *Interrogationes* and Ibn Ezra's other works on interrogations, each item in the second table is accompanied by a reference to *She'elot* I, *She'elot* II, and to the third part of the *Epitome totius astrologiae*, which deals with interrogations, if any.

The Sources of *Liber Electionum* and *Liber Interrogationum*

It goes without saying that Ibn Ezra, born in Muslim Spain, where he lived until the age of 50, and educated within the orbit of Arabic culture and language, drew his information from Arabic sources. Indeed, Ibn Ezra's astrological treatises are an excellent means for learning about the scientists and scientific texts available in al-Andalus in the twelfth century and earlier.[173] *Electiones* and *Interrogationes* provide a good example: whereas the former includes a fairly long list of names, most of them also mentioned in *Mivḥarim* I and *Mivḥarim* II,[174] the latter has the longest list of astrologers and scientists anywhere in Ibn Ezra's astrological corpus, some of them never or rarely mentioned elsewhere.[175] What follows here is not concerned with rarities but focuses on names or significant sources that are repeatedly mentioned, quoted, or paraphrased in both *Electiones* and *Interrogationes*.

(1) Ptolemy, the scientific authority most often cited in Ibn Ezra's Hebrew oeuvre, is referred to in two different ways: (a) *Baṭalmiyūs*, that is, "Ptolemy" in the Arabic pronunciation; or (b) *King Talmai* or *Talmai*, the post-biblical and talmudic Hebrew equivalent.[176] *Electiones* and *Interrogationes* can now be added to the second category, because both refer to "King Ptolemy."[177] *Electiones* and *Interrogationes* also refer to "Ptolemy" tout court, the former

[173] See tables of authorities and sources in Sela 2013, 498–504; Sela 2011, 543–551; Sela 2010, 319–322; Sela 2007, 353–356, and in the current volume, on pp. 588–596.

[174] This includes Dorotheus, the scientists of India, Ptolemy, Enoch, Māshā'allāh, and the Ancients. See Appendix 16, 588–596; cf. list of authorities in *Mivḥarim* I and *Mivḥarim* II, in Sela 2011, 543–545.

[175] This includes Abū 'Alī Al-Khayyāṭ; Ḥassān the Jew; al-Battānī ibn Jābir the Arab; Alihi; Buzurjmihr; the Persian king; King Enoch, the son of Jared; Scezen, Abū Ma'shar's disciple; Thābit ibn Qurra al-Ḥarrānī; and 'Umar b. al-Farrukhān al-Ṭabarī. See *Int*, I 1:7, I 2:1 and notes. For Scezen, Abū Ma'shar's disciple, see note on II i 6:10.

[176] For these two ways, see note on *El*, II vi 6:4.

[177] See *El*, II vi 6:4, and *Int*, I 2:1.

three times,[178] the latter two times.[179] In all five instances, *Electiones* and *Interrogationes* quote or paraphrase a Ptolemaic work that is not identical with the *Tetrabiblos*.[180] *Electiones* and *Interrogationes* disclose the title of this work: *Liber .c. verborum*, "Book of the 100 Statements,"[181] which is the pseudo-Ptolemaic *Centiloquium*, a work organized in 100 aphorism that in the Middle Ages was considered to be an authentic work by Ptolemy.

(2) The "Ancients," who are the next-most-quoted source,[182] are mentioned twice in *Electiones*[183] and twice in *Interrogationes*; in all these cases their identity and works are not specified. Who are these "Ancients"? Throughout his oeuvre, in fact, Ibn Ezra employs the term as a collective undefined epithet. However, closer scrutiny reveals that in several instances Ibn Ezra sets the "Ancients" against the "Modern," a collective pointer to Arabic science and astrology.[184] On one occasion Ibn Ezra numbers among them "the Babylonians, the scientists of Persia, India, and Greece, whose chief is Ptolemy."[185] It emerges, then, that the "Ancients" are the repositories of pre-Arabic science and astrology. Ibn Ezra was in all likelihood indebted to Abū Maʿshar for this collective name with this meaning.[186]

(3) Dorotheus, an astrologer who is to be identified as the author of the well-known *Pentabiblos*, is mentioned 32 times in *Electiones* and five times in *Interrogationes*.[187] In two places *Interrogationes* makes Dorotheus a king,[188] which indicates that Ibn Ezra was acquainted with the Arabic translations of Dorotheus' work, in which this astrologer is similarly enthroned.[189] Dorotheus is referred to so frequently because chapter six of *Electiones* makes him a source for the elections related to each of the 28 lunar mansions. The source on which Ibn Ezra drew for this information is probably the *Kitāb al-Bāriʿ fī aḥkām al-nujūm* by the Arab astrologer Ibn Abī l-Rijāl (late tenth and early eleventh centuries), or Ibn Abī l-Rijāl's

178 See *El*, I 2:4; I 5:5; and II i 2:8.

179 See *Int*, II i 15:3, and II xii 11:11.

180 Indeed, Ptolemy's *Tetrabiblos* does not address directly the doctrines of elections or interrogations.

181 See *El*, I 5:5, and *Int*, II i 15:3.

182 See s.v. "Ancients": Sela 2007, 353; Sela 2010, 319; Sela 2011, 543, 546, 551; Sela 2013, 499, 504; Sela 2017, 799, 801; Sela 2019, 524.

183 *El*, II vii 5:2; II xi 1:3.

184 See *ʿOlam* I, § 30:4, 72–73; § 48:14, 84–85; *Ṭeʿamim* II, § 8.2:2, 250–251.

185 See *Reshit ḥokhmah* § 1.12:1, 56–57; quoted in App. 5, Q. 43, 479.

186 See, for example, Abū Maʿshar, *Great Introduction*, ed. Burnett and Yamamoto 2019, VIII:1 5, 820–821 and VIII:2 3, 824–825.

187 See Appendix 16, s.v. "Dorotheus," 593.

188 See *Int*, I 1:7 and II i 13:2.

189 See *Int*, I 1:7 (s.v. "King Dorotheus") and note.

own source for this information, as we shall see. We do not know Ibn Ezra's source for the other passages in *Electiones* and *Interrogationes* where Dorotheus' unspecified works are quoted or paraphrased.

(4) Māshā'allāh, a Jewish astrologer who lived from the time of the Caliph al-Manṣūr (r. 754–775) to the time of the Caliph al-Ma'mūn (r. 813–833), is mentioned twice in *Electiones*[190] and four times in *Interrogationes*.[191] Ibn Ezra never mentions Māshā'allāh's Jewish origin, but *Interrogationes* makes Māshā'allāh an "Indian,"[192] an assignment that is also found in *Reshit ḥokhmah* and *Ṭeʿamim* I.[193] This curious notice about Māshā'allāh's Indian origins is probably due to the fact that Māshā'allāh was well acquainted with the work of Indian scientists. *Electiones* quotes or paraphrases some unspecified work by Māshā'allāh' in two places.[194] In one of them, though, *Mivḥarim* II assigns the same statement to Dorotheus, and *Mivḥarim* I to the scientists of India.[195] *Interrogationes* quotes or paraphrase some unspecified work by Māshā'allāh three times.[196] These quotations or paraphrases do not match anything in *She'elot le-Māshā'allāh*, whose Hebrew translation is assigned to Ibn Ezra, or anything in Māshā'allāh's works that survive in Latin translation.

(5) Enoch, as an astrological source, is mentioned three times in *Electiones*[197] and three times in *Interrogationes*.[198] The name *Enoc* or *Enoch*, not the Latinized form "Hermes," is used in six loci, a clear sign that *Electiones* and *Interrogationes* are ultimately Latin translations of a Hebrew source text. In *Electiones*, Enoch is very favorably invoked with respect to choosing the time of conception and birth,[199] and particularly concerning a method that uses the term of pregnancy to determine the time of birth, and vice versa.[200] As for the source, *Electiones* mentions only *Enoc in libro suo* ("Enoch in his book"),[201] without giving the title of this book. Determining the time of conception and birth is a topic more closely related to the doctrine of nativities than to the doctrine of elections. Hence it comes as

190 *El*, II ii 1:5; II iii 3:2.
191 *Int*, I 1:7; I 11:1; I 12:3; II vi 1:9.
192 *Int*, I 1:7.
193 See *Reshit ḥokhmah*, § 9.1:6, 234–235, and *Ṭeʿamim* I, § 2.18:2, 58–59.
194 *El*, II ii 1:5 and II iii 3:2.
195 See *El*, II iii 3:2, and note.
196 *Int*, I 11:1; I 12:3; II vi 1:9.
197 *El*, II v 1:2; II v 2:2,3.
198 *Int*, I 2:1; II vii 1:10,12.
199 See *El*, II v 1:2 and note.
200 See *El*, II v 2:2,3 and notes.
201 See *El*, II v 2:2 and note.

no surprise that *Moladot, Nativitates*, and *De nativitatibus* also cite Enoch favorably with respect to just these topics.[202] *Interrogationes* makes Enoch a king and the son of the biblical Jared.[203] This seems to be how Ibn Ezra refers to the "Ancient Enoch," the oldest of the "Triple Enoch," mentioned in different parts of *ʿOlam* I.[204] Finally, *Interrogationes* mentions and describes how to cast the "lot of husbands" according to Enoch. Here Ibn Ezra's source for the assignment of this lot to Enoch and for the description of this lot is Abū Maʿshar's *Great Introduction*.[205]

(6) Sahl the Jew, or simply Sahl, a leading Jewish astrologer of the early ninth century, is mentioned once in *Electiones* and once in *Interrogationes*.[206] Substantial parts of chapter 8 of *Reshit ḥokhmah* are translations from Sahl's *Nawādir al-qaḍā* (Maxims of judgment), a work organized in 50 aphorisms, although Ibn Ezra never mentions Sahl explicitly there.[207] Sahl's work on nativities is referred to repeatedly in *Moladot* and in *De nativitatibus*.[208] Neither *Mivḥarim* I nor *Mivḥarim* II mentions Sahl or his work, but *Electiones* is unique in that it includes a *verbatim* quotation from Sahl's *Book of Elections*.[209]

(7) *Electiones* stands out because of its quotation of authoritative Jewish sources for astrological purposes. *Interrogationes*, by contrast, has no Jewish material. Three biblical verses are quoted in *Electiones*: Psalms 148:6 and Ecclesiastes 3:14 to support a strong version of astral determinism, and, by contrast, Deuteronomy 30:15 to make the case for free will. But the quotation of authoritative Jewish sources is not unusual in *Mivḥarim* II.[210] *Electiones* is unparalleled in Ibn Ezra's astrological corpus in its explicit mention of the "Ancient rabbis, their memory for a blessing" as a source, though they are of course frequently invoked in his biblical commentaries and theological monographs. *Electiones* is also unique in that, as noted above, it quotes the Babylonian Talmud (*Moʿed Qaṭan* 28a): "length of life, children, and sustenance depend not on merit but rather on *mazzal*" to support a strong

---

202 See notes on *El*, II v 1:2 and *El*, II v 2:1–7 through *El*, II v 3:1–2.

203 *Int*, I 2:1.

204 See note on *Int*, I 2:1.

205 See *Int*, II vii 1:10,12 and note.

206 See *El*, II ii 2:2, and *Int*, I 1:7.

207 See *Reshit ḥokhmah* § 8.1:1 through § 8.3:1–21, 210–222 and notes.

208 See *Moladot*, III i 4, 8, 102–103; III ii 5, 4, 124–125; III v 6, 4, 146–147; III viii 4, 2, 166–167; and *De nativitatibus*, II iii 5:1,2, 298–299; II viii 4:1, 330–331.

209 See *El*, II ii 2:2; cf. Sahl's *Book of elections*, Paris, BnF, lat. 16204 491b (quoted in App. 3, P. 3, Q. 5, 411).

210 See *Mivḥarim* II, § 1:1–2, 142–143.

version of astral determinism.[211] Although this famous dictum is frequently cited in medieval Hebrew literature in support of astrology and is quoted several times by Ibn Ezra in his biblical commentaries, this is its sole occurrence in his astrological writings.

Special Features of *Liber Electionum* and *Liber Interrogationum*

Despite the aforementioned close similarities between *Electiones* and *Interrogationes*, on the one hand, and Ibn Ezra's other works on elections and interrogations, on the other hand, with respect to organization, contents, and sources, as may be expected in works on the same astrological traditions and composed by the same author, *Electiones* and *Interrogationes* display their own idiosyncratic features.

The bulk of the fifth chapter of *Electiones* (350 words in the Latin text) is an account of the *trutina Hermetis* or "balance of Hermes."[212] This curious term denotes a method that takes account of the duration of pregnancy for the "rectification of the nativity," that is, to find the ascendant of the natal horoscope when the time of birth is not known. Since this is the usual situation, and because it is impossible to cast the natal horoscope without knowing the ascendant at the time of birth, methods for the "rectification of the nativity" are an essential component of virtually every treatise on the doctrine of nativities.

Ibn Ezra deserves a special place in the history of the *trutina Hermetis*. This expression is nothing else than a translation of the Hebrew מאזני חנוך "Enoch's balance," first used in Ibn Ezra's *Moladot*, where we find a detailed description of this method.[213] The *trutina Hermetis* was subsequently transmitted to the Hebrew and Latin cultures through the diffusion of Ibn Ezra's astrological writings in Hebrew, Latin, and the European vernaculars, from the twelfth through the eighteenth century.[214] There are similar accounts of the *trutina Hermetis* in a section on nativities in *Mishpeṭei ha-mazzalot*,[215] and in Ibn Ezra's long commentary on Exodus 2:2, where he invokes it to take exception to a talmudic interpretation that Moses was born prema-

211 See *El*, I 1:6 and note.
212 See *El*, II v 2:1–7 and II v 3:1–2, and notes.
213 See *Moladot*, II 1:1; II 4:1–5, II 5:1–10, II 6:1–6, 88–95 (quoted in App. 3, P. 8, Q. 2, 415–417).
214 See Sela 2019 (c), 79–106.
215 See *Mishpeṭei ha-mazzalot* § 15:1–5, § 17:1–4, 500–505 (quoted in App. 3, P. 8, Q. 1, 414–415).

turely, after only six months in utero.[216] *De nativitatibus*, too, offers a very similar account of this method and attributes it to Hermes.[217] *Electiones* does not employ the term *trutina* but invokes *Enoc in libro suo* ("Enoch in his book") as a source for the method.[218] So too *Mishpeṭei ha-mazzalot*.[219]

The inclusion of the *trutina Hermetis* in a treatise on elections is a *unicum* in the astrological literature. Why does *Electiones* include a full account of the *trutina Hermetis*? Neither *Mivḥarim* I nor *Mivḥarim* II, in their fifth chapter, refers to this method, although both inquire there about determining the best time to beget sons.[220] *Electiones*, likewise, begins its fifth chapter inquiring "about an hour for conception."[221] It turns out, then, that Ibn Ezra saw the *trutina Hermetis* as the best solution for finding an hour for intercourse so that the woman will have a normal pregnancy and give birth to a healthy son. That Ibn Ezra attached great importance to the *trutina Hermetis* is indicated by the fact that he addressed this doctrine not only in treatises on nativities, its natural place, and in discussions related to nativities, but also in a treatise on elections.

Chapter six of *Electiones* is disproportionately long (1,800 out of 6,000 words) and constitutes a sort of treatise within a treatise. It does not begin with the formulation of any election, as all the other chapters, but with a theoretical introduction, based on the authority of the scientists of India, about the 28 lunar mansions:[222] detailing their size, explaining why the zodiac was divided into 28 segments, giving a value for the difference between their tropical and sidereal positions, sending the reader to consult one of the versions of *Sefer ha-ʿOlam*, and finally announcing that the rest of the chapter will address the significations according to the method of elections when the Moon lodges in each of the mansions.[223]

The rest of the sixth chapter is indeed made up of 28 sections, each headed by the Arabic name of the corresponding lunar mansion. The elections put forward there do not belong exclusively to the significations of the sixth horoscopic place, and the same election reappears in more than one lunar mansion and even within the same mansion. This is because the

216 See *Commentary on Exodus*, ed. Weiser (1976), long commentary on Exodus 2:2, II, p. 16, [Hebrew] (quoted in App. 3, P. 8, Q. 3, 4, 417–418).
217 *De nativitatibus*, I 5:1–2, 252–253 and I 7:1–7, 254–255.
218 See *El*, II v 2:2 and note.
219 See *Mishpeṭei ha-mazzalot*, § 15:4, 502–503 (quoted in App. 3, P. 8, Q. 1, § 1:4, 414).
220 See *Mivḥarim* I, § 5.1:1–4, 64–65 and *Mivḥarim* II, § 5.1:1–4, 158–159.
221 See *El*, II v 1:1–2 and note.
222 For this term, see note on *El*, II vi 1:1.
223 See *El*, II vi 1:1–6 and notes.

significations of the elections are given according to the scientists of India, according to Dorotheus, and in one instance according to King Ptolemy. The most frequent are the elections related to travel (34 times), to purchases (31 times), to forming a partnership (24 times), to release from prison (21 times), to taking a wife (19 times), to wearing new clothes (17 times), and to taking medicine (17 times).[224]

Neither *Mivḥarim* I nor *Mivḥarim* II includes an account of the Lunar mansions in relation to elections. What led Ibn Ezra to incorporate this long account in *Electiones*? Why does this account draw on the scientists of India and Dorotheus, what were Ibn Ezra's sources here,[225] and why did he place this long account in chapter six? One possible source for this chapter is the seventh part, on elections, of Ibn Abī l-Rijāl's *Kitāb al-Bāriʿ fī aḥkām al-nujūm*, already noted above,[226] or an earlier and unknown source on which both men drew. A long chapter at the end of the seventh part of the *Kitāb al-Bāriʿ* deals with "elections according to the motion of the Moon through the mansions." As in *Electiones*, the final chapter of the seventh part of the *Kitāb al-Bāriʿ* divides the account of the elections of the 28 lunar mansions into 28 sections, one each for the elections of one of the 28 mansions. Like *Electiones*, the *Kitāb al-Bāriʿ* gives the Arabic name of the lunar mansion first, and then presents the elections according to the Indians, on the one hand, and Dorotheus, on the other. As for the contents of the elections, *Electiones* and the *Kitāb al-Bāriʿ* are very close to each other, although not identical.[227]

Another source close to Ibn Ezra is the last chapter of the fourth part, on elections, of the *Epitome totius astrologiae*.[228] This chapter of the *Epitome*, the aforementioned chapter of the *Kitāb al-Bāriʿ*, and chapter six of *Electiones* are very similar. All three are divided into 28 sections, corresponding to the 28 lunar mansions. In each section, the *Epitome*, the *Kitāb al-Bāriʿ*

224 See *El*, II vi 1:1–2 through II vi 29:1–2, and notes.

225 For astrological texts applying the 28 lunar mansions to elections, see Burnett 2004, 48–55.

226 See *De iudiciis astrorum*, ed. Petri (1551), 342a–346b.

227 For the first section of this chapter, see *De iudiciis astrorum*, ed. Petri (1551), 342a–b (quoted in App. 3, P. 9, Q. 1, 421–422).

228 See *Epitome*, ed. Heller (1548), IV:18, S3r–T3v (first section quoted in App. 3, P. 9, Q. 2, 422–423). The last chapter on the elections of the lunar mansions occurs in the print edition of *Epitome totius astrologiae* alone (*Epitome*, ed. Heller (1548), IV:18, S3r–T3v) and in the oldest manuscripts of the *Epitome*: Venice, BNM, Fondo antico, MS lat. Z. 344 (1878) (13th c., "De electionibus indorum et Doronii secundum mansiones Lune"), fols. 28va–30va; Madrid, BN, MS 10063 (13th c., "electiones Indorum et Doronii"), fols. 11rb–12ra. This last chapter is missing from Madrid, BN, MS 10009 (13th c.) and Vienna, ÖNB, MS 5442 (14th c.).

and *Electiones* first present the name of the lunar mansion (the *Kitāb al-Bāriʿ* and *Electiones* the Arabic name, the *Epitome* its Latin translation), and then the elections according to the Indians, on the one hand, and according to Dorotheus, on the other. All in all, the *Epitome*, the *Kitāb al-Bāriʿ*, and *Electiones* present the same material, although there are no verbal parallels among them.[229]

As seen above, both the *Kitāb al-Bāriʿ* and the *Epitome* place the chapter on the elections of the 28 lunar mansions at the very end of the part dealing with elections. By contrast, the account of the elections of the lunar mansions appears at the very middle of *Electiones*, overlapping the chapter on the sixth place. Why did Ibn Ezra proceed in this manner? This brings us to the third and earliest source. Sahl's *Book of Elections*, like Ibn Ezra's treatises on elections, is organized in chapters that address the indications of the twelve horoscopic places. The sixth horoscopic place signifies diseases and slaves, and the whole sixth chapter of Sahl's *Book of Elections* is devoted to elections related to medical matters, such as choosing a time to take a medicine, and to slaves, such as choosing a time to purchase a slave. A special feature is that all the elections in this chapter of Sahl's *Book of Elections* are presented according to the position and condition of the Moon at the time of the election. For example, taking a medicine is said to be auspicious when the Moon is in Libra or in Scorpio; a cure of the head, when the Moon is in Aries or Taurus; and a cure of the body, when the Moon is in Capricorn, Aquarius, or Pisces.[230] In other words, although there is no explicit mention of the lunar mansions, the position of the Moon in the zodiacal signs is explicitly adduced. As we have seen, the second chapter of *Electiones* quotes *verbatim* a passage from Sahl's *Book of Elections*.[231] Hence it stands to reason that Ibn Ezra emulated that work when he decided to insert the elections of the 28 lunar mansions in the chapter corresponding to the sixth horoscopic place of *Electiones*, just as Sahl had done.[232]

The first chapter of *Interrogationes*, too, is disproportionately long (2,000 out of 8,500 words) and constitutes a sort of treatise within a treatise. In contrast to all the other chapters, the first chapter of *Interrogationes*

---

229 See *El*, II vi 2:1–4. Cf. the account of the first mansion in the seventh part of Abī l-Rijāl's *Kitāb al-Bāriʿ* (Ilnath: *De iudiciis astrorum*, ed. Petri (1551), 342a–b; quoted in App. 3, P. 9, Q. 1, 421–422) and in the fourth part of the *Epitome* (cornua Arietis: ed. Heller (1548), IV:18, S3r–T3v; quoted in App. 3, P. 9, Q. 2, 422–423).

230 See Sahl's *Book of Elections*, Paris, BnF, lat. 16204, 493a–495a.

231 See above, p. 36, *El*, II ii 2:2, and note.

232 Note that Sahl is also one of Abī l-Rijāl's explicit sources in the seventh part of *Kitāb al-Bāriʿ*, on elections. See *De iudiciis astrorum*, ed. Petri (1551), 298b.

does not address questions related to the corresponding horoscopic place and deals exclusively with the presentation of general principles related to the doctrine of interrogations. This includes the significations of various categories of signs (fixed, tropical, bicorporal), various horoscopic places (cardines, succedent and cadent of the cardines), various categories of planets (upper, lower, in their stations, in their position with respect the Sun), testimonies, the Moon, the significator, the ruler of the electional chart, and questions about which astrologers disagree (when the querent asks about himself, about two combatants, whether someone is alive or dead, the querent's lifespan).[233]

By contrast, *She'elot* II offers similar general principles for interrogations in its lengthy introduction;[234] *She'elot* I omits this topic altogether. Another preliminary general topic that does not overlap any particular question is that of reading the querent's thoughts, essential for knowing whether the querent is sincere in his question before the astrologer casts the interrogational horoscope. *She'elot* I and *She'elot* II address this topic in their introductions.[235] In sharp contrast, *Interrogationes* deals with this preliminary topic in four sections of its last chapter.[236] This peculiar feature of *Interrogationes*—incorporating general preliminary principles in unexpected places—has no parallel in the astrological literature on interrogations. To understand Ibn Ezra's modus operandi, we should recall his propensity, noticeable throughout his oeuvre, to interpolate a lengthy digression or excursus whenever he saw fit to enlarge the scope and discuss some burning issue.[237]

Linguistic Features of *Liber Electionum* and *Liber Interrogationum*

As said above, *Electiones* and *Interrogationes* are replete with Hebraisms and literal renderings of Ibn Ezra's Hebrew neologisms.[238] With the exception of the transliterations of the Arabic names of the lunar mansions in the sixth chapter of *Electiones*, which also occur in other of Ibn Ezra's

[233] See *Int*, II i 1:1–5 through II i 15:1–5, and notes.

[234] See *She'elot* II, § 2:1–3, 348–349 through § 8:1–5, 354–355.

[235] See *She'elot* I, § 4:1–5, 242–243 through § 11:1–3, 246–247, and *She'elot* II, § 9:1–3, 354–355 through § 10:1–6, 356–357.

[236] See *Int*, II xii 2:1–9 through II xii 5:1, and notes.

[237] For digressions in *Ṭe'amim* I and *Ṭe'amim* II, see Sela 2007, 345, 357. For digressions in *'Olam* I, see Sela 2010, 303–304.

[238] This is shown in two lists (see pp. 597–600.) and in the notes to the translations of *Electiones* and *Interrogationes*.

Hebrew astrological writings, *Electiones* and *Interrogationes* totally eschew Arabic transliterations (commonplace in medieval Latin astrological literature), just as Ibn Ezra does in his Hebrew work. By contrast, Pietro d'Abano and Arnoul de Quincampoix, in their translations of *Tractatus particulares*, do employ Arabic transliterations, such as *mubtazz*, which refers to the strongest planet in a horoscopic chart.[239] But *Electiones* and *Interrogationes* are not Hebrew into Latin translations of *Mivḥarim* III and *She'elot* III.

That *Electiones* and *Interrogationes* were produced via an intermediate French translation is proved by the four French words or phrases embedded in the Latin text of the former[240] and by the 16 French words or phrases embedded in the Latin text of the latter.[241] They are probably remnants of a translation *à quatre mains*: one scholar, probably a Jew, would read the Hebrew text and translate it orally into French; his collaborator translated what he heard into Latin and wrote it down. French words or phrases that the latter did not understand were left as is in the Latin text. That this is the case is suggested by the fact that no French remnants are found in the Latin text of the numerous translations of Ibn Ezra's treatises rendered into French by Hagin le Juif and transcribed in French by a certain Obers de Mondidier in Henry Bate's house in Mechelen, Flanders, at the end of 1273, which are extant in two manuscripts.[242]

That the names of the members of the team of Hebrew into French and French into Latin translators are not recorded in the two manuscripts in which *Electiones* and *Interrogationes* survive suggests that there was a behind-the-scene sponsor (or sponsors) of these two translations, who commissioned the teams (or team) that produced *Electiones* and *Interrogationes*. Note that when the sponsor of a translation is the translator himself, as in the cases of Henry Bate, Pietro d'Abano, and Arnoul de Quincampoix, the name of the Latin translator is explicitly specified in the manuscripts; but when the sponsor does not produce the translation himself, as in the case of Pierre de Limoges,[243] the name of the translator is absent. At present we do not know the circumstances in which *Electiones* and *Interrogationes* were produced, and therefore do not know the name of the translators or sponsor(s) of *Electiones* and *Interrogationes*.

---

239 See *Tp*, I i 7:1 and note. For the method of reference used in this volume to specific parts of *Tractatus particulares*, see below, "Editorial and Translation Principles," pp. 88–89.

240 See *El*, II iii 1:1; II vi 8:1,2; II ix 3:2.

241 See *Int*, II i 8:1; II i 14:2; II ii 2:8; II vi 2:3; II vii 1:2; II x 1:2; II x 1:3; II xi 1:7; II xii 4:1; II xii 5:1; II xii 6:4; II xii 6:5; II xii 8:3.

242 See Sela forthcoming (a).

243 See Sela 2019 (b).

A comparative scrutiny of the Latin texts of *Electiones* and *Interrogationes* strongly suggests that they were produced by the same team of translators. This emerges from the fact that in virtually every place where the same technical term is used in *Electiones* and *Interrogationes*, they employ the same Latin translation—no fewer than 133 items in the English-Latin Glossary of Technical Terms. To highlight this phenomenon, an asterisk is attached to the numbers assigned there to these 133 items. This includes the significant identical translations of the following terms:

- "Crooked signs" and "straight sign,"[244] rendered in *Electiones* and *Interrogationes* as *signa tortuosa* and *signa recta*,[245] calques of מזלות מעוותים and מזלות ישרים, used by Ibn Ezra to denote this term. *Nativitates* uses *torta* and *signa directa*.[246]
- "Author," rendered in *Electiones* and *Interrogationes* as *additor* or *addens*,[247] a calque of מחבר; whereas *De nativitatibus* has *auctor*.[248]
- "Give power,"[249] rendered in *Electiones* and *Interrogationes* as *dare fortitudinem*,[250] for לתת כח, frequently used by Ibn Ezra; *Tractatus particulares* uses *dare vim*.[251]
- "Hidden thing" and "hide," rendered in *Electiones* and *Interrogationes* as *absconditum* and *abscondere*, by contrast to *occultum* and *occultare*, used in *Tractatus particulares*.[252]
- "Indicate," rendered in *Electiones* and *Interrogationes* as *ostendere*; by contrast to *denotare*, used in *Tractatus particulares*.[253]
- "Places of dominion,"[254] rendered in *Electiones* and *Interrogationes* as *loci principatus*,[255] מקומות השררה, used by Ibn Ezra in some of his works to denote this term; by contrast to *loca principalia*, used in *De nativitatibus*.[256]

---

244 For these concepts, see note on *Int*, II iv 1:1.
245 See English-Latin Glossary, items 54 and 267, on pp. 543, 571.
246 See *Nativitates*, II iv 4:2–3, and note on Sela 2019, 226–227.
247 See English-Latin Glossary, item 19 on p. 538.
248 See *De nativitatibus*, II vi 9:1, 316–317.
249 For this concept, see note on *Tp*, I iv 1:2.
250 See English-Latin Glossary, item 99 on pp. 548–549.
251 See *Tp*, I iv 1:2, 3, 6, 7, 8, 9 et passim.
252 See *Tp*, I:3 and I i 5:7,8 et passim.
253 See *Tp*, I iii 1:3,4 et passim.
254 For this concept, see note on *Int*, II i 15:1.
255 See English-Latin Glossary, item 210, on p. 563.
256 See *De nativitatibus*, I 20:2, 268–269, et passim.

- "Zodiac,"[257] rendered in *Electiones* and *Interrogationes* as *circulus*,[258] for Hebrew גלגל, frequently used by Ibn Ezra to denote this term; *Tractatus particulares* has *zodiacus*.[259]

Moreover, in some places *Electiones* and *Interrogationes* provide not one but two identical alternative translations of the same technical term:

- "Astrologers," rendered in *Electiones* and *Interrogationes* as *sapientes iudiciorum signorum* and also as *sapientes signorum*,[260] represent חכמי משפטי המזלות and חכמי המזלות, both of them frequently used by Ibn Ezra to denote astrologers.
- "Trine,"[261] rendered in *Electiones* and *Interrogationes* as both *aspectus trinus* and *aspectus dilectionis*,[262] for the Hebrew מבט שלישית and מבט אהבה, both of them used by Ibn Ezra for this concept.
- "Malefic planet,"[263] rendered in *Electiones* and *Interrogationes* as *stella mala* and also as *stella malivola*,[264] for the Hebrew כוכב רע and כוכב מזיק, both frequently used by Ibn Ezra.
- "Country," rendered in *Electiones* and *Interrogationes* as both *patria* and *terra*,[265] representing the Hebrew מדינה and ארץ used by Ibn Ezra.
- "Planet," rendered in *Electiones* and *Interrogationes* as *stella* and also as *planeta*,[266] for כוכב and probably משרת, frequently used by Ibn Ezra.
- "To test," rendered in *Electiones* and *Interrogationes* as *temptare* and *probare*.[267] The dichotomy is possibly because both words can represent the Hebrew לנסות, frequently used by Ibn Ezra, which means both "to test" and "to try."

There are also cases in which only *Interrogationes*, or only *Electiones*, supplies a translation of some technical term, or in which *Electiones* and *Interrogationes* employ different Latin renderings of the same technical term. A scrutiny of these cases reveals that they are ultimately alternative transla-

257 For this concept, see note on *Tp*, I i 4:6.
258 See English-Latin Glossary, item 301, on pp. 576.
259 See *Tp*, I i 4:6.
260 See English-Latin Glossary, item 14, on p. 537.
261 For this concept, see *El*, II vii 1:3, s.v. "aspect of love."
262 See English-Latin Glossary, items 12 and 283, on pp. 537, 573.
263 For this concept, see note on *Int*, II i 9:5.
264 See English-Latin Glossary, item 171, on p. 557.
265 See English-Latin Glossary, item 51, on p. 543.
266 See English-Latin Glossary, item 211, on p. 563.
267 See English-Latin Glossary, item 279, on p. 573.

tions of technical terms for which *Electiones* and *Interrogationes* also use identical translations. In addition to showing how *Electiones* and *Interrogationes use* the same Latin translation for the same term, this also reveals interesting features about the modus operandi of the Latin translator(s) of *Electiones* and *Interrogationes* and of the lost Hebrew texts underlying *Electiones* and *Interrogationes*, which survive in part in the Modena fragments of *Mivḥarim* III and *She'elot* III. Here are some examples.

- (1) "Cardines"[268] is rendered in *Electiones* and *Interrogationes* as *anguli*,[269] the standard word for this term in Latin medieval astrological literature. But only *Interrogationes* also uses *caville*,[270] a calque of יתדות "pegs," which is Ibn Ezra's usual term. It is noteworthy that *Interrogationes* uses *caville* ten times, from its beginning until the second paragraph of the second chapter,[271] and that from then on it uses *anguli* more than 30 times,[272] as if the Latin translator suddenly became aware that the standard Latin *anguli* is more appropriate.[273]
- (2) A similar case is that of "cadent places,"[274] rendered in *Electiones* and *Interrogationes* as *domus cadentes*.[275] Once again, only in *Interrogationes* is it translated as *cadentes a cavillis*,[276] and then as *domus cadentes ab angulis*,[277] both of them representing נופלים מן היתדות "falling from the cardines," Ibn Ezra's usual way of denoting this term.
- (3) "Exaltation,"[278] rendered in *Electiones* and *Interrogationes* as *exaltatio*,[279] the common term in the Latin astrological literature. Only *Interrogationes* used *honor*,[280] a calque of כבוד, "honor," often employed by Ibn Ezra in this sense; while only *Electiones* uses *altitudo*[281] "highness," also employed by Ibn Ezra in some of his works for the same term.[282] As

---

268 For this concept, see note on *Int*, II xii 9:4.
269 See English-Latin Glossary, item 36 on p. 541, s.v., *anguli*.
270 See *Int*, II i 1:4,5; II i 3:2 et passim.
271 See English-Latin Glossary, item 36 on p. 541, s.v. *caville*.
272 See English-Latin Glossary, item 36 on p. 541, s.v. *anguli*.
273 Other possibilities, such as that there were two different underlying French words, or two Latin translators, are much less plausible in my opinion.
274 For this concept, see note on *Int*, II i 7:5.
275 See English-Latin Glossary, item 31 on p. 540.
276 See *Int*, II i 3:2.
277 See *Int*, II v 2:4; II vii 3:7.
278 For this concept, see notes on *Int*, II i 6:12 and II x 1:6.
279 See English-Latin Glossary, item 89 on p. 547.
280 See *Int*, II i 6:12.
281 See *El*, II ii 2:2.
282 See *El*, II ii 2:2 and note.

in the case of "cardines," *Electiones* and *Interrogationes* use first *altitudo* and *honor*, and then switch to *exaltatio*, as if there were three different underlying French words, or as if the Latin translator at certain stage became aware that the standard Latin rendering *exaltatio* is better than the unusual *altitudo* or *honor*.

- (4) "Fixed signs,"[283] rendered in *Electiones* and *Interrogationes* as *signa veridica*,[284] a calque of מזלות נאמנים "truthful signs," used in some of Ibn Ezra's works[285] and in the Modena fragment of *Mivḥarim* III and *She'elot* III to denote the fixed signs.[286] But only *Interrogationes* has *signa stabilia*,[287] possibly a calque of מזלות עומדים "stable signs," used in some of Ibn Ezra's works.
- (5) "Bicorporal signs"[288] is rendered in *Electiones* and *Interrogationes* as *signa bicorpora*.[289] Only *Interrogationes* is it translated at first as *domini duorum corporum*,[290] lords of two bodies, a misrendering of בעלי שני גופות "having two bodies," used in Ibn Ezra's work[291] and also in the Modena fragment of *Mivḥarim* III and *She'elot* III.[292] Later, *Interrogationes* switches to *signa bicorpora*, as if the Latin translator had realized that the standard Latin rendering *signa bicorpora* is to be preferred.
- (6) "Jupiter" appears in *Electiones* and *Interrogationes* as *Iupiter*,[293] the common Latin term. Only in *Interrogationes* do we find *stella Iovis*,[294] a calque of כוכב צדק "star of Jupiter," which Ibn Ezra sometimes uses for that planet.[295]
- (7) "Rays,"[296] is rendered in *Electiones* and *Interrogationes* as *radii*,[297] the standard term in the Latin astrological literature. Only *Interrogationes*

283 See note on *Int*, II iii 2:3.
284 See English-Latin Glossary, item 96 on p. 548.
285 See note on *Int*, II i 1:3.
286 See *Mivḥarim* III, II viii 1:1, 488–489 and *She'elot* III, II vi 2:2, 492, and corresponding Latin passages in *Electiones* and *Interrogationes*.
287 See *Int*, II viii 1:6.
288 See note on *Int*, II iii 2:3.
289 See English-Latin Glossary, item 26 on p. 539.
290 See *Int*, II i 4:1; II i 6:1,2.
291 See *Int*, II i 4:1 and note.
292 See *Mivḥarim* III, II vii 1:5, 485, and *She'elot* III, II vi 2:2, 492. But the Latin counterpart of these two loci reads *signa bicorpora*, a clear sign that the French into Latin or the Hebrew into French translator preferred the standard latinized form of this term.
293 See English-Latin Glossary, item 131 on p. 552.
294 See *Int*, II x 1:4.
295 See *Int*, II x 1:4 and note.
296 For this concept, see *El*, II vi 6:4, s.v. "number of its ray."
297 See English-Latin Glossary, item 225 on p. 565.

also has *claritas*,[298] a calque of אור "light," frequently used by Ibn Ezra in this sense, as well as *scintillatio*,[299] a calque of ניצוץ "spark," another term used by Ibn Ezra. Both אור and ניצוץ are found in the Modena fragment of *She'elot* III in this sense.[300] Put simply, the fact that several Latin words are used for "rays" reflects that Ibn Ezra used many different Hebrew words in this sense.

- (8) "Calculate," rendered in *Electiones* and *Interrogationes* as *computare*,[301] and in *Electiones* alone also as *preparare*,[302] a calque of לתקן, which means both "calculate" and "establish," used in Ibn Ezra's work as well as in the Modena fragment of *Electiones* to denote the same term.[303]
- (9) "Write," rendered in *Electiones* and *Interrogationes* as *scribere*,[304] and in *Interrogationes* alone also as *addere*,[305] a mistranslation of לחבר, which means both "combine" and "compose" (in the sense of write).
- (10) "Burning" is rendered in *Electiones* and *Interrogationes* as *combustio*,[306] the standard term in the Latin astrological literature. Only *Interrogationes* begins by using *inflammatio* and *reflammatio*,[307] before switching to *combustio* (for the usual reason). "Burnt," too, is rendered in *Electiones* and *Interrogationes* as *combustus*,[308] the standard term in the Latin astrological literature; but at first only *Interrogationes* has *reflammetur*[309] and later *combustus*.
- (11) "Upper planet" and "lower planet," rendered in *Electiones* and *Interrogationes* as *stella superior* and *stella inferior*,[310] representing כוכב עליון and כוכב שפל "upper" and "lower star." But the same terms are translated in *Interrogationes* as *planeta superior*[311] and *planeta inferior*,[312] representing משרת עליון and משרת שפל.[313]

---

298 See *Int*, II vi 1:3, s.v. "under the light of the Sun."

299 See *Int*, II ii 2:4 and II vii 1:3 and notes.

300 For אור, see *She'elot* III, II vi 1:3, 491, and corresponding Latin passage in *Interrogationes*; For ניצוץ, see *She'elot* III, II vii 1:3 and II vii 3:5, 493, 495, and corresponding Latin passages in *Interrogationes*.

301 See English-Latin Glossary, item 33 on p. 540.

302 See *El*, II v 1:1; II v 2:7; et passim.

303 See *Mivḥarim* III, II vii 1:6, 493, and corresponding Latin passage in *Electiones*.

304 See English-Latin Glossary, item 299 on p. 575.

305 See *Int*, I 3:1 and note.

306 See English-Latin Glossary, item 29 on p. 540.

307 See *Int*, II i 1:5 and II i 2:1 and notes.

308 See English-Latin Glossary, item 30 on p. 540.

309 See *Int*, II i 2:1.

310 See English-Latin Glossary, items 287 and 169, on pp. 574, 557.

311 See *Int*, II i 4:3 et passim.

312 See *Int*, II i 2:1 et passim.

313 See above, the case of the term "planet."

- (12) "Luminaries," rendered in *Electiones* and *Interrogationes* as *luminaria*,[314] is also translated in *Interrogationes* as *claritates*,[315] a calque of מאורות, the biblical term for the Sun and Moon, used in Ibn Ezra's work as well as in the Modena fragment of *Interrogationes* in the same sense.[316] Note that *Interrogationes* begins with *claritates* before adopting *luminaria*.
- (13) "Power" is rendered in *Electiones* and *Interrogationes* as *fortitudo*,[317] the standard term in the Latin astrological literature. *Electiones* begins with *potestas*[318] before switching to *fortitudo*.
- (14) "Add," "child," and "good fortune" are rendered in *Electiones* and *Interrogationes* as *addere*, *infans*, and *bonum*, respectively.[319] But *Electiones* employs *augere*, *puer*, and *fortuna*,[320] possibly on stylistic grounds.

The Modena fragments of *Mivḥarim* III and *She'elot* III also show that *Electiones* and *Interrogationes* employ Latin phrases that are identical with some Hebrew locutions typical of Ibn Ezra's style. This applies to (1) רק אם, meaning "unless," "only if" and "but if," and translated uniformly in *Electiones* and *Interrogationes* as *nisi*;[321] (2) ודע כי, meaning "know that," and translated uniformly in *Electiones* and *Interrogationes* as *et scias quod*;[322] and (3) הפך הדבר, meaning "vice versa" or "the opposite," and translated uniformly in *Electiones* and *Interrogationes* as *econtrario*.[323]

II. *TRACTATUS PARTICULARES*

The Latin translations of Ibn Ezra's astrological writings may be divided into three categories: (a) Latin translations whose Hebrew source-texts are

314 See English-Latin Glossary, item 170 on p. 557.
315 See *Int*, II i 9:1; II vi 9:1.
316 See *Mivḥarim* III, II vii 5:1,2 and II vii 6:5, 486–487; *She'elot* III, II vii 2:4, 494–495. The Latin translations of all these loci in *Electiones* and *Interrogationes* read *luminaria*.
317 See English-Latin Glossary, item 213 on p. 563.
318 See *El*, I 6:1.
319 See English-Latin Glossary, items 1, 38 and 101, on pp. 535, 541, 549.
320 See, respectively, *El*, I 1:2; II v 2:4; and I 6:1.
321 See, for example, *Mivḥarim* III, II vii 5:4,5 and *She'elot* III, II vii 3:3 and corresponding Latin text in *Electiones* and *Interrogationes*.
322 See, for example, *Mivḥarim* III, II vii 4:1 and *She'elot* III, II v 5:3 and corresponding Latin text in *Electiones* and *Interrogationes*.
323 See, for example, *Mivḥarim* III, II vii 4:2 and *She'elot* III, II vii 1:8 and corresponding Latin text in *Electiones* and *Interrogationes*.

extant today, like those that were mentioned in the first part of this introduction;[324] (b) Latin translations that have no surviving Hebrew counterpart but are obviously translations of texts by Ibn Ezra (*Electiones* and *Interrogationes*); and (c) Latin translations that have no surviving Hebrew counterpart in Ibn Ezra's astrological corpus and whose affiliation with Ibn Ezra is unclear. One example of this category is *De nativitatibus*, which was studied, edited, and translated in volume 6 of this series. Another specimen of the third category is the *Tractatus particulares*, a four-part work assigned to Abraham Ibn Ezra and extant in two Latin translations.

One of the translations—well known because it was printed by Petrus Liechtenstein in Venice in 1507[325] and transmitted in a large number of manuscripts—was carried out by Pietro d'Abano, during his stay in Paris (1293–1307). Below I will refer to Pietro d'Abano's translation of *Tractatus particulares* as *Tp*ᴬ. The second translation was carried out by Arnoul de Quincampoix and is preserved in a single manuscript, Ghent, MS Univ. 5 (416), whose contents were mentioned above.[326] Below I will refer to Arnoul de Quincampoix's translation of *Tractatus particulares* as *Tp*ᵠ. By contrast, the edition of *Tractatus particulares* found in this volume, based mainly on *Tp*ᴬ but with some input from *Tp*ᵠ, is denoted by *Tp* with no superscript.

Earlier Research on *Tractatus Particulares*

Moritz Steinschneider, in a list published first in 1880, did not include *Tractatus particulares* among Abraham Ibn Ezra's astrological writings.[327] In another list, though, published in 1897, Steinschneider remarked with great insight that although the name *Abraham Avenare* occurs at the end of *Tractatus particulares*,[328] the work includes parts that are not by Ibn Ezra. He suggested that the translator may have worked from a copy into which some inauthentic materials had found their way.[329]

Raphael Levy, in *The Astrological Works of Abraham Ibn Ezra*, published in 1927, mentioned *Tp*ᴬ and *Tp*ᵠ and their components only when he quoted the incipits and explicits of Pietro d'Abano's and Arnoul de Quincampoix's

324 See above, pp. 2–8. This is the most numerous of the three types and includes both credited and anonymous translations.

325 *Abrahe Avenaris* (Pietro d'Abano), ed. Liechtenstein (1507).

326 See above, p. 16.

327 Steinschneider 1880/1925, 493–498.

328 Steinschneider was certainly using the print edition of *Tractatus particulares*. See *Abrahe Avenaris* (Pietro d'Abano), ed. Liechtenstein (1507), sig. XCIv.

329 Steinschneider 1897, 138.

Latin translations of Ibn Ezra's astrological writings. Regarding the components of Tp^{Q}, Levy added that their attribution to Ibn Ezra "seems doubtful."[330] This seems to be his acknowledgement that he was unable to find the counterpart of Tp^{Q} (or Tp^{A}) in any of the Ibn Ezra's astrological works known to him. Lynn Thorndike, in his 1944 article, included Tp^{A} and Tp^{Q} among the Latin translations of astrological treatises by "Abraham Avenezra," listed seven manuscripts of Tp^{A}, and quoted their incipits and explicits.[331] Thorndike's aim was to identify manuscripts and texts and to examine their titles, incipits, and colophons; hence he did not describe the contents or try to identify the Hebrew source texts behind Tp^{A} or Tp^{Q}.

This was remedied to some extent by Renate Smithuis, who, in addition to briefly describing the contents of Tp^{A} and Tp^{Q}, took a significant step forward by asserting and demonstrating that "the entire text after the discussion of the twelve places in the *Liber Interrogacionum* is recycled in the first tract of the *Tractatus particulares*."[332] Smithuis's finding is fully corroborated in the present study of *Tractatus particulares*, as will be shown in due course. Another substantial contribution was made by David Juste, who detected the counterpart of two sections of the first part of Tp^{A} and Tp^{Q} in two Latin works that certainly are not by Ibn Ezra: the *Iudicia* ("judgments"), a pseudo-Ptolemaic Latin work on interrogations; and *Alchandreana*, a Latin collection of astrological texts translated and adapted from Arabic in the tenth century.[333] Juste's finding, too, is fully corroborated in the present study of *Tractatus particulares*.

But what about the Hebrew source texts of the reminding parts of the first treatise, and of the entire second, third and fourth treatises of Tp^{A} or Tp^{Q}, which, according to the incipits and explicits, were all by Ibn Ezra? The present study attempts to determine all the Hebrew source texts behind Tp^{A} and Tp^{Q}. It takes account of the evidence provided by virtually all the available manuscript and print witnesses of Tp^{A} or Tp^{Q}, on the one hand, and by the available Hebrew and Latin astrological literature, on the other. But first I look at the manuscript and print traditions as well as general features of Tp^{A} and Tp^{Q}, such as the names of the translations, the names of the translators, and the name of the presumptive author/authors of their source texts. I also attempt to determine the source language and

330 Levy 1927, p. 40, 46.
331 Thorndike 1944, pp. 293–302, esp. pp. 300–302.
332 Smithuis 2004, chapter 1, section 7.
333 See Juste 2007, 168–170, 274–275, 277 n. 230.

the general structure of Tp^{A} and Tp^{Q}. At the end of this part I describe the modus operandi of the originator of the Hebrew source text of Tp^{A} and Tp^{Q}, explain away why the two were attributed to Abraham Ibn Ezra, and reconstruct the circumstances in which a Hebrew astrological text such as that behind Tp^{A} and Tp^{Q} originated. The Hebrew source text behind Tp^{A} and Tp^{Q} is designated Tp^{H}.[334]

Manuscripts, General Features and Transmission of Tp^{A} and Tp^{Q}

The *Tractatus particulares* has been known to modern scholarship almost exclusively through the print edition of Tp^{A}, published in Venice in 1507 by Petrus Liechtenstein. Here I shed new light by taking account of all the available manuscripts of Tp^{A} and Tp^{Q} as well. I begin with a list, in the first column of the table below, of all the witnesses of Tp^{A} and Tp^{Q} known to me. The other columns of the table display main features of each witness of Tp^{A} and Tp^{Q} and give a succinct picture of their transmission across the centuries.

(1) The first column lists, from earliest to latest, all the manuscripts and print edition of Tp^{A} and Tp^{Q}, with their library designation (collection and shelfmark, etc.) and the date or century in which they were copied or printed. The siglum assigned to each begins with a capital letter suggestive of the library/collection/editor of the print edition. When more than one witness is held by the same library, a superscript number is appended to the letter. The next nine columns provide information about each witness:

(2) The name of the translator (A = Pietro d'Abano, Q = Arnoul de Quincampoix).

(3) The version of each witness. A scrutiny of all the available copies of Tp^{A} and Tp^{Q} reveals that they were transmitted in eight versions, as a function of the components included in each copy and their order of presentation, as follows: (i) Witnesses belonging to the first version, designated v^1, include all four treatises. (ii) Witnesses belonging to the second version, v^2, also include all four parts, but in a different order than v^1. (iii) Witnesses belonging to the third version, v^3, include only the second, third, and fourth parts found in v^1. (iv) Witnesses belonging to the fourth version, v^4, include only the first, second, and third parts found in v^1. (v) Witnesses belonging

334 For an earlier version of the present study of *Tractatus particulares*, see Sela 2019 (e).

to the fifth version, v^5, include only the fourth, second and third components of v^1. (vi) Witnesses belonging to the sixth version, v^6, include only the first component of v^1; (vii) Witnesses belonging to the seventh version, v^7, include only the third component of v^1; (viii) Witnesses belonging to the eighth version, v^8, include only the second component of v^1.

(4) The folios or pages of *Tp*^A or *Tp*^Q in the corresponding copy.

(5–10) Whether a manuscript or print edition that includes a copy of *Tp*^A or *Tp*^Q also contains a copy of another translation of Ibn Ezra's astrological writings carried out by Pietro or Arnoul. If a copy of any of these translations is in the manuscript or print edition, the corresponding folios/pages are indicated; otherwise the cell is left blank.

The table reveals the following features related to the transmission of *Tp*^A and *Tp*^Q:

(i) *Tp*^A was transmitted in 17 manuscripts plus one print edition; but *Tp*^Q is extant in only one manuscript.
(ii) Three of the manuscripts of *Tp*^A were copied in the fourteenth century; 12 manuscripts of *Tp*^A and the only one of *Tp*^Q were copied in the fifteenth century; two manuscripts of *Tp*^A were copied in the sixteenth century; the print edition of *Tp*^A was published at the beginning of the sixteenth century.
(iii) The majority of the witnesses of *Tp*^A (9 of 18) contain all seven translations of astrological treatises by Ibn Ezra carried out by Pietro d'Abano; the single witness of *Tp*^Q contains the two extant translations of astrological treatises by Ibn Ezra carried out by Arnoul de Quincampoix. Of the remaining witnesses of *Tp*^A, two contain four additional translations by Pietro d'Abano, one contains three additional translations, and another witness contains one translation. *Tp*^A occurs alone in four witnesses.
(iv) Eleven of the 18 witnesses of *Tp*^A include the version of *Tp*^A that incorporates all four components (v^1); two witnesses of *Tp*^A include only the third component of v^1 (v^7); the six other versions (v^2, v^3, v^4, v^5, v^6, v^8) are represented by a single witness.

We see, then, that *Tp*^A and *Tp*^Q were not transmitted in isolation but in tandem with collections of Pietro's and Arnoul's Latin translations of astrological treatises by Ibn Ezra. Moreover, in some cases (not detailed here) the same manuscript that contains *Tp*^A and Pietro's other translations of Ibn Ezra's astrological writings also includes translations of Ibn Ezra's astrological writings carried out by others, such as Henry Bate or anonymous

MSS and print editions	T	V	Tp^A or Tp^Q	*Reshit ḥokhmah*	*Moladot*	*Mivḥarim* II	*She'elot* II	*Ṭe'amim* II	*Me'orot*
D = Oxford, Bodl., Digby 212, 14th c.	A	v^1	53ra–56rb	34ra–48rb			63r–64r	56ra–63ra	
A = Oxford, Bodl., Ashmole 369, 14th c.	A	v^3	14r–17v						
V = Vienna, ÖNB, 5335, 14th–15th c.	A	v^1	54v–58v	1ra–20vb	28v–39r	43r–45v	39r–43r	20vb–28vb	46v–49r
E = Naples, BSOG, 15.11, 14th–15th c.	A	v^1	172vb–176rb	142ra–153ra	153ra–161vb	165va–167vb	162ra–165va		
K = Klagenfurt, ADG-BM, XXX b 7, 15th c.	A	v^1	209r–213r	159v–170v	180r–191v	196r–198v	191v–196r	170v–180r	200r–202v
C¹ = Oxford, Bodl., Canon. Misc. 190, 15th c.	A	v^1	72va–78va	1r–26r	36r–49r	53v–57r	110r–143v	27r–35r	59r–63v
P¹ = Paris, BnF, lat. 7336, 15th c.	A	v^1	109r–116v	21r–52r	64r–79v	86v–91r	79v–86r	52r–64r	93v–98v

MSS and print editions	T	V	Tp^A or Tp^Q	*Reshit ḥokhmah*	*Moladot*	*Mivḥarim* II	*She'elot* II	*Ṭeʿamim* II	*Me'orot*
P² = Paris, BnF, lat. 7438, 15th c.	A	v¹	168v–180v	1r–63v	87r–120r	130r–138v	118r–130r	63v–86v	142v–151r
P = Paris, BnF, lat. 10269, 15th c.	A	v²	102rb–110vb	1ra–38va	54ra–74rb	82va–87vb	74va–82rb	39ra–53vb	111ra–116ra
N = Vienna, ÖNB, 5309, 15th c.	A	v¹	264r–269v	187r–215v	228r–241r	247r–250v	241r–246v	216ra–226rb	252v–256r
Z = Zurich, ZB, B.244 (769), 15th c.	A	v¹	87ra–92rb	24ra–44vb	58a–69rb	74va–76rb	69va–74va	50vb–58rb	77vb–80va
B = Basel, UB, F.II.10, 15th c.	A	v¹	121ra–125va	91ra–121ra	149va–162rb		125va–130va	131ra–141vb	
V³ = Vienna, ÖNB, 3124, 15th c.	A	v⁶	196rb–198ra		129r–139v		193ra–196ra		
C² = Oxford, Bodl., Canon. Misc. 517, 15th c.	A	v⁷	33ra–35ra						

MSS and print editions	T	V	Tp^A or Tp^Q	*Reshit ḥokhmah*	*Moladot*	*Mivḥarim* II	*She'elot* II	*Ṭe'amim* II	*Me'orot*
U = Dublin, Trinity Coll., 368, 15th c.	A	v^5	37r–40v						
V⁴ = Vienna, ÖNB, 10534, 16th c.	A	v^7	186v–187r						
T = Gloucester, Cathedral Library 15, 16th c	A	v^8	123ra–123vb		39va–43rb				
L = Venice 1507, ed. P. Liechtenstein,	A	v^1	LXXXVrb–XCIvb	IIra–XXXIvb	XLIIIIva–LXva	LXVIIrb–LXXIrb	LXvb–LXVIIra	XXXIIra–XLIIIIrb	LXXIva–LXXvb
G = Ghent, Univ. 5 (416), 15th c.	Q	v^4	96v–103r			91v–96r	85r–91v		

translators.[335] The most frequent case is that of manuscripts that combine *Tp*^{A} with all six of Pietro's other translations of Ibn Ezra. This may explain the wide diffusion of *Tp*^{A} in the fourteenth and particularly in the fifteenth century, in contrast with the restricted dissemination of *Tp*^{Q}, which survives in a unique manuscript together with two other translations of astrological treatises by Ibn Ezra.

The transmission of *Tp*^{A} began immediately after Pietro d'Abano completed his translation at the end of the thirteenth or the beginning of the fourteenth century, but the number of witnesses increased considerably in the course of the fifteenth century. *Tp*^{Q} surfaced in the fifteenth century, in a single witness, and we have no trace of its earlier transmission. *Tp*^{A} and *Tp*^{Q} vanish from the scene after the sixteenth century: as far as I know, there are no further references to *Tp*^{A} or *Tp*^{Q} in Latin astrological literature after the print edition of *Tp*^{A} in 1507. The four-part version of *Tp*^{A} (v^{1}) is represented not only by the greatest number of witnesses but also by the earliest manuscripts, which indicates that this complete version is the closest to the Vorlage of *Tp*^{A} and to *Tp*^{H} as well.

Structure and General Features of *Tp*^{A} and *Tp*^{Q} according to Their Incipits and Explicits

Let us look at the general structure of *Tp*^{A} and *Tp*^{Q}. There is no better way to do this than to present a hierarchical chart of their incipits and explicits. For information about *Tp*^{A} I use **D** and **B**, two manuscripts that include all four parts of *Tp*^{A}. For *Tp*^{Q} I use **G**, the unique witness. All the incipits and explicits of *Tp*^{A} and *Tp*^{Q}, as well as the incipits or heading, explicits or codas, of each of their parts, are translated and indented hierarchically to highlight their role within the text.

Tp^{A}: Incipiunt quidam tractatus particulares. = Here begin certain particular tractates. [**D**, fol. 53ra, line 1]

Tp^{Q}: Liber Abrahe Iudei Avenezre. = Book by Abraham Ibn Ezra, the Jew. [**G**, fol. 97v, header, and in all the following headers on the verso of each folio]

335 One example is **D**. Besides *Tp*^{A} and Pietro d'Abano's translations of *Reshit ḥokhmah*, *She'elot* II, and *Ṭe'amim* II, **D** includes: (1) *Liber Abraham Iudei de nativitatibus* (fols. 30ra–33va); (2) *De planetarum conjunccionibus et annorum revolucionibus*, Henry Bate's translation of *'Olam* I (fols. 48v–52v); (3) *Electiones Abraham*, an anonymous translation of *Mivḥarim* II (fols. 64v–67v); (4) *Liber questionum*, an anonymous translation of *She'elot* II (fols. 67v–72r).

---

*Tp*A: [I] Liber hic quatuor continet capitula. = This book contains four chapters. [**D**, fol. 53ra, lines 2]

*Tp*Q: [I] Incipit liber Abrahe Evenezre Iudei de occultis. Iste liber dividitur in .4. capitula. = Here begins the *Book on Hidden Things* by Abraham Ibn Ezra. This book is divided into four chapters. [**G**, fol. 96v, lines 1–2]

*Tp*A: [I.i] Capitulum primum. = First chapter. [**B**, fol. 121ra, line 45]

*Tp*Q: [I.i] Capitulum primum de intentione. = First chapter on ⟨the querent's⟩ purpose. [**G**, fol. 96v, line 5]

[…]

*Tp*A and *Tp*Q: ----------

---

*Tp*A: [I.ii] Capitulum secundum. Si quis a te quesiverit de aliquo. = Second chapter. If someone asks you about something. [**B**, fol. 121vb, line 21]

*Tp*Q: [I.ii] Capitulum .2m. de intentione per dominos hore. = First chapter on ⟨the querent's⟩ purpose by means of the lords of the hour. [**G**, fol. 97r, line 28]

[…]

*Tp*A and *Tp*Q: ----------

---

*Tp*A: [I.iii] Capitulum tertium. = Third chapter. [**B**, fol. 122rb, line 17]

*Tp*Q: [I.ii] Capitulum .3m. de re absconsa. = Third chapter on the hidden thing. [**G**, fol. 98r, line 4]

[…]

*Tp*A and *Tp*Q: ----------

---

*Tp*A: [I.iv] Capitulum quartum. = Fourth chapter. [**B**, fol. 122va, line 44]

*Tp*Q: [I.ii] Capitulum .4. de fugitivo inveniendo. = Fourth chapter on finding a fugitive. [**G**, fol. 98v, line 9]

[…]

*Tp*A and *Tp*Q: ----------

Tp^{A}: Hic liber terminatur, post quem incipit liber significationis .7. planetarum in .13. generibus vel maneriebus. = This book is completed, and afterwards begins the *Book on the significations of the seven planets in 13 categories*. [**D**, fol. 54ra, lines 36–37]

Tp^{Q}: Explicit liber Abrahe dicti Evenesre de occultis. = This ends the *Book on Hidden Things* by Abraham called Ibn Ezra. [**G**, fol. 99r, line 8]

Tp^{A}: [II] Incipit tractatus de .13. maneriebus planetarum. De maneriebus .13. exponam significationem cuiuslibet planetarum .7. [**B**, fol. 123ra, lines 17–20] = Here begins the *Treatise on the 13 categories of the planets*. I will put forth the signification of each of the seven planets in 13 categories.

Tp^{Q}: [II] Incipit liber Abrahe Evenesre de significationibus 7 planetarum quem transtulit Arnulphus. Ego explanabo tibi significationem 7 planetarum 13 modis. = Here begins the *Book on the significations of the seven planets* by Abraham Ibn Ezra translated by Arnoul. I will explain to you the signification of the seven planets in 13 categories. [**G**, fol. 99r, lines 9–20]

[…]

Tp^{A}: Hic terminatur liber servorum, id est, .7. planetarum. = This completes the *Book of the servants*, that is, the seven planets. [**D**, fol. 55rb, lines 11–12]

Tp^{Q}: Explicit. = Here ends. [**G**, fol. 101r, line 32]

Tp^{A}: [III] Tractatus de significationibus planetarum in .12. domibus Abrahe Avenaris. = *Treatise on the significations of the planets in the 12 places* by Abraham Ibn Ezra. [**D**, fol. 55rb, lines 12–13]

Tp^{Q}: [III] Incipit liber Abrahe Evenezre de significationibus .7. planetarum et capitis et caude per .12. domos. = Here begins the *Book on the significations of the planets, and of the Head ⟨of the Dragon⟩ and ⟨its⟩ Tail, in the 12 places* by Abraham Ibn Ezra. [**G**, fol. 101r, lines 33–34]

[…]

Tp^{A}: ------------------

Tp^{Q}: Explicit. = Here ends. [**G**, fol. 103r, line 9]

Tp^{A}: [IV] Dogma universale in iudiciis. = General doctrine of judgments. [**D**, fol. 56ra, lines 32–33]

Tp^{Q}: [IV] ------------------

[…]

*Tp*A: ------------------

*Tp*Q: ------------------

---

*Tp*A: Finis quorundam tractatuum particularium Abrahe Avenare quos Petrus Paduanus transtulit de Gallico in latinum. = This is the end of certain particular tractates by Abraham Ibn Ezra which Pietro of Padua [i.e. Pietro d'Abano] translated from French into Latin. [**B**, fol. 125va, lines 4–6; cf. **D**, fol. 56ra, lines 32–33]

*Tp*Q: -------

With the help of this hierarchical chart of incipits and explicits I turn now to examine the general structure of *Tp*A and *Tp*Q, and some of their general features: their titles, the name of their translators, the name of their presumptive author, and their source language. A similar examination of the constitutive parts of *Tp*A and *Tp*Q, and especially their source texts, will be carried out in the next part of this study, based on the same hierarchical chart.

a. *General Organization*

Whereas *Tp*A includes four separate treatises, *Tp*Q incorporate only three: the fourth treatise of *Tp*A is missing in *Tp*Q. With the exception of the fourth treatise, *Tp*A and *Tp*Q have the same organization; this includes the first treatise, which is divided into the same four chapters in both translations. Despite their quadripartite and tripartite structures, *Tp*A and *Tp*Q seem to be translations of a self-contained source text and not of separate treatises. This impression is buttressed by the fact that *Tp*A and *Tp*Q have their own title, different from that of their constitutive parts, as we shall see next, and by their hierarchical organization.

b. *Name*

The two translations have different designations. *Tp*A is called *quidam tractatus particulares*, "certain particular tractates," a name that emphasizes that the whole work is made up of separate treatises. *Tp*Q is *Liber Abrahe Iudei Avenezre*, which highlights that the entire work is by one author: Abraham Ibn Ezra. The term *quidam tractatus particulares* occurs twice, in the initial incipit and again in the final colophon of *Tp*A, indicating that it designates a comprehensive work composed of several hierarchically inferior parts. Indeed, as shown in the hierarchical chart of incipits and explicits, each part of *Tp*A has its own implicit and explicit, and most of them have their own titles. *Tp*^{Q} is called *Liber Abrahe Iudei Avenezre* in all the verso running heads of *Tp*^{Q}. That *Liber Abrahe Iudei Avenezre* designates a comprehensive work that includes within it hierarchically inferior components is indicated by the fact that whereas the verso running heads of *Tp*^{Q} are identical and read *Liber Abrahe Iudei Avenezre*, those on the rectos change to indicate the title of the treatise on that folio. Note, however, that in the prologue to his translations, Arnoul de Quincampoix refers to *Tp*^{Q} as *Liber de inventione occultorum*, which is the name of the first treatise of *Tp*^{Q}.[336]

c. *Authorship*

Abraham Ibn Ezra is designated as the author of *Tp*^{A} and *Tp*^{Q}: *Abraham Avenare* in the final colophon of *Tp*^{A}, and *Abraham Avenezra* in all the verso running heads of *Tp*^{Q}. Moreover, as we shall see below, Abraham Ibn Ezra is cited again as the author of the components of *Tp*^{A} and *Tp*^{Q}, and even as the originator of specific ideas mentioned in the first treatise of *Tp*^{A} and *Tp*^{Q}. But the frequent name-dropping does not guarantee that Abraham Ibn Ezra was the author. For solid proof of Ibn Ezra's authorship we need to know the origins of *Tp*^{H}, a task addressed later in this study.

d. *Translator*

Petrus Paduanus, that is, Pietro d'Abano, is explicitly mentioned as the translator of *Tp*^{A} in the colophon of this translation. Pietro's responsibility for *Tp*^{A} is corroborated by the use of idiosyncratic terms and idioms found in his other translations.[337] Arnoul de Quincampoix is nowhere explicitly cited as the translator of the whole *Tp*^{Q}, but he is mentioned as the translator of the second treatise of *Tp*^{Q},[338] and in the prologue to his translations Arnoul informs readers that he intends to translate *Liber de inventione occultorum et forte alii* ("the Book on finding hidden things and perhaps other books").[339] This is a generic reference to the whole of *Tp*^{Q}, because *Liber de inventione occultorum* is the name of the first treatise of *Tp*^{Q} and *alii* "other" seems to be a reference to the other two treatises included in *Tp*^{Q}.

---

336 See below, p. 60.

337 This refers to terms such as *signum commune* to denote "bicorporal sign" (See *Tp*, I iii 1:3, et passim); *principator, principans, prelatus* to denote "ruler" (See *Tp*, II ii 13:3; II v 3:4 and II i 2:2 et passim); and the expression *rectum/rectus est* (See *Tp*, I i 4:9 et passim) to denote agreement with some opinion. See L, sig. LXXXVIva, line 27; sig. LXXXVIIIrb, line 3; sig. LXXXVIvb, line 20.

338 See above, Chart, *Tp*^{Q}, II, on p. 58.

339 See below, p. 61.

e. *Source Language*

B states explicitly that *Tp*^{A} was translated *de Gallico in Latinum*, "from French into Latin." The colophons of the other witnesses of *Tp*^{A} are silent as to the source language, but the use of a French intermediary between *Tp*^{A} and *Tp*^{H} is supported by the colophon of Pietro d'Abano's translation of *Reshit ḥokhmah*, which gives detailed information about Pietro's modus operandi in all his translations of Ibn Ezra and seems to serve as a methodological introduction for all of them. We read in this colophon that *cum Magister Petrus Paduanus invenisset in gallico idiomate, propter inperitiam transferentis ab ebraico, in pluribus defectivum vel corruptum necnon et aliquando inordinate transpositum … prout ei fuit possibile, latina lingua ad Abrahe priorem reduxit intellectum bene dictum omne, et textum et sententiam auctoris servando* = "When Pietro of Padua found ⟨this book⟩ in French, because of the unskillfulness of the translator from the Hebrew, defective in many ways, corrupt, and sometimes poorly arranged and failing to make sense … as far as he could he brought it back in the Latin tongue to Abraham's original meaning, everything well expressed, preserving the text and the meaning of the author."[340] A French intermediary is also attested to by the colophon of Pietro d'Abano's translation of *Moladot*, which states that *Petrus Paduanus ordinavit in latinum ex hebraico in ydeoma gallicum translatus*, "Pietro rendered it into Latin from a Hebrew into French translation."[341]

That *Tp*^{Q} was carried out through a Hebrew to French intermediary is supported by what Arnoul de Quincampoix himself says in the prologue to his translations of Ibn Ezra's astrological writings:

> Ego vero Arnulphus de Quiquenpoit, in scientia minimus, utilitati communi cupiens deservire, quosdam libellos Abrahe, dicti Evenesre Iudei, gloriosissimi et expertissimi astronomi, de gallico in quo prius per alium translati fuerant de hebreo, secundum quod meum ferre poterit ingenium prout melius et intelligibilius potero transferre disposui planius in latinum. … Libri autem quibus ad presens intendimus translationem facere sunt *Liber de questionibus*, *Liber de eleccionibus*, *Liber de inventione occultorum* et forte alii, qui libri valde sunt utiles et necessarii cum in eis racionabilis et compendiosior aliis tractatibus in huius sit processus. Librum autem questionum quia generalior et magis necessarius primitus, deinde *Librum de electionibus* et postea *Librum de occultorum inventionibus* ordinamus.[342]

---

340 Paris, Bibliothèque Sorbonne, MS 640 (13th c.), fol. 95rb, line 50–fol. 95va, line 6; this is the earliest witness of this translation; cf. *Abrahe Avenaris* (Pietro d'Abano), ed. Liechtenstein (1507), sig. XXXvb, lines 1–2.

341 Paris, BnF, MS lat. 10269 (14th c.), fol. 74rb, lines 5–8.

342 **G**, fol. 84v, line 32–fol. 85r, line 13.

> I, Arnoul de Quinquempoix, the least of men in knowledge, wishing to serve the public interest, intend to translate more clearly into Latin certain short books of Abraham called Ibn Ezra, the Jew, a most renowned and experienced astrologer, from French, in which they were previously translated from Hebrew by someone else, according to what my intelligence is able to comprehend and as far as I can do this in the best and most trustworthy way. … The books I intend to translate now are the *Book of Interrogations*, the *Book of Elections*, and the *Book on Finding Hidden Things*, and perhaps other books, which are very useful and necessary, because in them the development ⟨of the idea⟩ is more rational and more succinct than in other treatises. I translate first the *Book of Interrogations*, because it is more comprehensive and necessary, then the *Book of Elections*, and thereafter the *Book on Finding Hidden Things*.

The Hebrew into French intermediate of Tp^{A} and Tp^{Q} has not been found. That this French translation was produced by Hagin le Juif—commissioned by Henry Bate in 1273 to produce Hebrew to French translations of astrological writing by Ibn Ezra[343]—is suggested by the evidence we have that Pietro d'Abano and Arnoul de Quincampoix used Hagin le Juif's versions for some of their Latin translations of Ibn Ezra's astrological writings.[344]

Contents and Sources of Tp^{A} and Tp^{Q}

As seen above, Tp^{A} and Tp^{Q} are parallel Latin translations of a French intermediary translation (probably carried out by Hagin le Juif) of a Hebrew source text that the incipits and explicits of Tp^{A} and Tp^{Q} consistently assign to Abraham Ibn Ezra. Except for a portion of the first treatise of Tp^{A} and Tp^{Q}, however, modern scholarship has been unable to confirm, refute, or explain away this claim. I attempt now to reconstruct the origins of Tp^{H}. The only way to succeed in such an enterprise is to sequentially and meticulously examine the contents of all the components of Tp^{A} and Tp^{Q} and then to look for their counterpart in Ibn Ezra's extant astrological corpus, on the one hand, and in the available Hebrew and Latin medieval astrological literature, on the other. It is to this task that I turn now.

343 Sela forthcoming (a).
344 Sela 2019 (d).

I. *Liber de Occultis*

I begin with the first treatise of *Tp*^{A} and *Tp*^{Q}, designated *Liber de occultis* in the latter but unnamed in the former. For simplicity's sake I will designate it *Liber de occultis*, whether I am referring to the text of *Tp*^{A} or of *Tp*^{Q}. *Liber de occultis* is explicitly assigned to Abraham Ibn Ezra in the incipit and the explicit of *Tp*^{Q}, but not in *Tp*^{A}, although in both translations *Abraham*, presumably Ibn Ezra, is said to be the originator of some of the ideas presented. *Liber de occultis* is the longest of the four treatises of *Tp*^{A} and *Tp*^{Q} (approximately 3,000 out of 8,500 words in *Tp*^{A}). In both of them it is divided into four chapters, whose contents are described in both translations immediately after the incipits.[345] The four chapters of *Liber de occultis* study common topics of the astrological doctrine of interrogations. In what follows, I study the four chapters of *Liber de occultis* separately, briefly describing their contents and showing, as far as possible, its source.

I.1. *Reading Thoughts*

The first chapter of *Liber de occultis*, *De cogitatione hominis ac eius questione*,[346] henceforth *De cogitatione*, is the longest in *Liber de occultis* (approximately 900 out of 3000 words) and deals with "a man's thoughts and his question." This is an essential topic in the astrological doctrine of interrogations, because the astrologer can answer questions only if the querent's intentions are sincere. Since this doctrine presupposes that the astrologer may discover the querent's thoughts by studying the celestial configuration when the horoscope is cast, treatises on the doctrine of interrogations usually begin with a series of methods that allow the astrologer to "read" the querent's thoughts. This applies to *De cogitatione* as well.

I.1.i.

The first method presented in *De cogitatione* consists in determining the position and condition of the lord of the ascendant[347] at the time of the interrogation and relating the querent's thoughts to the indications of the horoscopic place in which the lord of the ascendant is located.[348] A close replica of this method in *Tp*^{A} and *Tp*^{Q} may be found in two Latin sources and one Hebrew source.

---

345 See *Tp*, I:1–4 and I:⟨⟨1–4⟩⟩.

346 See *Tp*, I:1.

347 For this concept, see note on *El*, I 2:2.

348 See *Tp*, I i 1:1–14 through I i 3:1–4. This technique is also briefly mentioned in *She'elot* I, § 5:1–2, 242–243 (assigned to Dorotheus), and in *She'elot* II, § 9:1–2, 354–355 (assigned to Māshā'allāh).

The two Latin sources are related treatises, variously attributed to Ptolesmy and Aristotle, known as Ptolemy's *Iudicia* and Aristotle's *Iudicia*. Each consists of two parts with the same contents: (a) an introduction to astrology including definitions of terms, descriptions of natives born under different planets and signs of the zodiac, etc.; (b) instructions on how to answer questions on a wide variety of topics posed to the astrologer by the querent and according to the position of the planet that functions as the lord of the ascendant in the twelve places of the natal horoscope. Ptolemy's *Iudicia* is extant in no fewer than 20 manuscripts, of which the earliest are from the twelfth century,[349] and was extensively used before 1141 by Raymond of Marseilles in his *Liber iudiciorum*. Aristotle's *Iudicia* is preserved in at least 15 manuscripts, of which the earliest is also from the twelfth century;[350] it is mentioned in the *Liber novem iudicum*, a Latin compilation of astrological texts said to have been translated from Arabic by Hermann of Carinthia and Hugo of Santalla in the middle of the twelfth century in northeastern Spain. The earliest witness of Ptolemy's *Iudicia* (MS Harley 5402) ascribes the work to *Alkanderinus*,[351] which recalls *Alchandreus*, a name associated with the late-tenth century Latin corpus of Arabic astrological material designated *Alchandreana* (see below, p. 70). The parallels between the subject matter, language, and style of Ptolemy's *Iudicia* and of the *Alchandreana* are so close that it has been suggested that they share a common source. Both include Arabic transliterations; hence it stands to reason that their ancestor was a tenth-century Arabic text, now lost, that was part of the aforementioned *Alchandreana*.[352]

The Hebrew counterpart of the first method in *De cogitatione* is *Kelal ha-She'elot le-divrei Talmai*, "All the questions according to Ptolemy" (henceforth *She'elot le-Talmai*), a pseudo-Ptolemaic work on interrogations, which, as a standalone treatise, is extant in at least 10 Hebrew manuscripts from the fifteenth through nineteenth centuries; some of them also contain collections of Ibn Ezra's Hebrew astrological works.[353] But the earliest copies

[349] London, British Library, MS Harley 5402 (before 1160), fols. 1r–15r; Paris, BnF, MS lat. 16208 (12th c.), fols. 59rb–65ra.

[350] BnF, lat. 16208, fols. 76ra–83vb.

[351] MS Harley 5402, fol. 1r.

[352] Burnett 2009, 39–62; Juste 2013, 145–164, esp. pp. 150–153.

[353] The earliest copy of *She'elot le-Talmai* is from the 15th century: Munich, Bayerische Staatsbibliothek, Cod. Hebr. 202, fols. 130a–137b [IMHM: F 1649 (IMHM = Institute for Microfilmed Hebrew Manuscripts, Jewish National and University Library, Jerusalem)]. The other nine copies were copied from the 17th to 19th centuries. See, for example, New York, Jewish Theological Seminary, MS 2583 (19th c.), fols. 86a–69b [IMHM: F 28836].

of *She'elot le-Talmai* are embedded within a work explicitly ascribed to Abraham Ibn Ezra, entitled *Sefer ha-She'elot*, "Book of interrogations," as if *She'elot le-Talmai* were by Ibn Ezra. This *Sefer ha-She'elot*, however, is an anthology of astrological fragments of diverse length and origin, some of them taken from texts by Ibn Ezra, and is not identical with any of the three versions of Ibn Ezra's *Sefer ha-She'elot*, as we shall see below.[354]

She'elot le-Talmai employs a peculiar terminology: on the one hand, the verb להדין "to judge," frequently found in Ibn Ezra's astrological corpus; on the other, מתכסה, lit. "be covered" or "be hidden," which intriguingly denotes the concept of "burnt" (Hebrew נשרף; Arabic محترق, Latin *combustus*) and was never used by Ibn Ezra. This means that *She'elot le-Talmai* could not have been written or translated by Ibn Ezra, but rather by someone familiar with his terminology. How can the use of מתכסה be accounted for? This weird term is in all likelihood a literal Hebrew rendering of منكسف, lit. "be covered" or "be hidden," but denoting the concept of being eclipsed. In an astrological context, to be "burnt" is one of the conditions of the planets vis-à-vis the Sun and takes place when the planet moves slightly away from conjunction with the Sun, that is, after the planet had been eclipsed by the Sun. This may explain the confusion between being "eclipsed" and being "burnt."[355] In any case, the use of מתכסה in *She'elot le-Talmai* indicates that this Hebrew work was translated from Arabic and not from either Latin *Iudicia*.

What is the relationship between *She'elot le-Talmai*, on the one hand, and Ptolemy's and Aristotle's *Iudicia*, on the other? A comparison shows that *She'elot le-Talmai*, as it survives today, is a close replica of the complete second part of the two *Iudicia* texts, but totally lacks the introduction to astrology found in them. In addition, *She'elot le-Talmai* lacks some short passages that occur in Tp^A and Tp^Q and in the *Iudicia*. Was the first method in *De cogitatione* derived from the *Iudicia* or from *She'elot le-Talmai*? Since Tp^A and Tp^Q are translations, via a French intermediary, of a Hebrew source

354 See Oxford, Bodleian Library, MS Opp. 707 [Neubauer 2025], fols. 114r–155v [IMHM: F 19310], copied in 1410. *She'elot le-Talmai* is on fols. 130v–138r. The header of *Sefer ha-She'elot* in this manuscript reads: "ספר השאלות. אמר רבי אברהם בר מאיר ן' עזרא הספרדי ז"ל סוד יי ליראיו ובריתו להודיעם." = "Book of interrogations. R. Abraham, the son of Meir Ibn Ezra, the Spaniard, of blessed memory, said: The counsel of the Lord is with them that fear Him; and His covenant, to make them know it [Ps. 25:14]." A second copy of *Sefer ha-She'elot* is in Munich, Bayerische Staatsbibliothek, MS Cod. Hebr. 45, fols. 478a–509b [IMHM: F 01139], copied in 1552. *She'elot le-Talmai* in this manuscript is fols. 491v–497v. For an account of *Sefer ha-She'elot*, see below, p. 79.

355 For this concept, see note on *El*, II i 1:5.

text, the second possibility is more plausible. However, because the last passage of the account of *Tp*^{A} and *Tp*^{Q} has its counterpart in Ptolemy's and Aristotle's *Iudicia* but not in *She'elot le-Talmai*,[356] the natural implication is that the surviving *She'elot le-Talmai* is a reduced version of an original translation into Hebrew from the same Arabic predecessor of the *Iudicia*, and perhaps included both parts of the *Iudicia* in full.

An appendix in Part Seven of this volume prints an entire section of *She'elot le-Talmai*, accompanied by an English translation, together with a complete section of Ptolemy's *Iudicia*, "Ptolemy's judgments," also accompanied by an English translation.[357] These two parallel sections of *She'elot le-Talmai* and Ptolemy's *Iudicia* were selected not only because they are virtually identical with each other but also with the whole section of *Tractatus particulares* (I i 1:1–14 through I i 3:1–4) that brings the first method in *De cogitatione*. For the correspondences between *Tractatus particulares*, *She'elot le-Talmai*, and Ptolemy's *Iudicia*, readers are invited to consult the notes to the English translation of the section of *Tractatus particulares* (I i 1:1–14 through I i 3:1–4) that presents the first method in *De cogitatione*.

I.1.ii.

Immediately after these instructions, *De cogitatione* has a passage, headed *Dicit quoque Abraham*, that is an alternative Latin translation of a passage from *She'elot* III, whose Hebrew original is lost but which survives in the last chapter of *Interrogationes*, which purportedly addresses interrogations related to the twelfth horoscopic place.[358] This passage presents four additional methods for reading the querent's mind, by observing: (i) the ninth-part[359] from the ascendant,[360] (ii) the Moon and the lot of Fortune,[361] (iii) the planet that has power in the five places of dignities, and the lord of the hour or the lord of the day,[362] and (iv) "the nature of whatever degree of the zodiac, according to what is written in the *Book Tamedas*." The fourth method is explained in further detail and completed by the statement that the *Book Tamedas* is a "valuable book."[363]

---

356 See *Tp*, I i 3:1–4 and note.

357 See below, "A section of *She'elot le-Talmai* and its counterpart in Ptolemy's *Iudicia*," on pp. 505–509.

358 See *Tp*, I i 4:1–10; Cf. *Int*, II xii 2:1–9.

359 For this concept, see note on *Int*, II xii 2:2.

360 See *Tp*, I i 4:1–3; cf. *Int*, II xii 2:1–2.

361 See *Tp*, I i 4:4; cf. *Int*, II xii 2:3. For the concept of lot of Fortune, see note on *Int*, II i 9:1.

362 See *Tp*, I i 4:5; cf. *Int*, II xii 2:4. For the concepts of "five places of dignities," "lord of the hour," and "lord of the day," see, respectively, notes to *Int*, II i 15:1, and *Tp*, I:3.

363 See *Tp*, I i 4:6–10; cf. *Int*, II xii 2:5–9.

We see, then, that the fourth method, "observing the nature of whatever degree of the zodiac," is mentioned in *De cogitatione* and in *Interrogationes* according to "what is written in the *Book Tamedas*." This method is explained in the passage quoted above in more detail than the other three methods, and, at the end, *De cogitatione* and *Interrogationes* say that this *Liber Tamedas* or *Liber Samechem* is a "valuable book." *Tamedas* is mentioned again in the second chapter of *Liber de occultis* in a passage that is an alternative Latin translation of a passage from the lost *She'elot* III that survives in *Interrogationes*.[364] The natural implication is that the originator of *Tp*^{H} (not Abraham Ibn Ezra himself) did not know *Tamedas* first hand but only through *She'elot* III. *Tamedas* is never mentioned elsewhere in Ibn Ezra's astrological corpus nor, as far as I know, in the Arabic and Latin astrological literature.

What is this *Tamedas*? A valuable clue is furnished by the description of the fourth method, in which *Tamedas* instructs the astrologer to "observe the nature of whatever degree of the zodiac" and "not to answer regarding thoughts unless he knows what each degree signifies." This is in all likelihood a reference to one of the two methods used in Arabic astrology to determine the "dodecatemoria," as described by Abū Maʿshar in his *Great Introduction*. The first divides each zodiacal sign into twelve equal parts of 2½° each; the first dodecatemorion is assigned to the ascendant sign, and the lord of this sign is the lord of this dodecatemorion; the subsequent dodecatemoria are assigned to the following signs, and the lords of these signs are the lords of the corresponding dodecatemoria.[365] The second method assigns the successive degrees of a certain sign to the 12 signs, in sequence; the lords of these signs, beginning with the ascendant sign, are the lords of these degrees or dodecatemoria.[366] Ibn Ezra describes the same method in similar terms and ascribes it to Hermes and the Ancients in *Reshit ḥokhmah*.[367] Abū Maʿshar, too, ascribes the method to Hermes and the ancient writers, and, at the end of his account, says that "Hermes mentioned in his book many judgments made according to each degree of each sign, in different kinds of topics in nativities and questions."[368] Note the

364 See *Tp*, I ii 8:1 and *Int*, II xii 3:1.

365 An account of the same method is found in *Tp*, I i 3:1–4. The first method is also described in al-Qabīṣī's *Introduction* (ed. Burnett et al. (2004), IV:15, 128–129). See also Bouché-Leclercq 1899, 299–304.

366 Abū Maʿshar's *Great Introduction*, ed. Burnett and Yamamoto (2019), V:18 [1–4], 520–523.

367 See *Reshit ḥokhmah*, § 2.1:46, 64–65.

368 See *Great Introduction*, ed. Burnett and Yamamoto (2019), V:18 [3], 521.

striking resemblance between "observing the nature of whatever degree of the zodiac" mentioned in the fourth method of *De cogitatione* and "making judgments according to each degree of each sign" as mentioned by Abū Maʿshar. The natural inference is that *Tamedas* is the book by Hermes that, according to Abū Maʿshar, contains the description of the second method for determining the dodecatemoria. Another possibility is that *Tamedas* is the 9th century *Kitāb al-daraj* (Book of the degrees), the bulk of which consists of a catalog of the characteristics of the seven planets and of all 360 degrees of the zodiac, intended to be used in interpreting a newborn's horoscope.[369]

I.1.iii.

The last section of *De cogitatione* is headed *Dicit Māshāʾallāh*, "Māshāʾallāh says," and is essentially a Latin translation of a passage from *Sefer ha-She'elot le-Māshāʾallāh*, "Book of interrogations by Māshāʾallāh," henceforth *She'elot le-Māshāʾallāh*, a popular Hebrew translation of the lost Arabic Book of Interrogations by Māshāʾallāh, extant in at least 19 Hebrew manuscripts, most of them from the fourteenth or fifteenth century.[370] A parallel Latin translation of this lost work, by Māshāʾallāh is variously entitled *Liber interpretationum, De inventione occultorum, De interpretationibus secundum Messahalam, De inventionibus occultorum, Libellus interpretationum*, etc. This translation dates from the first half of the twelfth century, was probably carried out by John of Seville, and is extant in at least 51 manuscripts.[371]

An appendix in Part Seven of this volume presents seven fragments from *She'elot le-Māshāʾallāh* whose Latin counterpart may be found in seven fragments of *Tractatus particulares*. These seven Hebrew fragments are accompanied by an English translation, together with their Latin counterpart in *Liber interpretationum*.[372] The first three fragments are a translation of

---

369 See Roberts 2013, 279–303.

370 These are the earliest witnesses of *She'elot le-Māshāʾallāh*, copied in the 14th and 15th centuries: Oxford, Bodleian, MS Opp. Add. Qu. 160 [Neubauer 2518] [IMHM: F 22230] (1367), fols. 154r–158r; Cambridge, University Library, MS Add. 481 [IMHM: F 16778] (14th c.), fols. 214v–218r; Paris, BnF, MS héb. 1055 [IMHM: F 14658] (14th c.), fols. 38v–40r; Cambridge, University Library, MS Add. 1517 [IMHM: F 17454] (14th–15th c.), fols. 61v–62v; Vatican, Biblioteca Apostolica Vaticana, MS ebr. 47 [IMHM: F 686] (14th–15th c.), fols. 81r–83v; Warsaw, Żydowski Instytut Historyczny, MS 255 [IMHM: F 10122] (1460), fols. 60v–62v; Munich, Bayerische Staatsbibliothek, Cod. Hebr. 202 [IMHM: F 01649] (15th c.), fols. 124r–127r; New York, Jewish Theological Seminary, MS 2625 [IMHM: F 28878] (15th c.), fols. 104r–106r; Paris, BnF, MS héb. 1045 [IMHM: F 33996] (15th c.), fols. 177r–180r; Cambridge, University Library, MS Add. 1563 [IMHM: F 17475] (15th c.), fols. 82v–85v.

371 See Juste 2016, 173–194, on 177, 190 (*Liber interpretationum*); Carmody 1956, 33–35; Thorndike 1956, 54–56. For an English translation, see *Hidden things*, trans. Dykes 2008.

372 See "Passages of *She'elot le-Māshāʾallāh* in *Tractatus particulares*," on pp. 497–504.

the last section of *De cogitatione*, which describes three significators for thoughts: (i) the lord of the ascendant and the receiver of its power;[373] (ii) the horoscopic place in which the significator is located;[374] (iii) the *mubtazz* of the ascendant, that is, the planet with the most dignities in the ascendant.[375]

At the end of the description of the third significator, *De cogitatione* and *She'elot le-Māshā'allāh* mention the dodecatemoria as the "strongest" significator. To clarify this point, *De cogitatione* and *She'elot le-Māshā'allāh* offer an identical example, in which each zodiacal sign is assigned 2½°.[376] This shows clearly that they are referring to the first of the aforementioned two methods for determining the dodecatemoria. This identical example epitomizes the dependence of Tp^{H} on *She'elot le-Māshā'allāh*. As we shall see below, this is not the only instance in which Tp^{H} follows *She'elot le-Māshā'allāh* closely.

She'elot le-Māshā'allāh was and still is associated with Abraham Ibn Ezra: in almost all the extant manuscripts it was copied together with various collections of Ibn Ezra's astrological writings; it shares common Hebrew terminology with Ibn Ezra's writings;[377] and prominent scholars such as Steinschneider thought it was executed by Ibn Ezra himself.[378] However, Ibn Ezra does not identify himself as the translator, as he does in the translations certainly carried out by him,[379] Ibn Ezra never quotes *verbatim* from *She'elot le-Māshā'allāh* in his own Hebrew work, and *She'elot le-Māshā'allāh* also evinces significant divergences from Ibn Ezra's terminology.[380] Therefore, it is more plausible that it was translated from the Arabic original after Ibn Ezra's death by one of Ibn Ezra's students or admirers and then incorporated into collections of Ibn Ezra's astrological writings copied from the thirteenth century on.[381]

---

373 See *Tp*, I i 5:1–4 and notes; Cf. *She'elot le-Māshā'allāh*, Passage 1, 1–4, 498.

374 See *Tp*, I i 6:1–2 and notes; Cf. *She'elot le-Māshā'allāh*, Passage 2, 1–2, 499.

375 See *Tp*, I i 7:1–3, and notes; Cf. *She'elot le-Māshā'allāh*, Passage 3, 1–3 499–500.

376 See *Tp*, I i 8:1–2, and notes; Cf. *She'elot le-Māshā'allāh*, Passage 4, 1–2, 500.

377 This refers to the following idiosyncratic terms used frequently by Ibn Ezra (the folios refer to MS Opp. Add. Qu. 160): כלי נחושת (154r) for the astrolabe; דינים (158r) for judgments; שר הפנים (154v) for lord of the decan; תקיף (154v) for the strongest planet; יתדות (155v) for the cardines of the horoscope; שליט (157r) for ruler.

378 Steinschneider 1880/1925, 127 (*Gesammelte Schriften*, 497).

379 *Ibn al-Muthannā's Commentary*, ed. Goldstein (1967), 302.

380 This refers, inter alia, to the following terms never used by Ibn Ezra (the folios refer to MS Opp. Add. Qu. 160): החלק הטוב (157r) for the lot of Fortune; שלטנות (157r) for rulership; נזור (157v) for retrograde; as well as the use of latinized names for the planets and other items.

381 Leicht 2012, 270.

I.2. *What Is the Querent Hiding in His Hand?*

The second chapter of *Liber de occultis*—"Quod illud est quod occultat in manu et de colore ipsius,"[382] henceforth *Quod occultat in manu*—covers approximately 770 out of the 3000 words of *Liber de occultis*, and addresses the question of how the astrologer can know what the querent is hiding in his hand and its color, a topic that may be found in other treatises on interrogations.[383] *Quod occultat in manu* is divided into two sections.

I.2.i.

The first section makes the answer depend on the time when the question is posed and provides a list of possible answers, as a function of whether the question was posed at the beginning, in the middle, or at the end of the hours during which each of the seven planets is in charge, every day of the week.[384] This entire section has a close counterpart in three texts of the so-called *Alchandreana*, an astrological corpus translated and adapted from Arabic in the tenth century, but including Hebrew and Latin sources as well. These three texts are *Epistola Argafalau ad Alexandrum*, *Proportiones competentes in astrorum industria*, and *Benedictum sit nomen domini*;[385] but the Hebrew source of this section of *Quod occultat in manu*, a Hebrew translation of the Arabic predecessor or the Hebrew source of one of these Latin texts, is now lost. An appendix in Part Seven of this volume presents a section of *Epistola Argafalau ad Alexandrum* that has a close counterpart in a whole part of *Tractatus particulares*.[386]

I.2.ii.

The second section assigns an alternative approach explicitly to *Abraham*, presumably Abraham Ibn Ezra, who is said to have taken it from the aforementioned *Book of Tamedas*. This approach takes into consideration the

---

382 See *Tp*, I:3 and I:⟨⟨4⟩⟩.

383 See *Int*, II xii 3:1 and *She'elot le-Talmai*, Oxford, Bodleian Library, MS Opp. 707 [Neubauer 2025], fol. 132v. (אם תרצה לדעת איזה דבר ביד אדם = "If you wish to know what a man holds in his hand").

384 See *Tp*, I ii 1:1–3 through I ii 7:1–3, and **G**, fol. 97r, line 29–fol. 97v, line 34. This method is based on the astrological theory that holds that the seven planets govern the hours of the seven weekdays in succession.

385 See, respectively, *Epistola Argafalau ad Alexandrum*, chapter 2, in *Alchandreana*, ed. Juste (2007), pp. 474–476; *Proportiones competentes in astrorum industria*, chapter 17, in *Alchandreana*, ed. Juste (2007), pp. 525–527, and *Benedictum sit nomen domini*, chapter 7, in *Alchandreana*, ed. Juste (2007), pp. 614–617. For the correspondences between *Tractatus particulares* and these three texts of the *Alchandreana*, see notes to *Tp*, I ii 1:1–3 through I ii 7:1–3.

386 See "Fragments of *Epistola Argafalau ad Alexandrum*," on pp. 531–534.

nature of the ascendant sign and its lord, the lord of the hour, the lord of the term, and the location of the Moon. This entire second section of *Quod occultat in manu* is a Latin translation of a passage from the twelfth and last chapter of the lost *She'elot* III, a parallel Latin translation of which survives in the twelfth chapter of *Interrogationes*.[387]

I.3. *Finding a Hidden Object*

The third chapter of *Liber de occultis, De re absconsa et loco eius*,[388] henceforth *De re absconsa*—approximately 690 out of the 3000 words of *Liber de occultis*—deals with finding the location of a hidden object or buried treasure, a common topic in treatises on interrogations.[389] Four methods are presented.

I.3.i.

The first method, assigned to Yaʿqub al-Kindī, consists of finding, first, whether the hidden object has been removed, then roughly establishing its location in the house, and finally identifying the precise place in the house. Such an approach occurs in *She'elot* I, where it is ascribed to Abū ʿAli, and in *She'elot* II, where it is ascribed to Yaʿqub al-Kindī.[390] However, the account in *De re absconsa* is a Latin translation of a passage from the twelfth chapter of *She'elot* III, an alternative Latin translation of which survives in the twelfth chapter of *Interrogationes*.[391]

I.3.ii.

Three additional methods for finding a hidden object are put forward in *De re absconsa*, all of them based on establishing correspondences between certain places in the interrogational horoscope and the predicted place of the hidden object. According to the first, ascribed to Māshā'allāh, the correspondence is between the location of the lord of the ascendant and the lord of the hour with respect to the four cardines[392] of the interrogational horoscope, on the one hand, and the cardinal direction in which the object

387 See *Tp*, I ii 8:1–2, I ii 9:1; I ii 10:1–2, a parallel Latin translation of which survives in *Int*, II xii 3:1, II xii 4:1, II xii 5:1–2.

388 See *Tp*, I:4 and I:⟨⟨5⟩⟩.

389 See, for example, *She'elot* I, §4.4:1–6 through §4.10:1–5, 258–263, and *She'elot* II, §12.5:1–5 through §12.7:1–4, 390–395.

390 See *She'elot* I, §4.7:1–3, 260–261 and *She'elot* II, Sela, §12.6:1–2, 392–303.

391 See *Tp*, I iii 1:1–6, a parallel Latin translation of which survives in *Int*, II xii 6:1–6.

392 For the concept of cardines, see note on *Int*, II xii 9:4.

is hidden, on the other. According to the second method, also ascribed to Māshā'allāh, the correspondence is between the location of the lord of the ascendant and the lord of the hour with respect to the four cardines of the interrogational horoscope, on the one hand, and the cardinal direction in which the object is hidden, on the other. According to the third method, ascribed to Ptolemy, the correspondence is between the cardinal direction of the sign[393] in which the lord of the hour is located, on the one hand, and the cardinal direction in which the object is hidden, on the other. The passage in *De re absconsa* where these three approaches are described is an alternative Latin translation of a passage from the aforementioned *She'elot le-Māshā'allāh*.[394]

I.4. *Finding a Fugitive*

The fourth chapter of *Liber de occultis*—*In loco fugitivi*[395]—is the shortest, at 550 words. It presents a number of methods for finding a fugitive, a common topic in treatises on interrogations.[396] *In loco fugitivi* is a Latin translation of the last section of the twelfth chapter of the lost *She'elot* III, an alternative Latin translation of which survives in the twelfth chapter of *Interrogationes*.[397]

II. *Liber Servorum*

The second treatise of *Tp*ᴬ and *Tp*ᵠ is also the second-longest (approximately 2,760 out of the 8,500 words of *Tp*ᴬ). It is explicitly ascribed to Abraham Ibn Ezra in the incipit of *Tp*ᵠ. The incipit in *Tp*ᴬ does not give Abraham Ibn Ezra as the author, but the corresponding coda designates the second treatise by the peculiar name *Liber servorum*, "Book of the Servants." *Mesharetim* (משרתים), literally "servants" but denoting the planets, may be

393 This approach takes into consideration that the astrologers divide the zodiacal signs into eastern, western, southern, or northern.

394 For these three methods, and their Hebrew counterpart in *She'elot le-Māshā'allāh*, see (1) *Tp*, I iii 2:1–6, and *She'elot le-Māshā'allāh*, Passage 5, 1–6, 500–501; (2) *Tp*, I iii 3:1–6, and *She'elot le-Māshā'allāh*, Passage 6, 1–7, 502–503; and (3) *Tp*, I iii 4:1–10 and *She'elot le-Māshā'allāh*, Passage 7, 1–10, 503–504.

395 See *Tp*, I:5 and I:⟨⟨6⟩⟩.

396 See, for example, *She'elot* I, § 7.8:1–8, 278–281; *She'elot* II, § 8.1:1–5, 376–377.

397 For the five sections of *In loco fugitivi* and their counterpart in *Interrogationes*, see: (1) *Tp*, I iv 1:1–10, and *Int*, II xii 7:1–10; (2) *Tp*, I iv 2:1–4, and *Int*, II xii 8:1–4; (3) *Tp*, I iv 3:1–4, and *Int*, II xii 9:1–4; (4) *Tp*, I iv 4:1–5, and *Int*, II xii 10:1–5; and (5) *Tp*, I iv 5:1–2, and *Int*, II xii 11:1–2. Cf. **G**, fol. 98v, line 10 through fol. 99r, line 7.

Ibn Ezra's most distinctive neologism.[398] Its use in the title of the second treatise of *Tp*^A not only betrays Ibn Ezra's alleged authorship but also indicates that its original Hebrew title was *Sefer ha-Mesharetim* (ספר המשרתים = Book of the planets). I will henceforth use *Liber servorum* to designate the second treatise of *Tp*^A and *Tp*^Q. *Liber servorum* is also called *Tractatus in tredecim maneriebus planetarum*, "Treatise on the 13 categories of the planets," in the incipit of *Tp*^A,[399] and *Liber Abrahe Evenezre, de significationibus septem planetarum*, "Book on the significations of the seven planets by Ibn Ezra," in the incipit of *Tp*^Q, which also states that it presents "the signification of the seven planets in 13 categories."[400]

Both *Tp*^A and *Tp*^Q present these "13 categories"—categories of astrological properties according to which the seven planets are described—immediately after the titles.[401] Ibn Ezra describes the properties of the seven planets in every one of his extant introductions to astrology, but never according to these "13 categories" or in the order in which these categories appear in *Liber servorum*.[402] This is probably why researchers failed to identify the source of *Liber servorum* in Ibn Ezra's astrological corpus. In fact, close scrutiny reveals that *Liber servorum* is simply a reworking of the account of the seven planets in Ibn Ezra's *Mishpeṭei ha-mazzalot*.

More precisely, the originator of the Hebrew source text of *Liber servorum* gleaned the building blocks of the account of the seven planets from discontinuous loci in *Mishpeṭei ha-mazzalot* and assembled them into *Liber servorum* according to the aforementioned 13 categories and in the order in which they appear in *Liber servorum*. It is worth noting that this applies to the bulk of *Liber servorum*, but there are a few passages whose counterpart I could not find in Ibn Ezra's *Mishpeṭei ha-mazzalot*, as this work is extant today. It cannot be ruled out that the originator of *Tp*^H used an early version of *Mishpeṭei ha-mazzalot* that is now lost,[403] although it is also possibly that these passages were added by the originator of *Tp*^H himself.

---

398 For this neologism, see note on *Tp*, II vii 14:1.

399 See *Tp*, II.

400 See *Tp*, II and II:⟨⟨1⟩⟩.

401 See *Tp*, II:2–14 and II:⟨⟨2–14⟩⟩.

402 *Reshit ḥokhmah*, § 4.1:1–2 through § 4.7:1–29, 146–183; *Mishpeṭei ha-mazzalot*, § 38:1–15 through § 44:1–9, 520–531; *Ṭeʿamim* I, § 4.1:1–7 through § 4.8:1–8, 68–81; *Ṭeʿamim* II, § 5.1:1–16 through § 5.9:1–5, 216–235.

403 In my edition of *Mishpeṭei ha-mazzalot* I presented evidence that the text of this work as we have it today is the result of interpolations and changes made either by Ibn Ezra in different stages of its composition or by copyists in the early stages of the transmission of the original text. See Sela 2017, 9–10.

An appendix in Part Seven of this volume contains all the relevant passages of the account of the seven planets in *Mishpeṭei ha-mazzalot* that are quoted or paraphrased in *Tractatus particulares*.[404] For the correspondences between *Liber servorum* and the account of the seven planets in *Mishpeṭei ha-mazzalot*, readers are invited to consult the notes to the English translation of *Liber servorum* in this volume.[405]

III. *De Significationibus Planetarum*

The third treatise of *Tp*^{A} and *Tp*^{Q} is also the third-longest (approximately 1650 words) and has similar titles in *Tp*^{A} and *Tp*^{Q}: *Tractatus de significationibus planetarum in duodecim domibus Abrahe Avenaris* in the former, and *Liber Abrahe Evenezre de significationibus septem planetarum et capitis et caude per duodecim domos* in the latter.[406] I will henceforth refer to it as *De significationibus*. Like the *Liber servorum*, *De significationibus* addresses the planets' astrological properties, but instead of describing them according to 13 categories it does so according to the 12 horoscopic places. Both *Tp*^{A} and *Tp*^{Q} explicitly ascribe *De significationibus* to Abraham Ibn Ezra. In fact, Ibn Ezra never organized his accounts of the planets' astrological properties according to the 12 horoscopic places.

Close scrutiny reveals that *De significationibus* is virtually identical with *Significationes planetarum in domibus*, henceforth *Significationes*, a popular Latin treatise extant in 65 manuscripts and a number of print editions, and credited to an unidentified author variously called Gergis, Iergis, or Girgith.[407] Nevertheless, *De significationibus* and *Significationes* are organized differently. *De significationibus* is organized in twelve sections (for each of the horoscopic places), each of them divided into nine paragraphs (for each of the seven planets, plus the Head and Tail of the Dragon); each paragraph presents the indications of the relevant planet or the Head/Tail of the Dragon in the relevant horoscopic place. By contrast, *Significationes* is organized in nine sections (for the seven planets and the Head/Tail of the Dragon), each of them divided into 12 paragraphs (for each of the twelve horoscopic places); each paragraph presents the indications of the relevant

---

404 See "The account of the seven planets in *Mishpeṭei ha-mazzalot*," on pp. 517–524.

405 See English translation of *Tp*, II i 1:1–5 through II vii 14:1, and notes, on pp. 293–314, 347–368.

406 See *Tp*, III.

407 See Juste 2016, 177, 187; Carmody 1956, 72. For an English translation, see *Significationes*, trans. Dykes 2008. For the Latin text, see Paris, BnF, MS lat. 16204, pp. 428b–432b.

planet, or of the Head/Tail of the Dragon in the relevant horoscopic place. In addition, *De significationibus* and *Significationes* take up the planets in a different order.[408]

The fourth treatise of *Tp*^A is missing from *Tp*^Q. Note, however, that **G** (the unique witness of *Tp*^Q) has a complete copy of *Significationes* immediately after *De significationibus*. This indicates that either Arnoul de Quincampoix, who produced *Tp*^Q, or Raphael de Marcatelle, who commissioned **G**, or the scribe who copied **G**, was aware of the close relationship between *De significationibus planetarum* and *Significationes planetarum in domibus* and therefore placed them one after the other in the manuscript.

The Hebrew source text of *De significationibus* is completely lost. The explicit of one manuscript of *Significationes* says that this text was translated by John of Spain *de hebreo in latinum*.[409] But there is no critical edition of *Significationes* and more research is needed to validate this statement. The available information suggests, however, that both *De significationibus* and *Significationes* are parallel Latin translations of the same lost Hebrew source. Whereas *Significationes* follows the wording and the organization of the lost Hebrew text closely, *De significationibus* follows the wording but considerably alters the structure. This should not come as a surprise, because the originator of *Tp*^H proceeded in the same way with *Liber servorum*: he kept the wording of Ibn Ezra's *Mishpeṭei ha-mazzalot* but dramatically changed its organization.

An appendix in Part Seven of this volume presents the complete Latin text of *Significationes planetarum in domibus* ascribed to Gergis.[410] For all the correspondences between *De significationibus* and *Significationes*, readers are invited to consult the notes to the English translation of the third part of *Tractatus particulares* in the current volume.[411]

---

408 *De significationibus* uses this order: Sun, Moon, Saturn, Jupiter, Mars, Venus, Mercury, Caput of the Dragon, Tail. By contrast *Significationes* uses this order: Sun, Venus, Mercury, Moon, Saturn, Jupiter, Mars, Caput of the Dragon, Tail.

409 Vicenza, Bibl. Civica Bertoliana, MS 208 (132), fol. 164v: "Explicit liber Alchabicii de significationibus .7^m. planetarum et capitis et caude draconis in .12. domibus a Ioanne Isanno interpretatus de hebreo in latinum." In addition, the copy of *Significationes* found in MS Gloucester, Cathedral Library, 15, fols. 154ra–154vb, assigns this work to *Abraham Avenesre*. See fol. 154ra, upper margin. The same manuscript includes an incomplete copy of *Tp*^A. See above, table on p. 55, MS T.

410 See "*Signsificationes planetarum in domibus ascribed to Gergis*," on pp. 510–516. An English translation of this text is found in *Significations*, trans. Dykes, 2008.

411 See *Tp*, III 1:2–10 through III 12:2–10, and notes.

IV. *Dogma Universale in Iudiciis*

Dogma universale is an almost complete Latin translation of a work by Māshā'allāh on reading thoughts, which was produced from a Hebrew source text of which only the first 26 words survive in all manuscripts that include copies of the aforementioned *She'elot le-Māshā'allāh*, just before the text of that work.[412] As noted, *She'elot le-Māshā'allāh* was traditionally associated with Ibn Ezra. That this 26-word fragment appears in all the extant manuscripts just before of *She'elot le-Māshā'allāh* indicates that the Hebrew translations of the two works by Māshā'allāh were produced by the same translator and copied together, but that at some stage of their transmission the first text was truncated. This may explain why the lost Hebrew translation of Māshā'allāh's work on reading thoughts was later associated with Ibn Ezra, just like *She'elot le-Māshā'allāh*. Moreover, as we will see, the Latin text of *Dogma universale* employs the Latin term *honor* to denote exaltation.[413] This is a literal translation of כבוד, used frequently by Ibn Ezra throughout his oeuvre to denote the astrological concept of exaltation.[414]

A complete alternative Latin translation of the same work by Māshā'allāh on reading thoughts, variously designated *De interpretatione cogitationis*, *De intentione*, or *De cogitationibus ab intentione* (henceforth *De interpretatione*), was translated from Arabic by John of Seville in the first half of the twelfth century, and is extant in at least in 40 copies.[415]

An appendix in Part Seven of this volume presents the 26-word fragment of the Hebrew translation of Māshā'allāh's work on reading thoughts, as well as the complete alternative Latin translation of the same work.[416] For all the correspondences between *Dogma universale* and the two texts included in this appendix, readers are invited to consult the notes to the English translation of the fourth part of *Tractatus particulares* in the current volume.[417]

---

412 See above, note 369.
413 See *Tp*, IV 3:2 and note.
414 See note to *Int*, II i 6:12.
415 See Juste 2016, 177, 191; Carmody 1956, 28–29; Thorndike 1956.
416 See "Māshā'allāh's Book on Reading Thoughts," on pp. 525–527.
417 See *Tp*, IV 1:1 through IV 10:1–3, and notes.

General Features of Tp^{H}

We now have a fairly complete picture of Tp^{H} and its sources. Our findings are summarized in the table the follows, where the main components of Tp^{A} and Tp^{Q} are in the left column and the sources of the constitutive parts of Tp^{H} in the right column.

I.1	De *cogitatione* hominis ac eius questione	
	I.1.i—*Tp*, I i 1:1–14 through I i 3:1–4	*She'elot le-Talmai*
	I.1.ii—*Tp*, I i 4:1–10	*She'elot* III → *Int*, II xii 2:1–9
	I.1.iii—*Tp*, I i 5:1–4 through I i 5:1–4	*She'elot le-Māshā'allāh*
I.2	*Liber* de *occultis*	
	I.2.i—*Tp*, I ii 1:1–3 through I ii 7:1–3	Hebrew source text of some text of the *Alchandreana*
	I.2.ii—*Tp*, I ii 8:1–2, I ii 9:1; I ii 10:1–2	*She'elot* III → *Int*, II xii 3:1, II xii 4:1, and II xii 5:1–2
I.3	De re absconsa et loco eius	
	I.3.i—*Tp*, I iii 1:1–6	*She'elot* III → *Int*, II xii 6:1–6
	I.3.ii—*Tp*, I iii 2:1–6 through I iii 4:1–10	*She'elot le-Māshā'allāh*
I.4	*In loco fugitivi*	*She'elot* III → *Int*, II xii 7:1–10
	Tp, I iv 1:1–10 through Tp, I iv 5:1–2	through II xii 11:1–2
II	*Liber servorum*	A reworking of *Mishpeṭei ha-*
	Tp, II i 1:1–5 through II vii 14:1	*mazzalot*, § 38:1–5 through § 44:1–9
III	*Tractatus de significationibus planetarum in duodecim domibus*	A reworking of a Hebrew source text on the significations of the
	Tp, III 1:2–10 through III 12:2–10	planets in the places, attributed to Gergis
IV	*Dogma universale in iudiciis*	Hebrew source text of a work by
	Tp, IV 1:1 through IV 10:1–3	Māshā'allāh on reading thoughts.

Several points emerge from this catalogue of the sources for the main components of Tp^{A} and Tp^{Q}. Let us begin with the authorship of Tp^{H}. We see that, despite the repeated claims in the incipits and explicits of Tp^{A} and Tp^{Q}, Tp^{H} cannot be a genuine work by Ibn Ezra or a collection of works by him. Why, then, do the incipits and explicits obstinately assign the whole work and its parts to Ibn Ezra? This is comprehensible for the parts derived from his *Mishpeṭei ha-mazzalot* and *She'elot* III. It is also understandable for the other parts of Tp^{H}, because they consist of Arabic to Hebrew translations carried out after Ibn Ezra's death and associated with him posthumously.

These translations employ his peculiar Hebrew astrological terminology, were transmitted in manuscripts together with works by him, and in some cases were explicitly said to have been authored by Ibn Ezra.

What was the modus operandi of the originator of Tp^{H}? He made good use of the state-of-the-art in Hebrew astrological literature available in the mid-thirteenth century. In sharp contrast with the slavish copying of whole works found in typical manuscripts collections of astrological texts, he never borrowed whole works as he found them but carefully selected sections of various length from them, reworked them, and incorporated them into Tp^{H} where he deemed them appropriate, using various methods. One remarkable method—used for the composition of the entire second and third parts of Tp^{H}, and thus the bulk of the whole work—consisted of extensive alteration of the organization of the original text while keeping its wording. Another method was to take a section from some source, divide it into individual passages, and embed them in discontinuous loci in Tp^{H}. This method was exploited in four nonconsecutive sections found in the first, second, third, and fourth chapters of the first part of Tp^{H}, which are based on a single continuous passage in the twelfth chapter of Ibn Ezra's *She'elot* III.[418] Another method was to take discontinuous passages from some source and embed them as discontinuous parts of Tp^{H}. This method was used for two passages from *She'elot le-Māshā'allāh*, which were embedded into the second and the third chapters of the first part of Tp^{H}.[419] Finally, another method was to take a single section from some source and embed it into Tp^{H}. This applies to the section from the first chapter of the first part of Tp^{H}, borrowed from *She'elot le-Talmai*.[420]

Was Tp^{H} created from the outset as a comprehensive multipart astrological work, a sort of medieval astrological encyclopedia, as suggested by the incipits and explicits of Tp^{A} and Tp^{Q}? Or did the parts of Tp^{H} originate as separate astrological treatises, which were collected by some later copyist or translator? What tips the scale in favor of the first possibility is that the same modus operandi employed in one part may be also detected in other parts of Tp^{H}. Moreover, what especially supports the first possibility is that Tp^{H}—according to its contents, organization, and method of composition—fits well into the Jewish intellectual climate of the mid-thirteenth century in general, and into one of the central genres of Hebrew medieval astrological literature that developed at this time, in particular.

---

[418] See I.1.ii; I.2.ii; I.3.i and I.4.

[419] See I.1.iii and I.3.ii.

[420] See I.1.i.

*Tp*H should be placed in the context of an increasing Jewish curiosity about astrology, which, in the wake of Ibn Ezra's astrological writings, sought further channels of expression. One of these was a vibrant stream of Hebrew translations of astrological texts, mainly from Arabic, which gathered momentum in the thirteenth century, concurrently with and as part and parcel of the larger movement of Hebrew translations of astronomical, mathematical, philosophical, and medical texts. Another channel for satisfying the growing Jewish curiosity about astrology was the composition of astrological encyclopedias, and this is the context in which *Tp*H should be placed. I will now outline the main features of two of these astrological encyclopedias and compare them with *Tp*H.

Sefer ha-She'elot, "Book of interrogations," is explicitly ascribed to Abraham Ibn Ezra, just like *Tp*H.[421] A look at its components reveals that it is an astrological encyclopedia composed of fragments of diverse length and origin, that some of them are taken from texts by Ibn Ezra, and that this *Sefer ha-She'elot* is not identical with any of the three versions of Ibn Ezra's *Sefer ha-She'elot*. It consists of an introduction (whose terminology indicates that it was not written by Ibn Ezra), a table of contents, and four parts, just like *Tp*H. The first part, "On the utilization of the zodiacal signs," consists of two sections. The first offers a series of categorizations of the zodiacal signs and the individual signs in each category, along with lists of the zodiacal signs that serve as planetary houses and exaltations. The second section of the first part studies the twelve signs, one by one, by means of long and discontinuous quotations from the second chapter of *Reshit ḥokhmah*, where the twelve zodiacal signs are also treated individually. The second part, "On the utilization of the planets," contains almost the entire fourth chapter of *Reshit ḥokhmah* and is similar to the third part of *Tp*H. The first section of the third part, "Properties of the houses," reviews the horoscopic places by means of miscellaneous fragments from the third chapter of *Reshit ḥokhmah*. Finally, in keeping with its title, the second section of the third part and the entire fourth part, entitled "Methods for interrogations," are devoted to the astrological doctrine of interrogations, just like the first and last parts of *Tp*H. This part of *Sefer ha-She'elot* incorporates the pseudo-Ptolemaic *She'elot le-Talmai*, also included in the first part of *Tp*H, and the full text of Ibn Ezra's first version of *Sefer ha-She'elot*.[422]

The second example is *Sefer ha-Kolel*, "Comprehensive book"—a vast Hebrew astrological and astronomical encyclopedia compiled in 1265 by an

[421] See above, n. 353.

[422] For the contents of *Sefer ha-She'elot*, see Sela 2010b, 46–48; Leicht 2012, 268–269.

anonymous and learned scholar who made clever selections, mainly from the works of Abraham Bar Ḥiyya (ca. 1065–ca. 1136) and Ibn Ezra, and interspersed them with articles and comments of his own. The title indicates that the author considered it to be an original and self-contained work, not a mere collection of texts, and recalls the way in which the title of *Tp*^A occurs in its incipit and explicit, and that of *Tp*^Q occurs in its headers. *Sefer ha-Kolel* consists of at least forty sections, of which only eight survive; and only four of these (§§ 32–35) have been studied.[423] Section 32 discusses the fixed stars. Section 33 presents the entire Jewish and universal astrological history incorporated by Abraham Bar Ḥiyya into his *Megillat ha-Megalleh* (Scroll of the Revealer). The same section also includes the last five chapters of the Hebrew translation of Māshā'allāh's *Book on the Eclipses*, commonly copied together with the aforementioned *She'elot le-Māshā'allāh*, two passages of which were included in the first part of *Tp*^H. Section 34 addresses the calculation of the twelve places of the horoscope. Section 35 explains typical astrological terms, addresses continuous horoscopy in nativities, and explains the lots. This is done by means of passages excerpted mainly from Ibn Ezra's astrological works. Particularly indicative of the author's methodology is how he organized the first article of this section as a smooth and clever combination of excerpts from Ibn Ezra's *Ṭeʿamim* I and *Ṭeʿamim* II, which, avoiding repetitions and redundancies, in fact creates a new version of *Sefer ha-Ṭeʿamim*. This is reminiscent of how the originator of *Tp*^H modified parts of Ibn Ezra's *Mishpeṭei ha-mazzalot* and of the lost Hebrew source text of *Significationes septem planetarum in domibus* assigned to Gergis and reshaped them as *Liber servorum* and *Tractatus de significationibus planetarum in duodecim domibus*, the second and third parts of *Tp*^A and *Tp*^Q.

[423] Sections §§ 32–35 of *Sefer ha-Kolel* are extant only in Paris, BnF MS 1058, fols. 50r–126r. I have recently located an additional portion of the same encyclopedia in Cambridge, MS Or. 2281 [not in IMHM], fols. 1a–76b, and in Oxford, Bodleian, MS Reggio 13 [Neubauer 2028] [IMHM: F 19313], fols. 1a–76b. This portion includes sections §§ 36–40. The following concise account of the contents of sections §§ 32–35 of *Sefer ha-Kolel* is based on Sela 2014, 189–241.

III. MANUSCRIPTS AND EDITORIAL PRINCIPLES

Manuscripts for the Critical Edition of *Liber Electionum* and *Liber Interrogationum*

The critical edition of *Electiones* and *Interrogationes* is based on the two currently available manuscripts for both texts. To identify the different copies of each text I have used capital letters that are suggestive of the archives that holds the manuscript:

E = Erfurt, MS Amplon. O.89, fols. 19v–30r (*Interrogationes*) and 39v–46v (*Electiones*): 8°, paper and parchment, second quarter of 14th c.

V = Vienna, Österreichische Nationalbibliothek, MS 5442, 180ra–186rb (*Interrogationes*) and 192vb–198va (*Electiones*): 80 × 200 mm, paper, 15th c.

Both manuscripts contain the same collection of Latin translations of Ibn Ezra's astrological writings (except for the first item), and in the same order, as follows: (1) *Liber Abraham de iudiciis signorum*, an anonymous translation of the bulk of Ibn Ezra's *Mishpeṭei ha-mazzalot* (E, fols. 5r–19v);[424] (2) *Liber interrogationum*, an anonymous translation of *She'elot* III (E, fols. 19v–30r; V, fols. 180r–186r); since V is later than E, the text of *Liber interrogationum* in V is a copy of that in E; (3) *Liber interrogationibus ab alio editus*, an anonymous translation of *She'elot* II (E, fols. 30r–39v; V, fols. 186r–192v); (4) *Liber electionum*, an anonymous translation of the lost *Mivḥarim* III (E, fols. 39v–46v; V, fols. 192v–198v); since V is later than E, the text of *Liber electionum* in V is a copy of that in E; (5) *Liber electionum ab Abraham Evenezre*, an anonymous translation of *Mivḥarim* II (E, fols. 46v–52v; V, fols. 198v–203v); (6) *Liber nativitatum*, an anonymous translation of the lost *Moladot* II, edited in volume 6 of this series (E, fols. 53r–68v; V, fols. 203v–217v); (7) *Liber revolucionum*, an anonymous translation *Tequfah* (E, fols. 69r–72r; V, fols. 218r–220v); (8) *Hec est Nativitas quedam ad instruendum te, et est de iudiciis Abraham*, a work on nativities ascribed to Ibn Ezra (E, fols. 73r–76r; V, fols. 221r–224r).

---

424 This anonymous translation omits the complete initial part of *Mishpeṭei ha-mazzalot*. The text of the translation corresponds to *Mishpeṭei ha-mazzalot* § 12:1 through § 76:4.

Witnesses for the Critical Edition of *Tractatus Particulares*

The critical edition of *Tractatus particulares* is based on seven manuscripts and one print edition, selected from the 19 surviving witnesses of *Tractatus particulares*.[425] These eight include seven witnesses of Tp^{A} (six manuscripts and the only print edition) and the sole manuscript of Tp^{Q}, as follows:

D = Oxford, MS Digby 212, fols. 53ra–56rb: parchment, 14th c. (the oldest surviving manuscript of *Tractatus particulares*), with a collection of Latin translations of Ibn Ezra's astrological writings: (1) fols. 34r–48r: Pietro d'Abano's translation of *Reshit ḥokhmah*; (2) fols. 48v–52v: Henry Bate's translation of *'Olam* I; (3) fols. 53r–56r: *Tractatus particulares*, ascribed to Ibn Ezra, translated by Pietro d'Abano; (4) fols. 56r–62r: Pietro d'Abano's translation of *Ṭe'amim* II; (5) fols. 63r–64r: Pietro's translation of *She'elot* II; (6) fols. 64v–67v: an anonymous translation of *Mivḥarim* II; (7) fols. 67v–72r: *Liber questionum*, an anonymous translation of *She'elot* II.

V = Vienna, Österreichische Nationalbibliothek, Cod. 5335, fols. 54v–58v, parchment and paper, 14th–15th c., with the following collection of Latin translations of Ibn Ezra's astrological writings: (1) fols. 1ra–20vb: Pietro d'Abano's translation of *Reshit ḥokhmah*; (2) fols. 20vb–28vb: Pietro d'Abano's translation of *Ṭe'amim* II; (3) fols. 28v–39r: Pietro d'Abano's translation of *Moladot*; (4) fols. 39r–43r: Pietro d'Abano's translation of *She'elot* II; (5) fols. 43r–45v: Pietro d'Abano's translation of *Mivḥarim* II; (6) fols. 46v–49r: Pietro d'Abano's translation of *Me'orot*; (7) 49r–54v: Henry Bate's translation of *'Olam* I; (8) fols. 54v–58v: Pietro d'Abano's translation of *Tractatus particulares*.

P = Paris, BnF, MS lat. 10269, fols. 102rb–110vb, paper, written in 1490, with the following collection of Latin translations of Ibn Ezra's astrological writings: (1) fols. 1ra–38va: Pietro d'Abano's translation of *Reshit ḥokhmah*; (2) fols. 39ra–53vb: Pietro d'Abano's translation of *Ṭe'amim* II; (3) fols. 54ra–74rb: Pietro d'Abano's translation of *Moladot*; (4) fols. 74va–82rb: Pietro d'Abano's translation of *She'elot* II; (5) fols. 82va–87vb: Pietro d'Abano's translation of *Mivḥarim* II; (6) fols. 88ra–99rb: Henry Bate's translation of *'Olam* I; (7) fols. 102rb–110vb: Pietro d'Abano's translation of *Tractatus particulares*. (8) fols. 111ra–116ra: Pietro d'Abano's translation of *Me'orot*.

---

[425] See table on pp. 53–55.

B = Basel, Universitätsbibliothek, F.II.10, fols. 121ra–125va, 15th c., paper, with the following collection of Latin translations of Ibn Ezra's astrological writings: (1) fols. 82ra–90rb: Henry Bate's translation of *ʿOlam* I; (2) fols. 91ra–121ra: Pietro d'Abano's translation of *Reshit ḥokhmah*; (3) fols. 121ra–125va: Pietro d'Abano's translation of *Tractatus particulares*; (4) fols. 125va–130va: Pietro d'Abano's translation of *Sheʾelot* II; (5) fols. 131ra–141vb: Pietro d'Abano's translation of *Ṭeʿamim* II;

N = Österreichische Nationalbibliothek, Cod. 5309, fols. 264r–269v, paper, 15th c., with the following collection of Latin translations of Ibn Ezra's astrological writings: (1) fols. 187r–215v: Pietro d'Abano's translation of *Reshit ḥokhmah*; (2) fols. 216ra–226rb: Pietro d'Abano's translation of *Ṭeʿamim* II; (3) fols. 228r–241r: Pietro d'Abano's translation of *Moladot*; (4) fols. 241r–246v: Pietro d'Abano's translation of *Sheʾelot* II; (5) fols. 247r–250v: Pietro d'Abano's translation of *Mivḥarim* II; (6) fols. 252v–256r: Pietro d'Abano's translation of *Meʾorot*; (7) fols. 256rb–264rb: Henry Bate's translation of *ʿOlam* I; (8) fols. 264r–269v: Pietro d'Abano's translation of *Tractatus particulares*.

Z = Zurich, Zentralbibliothek, B.244 (769), fols. 87ra–92rb, 15th c., with the following collection of Latin translations of Ibn Ezra's astrological writings: (1) fols. 50vb–58rb: Pietro d'Abano's translation of *Ṭeʿamim* II; (2) fols. 58a–69rb: Pietro d'Abano's translation of *Moladot*; (3) fols. 69va–74va: Pietro d'Abano's translation of *Sheʾelot* II; (4) fols. 74va–76rb: Pietro d'Abano's translation of *Mivḥarim* II; (5) fols. 77vb–80va: Pietro d'Abano's translation of *Meʾorot*; (6) fols. 80vb–87ra: Henry Bate's translation of *ʿOlam* I; (7) fols. 87ra–92rb: Pietro d'Abano's translation of *Tractatus particulares*.

G = Ghent, Universiteitbibliotheek, 5 (416), fols. 96v–103r, parchment, 15th c., the only manuscript with Arnoul de Quincampoix's Latin translations of Ibn Ezra's astrological writings, as follows: (1) fols. 85r–91: a Latin translation of *Sheʾelot* II; (1) fols. 91v–96r: a Latin translation of *Mivḥarim* II; (3) fols. 96v–103r: a Latin translation of *Tractatus particulares*.

L = *Abrahe Avenaris Iudei Astrologi peritissimi in re iudiciali opera ab excellentissimo philosopho Petro de Albano post accuratam castigationem in Latinum traducta* (Venice: Petrus Liechtenstein, 1507), sig. LXXXVra–XCIv2, with the following collection of Latin translations of Ibn Ezra's astrological writings: (1) sig. IIra–XXXIvb: Pietro d'Abano's translation of *Reshit ḥokhmah*; (2) sig. XXXIIra–XLIIIIrb: Pietro d'Abano's translation of *Ṭeʿamim* II; (3) sig. XLIIIIva–LXva: Pietro d'Abano's translation of *Moladot*; (4) sig. LXvb–LXVIIra: Pietro d'Abano's translation of *She'elot* II; (5) sig. LXVIIrb–LXXIrb: Pietro d'Abano's translation of *Mivḥarim* II; (6) sig. LXXIva–LXXvb: Pietro d'Abano's translation of *Me'orot*; (7) sig. LXXXVIra–LXXXra: Henry Bate's translation of *'Olam* I; (8) sig. LXXXVra–XCIv2: Pietro d'Abano's translation of *Tractatus particulares.*

Editorial and Translation Principles

From the two available manuscripts of *Electiones* and *Interrogationes*, I selected E as my copy text because it is the earliest. This means that when E and V diverge, the reading of E was usually preferred. However, V was useful not only to clarify difficult readings but also to correct erroneous readings of E, especially for numerical values. That V is a later and virtually identical copy of E explains why there are so few *variae lectiones* in the critical edition of *Electiones* and *Interrogationes*, as compared with *Tractatus particulares*. When both E and V proved unsatisfactory or wrong, the text here has been corrected according to the context. In the cases of serious conflict between the readings of the Latin texts of *Electiones* and *Interrogationes*, on the one hand, and the Hebrew texts of *She'elot* III and *Mivḥarim* III as rendered by the Modena fragments, on the other, I preferred a Latin translation of the latter.[426] In cases of serious conflict between parallel readings in *Tractatus particulares* and *Interrogationes*, I have preferred the former when I considered them more accurate.[427] To make cases in which the texts presented in the edition of *Electiones* and *Interrogationes* diverge from E clear to readers, the corresponding lemmas in the apparatus have been marked with an asterisk. The four French words or phrases embedded in the Latin text of *Electiones* and the 16 French words or phrases embedded in the Latin text of *Interrogationes*, and their corresponding English translations, have been enclosed in double angle brackets: ⟪ ⟫.

Since among the 19 surviving witnesses of *Tractatus particulares*, 18 are witnesses of Tp^{A} and only one of Tp^{Q}, the critical edition of *Tractatus particulares* offered here is basically an edition of Tp^{A}. However, Tp^{Q} has been also taken into account in crucial portions of the edition. Of the seven witnesses of Tp^{A}, **V** and **D**, the earliest among them, are the starting point. When **V** and **D** diverge I have preferred **V**, even though **D** is perhaps

---

[426] See. for example, readings in *Int*, II v 5:3, against corresponding readings in *She'elot* III, II v 5:3, or the reading in *Int*, II vii 1:1, against the corresponding reading in *She'elot* III, II vii 1:1.

[427] See readings in *Int*, II xii 2:2, against readings in *Tp*, I i 4:7.

the earlier, because **D** has multiple readings that are unique in all the 19 surviving witnesses and are probably interpolations by a hyperactive copyist rather than readings of the archetype of *Tractatus particulares*. All these interpolations of **D**, though, are recorded in the apparatus.

Regarding the incipits, explicits and titles of the various parts of *Tractatus particulares*, all the readings of **G**, the only one witness of Tp^{Q}, have been recorded in the edition, in parallel with the readings of the witnesses of Tp^{A}. In all those cases, the readings of **G** in the edition and their corresponding translations have been enclosed in double angle brackets: ⟪ ⟫. In all the cases in which the meaning of readings of the witnesses of Tp^{A} is confused, indeterminate, problematic, or marred by a lacuna, I have collated them with their counterpart in Tp^{Q}, if any. I also use **G** to substantiate problematic readings that are in substantial minority among the witnesses of Tp^{A}. I have recorded these cases, and in all these cases the number of the notes with reading of **G** is enclosed in curly braces: { }. I have preferred the readings of **G** when they are clearer than the readings in the witnesses of Tp^{A}, or fill lacunae there. In all these cases, the readings of **G** in the edition and their corresponding translations are enclosed in double angle brackets: ⟪ ⟫, and the numbers of the notes with reading of **G** are enclosed in curly braces: { }. To make cases in which the texts presented in the edition of *Tractatus particulares* diverge from **V** or **D** clear to readers, the corresponding lemmas in the apparatus have been marked with an asterisk. Problematic readings in the Latin text of *Interrogationes* and problematic translations in the English translation of this text are enclosed in curly braces: { }.

The critical apparatus offers the *variae lectiones* of *Electiones*, *Interrogationes*, and *Tractatus particulares* in the following format: first the lemma (as it appears in the text) followed by a square bracket (']') and by the sigla (or siglum) of the witnesses (or witness) that agree with this reading; then the sigla (or siglum) of the witnesses (or witness) that do not agree with this reading, followed by their corresponding diverging text (or texts). When only one witness disagrees with the reading in the body of the text, however, the lemma and bracket are followed only by the siglum of the deviant witness and its reading. This implies that all the other witnesses agree with the lemma. The critical apparatus is intended to offer a succinct indication of *all* the readings in the witnesses consulted that differ from text printed here. This is why I have recorded not only the sigla of the witnesses that present a different reading but also those of the witnesses that coincide with the body text. Where a siglum is omitted, the witness in question is illegible at this point.

To facilitate comprehension of *Electiones*, *Interrogationes*, and *Tractatus particulares*, I have added punctuation to their Latin texts; to facilitate references to specific parts of these works I have divided the Latin text into parts, chapters, sections, and sentences, in a way that reflects their subdivisions. Names of persons, planets, and zodiacal signs have been capitalized and names of books have been italicized. Ibn Ezra employs the word "house," Hebrew בית, to denote a disconcerting variety of astrological meanings: horoscopic house, zodiacal sign, planetary house, house of exaltation, etc. Following this usage, Latin translators rendered all these loci as *domus*. To partially disambiguate among these senses, I have rendered it as "place" (corresponding to the Greek *topos*) when the reference is to any of the twelve horoscopic houses, and as "house" in all the other cases. The spelling of proper names in *Electiones*, *Interrogationes*, and *Tractatus particulares* follows in principle the readings in their respective copy texts. However, I have always preferred *Abraham*, *Doroneus*, and *Ptholomeus*, over other forms. *Signat* for *significat* is disregarded. In conformity with the spelling conventions of the manuscripts, the diphthong *ae* is written and alphabetized as *e* (i.e., *Lune* instead of *Lunae*; *hec* instead of *haec*, etc.).

The translations are meant to help readers understand the Latin text and are not addressed only to those with no Latin. Ultimately, the translations are a gloss and commentary on the Latin text. The English is divided into the same parts, chapters, sections, and sentences as the Latin. The paragraph breaks and punctuation are virtually the same as in the Latin texts and may also be taken as interpretative. The numbers in the English translation refer to the notes that follow the texts. These notes are intended to illustrate the links among the works included here, as well as between them and other parts of Ibn Ezra's scientific corpus. They also serve to locate Ibn Ezra's views in the wider context of medieval astrological lore, to explain astrological or astronomical concepts and terms whenever necessary, and to identify sources. The notes to the English translations are full of references to primary sources. To make these notes more comprehensible, I have grouped most of these quotations thematically in appendixes whose title reflect the main topic addressed by the included texts.[428] The references to these quotations have the following formats:

[428] See "The Debate about Elections," on pp. 391–398; "The Debate about Interrogations," on pp. 399–405; "Elections," on pp. 406–430; "Interrogations," on pp. 431–464; "Planets, Signs and Horoscopic Places," on pp. 465–482.

- App. 1, Q. 4, 393 = Appendix 1 (which assembles quotations related to the debate about the validity of elections), quotation 4, on p. 393.
- App. 2, Q. 7, 401 = Appendix 2 (which assembles quotations related to the debate about the validity of interrogations), quotation 7, on p. 401.
- App. 3, P. 1, Q. 1, § 1:2, 406 = Appendix 3 (which assembles quotations related to elections), part 1 (which assembles quotations related to elections about taking a purgative), quotation 1, section1, sentence 2, on p. 406.
- App. 4, P. 22, Q. 1, 461 = Appendix 4 (which assembles quotations related to interrogations), part 22 (which assembles quotations related to interrogations about color), quotation 1, on p. 461.
- App. 5, Q. 47, 480 = Appendix 5 (which assembles quotations related to planets, signs and horoscopic places), quotation 47, on p. 480.
- App. 7, P. 1, 1–4, 498 = Appendix 7 (which brings passages from *She'elot le-Māshā'allāh*), passage 1, sentences 1–4, on p. 498.
- App. 8, *She'elot le-Talmai*, § 1:1–2, 505–506 = Appendix 8 (which brings a whole section of *She'elot le-Talmai* and its counterpart in Ptolemy's *Iudicia*), *She'elot le-Talmai* (which brings the section of *She'elot le-Talmai* and its English translation), paragraph 1, sentence 1–2, on pp. 505–506.
- App. 8, Ptolemy's *Iudicia*, § 1:1–2, 507–508 = Appendix 8 (which brings a whole section of *She'elot le-Talmai* and its counterpart in Ptolemy's *Iudicia*), Ptolemy's *Iudicia* (which brings the section of Ptolemy's *Iudicia* and its English translation), paragraph 1, sentence 1–2, on pp. 507–508.
- App. 9, Sol, § 1:1, 510 = Appendix 9 (which brings the complete text of *De significationibus planetarum in domibus*, ascribed to Gergis), Sol, § 1:1 (which brings the first part, on the Sun), section 1, sentence 1, on p. 510.
- App. 10, I: The Sun, 14–15, 517–518 = Appendix 10 (which brings passages of the account of the seven planets in *Mishpeṭei ha-mazzalot*), I: The Sun (which brings the brings the first part, on the Sun), sentences 14–15, on pp. 517–518.
- App. 11, I 1:2–4, 525 = Appendix 11 (which brings the fragment of the Hebrew translation and a complete Latin translation of a lost Arabic work by Māshā'allāh on reading thoughts), I (which brings the fragment of the Hebrew translation), section 1, sentences 2–4, on p. 525.
- App. 11, II 1:2–5, 525 = Appendix 11 (which brings the fragment of the Hebrew translation and a complete Latin translation of a lost Arabic work by Māshā'allāh on reading thoughts), II (which brings the Latin translation), section 1, sentences 2–5, on p. 525.
- App. 13, III: Mercury, 532 = Appendix 13 (which brings a section of *Epistola Argafalau ad Alexandrum*), III: Mercury (which brings the third part of this section, on Mercury), on p. 532.

Key to References to Liber Electionum

- The introduction: *El*, I 7:3 = *Electiones*, part I (introduction), section 7, sentence 3.
- The chapters on the twelve horoscopic places: *El*, II i 3:2 = *Electiones*, part II (the twelve horoscopic places), chapter i (addressing the first horoscopic place), section 3, sentence 2.

Key to References to Liber Interrogationum

- The introduction: *Int*, I 3:2 = *Interrogationes*, part I (introduction), section 3, sentence 2.
- The chapters on the twelve horoscopic places: *Int*, II vii 3:2 = *Interrogationes*, part II (the twelve horoscopic places), section vii (addressing the seventh horoscopic place), section 3, sentence 2.

Key to References to Tractatus Particulares

- The first chapter of the first part of *Tractatus particulares*: *Tp*, I i 7:2 = part I (the first part of *Tractatus particulares*), chapter i (addressing the first chapter of the first part of *Tractatus particulares*), section 7, sentence 2.
- The second chapter of the first part of *Tractatus particulares*: *Tp*, I ii 4:3 = part I (the first part of *Tractatus particulares*), chapter ii (addressing the second chapter of the first part of *Tractatus particulares*), section 4, sentence 3.
- The third chapter of the first part of *Tractatus particulares*: *Tp*, I iii 3:4 = part I (the first part of *Tractatus particulares*), chapter iii (addressing the third chapter of the first part of *Tractatus particulares*), section 3, sentence 4.
- The fourth chapter of the first part of *Tractatus particulares*: *Tp*, I iv 5:1 = part I (the first part of *Tractatus particulares*), chapter iv (addressing the fourth chapter of the first part of *Tractatus particulares*), section 5, sentence 1.
- The second part of *Tractatus particulares*, on the thirteen categories of the planets: *Tp*, II iii 4:1 = part II (the second part of *Tractatus particulares*), chapter iii (addressing the significations of Saturn), section 4 (addressing the fourth category of the significations of Saturn), sentence 1.
- The third part of *Tractatus particulares*, on the significations of the planets in the 12 horoscopic places: *Tp*, III 7:2 = part III (the third part of *Trac-*

tatus particulares), section 7 (addressing the significations of the seventh horoscopic place), sentence 2 (addressing the significations of the Sun in the seventh horoscopic place).
- The fourth part of *Tractatus particulares*: *Tp*, IV 2:3 = part IV ("General doctrine of judgments"), section 2, sentence 3.

Key to References to the Modena Fragments of Mivḥarim *III and* She'elot *III*

- *Mivḥarim* III, II vii 5:2, 486–487 = The Modena fragment of *Mivḥarim* III, part II (the twelve horoscopic places), chapter 7 (addressing the seventh horoscopic place), section 5, sentence 2, (the Hebrew source text of *Electiones*, II vii 5:2), on p. 486–487.
- *She'elot* III, II vii 3:2, 495 = The Modena fragment of *She'elot* III, part II (the twelve horoscopic places), chapter 7 (addressing the seventh horoscopic place), section 3, sentence 2, (the Hebrew source text of *Interrogationes* II vii 3:2), on p. 495.

The two treatises in this volume are highly specialized and technical texts. As a rule, the technical terms are explained in the notes when they first appear in the Latin text of *Electiones, Interrogationes*, and *Tractatus particulares*. To facilitate reference to these explanations from elsewhere in the two texts, I have added an index of astrological terms and major authorities. Each item in this index references the note where the corresponding term is explained.[429] *Electiones, Interrogationes*, and *Tractatus particulares* are based on Hebrew texts and exhibit idiosyncratic Latin technical vocabularies. To highlight this feature, the present volume includes an English-Latin and a Latin-English glossary of technical terms,[430] and, regarding *Electiones* and *Interrogationes*, lists of literal Hebrew to Latin translations.[431] The glossaries present the technical terms of *Electiones, Interrogationes*, and *Tractatus particulares* one next to the other. The same comparative approach is applied to the list of authorities and sources of *Electiones, Interrogationes*, and *Tractatus particulares*.[432]

429 See below, "Index of Technical Terms and Biographical Notes," on pp. 608–612.

430 See below, "English-Latin Glossary" on pp. 535–576, and "Latin-English Index to the English-Latin Glossaries," on pp. 577–587.

431 See below, "Literal Renderings of Hebraisms in *Electiones*," on pp. 597–598, and "Literal Renderings of Hebraisms in *Interrogationes*," on pp. 599–600.

432 See below, "Authorities and Sources," on pp. 588–596.

The abbreviations and short titles of works by Abraham Ibn Ezra and primary sources employed in this volume differ from those used in the previous volumes of this series: the short title is now followed by the name of the editor(s) of the text employed, after which comes the year of publication (in parentheses). I have adopted this method in order to do justice to the editors' significant contribution and to disambiguate the titles of some items in the bibliography.

Abbreviations and Sigla in the Latin Texts and Their Translations

<	In the apparatus: for a given lemma, the word(s) following the siglum are added in the indicated manuscript after the lemma
>	In the apparatus: For a given lemma, the word(s) following the siglum are added in the indicated manuscript before the lemma
⟨ ⟩	In *Electiones*, *Interrogationes*, and *Tractatus particulares* and in the English translations: word(s) added to clarify the meaning
[ ]	In the translations: paraphrase or gloss
{ }	Problematic readings in the Latin text of *Interrogationes* and problematic translations in the English translation of this text
⟪ ⟫	In *Electiones* and *Interrogationes*, and their English translation: Old French words or phrases
{ }	enclose notes with reading of **G** in *Tractatus particulares*

PART ONE

LIBER ELECTIONUM

LATIN TEXT AND ENGLISH TRANSLATION

⟨Liber electionum⟩

⟨I⟩

39v 1 (1) Abraham Additor.[1] Incipiam *Librum electionum.* (2) Communes sunt semper[2] gradatim succedentes et scientia eorum est fidelis, scientia autem singularium electionum, que non sunt stabiles in .1. puncto super una computatione, non est scientia, eo quod ipsa diversificatur secundum diversitatem eorum, et in electionibus suis et voluntate eorum. (3) Non enim possunt mutare cursum suum nec naturam suam, nam fortitudo Dei altissimi dedit eis consuetudinem quam numquam transibunt. (4) Et scio, quod hoc est scriptum, quod quidquid facit Deus super se vel respectu sui non minuitur nec augetur. (5) Et hec sunt divisiones, que divise sunt ex ore Dei altissimi de omni homine in puncto conceptionis et in puncto partus, quando venit ad aerem seculi. (6) Propter hoc dixerunt Antiqui, quorum rememoratio sit benedicta: vite, infantium hominum, et gubernationes non in bene operari dependent sed ex signo.

2 (1) Et propter hoc fuit quedam societas, item sapientes iudiciorum signorum, que dicit quod electiones sunt false et mentientes nec valent. (2) Nam si fuerit Saturnus in nativitate hominis in .9a. domo, in Cancro vel Scorpione vel Piscibus, et ipse aspiciat aspectu odii dominum ascendentis vel prepositum super natum, tunc transibit timor magnus in aqua. (3) Et si ita est, quid valet eligere punctum quo intrabit mare postquam ita divisum est in nativitate sua. (4) Et propter hoc dicit Ptholomeus: non facias electionem pro illo cuius nesciveris nativitatem, quia posset esse quod tu eligeres signum malum quod fuit ibi in nativitate sua. (5) Et ideo noceret ei talis electio et ipse nescit; ideo, abscondetur res electionis.

3 (1) Et ego, Abraham Additor, dico quod verum est quod non habet fortitudinem in tanto mutandi vias Dei honorabilis in verbis naturalibus. (2) Nam si eligerit homo tempus bonum contra sensum signorum ad faciendum, se cadere ipsemet in furno vel igne comburetur, et si fecerit se cadere a loco alto franget se. (3) Et ita, si intraverit mare et tormentum fuerit in eo,

[1]Abraham Additor] E^{m}V (before the incipit). [2]semper*] V; E super.

⟨Book of Elections⟩

⟨I⟩

1 (1) Abraham, the author.[1] I will begin the *Book of elections*. (2) ⟨The judgments about⟩ collectives always follow each other stepwise, and their knowledge is trustworthy, but the knowledge of the elections of individuals, which are unstable at any moment and in any computation, is not a ⟨sound⟩ knowledge because it varies according to their diversity, in their elections and in the exercise of their will.[2] (3) ⟨The stars⟩ cannot change their course or their nature, because the power of God, the Almighty, gave them a law they never transgress.[3] (4) "I know that," Scripture states, "whatsoever God doeth, ⟨it shall be forever;⟩ nothing can be added to it, nor any thing taken from it." (5) These are the decrees ⟨of the stars⟩ that were decreed by God, the Almighty, about every person at the moment of conception and at the moment of delivery, when he [the newborn] emerges into the air of the world.[4] (6) Therefore the Ancient ⟨rabbis⟩, their memory for a blessing, said: life, children of men and sustenance[5] depend not on merit but on the sign.[6]

2 (1) Therefore, there was certain group, also scholars in the judgments of the signs, who said that elections are false, deceiving, and worthless.[1] (2) For if Saturn is in the ninth place in a man's nativity, in Cancer, Scorpio or Pisces,[2] and it [Saturn] is itself in an aspect of hate[3] to the lord of the ascendant[4] or to the ruler of the native, then he [the querent] will experience strong fear ⟨when traveling⟩ by water.[5] (3) If so, of what avail is to choose a time at which he will set out by sea after ⟨the native's destiny⟩ has been decreed in his nativity. (4) Therefore Ptolemy[6] says: do not make an election for someone whose nativity you do not know, because it is possible that you will choose an inauspicious sign that was in his nativity there.[7] (5) Therefore, such an election will harm him [the querent] and he will not know ⟨why⟩; therefore, the object of the election will remain hidden.[8]

3 (1) I Abraham, the author,[1] say that it is true that ⟨an election⟩ does not have the power to change much of the ways of the Honorable God in natural matters. (2) For if a man chooses an auspicious time to do ⟨something⟩ against the intention of the signs, he will fall into an oven and be burnt in fire, and if he makes ⟨an election⟩, he will fall from a high place and smash himself. (3) Likewise, if he puts to sea and a storm breaks out there, he

patietur dolorem, quia electio non impediet rem communitatis, que procedit secundum viam iudiciorum signorum et planetarum, ad esse magnum ventum in die electionis in mari.

40r **4** (1) Et responsio huius interrogationis dure est difficilis,[1] | scilicet, utrum fortitudo sit in manibus hominis ad eligendum. (2) Et primo vidimus scriptum in lege: Vide quod ego dedi tibi hodie vitam et mortem bonum et malum [...] eliges[2] in vita tua. (3) Et iustum est quod omnes divisiones sint secundum modum recipientis, et propter hoc potest elector addere vel minuere.

5 (1) Exemplum: si acciderit homini, a nativitate sua,[3] quod in tali anno erit in periculo in itinere, eliges[4] in illo anno iter in quo non erit aliquod periculum et nullum, et transibit[5] super se dolor parvus. (2) Et si viderit quod Mars intraverit signum nativitatis sue et fuerit significator in nativitate sua, quod super corpus suum renovatum renovabitur infirmitas, et scietur quod infirmitas sua causatur a calore. (3) Et bibet infirmus potionem in principio ad refrigerandum corpus suum, nec comedet aliquid quod[6] sit in natura sua caro contra corpus hominis. (4) Et quando Mars intrabit signum nativitatis sue generabit super eum calorem, et rectificabitur corpus suum nec ledet eum nisi parvum. (5) Et ita dixerunt sapientes signorum quorum Ptholomeus[7] fuit caput. Item ipse dicit hoc in *Libro*[8] *.c. verborum.*

6 (1) Si nesciveris nativitatem hominis querentis ut ei eligas diem vel horam ad suas operationes, vide fortunam querentis et naturam suam, et vide que stella habet super ipsum potestatem, et equa illam stellam. (2) Et dicit Doroneus, sapiens magnus in iudiciis signorum: Si homo querat electionem super re operationis sue, accipe ab eo interrogationem; si fuerit rectificatum ei suum opus ad voluntatem suam, tunc eligas.

7 (1) Et ego dico si fuerit in nativitate hominis quod ei debet accidere dampnum in itinere et inceperit iter suum in hora bona, minuetur malum. (2) Et Luna est prepositus super principiis omniun rerum et omniun ope-

[1]difficilis] E; V difficilior. [2]eliges] E; V eligas. [3]sua] E; V om. [4]eliges] E; V eleges. [5]transibit] E; V transsibit. [6]quod] E; V om. [7]Ptholomeus] EV Tpholomeus; corrected according to *El*, I 2:4. [8]*Libro*] E; V> suo.

will suffer pain, because the election cannot annul the general rule,[2] which proceeds according to the method of the judgments of the signs and the planets, ⟨namely,⟩ for there to be a gale at sea on the day specified by the election.[3]

4 (1) The answer to this hard question, namely, whether human beings have the power to make a ⟨free⟩ choice, is difficult. (2) To begin with, we saw that it is written in the Torah: "See, I have set before thee this day life and death, good and evil ... and choose life."[1] (3) It is right that all the decrees ⟨of the stars⟩ be according to the disposition of the receiver ⟨of astrological influence⟩, and therefore the person who makes an election can augment or reduce ⟨what is signified by the stars⟩.[2]

5 (1) Example: If it falls out for some person, from his nativity, that in certain year he will be in danger in a journey, choose in this year a journey in which there will be no danger and he will suffer ⟨only⟩ a little pain.[1] (2) If he [the astrologer] sees that Mars ⟨in the electional horoscope⟩ enters the ⟨ascendant⟩ sign of his nativity and is the significator in his nativity, and ⟨if he sees⟩ that his [the querent's] body will be afflicted by disease, ⟨then⟩ it will be known that his [the querent's] disease is caused by heat. (3) ⟨Then⟩ the patient will drink a beverage at the beginning ⟨of the disease⟩ to cool his body, and will not eat something which is ⟨like⟩ flesh in its nature [i.e., hot] against the human body. (4) ⟨So,⟩ when Mars enters the ⟨ascendant⟩ sign of the nativity ⟨in the electional horoscope⟩ and makes him hot, his body will be healed and he will be afflicted only a little.[2] (5) This was said by the scholars of the signs, whose head was Ptolemy. He also says this in the *Book of the 100 statements*.[3]

6 (1) If you do not know the nativity of the querent, then, to choose for him a day or an hour for his undertakings, observe the fortune of the querent and his nature, and observe which planet exerts power over him, and calculate ⟨the position of⟩ this planet.[1] (2) Dorotheus, the great scholar in the judgments of the signs,[2] says: If a person asks ⟨you to make⟩ an election about his undertaking, ⟨first⟩ question him; if his undertaking is compatible with him according to his will, then make ⟨for him⟩ an election.[3]

7 (1) I say that if a man's nativity ⟨ determines⟩ that he will come to harm in a journey and he begins his trip at an auspicious hour, the misfortune will diminish.[1] (2) The Moon is the ruler of the beginnings of every undertaking

rum respectu signi ascendentis in illo puncto. (3) Et post .12. domos in *Libro nativitatum*, scripsi tibi capitulum .1. de electionibus, et non obliviscaris respicere in eo. (4) Nunc incipiam loqui de electionibus secundum .12. domos.

⟨II i⟩
Prima ⟨domus⟩

1 (1) Qui vult bibere potionem laxativam, eligat horam in nocte qua sit Luna in signo aqueo sola, et ratio quod non coniungatur cum alia mala vel bona nec aspiciat eas. (2) Et si non inveneris ita, pone aspectum Martis vel Saturni tertium vel .6lem. circuli. (3) Et omnes concordaverunt quod coniunctio Iovis et aspectus eius mali, et bene dicunt. (4) Et aspectus Veneris bonus et non coniunctio sua, et aspectus Mercurii est secundum tempera-
40v mentum | eius in loco suo. (5) Et vide quod Luna non sit combusta a Sole nec in opposito eius nec in .4o. aspectu, et alii aspectus sunt boni. (6) Et debes providere ne Luna sit in .6a. domo in puncto potionis respectu ascendentis et non in .8a. vel in .12a. (7) Et[1] si fuerit potio laxativa, et Luna det fortitudinem stelle existenti sub terra contra signum ascendentis in puncto quo accipitur potio, bonum est, et vide quod non det fortitudinem illi qui est super terram. (8) Et si fuerit potio ad vomendum, fac contrarium eorum que dicta sunt.

2 (1) Et si queris diem ad minuendum, vide quod non sit Luna in aspectu malo ad Martem vel ad Saturnum. (2) Et aspectus Martis trinus et sextilis sunt boni, et in hac re plus quam omnes aspectus Saturni. (3) Et coniunctio Solis vel Saturni vel Martis sunt mali, et aspectus Solis sunt mediocres. (4) Et coniunctio Veneris est melior quam Iovis, et aspectus ipsorum duorum sunt boni. (5) Et coniunctio Mercurii[2] et aspectus eius secundum temperamentum eius, si bene boni si male mali. (6) Et sententia omnium sapientum signorum et sapientum medicine est quod bonum est minuere in medietate

[1]Et] E; V vel. [2]Mercurii] E; V Saturni.

and every work with respect to the ascendant sign at this moment [i.e., the moment of the beginning of the undertaking].[2] (3) After ⟨the discussion of⟩ the 12 places in the *Book of nativities*, I have written for you a chapter on elections; do not forget to look at it.[3] (4) I will now begin to discuss the elections according to the 12 places.[4]

⟨II i⟩
The First Place

1 (1) One who wishes to drink a laxative potion should choose an hour in the night when the Moon is alone in a watery sign, meaning that it [the Moon] does not conjoin with either a malefic or benefic ⟨planet⟩[1] or aspect them [the planets].[2] (2) If you will not find it [the Moon] in this manner, put it in an aspect of trine or sextile of the circle with Mars or Saturn. (3) All agreed that conjunction with Jupiter or aspect with it are inauspicious, and they are right.[3] (4) An aspect with Venus is auspicious but not a conjunction with it, and an aspect with Mercury is according to its mixture in its position. (5) Make sure that the Moon is not burnt by the Sun[4] or in its opposition or in quartile, but the other aspects ⟨of the Moon to the Sun⟩ are auspicious. (6) You need to prevent the Moon from being in the sixth place with respect to the ascendant at the moment of ⟨taking⟩ the potion, and from being in the eighth or twelfth ⟨place⟩.[5] (7) If the potion is laxative, it is auspicious if the Moon gives power to a planet located below the Earth with respect to the ascendant sign at the moment the potion is taken, and make sure that it [the Moon] does not give power to a ⟨planet⟩ that is above the Earth.[6] (8) If the potion is vomitive, do the opposite of everything stated.[7]

2 (1) If you inquire about a day to reduce ⟨some humor⟩, make sure that the Moon is not in an inauspicious aspect with Mars or Saturn. (2) Trine and sextile ⟨of the Moon⟩ with Mars are auspicious, and in this matter ⟨they are⟩ more ⟨auspicious⟩ than all the aspects ⟨of the Moon⟩ with Saturn. (3) Conjunction ⟨of the Moon⟩ with the Sun, Saturn, or Mars is inauspicious, and the aspects ⟨of the Moon⟩ with the Sun are intermediate [i.e., neither auspicious nor inauspicious]. (4) Conjunction ⟨of the Moon⟩ with Venus is better than with Jupiter; the aspects of these two [Venus and Jupiter] ⟨with the Moon⟩ are auspicious. (5) Conjunction ⟨of the Moon⟩ with Mercury and its aspects are according to its [Mercury's] mixture: if ⟨the mixture is⟩ good, they are auspicious, if bad they are inauspicious.[1] (6) The opinion of all the scholars of the signs and the physicians is that it is auspicious to reduce

mensis ultima. (7) Et si fuerit causa periculosa non aspiciat eligere horam. (8) Et dicit Ptholomeus:[1] cave ne minuas Luna existente in Geminis quia periculosum est, eo quod ipsum habet de partibus membrorum hominis manus et brachia. (9) Et hanc regulam dicit Ptholomeus:[2] cave ne tangas membrum ferro Luna existente in signo illius membri, signum Arietis habet caput, Pisces pedes.

⟨II ii⟩
Secunda ⟨domus⟩

1 (1) Qui vult emere aliquid in quo lucretur ponat Lunam in parte parva circuli, que est a principio Aquarii usque ad finem Cancri, qui[3] est pars Lune. (2) Et est idoneum Lunam esse in aliquo angulorum vel succedentium contra signum ascendentis, excepta domo .8a., nec sit in aliqua cadentium, nisi in .3a., que est domus gaudii sui. (3) Et radix huius rei, magis quam totum quod ego dixi, est quod Luna non sit vaga sed det fortitudinem stelle bone in natura sua vel aspiciat eam quocumque aspectu; tamen amicabili stelle non bone in natura sua si ipsa est dominus ascendentis vel prepositus .5. locorum principatus vel quod fuerit stella in bono loco respectu gradus ascendentis. (4) Et cave ne Luna dederit fortitudinem stelle combuste vel retrograde nisi fuerit stella superior existens prope directionem in cursu suo. (5) Et dicit Mesahala:[4] semper respice quod dominus .2e. sit in bono loco vel Iupiter; et cave ne sit Mars in aliquo angulorum vel Saturnus, et si Luna sit combusta ibi nihil est peius.

2 (1) Et si vis thesaurum dare societati, vide quod Mars non sit in aliquo
41r angulorum | nec respiciat Lunam malo aspectu. (2) Et dicit Saal: si vis vendere, pone Lunam in altitudine sua vel in .3o. aspectu ad malos, sed quod non coniugas eam illis; hoc inveni ego.

[1]Ptholomeus*] V; E Tpholomeus. [2]Ptholomeus*] V; E Tpholomeus. [3]qui] E; V que. [4]Mesahala] E; V Mesehala.

⟨a humor⟩ in the last half of the month. (7) If his condition is dangerous, he should not look to choose an hour. (8) Ptolemy says: be careful not to reduce ⟨a humor⟩ when the Moon is in Gemini, because this is dangerous; the reason is that, among the parts of the body, it [the Moon] is in charge of the hands and the arm. (9) This rule is stated by Ptolemy: be careful not to touch a member with iron when the Moon is in a sign which signifies this member, ⟨like⟩ Aries, ⟨which is in charge of⟩ the head, and Pisces, the feet.[2]

⟨II ii⟩
The Second ⟨Place⟩

1 (1) One who wishes to buy something and make a profit from it should put the Moon in the smaller part of the zodiac, which is from the beginning of Aquarius to the end of Cancer, which is the Moon's part.[1] (2) It is appropriate for the Moon to be in one of the cardines, or the succedent places with respect to the ascendant sign, except for the eighth place, and for it [the Moon] not to be in any of the cadent ⟨places⟩, except for the third place, which is the place of its [the Moon's] joy. (3) The main thing, more than anything I have said, is that the Moon not be peregrine[2] but give power to a benefic planet in its nature or aspect it [the benefic planet] in any aspect; however, ⟨it is appropriate for the Moon to be⟩ in a friendly ⟨aspect with⟩ a planet that is not auspicious in its nature, if this ⟨planet⟩ is the lord of the ascendant or the ruler of the five places of dominion,[3] or if it is a planet in an auspicious position with respect to the ascendant degree.[4] (4) Be careful that the Moon does not give power to a planet that is burnt or retrograde,[5] except if it is a superior planet close to being direct in its course. (5) Māshā'allāh says: always take care that the lord of the second ⟨place⟩ or Jupiter be in an auspicious position; and be careful that Mars or Saturn is not in any of the cardines, but there is nothing worse than when the Moon is burnt there.[6]

2 (1) If you wish to lend money to a partnership, make sure that Mars is not in one of the cardines or aspects the Moon in an inauspicious aspect. (2) Sahl says: if you wish to sell, put the Moon in its exaltation[1] or in trine with malefics, but do not let it [the Moon] be in conjunction with them [the malefics]; this is what I found.[2]

⟨II iii⟩
Tertia ⟨domus⟩

1 (1) Qui querit ire viam parvam per terram, pone Lunam in loco bono et dominum .3e. domus et cum aspectu stelle bone, nec sit stella mala in domo .3a. vel in opposito eius ⟨⟨u e so quartement⟩⟩, et sit dominus ascendentis vel prepositus in loco bono, nec combustus nec retrogradus; et similiter si non fuerit in .3a. vel 9a. stella retrograda. (2) Dicit Doroneus quod fortitudo domini hore .9e. est sicut fortitudo domini ascendentis, et omnes concordant cum eo.

2 (1) Et si ad intrandum fluvium vel mare, omnes concordant unanimiter quod qui intrat navem in hora Saturni submergetur nisi fuerit Iupiter cum eo vel ipsum aspiciat ab aliquo angulorum, et Saturnum esse in aliquo angulorum durum. (2) Et Mars in mari, si fuerit in uno angulorum, non nocebit tantum quantum Saturnus; et econtrario Mars plus nocet in terra quam Saturnus.

3 (1) Et Doroneus dicit: cave ne intres navem in signo igneo, quia domus .8va., que est domus mortis, erit signum aqueum. Et bonum est quod unum eorum signum sit aqueorum ascendens, et si fuerit signum Cancri et Luna non fuerit in loco respiciente ascendentem, vide si fuerit Iupiter in bono loco et aspiciens; non dubitabis. (2) Et dicit Messehala: cave ne Luna sit in Piscibus, quia hoc est probatum nisi fuerit cum eo Iupiter vel Venus, vel dans fortitudinem eis et ipsa in bono loco respectu ascendentis; et econtra pone Lunam in aspectu Iovis vel Veneris, vel in aspectu Solis trino vel .6li. (3) Et[1] si quesieris horam eligendi ad intrandum mare ad bellandum infra mare vel ad rapiendum vel ad obsidendum aliquam villam, de hoc loquar aduc in .7. domo.

[1]et] E; V vel.

⟨II iii⟩
The Third ⟨Place⟩

1 (1) ⟨For⟩ one who inquires about setting off on a short overland journey, put the Moon in an auspicious position and the lord of the third place in an aspect with a benefic planet, and ⟨be careful⟩ that no malefic planet is in the third place or in opposition to it ⟨⟨…⟩⟩, and that the lord of the ascendant or the ruler is in an auspicious position, neither burnt nor retrograde; and the same applies if a retrograde planet is not in the third or ninth ⟨place⟩.[1] (2) Dorotheus says that the power of the lord of the ninth hour[2] is like the power of the lord of the ascendant, and everyone agrees with him.[3]

2 (1) If ⟨the election is about⟩ setting off ⟨on a journey⟩ by river or by sea, all agree unanimously that one who embarks on a ship at a Saturn's hour will drown unless Jupiter is with it [Saturn], or if it [Jupiter] itself aspects it [Saturn] from one of the cardines, and Saturn is harmful in one of the cardines. (2) Mars, ⟨for a journey⟩ by sea, if it is in one of the cardines, will not harm as much as Saturn; and on the contrary, Mars harms more than Saturn ⟨for a journey⟩ by land.[1]

3 (1) Dorotheus says: be careful not to embark on a ship in a fiery sign [i.e., when the ascendant sign is a fiery sign], because then the eighth place, which is the place of death, is a watery sign. It is auspicious if the ascendant is one of the watery signs, but if ⟨one of these signs⟩ is Cancer and the Moon is not in a position aspecting the ascendant, make sure that Jupiter is in an auspicious position and aspecting ⟨the ascendant⟩; do not be in doubt ⟨about this⟩.[1] (2) Māshā'allāh says: be careful that the Moon is not in Pisces, because this has been tested, unless Jupiter or Venus is with it [the Moon], or it [the Moon] gives power to them [Jupiter or Venus] and it [the Moon] itself is in a fortunate position with respect to the ascendant; on the other hand, put the Moon so that it aspects Jupiter or Venus, or aspects the Sun by trine or sextile.[2] (3) If you inquire about choosing an hour to set off by sea to fight at sea or to plunder or lay siege to some city, I will speak about this in ⟨the chapter on⟩ the seventh place.[3]

⟨II iv⟩
Quarta ⟨domus⟩

1 (1) Si queris horam querendi absconditum, cave ne sit stella bona vel mala retrograda in gradu ascendente vel sub termino combustionis, rursus quod non sit Saturnus in aliquo angulorum, et pone Lunam in loco in quo det fortitudinem stelle que sit super terram respectu gradus ascendentis nec sit combusta nec retrograda. (2) Et si vis abscondere aliquid, pone dominum ascendentis rursus Lunam sub termino combustionis, et si non potes fac ut dent ambo fortitudinem vel unus eorum stelle existenti sub terra. (3) Et signum Tauri melius est omnibus aliis signis in hac re, et post ipsum signum Aquarii nisi fuerit dominus signi combustus vel retrogradus.

2 (1) Et si ad fondendum murum et infortiandum villam, cave ne sit
41v dominus ascendentis in domo .7a. signi patrie, et pone dominum ville | in loco in quo non sit combustus nec retrogradus, nec cum stella mala, nec in aspectu ipsius, nec sit in domo cadente, et quod non sit malus aspectus inter ipsum et dominum ascendentem, precipue quod sit stella bona in ascendente quecumque sit illa, quia fortitudo eius est sicut fortitudo domini domus.

3 (1) Et si queris emere curiam vel vineam vel terram, pone stellam bonam in domo .4a. vel aspiciat eam vel stellam que est dominus .4e.; et si non possis, pone Saturnum in bono loco et Lunam similiter. (2) Et si potes ponere in domo .4a. de signis rectis, que[1] sunt a principio Cancri usque ad finem Sagittarii, fac, et similiter dominum .4e.

4 (1) Et si ad mutandum de loco ad locum, elige dominum hore quod non[2] sit in bono loco, similiter et gradus ascendentis et dominus eius. (2) Et non obliviscaris locum Lune, nam ipsa semper significat super principio rei, et stella cui dat fortitudinem significat[3] super finem rei. (3) Et si non dederit fortitudinem stelle alicui, scias finem rei per dominum domus et vide fortitudinem suam et ita iudicabis.

[1]que*] V; E qui. [2]non] E; V erased. [3]significat] E; V erased.

⟨II iv⟩
The Fourth ⟨Place⟩

1 (1) If you inquire about an hour to find something hidden, be careful that neither a benefic nor a malefic retrograde planet is in the ascendant degree or under the domain of burning, and also that Saturn is not in any of the cardines,[1] and put the Moon in a position in which it gives power to a planet that is above the Earth with respect to the ascendant degree and is neither burnt nor retrograde. (2) If you wish to hide something, put the lord of the ascendant and also the Moon under the domain of burning,[2] and if you cannot, proceed so that they both give, or one of them ⟨gives⟩, power to a planet below the Earth.[3] (3) Taurus is better than all the other signs in this matter, and after it Aquarius, unless the lord of the sign is burnt or retrograde.

2 (1) To lay the foundations of a wall and fortify a city, be careful that the lord of the ascendant is not in the seventh place ⟨counting⟩ from the sign of the country,[1,2] and put the lord of the city in a position in which it is neither burnt nor retrograde, nor with a malefic planet, nor in an aspect to it [the malefic planet], nor in a cadent place, and that there is not an inauspicious aspect between it [the lord of the city] and the rising lord, and especially ⟨take care⟩ that a benefic planet is in the ascendant, whichever it [the benefic planet] is, because its power is like the power of the lord of the place.

3 (1) If you seek to buy a manor-house, a vineyard, or a piece of land, put a benefic planet in the fourth place or see that it [the benefic planet] aspects it [the fourth place] or a planet that is the lord of the fourth place; but if you cannot, put Saturn in an auspicious position and likewise the Moon.[1] (2) If you can put in the fourth place one of the straight signs, which are from the cusp of Cancer to the end of Sagittarius, do ⟨this⟩, and ⟨proceed⟩ likewise regarding the lord of the fourth ⟨place⟩.

4 (1) To move from one place to another, choose a lord of the hour that is not in an auspicious position ⟨and proceed⟩ likewise regarding the ascendant degree and its lord. (2) Do not forget the position of the Moon, because it always signifies the beginning of some undertaking, and the planet to which it [the Moon] gives power signifies the end of the undertaking. (3) If it [the Moon] does not give power to any planet, know the end of the undertaking from the lord of the place, and observe its power, and judge accordingly.

⟨II v⟩
Quinta ⟨domus⟩

1 (1) Si queris horam ad recipiendum conceptionem, pone Iovem in loco bono respectu ascendentis, et si non[1] potes pone Venerem in loco suo, et cave ne stella malivola sit in aliquo angulorum nec in .5a. respectu ascendentis et prepara locum Lune. (2) Dicit Enoc quod fortitudo domini hore in hac domo est sicut fortitudo domini ascendentis.

2 (1) Et si sciveris tempus conceptionis tu poteris scire tempus partus, et econtrario. (2) Et hoc est sententia Enoc in libro suo; et hoc pluries temptavi, et inveni veritatem[2] si viderim iudicium .2. rerum, sicut explanabo aduc. (3) Et hec sunt verba Enoc: semper locus Lune in puncto conceptionis est gradus ascendentis hora partus, et gradus ascendentis hora conceptionis est locus Lune hora nativitatis. (4) Propter hoc dicit ipse: vide in puncto nativitatis, si fuerit Luna in gradu ascendente, certe mora pueri in utero erit .273. dierum et horarum .8. secundum propinquitatem; et si fuerit Luna in principio .7e. domus, quia semper ascendit de eo gradus vel pars gradus, certe mora erit .259. dierum; et si Luna est sub terra, precipue parva pars, erit mora .288. dierum. (5) Et si fuerit in aliis locis, vide si Luna fuerit sub terra et quanta est distantia sua a gradu ascendentis, et da cuilibet gradui .12. dies in approximatione; et si remanserint minus .6. gradus dimitte eos, et
42r si plus adde secundum dies in | approximatione et productum adde super .273. et tertiam diei; tunc enim invenies moram in approximatione. (6) Et si Luna est super terram, vide quanta est distantia sua a principio .7e. et fac sicud debes, et productum adde super moram parvam; et debes respicere aliquando in horis ad addendum vel minuendum propter diversitatem motus Lune. (7) Et ius est quod tu prepares loca stellarum et quod tu ponas locum Lune in nativitate gradu ascendentis.

3 (1) Et oportet aduc respicere quod si fuerit terminus propinquus et Mercurius intraverit in loco in quo decet ipsum esse, et sit ei fortitudo magna in illo loco, et ipse est de inferioribus a Sole, vel Mars, propter fes-

[1]non] E; V om. [2]veritatem] E; V unitatem (but veritatem above the line).

⟨II v⟩
The Fifth ⟨Place⟩

1 (1) If you inquire about an hour for conception, put Jupiter in an auspicious position with respect to the ascendant, but if you cannot ⟨do so⟩, put Venus in its [Jupiter's] place,[1] and be careful that no malevolent planet is in any of the cardines or in the fifth ⟨place⟩ with respect to the ascendant, and calculate the position of the Moon.[2] (2) Enoch says that the power of the lord of the hour in this place [the fifth place] is like the power of the lord of the ascendant.[3]

2 (1) If you know the time of conception you can know the time of birth, and vice versa. (2) This is Enoch's opinion in his book, and I tested this many times and found it true[1] if I take into account the judgment of two things, as I shall explain below. (3) This is what Enoch says: the position of the Moon at the moment of conception is always the ascendant degree at the time of parturition, and the ascendant degree at the time of conception is the position of the Moon at the time of birth.[2] (4) Therefore he says: observe, at the moment of birth, if the Moon is in the degree of the ascendant, the child's stay in the womb will certainly be 273 days and approximately 8 hours; and if the Moon is in the cusp of the seventh place, because it always ascends a degree and minute from it, the stay will certainly be 259 days; and if the Moon is beneath the Earth, especially a small part ⟨of the Earth⟩, the stay will be 288 days.[3] (5) If it [the Moon] is in other places, observe whether the Moon is below the Earth and find out its [the Moon's] distance from the degree of the ascendant, and assign one day to every 12° approximately;[4] if there is a remainder of less than 6°, ignore them, but if there is more ⟨than 6°⟩ convert them approximately into days and add the result to 273⅓ days; then you will find the stay approximately. (6) If the Moon is above the Earth, find its [the Moon's] distance from the cusp of the seventh ⟨place⟩ and proceed as you need, and add the result to the short stay [i.e., 259 days]; and sometimes you need to add or subtract hours because of the variability of the Moon's motion.[5] (7) It is right that you should calculate the positions of the planets and that you should put the Moon's position in the nativity at the degree of the ascendant.[6]

3 (1) It is also necessary to consider that if the term ⟨of the pregnancy⟩ is close and Mercury enters a position where it is suitable for it [Mercury] to be ⟨at the moment of birth⟩, and it [Mercury] exercises great power in this position, because it is one of the planets inferior to the Sun, or ⟨if⟩

tinationem nature sue, et dederit fortitudinem stelle existenti in loco predicto, exibit motus antequam attingat ad dictum locum, quia stella faciet opus Lune et hoc est probatum multotiens. (2) Et in tempore conceptionis computa quod Luna sit in gradu ascendentis tempore partus, et locus Lune tempore conceptionis gradus ascendentis in nativitate, et computa sicut debes.

4 (1) Dicit Doroneus quod hec domus significat super nuntios; et vide si fuerit dominus domus huius in bono aspectu cum domino .7e. et non sit dominus .7e. in .12. (2) Et prepara locum Lune, item locum Mercurii, quia fortitudinem habet in hac re. (3) Et si queris diem ad bibendum et ad faciendum gaudium, prepara locum Veneris nisi sit aliquis malus in aliquo angulorum vel succedentium.

⟨II vi⟩
Sexta domus

1 (1) Dixerunt sapientes Indie quod magna fortitudo est .28. mansionibus Lune in iudiciis signorum, et ego transferam verba eorum in qualibet mansione. (2) Et mansiones ita fecerunt: diviserunt gradus circuli, qui sunt .360., in .28. partibus, qui sunt mansiones[1] (sic) Lune. (3) Et ratio quod ipse sunt dies quibus videtur Luna super terram, et quod quelibet mansio habet .12. gradus et .6. septimas unius gradus, que sunt .51. partes prime, scilicet minuta, et .28. secunda, et non sunt inter eas[2] in fortitudine omnium graduum circuli nisi tertia pars prima, id est nisi .3. partes prime. (4) Et debes minuere in hiis diebus de loco Lune .9. gradus equales ad sciendum excessum cuiuslibet mansionis, et quod signum dividetur in .2. mansiones et .3am. mansionis. (5) Et in *Libro iudiciorum seculi*[3] explanabo formam mansionum. (6) Et hic explanabo illud quod dixerunt quando Luna est in aliqua mansione secundum viam electionum.

[1]mansiones] sic EV. [2]eas] E; V eos. [3]*Libro iudiciorum seculi*] EV *Libro iurium seculi*; corrected according to *El*, II vi 2:1.

Mars, because of the quickness of its nature, gives power to a planet situated in the aforementioned position, the movement ⟨of the fetus⟩ will become visible [i.e., the baby will be born] before it [Mercury or Mars] reaches the aforementioned position, because the planet behaves like the Moon, and this has been tested many time. (2) Calculate ⟨the position of⟩ the Moon at the time of conception so that it is in the degree of the ascendant at the time of birth, ⟨since⟩ the position of the Moon at the time of conception is the degree of the ascendant at birth, and calculate ⟨this⟩ as you need.[1]

4 (1) Dorotheus says that this place signifies messengers; and be sure that the lord of its place [i.e., the lord of the fifth place] is in an auspicious aspect with the lord of the seventh ⟨place⟩, and that the lord of the seventh ⟨place⟩ is not in the twelfth ⟨place⟩. (2) Calculate the position of the Moon, also the position of Mercury, because it exerts power in this matter.[1] (3) If you inquire about a day to drink and make merry, calculate the position of Venus, unless some malefic ⟨planet⟩ is in one of the cardines or the succedent ⟨places⟩.[2]

⟨II vi⟩
The Sixth Place

1 (1) The scientists of India said that the 28 mansions of the Moon have great power in the judgments of the signs,[1] and I will convey what they said about each mansion. (2) They made the mansions in this way: they divided the degrees of the zodiac, which are 360, into 28 parts, which are the mansions of the Moon. (3) The reason is that these are the days in which the Moon is seen above the Earth, and that each mansion extends 12° and 6⁄7 of one degree, which are 51 first parts, that is, minutes, and 28 seconds, and between them, in the power of all the degrees of the circle, there is only the third first part, that is, only 3 minutes.[2] (4) In the present day, you need to subtract 9 equal degrees from the position of the Moon in order to know the excess of every mansion,[3] and ⟨you need to know⟩ that the sign is divided into two mansions and one third of a mansion. (5) In the *Book of the judgment of the world*, I will explain the shape of the mansions.[4] (6) Here I will set forth what they say ⟨that will happen⟩ when the Moon is in some mansion, according to the method of elections.[5]

42v **2** (1) Prima signi Arietis, ahitaih in lingua Arabica, | et explanant in *Libro iudiciorum seculi.* (2) Dixerunt sapientes Indi: quando Luna est ibi, bonum est bibere potionem et emere[1] omnem rem equitaturam; et bonum ne foras nisi Luna fuerit in fine mansionis. (3) Dicit Doroneus: hec mansio est mala ad capiendum uxorem, aut ad[2] associandum cum homine, aut qui emet servum vel ancillam, ipsa fugiet. (4) Et concedit quod bona sit ad itenerandum per navem quia festinanter attingunt ad portum salutis, et bonum intromittere se[3] de rebus armorum, et plantare arbores et induere vestes novas.

3 (1) Secunda, albatin,[4] mala ad accipiendum uxorem; item mala ad associandum; et malum ire in mari et per terram bonum multum; et qui capietur in captivitate positus et in carcere; et Luna in hac mansione[5] elongabunt dies mali sui. (2) Dicit Doroneus: si potio sit laxativa, multum bonum est.

4 (1) Tertia altari.[6] Sapientes Indi dixerunt quod bonum est ire per mare vel per terram et non est bonum bibere potionem. (2) Dicit Doroneus: ire in siccitate melius est quam per mare quia impetus erit undarum; et est bonum emere equum; et multum malum emere oves et parva animalia, et capere uxorem, et associare, item plantare, et vestire novas vestes; et qui intrat carcerem non exibit cito; item malum emere servum vel ancillam.

5 (1) Quarta aldebaram. Sapientes Indi dixerunt: bonum est facere fundamentum, et edificare, et plantare, et bibere potionem, et vestire novos pannos. (2) Dicit Doroneus: malum est accipere uxorem, et associari; et ire in navi, evadet tamen post tormentum magnum; et si emat servum, erit fidelis; et bonum emere equitaturam; et captus vel incarceratus non exibit cito; item bonum est cavare putheos et foveas.

6 (1) Quinta alhata. Et dixerunt Sapientes Indi: bonum est accipere uxorem, et incipere librum vel addiscere, et ire in mari vel in sicco. (2) Dicit Doroneus: malum est se associare cum maiore suo quia finis erit malus; et captivus et incarceratus non exibit cito. (3) Et dixerunt quod bonum est emere servum vel ancillam. (4) Et Ptholomeus rex dicit regulam unam:

[1]emere] E; V om. [2]ad] E; V om. [3]se] E; V > debet. [4]Albatin] E; V ablatin. [5]hac mansione] E; V hanc mansionem. [6]Altari] E; V altaim.

2 (1) The first ⟨mansion⟩ of Aries is *al-naṭḥ* in Arabic, ⟨as⟩ they explain in the *Book of the judgment of the world*.[1] (2) The scientists of India said: when the Moon is there, it is auspicious to drink a potion and buy everything related to equitation; it is auspicious not ⟨to be⟩ outside unless the Moon is at the end of the mansion. (3) Dorotheus says: this mansion is inauspicious for taking a wife, for partnership with a man, or ⟨for⟩ one who buys a male or female slave, ⟨because⟩ she will run away. (4) He agrees that it is auspicious to travel by ship because they will quickly arrive in a safe harbor, and it is auspicious to occupy oneself with weaponry, to plant trees, and to put on new clothes.[2]

3 (1) The second ⟨mansion⟩, *al-buṭayn*, is inauspicious for taking a wife; also inauspicious for forming a partnership; it is inauspicious for travel by sea but very auspicious for travel by land; one who is held in captivity will be put in prison; when the Moon is in this mansion his bad days will be prolonged. (2) Dorotheus says: if the potion is a laxative, this is very auspicious.[1]

4 (1) The third is *al-thurayyā*. The scientists of India said that it is auspicious to travel by sea or by land but it is not auspicious to drink a potion. (2) Dorotheus says: to travel by land is better than by sea because there will be heavy waves; it is auspicious to buy a horse; very inauspicious to buy sheep and small livestock, to take a wife, to form a partnership, also to plant ⟨trees⟩, and to wear new clothes; one who enters prison will not get out soon; it is also inauspicious to buy a male slave or a female slave.[1]

5 (1) The fourth is *al-dabarān*. The scientists of India said: it is auspicious to erect foundations, to build, to plant, to drink a potion, and to wear new clothes. (2) Dorotheus says: it is inauspicious to take a wife, to form a partnership; one who travels by ship will however escape a great storm; if he buys a slave, he [the slave] will be loyal; it is auspicious to buy a horse for riding; one who is captured or imprisoned will not get out soon; it is also auspicious to dig wells and pits.[1]

6 (1) The fifth is *al-haqʿa*. The scientists of India said: it is auspicious to take a wife, to begin a book or study, and to travel by sea or by land. (2) Dorotheus says: it is inauspicious to form a partnership with someone who is older than himself because the outcome will be bad; one who is captured or imprisoned will not get out soon. (3) They said that it is auspicious to buy a male slave or a female slave.[1] (4) King Ptolemy[2] states one rule: it is

bonum est emere servum quando Luna est in uno signorum que sunt super formam filii hominis, cuius sunt Gemini, Virgo, Libra, et medietas Sagittarii, et signum Aquarii, dum tamen Luna non sit cum stella mala vel sub radiis; et veritas quod sit distans per .12. gradus, qui sunt quantitas radiationis eius.

43r **7** (1) Sexta alhana. Dixerunt | sapientes Indi: bonum est ponere in thesauro, et mittere in predam, et ponere obsidium circa villam aliquam; et malum seminare, et ire, et precipere preceptum. (2) Dicit Doroneus: incarceratus, nisi exiverit in die tertia, morabitur in domo incarceratorum diebus pluribus; et dicit quod bonum est ire in navi; et multum bonum associari; et malum bibere potionem, item malum vestire novum pannum.

8 (1) Septima aldaren. Dixerunt sapientes Indie: bonum est seminare, et[1] ⟪marchander⟫, et vestire novos pannos. (2) Dicit Doroneus: bonum est ire in mari vel in siccitate, item associari, et vestire novos pannos, et bibere potionem, et emere servos et equitaturas, et omnem rem inceptam consummare, et inceptio ⟪pourfitera⟫.

9 (1) Octava alnathra. Dixerunt sapientes Indie: bonum est vestire novos pannos, et loqui de peramatis, item ire; et si incipiat pluvia in gradu erit. (2) Et dicit Doroneus: bonum est associari quia lucrebunt multum; et malum accipere uxorem, rursum servum emere nam rebellis erit contra dominum suum; et bonum ire in navi; et incarcerato fiet demandatio.

10 (1) Nona achltas. Dixerunt sapientes Indie: malum est ire, seminare, vel commodare pecuniam, vel vincere alium (2) Dicit Doroneus: malum ire in siccitate et non in aqua;[2] et malum[3] vestire novum pannum; et sociorum quilibet decipiet alium; et bonum pendere hostia; et incarcerato festinabitur exitus.

11 (1) Decima algbha. Malum est acommodare thesaurus, rursus ire et seminare. (2) Et dicit Doroneus bonum est associari, et fondare[4] edificia, et vestire de novo; et incarceratus non cito exibit.

[1]et] E; V om. [2]aqua] E; V aliqua. [3]malum] E; V malis. [4]fondare] E; E fundare.

auspicious to buy a slave when the Moon is in one of the signs with human shape, which are Gemini, Virgo, Libra, half of Sagittarius, and Aquarius,[3] on condition that the Moon is not with a malefic planet or under the rays[4] ⟨of the Sun⟩; the truth is that the distance ⟨from the Sun⟩ should be up to 12°, which is the number ⟨of degrees⟩ of its [the Moon's] ray.[5,6]

7 (1) The sixth is *al-hanʿa*. The scientists of India said: it is auspicious to put ⟨objects⟩ in a treasury, to plunder, and to lay some city under siege; it is inauspicious to sow, to travel, and to give orders. (2) Dorotheus says: one who is imprisoned, unless he gets out on the third day, will remain in prison for many days; he says that it is auspicious to travel by ship; it is very auspicious to form a partnership; it is inauspicious to drink a potion and also to wear a new garment.[1]

8 (1) The seventh is *al-dhirāʿ*. The scientists of India said: it is auspicious to sow, ⟨⟨to trade⟩⟩, and to wear new garments. (2) Dorotheus says: it is auspicious to travel by sea or by land, also to form a partnership, to wear new garments, to drink a potion, to buy slaves and riding horses, to complete everything that has been begun, and the undertaking ⟨⟨will succeed⟩⟩.[1]

9 (1) The eighth is *al-nathra*. The scientists of India said: it is auspicious to wear new garments, to speak about those who persevere on love, also to travel; if it begins to rain it will be in the degree ⟨of the mansion⟩ [i.e., when the Moon enters the degrees of the mansion]. (2) Dorotheus says: it is auspicious to form a partnership because they will profit a lot; it is inauspicious to take a wife, also to buy a slave because he will be rebellious against his master; it is auspicious to travel by ship; there will be a delay ⟨in the release⟩ of one who is imprisoned.[1]

10 (1) The ninth is *al-ṭarf*. The scientists of India said: it is inauspicious to travel, to sow, to lend money, or to defeat someone else. (2) Dorotheus says: it is inauspicious to travel by land but not by water; it is inauspicious to wear a new garment; one of the partners will deceive the other; it is auspicious to put up doors; and the release of an imprisoned person will arrive sooner.[1]

11 (1) The tenth is *al-jabha*. It is inauspicious to lend money, also to travel and sow. (2) Dorotheus says: it is auspicious to form a partnership, to lay the foundation for buildings, and to wear new ⟨clothes⟩; one who is imprisoned will not get out quickly.[1]

12 (1) Undecima alzabda. Bonum est obsidere villam, et seminare; et qui fugit a domo carceris capietur. (2) Dicit Doroneus: bonum est fondare fondamentum, et emere terram, et associari, et vestire novo; et ire mediocre.

13 (1) Duodecima alserfa. Dixerunt sapientes Indie: bonum est edificare, et emere, et plantare, et seminare, et vestiri, et accipere uxorem, et ire in tertia principii mansionis. (2) Dicit Doroneus: malum est commodare, quia non revertetur thesaurus sibi, et si revertetur erit post lites; et qui vadit per mare erit in periculo; et bonum associari, et emere bestias; et dicit quod in tertia ultima huius mansionis bonum est emere servum vel[1] ancillam sed erit altus corde et multum bonus comestor.

14 (1) Tertia decima allahavaalahu. Dixerunt sapientes Indie: bonum est mercare, et ire per mare et per terram, et fodere, et seminare, et accipere
43v uxorem. (2) Dicit Doroneus: non est idoneum ducere | puellam vel viduam; item finis incarcerati est bonus; item ire in mari sed ibi morabitur; et bonum bibere potionem, et vestiri novo, et edificare, et gaudere, et intrare coram regibus et magnibus, et lavare caput.

15 (1) .14a., alchimeth. Dixerunt sapientes Indie: bonum est mercare, et accipere viduam non puellam, et plantare, et ire, rursus commodare pecuniam. (2) Dicit Doroneus: si accipit puellam non morabuntur in societate nisi parum; et accipere viduam bonum, item accipere servum vel ancillam, quia servus pius erit super dominum suum, ire per navem, item associari et lucrabitur multum; et incarceratus exibit cito a carcere.

16 (1) .15. algaphar. Dixerunt sapientes Indie: bonum est bibere potionem, et canare; et malum ire per mare et per siccitatem. (2) Dicit Doroneus: qui accipit uxorem cito erit lis inter eos; et malum associari, et emere servum vel ancillam vel bestiam, et commodare pecuniam quia non revertetur ad eum; et mutari de curia ad curiam bonum.

[1]vel] E; V et.

12 (1) The eleventh is *al-zubra*. It is auspicious to lay siege to a city and to sow; one who escapes from prison will be caught. (2) Dorotheus says: it is auspicious to lay the foundation ⟨of a building⟩, to buy land, to form a partnership, to wear new ⟨clothes⟩; to travel is intermediate.[1]

13 (1) The twelfth is *al-ṣarfa*. The scientists of India said: in the first third of the mansion it is auspicious to build, to buy, to plant, to sow, to get dressed, to take a wife, and to travel. (2) Dorotheus says: it is inauspicious to lend ⟨money⟩ because the money will not be returned to him, and if it is retuned it will be only after quarrels; one who travels by sea will be in danger; it is auspicious to form a partnership, to buy animals; he says that in the last third of the mansion it is auspicious to buy a male slave or female slave but he or she will be haughty and a very good glutton.[1]

14 (1) The thirteenth is *al-ʿawwāʾ*. The scientists of India said: it is auspicious to trade, to travel by sea and by land, to dig, to sow, and to take a wife. (2) Dorotheus says: it is not appropriate to marry a young woman or a widow; the end of one who is imprisoned will be good; it is also ⟨good⟩ to travel by sea but he will be delayed there; it is auspicious to drink a potion, to wear new ⟨clothes⟩, to build, to rejoice, to be in the presence of kings and magnates, and to wash the head.[1]

15 (1) The fourteenth is *al-simāk al-aʿzal*. The scientists of India said: it is auspicious to trade, to marry a widow but not a young woman, to plant, to travel, and to lend money. (2) Dorotheus says: if one marries a young woman they will remain together only a short time; it is auspicious to marry a widow, also to acquire a male slave or a female slave because he or she will be dutiful to his or her master, to travel by ship, also to form a partnership ⟨because⟩ he will make a great profit; one who is imprisoned will get out quickly.[1]

16 (1) The fifteenth is *al-ghafr*. The scientists of India said: it is auspicious to drink a potion and to sing; it is inauspicious to travel by sea and by dry land. (2) Dorotheus says: ⟨if⟩ one takes a woman, a quarrel will break out between them soon; it is inauspicious to form a partnership, to buy a male slave or a female slave or an animal, and to lend money because it will not be returned to him; it is auspicious to move from one manor-house to another.[1]

17 (1) .16a. alzabon. Dixerunt sapientes Indie: malum est ire, et bibere potionem, et seminare, et plantare, et mercare, et vestire novo. (2) Dicit Doroneus: malum est accipere uxorem, et associari; incarceratus exibit cito in brachiis.

18 (1) .17a. alkalis. Dixerunt sapientes Indie: bonum est emere bestiam, et vestiri novo, et obsidere villam. (2) Dicit Doroneus: malum est accipere puellam; et bonum edificare, et ire in navi et bibere potionem; et multum malum emere servum.

19 (1) .18a. alkalab. Dixerunt sapientes Indie: bonum est seminare et plantare; et si inceperit pluvia erit multa; et bonum ire; et malum accipere uxorem et emere servum. (2) Dicit Doroneus: bonum edificare; et malum associari, et vestiri novo, et bibere potionem.

20 (1) .19a. alsula. Dixerunt sapientes Indie: bonum est obsidere villam, ad bellandum et ad omnem viam, et semen, et plantationem. (2) Dicit Doroneus: si accipiat homo puellam et Luna sit in hac domo, parum erunt simul; et associari malum; et navis frangetur; et malum emere servum vel ancillam.

21 (1) .20a. alnasm. Dixerunt sapientes Indie: bonum est emere bestiam; ad motum in via, mediocre. (2) Dicit Doroneus: malum est associari; et captivi et incarcerati finis eorum erit malus.

22 (1) .21. albalda. Dixerunt sapientes Indie: bonum est seminare, et edificare, et plantare, et emere terram; et ire, mediocre. (2) Dicit Doroneus:
44r bonum est emere | bestiam; et mediocre emere servum et erit altus corde; et si moriatur dominus mulieris vel quod dimittat eam et Luna in hac mansione, numquam habebit alium maritum.

23 (1) .22. ayas aldeba. Dixerunt sapientes Indie: bonum est accipere uxorem; et bonum bibere potionem, et ire, et vestire novo. (2) Dicit Doroneus: Si homo ducet uxorem et Luna sit in hac mansione, dividentur antequam

17 (1) The sixteenth is *al-zubānā*. The scientists of India said: it is inauspicious to travel, to drink a potion, to sow, to plant, to trade, and to wear new ⟨clothes⟩. (2) Dorotheus says: it is inauspicious to take a wife and to form a partnership; one who is imprisoned will get out without delay.[1,2]

18 (1) The seventeenth is *al-iklīl*. The scientists of India said: it is auspicious to buy an animal, to wear new ⟨clothes⟩, and to lay siege to a city. (2) Dorotheus says: it is inauspicious to take a young woman; it is auspicious to build, to travel by ship and to drink a potion, and it is very inauspicious to buy a slave.[1]

19 (1) The eighteenth is *qalb al-ʿaqrab*. The scientists of India said: it is auspicious to sow and to plant; if it starts to rain, it will pour; it is auspicious to travel; it is inauspicious to take a wife and buy a slave. (2) Dorotheus says: it is auspicious to build; it is inauspicious to form a partnership, to wear new ⟨clothes⟩, and to drink a potion.[1]

20 (1) The nineteenth is *al-šawla*. The scientists of India said: it is auspicious to lay siege to a city, make war, and every trip, and seed and planting. (2) Dorotheus says: if a man takes a young woman when the Moon is in this place, they will seldom be together; it is inauspicious to form a partnership; the ship will be wrecked; it is inauspicious to buy a male slave or female slave.[1]

21 (1) The twentieth is *al-naʿāʾim*. The scientists of India said: it is auspicious to buy an animal; it is intermediate to set off on a trip. (2) Dorotheus says: it is inauspicious to form a partnership; the end of captives and the imprisoned will be bad.[1]

22 (1) The twenty-first is *al-balda*. The scientists of India said: it is auspicious to sow, to build, to plant, and buy land; it is intermediate to travel. (2) Dorotheus says: it is auspicious to buy an animal; it is intermediate to buy a slave, because he will be haughty; if the husband of a woman or her divorcé dies when the Moon is in this mansion, she will never have another husband.[1]

23 (1) The twenty-second is *saʿd al-dhābiḥ*. The scientists of India said: it is auspicious to take a wife; it is auspicious to drink a potion, to travel and to wear new ⟨clothes⟩. (2) Dorotheus says: If a man marries a woman when the Moon is in this mansion, they will separate before he takes her; if they

eam accipiat; et si coniugantur, morietur dominus ante .6. menses; et emere servum, scias quod fugiet cito non invenietur; nec est bonum associari; et incarceratus cito exibit; et ire in navi bonum post dolorem magnum transibit in mari.

24 (1) .23. seadblahi.[1] Dicunt sapientes Indie: bonum est bibere potionem, et vestire novum, et seminare, et commodare pecuniam, item ire. (2) Dicit Doroneus: malum est accipere uxorem quia mulier cogitat malum super maritum suum; et multum malum emere servum; et associari bonum; et incarceratus cito exibit.

25 (1) .24. sceadaltead. Dicunt sapientes Indie: malum est ad mercare, et vestire novum, et accipere uxorem; et bonum bibere potionem, et mittere predatores, et ire in navi mediocre. (2) Dicit Doroneus: malum est accipere uxorem, et emere servum quia erit vorax; et ire per terram malum, et similiter associari; et incarceratus cito exibit.

26 (1) .25. sciadakabe. Dicunt sapientes Indie: bonum est obsidere villam, et querere vindicam de inimicis, et mittere nuntios vel insidias, id est espies; et malum seminare, et accipere uxorem. (2) Dicit Doroneus: accipere uxorem est malum; et multum bonum emere servum, et edificare, et intrare in mari, nisi quod erit ibi ostensio; et finis bonum erit; et associari malum, et incarceratus numquam exibit.

27 (1) .26. alperalmakerem. Dicunt sapientes Indie: bonum est facere bonum; et malum bibere potionem. (2) Dicit Doroneus: malum est accipere uxorem; et bonum est emere servum quia pius erit domino, et bonum edificare, et ire in navi sed morabitur; et malum associari; et incarceratus ibi morietur.

28 (1) .27. alperagalmon. Dicunt sapientes Indie: bonum est seminare, et mercare, et bibere potionem, et accipere uxorem; et malum ire. (2) Dicit Doroneus: malum est emere servum; sed incarceratus ibi morietur.

[1]seadblahi] E; V seadblahii.

have had sexual intercourse, the husband will die before six months ⟨have passed⟩; ⟨as for⟩ buying a slave, know that he will run away soon and will not be found; it is inauspicious to form a partnership; one who is imprisoned will get out quickly; it is auspicious to travel by ship after he suffered a great grief on the sea.[1]

24 (1) The twenty-third is *saʿd al-bulaʿ*. The scientists of India say: it is auspicious to drink a potion, to wear new ⟨clothes⟩, to sow, to lend money, and to travel. (2) Dorotheus says: it is inauspicious to take a wife because the woman will think bad things about her husband; it is very inauspicious to buy a slave; it is auspicious to form a partnership; one who is imprisoned will get out soon.[1]

25 (1) The twenty-fourth is *saʿd al-suʿūd*. The scientists of India say: it is inauspicious to trade, to wear new ⟨clothes⟩, and to take a wife; it is auspicious to drink a potion and to send plunderers; it is intermediate to travel by ship. (2) Dorotheus says: it is inauspicious to take a wife, and to buy a slave because he will be voracious; it is inauspicious to travel by land, and likewise to form a partnership; one who is imprisoned will get out soon.[1]

26 (1) The twenty-fifth is *saʿd al-akhbiya*. The scientists of India say: it is auspicious to lay siege to a city, to seek vengeance against enemies, to send messengers or lay ambushes, that is, ⟨to send⟩ spies; it is inauspicious to sow, and take a wife. (2) Dorotheus says: it is inauspicious to take a wife, and very auspicious to buy a slave, to build, and to set off by sea unless there is there a scavage [i.e., tax levied on foreign merchants]; the outcome will be good; it is inauspicious to form a partnership; one who is imprisoned will never get out.[1]

27 (1) The twenty-sixth is *al-fargh al-awwal*. The scientists of India say: it is auspicious to do good; it is inauspicious to drink a potion. (2) Dorotheus says: it is inauspicious to take a wife; it is auspicious to buy a slave because he will be dutiful to the master; it is auspicious to build, to travel by ship but he will be delayed; it is inauspicious to form a partnership; one who is imprisoned will die there.[1]

28 (1) The twenty-seventh is *al-fargh al-thānī*. The scientists of India say: it is auspicious to sow, to trade, to drink a potion, and to take a wife; it is inauspicious to travel. (2) Dorotheus says: it is inauspicious to buy a slave; but one who is imprisoned will die there.[1]

29 (1) .28. berhenalhol. Dicunt sapientes Indie: bonum est bibere potionem, et seminare, et mercare; et malum commodare pecuniam. (2) Dicit Doroneus: bonum est accipere uxorem, et associari nisi quod finis non erit sicut principium; et malum emere servum; et incarceratus ibi morietur. [44v]

⟨II vii⟩
Septima domus

1 (1) Qui vult eligere horam despondi mulierem, videat ne Venus sit combusta, vel retrograda, vel coniuncta stelle malivole, vel[1] in opposito aspectu ad ipsam quando eliges horam Veneris. (2) Et si Venus sit in dispositione mala pones dominum hore Lunam. (3) Si fuerit crescens Lune, et si non inveneris, pones dominum hore Iovem, et si potes ponere .7m. respectu signi ascendentis in aspectu dilectionis ad dominum ascendentis; et si non aspexerit dominum, tunc melius. (4) Et si fuerit dominus .7e. in ascendente non combustus nec retrogradus, hoc est multum bonum. (5) Et si dominus ascendentis in .7a. et receptus sit in suo loco, est bonum. (6) Et si dominus electionis est ipsa mulier, prepara locum Solis vel Martis; et quicumque sit elector, mulier vel homo, non ponas Venerem in domo .7a. numquam contra ascendentem, quia ostendit lites.

2 (1) Et si queris associari, prepara locum Iovis et quod dominus .7e. sit in aspectu dilectionis ad dominum ascendentis vel ad ascendens, et quod non sit Luna sub radiis Solis et non cum stella malivola nec in aspectu .4o. ad eam nec in opposito.

3 (1) Et si ad eligendum regi vel principi horam eundi ad bellum, si inceperit bellum, pone Lunam separantem ab aspectu vel coniunctione stelle bone vel alte, et ratio unius stelle altioris quam Sol. (2) Et si potes ponere Lunam quod ipsa coniungat se stelle combuste vel retrograde, tunc erit electio bona et integra. (3) Et cave ne signum ascendens sit unum de domibus stellarum inferiorum, nam superiori est fortitudo magna, nec potest inferior

[1]vel] E; V et.

29 (1) The twenty-eighth is *baṭn al-ḥūt*. The scientists of India say: it is auspicious to drink a potion, to sow, to trade; it is inauspicious to lend money. (2) Dorotheus says: it is auspicious to take a wife and to form a partnership but the end will not be as the beginning; it is inauspicious to buy a slave; one who is imprisoned will die there.[1]

⟨II vii⟩
The Seventh Place

1 (1) One who wishes to choose an hour to betroth a woman, should make sure that Venus is not burnt, retrograde, or conjoining a malevolent planet, or in opposition to it when you choose Venus's hour. (2) If Venus is in an inauspicious configuration, put the Moon as the lord of the hour.[1] (3) If there is a crescent Moon and you do not find ⟨the lord of the hour⟩, put Jupiter as the lord of the hour, and, if you can, put the seventh ⟨sign⟩ with respect to the sign of the ascendant in an aspect of love[2] to the lord of the ascendant; and it is better if it [the lord of the ascendant] does not aspect the lord [Jupiter]. (4) If the lord of the seventh ⟨place⟩ is in the ascendant, neither burnt nor retrograde, this is very auspicious. (5) If the lord of the ascendant is in the seventh ⟨place⟩ and it is received in its position, this is auspicious. (6) If the subject of the election[3] is the woman herself, calculate[4] the position of the Sun and Mars;[5] no matter who is the person who makes the election, a woman or a man, do not put Venus in the seventh place with respect to the ascendant, because this indicates quarrels.[6]

2 (1) If you inquire about forming a partnership, calculate the position of Jupiter[1] and ⟨make sure⟩ that the lord of the seventh ⟨place⟩ is in an aspect of love with the lord of the ascendant or the ascendant, and that the Moon is not under the rays of the Sun,[2] or with a malevolent planet, or in quartile with it or in opposition.

3 (1) If ⟨one wishes⟩ to choose an hour for a king or a prince to go to war, if he begins the war, put the Moon where it separates from an aspect or a conjunction with a benefic planet or an upper ⟨planet⟩, and the meaning ⟨of upper planet⟩ is one higher than the Sun. (2) If you can put the Moon so that it itself conjoins a burnt or retrograde planet, the election will be auspicious and perfect.[1] (3) Be careful that the ascendant sign is not one of the houses of the lower planets, because an upper ⟨planet⟩ has great power,[2]

vincere superiorem, nisi fuerit inferior in angulo primo vel .10a. et superior in domo cadente. (4) Item, inferior sit fortificata ex parte Solis, et superior econtrario, et quod scilicet superior sit sub radiis Solis, item quod inferior sit directa et superior retrograda. (5) Et quod coniungantur inferiori multa bona et superior sit medio circuli, non poterit inferior vincere superiorem vinctu perfecto.

4 (1) Et scias si fuerit Iupiter in bona dispositione cum Sole et aspiciat Cancrum, pone ipsum sub Luna. (2) Et hoc est res scita, quod si fuerit dominus ascendentis in .7a., vincet eum in[1] initio; et econtrario, si fuerit dominus .7mi. in ascendente, vincetur inimicus, nisi quod si fuerit stella alta non vincetur vinctu perfecto. (3) Et in hoc defecerunt sapientes iudiciorum signorum si fuerit ascendens signum Tauri et Mars in ascendente. (4) Quidam dicunt quod iudicabis secundum fortitudinem Veneris domini ascendentis, et non iudicabis in testimonio Martis per ipsum. (5) Secundum quod
45r temptavi pluries dampnum accidet | ambobus bellatoribus secundum fortitudinem Martis et Veneris[2] a Sole; erit fortior ille qui erit dominus eius.

5 (1) Et scias quod .2. luminaria habent in hoc magnam fortitudinem, nam si unus eorum dederit fortitudinem domino ascendentis et non sit combustus nec retrogradus, ostendet quod; vincet et econtrario si dederit fortitudinem domino .7e.. (2) Et sententia Antiquorum est quod unus .2. luminarium non est bonum in ascendente ad incipiendum bellum. (3) Et ratio est quia natura Lune est contraria nature ascendentis, quia ipsa est sicut[3] natura Solis. (4) Propter hoc dixerunt ipsi quod gradus ascendentis scindit punctus (sic)[4] Lune, nisi quod si fuerit dominus vite, quod nativitas sit de nocte vel de die, et non Sol in loco idoneo ad querendam vitam de loco suo. (5) Et dixerunt quod illi planete est fortitudo, deest sub termino combustionis, nisi fuerit in ascendente malivolus, nisi fuerit signum ascen-

[1]in] E; V om. [2]Here lacuna in EV. [3]sicut] E; V sicud. [4]ductum*] EV punctus; corrected according to the Hebrew original = ניהוג; see *Mivḥarim* III, II vii 5:4.

and a lower ⟨planet⟩ cannot be victorious over an upper ⟨planet⟩ unless the lower ⟨planet⟩ is in the first or the tenth cardo [i.e., the tenth house] and the upper ⟨planet⟩ is in a cadent place. (4) Likewise, ⟨a lower planet can be victorious over an upper planet because⟩ the lower ⟨planet⟩ is strengthened by the Sun, and the opposite applies to the upper ⟨planet⟩, that is, when the upper ⟨planet⟩ is under the rays of the Sun, and also when the lower ⟨planet⟩ is direct ⟨in its motion⟩ and the upper ⟨planet⟩ is retrograde. (5) Even if many dignities are assigned to the lower ⟨planet⟩ but the upper ⟨planet⟩ is in the middle of the zodiac,[3] the lower ⟨planet⟩ cannot be completely victorious over the upper ⟨planet⟩ either.[4,5]

4 (1) Know that if Jupiter is in an auspicious configuration with the Sun and it aspects Cancer, put it [Jupiter] instead[1] of the Moon.[2] (2) It is known that if the lord of the ascendant is in the seventh ⟨place⟩, he [i.e., his enemy] will defeat him at first; and on the contrary, if the lord of the seventh ⟨place⟩ is in the ascendant, the enemy will be defeated, but if it [the lord of the seventh place] is an upper planet, it [the enemy] will not be defeated completely. (3) The scholars in the judgments of the signs were confused in this matter [i.e., about who is victorious] if the ascendant sign is Taurus and Mars is in the ascendant. (4) Some say that you should judge according to the power of Venus ⟨as⟩ the lord of the ascendant, and that you should not judge on the basis of Mars's testimony alone. (5) According to what I have tested many times, harm will befall both combatants according to the power of Mars and Venus coming from the Sun; the stronger [i.e., of Mars and Venus] is the one which is its lord [i.e., the lord of the ascendant].[3,4]

5 (1) Know that the two luminaries have great power in this matter, for if one of them gives power to the lord of the ascendant, and it is neither burnt nor retrograde, it indicates that he [the side that begins the war] will be victorious, and the opposite applies if it gives power to the lord of the seventh ⟨place⟩. (2) The opinion of the Ancients is that ⟨if⟩ one of the two luminaries is in the ascendant, ⟨it⟩ is not auspicious to start a war. (3) The reason is that the Moon's nature is the opposite of the ascendant's nature, because it [the ascendant's nature] is like the Sun's nature.[1] (4) Therefore they said that the degree of the ascendant cuts the point of the Moon, except if it [the Moon] is the lord of life in a nocturnal or diurnal nativity, and the Sun is not in an appropriate position to inquire from its position about ⟨the length of⟩ life. (5) They said that this planet has power, ⟨but this power⟩ is not there in the domain of burning, unless there is a malevolent

dens Aries qui est domus exaltationis eius vel Leo qui est domus eius. (6) Et dico: si fuerit ita non vincet inceptor belli, nisi fuerit Saturnus combustus in termino combustionis vel fuerit retrogradus.

6 (1) Et scias quod dominus domus .2e. ab ascendente significabit super exercitum exeuntem, et dominus .8e. domus significabit super exercitum inimici. (2) Et si unus aspexerit alium aspectu opposito vel .4o. erit bellum forte, et secundum dominum domus ostendet victum. (3) Et si ambo fuerint coniuncti tunc erit bellum valde durum et forte; tunc respicias quis eorum vincet secundum quod dixi tibi in *Libro primo de sensu*. (4) Et si dominus .8e. dederit fortitudinem domino ascendentis, effugient ab exercitu inimici et revertentur ad illum[1] qui incipit bellum. (5) Et tu debes respicere ad revolutionem anni mundani quomodo aspicient luminaria Martem, vel in sua coniunctione, vel quod attinget signum finis coniunctionis loci vel principium triplicitatis ad locum Martis aut signum finis .20. annorum, sicut explanavi in *libro iudiciorum*, id est, *revolutionum mundi*.

7 (1) Et si queris horam ire predatum in mari vel ponere obsidium circa villam, si fuerit Mars, elige illi qui vadit Scorpionem, quia melius est inter signa aquea. (2) Et si fuerit Iupiter fortis versus Solem et versus signum ascendentem, signum Cancri, et si potes ponere quod Luna det fortitudinem Iovi, hoc est bonum. (3) Et cave ne det fortitudinem Saturno vel Marti et precipue si fuerit aliquis eorum fortis, quia dampnum veniret domino electionis. (4) Signum Piscium bonum si Iupiter in loco bono vel Venus; et
45v si fuerit Mercurius combustus | vel retrogradus, tunc erit electio bona. (5) Et cave ne Saturnus sit in .10a. in electione itineris marini, nec in .4a., similiter nec Mars. (6) Et si scis signum loci ad quem elector vult ire vel obsidere vel predare, cave ne eligas signum illius loci; et si fuerit .7m., tunc melius si fuerit in domo aliqua superiorum. (7) Et scias quod omnis stella que est in domo prima—nisi fuerit combusta vel retrograda et ipsa in termino suo vel

[1]illum] E; V illud.

⟨planet⟩ in the ascendant, ⟨and⟩ unless the ascendant sign is Aries, which is its [the Sun's] house of exaltation,[2] or Leo, which is its [the Sun's] house.[3] (6) ⟨But⟩ I say: if this is so, one who starts a war will not be victorious unless Saturn is burnt in the domain of burning or is retrograde.[4]

6 (1) Know that the lord of the second house ⟨counting⟩ from the ascendant signifies the departing army, and the lord of the eighth house signifies the enemy's army. (2) If one aspects the other in opposition or quartile the war will be fierce, and it indicates victory according to the lord of the house. (3) But if both are in conjunction the war will be very intense and fierce; then find out which of them is victorious according to what I told you in the *Book of the beginning of wisdom*.[1] (4) If the lord of the eighth ⟨place⟩ gives power to the lord of the ascendant, ⟨soldiers⟩ from the enemy's army will run away and go over to the one that began the war.[2] (5) You need to observe the revolution of the world-year[3] ⟨and find out⟩ in what way the luminaries aspect Mars—whether conjunction with it, or whether the terminal sign[4] from the place of conjunction or the beginning of the triplicity reaches the place of Mars or ⟨reaches⟩ the terminal sign of twenty years,[5] as I have explained in the *Book of judgments*, that is, ⟨the *Book of judgments*⟩ of the *revolutions of the world*.[6,7]

7 (1) If you inquire about an hour to go to sea and plunder or to lay siege to a city, if Mars is ⟨in the seventh place⟩, choose Scorpio for the one who is going ⟨to plunder or lay siege⟩, because it is the best among the watery signs.[1] (2) If Jupiter is strong with respect to the Sun and with respect to the ascendant sign, ⟨choose for the one who is going to plunder or lay siege⟩ Cancer, and it is auspicious if you can put the Moon so that it gives power to Jupiter.[2] (3) Be careful that it [the Moon] does not give power to Saturn or Mars, especially if one of them is strong, because harm will come to the subject of the election. (4) Pisces is auspicious if Jupiter or Venus is in a good position; if Mercury is burnt or retrograde the election will be auspicious.[3,4] (5) In an election about a sea voyage, be careful that Saturn is not in the tenth place or in the fourth place, and likewise for Mars. (6) If you know the sign of the place that the person who makes the election wants to besiege or plunder,[5] be careful not to choose the sign of that place; if it is the seventh ⟨sign⟩ [i.e., counting from the sign of the city], then it is more auspicious if it [the 7th sign] is in the house of one of the upper ⟨planets⟩. (7) Know that any planet that is in the first place—if it is neither burnt nor retrograde, and if it is in its term or if it is the lord of the house of the Sun

sit dominus domus Solis vel Lune—computa ipsam sicut dominum domus, quia fortitudo magna inest ei et precipue si fuerit dominus hore. (8) Et ita iudicabis si fuerit stella in domo .7a.

⟨II viii⟩
Octava ⟨domus⟩

1 (1) Si vis eligere horam querendi rem furatam vel perditam, quere stellam que est domina signi fortis,[1] et Sol vel Luna dederint ei fortitudinem vel in aspectu ad ipsam; et illi qui est timorosus de nocte dederit dominus .8e. fortitudinem, vel quod sit in aliquo angulorum. (2) Et si potes, parare quod dominus hore sit dominus .2e. domus, vel Iupiter si non sit combustus vel retrogradus, vel in aliquo malo aspectu ad aliquam malam stellam. (3) Et si potes ponere dominum .7e. domus in ascendente vel respiciat dominum ascendentis, tunc erit melius. (4) Et cave ne dominus hore sit dominus .7e. domus. (5) Et signa mobilia et bicorpora sunt meliora quam veridica.

⟨II ix⟩
Nona ⟨domus⟩

1 (1) Qui querit eligere horam ad scribendum, vel ad discendum, vel scribendum librum, et ad aperiendum cor, ponas semper Lunam in aliqua domorum Mercurii et non sit Mercurius retrogradus. (2) Et si sit in .1. gradu cum Sole, tunc bonum. (3) Et si fuerit Mercurius in domo prima vel cum domino ascendentis vel dominus hore fuerit tunc Mercurius, tunc melius. (4) Et si sit dominus hore Saturnus, tunc est durum, quia ipse significat super pigritia. (5) Et si dominus hore fuerit Mars, complebit voluntatem suam, et si Venus aut Sol est mediocriter.

2 (1) Ad eligendum horam ad eundum viam longam, videbis quod non sit in loco malo dominus .9e. (2) Item nec sit ibi stella mala. (3) Et Mars econtra in terra non est durus[2] plus quam Saturnus, et econtrario in mari. (4) Et si Sol est in .9a., bonum, quoniam ipsa est domus gaudii sui. (5) Et

[1]signi fortis] E; V fortis signi. [2]durus] E; V dominus.

or the Moon—think of it as if were itself the lord of the place, because it has a great power especially if it is the lord of the hour. (8) Judge likewise if the planet is in the seventh house.[6]

⟨II viii⟩
The Eighth ⟨Place⟩

1 (1) If you wish to choose an hour to look for something stolen or lost, try to find a planet that is the lord of the sign and is strong ⟨there⟩ and the Sun or the Moon give power to it or aspect it [the planet]; and, for one who is afraid at night, ⟨when⟩ the lord of the eighth ⟨place⟩ gives power ⟨to it⟩ [the planet], or ⟨when⟩ it [the planet] is in one of the cardines. (2) If you can, arrange that the lord of the hour be the lord of the second place, or that Jupiter be neither burnt nor retrograde, nor in an unfortunate aspect with one of the malefics. (3) And if you can put the lord of the seventh place in the ascendant or in an aspect with the lord of the ascendant, then this is even more auspicious. (4) Be careful that the lord of the hour is not the lord of the seventh place. (5) The tropical and the bicorporal signs are more auspicious than the fixed ⟨signs⟩.[1,2]

⟨II ix⟩
The Ninth ⟨Place⟩

1 (1) ⟨For⟩ one who inquires about an hour to write, or to study or to write a book, and to open the heart, always put the Moon in one of Mercury's houses when Mercury is not retrograde. (2) If it is in the same degree with the Sun, this is auspicious.[1] (3) If Mercury is in the first place or with the lord of the ascendant, or if the lord of the hour is then Mercury, this is more auspicious. (4) But if Saturn is the lord of the hour, this is harmful because it signifies sluggishness (5) If Mars is the lord of the hour,[2] he will fulfill his wish, and if Venus or the Sun ⟨is the lord of the hour⟩, ⟨the outcome⟩ will be intermediate.

2 (1) For choosing an hour to set off on a long journey, make sure that the lord of the ninth ⟨place⟩ is not in an inauspicious position. (2) Also ⟨make sure that⟩ a malefic planet is not there [in the ninth place]. (3) On the other hand, for ⟨a journey⟩ by land Mars is not more harmful than Saturn, and the opposite ⟨for a journey⟩ by sea. (4) It is auspicious if the Sun is in the ninth ⟨place⟩, because it [the ninth place] is the house of its [the Sun's] joy.[1] (5)

debes respicere quod sit in .9a. domo secundum divisionem ascencionum, et si fuerit in .9a. respectu graduum signorum, tunc est melius.

3 (1) Et vide radicem, et cursum suum ad quam vadit, et prepara locum
46r stelle que est idonea. | (2) Quoniam si vadet ad videndum ⟨⟨seniure⟩⟩, vel ad emendum terram, vel ad querendum absconditum, prepara locum Saturni. (3) Si ad mercaturam vel ad emendum thesaurum, prepara locum Iovis. (4) Et si ad bellum, prepara locum Martis. (5) Et si ad videndum facies regum, prepara locum Solis. (6) Et si pro muliere prepara locum Veneris. (7) Et si pro sapientibus prepara locum Mercurii.

4 (1) Omnes sapientes signorum dicunt quod si fuerit Luna vaga et nulla stella eam aspiciat, non proficiet itinerans in itinere suo nec faciet voluntatem suam secundum propositum suum. (2) Et cave ne sit in ascendente stella retrograda, precipue sit ipsa bona non combusta nec intrans sub radiis nisi fuerit de altis et ipse orientales et transiverit terminum combustionis.

⟨II x⟩
Decima ⟨domus⟩

1 (1) Qui querit obsidere super obsidio regni, si scis nativitatem eius, eligas ei domum .10am. nisi ibi fuerit stella malivola. (2) Et si ibi fuerit, quere quod non sit gradus ascendens donec transacti fuerint .10. gradus loci in quo est malivola, tunc enim elige ei locus Solis, si fuerit in loco bono respectu ascendentis. (3) Et cave ne Luna sit in .7a. domo vel in opposito domini ascendentis, et quod Mars non sit in aliquo angulorum. (4) Et si sit combustus non dubita de eo, et pone dominum hore orientalem a Sole, si fuerit superior planeta, vel occidentalem, si fuerit inferior. (5) Et signa veridica meliora sunt in hac re signis bicorporis, et bicorpora meliora sunt mobilibus, et recta meliora sunt tortuosis. (6) Et si non potes,

You need to be careful that it [the Sun] is in the ninth place according to the division of rising times,[2] but if it is in the ninth ⟨place⟩ according to the degrees of the signs, this is more auspicious.

3 (1) Find out the reason ⟨for the journey⟩ and the direction in which he travels, and calculate the position of the suitable planet. (2) Because if he travels to see an ⟪old man⟫, to buy land, or to look for something hidden, calculate the position of Saturn. (3) If ⟨he travels⟩ to trade or to buy something valuable, calculate the position of Jupiter. (4) If ⟨he travels⟩ to wage war, calculate the position of Mars. (5) If ⟨he travels⟩ to meet kings, calculate the position of the Sun. (6) If ⟨he travels⟩ for the sake of a woman, calculate the position of Venus. (7) If ⟨he travels⟩ for the sake of scholars, calculate the position of Mercury.[1,2]

4 (1) All the scholars of the signs say that if the Moon is peregrine and no planet aspects it [the Moon], the traveler will not profit in his journey nor effect his wish according to his purpose. (2) Be careful that no retrograde planet is in the ascendant, especially ⟨be careful that in the ascendant⟩ there is a benefic ⟨planet⟩ which is not burnt and does not enter under the rays ⟨of the Sun⟩, unless it is one of the upper planets and oriental ⟨of the Sun⟩ and goes past the domain of burning.

⟨II x⟩
The Tenth ⟨Place⟩

1 (1) One who inquires about taking possession of a kingdom: if you know his nativity, choose for him ⟨as the ascendant of his electional horoscope⟩ the tenth place ⟨of his natal horoscope⟩, unless a malevolent planet is there. (2) If ⟨a malevolent planet⟩ is there, be careful ⟨not to put this position as⟩ the ascendant degree ⟨of the electional horoscope⟩ until 10° have passed from the position in which a malevolent ⟨planet⟩ is located, then choose for him the position of the Sun, if it is in an auspicious position with respect to the ascendant. (3) Be careful that the Moon is not in the seventh place or in opposition to the lord of the ascendant, and that that Mars is not in any of the cardines. (4) If it [Mars] is burnt, do not doubt about this, and put the lord of the hour so that it is oriental of the Sun if it is an upper planet, or occidental ⟨of the Sun⟩ if it is a lower ⟨planet⟩. (5) In this matter, the fixed signs are better than the bicorporal, and the bicorporal signs are better than the tropical, and the straight ⟨signs⟩ are better than the crooked ⟨signs⟩. (6)

pone dominum .4am. in divisione ascensionum signorum rectorum. (7) Et quod Luna non sit in domo .12., nam ipsa significat quod congregabuntur homines terre sue super eum et odio habebunt eum.

2 (1) Et si ad intrandum ad regem vel principem magnum, pone Solem in aspectu bono cum gradu ascendente. (2) Et pone prepositum quod sint ei fortitudines multe in .5. locis principatus nec sit ipse prepositus intrans sub radiis Solis et precipue sicut in termino combustionis et in uno gradu. (3) Et sit stella directa, multum bonum, et cave ne Sol sit in .7a. domo vel .12a.[1]

⟨II xi⟩
Undecima ⟨domus⟩

1 (1) Qui querit amorem hominis, respiciat stellam que est prepositus
46v super similitudine sua, et pones super eam | in bono loco. (2) Et associabis cum eo dominum .11e. domus, nec sit dominus hore Mars vel Saturnus vel Mercurius, si sit in mixtione mala cum aliquo malorum. (3) Et dixerunt Antiqui quod item hora Solis in hac re non est bona nisi quando Leo est[2] ascendens.

⟨II xii⟩
Duodecima ⟨domus⟩

1 (1) Si eligis horam emendi equum, prepara locum Solis nec sit dominus .12e.[3] in .7a. nec dominus ascendentis. (2) Et si ad emendum mulam, prepara locum Martis; et si ad asinum, locum Saturni; et si ad camelum, locum Veneris; et si ad bestiam parvam sicut est ovis, locum Mercurii; et si ad bovem, prepara locum Lune respectu ascendentis locus. (3) Dico quod non sit minuens Lune, et si ipsa est in parte sua clara quod est in medietate

[1] vel .12a.] E; V om. [2] est] E; V sit. [3] .12e.] V; E .12.

If you cannot ⟨do this⟩, put ⟨the lord of the hour so that it is⟩ the lord of the fourth ⟨place⟩ in the division of the rising times of the straight signs. (7) And ⟨be careful⟩ that the Moon is not in the twelfth place, because it signifies that people of his country will assemble against him and hate him.[1]

2 (1) If ⟨one inquires about when⟩ to be introduced to the king or a great prince, put the Sun in an auspicious aspect to the ascendant degree. (2) Put ⟨a planet⟩ that has the most powers in the five places of domination as the ⟨querent's⟩ ruler, ⟨but be careful⟩ that this ruler does not enter under the rays of the Sun, and especially in the domain of burning, and in the same degree ⟨with the Sun⟩. (3) If the planet is direct ⟨in its motion⟩, this is very auspicious, and be careful that the Sun is not in the seventh or the twelfth place.[1]

⟨II xi⟩
The Eleventh ⟨Place⟩

1 (1) If one inquires about love for a person, he should find the planet that is the ruler over his [the querent's] likeness, and put ⟨the planet⟩ in charge of it [his likeness] in an auspicious position. (2) Associate with it [the ruler] the lord of the eleventh place, and ⟨be careful⟩ not to put Mars, Saturn, or Mercury as the lord of the hour, if ⟨any of them⟩ is in an inauspicious mixture with any of the malefic planets. (3) The Ancients also said that in this matter the Sun's hour is not auspicious, unless Leo is rising.[1]

⟨II xii⟩
The Twelfth ⟨Place⟩

1 (1) If you are choosing an hour to buy a horse, calculate the position of the Sun so that the lord of the twelfth ⟨place⟩ is not in the seventh ⟨place⟩ and is not the lord of the ascendant. (2) For buying a mule, calculate the position of Mars; for ⟨buying⟩ a donkey, ⟨calculate⟩ the position of Saturn; for ⟨buying⟩ a camel, ⟨calculate⟩ the position of Venus; for ⟨buying⟩ small livestock, like sheep, ⟨calculate⟩ the position of Mercury; for ⟨buying⟩ an ox, calculate the position of the Moon with respect to the position of the ascendant. (3) I say that the Moon should not be waning, and it if it is in its bright part it is better when it is in the half of the short circle which is from

circuli brevis que a capite Cancri usque ad finem Sagittarii et tunc melius. (4) Et quod dominus hore sit in bono loco respectu ascendentis.

2 (1) Explicit *Liber electionum* Abraham.

the head of Cancer to the end of Sagittarius. (4) ⟨It is auspicious⟩ for the lord of the hour to be in an auspicious position with respect to the ascendant.[1]

2 (1) This ends the *Book of elections* by Abraham.

PART TWO

NOTES TO *LIBER ELECTIONUM*

⟨I 1⟩

[1]**1: Abraham, the author, Latin: *Abraham Additor, lit.* “Abraham, who adds/combines.”** This renders אברהם המחבר “Abraham, the author,” which is one of the ways in which Ibn Ezra refers to himself in his monographs and biblical commentaries, usually in their prefaces. See *Yesod Mora’*, ed. Simon (2007), 64, line 11; *Neḥoshet* I, 148r; *Neḥoshet* II, 188r; *Ṭeʿamim* I, § 1.5:5, 34–35; *Mispar*, ed. Silberberg (1895), 25. The Hebrew root חבר denotes “combination,” “addition,” or “binding,” but the derived noun מחבר means “author.” Thus “Abraham additor” = “Abraham, the author” renders אברהם המחבר. “Abraham Additor,” as a translation of אברהם המחבר, appears as the author in *Nativitates*, I 1:2, 80–81; a slightly different name, “Abraham Addens,” also a translation of אברהם המחבר, is given as the author in *Int*, II i 2:1. By contrast, in his translation of *Ṭeʿamim* I (§ 1.5:5, 34–35), Henry Bate renders אברהם המחבר as *Abraham Compilator*. See Leipzig, MS Univ. 1466, fol. 61vb. This indicates that Bate could not have been the translator of *Electiones*, *Interrogationes*, or *Nativitates*.

[2]**2: ⟨The judgments about⟩ collectives ... their will.** In the current passage, “general rules” (Latin *communes*), which apply to collectives, are set against the “knowledge of the elections of individuals” (*scientia singularium electionum*). This statement is grounded in the principle that astrological judgments that include human beings in larger social and geographical units take precedence over judgments that refer to individuals and their particular destiny. The ultimate source for this idea is *Tetrabiblos*, ed. Robbins (1980), II:1, 117–119 (quoted in App. 1, Q. 4, 393). This principle is predicated in *Electiones* upon the doctrine of elections, but Ibn Ezra applies the same idea in relation to other branches of astrology, particularly the doctrine of nativities. See above, p. 25, n. 129.

[3]**3: ⟨The stars⟩ cannot change ... never transgress.** This conveys a strong version of astral determinism via a paraphrase of Psalms 148:6: וַיַּעֲמִידֵם לָעַד לְעוֹלָם חָק־נָתַן וְלֹא יַעֲבוֹר = “He made them endure forever establishing an order that shall never change.” Ibn Ezra quotes this verse in his commentary on Job 38:33 (quoted in App. 1, Q. 5, 393), to support a strong version of astrology.

[4]**4–5: “I know that,” ... air of the world.** This passage continues the presentation of a strong version of astral determinism via a quotation of Ecclesiastes 3:14: יָדַעְתִּי כִּי כָּל־אֲשֶׁר יַעֲשֶׂה הָאֱלֹהִים הוּא יִהְיֶה לְעוֹלָם עָלָיו אֵין לְהוֹסִיף

וּמִמֶּנּוּ אֵין לִגְרֹעַ = "I realized, too, that whatever God has brought to pass will recur evermore: Nothing can be added to it and nothing taken from it." The same verse, in a similar setting, is quoted in *Mivḥarim* II, § 1:2, 142–143 (quoted in App. 1, Q. 6, 2, 393–394).

[5]**6: Sustenance, Latin: *gubernationes*.** Here the Latin translator, probably misled by a French intermediary, misrendered the Aramaic מזוני, "sustenance" or "nourishment," which is part of the talmudic passage quoted in *El*, I 1:6. See next note. The English translation ignores the literal meaning of the Latin and restores the original meaning of the term.

[6]**6: Therefore the Ancient … on the sign.** This passage completes the presentation of a strong version of astral determinism by quoting a passage from *Moʿed Qaṭan* 28a (quoted in App. 1, Q. 7, § 1:2, 394). In this passage the Babylonian Talmud reports that two saintly rabbis, Rabbah and R. Ḥisda, both "prayed for rain and it came," despite their markedly contrasting fortunes: the former passed away at forty, there were sixty bereavements in his family, and there was only barley bread for people to eat, and that in scant amounts; the latter lived to the age of ninety-two, celebrated sixty wedding feasts in his house, even the dogs ate the finest wheat bread, and there was so much that some went to waste. This passage from *Moʿed Qaṭan* is frequently quoted in medieval Hebrew literature. Aside from the present locus, Ibn Ezra quotes and comments on it only in his biblical commentaries. See, in particular, the long commentary on Exodus 32:32 (quoted in App. 1, Q. 8, 394); see also the long commentary on Exodus 20:14 and the commentary on Ecclesiastes 2:21.

⟨I 2⟩

[1]**1: Therefore, there was … deceiving, and worthless.** Here Ibn Ezra seems to have been inspired by Sahl Ibn Bashr, a Jewish astrologer well known to him, in his *Book of Elections*, which survives in Latin translation. See Paris, BnF, MS lat. 16204, *Liber electionum*, 488b (quoted in App. 1, Q. 9, 394–395).

[2]**2: Cancer, Scorpio or Pisces.** These three signs belong to the category of the watery signs, so called because "water," one of the four elements of the sublunar domain, is considered to be their common "nature." They are part of a quadripartite classification that ascribes one of the four elements of the sublunar domain to each of the four groups. See note on *Tp*, III 4:9.

[3]**2: Aspect of hate, Latin: *aspectus odii*.** This is a calque of מבט איבה, "aspect of antagonism," a locution Ibn Ezra employs for the aspect of quartile, when the angular relationship between planets, zodiacal signs, and other celestial objects is 90°. For the concept of aspect, see note on *Tp*, I i 4:7. The aspect of quartile is considered to be disharmonious and unfortunate.

[4]**2: Ascendant.** As the zodiac moves with the diurnal motion, it may be seen at any given moment as a wheel constantly rising above the eastern horizon. The ascendant is the degree of the zodiac, or the zodiacal sign, that rises above the eastern horizon at the time the horoscope is cast; it plays the crucial role of the starting point from which the zodiac is divided into the twelve places of the horoscope. For the indications of the twelve horoscopic places, see above, pp. 18–19.

[5]**2: For if Saturn ... by water.** This property of Saturn is mentioned in several of Ibn Ezra's works. See (1) *Mivḥarim* II, § 9.1:2, 168–169 (quoted in App. 1, Q. 10, 395); (2) *'Olam* I, § 55:1, 86–87 (quoted in App. 1, Q. 11, 395); and (3) *Nativitates*, II vi 8:4, 136–137 (quoted in App. 1, Q. 12, 395).

[6]**4: Ptolemy.** See note on *El*, II vi 6:4.

[7]**4: Therefore Ptolemy says ... his nativity there.** The same idea is assigned to Ptolemy in *Mivḥarim* II, § 1:5, 142–143 (quoted in App. 1, Q. 6, 5, 393–394). The present statement is based on aphorism 6 of Pseudo-Ptolemy's *Centiloquium* (quoted in App. 1, Q. 14, 395–396). In *Tetrabiblos*, however, the "real" Ptolemy gives instructions for making "derived" or "extracted" horoscopes for the father, mother, or brothers by considering the horoscopic place of the relative as an ascendant and then examining "the remaining topics as though it were a nativity of the parents themselves" or "by taking the planet which gives brethren as the horoscope and dealing with the rest as in a nativity." See *Tetrabiblos*, ed. Robbins (1980), III:4, 249 and III:5, 255. By contrast, *Mivḥarim* I, § 1.3, 46–47 (quoted in App. 1, Q. 15, 3, 396), assigns a similar statement to Dorotheus. Such a statement is not to be found in the fifth book of Dorotheus' *Pentabiblos*, which deals with interrogations and elections, but in that work Dorotheus repeatedly enjoins the astrologer to look at the natal horoscope of the person for whom an election or an interrogation is to be made (*Carmen astrologicum*, ed. Pingree (1976), V:16, p. 273, 274; V:31, p. 291; V:32, p. 292), or proceeds on the assumption that the details of the natal horoscope are known to the astrologer (*Carmen*

astrologicum, ed. Pingree (1976), V:5, p. 264; V:25, p. 284; V:26, p. 286, 287; V:35, p. 297; V:41, p. 319).

[8]**5: The object of the election will remain hidden, Latin: *abscondetur res electionis*.** Here the peculiar expression *abscondetur res electionis* ("the object of the election will remain hidden") denotes the idea that when there is a contradiction between the natal and the electional horoscopes, the election will remain ineffective because it is not as strong as the former. *Mivḥarim* II § 1.5, 142–143 (quoted in App. 1, Q. 13, 395) uses similar terms to convey the same idea. In particular, *Mivḥarim* II states that when the natal and the electional horoscopes are in conflict, "the power of the favorable configuration of the stars that you choose for him *will not be seen* against the power of what is signified by the natal horoscope" (כח המזל הטוב שתבחר לו לא יראה כנגד כח מה שיש במולד); but when the natal and electional horoscopes are in harmony, "the election may be useful and its power *may be seen*" (יועיל המבחר ויראה כחו).

⟨I 3⟩

[1]**1: Abraham, the author, Latin: *Abraham additor*,** *lit*. "Abraham, who adds or combines." For this name, see note on *El*, I 1:1.

[2]**3: The election cannot annul the general rule.** This corresponds to *Mivḥarim* I, § 1:1, 46–47 (quoted in App. 1, Q. 15, 1, 396).

[3]**1–3: I Abraham ... by the election.** This passage echoes the seventh way of the preface to *Moladot* I § 8:1–2, 86–89 (quoted in App. 1, Q. 1, § 2:1–4, 391–392), which converts weather into a powerful principle that cancels out the outcome of the electional horoscope. The same idea is found in *Mivḥarim* I, § 1:2, 46–47 (quoted in App. 1, Q. 15, 2, 396), and in *Mivḥarim* II, § 1:5, 142–143 (quoted in App. 1, Q. 6, 5, 393–394).

⟨I 4⟩

[1]**1–2: The answer ... and choose life.** The same idea, making the case for free will (the ability to choose between good and evil) by quoting Deuteronomy 30:15, and highlighting the possibility that human beings can modify their own destiny slightly, that is, augment or reduce what is signified by the stars, occurs in *Mivḥarim* II, § 1:1–3, 142–143 (quoted in App. 1, Q. 6, 1–3, 393–394).

[2]**3: It is right ... ⟨what is signified by the stars⟩.** For an explanation of this passage, see above, pp. 27–28. The idea that the doctrine of elections allows a partial escape from the decrees of the stars is expressed in *Mivḥarim* I, § 1:1, 46–47 (quoted in App. 1, Q. 15, 1, 396); and *Mivḥarim* II, § 1:3, 142–143 (quoted in App. 1, Q. 6, 3, 393–394).

⟨I 5⟩

[1]**1: Example ... little pain.** An identical example is offered in *Mivḥarim* I, § 1:2, 46–47 (quoted in App. 1, Q. 15, 2, 396).

[2]**2–4: If he [the astrologer] ... afflicted only a little.** This passage echoes one of the examples offered in the eighth way of the preface to *Moladot*, I 9:2–2, 88–89 (quoted in App. 1, Q. 1, § 2:1–3, 391), where Ibn Ezra attempts to demonstrate that a rational and scientific methodology allows human being to rectify some of the physical harm inflicted by the stars.

[3]**5: This was said ... in the *Book of the 100 Statements*.** This corresponds to aphorism 5 of Pseudo-Ptolemy's *Centiloquium* (quoted in App. 1, Q. 19, 397).

⟨I 6⟩

[1]**1: If you do not know ... this planet.** *Mivḥarim* I, *Mivḥarim* II, and *Epitome* call explicit attention to two methods for elections, which *Electiones* does not. The present passage tallies with the description of the second method for elections in *Mivḥarim* I, *Mivḥarim* II, and *Epitome*, which assumes that the querent's nativity is not known. See *Mivḥarim* I, § 5:1–2, 48–49 (quoted in App. 1, Q. 20, 397); *Mivḥarim* II, § 5:1–3, 146–147 (quoted in App. 1, Q. 21, 397–398); and *Epitome*, ed. Heller (1548), IV:1, R3r–v.

[2]**2: Dorotheus, the great scholar in the judgments of the signs.** See note on *Int*, I 1:6.

[3]**2: Dorotheus ... ⟨for him⟩ an election.** This corresponds closely to (1) *Mivḥarim* I, § 1:3, 46–77 (quoted in App. 1, Q. 15, 3, 396), which also mentions Dorotheus as the originator; (2) *Mivḥarim* I, § 3.2:5, 58–59, which repeats

the same statement but does not mention Dorotheus; and (3) Sahl Ibn Bashr's *Book of Elections* (quoted in App. 1, Q. 22, 398), which repeats the same statement but also does not mention Dorotheus.

Why do the current locus and the three aforementioned passages make the election conditional on an interrogation? The doctrine of interrogations posits that the astrologer can answer questions only if the querent's intentions are sincere and presupposes that the astrologer may discover the querent's thoughts by studying the celestial configuration when the horoscope is cast. See above, pp. 30–31. Thus, making the election conditional on the querent's undertaking's being "compatible with him according to his will" seems to mean that, when the nativity is not known, it is necessary, by reading the querent's thought, to discover the real intention of the election according to the celestial configuration when the interrogational horoscope is cast. Only if the querent's intentions are sincere should an electional horoscope be cast for him.

⟨I 7⟩

[1]**1: I say that ... misfortune will diminish.** This corresponds closely to *Mivḥarim* I, § 1:2, 46–47 (quoted in App. 1, Q. 15, 2, 396), and to *Mivḥarim* II, § 1:4, 142–143 (quoted in App. 1, Q. 6, 4, 393–394).

[2]**2: The Moon is the ruler ... [i.e., the moment of the beginning of the undertaking].** Such a statement is ubiquitous in Ibn Ezra's oeuvre and in the Latin works associated with him: See: *Mivḥarim* II, § 6:1, 146–147: ולעולם יש לנו לתקן מקום הלבנה, כי היא האמצעית בין העולם העליון ובין העולם השפל, והיא תורה על כל דבר שיחל האדם = "We should always determine the position of the Moon, because it is in the middle between the upper world and the lower world and signifies anything initiated by man"; *Mishpeṭei ha-mazzalot* § 39:3, 522–523: והיא תורה על כל דבר שיחל האדם = "It portends everything that a person begins"; *De rationibus tabularum*, ed. Millás Vallicrosa (1947), 97: *ipsa dominium habet in omnibus inchoandis, scilicet initiamentis rerum* = "It [the Moon] has rulership over all the beginnings, that is, the commencement of undertakings"; *Epitome*, ed. Heller (1548), XIV, D1r: *Luna ... significat ... in rerum exordiis* = "The Moon ... signifies ... in the beginning of undertakings."

[3]**3: After ⟨the discussion of⟩ the 12 places in the *Book of Nativities*, I have written to you a chapter on elections; do not forget to look at it.** This refers

to the last section of *Nativitates*, the Latin translation of the lost *Moladot* II, which follows the twelve chapters on the horoscopic places. It deals with the special case of elections in which the querent knows his nativity and addresses general principles on elections in which the interpretation of the electional horoscope depends on the features of the querent's natal horoscope. This entire section is quoted in App. 12, 528–530. Given that *Moladot* II was composed in 1158 (see *Nativitates*, II i 7:1, 110–111 and Sela 2019, 27, 43), this past tense cross-reference means that 1158 is the *terminus post quem* of *Mivḥarim* III, which makes *Mivḥarim* III the latest datable astrological treatise by Ibn Ezra.

[4]**4: I begin now … 12 places.** This corresponds to *Int*, I 3:2. See note there.

⟨II i 1⟩

[1]**1: Malefic or benefic ⟨planet⟩.** For these categories of planets, see note on *Int*, II i 9:5.

[2]**1: One who wishes … [the planets].** This corresponds closely to (1) *Mivḥarim* I, § 1.3:2, 52–53 (quoted in App. 3, P. 1, Q. 1, § 1:2, 406); (2) *Mivḥarim* II, § 1.1:1–2, 150–151 (quoted in App. 3, P. 1, Q. 2, § 1:1–2, 407); and (3) *Epitome*, ed. Heller (1548), IV:2, R4r (quoted in App. 3, P. 1, Q. 3, 407). The ultimate source is aphorism 21 of Pseudo-Ptolemy's *Centiloquium* (quoted in App. 3, P. 1, Q. 4, § 1:1, 407–408).

[3]**3: All agreed … they are right.** This corresponds to (1) *Mivḥarim* I, § 1.5:1, 52–53 (quoted in App. 3, P. 1, Q. 1, § 2:1, 406), which assigns the statement to Ptolemy; (2) *Mivḥarim* II, § 1.2:1, 150–151 (quoted in App. 3, P. 1, Q. 2, § 1:1–2, 407); and (3) *Epitome*, ed. Heller (1548), IV:2, R4r (quoted in App. 3, P. 1, Q. 3, 1, 407). The ultimate source is aphorism 19 of Pseudo-Ptolemy's *Centiloquium* (quoted in App. 3, P. 1, Q. 4, § 2:1, 407–408).

[4]**5: Burnt by the Sun, Latin: *combusta a Sole*.** Being "burnt" (Hebrew נשרף; Arabic محترق), or "in the domain of burning" (Hebrew בגבול השריפה; Latin *in termino combustionis*; see note to *El*, II iv 1:1) is one of the conditions of planets relative to the Sun. In these conditions, to which Ibn Ezra devoted a section of chapter 6 of *Reshit ḥokhmah* (§ 6.6:1–21, 192–195; § 6.7:1–10, 194–195; § 6.8:1–14, 194–197), a section of *Mishpeṭei ha-mazzalot*

(§ 25:1–12, 508–511; § 26:1–4, 510–511; § 29:1–5, 512–515; § 30:1–4, 514–151), and a section of *ʿOlam* II (§ 17:1–17, 168–169; § 18:1–12, 168–169), a planet, after being in conjunction with the Sun, gradually moves away from and then approaches it until it again conjoins the Sun. In this process, the planet's power waxes and wanes. Thus, according to *Reshit ḥokhmah*, Saturn and Jupiter are "burnt" (נשרפים) or in the "domain of burning" (בגבול השרפה) when between 16′ and 6° from the Sun; Mars, between 16′ and 10°; Venus and Mercury, between 16′ and 7°; and the Moon, between 16′ and 6°. For the conditions of Saturn, Jupiter, and Mars with respect to the Sun, see *Reshit ḥokhmah* § 6.5:1–4, 190–193; § 6.6:1–21, 192–195; *Mishpeṭei ha-mazzalot* § 25:1–12, 508–511; and *ʿOlam* II, § 17:1–15, 168–169. For the conditions of Venus and Mercury with respect to the Sun, see *Reshit ḥokhmah* § 7.7:1–10, 200–203; *Mishpeṭei ha-mazzalot* § 29:1–6, 512–515; and *ʿOlam* II, § 17:16–17, 168–169. For the conditions of the Moon with respect to the Sun, see *Reshit ḥokhmah* § 6.8:1–14, 194–197. *Reshit ḥokhmah* § 6.6:5–6, 192–193 (quoted in App. 5, Q. 4, 466), also gives an account of the planets' powers in these conditions. For the testimony of the planets in these conditions, see *Meʾorot* § 14:1, 464–465.

[5]**6: Sixth place ... eighth or twelfth ⟨places⟩.** This refers to the unfortunate horoscopic places. *Moladot*, IV 26:1–2, 200–201 (quoted in App. 5, Q. 1, 465) defines them together with the fortunate and intermediate horoscopic places in the context of an application of the doctrine of elections. The inauspicious character of the sixth, eighth, and twelfth places derives, in all likelihood, from the fact that none of them is in any aspect to the degree of the ascendant. It is for this reason that *Ṭeʿamim* I (§ 3.5:10,12, 64–65) describes the sixth and twelfth places as "the most malefic of all" and characterizes the eighth place negatively. These three inauspicious horoscopic places are referred to as distinct group throughout Ibn Ezra's astrological corpus. See *El*, II v 1:3, II v 2:2; II vi 1:9; *Int*, II v 1:3, II v 2:3, II i 3:1; II vi 1:9; II viii 1:2; II xii 9:2; *Nativitates*, I viii 1:3, 94–95; II i 5:5, 110–111; III i 2:1, 156–157; *Mivḥarim* I, § 2:1, 46–47; *Mivḥarim* II, § 3:2, 144–145; *Sheʾelot* I, § 5.2:3, 264–265; § 7.6:6, 276–277; § 7.8:8, 286–287; § 8.1:2, 282–283; § 12.1:6, 294–295; *Sheʾelot* II, § 1.5:1, 360–361; § 7.6:4–5, 373–375; § 8.3:3, 378–379; et passim.

[6]**7: If the potion ... above the Earth.** This corresponds to *Mivḥarim* I, § 1.3:3–4, 52–53 (quoted in App. 3, P. 1, Q. 1, § 1:3–4, 406); and *Mivḥarim* II, § 1.2:4, 150–151 (quoted in App. 3, P. 1, Q. 2, § 2:4, 407)

[7]**1–8: One who wishes ... everything stated.** This corresponds closely to *Mivḥarim* I, § 1.3:1–4, § 1.5:1–3, 52–55 (quoted in App. 3, P. 1, Q. 1, § 1:1–4, § 2:1–3, 406), and *Mivḥarim* II, § 1.1:1–2, § 1.2:1–4, 150–151 (quoted in App. 3, P. 1, Q. 2, § 1:1–2, § 2:1–4, 407).

⟨II i 2⟩

[1]**1–5: If you inquire ... are inauspicious.** This corresponds to (1) *Mivḥarim* I, § 1.6:1–2, 54–55 (quoted in App. 3, P. 2, Q. 1, § 1:1–2, 408); (2) *Mivḥarim* II, § 1.3:2, 150–151 (quoted in App. 3, P. 2, Q. 2, § 1:1, 408); and (3) *Epitome*, ed. Heller (1548), IV:3, R3v (quoted in App. 3, P. 2, Q. 3, 2–4, 409).

[2]**8–9: Ptolemy says ... Pisces, the feet.** This corresponds to *Mivḥarim* I, § 1.8:1–3, 54–55 (quoted in App. 3, P. 2, Q. 1, § 2:1–3, 408), *Mivḥarim* II, § 1.3:3, § 1.4:1–3, 150–153 (quoted in App. 3, P. 2, Q. 2, § 1:2, § 2:1–3, 408–409), and *Epitome*, ed. Heller (1548), IV:2, R3v (quoted in App. 3, P. 2, Q. 3, 5, 409). The ultimate source of these statement is aphorism 20 of Pseudo-Ptolemy's *Centiloquium* (quoted in App. 3, P. 2, Q. 4, 409). The mention in the latter passage of "the Moon located in a sign assigned to some member" is a reference to the doctrine of melothesia, which distributes the parts of the body among the zodiacal signs. This doctrine is presented in *Mishpeṭei ha-mazzalot* § 19:1–3, 504–505 (quoted in App. 5, Q. 2, 465). The rationale behind the theory is provided in two of Ibn Ezra's introductions to astrology, *Ṭeʿamim* I, § 2.3:2, 40–41, and *Ṭeʿamim* II, § 2.4:20–21, 194–195 (quoted in App. 5, Q. 3, 465). References to the theory of melothesia, either in lists or as part of separate descriptions of the properties of each sign, are common in ancient and medieval introductions to astrology. See *Carmen astrologicum*, ed. Pingree (1976), IV:1, 251; *Astronomica*, ed. Goold (1977), II:453, 119, *Anthologiae*, ed. Riley (1995), 109K–111K, *Matheseos*, ed. Bram (1975), II, xxiv, 56, *Introduction*, ed. Burnett et al. (2004), I:25–36, 35–37, *Abbreviation*, ed. Burnett et al. (1994), I:9–81, 15–25, *Great Introduction*, ed. Burnett and Yamamoto (2019), VI:12, 506–508, and *Elements*, ed. Ramsay Wright (1934), § 359, 216.

⟨II ii 1⟩

[1]**1: One who wishes ... Moon's part.** This corresponds closely to the following loci: (1) *Mivḥarim* II, § 2.1:1, 152–155 (quoted in App. 3, P. 3, Q. 1, 1, 409–410); (2) *Mivḥarim* I, § 2.1:1–2, 54–55 (quoted in App. 3, P. 3, Q. 2, 1–2, 410), where such a statement is assigned to Ptolemy; (3) *Ṭeʿamim* I, § 2.5:4–

44–45 (quoted in App. 3, P. 3, Q. 3, 4–5, 410) where such a statement is assigned to the "scholars who rely on experience"; (4) *Epitome*, ed. Heller (1548), IV:4, sig. R4r (quoted in App. 3, P. 3, Q. 4, 411), where the Moon's smaller domain of the circle is interchanged with the Sun's larger domain of the circle; and (5) *She'elot* I, § 2.4:2, 252–253 and *She'elot* I, § 2.2:2, 360–361, where such a statement is attributed to an unknown astrologer named Saʿīd.

The rationale behind the division of the zodiac into a "smaller domain," assigned to the Moon, and a "larger domain," assigned to the Sun, is revealed in *Ṭeʿamim* I, § 2.5:1–4, 44–45 (quoted in App. 3, P. 3, Q. 3, 1–4, 410). Similar explanations are offered in *Ṭeʿamim* II, § 8.1:1–4, 248–249 and in al-Qabīṣī's *Introduction* (ed. Burnett et al. (2004), I:10, 21–22). Brief explanations are offered in *Mishpeṭei ha-mazzalot* § 2:7, 490–491 and *De rationibus tabularum*, ed. Millás Vallicrosa (1947), 98 (quoted in App. 5, Q. 5, 466). See also *Tetrabiblos*, ed. Robbins (1980), I:17, 79 and *Elements*, ed. Ramsay Wright (1934), § 440, 256.

[2]3: **Peregrine, Latin:** ***vaga***. As explained in *Tp*, IV 3:2, a planet is said to be "peregrine" (Latin: *vagus* or *peregrinus*) when in it is not in its house, exaltation, or triplicity.

[3]3: **Ruler of the five places of dominion, Latin:** ***prepositus .5. locorum principatus***. See note on *Int*, II i 15:1.

[4]2–3: **It is appropriate ... ascendant degree**. This corresponds to *Mivḥarim* II, § 2.1:2–3, 152–155 (quoted in App. 3, P. 3, Q. 2, 2–3, 410).

[5]4: **Retrograde**. The planets generally move from west to east, in "direct motion" (in the direction of increasing ecliptical longitude), but sometime from east to west, in "retrograde motion" (opposite the direction of increasing ecliptical longitude) and seem to be moving backward.

[6]5: **Māshāʾallāh says ... burnt there**. The work by Māshāʾallāh from which this passage was presumably taken is not known. It corresponds to *Mivḥarim* II, § 10.1:2, 170–171.

⟨II ii 2⟩

[1]2: **Exaltation, Latin:** ***altitudo***. This translates גבהות, lit. "highness," to denote the astrological concept of exaltation. To denote this concept Ibn

Ezra usually uses כבוד, "honor." See *Int*, II i 6:3 and note. Precisely the same terminological phenomenon occurs in *Nativitates*, II vii 3:8, 140–141, and in *Me'orot*. See *Me'orot* § 2:2, 454–455 and § 10:2, 462–463, and corresponding notes. This creates a terminological link between *Electiones*, *Nativitates*, and *Me'orot*.

[2]**2: Sahl says ... what I found**. A perfect match of this passage may be found in Sahl's *Book of Elections*, Paris, BnF, lat. 16204, 491b (quoted in App. 3, P. 3, Q. 5, 411).

⟨II iii 1⟩

[1]**1: ⟨For⟩ one who inquires ... ninth ⟨place⟩**. This corresponds loosely to *Int*, II iii 1:1 and *Mivḥarim* I, § 3.1:1, 58–59.

[2]**2: Lord of the hour**. For this concept, see note to *Tp*, I:3.

[3]**2: Dorotheus says ... agrees with him**. The source text behind this reference to Dorotheus is not known.

⟨II iii 2⟩

[1]**1–2: If ⟨the election is about⟩ setting off ... ⟨for a journey⟩ by land**. This corresponds to *Mivḥarim* II, § 3.2:1–3, 156–157 (quoted in App. 3, P. 4, Q. 1, 1–3, 411). For similar comparisons between Mars and Saturn regarding a journey by land or sea, see *Mivḥarim* I, § 3.3:1, 60–61, where a similar statement is ascribed to Māshā'allāh; and *She'elot* I, § 9.3:2, 284–287, and *She'elot* II, § 9.1:3, 378–379, where the statements are ascribed to Dorotheus and Ptolemy, respectively, with respect to the ninth place.

⟨II iii 3⟩

[1]**1: Dorotheus says: ... doubt ⟨about this⟩**. This corresponds to *Mivḥarim* I, § 3.5:1–3, 60–61 (quoted in App. 3, P. 4, Q. 2, 1–3, 412–413). It also corresponds to *She'elot* I, § 9.3:1, 284–285. Note that Dorotheus is not mentioned in either place.

[2]**2: Māshāʾallāh says … trine or sextile.** This corresponds closely to *Mivḥarim* II, § 9.2:1–2, 168–171 (quoted in App. 3, P. 4, Q. 3, 412), where a similar statement is attributed to Dorotheus, and to *Mivḥarim* I, § 3.4:1, 60–61 (quoted in App. 3, P. 4, Q. 4, 412), where a similar statement is assigned to the scientists of India.

[3]**3: If you inquire … seventh place.** This refers to *El*, II vii 7:1–8.

⟨II iv 1⟩

[1]**1: If you inquire … any of the cardines.** This corresponds to *Mivḥarim* I, § 4.5:2, 64–65 (quoted in App. 3, P. 5, Q. 1, 2, 412).

[2]**2: Under the domain of burning, Latin: *sub termino combustionis*.** This term refers to one of the conditions of the planets with respect to the Sun. See note to *El*, II i 1:5, s.v. "burnt." According to *Reshit ḥokhmah* (§ 6.6:6, 192–193; § 6.7:6,194–195; § 7.4:8, 200–201), Saturn and Jupiter are in the "domain of burning" when between 16′ and 6° from the Sun; Mars, between 16′ and 10°; Venus and Mercury, between 16′ and 7°; and the Moon, between 16′ and 6°. The Latin term *terminus combustionis* is a literal translation of גבול השריפה "domain of burning," used throughout Ibn Ezra's Hebrew astrological corpus. See, for example, *Ṭeʿamim* I, § 1.5:2, 34–35; § 6.2:5, 86–87; *Reshit ḥokhmah* § 6.6:6, 192–193; § 6.7:6,194–195; § 7.4:8, 200–201; *ʿOlam* II, § 17:14, 168–169; *Mivḥarim* III, § 7.3:4,5, 220–221; *Meʾorot* § 23:4, 468–469.

[3]**2: If you wish to hide … below the Earth.** This corresponds to *Mivḥarim* I, § 4.5:1, 64–65 (quoted in App. 3, P. 5, Q. 1, 1, 412). Both the present passage and *Mivḥarim* I mention the lord of the ascendant and the Moon; but whereas the former refers to them as being "under the domain of burning," a condition of the planets with respect to the Sun, the latter refers to them as being "under the ray of the Sun," another condition of the planets with respect to the Sun. For the condition of being "under the domain of burning," see note to *El*, II iv 1:1; for the condition of being "under the ray of the Sun," see note to *Int*, II vi 1:3.

⟨II iv 2⟩

[1]**1: Sign of the country, Latin: *signum patrie*.** This concept is defined in *ʿOlam* II 15:1–25, 164–167 (quoted in App. 5, Q. 6, 1–25, 466–467), which

also offers a similar list of 23 countries/cities. *ʿOlam* I, § 38:1–24, 76–79, presents a list of 22 countries/cities and their respective zodiacal signs. Both versions of *ʿOlam* list many applications of the sign of the country or city in world astrology. See *ʿOlam* I, § 25:1–5, 68–69; § 34:1–7, 74–75; § 35:1–7, 74–77; § 53:1–7, 86–87; § 68:1, 96–97; *ʿOlam* II, § 9:6, 162–163; § 20:1–7, 170–171; § 23:1–3, 170–173. The sign of the country or city is also applied in elections (see *Mivḥarim* II, § 4.2:8, 158–159) and interrogations (see *She'elot* I, § 7.5:1, 274–275).

[2]**1: To lay the foundations ... sign of the country.** This corresponds closely to *Mivḥarim* II, § 4.2:8, 158–159 (quoted in App. 3, P. 6, Q. 1, 413).

⟨II iv 3⟩

[1]**1: If you seek ... likewise the Moon.** This corresponds to *Mivḥarim* II, § 4.1:1–4, 156–157 and *Mivḥarim* I, § 4.4:1–3, 64–65.

⟨II v 1⟩

[1]**1: If you inquire ... [Jupiter's] place.** Although not stated explicitly, the use of Jupiter and Venus here implies that the real objective of this election is to find a proper time to impregnate a woman and beget sons. This is corroborated by *Mivḥarim* I, § 5.1:1,2,6, 64–67 (quoted in App. 3, P. 7, Q. 1, 413), and *Mivḥarim* II, § 5.1:4, 158–159 (quoted in App. 3, P. 7, Q. 2, 413). The role of Jupiter in the same context is also mentioned in *Int*, II v 1:6; *She'elot* I, § 5.2:2, 262–265; *She'elot* II, § 5.1:2, 364–365 and *Epitome*, ed. Heller (1548), IV:9, S1r.

[2]**1: Be careful that no malevolent planet ... position of the Moon.** This statement refers to the special case when one is trying to avoid a miscarriage. This is substantiated by *Mivḥarim* I, § 5.1:5, 64–65 (quoted in App. 3, P. 7, Q. 3, 413).

[3]**2: Enoch says ... lord of the ascendant.** The source text behind this quotation is not known; but all the works on nativities authored by or assigned to Ibn Ezra cite Enoch or Hermes as making statements in which the lord of the hour plays an important role. See *Moladot*, III v 1:1, 142–143; IV 17:1, 196–197; *Nativitates*, II iii 3:2–3, 124–125; *De nativitatibus*, II iii 3:1–2, 296–297.

⟨II v 2⟩

[1]**2: This is Enoch's opinion … found it true.** The same book by Enoch is mentioned in *Mishpeṭei ha-mazzalot* § 15:1, 500–501 (quoted in App. 3, P. 8, Q. 1, § 1.1:1, 414). Ibn Ezra's very positive opinion about this method and his use of empirical experience to validate it are mentioned in all the accounts of the *trutina Hermetis* in Ibn Ezra's Hebrew oeuvre and even in one of the Latin works associated with him. See *Mishpeṭei ha-mazzalot*, § 15:4, 502–503 (quoted in App. 3, P. 8, Q. 1, § 1:4, 414); *Moladot*, II 4:5, 92–93 (quoted in App. 3, P. 8, Q. 2, § 2:5, 415–416); long commentary on Exodus 2:2 (quoted in App. 3, P. 8, Q. 3, 4, 417–418); *Ṭeʿamim* II, § 6.1:5, 234–235 (quoted in App. 3, P. 8, Q. 4, 5, 418–419); and *De nativitatibus*, I 5:2, 252–253 (quoted in App. 3, P. 8, Q. 5, § 2:2, 419–420).

[2]**3: This is what Enoch says … time of birth.** Virtually the same succinct formulation of Enoch's method appears in all the accounts of the *trutina Hermetis* in Ibn Ezra's Hebrew and even in Latin works associated with him. See: (1) *Mishpeṭei ha-mazzalot*, § 15:1, 500–501 (quoted in App. 3, P. 8, Q. 1, § 1:1, 414); (2) *Moladot*, II 5:1, 92–93 (quoted in App. 3, P. 8, Q. 2, § 3:1, 415–416); (3) long commentary on Exodus 2:2 (quoted in App. 3, P. 8, Q. 3, 3, 417–418); (4) *De nativitatibus*, I 5:1, 252–253 (quoted in App. 3, P. 8, Q. 5, § 2:1, 419–420); and (5) *Epitome*, ed. Heller (1548), II:1, H3r–H3v (quoted in App. 3, P. 8, Q. 6, 3, 420–421). However, procedures that involve the gestational period to rectify the nativity and similar succinct formulations of this method can be traced to astrological literature preceding the twelfth century. One example is Pseudo-Ptolemy's aphorism 51 (quoted in App. 3, P. 8, Q. 7, 421).

[3]**4: Observe, at the moment of birth … 288 days.** The same three numbers of days, corresponding to the various periods of pregnancy when the Moon is in the cardines of the natal horoscope, are found in all the detailed accounts of the *trutina Hermetis* authored by Ibn Ezra or assigned to him. See: *Mishpeṭei ha-mazzalot*, § 15:2, 500–503 (quoted in App. 3, P. 8, Q. 1, § 1:2, 414); *Moladot*, II 5:4, 92–93 (quoted in App. 3, P. 8, Q. 2, § 3:4, 415–416); long commentary on Exodus 2:2 (quoted in App. 3, P. 8, Q. 3, 4, 417–418); *De nativitatibus*, I 7:2–4, 254–255 (quoted in App. 3, P. 8, Q. 5, § 3:2–4, 419–420); *Epitome*, ed. Heller (1548), II:1, H3r–H3v (quoted in App. 3, P. 8, Q. 6, 3, 420–421).

[4]**5: Assign one day to every 12° approximately, Latin: *da cuilibet gradui .12. dies in approximatione*.** The translation of this passages has been corrected according to *Mishpeṭei ha-mazzalot* § 17:1–2, 502–503 (quoted in

App. 3, P. 8, Q. 1, § 2:1, 414) and *Moladot*, II 5:7–8, 94–95 (quoted in App. 3, P. 8, Q. 2, § 3:7–8, 415–416).

[5]**5–6: If it [the Moon] ... Moon's motion.** Similar accounts of how to determine the duration of the pregnancy when the Moon is not in the cardines of the natal horoscope are found in most of the detailed accounts of the *trutina Hermetis* authored by Ibn Ezra or assigned to him. As in *Electiones*, these accounts consider two cases, namely, that the Moon is above or below the Earth. In the former case, the correction is added to the period of 273 days (when the Moon is in the ascendant); in the latter case, the correction is added to the period of 259 days (when the Moon is in the descendant). See: *Mishpeṭei ha-mazzalot*, § 17:1–4, 502–505 (quoted in App. 3, P. 8, Q. 1, § 2:1–4, 414); *Moladot*, II 5:7–10, 94–95 (quoted in App. 3, P. 8, Q. 2, § 3:7–10, 415–416); *De nativitatibus*, I 7:3–4, 254–255 (quoted in App. 3, P. 8, Q. 5, § 3:3–4, 419–420); *Epitome*, ed. Heller (1548), II:1, H3r–H3v (quoted in App. 3, P. 8, Q. 6, 7–8, 420–421).

[6]**1–7: If you know the time of conception ... degree of the ascendant.** This section deals with Enoch's approach to the "rectification of the nativity," a topic concerned chiefly with determining the ascendant of the natal horoscope when the time of birth is unknown. This is a matter of fundamental importance, because it is the situation in the vast majority of cases, but it is impossible to cast the natal horoscope without knowing the ascendant at the time of birth. Ibn Ezra deserves a special place in the history of the transmission of Enoch's approach not only because he integrated accounts of this method in many of his works, but also because of his impact on Jewish and Christian readers after his death. The Hebrew מאזני חנוך *mo'znei Ḥanok̲*, "Enoch's balance," and the Latin *trutina Hermetis*, "Hermes' balance," were first used in Ibn Ezra's Hebrew astrological treatises to designate a procedure that utilizes the duration of pregnancy for the rectification of the nativity. Subsequently these two terms were transmitted to the Hebrew and Latin cultures through the diffusion of Ibn Ezra's astrological writings in Hebrew, Latin, and the European vernaculars from the twelfth through the eighteenth century.

That Ibn Ezra attached great importance to the *trutina Hermetis* is indicated by the fact that he wrote about it not only in treatises on nativities, its natural place, but also in other astrological contexts. An excellent example is the present section of *Electiones*. Why should the *trutina Hermetis* be incorporated into a treatise on the doctrine of elections, which is concerned with finding the best time to begin a particular activity? The reason for its inclusion in *Mivḥarim* III is that the fifth horoscopic place indicates children, and the first topic addressed in the fifth chapter is finding the appropriate time to have intercourse so that the woman will have a normal pregnancy and give birth to a healthy child. The *trutina Hermetis* is supposed to be useful for this. At a time when childbirth was often dangerous to both mother and infant, the *trutina Hermetis*' promise of astral favor if the time of conception was planned must have been viewed as a source of hope.

A clear account of the principle underlying Enoch's approach to the rectification of the nativity is found in aphorism 51 of Pseudo-Ptolemy's *Centiloquium* (quoted in App. 3, P. 8, Q. 7, on p. 421). The same principle is clearly formulated in the *Anthologiae* by Vettius Valens (ed. Riley (1995), III, 67). Māshā'allāh (ca. 740–ca. 815), according to the evidence provided by *Liber Aristotilis* (composed in the twelfth century by Hugo de Santalla), follows Valens' tradition and mentions two gestation periods, 258 days (258 = 273 – 15) and 288 days (288 = 273 + 15). See *Liber Aristotilis*, ed. Burnett and Pingree (1997), III i 10, 21–24, 43–44 and note on p. 144. Abū Bakr al-Ḥasan b. al-Khaṣib (ninth century), in the *Kitāb al-Mawālid* (*De nativitatibus*, ed. Petreius (1540), III, sig. B4v), endorses Valens' traditions and mentions three periods of 258, 273, and 288 days. Al-Bīrūnī's *Kitāb al-Tafhīm* (*Elements*, ed. Ramsay Wright (1934), § 526, 329–331) employs the same principle, without mentioning the aforementioned gestation periods, and informs readers that astrologers use this theory to determine the native's temperament, constitution, and form.

A full account of Enoch's rectification of the nativity is offered in *Mishpeṭei ha-mazzalot*, § 15:1–5, § 17:1–4, 500–505 (quoted in App. 3, P. 8, Q. 1, § 1:1–5, § 2:1–4, 414–415). As in the present passage of *Electiones*, *Mishpeṭei ha-mazzalot* cites Enoch's book as its main source and does not mention the *trutina Hermetis*, "Hermes' balance." The fullest account of Enoch's rectification of the nativity is offered in *Moladot* (II 1:1; II 4:1–5, II 5:1–10, II 6:1–6, 88–95; quoted in App. 3, P. 8, Q. 2, § 1:1, § 2:1–5; § 3:1–10, § 4:1–6, 415–417). An equally detailed account of Enoch's rectification of the nativity is found in *De nativitatibus* (I 2:1–3, I 5:1–2, I 7:1–7, 250–255; quoted in App. 3, P. 8, Q. 5, § 1:1–2, § 2:1–2, § 3:1–7, 419–420), where this method of rectification is designated *trutina* and ascribed to Hermes, and in *Epitome* (ed. Heller (1548), II:i, sig. H3r–H3v; quoted in App. 3, P. 8, Q. 6, 1–8, 420–421), a work whose contents are closely related to Ibn Ezra's astrological oeuvre. *Ṭeʿamim* II (§ 6.1:1–5, 234–235; quoted in App. 3, P. 8, Q. 4, 1–5, 418–419) refers to Enoch's method of rectification in highly favorably terms, in a discussion where Māshā'allāh's and Ptolemy's methods of rectification of the nativity are described and criticized. As far as I know, Enoch/Hermes is explicitly mentioned in the Middle Ages as the originator of this method of rectification only in astrological treatises that were written by Ibn Ezra or are closely related to his astrological oeuvre, such as the *Epitome*. The work by Enoch/Hermes in which the method of rectification is mentioned, or Ibn Ezra's source for this information, has not been identified. Ibn Ezra repeats the technical details of Enoch's method (although without mentioning Enoch's name because the ascription is not germane) in his long commentary on Exodus 2:2 (quoted in App. 3, P. 8, Q. 3, § 1–4, 417–418), to take exception to the talmudic statement (B *Sotah* 12a) that Moses was born prematurely (after six full months of pregnancy) and buttress the argument that Moses must have been born after a normal gestation of nine months.

⟨II v 3⟩

[1]**1–2: It is also necessary … as you need.** The same corrections to the *trutina Hermetis* occur in *Moladot*, II 6:1–6, 94–95 (quoted in App. 3, P. 8, Q. 2, § 4:1–6, 415–417). *De nativitatibus* was transmitted in four different versions. Only one of them, which included long passages from Pietro d'Abano's Latin translation of *Sefer ha-moladot*, also includes a succinct account of the corrections found in *Moladot*, II 6:1–6, 94–95. See *De nativitatibus* I 7:7, 254, note 24.

⟨II v 4⟩

[1]**1–2: Dorotheus says … power in this matter.** The topic of messengers is not addressed in *Mivḥarim* I or *Mivḥarim* II, in contrast with *She'elot* I (§ 9.2:1–4, 284–285) and *She'elot* II (§ 9.3:1–2, 380–381), which do so in the context of the ninth place. That the fifth place signifies messengers, as stated here by Dorotheus in an otherwise unknown work, is commonplace. See: *Reshit ḥokhmah* § 3.9:1, 144–145; al-Qabīṣī's *Introduction*, ed. Burnett et al. (2004), I:61, 50–51.

[2]**3: If you inquire … succedent ⟨places⟩.** This corresponds to *Mivḥarim* I, § 5.3:1–2, 66–67 and *Mivḥarim* II, § 5.3:1, 160–161

⟨II vi 1⟩

[1]**1: The scientists of India ... judgments of the signs:** Throughout history, various civilizations have divided the zodiac into 28 parts that are relevant to weather forecasting and astrology. The Indians divided the ecliptic into 28 divisions associated with diverse deities, called *nakṣatra*. In pre-Islamic times, the Arabs distinguished 28 fixed stars, each of them a *naw*ʾ (plural *anwā*), whose rising and settings divided the solar year of 365 days into roughly 28 periods of thirteen days, each with its own characteristic weather. Also ascribed to the Indians and the Arabs are the 28 lunar mansions (Arab. *manāzil al-qamar*), which have a special relevance for rainfall. Because the lunar month has approximately 28 days, each lunar mansion was taken to be the place where the Moon "lodges" on one day of the lunar month. In Arabic sources the *anwā* are related to the lunar mansions. Texts attributed to Hermes Trismegistus prescribe the activities to be undertaken when the Moon is located in each of these 28 constellations. See Bos and Burnett 2000, 19–20. Al-Bīrūnī (*Elements*, ed. Ramsay Wright (1934), § 166, 87) points out that the *anwā* are associated with the rains because the times of their occurrence are related to the setting of the mansions in the west in the morning. The lunar mansions are frequently mentioned, catalogued, and described in Arabic (mainly translated into Hebrew and Latin) and Latin sources, generally in close connection with weather or rain forecasting. See al-Kindī's *Letter* II, 83–107 ("On the causes attributed to the higher bodies which indicate the origin of rains," al-Kindī, ed. Bos and Burnett (2000), 253–256); Jafar Indus, *Liber imbrium* 44–51, and the parallel sections in *Sapientes Indi*, 44–47 (al-Kindī, ed. Bos and Burnett (2000), 368–369); *Elements*, ed. Ramsay Wright (1934), § 164–166, 81–87; *Tractatus pluviarum*, ed. Burnett (2008), 68–101, 249–254; *Epitome*, ed. Heller (1548), I:11, H1v–H3v; IV:17, sig. S3r–T3r.

The 28 lunar mansions feature prominently throughout Ibn Ezra's oeuvre. In his commentary on Ecclesiastes 3:1 and the long commentary on Exodus 26:2 he harshly criticizes anonymous (presumably Jewish) commentators who associated the 28 lunar mansions with the 28 varieties of time enumerated in Ecclesiastes 3:2–8 and with the 28 cubits of the curtains of the sanctuary (Ex. 26:2). In the introduction to his short commentary on the Pentateuch, however, Ibn Ezra notes without comment that the 28 letters of the Hebrew alphabet correspond to the 28 lunar mansions. Ibn Ezra devoted complete chapters to the 28 lunar mansions in *Neḥoshet* I (156v–157r) and *Neḥoshet* II (193r–194r), where he invokes the authority of the Ancients. In these two chapter he defines the lunar mansions, gives instructions for finding the Moon in the mansions with respect to the place of the Sun at the beginning of the month, and offers a complete catalogue of the 28 lunar mansions, including their Arabic names, translation into Hebrew, and the number and size of the stars thereof. In *Neḥoshet* II he adds the graphical representation of each asterism. Ibn Ezra also devoted entire sections to the 28 lunar mansions in *'Olam* I (§ 62:1–5, 92–93; § 63:1–11, 92–95) and *'Olam* II (§ 37:4, 180–181; § 43:1–4, 184–185; § 44:1–3, 184–185; § 45:1–4, 184–185; § 49:6, 188–189). These sections provide only incomplete lists of the lunar mansions and focus on the calculation of their positions. This is because these sections in *'Olam* I and *'Olam* II deal only with the lunar mansions that have a bearing on weather, particularly rainfall, and divides them into "moist," "dry" and "rainy." Like *Electiones* in the current locus, both *'Olam* I (§ 62:1, 92–93) and *'Olam* II (§ 44:1, 184–185) ascribe the lunar mansions to the scientists of India.

[2]**2–3: They made the mansions ... only 3 minutes.** Ibn Ezra offers four separate explanations of the lunar mansions—in *Neḥoshet* I, 156v–157r; *Neḥoshet* II; 193r–194r; *'Olam* I, 62:1–5, 92–93; and *'Olam* II, § 45:1–4, 184–185. Of these four, the account in *Neḥoshet* II is consistent with that offered here (although the lunar mansions in *Neḥoshet* II are not ascribed to the Indian scholars but to the Arabs). See *Neḥoshet* II, 193v (quoted in App. 3, P. 9, Q. 3, 423)

[3]**4: In the present days ... every mansion.** Like the present passage, *'Olam* I (§ 62:1, 92–93) and *'Olam* II (§ 44:1, 184–185) maintain that a certain interval must be subtracted in order to calculate the position of every mansion. The closest account is *'Olam* I (§ 62:3, 92–93), which specifies subtracting 8° from the position of the Moon; *'Olam* II (§ 45:3–4, 184–185) specifies a distance of 9° to subtracted from the place of the Sun. No excess interval is specified in the accounts of the lunar mansions in *Neḥoshet* I or *Neḥoshet* II.

[4]**5: In the *Book of the Judgement of the World*, I will explain the shape of the mansions; Latin: *Et in Libro iudiciorum seculi explanabo formam mansionum*.** In the present passage, *Liber iudiciorum seculi* is the translation of ספר משפטי העולם, one of the names for Ibn Ezra's *Sefer ha-'Olam*. This future-tense cross-reference points to a passage of the lost *'Olam* III, because neither *'Olam* I nor *'Olam* II includes a full list of the lunar mansions or any reference to *formam mansionum*, "the shape of the mansions," an expression which in this context means a graphical representation of

the asterisms of each mansion. A hitherto unknown Latin translation of the lost *ʿOlam* III was recently identified in Vatican, BAV, MS Pal. lat. 1407, 14th–15th c., fols. 55r–58r, where it precedes Henry Bate's translation "de Hebreo in Latinum," produced in Mechelen in 1278, of two treatises assigned to al-Kindī (fols. 58r–62r). In all likelihood, Bate was also responsible for the Latin translation of *ʿOlam* III. That the text on fols. 55r–58r of the Vatican manuscript is a Latin translation of *ʿOlam* III is shown by the following. (1) The Latin text on fols. 55r–58r of that manuscript deals predominantly with world astrology and evinces striking similarities with the ideas on world astrology developed by Ibn Ezra elsewhere in his astrological oeuvre. (2) A complete list of the 28 lunar mansions appears in the middle of the Latin text of the Vatican manuscript (fols. 56r–56v), and each item is accompanied by a graphical representation of the asterisms of the corresponding lunar mansion. This list of mansions is the target of the cross-reference in *El*, II vi 1:5. (3) The account of the lunar mansions in this Latin translation is followed by a note in which the Latin translator explicitly assigns part of the account of the lunar mansions in this text to Ibn Ezra. That *ʿOlam* III was composed after 1158, in the last phase of Ibn Ezra's career, follows from the fact that *Electiones* was certainly written in 1158 or after and the present cross-reference here is in the future tense. See above, pp. 23–24. An edition of the Latin translation of *ʿOlam* III, accompanied by an English translation and an introductory study, has been recently published. See Sela et al. (2020).

[5]**6: Here I will set forth ... method of elections.** Using the lunar mansions for elections is not routine in astrological literature, where they are typically used instead for weather forecasting. *Mivḥarim* I and *Mivḥarim* II, for example, are totally silent about the lunar mansions. However, there are astrological texts that use the lunar mansions for elections. See Burnett 2004, 48–55. *Electiones* divides the sixth chapter into 28 sections, each addressing the elections made when the Moon lodges in one of the 28 lunar mansions. In each section, *Electiones* first states the elections according to the scientists of India, and then the elections according to Dorotheus. Ibn Ezra's source may be the last section of the seventh part, on elections, of the *Kitāb al-Bāriʿ fī aḥkām al-nujūm* by the Arab astrologer Ibn Abī l-Rijāl (see *De iudiciis astrorum*, ed. Petri (1551), 342a–346b), or an earlier unknown source on which Ibn Abī l-Rijāl and Ibn Ezra drew. The final section of the fourth part of the *Epitome*, on elections, is also very close to *Electiones* and the *Kitāb al-Bāriʿ*. Ibn Ezra may have emulated Sahl's *Book of Elections* when he placed the account of the elections based on the lunar mansions in the sixth chapter of *Electiones*. For the details, see above, p. 40.

⟨II vi 2⟩

[1]**1: *Al-naṯḥ* in Arabic, ⟨as⟩ they explain in the *Book of the Judgment of the World*; Latin: *ahitaih in lingua Arabica, et explanant in Libro Iudiciorum Seculi*.** As in *El*, II vi 1:5 (see note there), this present tense cross-reference to *Liber iudiciorum seculi*—the translation of ספר משפטי העולם, one of the names for Ibn Ezra's *Sefer ha-ʿOlam*—points in all likelihood to a passage of the lost *ʿOlam* III, a hitherto unknown Latin translation of which was recently identified in Vatican, BAV, MS Pal. lat. 1407. This text includes two complete lists of lunar mansions which, besides the transliteration of their Arabic name, present their astronomical and astrological features. For *al-naṯḥ*, the first lunar mansion, in one of these two lists, see Vatican, BAV, MS Pal. lat. 1407, fol. 56r (quoted in App. 3, P. 9, Q. 5, 423). Note that *ʿOlam* I, § 62:4, 92–93, too, includes a succinct note about *al-naṯḥ*. By contrast, *Olam* II does not refer to *al-naṯḥ*.

[2]**1–4: The first ⟨mansion⟩ of Aries is *al-naṯḥ* … new clothes.** This corresponds to the account of the first mansion in the seventh part of Abī l-Rijāl's *Kitāb al-Bāriʿ* (*ilnath* [*De iudiciis astrorum*, ed. Petri (1551), 342a–b; quoted in App. 3, P. 9, Q. 1, 421–422]) and in the fourth part of the *Epitome* (*cornua Arietis* [ed. Heller (1548), IV:18, S3r–T3v; quoted in App. 3, P. 9, Q. 2, 422–423]).

⟨II vi 3⟩

[1]**1–2: The second ⟨mansion⟩, *al-buṭayn* … is very auspicious.** This corresponds to the account of the second mansion in the sixth part of Abī l-Rijāl's *Kitāb al-Bāriʿ* (*albethain* [*De iudiciis astrorum*, ed. Petri (1551), 342b]) and in the fourth part of the *Epitome* (*venter Arietis* [ed. Heller (1548), IV:18, S3v])

⟨II vi 4⟩

[1]**1–2: The third is *al-thurayyā* … female slave.** This corresponds to the account of the third mansion in the sixth part of Abī l-Rijāl's *Kitāb al-Bāriʿ* (*althoraie* [*De iudiciis astrorum*, ed. Petri (1551), 342b]) and in the fourth part of the *Epitome* (*caput Tauri* [ed. Heller (1548), IV:18, S3v]).

⟨II vi 5⟩

[1]**1–2: The fourth is *al-dabarān* ... wells and pits.** This corresponds to the account of the fourth mansion in the sixth part of Abī l-Rijāl's *Kitāb al-Bāriʿ* (*addavennam* [*De iudiciis astrorum*, ed. Petri (1551), 342b–343a]) and in the fourth part of *Epitome* (*oculus Tauri* [ed. Heller (1548), IV:18, S3v]).

⟨II vi 6⟩

[1]**1–3: The fifth is *al-haqʿa* ... female slave.** This corresponds to the account of the fifth mansion in the sixth part of Abī l-Rijāl's *Kitāb al-Bāriʿ* (*alhathaya* [*De iudiciis astrorum*, ed. Petri (1551), 343a]) and in the fourth part of *Epitome* (*caput canis validi* [ed. Heller (1548), IV:18, S4r]).

[2]**4: King Ptolemy.** Ibn Ezra cites Claudius Ptolemy as a scientific source more often than any other scientist or astrologer. See the tables of authorities and sources in the editions of the Hebrew astrological works of Ibn Ezra: Sela 2007, 355; Sela 2010, 321; Sela 2011, 545, 548, 551; Sela 2013, 502, 504; Sela 2017, 800, 801; Sela 2019, 527, 528. The person known to Ibn Ezra, however, is not the historical scientist of classical antiquity but a compound of legend and myth. This is reflected in the fact that Ibn Ezra refers to him in two different ways in his Hebrew astrological, scientific, and nonscientific works. He is *Baṭalmiyūs*, that is, the Arabic form of "Ptolemy," in all the astrological works we are certain were part of the astrological encyclopedia composed in Béziers in 1148. *King Talmai*, or *Talmai*, the post-biblical or talmudic Hebrew equivalent of "King Ptolemy," is used in all the other astrological works: *Mishpeṭei ha-mazzalot* (see table of authorities, s.v. "King Ptolemy" and "Ptolemy," Sela 2017, 800, 801), *She'elot* II (table of authorities, s.v. "Ptolemy," Sela 2011, 548), *Mivḥarim* II (table of authorities, s.v. "King Ptolemy" and "Ptolemy," Sela 2011, 545), *ʿOlam* II (table of authorities, s.v. "King Ptolemy," Sela 2010, 321), *Ṭeʿamim* II (table of authorities, s.v. "King Ptolemy" and "Ptolemy," Sela 2007, 355), *Me'orot* (table of authorities, s.v. "King Ptolemy," Sela 2011, 551), and *Tequfah* (table of authorities, s.v. "Ptolemy," Sela 2013, 504). "King Talmai" is also used in *Neḥoshet* I, 151v, *Neḥoshet* II, 189r, *ʿIbbur* (2011, 81, 88), and *Mispar*, ed. Silberberg (1895), 45.

Ibn Ezra probably inherited the mythical King Ptolemy from Abū Maʿshar's *Kitāb al-Mudkhal al-kabīr*. See *Great Introduction*, ed. Burnett and Yamamoto (2019), IV:1, [4]:346–347. Abū Maʿshar reports that there were ten Greek kings who succeeded Alexander of Macedon, each of whom was known as Ptolemy. They lived in Egypt and their rule lasted 275 years (i.e., 305–30 BCE). One of them composed the *Almagest*; another wrote a book on astrology (i.e., the *Tetrabiblos*) and attributed it to the author of the *Almagest*. At the end of this passage, Abū Maʿshar adds that some say that the very learned man who wrote the *Tetrabiblos* also wrote the *Almagest*. Ibn Ezra in turn created a new mythical King Ptolemy who sponsored the translation of the Septuagint. See Sela 2003, 296–313; cf. long comm. on Ex. 33:21, in *Commentary on Exodus*, ed. Weiser (1976), 217. For a parallel Latin tradition about King Ptolemy, see Burnett 1998, 340–342.

[3]**4: Signs with human shape ... Sagittarius and Aquarius.** All the signs in this category (Virgo, Gemini, Libra, half of Sagittarius, and Aquarius) are listed and dubbed צורת האדם "human shape" in *Mishpeṭei ha-mazzalot* § 2:14, 490–491. *Ṭeʿamim* II (§ 2.4:15, 194–195) explains that all the signs with a human shape are sterile, because human beings produce few children. This category is mentioned in *Tetrabiblos*, ed. Robbins (1980), IV:6, 409 (where only Leo and Virgo are listed), and in Arabic introductions to astrology, where the sterile signs do not precisely coincide with those that have a human shape. See *Great Introduction*, ed. Burnett and Yamamoto (2019), VI:16, [5]:896–897; *Abbreviation*, ed. Burnett et al. (1994), I:24, 15 et passim; *Elements*, ed. Ramsay Wright (1934), § 354, 214; *Introduction*, ed. Burnett et al. (2004), I:24, 33.

[4]**4: Under the rays, Latin: *sub radiis*.** Being "under the rays" is one of the condition of the planets with respect to the Sun. For this concept, see note on *El*, II vii 1:1.

[5]**4: Number of its ray; Latin: *quantitas radiationis eius*.** The expression "number of its ray" = *quantitas radiationis eius* refers to a certain number of degrees in the zodiac, ahead of or behind the planet, where its influence is still felt. In particular, the 12° mentioned in *Int*, II vi 6:4 is the extent of the Moon's ray. Ibn Ezra uses this concept frequently in his astrological corpus, because where a planet's influence is felt in the zodiac is used to determine the planet's relative power during the analysis of a specific horoscopic chart. The planets' rays are enumerated in *Mishpeṭei ha-mazzalot* § 24:1, 508–509 (quoted in App. 5., Q. 7, 467). *Mishpeṭei ha-mazzalot* uses ניצוץ, "spark," to denote this concept. The same term is used in *Sefer ha-Tequfah* (§ 13:1, 380–381 et passim). It is designated כח הגוף, "power of the body," or אור הגוף, "light of the body," throughout *Reshit ḥokhmah* (see § 4.1:37, 154–155 et passim), *Ṭeʿamim* I (§ 4.2:12, 74–75 et passim), *Moladot* (III i 15,

4, 120–121 et passim), *She'elot* I (§ 7.4:9, 272–273), and *Mivḥarim* I (§ 3:2, 48–49). For the latter usage Ibn Ezra was indebted to Abū Maʿshar, who employed قوّة جرم "power of the body" for this property (*Great Introduction*, ed. Burnett and Yamamoto (2019), VII:3, [1]:201–202 et passim; but also *Abbreviation*, ed. Burnett et al. (1994), II:11–12, 34–34, and *Introduction*, ed. Burnett et al. (2004), II:5, 64, line 26 et passim). In other astrological treatises, Ibn Ezra uses the kindred term אור "light" for this property. See *Ṭeʿamim* II (§ 4.2:1–4, 208–209), *She'elot* II (§ 6.1:8, 368–369; § 7.6:6, 372–373 et passim), *Mivḥarim* II (§ 2:3, 144–145), and *Me'orot* (§ 25:4, 472–473). Ibn Ezra probably took ניצוץ and אור from the preface to Sahl Ibn Bishr's *Introduction* (*Kitāb Sahl Ibn Bishr al-Isra'īlī fī ʿilm al-falak wa l-burūj wa l-a ḥām al falakiyya ʿalā l-tamām wa l-kamāl*, New Haven, Yale University Library, MS Arabic 532, fol. 24a–b), where this astrological property is designated انوار الكواكب السبعة "the lights of the seven planets." Some Arabic introductions to astrology, including *Mishpeṭei ha-mazzalot* deal with this topic and assign these numbers of degrees to each of the planets in a single section. See: *Kitāb Sahl Ibn Bishr al-Isra'īlī*, fol. 24a–b; *Great Introduction*, ed. Burnett and Yamamoto (2019), VII:3, [2]:203–211; *Abbreviation*, ed. Burnett et al. 1994, II:11–12, 34–35; *Elements*, ed. Ramsay Wright (1934), § 436, 255.

[6]**4: King Ptolemy stated … [the Moon's] ray**. This portion of the account of the fifth mansion ascribed to King Ptolemy is absent from the sixth part of Abī l-Rijāl's *Kitāb al-Bāriʿ* and from the fourth part of *Epitome*. It may be Ibn Ezra's own addition to *She'elot* III.

⟨II vi 7⟩

[1]**1–2: The sixth is *al-hanʿa* … new garment**. This corresponds to the account of the sixth mansion in the sixth part of Abī l-Rijāl's *Kitāb al-Bāriʿ* (*alhana* [*De iudiciis astrorum*, ed. Petri (1551), 343a–b]) and in the fourth part of *Epitome* (*sidus parvum* [ed. Heller (1548), IV:18, S4r]).

⟨II vi 8⟩

[1]**1–2: The seventh is *al-dhirāʿ* … ⟨⟨will succeed⟩⟩**. This corresponds to the account of the seventh mansion in the sixth part of Abī l-Rijāl's *Kitāb al-Bāriʿ* (*addirach* [*De iudiciis astrorum*, ed. Petri (1551), 343b]) and in the fourth part of *Epitome* (*brachium Leonis* [ed. Heller (1548), IV:18, S4v]).

⟨II vi 9⟩

[1]**1–2: The eighth is *al-nathra* … who is imprisoned.** This corresponds to the account of the eighth mansion in the sixth part of Abī l-Rijāl's *Kitāb al-Bāriʿ* (*aluayra* [*De iudiciis astrorum*, ed. Petri (1551), 343b]) and in the fourth part of *Epitome* (*nebula* [ed. Heller (1548), IV:18, S4v]).

⟨II vi 10⟩

[1]**1–2: The ninth is *al-ṭarf* … will arrive sooner.** This corresponds to the account of the ninth mansion in the sixth part of Abī l-Rijāl's *Kitāb al-Bāriʿ* (*attraof* [*De iudiciis astrorum*, ed. Petri (1551), 343b–344a]) and in the fourth part of *Epitome* (*oculus Leonis* [ed. Heller (1548), IV:18, S4v]).

⟨II vi 11⟩

[1]**1–2: The tenth is *al-jabha* … get out quickly.** This corresponds to the account of the tenth mansion in the sixth part of Abī l-Rijāl's *Kitāb al-Bāriʿ* (*algebhe* [*De iudiciis astrorum*, ed. Petri (1551), 344a]) and in the fourth part of *Epitome* (*frons Leonis* [ed. Heller (1548), IV:18, T1r]).

⟨II vi 12⟩

[1]**1–2: The eleventh is *al-zubra* … travel is intermediate.** This corresponds to the account of the eleventh mansion in the sixth part of Abī l-Rijāl's *Kitāb al-Bāriʿ* (*azobrach* [*De iudiciis astrorum*, ed. Petri (1551), 344a]) and in the fourth part of *Epitome* (*capillus* [ed. Heller (1548), IV:18, T1r]).

⟨II vi 13⟩

[1]**1–2: The twelfth is *al-ṣarfa* … very good glutton.** This corresponds to the account of the twelfth mansion in the sixth part of Abī l-Rijāl's *Kitāb al-Bāriʿ* (*azarfa* [*De iudiciis astrorum*, ed. Petri (1551), 344a]) and in the fourth part of *Epitome* (*cauda Leonis* [ed. Heller (1548), IV:18, T1r]).

⟨II vi 14⟩

[1]**1–2: The thirteenth is *al-ʿawwāʾ* ... to wash the head.** This corresponds to the account of the thirteenth mansion in the sixth part of Abī l-Rijāl's *Kitāb al-Bāriʿ* (*aloce* [*De iudiciis astrorum*, ed. Petri (1551), 344b]) and in the fourth part of *Epitome* (*canis* [ed. Heller (1548), IV:18, T1r]).

⟨II vi 15⟩

[1]**1–2: The fourteenth is *al-simāk al-aʿzal* ... get out quickly.** This corresponds to the account of the fourteenth mansion in the sixth part of Abī l-Rijāl's *Kitāb al-Bāriʿ* (*azimech* [*De iudiciis astrorum*, ed. Petri (1551), 344b]) and in the fourth part of *Epitome* (*spica* [ed. Heller (1548), IV:18, T1v]).

⟨II vi 16⟩

[1]**1–2: The fifteenth is *al-ghafr* ... manor-house to another.** This corresponds to the account of the fifteenth mansion in the sixth part of Abī l-Rijāl's *Kitāb al-Bāriʿ* (*algarf* [*De iudiciis astrorum*, ed. Petri (1551), 344b]) and in the fourth part of *Epitome* (*cooperta* [ed. Heller (1548), IV:18, T1v]).

⟨II vi 17⟩

[1]**2: Without delay, Latin: *cito in brachiis*.** The phrase *in brachiis* ("on the hands") seems to be a mistranslation of מיד, literally "from the hand" but meaning "without delay."

[2]**1–2: The sixteenth is *al-zubānā* ... without delay.** This corresponds to the account of the sixteenth mansion in the sixth part of Abī l-Rijāl's *Kitāb al-Bāriʿ* (*azebone* [*De iudiciis astrorum*, ed. Petri (1551), 345a]) and in the fourth part of *Epitome* (*cornua* [ed. Heller (1548), IV:18, T1v]).

⟨II vi 18⟩

[1]**1–2: The seventeenth is *al-iklīl* ... buy a slave.** This corresponds to the account of the seventeenth mansion in the sixth part of Abī l-Rijāl's *Kitāb al-Bāriʿ* (*alidil* [*De iudiciis astrorum*, ed. Petri (1551), 345a]) and in the fourth part of *Epitome* (*corona* [ed. Heller (1548), IV:18, T1v]).

⟨II vi 19⟩

[1]**1–2: The eighteenth is *qalb al-ʿaqrab* ... drink a potion.** This corresponds to the account of the eighteenth mansion in the sixth part of Abī l-Rijāl's *Kitāb al-Bāriʿ* (*alcalb* [*De iudiciis astrorum*, ed. Petri (1551), 345a]) and in the fourth part of *Epitome* (*cor Scorpionis* [ed. Heller (1548), IV:18, T2r]).

⟨II vi 20⟩

[1]**1–2: The nineteenth is *al-šawla* ... female slave.** This corresponds to the account of the nineteenth mansion in the sixth part of Abī l-Rijāl's *Kitāb al-Bāriʿ* (*yenla* [*De iudiciis astrorum*, ed. Petri (1551), 345b]) and in the fourth part of *Epitome* (*cauda Scorpionis* [ed. Heller (1548), IV:18, T2r]).

⟨II vi 21⟩

[1]**1–2: The twentieth is *al-naʿāʾim* ... will be bad.** This corresponds to the account of the twentieth mansion in the sixth part of Abī l-Rijāl's *Kitāb al-Bāriʿ* (*alimain* [*De iudiciis astrorum*, ed. Petri (1551), 345b]) and in the fourth part of *Epitome* (*trabs* [ed. Heller (1548), IV:18, T2r]).

⟨II vi 22⟩

[1]**1–2: The twenty-first is *al-balda* ... another husband.** This corresponds to the account of the twenty-first mansion in the sixth part of Abī l-Rijāl's *Kitāb al-Bāriʿ* (*albeda* [*De iudiciis astrorum*, ed. Petri (1551), 345b]) and in the fourth part of *Epitome* (*desertum* [ed. Heller (1548), IV:18, T2v]).

⟨II vi 23⟩

[1]**1–2: The twenty-second is *saʿd al-dhābiḥ* ... on the sea.** This corresponds to the account of the twenty-second mansion in the sixth part of Abī l-Rijāl's *Kitāb al-Bāriʿ* (*sahaddadebe* [*De iudiciis astrorum*, ed. Petri (1551), 345b]) and in the fourth part of *Epitome* (*pastor* [ed. Heller (1548), IV:18, T2v]).

⟨II vi 24⟩

[1]**1–2: The twenty-third is *sa'd al-bula'* ... get out soon.** The Hebrew source text of the present passage is extant in the parchment bifolium 368.2 found in the Archivio di Stato, Modena. See *Mivḥarim* III, II vi 24:1–2, 484. This corresponds to the account of the twenty-third mansion in the sixth part of Abī l-Rijāl's *Kitāb al-Bāriʿ* (Zadebolal [*De iudiciis astrorum*, ed. Petri (1551), 345b–346a]) and in the fourth part of *Epitome* (*deglutiens* [ed. Heller (1548), IV:18, T2v]).

⟨II vi 25⟩

[1]**1–2: The twenty-fourth is *sa'd al-su'ūd* ... get out soon.** This corresponds to the account of the twenty-fourth mansion in the sixth part of Abī l-Rijāl's *Kitāb al-Bāriʿ* (*zaadescod* [*De iudiciis astrorum*, ed. Petri (1551), 346a]) and in the fourth part of *Epitome* (*fortuna* [ed. Heller (1548), IV:18, T2v]).

⟨II vi 26⟩

[1]**1–2: The twenty-fifth is *sa'd al-akhbiya* ... never get out.** This corresponds to the account of the twenty-fifth mansion in the sixth part of Abī l-Rijāl's *Kitāb al-Bāriʿ* (*sadalabbia* [*De iudiciis astrorum*, ed. Petri (1551), 346a]) and in the fourth part of *Epitome* (*papilio* [ed. Heller (1548), IV:18, T3r]).

⟨II vi 27⟩

[1]**1–2: The twenty-sixth is *al-fargh al-awwal* ... will die there.** This corresponds to the account of the twenty-sixth mansion in the sixth part of Abī l-Rijāl's *Kitāb al-Bāriʿ* (*fargalmocaden* [*De iudiciis astrorum*, ed. Petri (1551), 346a–b]) and in the fourth part of *Epitome* (*hauriens* [ed. Heller (1548), IV:18, T3r]).

⟨II vi 28⟩

[1]**1–2: The twenty-seventh is *al-fargh al-thāni* ... will die there.** This corresponds to the account of the twenty-seventh mansion in the sixth part of Abī l-Rijāl's *Kitāb al-Bāriʿ* (*alfargamahar* [*De iudiciis astrorum*, ed. Petri (1551), 346b]) and in the fourth part of *Epitome* (*secundus hauriens* [ed. Heller (1548), IV:18, T3r]).

⟨II vi 29⟩

[1]**1–2: The twenty-eighth is *baṭn al-ḥūt* ... will die there.** This corresponds to the account of the twenty-eighth mansion in the sixth part of Abī l-Rijāl's *Kitāb al-Bāriʿ* (*bathnealoth* [*De iudiciis astrorum*, ed. Petri (1551), 346b]) and in the fourth part of *Epitome* (*piscis* [ed. Heller (1548), IV:18, T3v]).

⟨II vii 1⟩

[1]**1–2: One who wishes ... lord of the hour.** This corresponds to *Mivḥarim* I, § 7.6:1–2, 74–75 and *Epitome*, ed. Heller (1548), IV:13, S2r. Cf. *Mivḥarim* II, § 7.4:1–6, 166–167.

[2]**3: Aspect of love, Latin: *aspectus dilectionis*.** This is a calque of מבט אהבה, "aspect of love," a locution used by Ibn Ezra to denote the aspect of trine, when there is an angular relationship of 120° between planets, zodiacal signs, and other celestial objects. For the concept of aspect, see note on *Tp*, I i 4:7. The aspect of trine is considered to be harmonious and fortunate.

[3]**6: Subject of the election.** The Latin reading here, *dominus electionis*, lit. "lord of the election," is a literal mistranslation of the Hebrew in the corresponding place in the Modena fragment, בעל המבחר, meaning "the subject of the election," but with the alternate possible sense "lord of the election." See *Mivḥarim* III, II vii 1:6, 485.

[4]**6: Calculate.** The Latin reading here, *prepara*, *lit.* "make ready" or "prepare," is a somewhat inaccurate translation of the Hebrew in the corresponding place in the Modena fragment, תקן, which Ibn Ezra frequently uses with the sense of "calculate." See *Mivḥarim* III, II vii 1:6, 485. I have used the appropriate meaning of the Hebrew original for the translation of this passage as well as of all the other loci where the Latin verb *preparare* occurs.

[5]**1–6: One who wishes ... position of the Sun and Mars.** The Hebrew source text of the present passage is extant in the Modena fragment of *Mivḥarim* III. See *Mivḥarim* III, II vii 1:1–6, 485.

[6]**6: If the subject of the election ... indicates quarrels.** This corresponds to *Mivḥarim* I, § 7.6:9, 76–77 (quoted in App. 3, P. 10, Q. 1, 423)

⟨II vii 2⟩

[1]**1: If you inquire ... position of Jupiter.** This corresponds to *Mivḥarim* I, § 7.7:1, 76–77 and *Mivḥarim* II, § 7.5:1, 166–167.

[2]**1: Under the rays of the Sun, Latin: *sub radiis Solis*.** For this condition of the planets with respect to the Sun, see note on *Int*, II vi 1:3.

⟨II vii 3⟩

[1]**1–2: If ⟨one wishes⟩ to choose ... auspicious and perfect.** This corresponds to *Mivḥarim* I, § 7.4:1–2, 72–73 (quoted in App. 3, P. 11, Q. 1, 424), which makes a similar statement on the authority of Māshā'allāh.

[2]**3: Be careful ... great power.** This corresponds to the following loci: (1) *Mivḥarim* I, § 7.1:2, 70–71 (quoted in App. 3, P. 11, Q. 2, 424); (2) *She'elot* I, § 7.3:3, 270–271 (quoted in App. 4, P. 11, Q. 2, 3, 445); (3) *She'elot* II, § 7.1:2, 368–369 (quoted in App. 4, P. 11, Q. 1, 2, 445); (4) *Epitome*, ed. Heller (1548), IV:11, S1v (quoted in App. 3, P. 11, Q. 3, 424); (5) Sahl Ibn Bishr's *Book of Elections* (quoted in App. 3, P. 11, Q. 4, 424).

[3]**5: In the middle of the zodiac, Latin: *medio circuli*.** This refers to the middle of the zodiac, that is, the ecliptic. Note that the Hebrew counterpart of this phrase is **אמצעי** "intermediate." It follows that either the Latin translation depends on a variant Hebrew manuscript or is an explanatory expansion of the Hebrew.

[4]**3–5: Be careful that the ascendant sign ... upper ⟨planet⟩ either.** For the astrological concept of a planet as "victorious" over another planet, see note on *El*, II vii 6:3. This corresponds to *She'elot* II, § 7.1:2–4, 368–369 (quoted in App. 4, P. 11, Q. 1, 2–4, 445) and *She'elot* I, § 7.3:3–5, 270–271 (quoted in App. 4, P. 11, Q. 2, 3–5, 445).

[5]**3–5: Has great power, and a lower ⟨planet⟩ ... over the upper ⟨planet⟩ either.** The Hebrew source text of the present passage is extant in the Modena fragment of *Mivḥarim* III. See *Mivḥarim* III, II vii 3:1–5, 485–486.

⟨II vii 4⟩

[1]**1: Instead, Latin:** ***sub***. The Hebrew counterpart of this passage has תחת, *lit.* "below" but also denoting "instead." Thus here *Electiones* mistranslates the Hebrew. I have gone with the correct sense of the Hebrew.

[2]**1: Know that if Jupiter … instead of the Moon**. This corresponds to *Mivḥarim* I, § 7.5:6, 74–75 (quoted in App. 3, P. 12, Q. 1, 6, 425–426) and *Mivḥarim* II, § 7.1:5, 162–163 (quoted in App. 3, P. 12, Q. 2, 5, 426).

[3]**2–5: It is known … its lord [i.e., the lord of the ascendant]**. This corresponds closely to the following loci: (1) *Int,* II vii 5:1, which mentions Abū Maʿshar as a source; see note there; (2) *She'elot* II, § 7.4:1–3, 370–373 (quoted in App. 4, P. 12, Q. 4, 1–3, 447–448); (3) *Mivḥarim* I, § 7.2:1–4, 70–71 (quoted in App. 4, P. 12, Q. 5, 1–4, 448); (4) *Mivḥarim* II, § 7.3:1–2, 166–167 (quoted in App. 4, P. 12, Q. 6, 1–2, 448–449); and (5) *Epitome*, ed. Heller (1548), III:12, Q2r (quoted in App. 4, P. 12, Q. 7, 449). The "confusion" of the astrologers, presented at *Int,* II vii 4:3–4, is caused by the following contradiction: (a) On the one hand, Taurus is the ascendant and Mars is in Taurus; consequently, Mars, which is the lord of the seventh place, is in the ascendant, and therefore "the enemy will be defeated" (II vii 4:2); (b) on the other hand, Mars is an upper planet and thus, according to II vii 4:2, the enemy "will not be defeated completely." Note that in *She'elot* II, § 7.4:3, 370–373 (quoted in App. 4, P. 12, Q. 4, 3, 447–448), and *Mivḥarim* II, § 7.3:1–2, 166–167 (quoted in App. 4, P. 12, Q. 6, 1–2, 448–449), Ibn Ezra presents the same solution as here: "harm will befall both warring sides."

[4]**1–5: Know that if Jupiter … its lord [i.e., the lord of the ascendant]**. The Hebrew source text of the present passage is extant in the Modena fragment of *Mivḥarim* III, Modena. See *Mivḥarim* III, II vii 4:1–5, 486.

⟨II vii 5⟩

[1]**2–3: The opinion of the Ancients … Sun's nature**. This corresponds to *Nativitates,* I x 8:1–2, 102–103 (quoted in App. 3, P. 11, Q. 5, 425). A similar rule is found in *Mivḥarim* I § 8:1–2, 50–51 (quoted in App. 3, P. 11, Q. 6, 425). The reason is explained in *Ṭeʿamim* II, § 7.1:2, 242–345 (quoted in App. 3, P. 11, Q. 7, 425).

[2]**5: House of exaltation.** Here the Hebrew source text of the present passage reads בית כבוד, *lit.* "house of honor." See *Mivḥarim* III, II vii 5:5, 486–487. The Latin translation, though, is *domus exaltationis*, "house of exaltation," which is consistent with the common usage in Latin astrological contemporaneous literature, but diverges from *domus honoris*, frequently used in other Latin translations of Ibn Ezra's astrological works. See, for example, *Int*, II i 6:12, and *Tp*, IV 3:2.

[3]**5: Unless there is a malevolent ... its [the Sun's] house.** This corresponds to Mivḥarim I, § 7.3:2, 72–73 (quoted in App. 5., Q. 8, 467).

[4]**1–6: Know that the two luminaries ... burning or is retrograde.** The Hebrew source text of the present passage is extant in the Modena fragment of *Mivḥarim* III. See *Mivḥarim* III, II vii 5:1–6, 486–487.

⟨II vii 6⟩

[1]**3: Find out which ... *Book of the Beginning of Wisdom*.** There is no explicit discussion of this topic in *Reshit ḥokhmah*, but the topic is addressed in *Ṭeʿamim* II (§ 4.4:1–3, pp. 210–211), which is a commentary on *Reshit ḥokhmah* II. This suggests that the current reference is to *Reshit ḥokhmah* II, a fragment of which was discovered recently (see Sela 2010b, 43–66). There is an analogous reference to *Sefer Reshit ḥokhmah*, apropos of the same subject matter, in *Sheʾelot* II, § 7.2:2, 370–371 (quoted in App. 5., Q. 9, 467).

Discussions of how to find out which of two conjoining planets "governs and rules" the other or is "victorious" over the other are common in Ibn Ezra's astrological corpus. They usually entail a comparison of two factors: (1) proximity to the apogee on the epicycle; (2) location on the ecliptic or at the higher ecliptical latitude. See *Ṭeʿamim* I, § 7.1:4–10, 88–89; *Ṭeʿamim* II, § 4.4:1–3, 210–211; *Moladot* III, vii 4, 1–11, 160–163; *ʿOlam* I, § 21:1–4, 64–67; *Meʾorot* § 30:1–7, 474–475; *Sheʾelot* I § 7.3:10–19, 270–271; *Sheʾelot* II § 7.2:2, 370–371; *Mishpeṭei ha-mazzalot* § 33:1–7, 516–518; § 34:1–5, 518–519. See also *Epitome*, ed. Heller (1548), XXIII, D3v. Ibn Ezra's ultimate source for this doctrine is Abū Maʿshar's *Great Introduction* (ed. Burnett and Yamamoto (2019), VII:4, [8]:282–288). See also Al-Bīrūnī's *Elements* (ed. Ramsay Wright (1934), § 495, 307–308).

[2]**4: If the lord of the eighth ... began the war.** This corresponds to *Mivḥarim* I, § 7.5:1–2, 74–75 (quoted in App. 3, P. 12, Q. 1, 1–2, 425–426), where such a statement is ascribed to Abū Maʿshar.

[3]5: **Revolution of the world-year, Latin:** ***revolutio anni mundani.*** This term refers to a special type of horoscope, cast each year when the Sun enters Aries, in order to forecast world affairs during the coming year. See note on *Tp*, II i 2:1.

[4]5: **Terminal sign, Latin:** ***signum finis.*** The doctrine of the terminal sign derives from two related concepts found in the work of Ptolemy and Dorotheus and developed further by Arabic astrologers: (a) the "chronocrator" or "lord of [the] time," which, according to Ptolemy, is found by counting around the zodiac from each of the prorogative places (ascendant, Sun, Moon, lot of Fortune, and midheaven, each of them linked to specific domains of the native's life): "one year to each sign" in order to determine the lord of the years; "twenty-eight days to a sign" in order to determine the lord of the months; and "two and a third days to a sign" in order to determine the lord of the days (*Tetrabiblos*, ed. Robbins (1980), IV:10, 453); (b) the "prorogation" or "direction," a procedure in which a zodiacal point is launched and moved around the zodiac at a specified rate until it reaches another zodiacal position; see note on *Int*, I 1:3.

To denote the astrological concept of terminal sign, Ibn Ezra coined two similar expressions—מזל הסוף, "terminal sign" and בית הסוף, "terminal house"—and used them throughout his astrological corpus in applications related to continuous horoscopy. See, for example, *Moladot*, IV 13:1,4,5 and IV 14:1 for the use of מזל הסוף, "terminal sign," and *Moladot*, IV 22:1,2,3 and IV 24:3 for the use of בית הסוף, "terminal house."

[5]5: **Twenty years.** This is the cycle of the small conjunction of Saturn-Jupiter, as explained, for example, in *'Olam* I, § 8:1–2, § 10:1, 56–57 (quoted in App. 5, Q. 10, 467).

[6]5: **As I have explained in the** ***Book of Judgments,*** **that is, ⟨the** ***Book of Judgments*****⟩ of the** ***Revolutions of the World*****; Latin:** ***sicut explanavi in Libro Iudiciorum, id est, Revolutionum Mundi.*** This is a further reference to Ibn Ezra's *Sefer ha-'Olam*. According to the Modena fragment of *Mivḥarim* III, the name of the book is ספר משפטי העולם, "Book of the Judgments of the World." See *Mivḥarim* III, II vii 6:5, 487. This is precisely the name of *'Olam* I that appears in that book's explicit. See *'Olam* I, § 70:7, 96–97: נשלם ספר משפטי העולם ובו נשלמו ספרי הדינים כלם. = "This completes the *Book of the Judgments of the World,* which is the last of all the books of judgments." But here the Latin translator seems to have been confused regarding the name of Ibn Ezra's book and supplies what seem to be two alternative names. Note

also that while in *El*, II vi 1:5, the reference is in the future tense and the book referred to is designated *Liber iurium seculi*, and in *El*, II vi 2:1 the reference is in the present tense and the book cited is *Liber iudiciourum seculi*, here the reference is the past tense and to *Liber iudiciourum id est revolutionum mundi seculi*. This indicates that in the present reference is to one of the two extant versions of *Sefer ha-ʿOlam*. Indeed, judging on the basis of the contents of this cross-reference, it may well point to *ʿOlam* I, § 39:1–9, 78–79 (quoted in App. 5, Q. 11, 468). See corresponding notes in Sela 2010, 131–132.

[7]**1–5: Know that the lord ... *Revolutions of the World*.** The Hebrew source text of the present passage is extant in the Modena fragment of *Mivḥarim* III. See *Mivḥarim* III, II vii 6:1–5, 487.

⟨II vii 7⟩

[1]**1: If you inquire ... choose Scorpio ... watery signs.** Scorpio is to be chosen because it is Mars's house. This corresponds to *Mivḥarim* I, § 7.5:3, 74–75 (quoted in App. 3, P. 12, Q. 1, 3, 425–426), and *Mivḥarim* II, § 7.1:3, 162–163 (quoted in App. 3, P. 12, Q. 2, 3, 426).

[2]**2: If Jupiter is strong ... power to Jupiter.** Cancer is to be chosen because it is Jupiter's exaltation. This corresponds to *Mivḥarim* I, § 7.5:6, 74–75 (quoted in App. 3, P. 12, Q. 1, 6, 425–426), and *Mivḥarim* II, § 7.1:5, 162–163 (quoted in App. 3, P. 12, Q. 2, 5, 426).

[3]**3–4: Be careful ... be auspicious.** This passage has no counterpart in the Modena fragment of *Mivḥarim* III. This proves that the text of the Hebrew manuscript used to produce *Electiones* was not identical with that of *Mivḥarim* III found in the Modena fragment

[4]**4: Pisces is auspicious ... will be auspicious.** This corresponds to *Mivḥarim* I, § 7.5:4–5, 74–75 (quoted in App. 3, P. 12, Q. 1, 4–5, 425–426), and *Mivḥarim* II, § 7.1:4, 162–163 (quoted in App. 3, P. 12, Q. 2, 4, 426).

[5]**6: The sign of the place ... to besiege or plunder.** This is a reference to the sign of the country or city. For this concept, see note on *El*, II iv 2:1.

[6]**1–8: If you inquire ... seventh house.** The Hebrew source text of the present passage, with the exception of sentences 3 and 4, is extant in the Modena fragment of *Mivḥarim* III. See *Mivḥarim* III, II vii 7:1–8, 487–488.

⟨II viii 1⟩

[1]**5: Fixed ⟨signs⟩, Latin: *veridica*, lit. truthful.** This translates, through a French intermediary, the Hebrew נאמן, which has both the concrete sense "steady, unwavering" and the (more common) metaphorical sense "faithful, truthful," to denote the fixed signs (Taurus, Leo, Scorpio, Aquarius). *Interrogationes* (II i 1:3,4,5; II i 6:2,4; II iii 2:3; II vi 2:2; II ix 2:3; II x 2:4; II xii 1:5; II xii 6:3; II xii 9:4) and *Tractatus particulares* (I iii 1:3), too, use *signa veridica* to denote the fixed signs. *Nativitates* (II ii 5:9, 122–123), the Latin translation of *Moladot* II, employs *signum verax*, which is a variant literal translation of the Hebrew נאמן. Ibn Ezra generally writes מזלות עומדים "stationary signs," but occasionally uses נאמנים to denote them. See *Mishpeṭei ha-mazzalot* § 2:3, 488–489; *Tequfah*, § 18:1, 386–387; *Me'orot*, § 17:1, 466–467; *Mivḥarim* III, § 8.1:4, 222–223, and *She'elot* III, § 6.2:2, 440–441. This terminology links *Electiones* to the treatises of this group as well as to *Interrogationes* and *Tractatus particulares*.

[2]**1–5: If you wish to choose ... fixed ⟨signs⟩.** This corresponds to *Mivḥarim* II, § 8.1:1–2, 168–168. The Hebrew source text of the present passage is extant in the Modena fragment of *Mivḥarim* III. See *Mivḥarim* III, II viii 1:1–5, 488–489.

⟨II ix 1⟩

[1]**1–2: ⟨For⟩ one who inquires ... this is auspicious.** This corresponds closely to *Mivḥarim* I, § 9.3:1, 80–81 (quoted in App. 3, P. 13, Q. 1, 427).

[2]**1–5: ⟨For⟩ one who inquires ... lord of the hour.** The Hebrew source text of the present passage, with the exception of *El*, II xi 1:3, is extant in the Modena fragment of *Mivḥarim* III. See *Mivḥarim* III, II ix 1:1–5, 489.

⟨II ix 2⟩

[1]**4: Because it [the ninth place] is the house of its [the Sun's] joy.** This refers to the ninth horoscopic place, where the Sun is said to have its "joy" or "rejoices." For this concept, see note on *Int*, II iii 2:2.

[2]**5: Rising times, Latin: *ascensiones*.** This term refers to the arc on the equator that rises above the horizon in the same time as a given arc on the ecliptic. In the special case where the observer is at the terrestrial equator,

that is, when the celestial equator is perpendicular to the local horizon, the rising times or ascension are said to be at *sphaera recta* ("the right sphere"). In all other cases, reference is made to oblique rising times or ascensions, which depend on the obliquity of the ecliptic and the observer's geographical latitude. For this term and its implementation in medieval astronomical tables, see Kennedy 1956, p. 140; Chabás and Goldstein, 2012, pp. 24–29.

⟨II ix 3⟩

[1]**7: If ⟨he travels⟩ … position of Mercury**. This corresponds to *Int*, II x 2:1. See note there.

[2]**1–7: Find out the reason … position of Mercury**. This corresponds to *Mivḥarim* I, § 9.2:1–8, 80–81 (quoted in App. 3, P. 14, Q. 1, 427) and *Mivḥarim* II, § 10.3:1–5, 172–173 (quoted in App. 3, P. 14, Q. 2, 427–428). See also the chapter corresponding to the ninth horoscopic place in Sahl Ibn Bashr's *Book of Elections* (Paris, BnF, MS lat. 16204, 497a–b).

⟨II x 1⟩

[1]**1–7: One who inquires … against him and hate him.** Corresponds loosely to *Epitome*, ed. Heller (1548), IV:16, S2v–S34 and Sahl Ibn Bishr's *Book of elections*, BnF, lat. 16204, 498b–499a.

⟨II x 2⟩

[1]**1–3: If one inquires … twelfth place.** This corresponds to *Mivḥarim* II, § 10.2:1–2, 172–173 (quoted in App. 3, P. 15, Q. 1, 428). It also corresponds to *Mivḥarim* I, § 10.1:2–5, 80–83.

⟨II xi 1⟩

[1]**1–3: If one inquires … Leo is rising.** This corresponds closely to *Mivḥarim* I, § 11.1:1–3, 86–87 (quoted in App. 3, P. 16, Q. 1, 428–429) and to *Mivḥarim* II, § 11.2:1–4, 174–175 (quoted in App. 3, P. 16, Q. 2, 429).

⟨II xii 1⟩

[1]**1–2: If you are choosing ... respect the ascendant.** This corresponds closely to the following loci: (1) *Mivḥarim* I, § 12.1:3, 56–57 (quoted in App. 3, P. 17, Q. 1, 429); (2) *Mivḥarim* II, § 12.1:3–4, 176–177 (quoted in App. 3, P. 17, Q. 2, 429–430); and (3) *Epitome*, ed. Heller (1548), IV:17, S3r (quoted in App. 3, P. 17, Q. 3, 430). For the association between this place and animals that men ride on, see *Ṭeʿamim* I, § 3.3:16, 68–69 (quoted in App. 3, P. 17, Q. 4, 430). See also *Ṭeʿamim* II, § 3.3:5, 206–207.

PART THREE

LIBER INTERROGATIONUM

LATIN TEXT AND ENGLISH TRANSLATION

⟨I⟩

19v **1** (1) In nomine illius qui scit abscondita et aperta, incipiam *Librum Interrogationum.* (2) Et diviserunt se sapientes iudiciorum signorum in .2. societates. (3) Una societas dixit quod iura sunt experta in capite clavium: adesse gradus .2000.; et signa super .2000.;[1] rursus[2] centha et 20, et id est et cum[3] 120[4] modis coniunctionum planetarum; et in principio quorumlibet 75 annorum, et coniunctionum Saturni cum Marte in signo Cancri, que est in signo seculi; in fine decursus[5] totius anni; et partes et ductus; et iura singularium cum dispositione signi ascendentis et tempore nativitatis cum revolutionibus annorum nati; et ductus et partes. (4) Rursus ipsi dicunt quod iura interrogationum rursus ipsa iura, et radix locus Lune, et gradus ascendentis, et cum hiis stella que est prepositus. (5) Et dixerunt quod non interrogabit interrogans nisi rem decentem, qua significabit tempus super ipsam, super hoc potuerunt scire interrogationem interrogantis non sit deridens vel temptator, imo[6] teneat semet ipsum in hora qua ascendet cogitatio in corde suo ad accipiendum punctum hore ut sciat gradum ascendentem. (6) Et aliqui eorum dicunt quod ipsi ponent signa quando erit ita, quando videbunt hominem solum, tunc petet ab eo homo[7] super verbo scito, accipiat tunc punctum hore. (7) Et homines huius societatis sunt multi: Doronius[8] rex; Canba Aliendi; Mesehalla Halehendi; et Bugam, rex persicus; Aomar Tiberiadis; et Sahal Iudeus; et Even Mahasar Sarracenus; et Jacob Alkindi; et Even Aeli Alkahi. (8) Et isti sunt sapientes magni qui addiderunt libros
20r multos | et ipsi sunt illi qui inveniuntur in lingua sarracenaca.

2 (1) Et societas secunda,[9] cuius caput est Enoch, filius Ige, rex; et Bartholomeus rex; et Thebit, filius Kha Alharani; Albategni Gehii Sarraceni;

[1]et signa super .2000.] E; V[m]. [2]rursus] EV russus. [3]cum] E; V om. [4]120*] V; E .720. [5]fine decursus*] corrected according to the context; E finis decursos; V finis decrusos. [6]imo] E; V ymo. [7]homo] E; V hoc. [8]Doronius] E; V Doroteus. [9]secunda] E; V om.

⟨Book of Interrogations⟩

⟨I⟩

1 (1) In the name of the One who knows what is concealed and what is exposed, I will begin the *Book of interrogations*. (2) The scholars of the judgments of the signs divided themselves into two groups.[1] (3) One group said that the doctrines ⟨of astrology⟩ are known by experience under the heading of general rules: the degrees are with ⟨cycles of⟩ 2,000 ⟨years⟩; the signs are with ⟨cycles of⟩ 2,000 ⟨years⟩;[2] ⟨there are⟩ also 120, that is, 120 modes of planetary conjunctions;[3] at the beginning of any ⟨cycle⟩ of 75 years[4] and of the conjunctions of Saturn and Mars in Cancer, which is the sign of the world;[5] at the end of a whole year; ⟨there are⟩ lots[6] and directions[7] ⟨related to these conjunctions⟩; ⟨there are⟩ doctrines related to individuals according to the configuration of the ascendant sign at the time of birth, with the revolutions of the years of the newborn;[8] and ⟨there are⟩ directions an lots ⟨related to these doctrines about individuals⟩. (4) They also say that the doctrines related to interrogations are themselves ⟨true⟩ doctrines, and ⟨that their⟩ root is the position of the Moon, the degree of the ascendant, and with them the planet that is the ruler.[9] (5) They said that the querent should not pose a question except if it is about an appropriate matter, that the time ⟨of the question⟩ signifies ⟨the matter of the question⟩, ⟨a time⟩ according to which they can know that he [the querent] is not mocking or cheating, indeed a ⟨question⟩ that he [the querent] has at the time the thought ⟨of the question⟩ rises in his heart, so that ⟨the astrologer⟩ takes the moment and ⟨from it he⟩ can know the ascendant degree ⟨of the interrogational horoscope⟩.[10] (6) Some of them say that they imagine a sign when this happens, when they see that the man [the querent] is alone, then the man [the querent] asks him [the astrologer] about the aforesaid thing, then he [the astrologer] uses that moment ⟨to cast the interrogational horoscope⟩. (7) There are many men in this group: King Dorotheus;[11] Kanakah the Indian;[12] Māshā'allāh the Indian;[13] Buzurjmihr?, the Persian king;[14] ʿUmar ⟨b. al-Farrukhān⟩ al-Ṭabarī;[15] Sahl the Jew;[16] Abū Maʿshar the Arabian;[17] Yaʿqub al-Kindī;[18] and Abū ʿAlī ⟨Yaḥyā ibn Ghālib⟩ al-Khayyāṭ.[19] (8) These are great scholars who wrote many books, which were found written in the Arabic language.

2 (1) The second group is headed by King Enoch, the son of Jared;[1] King Ptolemy;[2] Thābit ibn Qurra al-Ḥarrānī;[3] al-Battānī ibn Jābir the Arab;[4]

et Hessen Iudeus, et Alihi. (2) Et ipsi fatentur in verbis donorum planetarum, et coniunctionum Saturni cum Marte in domo Lune, et derident se super verbis computationum et finium[1] de 75 annis, et verbis[2] partium in singularibus et universalibus. (3) Et confitentur in verbis nativitatum et revolutiones earum, et diminutionantur verba interrogationum et dicunt quod ipse sunt quasi verba sortium.

3 (1) Et ego Abraham, qui addo hunc librum, concordo me verbis societatis secunde, sicut pluries temptavi. (2) Rursus semper temptavi in verbis interrogationum et ipse sunt radices et probate, si fuerit acceptus punctus quo iam ascendit cogitatio in corde cogitantis qua[3] non retinebit. (3) Quia si remansit gradus ascendens poterit esse quod ibi erit stella, et propter recentionem suam usquequo ibit[4] interrogans ad domum sapientis signorum ad accipiendum tunc horam erit stella in parte .12. domus. (4) Et veritatem dixerunt quod non debet se ponere sapiens in verbis temptatoris.

4 (1) Nunc incipiam loqui super interrogationibus. (2) Ad alleviandum super discipulos mentionem feci cuiuslibet interrogationis in domo decente, scilicet cum manieribus domorum quorum mentionem feci in *Principio libri de sensu*.

⟨II i⟩
Domus prima

1 (1) Secundum quod dixerunt sapientes qui est gradus ascendens—qui fuit sub terra antequam inciperet ascendere, et ipse incipit ascendere super[5] superficiem terre in oppositio habitantium—ipse assimilabitur infanti exeunti[6] de utero[7] matris sue ad aerem seculi, et ita illud quod erit in corde cogitantis absconditum. (2) Dixerunt ipsi respice semper ad tria: unum est ad signa; secundum est ad dispositionem domorum respectu gradus ascendentis; tertium est ad dispositionem planetarum respectu Solis. (3) Et scias quod signa veridica significant super illud quod debet esse res interrogata, et erit disposita et probata et vera, et longitudi-

[1]finium*] corrected; EV finem. [2]verbis*] corrected; EV verba. [3]qua] E; V et. [4]ibit*] V; E ibi. [5]Super] E; V om. [6]exeunti] E; V exeunte. [7]utero] E; V ventre.

Ḥassān the Jew;[5] and Alihi.[6] (2) They acknowledge matters related to the effects of the planets, and to the Saturn-Mars conjunctions in the Moon's house, but they laugh at matters related to the computations of the ends ⟨of the cycles⟩ of 75 years, and matters concerning the lots related to individuals and groups.[7] (3) They acknowledge matters related to nativities and their revolutions, and they disparage matters related to interrogations and say that they are like matters related to divination.[8]

3 (1) I, Abraham, who authored this book,[1] agree with the statements of the other group, as I have tested ⟨them⟩ many times. (2) I also have always tested matters related to interrogations and ⟨found them⟩ to be roots and tested, on condition that the moment taken ⟨for the interrogational horoscope⟩ is when the thought ⟨of the question⟩ rose in the heart of the person who thinks ⟨about the question⟩ and that he does not delay it. (3) Because if the ⟨appropriate⟩ ascendant degree is ignored it may be that a planet was there [in the ascendant degree], but as a result of the delay until ⟨the querent⟩ goes to the house of the scholar of the signs to take then the time ⟨of the question⟩, the planet will be in the 12th ⟨horoscopic⟩ place.[2] (4) They said that the truth is that a wise person should not be tricked by the statements of one who cheats.[3]

4 (1) I will now begin to discuss interrogations. (2) To make it easier for students, I mention each question in the appropriate ⟨horoscopic⟩ place, according to the properties of the places which I mentioned in the *Book of the beginning of wisdom* [*lit.* in the beginning of the Book of Wisdom].[1,2]

⟨II i⟩
The First Place

1 (1) According to what the astrologers said, the ascendant degree—which was below the Earth before it began to rise, and starts to rise above the surface of the Earth facing the inhabitants ⟨of the Earth⟩—is like the child who emerges from the womb of his mother into the air of the world, and so is the thing hidden in the heart of the person who thinks.[1] (2) They said to always observe these three: first, the signs; second, the configuration of the ⟨horoscopic⟩ places with respect to the ascendant degree; third, the configuration of the planets with respect to the Sun.[2] (3) Know that the fixed signs[3] signify what should be the matter of the question, and ⟨that the matter of the question⟩ will be arranged, proved and true, and ⟨what

nem termini. (4) Et ista ostendunt .4or. caville sicut faciunt signa veridica. (5) Et similiter locus in dispositione Solis, quia reflammatio stelle servientis
20v et dispositio sui motus et sua coniunctio cum Sole in uno gradu, ostendunt | sicut faciunt signa veridica et caville.

2 (1) Et ego Abraham Addens confiteor illis inflammatione planete, et ratio est propter hoc quod ipse ascendit in orientem antequam reflammetur {Sole}[1] si fuerit planeta superior e directo circuli Solis et si fuerit planeta inferior occidentali fortior est quam si sit orientalis. (2) Si Venus aut Mercurius coniungantur cum Sole in uno gradu et ipsi sint retrogradi non erit res integra.

3 (1) Et signa mobilia significant quod non erit res et non levabit nisi quod significant super motionem interrogantis a suo gradu, vel super cupiditatem cordis et desiderium eius super rem que non erit, et super commotionem eius a suo loco, et super expavescentia et timore (sic), et non erit firmum bonum quod cogitabit vel malum. (2) Et idem significant domus cadentes a cavillis que sunt .3a. .6a. .9a. .12a. (3) Et si interrogatio fuerit super re bona non adveniet, et si super mala re adveniet si fuerit planeta in .6a. vel .12.[2] domo. (4) Si ad monendum fuerit interrogatio facta scilicet,[3] vel ad timorem quin[4] aufferatur quis a suo gradu, significabit super ipsum domus .3a. et[5] nona. (5) Et ita significabunt verba combustionis stelle a Sole et retrogradatio planete ab opposito Solis, sicut significant signa mobilia et domus cadentes.

4 (1) Et signa que sunt domini[6] duorum corporum et domus succedentes, que sunt .2a. .5a. .8a. .11a., significant super illiud quod debet esse verbum quesiti post spem, et quod duplicabitur res, et revertentur alias, et excrementum erit. (2) Et .2a. et .8a. significant super illud quod debet esse res sed non super via cogitationis quam cogitabit, et cadet propter hoc quod non est aspectus inter illas domos et gradus ascendentis. (3) Et ita ostendent planete superiores quando ipsi sunt occidentales aut quando sunt in aliqua stationum suarum.

[1]sole] corrected; EV Sol. [2].12.] E; V^{m}. [3]fuerit interrogacio facta scilicet*] V; E^{m}. [4]quin*] E; V quando. [5]et] E; V vel. [6]domini] E; V om (erased).

will be⟩ the length of the duration ⟨of the matter of the question⟩. (4) The four cardines indicate these things just as the fixed signs do. (5) Likewise, the position ⟨of the planet⟩ in ⟨its⟩ configuration with the Sun, because the burning[4] of the planet,[5] the configuration of its motion, and its conjunction with the Sun in one degree, ⟨all these⟩ indicate ⟨the same thing⟩ as the fixed signs and the cardines do.[6]

2 (1) I Abraham, the author,[1] admit these things owing to the burning[2] of the planet, and the reason is because it [the planet] ascends in the east before it is burnt by the Sun if the planet is above the line of the Sun's orb, and if the planet is lower this is stronger when it is occidental ⟨of the Sun⟩ than when it is oriental ⟨of the Sun⟩. (2) If Venus and Mercury are in conjunction with the Sun in one degree and they are themselves retrograde, ⟨the outcome of⟩ the matter will not be full.[3]

3 (1) The tropical signs signify that the thing ⟨asked about⟩ will not come to be or arise unless they signify the demotion of the querent from his rank, or greed and his desire for something that will not come to be, and his removal from his location, ⟨his⟩ terror and fear, and that what he thinks will not be permanent for good or for evil. (2) The places which are cadent from the cardines, which are the third, sixth, ninth, and twelfth,[1] signify the same. (3) If the question is about a fortunate matter it will not come to pass, and if about an unfortunate thing it will come to pass if the planet is in the sixth or twelfth place. (4) If the question is about a warning, or about the fear that someone will be removed from his rank, this is signified by the third and ninth places. (5) They also signify things related to the burning[2] of the planet by the Sun and by the retrogradation of a planet from opposition to the Sun, just as the tropical signs and the cadent places do.[3]

4 (1) The bicorporal signs[1] and the succedent ⟨horoscopic⟩ places, which are the second, fifth, eighth, and eleventh, signify that the thing asked about will come to pass after hope ⟨is lost⟩, that the thing ⟨asked about⟩ will happen twice, that other things will come back, and that there will be an increase ⟨of the thing asked about⟩. (2) The second and eighth ⟨places⟩ signify that the thing will happen but not in the way that was in the ⟨querent's⟩ mind, and that it will happen because there is no aspect between these places and the ascendant degree. (3) The upper planets indicate the same when they are occidental ⟨of the Sun⟩ or when they are in one of their stations.[2,3]

5 (1) Dicit Abraham subtiliter:[1] quando planeta superior fuerit in statione sua secunda, tunc erit verbum alia recordatio et cogitatio que non erit. (2) Sed si fuerit in statione prima, fere erit cogitatio integra sed tamen parate sunt occasiones, et renovabuntur opera per que resistet res, et non erit firma, scilicet et non firmabitur. (3) Et in via stationis se erit in fortitudine,
21r similiter est[2] fortitudo superioris planete si fuerit orientalis | a Sole et fuerint inter eos .9. gradus, et etiam ita est fortitudo planetarum inferiorum si fuerint occidentales a Sole et fuerint inter eos .12. gradus.

6 (1) Et scito quod domini corporum significant super terminum mediocrem, et signa mobilia super terminos multum propinquos (2) Et si fuerint signa veridica super annis, significabunt domini corporum super mensibus et mobilia signa super diebus; et si signa veridica significaverint menses, domini corporum significabunt septimanas et mobilia signa horas cum natura rei interrogate. (3) Et scias quod stelle inferiores significant super festinationem et superiores super dilationem cum ascencione ipsorum in circulo suo et ita domus earum. (4) Propter hoc signum Aquarii verius est quam alia[3] tria veridica scilicet.[4] (5) Et post ipsum Leo propter hoc[5] quod Sol est altus. (6) Et quia Taurus est signum terreum ipsum est verius quam Scorpio. (7) Et Scorpio omnibus propter festinationem domini signi est minus verax, scilicet, et hanc falsitatem et festinationem. (8) Et propter hoc dicunt ipsi quod est signum falsitatis; et nullam interrogationem quam interrogabit interrogans iudices cuius ascendens fuerit Scorpio quia falsum erit tuum iudicium. (9) Et non poteris scire veritatem rei quam demonstrabit Mars in figura et ita erit si fuerit Mars in aliqua cavillarum, dum tamen hoc sit super verbis bellorum et malorum. (10) Et ita dicit Even Maasar Scezen discipulus eius se semper de rebus regalibus in interrogationibus ut in pluribus non iudices si Scorpio fuerit ascendens vel Mars. (11) Et non est ita de signo Arietis, quando ipsum est signum iusti, quando dies et nox equantur in capite suo in omni loco, et propter hoc significat ipsum super locis servicii dei. (12) Et adhuc ipsum est domus honoris claritatis magne et non ita Scorpio quia ipsum est domus vilitatis claritatis parve scilicet Lune.[6] (13) Et domus Mercurii sunt festinantiores quam domus Iovis qui est altus. (14) Nec est in signis mobilibus levioribus Cancro, eo quod ipsum est domus Lune.

[1]subtiliter*] corrected according to the context; EV subtilis. [2]est] E; V et. [3]alia] E; V > signa. [4]veridica scilicet*] V, E^m. [5]hoc] E; V om. [6]scilicet lune] E above the line; V om.

5 (1) Abraham says with fineness of judgment: when an upper planet is in its second station, then the thing ⟨asked about⟩ will come to pass ⟨after⟩ another memory and the thought that it will not come true. (2) But if it is in the first station, the thing thought about will come to pass almost completely, although circumstances will cause that new things will happen by which the thing ⟨asked about⟩ will be thwarted, and will not be certain, that is, will not take place.[1] (3) Between the stations it [the planet] will be in ⟨its⟩ power; the same applies to the power of the upper planet if it is oriental of the Sun and there is 9° between them [the upper planet and the Sun], and so too the power of the lower planets if they are occidental of the Sun and there are 12° between them.

6 (1) Know that the bicorporal signs[1] signify an intermediate period ⟨of time⟩, the tropical signs ⟨signify⟩ periods ⟨of time in the⟩ very near ⟨future⟩. (2) If the fixed signs indicate years, the bicorporal signs signify months and the tropical signs ⟨signify⟩ days; and if the fixed signs indicate months, ⟨then⟩ the bicorporal signs signify weeks and the tropical signs ⟨signify⟩ hours in connection with the nature of the requested matter.[2] (3) Know that the lower planets indicate quickness and the upper ⟨planets⟩ delay in connection with their ascension in their circle and also their ⟨horoscopic⟩ place. (4) In regard to this, the sign of Aquarius is more truthful than the other three fixed ⟨signs⟩. (5) After it [Aquarius] comes Leo, because the Sun [i.e., the lord of Leo] is high. (6) Since Taurus is an earthy sign it is more truthful than Scorpio. (7) Scorpio is the least truthful of all because of the quickness of the lord of the sign [i.e., Mars], that is, ⟨because of its⟩ falsehood and quickness. (8) Consequently they say that it [Scorpio] is the sign of falsehood; do not pronounce judgment on any question asked by a querent in which it [Scorpio] is the ascendant, because your judgment will be false. (9) You cannot know the truth of what Mars shows in a configuration, and the same applies if Mars is in one of the cardines, on condition that this relates to wars and disasters.[3] (10) Accordingly, Scezen, Abū Ma‘shar's disciple,[4] says: always, in affairs related to kings, in many questions, do not pronounce judgment if Scorpio or Mars is ascending.[5] (11) But this is not so regarding Aries, since it is a just sign, because the day and the night become equal in every place ⟨on Earth⟩ ⟨when the Sun enters⟩ its [Aries's] head, and consequently it signifies the places of divine worship.[6] (12) Besides, it [Aries] is the house of exaltation[7] of the great luminary [the Sun], and not so Scorpio, because it is the house of dejection[8] of the lesser luminary, that is, the Moon. (13) Mercury's houses speed up things more than Jupiter's houses, which is an upper ⟨planet⟩.[9] (14) Cancer is not one of the more harmful of the tropical signs, because it is the Moon's house.

7 (1) Et debes respicere in omni interrogatione ad tria memorata, scilicet, signa, domus, planetas, quod si coniungantur illa tria scias quod tu iudicabis interrogationem integram et perfectam sine diminutione quoniam
21v tu habes 3 testimonia. (2) | Et si fuerint .2. testimonia, eveniet maior pars rei et minuetur parvum. (3) Et non iudices per os testimonii unius,[1] scilicet,[2] et si fuerit testimonium forte multum erit parvum de re quesita. (4) Et demonstrant hoc et super interrogationem, dominus signi ascendentis, rursus Luna, quoniam ipsa demonstrat super omni interrogatione quia ipsa assimilatur[3] nato et omni interrogationi ascendenti in cor (sic!) in principio hore. (5) Et si unus eorum aspiciat gradum ascendentem et alius[4] est cadens, accipe aspicientem. (6) Et si ambo aspiciunt, scilicet, ascendentem, illud quod est forte in loco suo. (7) Et si ambo sunt fortia, antecede Lunam et associa cum signo ascendente. (8) Et si ambo eorum fuerint cadentia et unum eorum aspiciat stellam que est in ascendente aut que aspicit ipsum, accipe aspiciens, et melius est si ipsum habet fortitudinem aliquam in ascendente.

8 (1) Et si fuerit Luna ostensor, id est significator, accipe dominum signi quod est ibi ad sciendum finem et ⟨⟨lemploias⟩⟩. (2) Et si dominus ascendentis fuerit ostensor, quere dominum .4e. domus, id est, in quo est Luna, ad sciendum finem, in ascencionibus tabule terre. (3) Et similiter si fuerit Luna in signo Cancri, et si dederit dominus ascendentis vel Luna fortitudinem stelle aspicienti, scias quod ipsa significabit super finem. (4) Et si fuerit eidem stelle planeta aspicientia, scias quod ultimum significabit super finem.

9 (1) Dicit Abraham Additor: semper respice ad prepositum cui insunt plures fortitudines in gradu ascendente, et in locis claritatum, et in locis coniunctionum vel oppositionum eorum qui transierunt, et respice scilicet[5] partem gratie et dominum diei et dominum hore. (2) Et ipsi demonstrant illud si aspexerunt gradum ascendentem vel dominum rei quesite. (3) Et

[1]unius] V; E above the line. [2]scilicet] E above the line; V om. [3]assimilatur] E; V assignatur. [4]alius] corrected according to the context; E alius alius; V aliud. [5]respice scilicet] E (above the line); V om.

7 (1) In every question you need to consider the aforementioned three, that is, the signs, the ⟨horoscopic⟩ places, ⟨and⟩ the planets,[1] for, if these three agree, know that you will pronounce judgment about a complete and perfect question, without any reduction, because you have three testimonies. (2) If there are two testimonies, the greater part ⟨of the question⟩ will come to pass and will be reduced a little. (3) Do not pronounce judgment according to one testimony ⟨alone⟩,[2] but if the testimony is very strong a small part of the thing asked about will come to pass. (4) The lord of the ascendant sign, as well as the Moon, signifies this [i.e., the thing asked about] and the question; ⟨the Moon⟩ because it signifies every question, since it [the Moon] resembles the native and every question that rises into the heart at the beginning of the hour ⟨of the question⟩. (5) If one of them [i.e., the lord of the ascendant or the Moon] aspects the ascendant degree and the other is cadent,[3] take the one that aspects. (6) If both are aspecting, that is, the ascendant, ⟨take⟩ the one that is strong in its position. (7) If both are strong, give preference to the Moon and associate ⟨it⟩ with the ascendant sign. (8) If both are cadent and one of them aspects a planet that is in the ascendant or that aspects it [the ascendant], take the one that aspects, and it is better if it has some power in the ascendant.[4]

8 (1) If the Moon is the indicator, that is, the significator, take the lord of the sign where it [the Moon] is located to know the outcome and ⟨⟨use it⟩⟩. (2) If the lord of the ascendant is the indicator, find out the lord of the fourth place ⟨from the ascendant⟩, that is, in which the Moon is, according to the rising times of the tables for the country, to know the outcome. (3) Likewise, if the Moon is in Cancer, and if the lord of the ascendant or the Moon gives power to a planet that forms an aspect ⟨with the ascendant⟩, know that it [the planet that forms an aspect with the ascendant] signifies the outcome. (4) If there is a planet aspecting this star [the planet that forms an aspect with the ascendant], know that the latter [the planet aspecting the planet that forms an aspect with the ascendant] signifies the outcome.[1]

9 (1) Abraham, the author, says: always observe the ruler to which are assigned most of the powers in the ascendant degree, in the positions of the luminaries, in the positions of the conjunctions or the oppositions ⟨of the luminaries⟩ which have taken place, and observe the lot of Fortune,[1,2] and the lord of the day, and the lord of the hour.[3] (2) These signify this [i.e., the object of the querent's interrogation] if they have aspected the ascendant degree or the lord of the thing asked about. (3) Know that the

scias quod fortitudo domini hore est sicut dominus domus. (4) Et si fuerit dominus in una cavillarum, vel Luna et fuerit ei significator, id est, fuerit significator rei, scias quod interrogatio est super magna re. (5) Et si coniungatur significator vel det fortitudinem stelle bone vel male existenti in .6a. domo vel .12., non surget res, et aspectus .4us. similiter oppositio ambo mali, insimul stelle dampnificantes. (6) Et si dederit significator fortitudinem vel quod coniungatur cum stella mala in malo aspectu, et significator
22r fuerit in aliqua cavillarum, et insit fortitudo stelle male in loco significatoris; vel quod coniungatur significator vel det fortitudinem stelle retrograde, et insit eidem stelle fortitudo in loco significatoris, qui est dominus alicuius cavillarum, erit res quesita post desperationem.[1]

10 (1) Dicit Abraham: hoc est rectum et probatum: si fuerit stella postquam ipsa transierit oppositum Solis, et si fuerit significator in domo .4a. et ipsa sit scilicet[2] signum mobile, et interogatio scilicet fuerit super re potente, non surget. (2) Dicit Abraham: hoc est iustum quod iudicaverunt sapientes signorum propter hoc quod domus .4a. est in opposito domus .10e., que ostendit super honorem, et quarta ostendit super locum imum et profundum, et carcerem, in quo non est claritas, et foveam super locum imum, quia .10a. ostendit, in *Libro nativitatum* in domo sexta, super mast.

11 (1) Dicit Mesehala: semper respice ad tria: unum est signum ascendens et dominus eius, et domus in qua est res quesita et dominum eius, et significatorem, quod est Luna et dominum eius, et ratio est dominus domus eius. (2) Est autem contentio in verbis interrogationum, et veritas est illa que tibi dicam. (3) Nam si interrogator interrogat de se ipso, pone signum ascendens quemadmodum signum nativitatis sue; et si ipse interrogat pro re thesauri sui, pone domum secundam et dominos eius; et si super rebus fratrum suorum in via propinqua, quere .3am. domum; et ita de omnibus domibus sicut ostendunt sicut scriptum est in *Principio libri de sensu*. (4) Et si interrogaverit super rege, qui erit, respice ad locum Solis et domum ascendentem et dominos eius; et si pro latrone, locum Martis et .7am. domum.

[1]desperationem] E; V disperacionem. [2]scilicet] E; V vel.

power of the lord of the hour is like ⟨the power of⟩ the lord of the house.[4] (4) If the lord is in one of the cardines or the Moon is its significator, that is, the significator of the thing ⟨asked about⟩, know that that the question is about a great thing. (5) If the significator is in conjunction with or gives power to a benefic or malefic planet[5] located in the sixth or twelfth place, the thing ⟨asked about⟩ will not come to pass, and quartile and opposition are both inauspicious, just like the harmful planets. (6) If the significator gives power to or is in conjunction with a malefic planet in an inauspicious aspect, and the significator is in one of the cardines, the power of the malefic planet is exerted instead of that of the significator; or ⟨if⟩ the significator is in conjunction with or gives power to a retrograde planet, and the power of this planet is exerted instead of that of the significator, which is the lord of one of the cardines, the thing asked about will come to pass after despair.

10 (1) Abraham says: this is right and has been tested: if a planet has passed opposition to the Sun, and if the significator is in the fourth place and it [the fourth place] is [i.e., coincides with] a tropical sign, and the question is about a powerful matter, it [the thing asked about] will not come to pass. (2) Abraham says: what the scholars of the signs judged is correct because the fourth place is in opposition to the tenth place, which signifies honor, and ⟨because⟩ the fourth ⟨place⟩ signifies the lowest and deep place, and prison, in which there is no light, and the pit above the lowest place, ⟨and⟩ because the tenth ⟨place⟩ signifies the mast in the ⟨chapter on the⟩ sixth place of the *Book of nativities*.[1]

11 (1) Māshā'allāh says: always observe ⟨these⟩ three: one is the ascendant sign and its lord, ⟨the second is⟩ the place in which is the thing asked about and its lord, and ⟨the third is⟩ the significator, which is the Moon, and its lord, meaning the lord of its [the Moon's] house.[1] (2) There is a dispute about matters related to interrogations, and the truth is what I shall tell you ⟨now⟩. (3) For if the querent asks about himself, put the ascendant sign ⟨of the interrogational horoscope⟩ in the same way as his nativity; and if he asks about his money, put the second place ⟨of the interrogational horoscope⟩ and its lords; and if ⟨he asks⟩ about his brothers in a short journey, seek the third place ⟨of the interrogational horoscope⟩; and likewise for all the places according to what they signify,[2] as written in the *Book of the beginning of wisdom*.[3] (4) If he asks about a king, whoever he may be, observe the position of the Sun and the ascendant place and its lords; and if about a thief, ⟨observe⟩ the position of Mars and the seventh place.

12 (1) Et super duobus bellatoribus, unus contra alterum, de hoc est contentio. (2) Dicit Even Maasar: pone signum ascendens et dominum eius pro parvo in annis, id est iuniori, et .7m. pro magno in annis, id est seniori in annis. (3) Et Mesehalla dicit pones ascendens pro illo quem diligis et .7m. pro inimico. (4) Et verum est si fuerit unus eorum interrogans ad dominum signorum, quem ostendit gradus ascendens sibi et .7m. ad inimicum suum. (5) Et si nullus eorum fuerit interrogans, ipse debet cogitare in corde suo in principio pro quo eorum ipse ponet ascendens et .7m. erit pro adversario suo.

22v **13** (1) Et si interrogaverit | ad dominum signorum pro homine alio, utrum scilicet sit vivus vel mortuus, respice ad signum ascendens et dominos eius et significatorem qui eius est Luna. (2) Dicit Doronius rex: si quis homo[1] interrogat de se ipso, et ratio sit pro opere suo, pone ascendens pro interrogante. (3) Si fuerit aspiciens vel coniungens se cum domino domus, res interrogata surget dum tamen[2] receptor fortitudinis non fuerit in .6a. domo vel .12. aut combustus vel retrogradus. (4) Et si fuerit aspectus coniunctionis inter dominum ascendentis et dominum domus rei quesite in loco bono respectu ascendentis et respectu Solis, et receptus fuerit in loco suo, erit res. (5) Et ita iudicabis si fuerit significator eius, est[3] Luna, aspiciens vel coniungens se cum domino domus rei quesite. (6) Et si videris quod res fuerit recta propter aspectum vel coniunctionem, respice quot gradus sumitur inter illos .2. planetas, et da cuilibet gradui horam vel diem vel septimanam vel mensem vel annum secundum naturam rei quesite, vel quando attinget stella in semet ipsa ad locum stelle alterius in motu suo qui mutatur in circulo suo aut ad locum finis aspectus stelle, sive fuerit aspectus .6lis. dester vel sinister sive aspectus .4us. vel trinus.

14 (1) Et non obliviscaris scire naturam stellarum planetarum quoniam propinquiores terre in circulo suo festinantiores sunt, rursus cum hoc locus planete respectu Solis. (2) Et si fuerit interrogatio suspecta, ipse respondet ad hoc quod ipse dixit si res fuerit recta ⟪sil le vera sil non regarde⟫[4] dominum .11e. domus utrum fuerit in ascendente receptus, eveniet res.

[1]homo] E; V hoc. [2]tamen] E; V om. [3]est] E; V scilicet. [4]sil le vera sil non regarde] E underlined with a red line.

12 (1) There is a dispute about two combatants, one against the other. (2) Abū Maʿshar says: put the ascendant sign and its lord for the fewer in years, that is, the younger, and the seventh ⟨place⟩ for the one with more years, that is, the older in years. (3) Māshāʾallāh says: put the ascendant ⟨of the interrogational horoscope⟩ for the one you love and the seventh place for the enemy.[1] (4) This is true if one of them [i.e. one of the two combatants] is the one who poses the question to the expert in astrology,[2] and ⟨in this case⟩ this one is signified by the ascendant degree and his enemy ⟨is signified⟩ by the seventh ⟨place⟩. (5) But if none of them poses the question, ⟨the querent⟩ himself should think in his heart at the beginning which of them he would put the ascendant for, and the seventh ⟨sign⟩ will be assigned to his opponent.[3]

13 (1) If he poses a question to the expert in astrology on behalf of someone else, whether he is alive or dead, observe the ascendant sign and its lord and its significator, which is the Moon.[1] (2) King Dorotheus says: if someone poses a question about himself, meaning about his own deeds, put the ascendant for the querent.[2] (3) If it [the ascendant] is in an aspect or in conjunction with the lord of the house, the thing asked about will come to pass on condition that the receiver of power[3] is not in the sixth or twelfth place,[4] and is not burnt or retrograde. (4) If an aspect of conjunction is formed in an auspicious position with respect to the ascendant and the Sun between the lord of the ascendant and the lord of the place ⟨signifying⟩ the thing asked about, and the ⟨planet that is⟩ received is in its place, the thing ⟨asked about⟩ will come to pass. (5) Judge in this way if its significator, the Moon, is in an aspect or in conjunction with the lord of the place ⟨signifying⟩ the thing asked about. (6) If you see that the thing is suitable because of an aspect or a conjunction, observe how many degrees are between the two planets, and assign to each degree an hour, day, week, month, or year according to the nature of the thing asked about,[5] or ⟨take into account⟩ when the planet arrives at the position of the other planet in its motion along its circle or at the position of the end of the aspect of the planet, whether the aspect is of right or left sextile, quartile, or trine.

14 (1) Do not forget to know the nature of the planets,[1] because the closer their circle is to the Earth, the quicker they are; furthermore, together with this, ⟨know⟩ the position of the planet with respect to the Sun. (2) If the question is suspicious, he [the querent] will answer to what he himself said if the thing ⟨asked about⟩ ⟨⟨was suitable; if not observe⟩⟩ the lord of the eleventh place; if it is received in the ascendant, the thing ⟨asked about⟩

(3) Et si dederit fortitudinem alie stelle respice ad locum stelle alterius; et ita iudicabis super finem res quesite.

15 (1) Et si interrogaverit interrogator pro vita sua respice in .5. locis principatus et fac sicut precepi tibi in *Libro nativitatum*. (2) Sed tu debes advertere quod non des annos stelle magnos magnis in annos, id est, senibus, quoniam si fuerit stella in loco significante super annis magnis da ei annos mediocres, et si in loco significante super mediocribus da ei minores, et radi-
23r cem ductuum. (3) Dicit | Ptholomeus[1] in *Libro .c. verborum*: si fecerit homo[2] interrogationem pro se ipso, ipsa est sicut nativitas; et ab illo tempore et deinceps scias revolutionem cuilibet anni. (4) Et ita si interrogaverit super villa aliqua et patria que venierit super ipsam (5) Et super serviente scito et super finem omnis res ipse, videbit revolutionem eorum de anno in annum quemadmodum fuisse in puncto etatis ville.

⟨II ii⟩
Domus secunda

1 (1) Si interrogator interrogat super diviciis, si ei assueverint, vide si fuerit dominus ascendentis aut prepositus aspiciens vel coniungens se cum domino secunde domus, aut et prepositus sit in domo secunda vel Luna aspiciens ipsum vel coniungens se cum eo; surget res. (2) Et dominus secunde domus fuerit in ascendente, divicie sibi deerunt sine labore, et ita iudicabis si fuerit in aliqua cavillarum et fuerit receptus in loco suo nec fuerit combustus a Sole nec retrogradus. (3) Et si invenias significatorem aut prepositum aspicientem stellam cui dederit fortitudinem dominus secunde domus, vel coniungentem se cum ea sive aspiciendo sive coniungendo, erit res quesita, hoc est thesaurum, per manum mediam vel mediocrem secundum naturam stelle mediocris quemadmodum scriptum est in *Libro capitis sensus*.

2 (1) Et ille qui interrogat super re emali vel venali, pone ascendens pro venditore et .7m. pro emptore.[3] (2) Si fuerit inter eos aspectus vel coniunc-

[1]Ptholomeus] V; E Tpholomeus. [2]homo] E; V hoc. [3]emptore] E; V empcione.

will come to pass. (3) If it gives power to another planet, observe the place of the other planet; judge in this way about the outcome of the thing asked about.

15 (1) If the querent poses a question about his lifespan, consider the five places of dominion[1] and proceed as I instructed you in the *Book of nativities*.[2] (2) But be careful not to assign the great years of a planet to ⟨those who are⟩ great in years, that is, the elderly, because if the planet is in a position which signifies the great years you should assign him [the elderly querent] the middle years,[3] and if in a position which signifies the middle ⟨years⟩ assign him the least ⟨years⟩ and the root of the directions.[4,5] (3) Ptolemy says in the *Book of the 100 statements*: if someone poses a question about himself, this is like a nativity;[6] from this time on you should know the revolution of each year.[7] (4) The same applies if he poses a question about a city and a country to which he comes.[8] (5) About a suitable servant and about the outcome of everything he should observe their revolution from year to year, just as in any moment of the history of a city.

⟨II ii⟩
The Second ⟨Place⟩

1 (1) If the querent poses a question about riches, whether he will be accustomed to them, observe whether the lord of the ascendant or the ruler is in an aspect or in conjunction with the lord of the second place, or if the ruler is in the second place, or if the Moon aspects it [the ruler] or is in conjunction with it; ⟨in this case⟩ the thing ⟨asked about⟩ will come to pass. (2) ⟨If⟩ the lord of the second place is in the ascendant, riches will be at his disposition without effort,[1,2] and judge in this manner if it [the lord of the second place] is in one of the cardines or is received in its position and is neither burnt nor retrograde. (3) If you find the significator or the ruler aspecting a planet to which the lord of the second place gives power, or applying to it [the lord of the second place] in an aspect or in conjunction, the thing asked about, that is, the money, will be by an intermediary according to the nature of the intermediate planet, as is written in the *Book of the beginning of wisdom*.[3]

2 (1) ⟨For⟩ one who poses a question about buying or selling, put the ascendant for the seller and the seventh ⟨place⟩ for the buyer. (2) If there is an aspect or a conjunction between them, the sale will be made. (3) If

tio, erit peracta venditio. (3) Et si stella dederit scintillationem prima secunde, erit per manum mediocrem, et si non non vendetur. (4) Et associa in re ipsa Lunam, si fuerit ei aliud prepositure in ascendente, et scias cuius stelle sua scintillatio fuerit supra et cui dederit fortitudinem, quia prima ostendit super venditore et secunda super emptore. (5) Et vide etiam si stella prima aspexerit secundam vel coniunxerit se cum ea, tunc enim interrogabit venditionem et levabit, et si non aspexerit hic illum, non levabit.[1] (6) Et si interrogaverit super re si per⟨h⟩abitur vel totaliter vendetur in foro, vide si fuerit dominus ascendentis in cavilla; non vendetur nisi invite.
23v (7) Et si fuerit stella dampnificans | in cavillis et fuerit in loco cui non est prepositura, ostendet quod non vendetur; et si fuerit in cavilla prima erit recentio aperte; et si in .7o. ex parte emptoris; et si in .10o. ex parte vilitatis; et si in .4a. et ipsa signum mobile, exibit sub manu illius qui potestatem habet super ipsa re. (8) Et si fuerit in ascendente stella, ⟨⟨est mein est montant⟩⟩, ostendet super recentione et perditione. (9) Et si fuerit dominus secunde domus ante dominum ascendentis vel econtrario, ostendet quod recentio erit a domino illius res et una vice tota vendetur.

3 (1) Et in re furata vel perdita, .4or. possunt sciri vel interrogari: unum, utrum inveneris furtum; secundum, utrum non inveneris ipsum; tertium, utrum capietur latro; quartum, utrum evasit latro. (2) Et ita facies: vide si fuerit dominus .7. dans fortitudinem domino ascendentis aut stelle existenti in ascendente; latro reddet latrocinium dominis suis. (3) Et similiter, si fuerit dominus .7a. sub claritate Solis et dederit fortitudinem domino ascendentis, revertetur furtum per timore regis. (4) Et similiter, si stella dederit fortitudinem scintillationis Solis, scintillationis domini domus .7e., aut scintillationis stelle in .7a., domino[2] ascendentis aut stelle existenti in ascendente, ostendet quod rex adiuvabit dominum rei furtate. (5) Si Sol aspexerit dominum ascendentis aspectu amicabili et ita erit si dominus .10e. aspexerit ascendens, rursus ostendet revertionem latrocinii. (6) Si fuerit dominus .2e.

[1]et si non aspexerit hic illum non levabit] E; V om. [2]domino] E; V domo.

the planet gives the spark from the first [i.e., the ascendant] to the other [i.e., the seventh place],[1] this will be through an intermediary, and if not ⟨the thing⟩ will not be sold.[2] (4) Associate for the same matter the Moon, if it has another rulership in the ascendant, and know under the spark of which planet it [the Moon] is[3] and to which ⟨planet⟩ it [the Moon] gives power, because the first indicates the seller and the second the buyer.[4] (5) Observe in addition whether the first planet aspects the second or is in conjunction with it, then he will pose a question about selling and ⟨the sale⟩ will take place, and if ⟨the first planet⟩ does not aspect it [the second], ⟨the sale⟩ will not take place. (6) If he poses a question about whether he will own something in perpetuity or whether all of it will be sold in the market, observe whether the lord of the ascendant is in a cardo; ⟨in this case⟩ it will be sold only reluctantly. (7) If a harmful planet is in the cardines in a position where ⟨it does⟩ not have rulership, this indicates that it will not be sold; if it is in the first cardo, the retention ⟨of the merchandise⟩ will be manifest; if in the seventh ⟨cardo⟩, ⟨this will be done⟩ by the buyer; if in the tenth ⟨cardo⟩, because of the low quality; if in the fourth ⟨cardo⟩[5] and it coincides with a tropical sign, ⟨the merchandise⟩ will leave the hands of its owner. (8) If the planet is in the ascendant, ⟨⟨either in perigee or in apogee⟩⟩, it indicates retention ⟨of the merchandise⟩ and destruction. (9) If the lord of the second place is ahead of the lord of the ascendant or vice versa, this indicates that the retention ⟨of the merchandise⟩ is by its owner and that all of it will be sold at once.

3 (1) Regarding a stolen or lost article, four ⟨things⟩ may be known or asked about: first, whether you will find the stolen article; second, whether you will not find it; third, whether the thief will be caught; four, whether the thief will escape. (2) Proceed in this manner: observe whether the lord of the seventh ⟨place⟩ gives power to the lord of the ascendant or to a planet located in the ascendant; ⟨in this case⟩ the thief will return the stolen article to its owners. (3) Likewise, if the lord of the seventh ⟨place⟩ is under the light of the Sun and gives power to the lord of the ascendant, the stolen article will be returned as a result of fear of the king. (4) Likewise, if a planet gives the power of the spark of the Sun, ⟨or the power of⟩ the spark of the lord of the seventh place, or ⟨the power of⟩ the spark of a planet in the seventh ⟨place⟩, to the lord of the ascendant or to a planet located in the ascendant,[1] this indicates that the king will assist the owner of the stolen article. (5) If the Sun forms an aspect of love with the ascendant, and so too if the lord of the tenth ⟨place⟩ aspects the ascendant, it also indicates the return of the stolen article. (6) If the lord of the second place is in the ascendant,

domus in ascendente, et similiter si aspexerit dominus .7e., rursus dominum secunde, revertetur {partem secundam aut unius non habito} respectu ad dominum ascendentis. (7) Et ita erit si dederit dominus .8e. domus fortitudinem domino secunde domus et dominus ascendentis aspiciat illos .2. (8) Et similiter, si fuerit dominus .7. rursus secunde in una cavillarum, ostendet quod latro non exibit villam et quod non detulit furtum extra. (9) Rursus hoc est signum bonum si Luna dederit fortitudinem Soli vel domino ascendentis. (10) Et ostendet quod non invenietur furtum si fuerit dominus secunde domus dans fortitudinem domino ascendentis et ipse in domo cadente, et similiter si fuerit dominus .8e. dans fortitudinem domino .7e. (11) Et si dominus .2e. dederit fortitudinem domino .3e. domus aut .9e.,
24r scias quod iam detulit latro thesaurum extra villam. (12) | Et si dominus .7e. dederit fortitudinem domino .10e., ostendet quod rex adiuvabit latronem et non redibit latocinium. (13) Et ita si dederit Luna fortitudinem domino .7e., et ita erit si dominus .2e. dederit fortitudinem domino .7e.

4 (1) Et iudicium quando capietur latro. (2) Si inveneris dominum .7e. dantem fortitudinem suam domino ascendentis, et dominus .7m. fortitudinem stelle existenti in cavilla, et precipue in .10a., et similiter si dederit stella fortitudinem stelle dampnificanti, et similiter si dominus .7e. domus fuerit combustus in claritate Solis, accipiet eum rex.

5 (1) Et iudicium quando non invenietur latrocinium. (2) Si dederit dominus .7e. fortitudinem stelle et ipsa in domo cadente non respiciat dominum ascendentis, et similiter si dederit Luna fortitudinem planete bono, si fuerit dominus .7e. dans fortitudinem domino .10e., significat quod rex adiuvabit eum. (3) Et si dominus .7e. fuerit retrogradus ab[1] aspectu domimi ascendentis, et dederit fortitudinem stelle existenti in domo cadente, iudicabis quod latro evadet. (4) Et ita iudicabis si dederit dominus .7e. fortitudinem domino .3e. domus et .9e., aut stelle ibi existenti, aut quod fuerit ibi domi-

[1]ab] E; V om.

and likewise if the lord of the seventh ⟨place⟩ aspects ⟨the ascendant⟩ and also ⟨it aspects⟩ the lord of the second ⟨place⟩, ⟨the stolen article⟩ will be returned {…} with respect to the lord of the ascendant. (7) The same applies if the lord of the eighth place gives power to the lord of the second place and the lord of the ascendant aspects these two [the lord of the eighth place and the lord of the second place]. (8) Likewise, if the lord of the seventh ⟨place⟩, also of the second ⟨place⟩, is in one of the cardines, it indicates that the thief has not yet left the city and did not take the stolen article out ⟨of the city⟩. (9) It is also an auspicious sign if the Moon gives power to the Sun or to the lord of the ascendant. (10) If the lord of the second place gives power to the lord of the ascendant and it itself [the lord of the second place] is in a cadent place, and likewise if the lord of the eighth ⟨place⟩ gives power to the lord of the seventh ⟨place⟩, it signifies that the stolen article will not be found (11) If the lord of the second ⟨place⟩ gives power to the lord of the third place or the ninth ⟨place⟩, know that the thief already took the money out of the city. (12) If the lord of the seventh ⟨place⟩ gives power to the lord of the tenth ⟨place⟩, it indicates that the king will assist the thief, who will not give back the stolen article. (13) The same applies if the Moon gives power to the lord of the seventh ⟨place⟩, and likewise if the lord of the second ⟨place⟩ gives power to the lord of the seventh ⟨place⟩.[2]

4 (1) Judgment on when the thief will be captured. (2) If you find that the lord of the seventh ⟨place⟩ gives its power to the lord of the ascendant, and the lord of the seventh ⟨place gives⟩ power to a planet located in a cardo, particularly in the tenth, and likewise if a planet gives power to a harming planet, and likewise if the lord of the seventh place is burnt under the light of the Sun, the king will capture him [the thief].[1]

5 (1) Judgment about when the thief will not be found. (2) If the lord of the seventh ⟨place⟩ gives power to a planet which is in a cadent place and does not aspect the lord of the ascendant, and likewise if the Moon gives power to a benefic planet, ⟨and⟩ if the lord of the seventh ⟨place⟩ gives power to the lord of the tenth ⟨place⟩, it signifies that the king will help him [the thief]. (3) If the lord of the seventh ⟨place⟩ is retrograde from an aspect with the lord of the ascendant, and gives power to a planet located in a cadent place, judge that the thief will escape. (4) Judge in this way if the lord of the seventh ⟨place⟩ gives power to the lord of the third and ninth place, or to a planet located there [the third or ninth place], or if the lord of seventh ⟨place⟩ is there [the third or ninth place]; ⟨in these cases⟩ judge

nus .7e., iudicabis quod evadet latro. (5) Et si interrogatum fuerit si latro fuerit ante se, respice si ascendens in .10a. vel in .7a. Hoc inveni.

⟨II iii⟩
Tertia domus

1 (1) Qui petit super via sua, si paraverit eam, utrum sit bonum vel malum, vide: si fuerit dominus ascendentis coniungens se cum domino .3e. vel .9e., aut quod respiciat ipsos et det fortitudinem eis, ibit. (2) Et iudicabis quemadmodum essent, cum domino .3e. domus vel .9e., et quemadmodum locus eius exibit[1] respectu Solis. (3) Et ita iudicabis si fuerit dominus ascendentis, aut prepositus, aut significator quod est Luna, in domo .3a. vel .9a., et ita iudicabis si unus istorum duorum fuerit in ascendente.

2 (1) Dixerunt Antiqui quod hec domus demonstrat super gaudium. (2) Propter hoc quod gaudium Lune est in ista domo dixerunt: si Luna dederit fortitudinem stelle existenti in angulo primo, res ipsa est vera et discooperietur; et si in .10a. ipsum est discoopertum; et si in .7a. adhuc veniet alia ei similiter fortificans ipsum; et si in .4a. ipsa est vera et abscondetur a pluribus. (3) Et associate cum ipsa re signum ⟨quod⟩ est ⟨ibi⟩, si veridicum vel mobile vel bicorporum, quoniam ipsa demonstrabunt partes gaudii esse
24v prestitas sed non totum; et associate semper in re ipsa dominum hore, | et iudicabis secundum locum suum et signum quod est ibi. (4) Et ad sciendum quid est in scripto, si ipsa aut bene aut male se habuerit ad Lunam et ad[2] aspicientes ipsam, et associate in hac re dominum hore ad mulierem que nunciat suas abscontiones.

[1]exibit*] V; E exigit. [2]ad] E; V om.

that the thief will escape.[1] (5) If ⟨the astrologer⟩ is asked whether the thief was before him [in the querent's presence], find out whether the ascendant ⟨of the interrogational horoscope⟩ is in [i.e., coincides with] the tenth or seventh ⟨place of the querent's natal horoscope⟩. This is what I found.

⟨II iii⟩
The Third Place

1 (1) If one arranges a journey and asks whether it is auspicious or inauspicious ⟨to take it⟩, observe: if the lord of the ascendant is in conjunction with the lord of the third or ninth ⟨place⟩, or aspects them and gives them power, he will go. (2) Judge according to how they are, ⟨the lord of the ascendant⟩ with the lord of the third or ninth ⟨place⟩, and according to how its [the lord of the ascendant] position moves away with respect to the Sun. (3) Judge in this way if the lord of the ascendant, either the ruler or the significator, which is the Moon, is in the third or ninth place, and judge in this manner if one of the two [the ruler or the significator] is in the ascendant.[1]

2 (1) The Ancients said that this place indicates joy. (2) Since the Moon's joy is in this place[1] they said: if the Moon gives power to a planet located in the first cardo, the thing ⟨asked about⟩ itself is true and will be disclosed; if ⟨the Moon gives power to a planet⟩ in the tenth ⟨cardo, the thing⟩ itself has been disclosed; and if in the seventh ⟨cardo⟩[2] something else similar to it [i.e., the thing asked about] and strengthening it will also come about; and if in the fourth ⟨cardo the thing⟩ itself is true but is hidden from many people. (3) Associate with it [the Moon] the sign ⟨which⟩ is ⟨there⟩, whether fixed, tropical or bicorporal,[3] because they indicate that the joy is felt partly but not completely; and always associate with the same thing the lord of the hour, and judge according to its position and the sign it is in. (4) To know the content of a letter, ⟨find out⟩ if it [i.e., the lord of the hour] is in an auspicious or inauspicious position with respect to the Moon and to those aspecting it [the Moon], and associate in this matter the lord of the hour for a woman who is revealing her secrets.

⟨II iv⟩
Quarta domus

1 (1) Ille qui petit de re, quis erit eius finis, respice domum .4am., si est recta vel tortuosa, et que stella fuerit in ea, aut respiciet eam aut locum domorum suorum, et quo modo[1] ipse se habet, et utrum sit directus in cursu suo, et stellam cui dederit significator fortitudinem, et dominum sue domus, et ita iudicabis.

2 (1) Et scias si fuerit interrogator rex et interrogaverit super aliquam patriarum suarum vel villarum, utrum fuerit ei rebelles, pone ascendens pro rege et dominum .4e. domus pro hominibus patrie vel stellam que erit ibi; secundum dispositionem eius a gradu ascendente et ad dominos, ita iudicabis. (2) Rursus pones Solem pro rege et Lunam pro hominibus patrie, et secundum quod videbis iudicabis. (3) Et plures dicunt quod si interrogaverit interrogator super hominibus, utrum erunt rebelles regi, quod ponet ascendens pro hominibus ipsius ville et .10m. regi. (4) Et hoc non est iustum nisi tamen quod si fuerit interrogator hominem rex, et erit princeps magnus; tunc iudicabis secundum prepositum super ascendente et loco Lune et regi .10m et quintum.

⟨II v⟩
Quinta domus

1 (1) Si interrogator interrogaverit si habebit filium mihi videtur quod explanat masculum; ea que ostendunt si habebit filium sunt ista. (2) Si dominus .5e. domus dederit fortitudinem domino ascendentis aut econtrario. (3) Et etiam si fuerit dominus ascendentis in angulo et non dederit fortitudinem stelle existenti in .6a. .8a. vel .12a. (4) Similiter si fuerit dominus hore in aliquo angulorum et receptus sit in suo loco. (5) Et item si fuerit ei potestas in domo .5a. .11a. vel .9a. (6) Et similiter si fuerit Jupiter in ascendente et non fuerit combustus nec retrogradus nec cum stella dampni-

[1]modo] E; V om.

⟨II iv⟩
The Fourth Place

1 (1) ⟨For⟩ one who asks about the outcome of something, observe the fourth place, whether it is straight or crooked[1] [i.e., whether it coincides with a straight or a crooked sign], and which planet is in it [i.e., the fourth place], or aspects it, or ⟨aspects⟩ the position of its [i.e., the planets'] ⟨two⟩ houses, and how it [i.e., the planet] behaves, and whether it [i.e., the planet] is direct in its course, and to which planet the significator [i.e., the Moon] gives power, and ⟨which is⟩ the lord of its house, and judge accordingly.[2]

2 (1) Know that if the querent is a king and poses a question about one of his countries or cities, whether they will rebel against him, assign the ascendant to the king and the lord of the fourth place or the planet that is there [i.e., in the fourth place] to the people of the country; judge according to its [the planet in the fourth place] configuration with respect to the ascendant degree and the lords [i.e., the lords of the ascendant and of the fourth place]. (2) Also assign the Sun to the king and the Moon to the people of the country, and judge according to what you observe. (3) Many say that if the querent asks about people, whether they will rebel against the king, assign the ascendant to the people of the city and the tenth ⟨place⟩ to the king. (4) But this is not correct unless the one who asks the astrologer is the king, and is a great prince; then judge according to the ruler of the ascendant and ⟨the ruler⟩ of the position of the Moon, and ⟨assign⟩ the tenth and fifth ⟨places⟩ to the king.[1]

⟨II v⟩
The Fifth Place

1 (1) If the querent asks whether he will have a son, it seems to me clear what makes plain that it might be a male; these are ⟨the signs⟩ which indicate that he will have a son. (2) If the lord of the fifth place gives power to the lord of the ascendant or vice versa. (3) Also if the lord of the ascendant is in a cardo and does not give power to a planet located in the sixth, eighth, or twelfth ⟨place⟩.[1] (4) Likewise, if the lord of the hour is in one of the cardines and it is received in its position. (5) Also if it [i.e., the lord of the hour] has a dignity in the fifth, eleventh, or ninth ⟨place⟩.[2] (6) Likewise, if Jupiter is in the ascendant and is neither burnt nor retrograde nor with a malefic planet,

ficante et etiam quando erit in domo radicis sterilis. (7) Et similiter ostendit
25r si fuerit dominus ascendentis | in quinta.

2 (1) Et ea que demonstrant quod non habebit filium sunt ista. (2) Si non fuerit aspectus aut coniunctio inter dominum ascendentis et dominum .5e. (3) Et si fuerit dominus hore in .6a. vel .8a. vel .12a., aut quod non aspiciat dominum hore, rursus dominus .5e. dominum ascendentis. (4) Et peius si fuerit dominus hore aut dominus .5e. in aliqua trium domorum cadentium ab angulis.

3 (1) Et si interrogatio fuerit si mulier est pregnans, respice et dic quod ita si fuerit significator dans fortitudinem suam stelle existenti in angulo. (2) Et ita fuerit dominus hore in angulo. (3) Et etiam quando ibi fuerit Iupitter vel Venus. (4) Et similiter si fuerit significator receptus in loco suo. (5) Et similiter si fuerit ascendens dans fortitudinem stelle in .5a. (6) Et similiter si fuerit signum ascendens signum bicorporum.

4 (1) Et hoc ostendet quod non est pregnans: (2) Si significator dederit fortitudinem stelle existenti in domo cadente. (3) Et similiter si ascendens fuerit signum mobile. (4) Et si fuerit stella dampnificans in aliquo angulorum, quia tunc ostendet quod mulier erit impotens. (5) Et ita si dederit dominus .5e. fortitudinem stelle male, ita quod non sit ei potestas in ascendente vel in .5a., (6) Et ita iudicabis si significator non aspexerit dominum ascendentis et domum .5a.

5 (1) Et si interrogatum fuerit utrum masculum aut femellam[1] pariet mulier, vide dominum ascendentis vel prepositum aspicientem, utrum scilicet sit masculinus aut femininus[2] in natura sua, et utrum in parte masculina vel in opposito[3] respectu gradus ascendentis, rursus contra dispositionem ad Solem. (2) Et vide signum in quo fuerit, utrum masculinum vel feminum, rursus similiter domum .5am. et[4] dominum eius, et dominum hore, et signum Lune et locum eius, et dominum hore et naturam suam. (3) Et scias quod hora in qua nascitur est par[5] in fortitudine masculorum et quod

[1]femellam] E; V feminam. [2]masculinus aut femininus] E; V masculus aut feminus. [3]vel in opposite] VE; Hebrew text om; see *She'elot* III, II v 5:1. [4]et] E; V > similiter. [5]par] E; V impar; Hebrew: זוג; see *She'elot* III, II v 5:3.

nor when it is in a place of barren root.[3] (7) The same is indicated if the lord of the ascendant is in the fifth ⟨place⟩.[4]

2 (1) These are ⟨the signs⟩ which indicate that he will not have a son. (2) If there is no aspect or conjunction between the lord of the ascendant and the lord of the fifth ⟨place⟩.[1] (3) If the lord of the hour is in the sixth, eighth, or twelfth ⟨place⟩, or ⟨the lord of the fifth place⟩ does not aspect the lord of the hour, ⟨or⟩ in addition the lord of the fifth ⟨place does not aspect⟩ the lord of the ascendant.[2] (4) It is worse if the lord of the hour or the lord of the fifth ⟨place⟩ is in any of the three places cadent from the cardines.[3,4]

3 (1) If the question is whether a woman is pregnant, you should observe and say that this is so [i.e., the woman is pregnant] if the significator gives its power to a planet that is in a cardo. (2) This is so if the lord of the hour is in a cardo. (3) Also when Jupiter and Venus are there. (4) Likewise if the significator is received in its position. (5) Likewise if the ascendant gives power to a planet that is in the fifth ⟨place⟩. (6) Likewise if the sign of the ascendant is a bicorporal sign.[1]

4 (1) This indicates that ⟨the woman⟩ is not pregnant: (2) If the significator gives its power to a planet located in a cadent place. (3) Likewise if the ascendant is a tropical sign. (4) If a harmful planet is in one of the cardines, for then it indicates that the woman will have an abortion.[1] (5) Likewise if the lord of the fifth place gives power to a malefic planet that has no dignity in the ascendant or in the fifth place. (6) Judge in the same way if the significator does not aspect the lord of the ascendant or ⟨the lord of⟩ the fifth place.[2]

5 (1) If ⟨the astrologer⟩ is asked whether the woman will give birth to a boy or a girl, observe the lord of the ascendant or the ruler that aspects ⟨the ascendant⟩, ⟨and find out⟩ whether it is masculine or feminine in its nature, whether on a masculine side or the opposite with respect to the ascendant degree, also in relation to the configuration with the Sun. (2) Observe the sign in which it [the lord of the ascendant] is, whether it [the sign] is masculine or feminine, also ⟨proceed⟩ similarly [i.e., find out whether the sign is masculine or feminine] ⟨regarding⟩ the fifth place and its lord, the lord of the hour, the sign of the Moon and its position ⟨with respect to the Sun⟩, and ⟨the sign of⟩ the lord of the hour and its nature. (3) Know that an even-numbered hour of birth is under the power of the males, and an

ipsa est impar[1] in fortitudine femellarum. (4) Et computa omnes tuas fortitudines et iudica secundum maiorem partem in computatione.

⟨II vi⟩
Sexta ⟨domus⟩

1 (1) Si morietur quis aut sanabitur, vel diu infirmabitur vel cito sanabitur. (2) Hec sunt que ostendunt si vivet. (3) Si fuerit dominus ascendentis in loco bono contra ascendentem et non sit combustus, vel intraverit sub claritate
25v Solis secundum computationem | qua dixi in *Libro principii sensuum*, nec sit in aspectu stelle male. (4) Et ita si fuerit dominus ascendentis aspiciens vel coniungens se cum stella bona existente in aliquo angulorum. (5) Et ita iudicaverunt Antiqui, et ego Abraham temptavi multotiens quod si fuerit dominus ascendentis dans fortitudinem aut coniungatur cum stella in .4a., morietur infirmus quia ipsa est domus[2] fovee. (6) Et si significator in .4a.[3] et sit accrescens Lune, alleviabitur a malo quia festina est ipsa. (7) Dixerunt Antiqui: respice fortitudinem planetarum, si ipsi in altum et fuerit stella diurna, et econtrario in planeta qui est stella nocturna, rursus associa in hac re significatorem, quia habet magnam fortitudinem in hac re. (8) Et dicit Doronius quod associas semper cum domino ascendentis, a significatore, dominum triplicitatis prime in ascendente, quia ipse habet fortitudinem magnam. (9) Et Mesehala[4] dicit: item associa cum illis .3. significatoribus dominum hore, et non iudices quod morietur nisi postquam coniungetur illi .4. vel .3. vel .2., si fuerint multum fortes. (10) Et iudicabis quod morietur homo si fuerit dominus ascendentis in .6a. vel .8a. vel in .12., vel quod dampnificet se, vel in aspiciendo vel in coniungendo se cum aliquo dominorum ipsarum .3m. domorum. (11) Et dominus .8e. domus, si in ascendente fuerit, significat malum, sive fuerit stella bona sive mala. (12) Et aspectus dampnificans, scilicet .4us. vel oppositionis ascendentis, ad suos dominos vel ad significatorem, significat malum.

[1]impar*] corrected according to the Hebrew: לא זוג; EV par; see *She'elot* III, II v 5:3. [2]domus*] corrected according to the Hebrew; EV dominus; see *She'elot* III, II vi 1:5. [3].4.] E; V 9. [4]Mesehala] E; V Mesehalla.

odd-numbered hour of birth is under the power of the females. (4) Count all these powers and pass judgment in accordance with the larger number ⟨of masculine or feminine powers⟩.[1]

⟨II vi⟩
The Sixth Place

1 (1) ⟨A question about a sick person,⟩ whether he will die or recover, whether he will be ill for a long time or will recover quickly. (2) These are ⟨the things⟩ that signify that he will live. (3) If the lord of the ascendant is in an auspicious position with respect to the ascendant, and it is not burnt, and does not enter under the light of the Sun[1] according to the computation I have mentioned in the *Book of the beginning of wisdom*,[2] nor does it aspect a malefic planet.[3] (4) The same applies if the lord of the ascendant is in an aspect or in conjunction with a benefic planet located in one of the cardines. (5) The Ancients judged in this way and I, Abraham, have tested many times that if the lord of the ascendant gives power or is in conjunction with a planet in the fourth ⟨place⟩, the sick person will die because this is the place of the grave. (6) If the significator is in the fourth ⟨place⟩ and the Moon is increasing, he [the sick person] will be relieved of his misfortune because it [the Moon] is moving rapidly. (7) The Ancients said: observe the power of the planets, if they are above ⟨the Earth⟩ and there is a diurnal planet, and conversely ⟨if there is⟩ a nocturnal planet, also associate in this matter the significator, because it has a great power in this matter. (8) Dorotheus says that you must always associate the lord of the ascendant with the significator and the lord of the first triplicity,[4] because it has a great power.[5] (9) Māshā'allāh says: also associate the lord of the hour with these three significators [i.e., the lord of the ascendant, the significator (the Moon), and the first lord of the triplicity], and do not judge that ⟨the sick person⟩ will die except after four, three, or two are in conjunction, if they are very strong.[6] (10) Judge that the person will die if the lord of the ascendant is in the sixth, eighth, or twelfth ⟨place⟩, or if it [the lord of the ascendant] is harmed, either in aspect or in conjunction with the lords of any of these three places.[7] (11) The lord of the eighth place, if it is in the ascendant, signifies bad fortune, whether it is a benefic or malefic planet. (12) A harmful aspect, that is, quartile or opposition to the ascendant, to its lords, or to the significator, signifies bad fortune.[8]

2 (1) Et scias quod infirmitas prolongabitur si fuerit significator tardus in suo cursu, et similiter si dominus ascendentis vel prepositus scilicet fuerint tardi vel quod fuerint retrogradi. (2) Et signa veridica sunt multum dura, et signa bicorpora ostendunt quod revertetur infirmitas vel renovabitur super ipsum infirmitas alia, et mobilia signa significant super festinationem ad vitam vel ad mortem. (3) Et si fuerit stella, dampnificans an ⟪germinant⟫ an ⟪a ses signeurs⟫, velox in curso suo et exierit velociter ad aliud signum, ipse erit medicinatus. (4) Et si invenias dominum ascendentis in gradu quando
26r exierit de domo, sanabitur, vel quando ipsum aspiciet stella bona vel ei | coniungetur, vel quando erunt in gradu longitudinis uniti in fine meridiei vel in fine septentrionis. (5) Et diem mortis quando dominus ascendentis est in aliquo angulorum et in fine aspectus domini .8e. domus, aut quando coniungentur insimul vel quando ipse attinget ad locum domini .8e. domus. (6) Et si fuerit stella signatrix, qui sit dominus ascendentis, in loco cui non sit aspectus, respice signum secundi succedentis, et duc eum. (7) Et si sciveris locum Lune ad horam qua concubuit infirmus in lecto suo, tunc erit magis peractum, sicut scriptum est in *Libro claritatum* et in diebus terminorum. (8) Ad sciendum utrum homo sit infirmus, respice dominum .6e., si ipse in .12. infirmus est, quia domus .12. domus carceris est et prisionis. Hoc adinveni.

⟨II vii⟩
Septima domus

1 (1) Habet in se .4.[1] (2) Super rebus sponsalium mulierum, vide si dominus ascendentis dederit fortitudinem in aspectu vel in coniunctione domino .7e.; ⟪le signeur il amant et le requirant,⟫ et contrarium huius levabit rem. (3) Et si fuerit stella capiens scintillationem et ipsa dederit eam alii, vel receperit scintillationem ab illis duobus, erit integra res ipsa per manus mediatorum. (4) Et similiter, erit integra si fuerit Luna dans fortitudinem

[1].4.*] corrected according to the Hebrew; EV .12; see *She'elot* III, II vii 1:1.

2 (1) Know that the disease will be prolonged if the significator is slow in its course, and the same applies if the lord of the ascendant or the ruler is slow or retrograde.[1] (2) The fixed signs are very harmful, the bicorporal ⟨signs⟩ indicate that the disease will return or that he [the sick person] will contract another disease, and the tropical signs signify quickness ⟨in the development of the disease⟩ either towards life or death.[2] (3) If a planet, which is harming either the ascendant or its lords, is quick in its motion and moves rapidly to another sign, ⟨the sick person⟩ will be cured.[3] (4) If you find the lord of the ascendant in the degree[4] when it moves away from the place, ⟨the sick person⟩ will recover,[5] either when it [the lord of the ascendant] aspects a benefic planet, or when it is in conjunction with it [the benefic planet], or when they [the lord of the ascendant and the benefic planet] are in the same degree of longitude from the extreme north or the extreme south [i.e., in degrees whose distance from the cusp of Cancer and the cusp of Capricorn is the same]. (5) ⟨You may find⟩ the day of death when the lord of the ascendant is in one of the cardines and is at the end of an aspect with the lord of the eighth place, or when they [the lord of the ascendant and the lord of the eighth place] conjoin with it, or when it [the lord of the ascendant] reaches the place of the lord of the eighth place.[6] (6) If the planet that is the significator, which is the lord of the ascendant, is in a position where it does not form any aspect, observe ⟨the aspects to⟩ the next sign, and direct it. (7) If you know the position of the Moon at the moment when the sick person fell ill, this is more correct, as is written in the *Book of the luminaries* regarding the critical days.[7,8] (8) To know if someone is ill, observe the lord of the sixth place; if it is in the twelfth place, he is ill, because the twelfth place is the place of prison and jail.[9] This is what I found.[10]

⟨II vii⟩
The Seventh Place

1 (1) ⟨This place⟩ includes four questions. (2) Regarding the betrothal of women, observe whether the lord of the ascendant gives power by aspect or conjunction to the lord of the seventh place; ⟨in this case⟩ ⟨⟨the husband will love and court her,⟩⟩ but ⟨otherwise⟩ the opposite will be the case.[1] (3) If a planet [A] takes the spark ⟨of some planet [B]⟩ and gives it to another ⟨planet [C]⟩, or receives the spark from these two[2] [B and C], the matter will be completed by means of an intermediary.[3] (4) Likewise, ⟨the matter⟩ will be completed if the Moon gives power to the lord of the ascendant and there

domino ascendentis et Lune insit fortitudo in .7a. domo. (5) Et similiter si fuerit Venus in via Lune et dominus ascendentis in aliquo angulorum et melius in .10a. quam in aliis. (6) Et si dominus ascendentis fuerit in .7a., non combustus nec retrogradus, et non sit stella malivola, ita iudicabis. (7) Et si fuerit dominus .7e. aut Venus vel Luna in ascendente et non sit impeditus, levabit rem. (8) Et vide si non fuerit dominus .7e. in loco suo receptus a domino ascendentis vel econtrario, non levabitur res ad ultimum. (9) Et scias quod Mercurius facit lites, et vide si fuerit ipse in aliquo angulorum et non levabit res ad ultimum. (10) Dicit Enoch: respice pro manerie mulieris qua accipies distantiam Saturni a signo Veneris et adde eam super gradum ascendentem nam fortitudo inest ei in .7a. domo. (11) Et Doronius dicit accipe dominum hore pro interrogatore et dominum .7e. pro muliere, et si mulier fuerit interrogans pone ascendens pro ipsa et .7m. pro domino sua,[1] scilicet marito,[2] et associa cum hiis Solem sicut fecisti Lunam. Et Doronius
26v dicit quod associes item Martem, quia ipse est sicut Venus. (12) Et Enoch | dicit quod tu associes dominum partis dominorum et ita sciet interrogator, quod tu accipies distantiam gradus Veneris a gradu Saturni, et adde gradibus ascendentis equalibus, et secundum fortitudinem dominum partis si fuerit ei aspectus iudicabis.

2 (1) Interrogatio secunda est super verbis litis vel contentionis. (2) Si dominus litis sit interrogator, pone ascendens pro ipso et dominum .7e. pro illo cum quo querit litigare. (3) Et si homo interrogaverit pro alio a se, pone ascendens pro illo qui incipit litigare, vel pro illo quem primus posuisti in corde tuo ante interrogationem, et vide si dominus ascendentis vel significator fuerit in aliquo angulorum vel in .11ma. domo, et dominus .7e. in cadente vel sit combustus ante retrogradus; vincet inceptor vel interrogator et ille quem posuisti in corde tuo. (4) Et contrarium huius eveniet si fuerit dominus .7e. in aliquo angulorum, et precipue in .7o. vel .4o. vel in 5a. domo, et dominus ascendentis in loco malo, et quicumque aspiciet aliud luminarium est ali tenue. (5) Et ita unus eorum cum quo coniuncta est stella bona

[1]sua*] corrected according to the context; EV suo. [2]scilicet marito] EV; E above the line.

is power to the Moon in the seventh place. (5) The same applies if Venus is in the path of the Moon and the lord of the ascendant is in one of the cardines, and the tenth ⟨cardo⟩ is better than the others. (6) Judge in the same way if the lord of the ascendant is in the seventh ⟨cardo⟩,[4] neither burnt nor retrograde, and no malefic planet is there. (7) If the lord of the seventh ⟨place⟩ or Venus or the Moon is in the ascendant and is not hindered, the matter will be realized.[5] (8) Observe: the matter will not be realized in the end if the lord of the seventh ⟨place⟩ is not received in its position by the lord of the ascendant or vice versa. (9) Know that Mercury causes quarrels,[6] and observe that the matter will not be realized in the end if it [Mercury] is in one of the cardines. (10) Enoch says: for matters related to woman observe and take the distance between Saturn and the sign of Venus and add it to the ascendant degree, because it has power in the seventh place. (11) Dorotheus says that you should also take the lord of the hour for the querent and the lord of the seventh ⟨hour⟩[7] for the woman, and if the querent is the woman, assign her the ascendant and the seventh ⟨place⟩ for her lord, that is, ⟨her⟩ husband,[8] and associate the Sun with them as you have done regarding the Moon. Dorotheus says that you should associate Mars, too, because it is like Venus.[9] (12) Enoch says that you should associate the lord of the lot of husbands, and the querent will know it in this way: take the distance from the degree of Venus to the degree of Saturn, and add it to the equal degrees of the ascendant, and judge according to the power of the lord of the lot, if it forms an aspect.[10,11]

2 (1) The second question is about matters related to quarrels and strife. (2) If the person involved in the quarrel is the querent, assign to him the ascendant, and the lord of the seventh ⟨place⟩ to the one with whom he [the querent] seeks to quarrel.[1] (3) If a person poses a question on behalf of someone else, assign the ascendant to the person who started quarreling, or to the person you first have had in your heart before the question, and observe whether the lord of the ascendant or the significator is in one of the cardines or in the eleventh place, and the lord of the seventh is in a cadent ⟨place⟩ or is burnt or retrograde; ⟨in this case⟩ the one who started ⟨the quarrel⟩ or the one who you have had first in your heart will win. (4) The opposite will happen if the lord of the seventh ⟨place⟩ is in one of the cardines, and especially ⟨if it is⟩ in the seventh or fourth ⟨cardo⟩,[2] or in the fifth place, and ⟨if⟩ the lord of the ascendant is in an inauspicious position, and ⟨if⟩ whichever ⟨of the luminaries⟩ that aspects the other luminary is weaker than the other. (5) The same applies ⟨if⟩ one of them

vel aspiciens ipsum aspectu oppositionis vel .4o. vel coniunctionis cum eo. (6) Et si fuerit dominus ascendentis aspiciens aspectu amicabili dominum .7e., faciet pacem inter eos. (7) Et ita si fuerit in eodem loco et quilibet sit receptus a socio suo, et ille cui significaverit significator festinus in cursu suo; ipse queret pacem, et ita si fuerit cadens ab angulo et alius in uno angulorum vel in succedente domo. (8) Et si inter dominum ascendentis et .7e. fuerit aspectus .4us. vel oppositionis, vel quod fuerit insimul quilibet stella mala vel in domo vilitatis sue vel belli sui, vel quod non aspiciant se ad invicem, non est pax inter eos, et illum quem aspiciet dominus .10e. in aspectu amicabili vel Sol[1] significabit quod rex iuvabit eum. (9) Et si dominus .10e. sit retrogradus, significat quod rex faciet iudicium inequitatis. (10) Et si fuerit iudicium super thesaurum, faciet iudex sicut dictum est de rege.

3 (1) Tertia interrogatio est super bello. (2) Ad sciendum verba bellorum, fac quemadmodum fecisti pro litigantibus ad invicem. (3) Et vide si fuerit dominus ascendentis stella inferior et dominus septime .7e. superior; non
27r poterit inceptor | vincere alium victu perfecto, precipue si fuerit in domo prima vel .10a., nisi quod si .4or. affuerint domino .7e. (4) Unum est si fuerit in domo cadente. (5) Secundum si combustus vel sub radiis vel retrogradus. (6) Et tertium si fuerit in simul stella malivola vel in aspectu malo stelle malivole. (7) Et .4m. est quod sit stella malivola in domo .7a.

4 (1) Et si fuerit stella in ascendente, vide utrum inferior vel superior, et da medietatem fortitudinis ei et medietatem domino domus, si aspexerint se vel preposito aspiciente. (2) Et si fuerit dominus ascendentis in .7a., devictus erit si fuerit inferior planeta, et si superior planeta fuerit non erit devictus victoria perfecta, et ita iudicabis de domino .7e. domus. (3) Et si illi duo domini coniugantur, vide fortiorem et vide ad latitudenem ipsorum. (4) Si fuerit latitudo unius sinistra et alterius meridionali, vincet sinistra. (5) Et si ambe[2] sinistre vel septentrionales vincet ille cuius latitudo fuerit maior.

[1]Sol] E; V Solis. [2]ambe] E; V ambo.

is in conjunction with a benefic planet or aspects it [the benefic planet] in an aspect of opposition, quartile, or conjunction with it. (6) If the lord of the ascendant aspects the lord of the seventh place in an aspect of love, this will make peace between them. (7) The same applies if it [the lord of the ascendant] is in this position and any of them is received by its partner, and the one which is signified by the significator is quick in its motion; ⟨in this case⟩ he himself [the quarreler] will seek peace, and the same applies if it is cadent from the cardo and the other is in one of the cardines or in a succedent place. (8) If there is quartile or opposition between the lord of the ascendant and ⟨the lord of⟩ the seventh ⟨place⟩, or ⟨if⟩ at the same time there is an inauspicious planet in its house of dejection or in its house of war,[3] or ⟨if⟩ they do not aspect each other, there will be no peace between them, and the one [planet] which is aspected in an aspect of love by the lord of the tenth ⟨place⟩ or by the Sun signifies that the king will help him [the disputant]. (9) If the lord of the tenth ⟨place⟩ is retrograde, it signifies that the king will judge unjustly. (10) If the judgment is about money, the judge will do as he is told by the king.[4]

3 (1) The third question is about war. (2) To know matters related to wars, proceed in the same way as you did regarding disputants one against the other. (3) Observe whether the lord of the ascendant is a lower planet and the lord of the seventh is an upper ⟨planet⟩; ⟨in this case⟩ the initiator ⟨of the war⟩ cannot be completely victorious over the other, especially if it is in the first or tenth place, unless four ⟨things⟩ pertain to the lord of the seventh ⟨place⟩. (4) The first is that it is in a cadent place. (5) The second is that it is burnt or under the rays ⟨of the Sun⟩[1] or retrograde. (6) The third is that it is together with a malefic planet or forms an inauspicious aspect with a malefic planet. (7) The fourth is that a malefic planet is in the seventh place.[2]

4 (1) If the planet is in the ascendant, observe whether it is below or above ⟨the Sun⟩, and assign half of the power to it and half ⟨of the power⟩ to the lord of the place, if they aspect each other, or to the aspecting ruler. (2) If the lord of the ascendant is in the seventh ⟨place⟩, he [the initiator of the war] will be defeated if it [the lord of the ascendant] is a lower planet, but if it is an upper planet he will not be completely defeated; and judge in the same way regarding the lord of the seventh place. (3) If the two lords are in conjunction, find out the stronger and their latitude. (4) If one has northern latitude and the other southern, the northern is victorious. (5) If both are on the "left side" or northern,[1] the one with the greatest latitude

(6) Et si ambe meridionales, vincet ille cuius latitudo fuerit parva. (7) Et si unus est in linea signorum et alius sinister, vincet sinister, et si meridionalis[1] vincet meridionalis.[2]

5 (1) Dicit Even Maasar: si fuerit Scorpio ascendens et Mars in septima, magnum malum eveniet ambobus bellatoribus, et finis illi qui est receptus et aspexerit bonam stellam, et contrarius huius si aspexerit malam.

6 (1) Et si interrogatum fuerit super .4a. interrogationem, sicut de societate, vide: si fuerit aspectus amicabilis inter dominum ascendentis vel .7m. et stella bona in angulo, significat super proficium, et si malivola, econtrario. (2) Et Mars significat super diminutionem fidei et litem magnam in aliquo sociorum.

⟨II viii⟩
Octava ⟨domus⟩

1 (1) Qui timet se in loquendo quando vocatur et qui timet de re ne sibi accidat, vide: si fuerit dominus ascendentis aspiciens ascendens et non aspexerit cum stella malivola nec coniungatur ei nec sit sub radiis Solis; nec accidet illud de quo timet. (2) Et si fuerit dominus ascendentis in domo .6a. .8a. .12a. et non aspexerit eum stella malivola existens in aliquo angulorum et non in ascendente, non accidet ei malum nisi timor anime et cognitionis; et ratio est quia ille domus non aspiciet ascendens et tunc nec significator dominum ascendentis omnino. (3) Et si fuerit malivola in aliquo angulorum
27v aspiciens eum vel ascendens, accidet | ei malum de quo timet. (4) Et si malivola non fuerit dominus domus male, non accidet ei malum illud totum de quo timet nisi in parte. (5) Et si stella bona aspiciat, evadet a malo. (6) Et respice ad signa mobilia nam ipsa significant quod festinanter accidet timor, et stabilia vel bicorpora dura, et secundum naturam signi in quo est malivola, quod si fuerit in signis aqueis, hoc erit in partibus aque.

[1]meridionalis] E; V meridionales. [2]meridionalis] E; V meridionalem.

will be victorious. (6) If both are southern, the one with the smallest latitude will be victorious. (7) If one of them is in the line of the signs [the ecliptic] and the other is northern, the northern is victorious, and if ⟨the other⟩ is southern, the southern is victorious.[2,3]

5 (1) Abū Maʿshar says: if Scorpio is ⟨in⟩ the ascendant and Mars is in the seventh ⟨place⟩, a great misfortune will happen to both combatants, and the ⟨final⟩ outcome ⟨of the war⟩ depends on the one which is received and aspects a benefic planet, and the opposite applies if it aspects a malefic ⟨planet⟩.[1]

6 (1) If ⟨the astrologer⟩ is asked about the fourth question, that is, about a partnership, observe: if there is an aspect of love[1] between the lord of the ascendant or the ⟨lord of⟩ seventh ⟨place⟩ and a benefic planet in a cardo, ⟨this⟩ signifies success, and if a malefic ⟨planet⟩, the opposite. (2) Mars signifies the decrease of trust and a great quarrel for any of the partners.[2]

⟨II viii⟩
The Eighth Place

1 (1) ⟨For⟩ one who is afraid when he is called to speak and ⟨for⟩ one who is afraid lest something happen to him, observe: if the lord of the ascendant aspects the ascendant and does not aspect a malefic planet, and is not in conjunction with it, or under the ray of the Sun; ⟨in this case⟩ what he is afraid of will not happen to him. (2) If the lord of the ascendant is in the sixth, eighth, ⟨or⟩ twelfth ⟨place⟩ and is not aspected by a malefic planet in one of the cardines or in the ascendant, no misfortune will befall him except for fear in the soul and awareness ⟨of fear⟩; the reason is that this place [i.e., the sixth, eighth, or twelfth] does not aspect the ascendant and then the significator does not ⟨aspect⟩ the lord of the ascendant in any way. (3) If a malefic ⟨planet⟩ is in one of the cardines aspecting it [the lord of the ascendant] or the ascendant, the misfortune he is afraid of will happen to him. (4) If the malefic ⟨planet⟩ is not the lord of an inauspicious place, the misfortune will befall him only in part but not in full. (5) If a benefic planet is aspecting, he will escape the misfortune. (6) Observe the tropical signs because they signify that what he is afraid of will occur quickly, and the fixed and bicorporal signs are harmful, and ⟨the signification⟩ is according to the sign in which the malefic ⟨planet⟩ is, for if it is in one of the watery signs, it [what the querent is afraid of] will be in water.[1]

2 (1) Et qui petit pro alio homine, utrum sit vivus vel mortuus, vide si fuerit princeps ascendentis in .8va., vel in quocumque loco sub radiis Solis, vel in quarta domo cum stella mala; scias quod mortuus est. (2) Et si fuerit dominus .8e. in ascendente, quicumque stella sit, et dominus ascendentis in .6a. vel in .12., item est mortuus, et si non fuerit ita est vivus. (3) Et debes associare in hac re locum Lune, nam si dederit fortitudinem illi qui est sub terra in puncto interrogationis, item est mortuus, et si dederit fortitudinem illi qui est supra, quicumque sit illa stella, ipse est vivus. (4) Et sicut significat Luna ita iudicabis de domino hore.

⟨II ix⟩
Nona domus

1 (1) Si quis petierit a te pro itinere terreno vel marino, utrum aderit ei et proficiet, vide si fuerit dominus .3e. vel .9e. in ascendente et non retrogradus; proficiet iter suum. (2) Et ita si fuerit significator vel dominus ascendentis in domibus dictis, scilicet, .3a. vel .9a. (3) Et inter significatorem vel inter prepositum, et secundum naturas stellarum in .4or. domibus iudicabis, et scias naturam[1] signorum. (4) Et si inveneris stellam bonam in .7a., inveniet bonum in loco ad quem ibit, et si mala malum. (5) Et si petierit que pars est ei bona, scias[2] loca stellarum bonarum et malarum, in qua parte sunt respectu ascendentis et respectu dispositionis earum ad Solem.

2 (1) Et si interrogaverit te pro homo qui iam ivit—transactis aliquot[3] diebus vel mensibus vel annis—ad sciendum si revertetur et quando, vide si inveneris dominum ascendentis et significatorem in aliquo angulorum, vel quod aliquis eorum dans fortitudinem stelle existenti in angulo primo vel .10o., vel quod dominus ascendentis aspiciat ascendens et retrogradus; significabit quod morabitur in loco suo. (2) Et si inveneris dominum ascendentis velocem in cursu et non aspiciat ascendens, vel quod dederit fortitudinem stelle in .3a. vel .9a., vel quod dederit significator fortitudinem

[1]naturam] E; v naturas. [2]scias] E; V scies. [3]Aliquot] E; V aliquod.

2 (1) ⟨If⟩ someone asks about another person, whether he is alive or dead, observe whether the lord of the ascendant is in the eighth ⟨place⟩, or in any other position under they rays of the Sun, or in the fourth place with a malefic planet; ⟨in this case⟩ know that he is dead. (2) If the lord of the eighth ⟨place⟩ is in the ascendant, no matter which planet it is, and the lord of the ascendant is in the sixth or twelfth ⟨place⟩, he is dead, and otherwise he is alive. (3) You should associate in this matter the position of the Moon, for if it [the Moon] gives power to some ⟨planet⟩ that is below the Earth at the moment of the question, he is dead, and if it [the Moon] gives ⟨power to some planet which is⟩ above ⟨the Earth⟩, no matter which planet it is, he is alive.[1] (4) Judge by means of the lord of the hour as signified by the Moon.

⟨II ix⟩
The Ninth Place

1 (1) If someone asks you about a journey by land or by sea, whether it will be propitious for him and he will succeed, observe whether the lord of the third or ninth ⟨place⟩ is in the ascendant and is not retrograde; ⟨in this case⟩ his journey will be successful. (2) The same applies if the significator or the lord of the ascendant is in the aforementioned places, namely, the third or the ninth ⟨place⟩. (3) Judge ⟨choosing⟩ between the significator and the ruler, and according to the nature of the planets in the four places [i.e., the four cardines], and know the nature of the signs.[1] (4) If you find a benefic planet in the seventh ⟨place⟩, he will find good fortune in the place to which he is going, and if ⟨you find⟩ a malefic ⟨planet in the seventh place, he will find⟩ misfortune ⟨in the place to which he is going⟩. (5) If he asks which part ⟨of the journey⟩ is fortunate for him, know the positions of the benefic and malefic ⟨planets⟩, in which part ⟨of the zodiac they are⟩ with respect to the ascendant and with respect to their configuration with the Sun.

2 (1) If he asks you on behalf of a man who has already gone—a number of days, months or years having already elapsed—to know whether he will return and when, observe whether you find the lord of the ascendant and the significator in one of the cardines, or whether one of them gives power to a planet located in the first or tenth cardo, or whether the lord of the ascendant aspects the ascendant and is retrograde; ⟨in these cases⟩ it signifies that he will be delayed in his place. (2) ⟨The same applies⟩ if you find that the lord of the ascendant is quick in ⟨its⟩ motion and does not aspect the ascendant, or that it gives power to a planet in the third or ninth

28r domino ascendentis | vel domino .7e. si fuerit in .7a. (3) Et signa veridica significant super terminum longum, et significat bicorporum super mediocrem et mobilia super velocem. (4) Et significabit significator super festinatione adventus si dederit significator fortitudinem domino ascendentis et ipse in ascendente. (5) Et ita dominus hore in aliquo angulorum; et dixerunt quod angulus primus significat super horas et .10. super dies et .7a. super menses et quartus super annos. (6) Ego inveni si dominus .9e. et .3e. fuerint retrogradi loquentur de motione eius, id est, itinere, sed non veniet ad opus, vel movebuntur bis vel ter et revertentur. (7) Et si dominus ascendentis et dominus loci Lune, ibunt et proficient.

⟨II x⟩
Decima domus

1 (1) Si petierit super valore, utrum erit ei a rege vel a principe, respice semper ad dominum ascendentis et significatorem: utrum inter eum et dominum decime fuerit aspectus dilectionis et recipiatur ab eo et dominus .10e. in aliquo angulorum, erit res ad voluntatem suam, et si fuerit in aliqua succedentium que aspiciunt ascendens, erit pars rei quesite et non tota. (2) Et ita iudicabis si fuerit significator vel dominus ascendentis aspiciens prepositum, et ipse in aspectu bono ad Solem, et Sol in aliquo angulorum—et ⟨⟨la .10.⟩⟩ melior quam ascendens, et ascendens melior quam .7a., item melior quam .4a.[1] (3) Et ita iudicabis si fuerit prepositus cum Sole in uno gradu et ipse directus in cursu suo, et si fuerit retrogradus non accedet res tota. (4) Et super hoc vide pro illo qui queret ex parte valorem iudicum et emptorum stellam Iovis, utrum ipsa in aliquo angulorum; et similiter pro querente ex parte valorem regine vel domine alique, ad locum Veneris, item Lunam si est in medietate mensis prima. (5) Et si valorem de femine, respice Saturnus, et si a domino bellorum, Martem. (6) Et debes advertere

[1] .4a.] E; V .9.

⟨place⟩, or that the significator gives power to the lord of the ascendant or to the lord of the seventh ⟨place⟩ if it is in the seventh ⟨place⟩. (3) The fixed signs signify a long period, a bicorporal ⟨sign signifies⟩ an intermediate ⟨period⟩, and a tropical ⟨sign signifies⟩ a quick ⟨return⟩. (4) The significator signifies the quickness of the arrival if the significator gives power to the lord of the ascendant and it [the significator] is itself in the ascendant. (5) The same applies to the lord of the hour in one of the cardines; ⟨the astrologers⟩ said that the first cardo signifies hours, the tenth days, the seventh months, and the fourth years. (6) I found that if the lords of the ninth and third ⟨places⟩ are retrograde they speak of his motion, that is, ⟨his⟩ journey, but ⟨in this case the journey⟩ will not be carried out, or they [the travelers] will be moved two or three times and they will be returned. (7) If the lord of the ascendant and the lord of the position of the Moon ⟨speak of their motion⟩, they [i.e., the travelers] will go and succeed.[1]

⟨II x⟩
The Tenth Place

1 (1) If someone asks about wealth, whether he will get it from a king or a prince, always observe the lord of the ascendant and the significator: if there is an aspect of love[1] between it [i.e., the lord of the ascendant or the significator] and the lord of the tenth ⟨place⟩, and it [i.e., the lord of the ascendant or the significator] is received by it [i.e., the lord of the tenth place] and the lord of the tenth ⟨place⟩ is in one of the cardines, the thing ⟨asked about⟩ will be according to his wish, and if it is in one of the succedent ⟨places⟩ which aspect the ascendant, the thing asked about will come to pass but not fully. (2) Judge in the same way if the significator or the lord of the ascendant aspects the ruler, and it [the ruler] is itself in an auspicious aspect with the Sun, and the Sun is in one of the cardines—the tenth is better than the ascendant, and the ascendant is better than the seventh, which is better than the fourth. (3) Judge in the same way if the ruler is with the Sun in one degree and it [the ruler] is direct in its motion, but if it is retrograde the thing ⟨asked about⟩ will not take place completely.[2] (4) For one who seeks wealth from judges and buyers observe Jupiter,[3] whether it is in one of the cardines; likewise, for someone who seeks wealth from the queen or some lady, ⟨observe⟩ the position of Venus, as well as the Moon if it is in the first half of the month. (5) If the wealth comes from a woman, observe Saturn, and if ⟨the wealth comes⟩ from a warlord, ⟨observe⟩ Mars. (6) You have to pay attention that if Saturn or Mars

si fuerit Saturnus vel Mars in aliquo angulorum et si orientales a Sole non significabunt bonum nisi fuerint masculini in aspectu stelle, vel quod essent in exaltationibus suis, vel in domibus suis, vel erunt insimul coniuncti. (7) Et si fuerit dominus domus bone in opposito ascendentis in interrogatione, ostendet quod res quesita erit cum pena et difficultate et labore, et si non fuerit dominus domus bone, non significabit in seculo super bonum, et si fuerit dominus domus male contra ascendens, tunc significabit malum.

2 (1) Et si interrogaverit si addiscet a sapiente, vide Mercurius et secun-
28v dum | fortitudinem suam iudicabis. (2) Si fuerit significator vel prepositus dabit ei fortitudinem et si fuerit stella dans ei fortitudinem directa, ostendet super hoc quod debet esse res quesita. (3) Et si fuerit retrograda, non[1] erit res nec accidet nisi fuerit ipsa stella propinque stationem suam secundam; tunc enim erit res post[2] desperationem.[3] (4) Et si fuerit in signo veridico, stabit res diu; et si in mobili non morabitur nisi parum; et signa bicorpora super temporem mediocrem si fuerit in domo mala.

⟨II xi⟩
Undecima domus

1 (1) Si petierit super amore, vide stellam que ostendit super re petita, sicut Venus super mulieribus et Sol super principibus magnis. (2) Item aspice ad dominum .11me. et secundum locum eius et aspectum significatoris, vel dominum ascendentis vel prepositi .5. locorum principatus ad ipsum iudicabis, secundum naturam planete existentis tunc in puncto interrogationis in .11ma. domo, vel domum ascendentis vel prepositi, et secundum locum eius et aspectum significatoris. (3) Et scias quod Mars ⟨⟨delibra⟩⟩[4] dilectionem si fuerit in aliquo angulorum vel in .11ma. domo et non ita Saturnus nisi fuerit dominus male domus in opposito vel respectu gradus ascendentis.

[1]non] E; V om. [2]res post] E; V respectus. [3]non erit res post desperacionem] E; V non erit res respectus desperacione. [4]delibra] V; desibra E.

is in one of the cardines and oriental of the Sun, they will not signify good fortune unless they are masculine ⟨and⟩ in aspect ⟨with⟩ a planet, or are in their exaltations[4] or in their houses, or are in conjunction. (7) If the lord of an auspicious place is in opposition to the ascendant in the question [i.e., the interrogational horoscope], it indicates that the thing asked about will be obtained with sorrow, difficulty, and hardship, but if it is not the lord of an auspicious place, it will never signify good fortune, and if it is the lord of an inauspicious place with respect to the ascendant, then it will signify bad fortune.

2 (1) If someone asks whether he will learn from a scholar, observe Mercury and judge according to its [Mercury's] power.[1] (2) If the significator or the ruler gives it [Mercury] power, and if the planet which gives it [Mercury] power is direct ⟨in its course⟩, it indicates that the thing asked about must be fulfilled. (3) But if it is retrograde, the thing ⟨asked about⟩ will not be nor will it happen, unless this planet is close to its second station; then the thing ⟨asked about⟩ will happen after despair. (4) If it is in a fixed sign, the thing ⟨asked about⟩ will be postponed for a long time; if in a tropical ⟨sign⟩ it will be delayed for only a short time; the bicorporal signs ⟨indicate⟩ an intermediate period if it [the planet] is in an inauspicious place.

⟨II xi⟩
The Eleventh Place

1 (1) If someone asks about love [i.e., finding favor with another person], observe the planet that indicates the thing asked about, such as Venus regarding women and the Sun regarding great princes. (2) Also observe the lord of the eleventh ⟨place⟩ and judge according to its position and the aspect of the significator, or ⟨according to⟩ the ⟨horoscopic⟩ place of the ascendant or of the ruler of the five places of dominion to it [the lord of the eleventh place], ⟨and⟩ according to the nature of the planet located at the moment of the question in the eleventh place, or ⟨according to⟩ the ⟨horoscopic⟩ place of the ascendant or of the ruler, and according to its position and the aspect of the significator. (3) Know that Mars {removes} love if it is in one of the cardines or in the eleventh place, but not so Saturn unless it is the lord of an inauspicious place in opposition to the ascendant or retrograde.[1]

⟨II xii⟩
Duodecima ⟨domus⟩

1 (1) Si petierit quis pro homine incarcerato vel captivo in manibus hominis, vide si fuerit dominus ascendentis et significator veloces in cursu suo et in signo mobili; significabit super festinatione exitus eius. (2) Et ita si fuerint in aliquo angulorum et dederint fortitudinem in aspectu stelle in .3a. vel .9a. existente, et similiter si dederint fortitudinem dominis illarum domorum et ipse in .4a. feminina, significat super revertione sua. (3) Et si fuerit prepositus vel significator in angulo, aut domini anguli in uno angulorum, aut fuerit dominus ascendentis in domo domini .12., vel econtrario, vel dominus ascendentis in .4a. que est dura, vel quod fuerit stella que est tunc in angulo dominorum domus male, et precipue si fuerit stella malivola in natura sua, et similiter si fuerit stella malivola dominus .12e. coniungens se cum domino ascendentis, tunc malum perfectum. (4) Si dederit fortitudinem dominus ascendentis stelle existenti in angulo, vel stelle impedite a malivola vel a Sole, et fuerit cum ipsa impedita vel malivola in .8a., quia
29r tunc ostendit incarceratus | esse in carcere et captum in captivitate sua; et datio fortitudinis significatoris domino ascendentis item[1] mala. (5) Et signa veridica mala etiam in hac re, et signa bicorpora significant super exitum et item revertetur una vice. (6) Et si dominus ascendentis dederit fortitudinem domino .3e. vel .9e. et ipsi in .3a. vel .9a., vel .4a. feminina, et ipsi et unus eorum det fortitudinem stelle existenti in angulo, tunc ostendet quod fugiet, vel exibit et capietur alias. (7) Et respice ad incarcerantem vel ⟪lepecinement⟫ dominum .7e.; si fuerit in aspectu bono vel ascendens vel ad dominum eius, significabit super amore et quod ei faciet bonum, et si in aspectu malo, iudica contrarium. (8) Et si fuerit stella malivola in natura sua ostendet super ictus et doloribus magnis. (9) Et si fuerit significator dans fortitudinem stelle in .8a. vel .2a., ostendet super doloribus quos patietur postquam exierit. (10) Et si fuerit stella retrograda, capietur secunda vice et revertetur in carcerem.

[1] item] E; V iterum.

⟨II xii⟩
The Twelfth ⟨Place⟩

1 (1) If someone asks about a man in jail or held captive by men, observe whether the lord of the ascendant and the significator are quick in their motion and in a tropical sign; ⟨this⟩ signifies the quickness of his release. (2) If they [i.e., the lord of the ascendant and the significator] are in one of the cardines and give power by aspect to a planet located in the third or ninth ⟨place⟩, and likewise if they give power to the lords of these places and it itself is in a feminine quadrant, it signifies his return ⟨to jail⟩. (3) If the ruler or the significator is in a cardo, or ⟨if⟩ the lords of the cardo are in one of the cardines, or ⟨if⟩ the lord of the ascendant is in the house of the lord of the twelfth ⟨place⟩, or vice versa, or ⟨if⟩ the lord of the ascendant is in an inauspicious quadrant, or ⟨if⟩ a planet, which is then in a cardo, is one of the lords of an inauspicious place, and particularly if the planet is a malefic in its nature, and likewise if the malefic planet is the lord of the 12th ⟨place⟩ when it is conjoining the lord of the ascendant, then the misfortune is complete. (4) If the lord of the ascendant gives power to a planet in a cardo, or to a planet harmed by a malefic or by the Sun, and ⟨if⟩ it [the lord of the ascendant] is together with the harmed ⟨planet⟩ itself or the malefic ⟨planet⟩ is in the eighth ⟨place⟩, then it signifies that he will be put in jail and held in his captivity; the significator's giving of power to the lord of the ascendant is also inauspicious. (5) The fixed signs are also inauspicious for this matter, and the bicorporal signs signify release ⟨from jail⟩ and also that he will be jailed again. (6) If the lord of the ascendant gives power to the lord of the third or ninth ⟨place⟩ and they themselves are in the third or ninth ⟨place⟩, or in a feminine quadrant, and they themselves and each of them gives power to a planet located in a cardo, then it signifies that he will escape, or ⟨that he will⟩ be released and captured again. (7) For the person who put him in prison or the {...} observe the lord of the seventh ⟨place⟩; if it is in an auspicious aspect to the ascendant or to its lord, it signifies love and that he [the person who has imprisoned him] will do good to him [the prisoner], but ⟨if it is⟩ in an inauspicious aspect, judge the opposite. (8) If the planet is malefic in its nature, it signifies a blow and great pains. (9) If the significator gives power to a planet in the eighth or second ⟨place⟩, it indicates pains that he [the prisoner] will suffer after he is released ⟨from jail⟩. (10) If ⟨the significator⟩ is a retrograde planet, he [the prisoner] will be captured a second time and returned to jail.[1]

2 (1) Dicit Abraham additor: scias quod sapientes interrogationum iudiciorum dixerunt quod homo[1] potest scire quid in corde interrogantis est. (2) Et quidam ipsorum satis defecerunt, quoniam quidam dicit quod semper respiciet ad .9am. a gradu ascendente eius domus ipsa est. (3) Et alii dicunt quod semper aspicient ad significatorem et ad partem gratie. (4) Et alii dicunt quod semper aspiciat ad prepositum .5. locorum principatus, et dominum hore, item dominum diei. (5) Et propinquius veritati si sciveris naturam omnium graduum circuli sicut scriptum est in *Libro Samechem*. (6) Et associabis cum hoc dominum ascendentis, vel si aspiciat eum, vel quecumque stella associata ei in ascendente. (7) Item[2] associabis semper[3] stellam que est tunc in ascendente, et scies que est eius naturam, et semper[4] qua domo qua ascendens qui aspiciet eum, vel cui inest potestas super eum. (8) Et rectum est quod non debet facere animam hominis intrare in suspectionem nisi fuerit qui ostenderit ei quemlibet gradus. (9) Et ipse liber est honoratus.

3 (1) Et ita dixerunt quod poterit sapiens scire quid est in manu interrogantis ex parte libri dicti, et secundum naturam signi ascendentis et domini eius et illius qui tunc est in ascendente.

4 (1) Et dominus hore ostendet super visione, sicut Saturnus qui ostendit super denigratione, et Iupitter super viride, et Mars super rubeo, et Sol super russo et Venus super oculo clangente, et Mercurius super oculo ⟪tenibret⟫ et Luna super albedine qui non est munda.

5 (1) Et dicunt quod dominum terminorum significat super rem que est
29v ⟪recitee⟫ | vetus vel nova secundum dispositionem eius ad Solem. (2) Et alii dixerunt: respice semper ad locum significatoris.

6 (1) Et ita dixerunt quod potuerunt trahere abscondita. (2) Respicient: si fuerit aliqua malivola in aliquo angulorum, indicabunt quod[5] fuit ibi et quod attraxerunt, et si ibi fuerit stella bona, ibi est in vicinitate. (3) Et ad sciendum locum eius, dixerunt quod signum veridicum significat quod est sub terra, et signa bicorpora in pariete, et mobilia in coopertorio vel tecto. (4) Et dixerunt quod Sol ostendit infra terram vel in medio domus; et Luna prope portam vel hostium; et Mars super domum, in qua sit ignis, vel super

[1]homo] E; V hoc. [2]item] E; V iterum. [3]semper*] corrected according to *Tp*, I i 4:7; EV super. [4]semper*] corrected according to *Tp*, I i 4:7; EV super. [5]quod] E; V quid.

2 (1) Abraham the author says: know that the scholars of the judgments of interrogations said that a man can know what the querent has in his heart. (2) Some of them were very confused because one says that one should always observe the ninth-part[1] from the ascendant ⟨to find⟩ where its ⟨horoscopic⟩ place is.[2,3] (3) Others say that they [the astrologers] should always observe the significator and the lot of Fortune.[4,5] (4) Others say that he [the astrologer] should always observe the ruler of the five places of dominion, and the lord of the hour, also the lord of the day.[6] (5) It is closer to the truth if you know the nature of every degree of the zodiac, as written in the *Book Samechem*.[7] (6) Associate with this the lord of the ascendant, or ⟨any planet⟩ if it aspects it [the lord of the ascendant], or any planet associated with it [the lord of the ascendant] in the ascendant. (7) Also always associate the planet that is then in the ascendant, and know its [the planet's] nature, and always ⟨know⟩ which place aspects ⟨the planet that⟩ is in the ascendant,[8] or which ⟨planet⟩ exerts dignity over it.[9] (8) It is proper not to be in doubt regarding what a man has in his mind only if one knows what each degree signifies. (9) That is a noble book.[10,11]

3 (1) They said that in this way the astrologer may know what is in the querent's hand on the basis of the aforementioned book, and according to the nature of the ascendant sign, its lord, and ⟨the planet⟩ which is then in the ascendant.[1]

4 (1) The lord of the hour[1] signifies the color, like Saturn which signifies grey; Jupiter ⟨which signifies⟩ green; Mars, red; the Sun, crimson; Venus, a brilliant color; Mercury, a ⟪mixed⟫ color; the Moon, white but not pure.[2]

5 (1) They say that the lord of the terms[1] signifies whether the ⟪hidden⟫ thing is old or new according to its configuration with respect to the Sun. (2) Others said: always observe the position of the significator.[2]

6 (1) They said that in this way they can find a hidden thing. (2) They observed: if a malefic ⟨planet⟩ is in one of the cardines, they indicate that it [the hidden thing] was there but it has been ⟨already⟩ taken, and if a benefic planet is there, it is there nearby.[1] (3) To find out the place, they said that a fixed sign signifies that it is below ground, and the bicorporal signs ⟨indicate that it is⟩ in a wall, and the tropical ⟨indicate that it is⟩ in a covered place or in the roof.[2] (4) They said that the Sun signifies ⟨that the hidden thing is⟩ underground or inside the house; the Moon ⟨signifies that the hidden thing is⟩ near the door or the entrance; Mars ⟨signifies⟩ the room, in which

locum furni in domo; et Jupiter super domum honoratam, in curia, et super locum bonum in domo que est munda, sicut locum orationis; et Venus super domum mulierum, in loco concubitus; et Mercurius super domum librorumm, vel domum in qua sunt libri, vel locum pictum; et Saturnus super latrinam vel locum inmundum vel ⟪affondement bo⟫, item similiter super lectum obscurum in domo. (5) Item hee domus non sunt ⟪aigies⟫ super ⟪fondamentum⟫ bonum, item quidquid dictum est in hac re dicit Jacobus Alkindi in libris suis. (6) Et bonum est et iustum homini scire quod non debet intrare in hoc verba.

7 (1) Et adhuc dixerunt quod fugit a domino suo. (2) Si dominus ascendentis dederit fortitudinem stelle malivole vel stelle retrograde, revertetur servus per semet ipsum ad dominum suum. (3) Et si dederit fortitudinem vel coniungatur domino .7e., vel dominus ascendentis aut dominus gratie domino secunde, inveniet fugitivum. (4) Et dominus ascendentis coniungatur domino .7e., dominus eius inveniet eum. (5) Et respice stellam a qua separatur Luna ex aspectu suo et stellam cui dabit Luna fortitudinem, aspiciendo vel coniungendo; aut quod aspiciat Solem, invenietur[1] fugitivus. (6) Et si significator dat fortitudinem domino ascendentis vel domino .7e., significat quod invenietur per nuntios. (7) Et si dominus .7e. dederit fortitudinem stelle bone non retrograde, evadet fugitivus. (8) Et similiter si non aspexerit dominus .7e. dominum ascendentis, vel quod stella retrograda non aspiciat significatorem ex suo aspectu vel coniunctione sua cum stella cui dat significator fortitudinem in aspectu vel in coniunctione. (9) Et si significator det fortitudinem stelle combuste, morietur fugiens. (10) Et ita si significator fuerit combustus a Sole, invenietur fugitivus tamen mortuus.

8 (1) Item vide: ⟨si⟩ significator dederit fortitudinem stelle existenti in
30r quarta feminina, iudicabis quod iam[2] exivit | fugitivus a loco in quo existit vel erat. (2) Et si stella cui[3] dabit Luna fortitudinem fuerit in .4a. masculina, ostendit quod fugitivus est adhuc propinque locus fugationis sue. (3) Et si Luna dederit fortitudinem stelle malivole et recipiatur ab ea, item malivola sit recepta in loco suo, ostendet quod fugitivus est prope ⟪lmaguium⟫ suum

[1]invenietur] E; V inveniet. [2]iam] E; V om. [3]cui] E; V om.

there is a fire, or the place of the oven in the house; Jupiter ⟨signifies⟩ an honorable room, in the hall, and a good place in the house which is clean, like the place of prayer; Venus ⟨signifies⟩ the room of women, in the place for sexual intercourse; Mercury ⟨signifies⟩ the room of books, or the room where there are books, or the place of pictures; Saturn ⟨signifies⟩ the toilet or a filthy place or the basement, also a hidden bed in the house.[3] (5) ⟨The explanation of⟩ these ⟨places of the⟩ houses are not grounded on a sound foundation, and ⟨the same applies to⟩ everything said on this matter by Yaʿqub al-Kindī in his books. (6) It is just and proper to know that no one should go into these matters.

7 (1) In addition, this is what they said regarding someone who escaped from his master. (2) If the lord of the ascendant gives power to a malefic planet or to a retrograde planet, the slave will return to his master on his own.[1] (3) If it gives power to or conjoins the lord of the seventh ⟨place⟩, or the lord of the ascendant or the lord of the ⟨lot of⟩ Fortune ⟨gives power to or conjoins⟩ the lord of the second ⟨place⟩, he [the master] will find the fugitive.[2] (4) ⟨If⟩ the lord of the ascendant conjoins the lord of the seventh ⟨place⟩, his master will find him.[3] (5) Observe the planet from which the Moon has separated from its aspect and the planet to which the Moon gives power, either by aspect or by conjunction; if ⟨any of them⟩ aspects the Sun, the fugitive will be found. (6) If the significator gives power to the lord of the ascendant or to the lord of the seventh ⟨place⟩, this signifies that ⟨the slave⟩ will be found by messengers.[4] (7) If the lord of the seventh ⟨place⟩ gives power to a benefic planet that is not retrograde, the fugitive will escape. (8) The same applies if the lord of the seventh ⟨place⟩ does not aspect the lord of the ascendant, or ⟨if⟩ a retrograde planet does not aspect the significator with respect to its aspect or its conjunction with a planet to which the significator gives power by aspect or by conjunction. (9) If the significator gives power to a burnt planet, the fugitive will die.[5] (10) Likewise, if the significator is burnt by the Sun, the fugitive will be found but dead.[6,7]

8 (1) Also observe: ⟨if⟩ the significator gives power to a planet located in a feminine quadrant, judge that the fugitive has already left the place in which he appeared or was. (2) If the planet to which the Moon gives power is in a masculine quadrant, this indicates that the fugitive is still near the place of his escape.[1] (3) If the Moon gives power to a malefic planet and it [the malefic planet] is received by it [the Moon], and also ⟨if⟩ the malefic is received in its position, this indicates that the fugitive is near his family

et parentes suos. (4) Et si malivola non recipiatur nec recipiat, ostendet quod fugitivus est deprope hominibus vacuis expavescentibus.

9 (1) Et clavis est quod Luna significat super locum fugitivi. (2) Si dederit fortitudinem stelle que est dominus .6e. domus vel .8e. vel .2e., scias quod capietur fugitivus et quod revertetur ad dominum suum. (3) Et poteris scire terminum per grados qui sunt inter locum Lune et locum aspectus, vel locum coniunctionis aut quod erit significator vel dominus ascendentis insimul in loco domini .7e. domus. (4) Et stella velox cursu ostendit festinationem secundum naturam signi in quo est stella recipiens fortitudinem, si fuerit veridicum, et per planetam, si fuerit altus vel inferior, si est in angulis, vel in succedentibus, vel in cadentibus, et secundum dispositionem eius ad Solem.

10 (1) Et omne illud quod ego dixi est si interrogaverit homo pro homine fugiente a domino suo. (2) Et si dominus met interrogat, pone ascendens pro domino et .7m. vel stellam in ea existentem pro fugitivo et sicut videbis iudicabis. (3) Et dixerunt quod locus fugientis est contra angulum in quo est dominus ascendentis, et si non interrogaret dominus suus (4) Sed ipse dominus suus, accipe locum domini .7e. et ⟨⟨concecɔ e cocce⟩⟩ signum ascendens in puncto interrogationis. (5) Quod pones a principio gradus ascendentis usque ad principium .4e.[1] domus ad orientem, et a principio .4e. usque ad principium .7e. ad septentrionem, et a principio .7e. usque ad principium .10e. ad[2] occidentem, et a principio .10e. usque ad principium prime ad meridiem.

11 (1) Dicit Abraham multum honorantur verba Ptholomei[3] in *Libro .C. Verborum*. (2) De te et de illis, item id radix magna.

12 (1) Explicit Liber de interrogationibus editus ab Abraham Iudeo quodam.

[1].4e.] E; V .9e. [2]ad] E; V om. [3]Ptho⟨lome⟩i] V; E Tpho⟨lome⟩i.

and relatives. (4) If the malefic is not received and does not receive ⟨another planet⟩, this indicates that the fugitive is close to worthless and frightened people.[2,3]

9 (1) The general rule is that the Moon signifies the place of the fugitive. (2) If it [the Moon] gives power to a planet that is the lord of the sixth, eighth, or second place, know that the fugitive will be captured and returned to his master.[1] (3) You can know the period ⟨of time after which the fugitive will be returned to his master⟩ by the degrees between the position of the Moon and the position of the aspect or the position of the conjunction, or ⟨of the position⟩ where the significator or the lord of the ascendant was located together in the position of the lord of the seventh place.[2] (4) A planet that is quick in ⟨its⟩ motion indicates quickness according to the nature of the sign in which the planet that receives power is located, if it is a fixed ⟨sign⟩, or according to the planet, if it is above or below ⟨the Sun⟩, if it is in the cardines, or in the succedent or the cadent ⟨places⟩,[3] or according to its configuration with respect to the Sun.[4]

10 (1) All I have said is ⟨valid⟩ if someone poses a question about a man who is running away from his master. (2) If the master himself is the querent, assign the ⟨lord of the⟩ ascendant to the master and ⟨the lord of⟩ the seventh place or the planet located in it [the seventh place] to the fugitive, and judge according to what you see. (3) They said that the fugitive's location is opposite the cardo in which the lord of the ascendant is, if his [the fugitive's] master is not asking. (4) But ⟨if⟩ the [fugitive's] master ⟨is asking⟩, take the position of the lord of the seventh ⟨place⟩, and all this with respect to the ascendant sign at the time of the question. (5) Assign the east to the ⟨interval⟩ between the beginning of the ascendant degree and the cusp of the fourth place; ⟨assign⟩ the north to ⟨the interval⟩ between the cusp of the fourth ⟨place⟩ and the cusp of the seventh ⟨place⟩; ⟨assign⟩ the west to ⟨the interval⟩ between the cusp of the seventh ⟨place⟩ and the cusp of the tenth ⟨place⟩, ⟨and assign⟩ the south to ⟨the interval⟩ between the cusp of the tenth ⟨place⟩ and the cusp of the first ⟨place⟩.[1,2]

11 (1) Abraham says: Ptolemy's statements in the *Book of the 100 statements* are much to be praised. (2) ⟨Ptolemy says⟩ from you and from them, and this is also a great principle.[1,2]

12 (1) Here ends the *Book of interrogations* written by a certain Abraham the Jew.

PART FOUR

NOTES TO *LIBER INTERROGATIONUM*

⟨I 1⟩

[1]**2: The scholars of the judgments of the signs divided themselves into two groups.** *She'elot* I and *She'elot* II, too, in their opening sentences, present the same division of opinion among the astrologers regarding the reliability and trustfulness of the doctrine of interrogations. While *She'elot* I (§ 1:2–7, § 2:1–3, 240–241; quoted in App. 2, Q. 1, § 1:1–7, § 2:1–3, 399) speaks of two opposing schools of thought, *She'elot* II (§ 1:1–4, 348–349; quoted in App. 2, Q. 2, 1–4, 400), mentions two leading astrologers, who were also kings. For this twofold division, see the beginning of Ibn Abī l-Rijāl's *Kitāb al-Bāriʿ* (quoted in App. 2, Q. 3, 400–401).

[2]**3: The degrees ... 2,000 ⟨years⟩.** Cycles of 2000 years in relation to the degrees of the zodiac and to the zodiacal signs are not found anywhere in Ibn Ezra's extant Hebrew works. However, they are mentioned in the recently identified Latin translation of *Olam* III (see note on *El*, II vi 1:5), preserved in Vatican, BAV, MS Pal. lat. 1407, fol. 56r, and quoted in App. 5, Q. 46, 480.

[3]**3: .120., that is, .120. modes of planetary conjunctions.** This passage presents the pattern of the "120 planetary conjunctions," that is, the sum total of the combinations (involving at least two planets) of seven planets, from high to low, when the order in which the planets are taken is insignificant and no planet may appear more than once in any particular combination. Ibn Ezra borrowed this numerical-cosmological pattern from aphorism 50 of Pseudo-Ptolemy's *Centiloquium* (quoted in App. 2, Q. 6, 401). This pattern is the first topic addressed in *ʿOlam* I (§ 2:1–4 through § 6:1–7, 52–55), and *ʿOlam* II (§ 1:7, 156–157). The lengthy explanation in *ʿOlam* I constitutes Ibn Ezra's original attempt to provide a mathematical demonstration of each of the partial combinations of two, three, four, five, six, and seven planets. A passage in the introduction of *Nativitates* (I iv 1:1–7, 84–86) presents the partial combinations in descending order but without explaining how they are computed. In his biblical commentaries Ibn Ezra repeatedly highlights the cosmological connotations of the pattern of the 120 planetary conjunctions but does not explain how the number is obtained. See long commentary on Ex. 3:15; long commentary on Daniel 10:21; long commentary on Gen. 1:14; commentary on Eccles. 1:3. The theological-scientific excursus in Ibn Ezra's long commentary on Ex. 33:21 is a remarkable exception to this rule. See Sela 2003, 313–323.

[4]**3: Any ⟨cycle⟩ of 75 years.** This passage refers to the "years of the *fardār*," a theory used in nativities that takes an interval of human life of 75 years and divides it into nine periods, ruled by the seven planets in the order of their orbs, followed at the end by the Head and Tail of the Dragon. *Moladot* (IV 12:1–17, 190–193) and *Tequfah* (§ 14:1–11, 382–385) offer long and detailed explanations of the method of allocation of *fardār*ships. By contrast with *Nativitates* (II ii 4:1, 120–121), where this doctrine is assigned to the scientists of India, Ibn Ezra frequently mentions the contribution of the Persian scientists to the *fardār* (*Moladot*, III ii 7: 12, 128–129; *'Olam* I, § 23:1, 66–67; § 24:1, 68–69; *'Olam* II, § 30:1, 174–175; § 32:1, 176–177; *De nativitatibus*, II ii 7:1–6, 292–295). He adds, however, that they did not provide explanations and relied for this doctrine on empirical evidence (*Ṭe'amim* II, § 5.12:13, 218–219; § 5.5:12, 230–231; § 5.8:13, 234–235; § 6.6:1, 240–241). The *fardār*, which appears in medieval Arabic, Hebrew, and Latin texts, is used in both nativities and historical astrology. In nativities, the *fardār* refers to a period of 75 years, which corresponds to the natural span of human life and is distributed into nine ages ruled by the seven planets and the lunar nodes. The earliest source for the *fardār* in nativities is al-Andarzagar, whom the Arabs associated with Persian astrology (although he may have been post-Sassanid). See *Andarzaghar* 1991, 338–359, and *Liber Aristotilis*, ed. Burnett and Pingree (1997), IV 17–25, 113–121. The *fardār* in nativities appears frequently in subsequent Arabic astrology. A similar doctrine, also called *fardār*, is applied in world astrology. Although it too posits a span of 75 years divided into nine periods, and the planets and the two lunar nodes are assigned the same number of years as in the version applied in nativities, their *fardār*ships follow the order of their exaltations and not of their orbs. See *Kitāb al-Ulūf*, ed. Pingree (1968), 60–63.

[5]**3: Conjunctions of Saturn and Mars in Cancer, which is the sign of the world.** Throughout his astrological corpus Ibn Ezra refers to Cancer as the "sign of the world." *Reshit ḥokhmah* (§ 2.4:34, 82–83) and *Nativitates* (I i 3:1, 82–83) ascribe this idea to Enoch. *Ṭe'amim* I (2.4:4, 42–43, quoted in App. 5, Q. 12, 468), besides mentioning Enoch as the originator, explains why astrologers pay special attention to the Saturn-Mars conjunction in Cancer. With regard to world affairs, the Saturn-Mars conjunctions in Cancer are mentioned separately in *'Olam* II (§ 4:1, 156–157) and *'Olam* I (§ 27:1, 70–71). One source is Abū Ma'shar's *Great Introduction*, (ed. Burnett and Yamamoto (2019), V:7, [7]:358–359). Māshā'allāh mentions the Saturn-Mars conjunction for world affairs in his *Book on Eclipses* (ed. Sela (2010), § 11:1–4, 256–257). Al-Kindī (ed. Bos and Burnett (2000), App. III,

[4]–[11, [17]–[35], 529–533, 535–541) and Abū Maʿshar (*Book of Religions and Dynasties*, ed. Yamamoto and Burnett (2000), § 2.8:3–6, 123–131) offer two parallel accounts of the conjunctions of the two malefics in Cancer and their sway over Islamic history.

[6]**3: Lots.** These are ecliptical points, influential in the horoscope, that are calculated on the basis of three horoscopic entities. The distance between two of them (place of the planets, cusps of horoscopic places, etc.) is added to the position of the third, usually the ascendant. Ibn Ezra explains this concept in *Reshit ḥokhmah* § 9.24:1–3, 264–265 (quoted in App. 5, Q. 13, 469).

[7]**3: Directions; Latin: *ductus*.** This term denotes a procedure in which an imaginary clock-hand or pointer is set in motion, starting at some zodiacal position, and moved around the zodiac at some specified rate until it reaches another zodiacal position. The arc drawn between these two zodiacal positions, usually projected onto the equator, is then converted into a corresponding number of years, months, and days, which is used for a variety of astrological predictions. The ultimate source is *Tetrabiblos*, where Ptolemy reports how this procedure is applied in nativities, on the one hand, and in continuous horoscopy, on the other. In the third part of *Tetrabiblos* (ed. Robbins (1980), III:10, 271–307), life is represented as a continuous progression of an initial zodiacal point, the "prorogator" or "prorogative" place, until it reaches one or several destructive points in the zodiac, the "anaeretic" places, which symbolize threats to the native's life and, ultimately, the native's death. By contrast, in the fourth part of *Tetrabiblos* (ed. Robbins (1980), IV:10, 447–449), the prorogation is launched simultaneously from five prorogatory places (the ascendant, the Sun, the Moon, the lot of Fortune, and midheaven, each of them linked to specific domains of the native's life) and moved from one zodiacal sign to the next at three different rates: one zodiacal sign in one year, in one month, or in one day. This makes it possible to identify the chronocrators or rulers of the native's years, months, and days. The procedure of directions is also used in world astrology in a great variety of cycles, as shown, for example, in chapter 10 of *Reshit ḥokhmah* (§ 10.2:1–11, § 10.3:1–7, 268–271).

[8]**3: Revolutions of the years of the newborn, Latin: *revolutiones annorum nati*.** This term refers to a horoscope cast at the anniversary of the native's birth, that is, at the time "when the Sun returns to the degree in the sign where it was at the moment of the birth, and the same minutes," as stated at the start of *Sefer ha-Tequfah* (§ 1:1, 372–373). *Revolutio anni* in the cur-

rent passage is a Latin translation of Ibn Ezra's תקופת השנה, or תקופה tout court. This biblical locution (Ex. 34:22; 2 Chron. 24:23) conveys the idea of the beginning or completion of some unspecified cycle. But תקופת השנה to denote the revolution of the year is not Ibn Ezra's coinage. Abraham Bar Ḥiyya preceded him with an elaborate explanation of this concept in chapter 19 of *Ḥeshbon mahalakhot ha-kokhavim* (ed. Millás Vallicrosa (1959), 106–107, Hebrew part). Note that *Interrogationes* uses various expressions to denote the same concept: *revolutiones nativitatum* = "revolutions of the nativities" (I 2:3); *revolutiones cuilibet anni* = "revolutions of each year" (II i 15:3); and *revolutiones de anno in anno* = "revolution from year to year" (II i 15:4).

[9]**4: ⟨Their⟩ root is the position ... planet that is the ruler.** Corresponds to *Epitome*, ed. Heller (1548), III:2, O4r (quoted in App. 2, Q. 4, 401) and Sahl's *Book of Interrogations* (quoted in App. 2, Q. 5, 401).

[10]**4–5: They also say ... degree ⟨of the interrogational horoscope⟩.** This passage echoes the position of the school that supports the reliability of the doctrine of interrogations, as represented by Māshā'allāh in *She'elot* I (§ 3:1–2, 240–241; quoted in App. 2, Q. 1, § 3:1–2, 399–400) and by Dorotheus in *She'elot* II (§ 1:3, 348–349; quoted in App. 2, Q. 2, 3, 400). They both warn the astrologer not to pronounce judgment on any interrogation if the querent is cheating or scoffing.

[11]**7: King Dorotheus, Latin: *Doronius rex*.** Dorotheus is mentioned in *She'elot* II (§ 1:1, 348–349; quoted in App. 2, Q. 2, 1, 400), also with the designation of "king," and in *She'elot* I (§ 2:1, 240–241; quoted in App. 2, Q. 1, § 2:1, 399–400), without the designation of "king." In both cases Dorotheus is the head of the astrological school that supports the trustfulness of the doctrine of interrogations. This astrologer is to be identified with Dorotheus of Sidon, author of the well-known *Pentabiblos* (*Carmen astrologicum*, ed. Pingree (1976)). The Hebrew originals of Ibn Ezra's astrological writings usually spell this name Doroneus or Doronius, a mistake produced by a mispointing of the Arabic text. "Doronius" as an explicit appellation for Dorotheus of Sidon is found in *Liber Aristotilis* (ed. Burnett and Pingree (1997), prologus, 24, 15 et passim), an early twelfth-century astrological treatise by Hugo of Santalla. *Liber Aristotilis* ascribes 13 works of astrology to Doronius, one of which is on interrogations (ibid., 1, 4, 15). But in a Byzantine translation of a bibliography, Māshā'allāh ascribes 11 works to Dorotheus, three of which are on interrogations (ibid., 4, 201–214). Dorotheus' *Pentabiblos* was

translated into Arabic by ʿUmar b. al-Farrukhān al-Ṭabarī and Māshāʾallāh from a previous translation into Pahlavī (Pingree 1997, 46). That Ibn Ezra was acquainted with the Arabic translations of Dorotheus's work, which were contaminated with Sassanian material and references to Hermes and other astrologers, is suggested by the fact that in the current passage, as well as in *Sheʾelot* II (§ 1:1, 348–349), *ʿOlam* I (§ 32:1, 72–73), *ʿOlam* II (§ 24:1, 172–173), and *Ṭeʿamim* I (§ 2.18:2, 58–59), Dorotheus is referred to as a king, just as in the translation of Dorotheus's work (*Carmen astrologicum*, ed. Pingree (1976), 262).

[12]**7: Kanakah, the Indian, Latin: *Canba Aliendi*.** Ibn Ezra, in his introduction to his Arabic-to-Hebrew translation of *Ibn al-Muthannā's Commentary on the Astronomical Tables of al-Khwārizmī* (ed. Goldstein (1967), 301–302; quoted in App. 5, Q. 14, 469), presents Kanakah as the Indian scientist who first acquainted the Arabs with the main elements of Hindu science. Al-Bīrūnī (*India*, ed. Sachau (1888), vol. II, 15) gives a similar account: a Hindu came to Baghdad as the member of an Indian scientific mission to the caliph al-Manṣūr in 771. Subsequently, Kanakah the Indian (Kankah al-Hindī, in Arabic) came to symbolize for Arabic intellectuals the partial dependence of some of their science on Sanskrit sources. See Pingree 1997, 51–62. *Reshit ḥokhmah* (§ 2.1:23, 60–61) begins the account of the *paranatellonta* of the first decan of Aries according to the Indians with a mention of "Kanakah, their scientist."

[13]**7: Māshāʾallāh, the Indian, Latin: *Mesehalla Halehendi*.** Māshāʾallāh is mentioned in *Sheʾelot* I (§ 3:1, 240–241; quoted in App. 2, Q. 1, § 3:1, 399–400) and in *Sheʾelot* II (§ 1:4, 348–349; quoted in App. 2, Q. 2, 4, 400) as a key member of the astrological school that sees the doctrine of interrogations as trustworthy. Māshāʾallāh, according to Ibn al-Nadim (d. 995 or 998) in his *Fihrist* (1970, II, 650–651), was a Jew who lived from the time of the caliph al-Manṣūr (r. 754–775) to the time of the caliph al-Maʾmūn (r. 813–833), "a man of distinction and during his period the leading person for the science of judgments of the stars," who left behind a long list of works, most of them on astrology. Only a few of Māshāʾallāh's numerous works survive in Arabic; more of them are extant in Latin, Hebrew, and Persian. In the current locus, in *Reshit ḥokhmah* (§ 9.1:6, 234–235), and in *Ṭeʿamim* I (§ 2.18:2, 58–59), Ibn Ezra reports that Māshāʾallāh was from India. This curious notice about Māshāʾallāh's Indian origins is probably due to the fact that Māshāʾallāh was well acquainted with the work of Indian scientists, such as Kanakah (see *Reshit ḥokhmah* § 2.1:23, 60–61 and note), who visited

the courts of al-Manṣūr and Hārūn al-Rashīd. The Hebrew translations of two of Māshā'allāh's works are ascribed to Ibn Ezra: the ספר למשאללה בקדרות הלבנה והשמש, וחיבור הכוכבים, ותקופות השנים = *Māshā'allāh's Book on the Eclipses of the Moon and the Sun, the Conjunctions of the Planets, and the Revolutions of the Years* (see *Book on Eclipses*, ed. Sela (2010)) and ספר השאלות למאשא אללה = *Māshā'allāh's Book of Interrogations*, a popular Hebrew translation of the lost Arabic Book of Interrogations by Māshā'allāh, extant in at least 19 Hebrew manuscripts, most of them from the fourteenth or fifteenth century.

[14]7: **Buzurjmihr?, the Persian king, Latin: *Bugam rex persicus*.** This is probably a reference to Buzurjmihr, a sixth-century Sassanian scholar who translated the *Pancatantra* into Pahlavī (thereby introducing the tales of *Kalīla wa Dimna* to the Sassanid court), introduced chess (caturanga) to Sassanian Iran, and composed a commentary on the *Anthologies* of the Greek astrologer Vettius Valens. See Pingree 1989, 231; *Andarzaghar*, ed. Burnett and al-Hamdi (1991), 294–295. The same astrologer is mentioned in *De nativitatibus*, II iv 1:3, 300–301.

[15]7: **'Umar ⟨b. al-Farrukhān⟩ al-Ṭabarī, Latin: *Aomar Tiberiadis*.** This is the only place where this astrologer is mentioned in Ibn Ezra's work. 'Umar first appears on the scene as one of the group of astrologers, including Nawbakht, Māshā'allāh, and al-Fazārī, whom al-Mansūr asked to select an auspicious time for the foundation of Baghdad: they chose July 30, 762. The latest date we have for him is June 15–July 13, 812, when he finished his version of Ptolemy's *Kitāb al-arba'a* (*Tetrabiblos*). Of 'Umar's personal life nothing is known save that he had a son, Abā Bakr Muhammad, who also wrote extensively on astrology and astronomy. 'Umar's works include a *tafsīr* or paraphrase of Ptolemy's *Tetrabiblos* completed, as noted, in July 812; a *tafsīr* of the astrological work of Dorotheus of Sidon, based on a Pahlavī recension of the early fifth century; *Mukhtasar masā'il al-Qaysarānī* (Abridgment of the Caesarean [?] interrogations) in 138 chapters; *Kitāb fi'l-mawālīd* (Book on nativities), a short treatise on genethlialogy that is probably identical with the Latin *De nativitatibus secundum Omar* in three books, translated by Iohannes Hispalensis; *Kitāb al-'ilal*, a work known to us only through a citation by al-Bīrūnī in his treatise on the solar equation. See Pingree 2019.

[16]7: **Sahl, the Jew, Latin: *Sahal Iudeus*.** This refers to Sahl Ibn Bishr al-Yahūdī, a leading Jewish astrologer of the early ninth century (*Fihrist* 1970,

II, 651–652), well known in the Middle Ages and early modern period, mainly through John of Seville's Latin translations of five of his works. Ibn Ezra knew Sahl in the original Arabic. In *El*, II ii 2:2 (see note there), Ibn Ezra quotes *verbatim* from Sahl's *Book of Elections*; in the current passage he refers to Sahl's work on interrogations. Although Ibn Ezra never mentions Sahl explicitly in *Reshit ḥokhmah*, substantial parts of chapter 8 of the latter work are translations from Sahl's *Nawādir al-qaḍā* (Maxims of judgment), a work organized in 50 aphorisms. See *Reshit ḥokhmah* § 8.1:1 through § 8.3:1–21, 210–222 and notes. Sahl's work on nativities is repeatedly referred to in *Moladot* (III i 4, 8, 102–103; III ii 5, 4, 124–125; III v 6, 4, 146–147; III viii 4, 2, 166–167) and in *De nativitatibus* (II iii 5:1,2; II viii 4:1).

[17]**7: Abū Maʿshar, the Arabian, Latin:** ***Even Mahasar Sarracenus.*** Born in Balḥ in the Persian province of Ḥurāsān in 787 CE; died in al-Wāsiṭ in central Iraq in 886. Abū Maʿshar was the most prominent astrologer of the Middle Ages. He formulated the standard expression of Arabic astrology in its various branches, creating a synthesis of the Indian, Persian, Greek, and Ḥarranian theories current in his day. See *Fihrist* 1970, II, 656–658; Lemay 1962, 1–132; Pingree 1970, 32–39; Pingree 1990, 298–298. Ibn Ezra's attitude towards Abū Maʿshar varies: (a) He takes an approving attitude towards his work on interrogations (*She'elot* I, § 3:6–7, 242–243; § 7.4:5, 272–273; *She'elot* II, § 9.2:7, 380–381; cf. *Int*, II i 12:2; II vii 5:1). (b) He adopts a neutral attitude towards his work on nativities and elections (*Moladot*, III ii 4:2, 124–125; III iv 5: 2, 142–143; III xii 4:1, 142–143; *Mivḥarim* I, § 1.2:2, 52–53; § 1.9:1–2, 54–55; § 5.4:3, 66–67; § 7.2:4, 70–71; § 7.5:1, 74–75; § 12.1:3, 88–89). (c) He refers disapprovingly to Abū Maʿshar's work on historical astrology in *'Olam* I (§ 1:1–2, 52–53; § 61:1–5, 92–93). (d) He draws heavily on Abū Maʿshar's introductions to astrology without mentioning his name: substantial parts of *Reshit ḥokhmah* (chapters 5–7) are paraphrases or *verbatim* translations of Abū Maʿshar's *Great Introduction*. See Sela 2017, 10–12.

[18]**7: Yaʿqub al-Kindī, Latin:** ***Jacob Alkindi.*** Known as the "philosopher of the Arabs," al-Kindī (d. after 866) wrote on the Greek philosophy that was being introduced to the Muslim world. Although he criticized the inconsistent views of astrologers, al-Kindī wrote extensively on all branches of contemporary astrology (see Burnett 1993, 77–117; Adamson 2007, 181–206). Ibn Ezra frequently quotes from al-Kindī's astrological oeuvre, usually without specifying the title, in his introductions to astrology (*Ṭeʿamim* I, § 1.4:2, pp. 32–33; § 2.13:9, pp. 53–53; § 3.1:2, pp. 58–59; § 10.1:5, pp. 96–97; *Ṭeʿamim* II, § 2.1:6, pp. 184–185; § 4.8:1, pp. 212–213; § 8.5:2, pp. 252–253),

and in his works on nativities (*Moladot*, III iv 3:1, 138–139; III v 2:1, 144–145; III vi 12:4, 156–157; III vii 2:3, 158–159; III viii 4:3, 166–167; III x 1:8, 172–173; *De nativitatibus*, II ii 2:1, 286–287), interrogations (*She'elot* I, § 7:1, 244–245; § 4.8:1, 260–261; § 5.3:1, 264–265; *She'elot* II, § 12.5:1; § 12.6:1, 390–393; *Int*, I 1:6; II xii 6:5), elections (*Mivḥarim* I, § 1.7:1; § 7.6:10, 54–55, 76–77; *Mivḥarim* II, § 1.3:1, 151–151), and general astrology (*'Olam* I, § 44:1–6, § 60:1–2, 82–83, 90–91).

[19]**7: Abū 'Alī Al-Khayyāṭ, Latin:** ***Even Aeli Alkahi.*** This is a reference to Abū 'Alī Yaḥyā ibn Ghālib Al-Khayyāṭ, an Arabophone astrologer who flourished in the first half of the ninth century. According to Ibn al-Nadim (d. 995 or 998) in his *Fihrist* (1970, II, 655), he was a student of Māshā'allāh, "one of the most excellent of the astrologers," and composed the following works: *The Introduction*; *Questions*; *The Meaning*; *Governments* (Dynasties); *Nativities*; *Revolution of the Years of the Nativities*; *The Prism*; *The Rod of Gold*; *Revolution of the Years of the World*; *Al Nukat*. In Latin sources he is known as Albohali, mainly thanks to a work on nativities entitled *Liber Albohali de iudiciis nativitatum*, which was translated into Latin by Plato of Tivoli in 1136 and again in 1153 by Johannes Hispalensis. It is in all likelihood to this work by Abū 'Alī on nativities that Ibn Ezra refers in *Moladot* (III ii 4:3, 124–125; III vi 10:2,5, 154–155; III xii 3:1, 180–181). Ibn Ezra also refers to Abū 'Alī's work on interrogations in general in *Int*, I 1:6, and in particular in *She'elot* I, § 4.7:1, 260–261; § 7.4:4, 272–273 and *She'elot* II, § 1.5:2, 360–361.

⟨I 2⟩

[1]**1: King Enoch, the son of Jared.** Enoch is also mentioned in *She'elot* I (§ 1:2, 240–241; quoted in App. 2, Q. 1, § 1:2, 399), without the designation "king" and, together with Ptolemy and many of the Ancients, as the head of the astrological school that rejects the trustworthiness of the doctrine of interrogations. The current passage is the only locus in Ibn Ezra's entire corpus where Enoch is designated "king." Note that in Dorotheus's *Pentabiblos* or *Carmen astrologicum* (ed. Pingree (1976), 224) and in Abū Ma'shar's *Kitāb al-Ulūf* (ed. Pingree (1968), 9–11), Enoch, or Hermes, is designated king of Egypt and son of Dorotheus. Enoch or Hermes is a legendary figure, an incarnation of the god Hermes Trismegistus, an avatar of the Egyptian Thoth, and held to be the author of treatises on philosophy, science, and magic. In the Muslim world he was split in three: the first, who originated the sciences before the Flood; the second, Babylonian, who recovered the

knowledge lost in the Flood; and the third, who lived in Egypt at a later date (Bladel 2009, 121–163; *Kitāb al-Ulūf*, ed. Pingree (1968), 14–19; *Tabaqāt al-ʾumam*, ed. Salem and Kumar (1991), 19, 36; Burnett 1976, 231–234; Plessner 1954; Plessner 1971, 45–59). Ibn Ezra follows this tradition and refers to the triple Enoch in three different sections of *ʿOlam* I: "the ancient Enoch" (§36:1–2, 76–77), "Enoch the Egyptian" (§37:1–2, 76–77), and "Enoch the First" (§56:1–15, 88–89). Ibn Ezra frequently refers to Enoch's astrological and astronomical work, usually in an approving tone and with no accompanying epithet. See, for example, *Ṭeʿamim* I (§2.4:3, 42–43; §2.5:1, 44–45). According to *Ṭeʿamim* I (§1.2:3, 30–31), Ibn Ezra believed that Enoch lived 1,700 years before his own time, as indicated by the position he supposedly reported for the star Cor Leonis. See Sela 2003, 184–185.

[2]**1: King Ptolemy**. Ptolemy is mentioned in *Sheʾelot* II (§1:1–2, 348–349; quoted in App. 2, Q. 2, 1–2, 400), also with the designation "king", and in *Sheʾelot* I (§1:2, 240–241; quoted in App. 2, Q. 1, §1:2, 399), without the designation "king" but together with Enoch and many of the Ancients as the head of the astrological school that rejects the trustworthiness of the doctrine of interrogations. *Sheʾelot* I also puts forward Ptolemy's arguments (§1:3–6, 240–241; quoted in App. 2, Q. 1, §1:3–6, 399) for the rejection of the doctrine of interrogations. For Ptolemy and "King Ptolemy," see note on *El*, II vi 6:4.

[3]**1: Thābit ibn Qurra al-Ḥarrānī.** Al-Ṣābiʾ Thābit ibn Qurra al-Ḥarrānī (826–901) was a mathematician, physician, astronomer and translator who lived in Baghdad in the second half of the ninth century. Ibn Qurra made important discoveries in algebra, geometry, and astronomy. In astronomy, Thābit is considered one of the first reformers of the Ptolemaic system. Thābit ibn Qurra belonged to the Sabian (Mandaean) sect, but the *Liber de rationibus tabularum* (ed. Millás Vallicrosa (1947), 76) informs that he was an outstanding Christian philosopher: *Tebit Bencore christianorum summus philosophorum fuit*. = "Thābit ibn Qurra was an outstanding Christian philosopher." This may be a reference to the Christiam philosopher Theodore Abū Qurra. Thābit ibn Qurra is mentioned in relation to an astrological topic in *Moladot* III iv 2:3, 138–139, and in relation to astronomical topics in *Moladot* IV 1:3, 182–183, *Liber de rationibus tabularum* (ed. Millás Vallicrosa (1947), 76, 79, 81,82, 83), and in the introduction to Ibn Ezra's translation of Ibn al-Muthannā's *Commentary on the Astronomical tables of al-Khwārizmī* (ed. Goldstein (1967), 150, 300).

[4]**1: Al-Battānī ibn Jābir the Arab, Latin.** Al-Battani (ca. 858–929) is also mentioned in *Moladot* (IV 1:7, 182–183) and *Liber de rationibus tabularum* (ed. Millás Vallicrosa (1947), 76) as one of the great Arabic scientists who followed in Ptolemy's footsteps. Al-Battani was the son of a maker of astronomical instruments in Harran but worked mainly in Raqqah on the Euphrates. He was basically a follower of Ptolemy, devoting himself to refining and perfecting the work of his master. Al-Battānī's major work is *Kitāb az-Zīj* (Book of astronomical tables). It was largely based on Ptolemy's theory and other Greco-Syriac sources, while showing little Indian or Persian influence. His work was widely known in the Middle Age, having been translated by Plato of Tivoli in about 1120 as *De motu stellarum* (On stellar motion), which was finally published in Nuremberg in 1537.

[5]**1: Ḥassān the Jew.** This otherwise unknown Jewish savant may be identical with "Ben Ḥassān, the Spaniard," scornfully referred to in *'Ibbur* (ed. Goodman (2011), 127, English part; 70, Hebrew part), where Ibn Ezra writes that he wrote three treatises on the Jewish calendar "of no great import." This Ben Ḥassān, in his turn, is in all likelihood identical with Mar Ḥassān, who in Ibn Ezra's second commentary on Genesis 1:6 endorses the same cosmological arguments held by a "prominent Spaniard sage" in Ibn Ezra's first commentary on Genesis 1:14: the firmament (*raqia'*) referred to in Genesis 1:14 is divided into eight parts, seven for the seven planets and one for the orb of the zodiacal signs. See Sela 2003, 332–335. Mar Ḥassān was also sarcastically referred to by Abraham Bar Ḥiyya in his own *Sefer ha-'Ibbur* (ed. Philipobsky (1851), 54, 94).

[6]**1: Alihi.** This name is never mentioned elsewhere in Ibn Ezra's work.

[7]**2: They laugh at matters … individuals and groups.** The current passage reflects the fact that, according to Ibn Ezra, Ptolemy left out all the lots, except for the lot of Fortune. See especially *Ṭe'amim* II, § 7.1:1, 242–243 (quoted in App. 5, Q. 15, 469), *Ṭe'amim* I, § 9.1:1–2, 92–93, and *De nativitatibus*, I 13:1, 258–259. The same omission of the lots applies to al-Bīrūnī's *Elements* (ed. Ramsay Wright (1934), § 476, 282) and Ptolemy's *Tetrabiblos* (ed. Robbins (1980), III:10, 275–277).

[8]**1–3: The second group … related to divination.** The same school that was skeptical about the doctrine of interrogations is presented in the opening sentences of *She'elot* I (§ 1:2–7, quoted in App. 2, Q. 1, § 1:2–7, 399) and *She'elot* II (§ 1:2, 348–349; quoted in 2, Q. 2, 2, 399–400). *She'elot* I says that

this school is represented by Enoch, Ptolemy, and many of the Ancients, who maintain that the celestial bodies give no indication about the human thoughts or interrogations. By contrast, *She'elot* II (§ 1:2, 348–349; quoted in App. 2, Q. 2, 2, 400) mentions only King Ptolemy and says only that he did not agree that interrogations are accurate.

⟨I 3⟩

[1]**1: I Abraham, who authored this book, Latin:** ***Et ego Abraham, qui addo hunc librum.*** The name *Abraham Addens*, a translation of אברהם המחבר "Abraham the author," occurs in *Int*, II i 2:1, as the name of the author of this book. From *Abraham Addens* the Latin translator of *Interrogationes* derived the verb *addere* with the meaning of writing a book. This is so because the Hebrew root חבר denotes "combination," "addition," or "binding," but the derived noun מחבר means "author" and the derived infinitive לחבר means "to author."

[2]**3: The planet will be in the 12th ⟨horoscopic⟩ place.** Due to the counterclockwise motion of the zodiac with respect to the Earth, the next horoscopic place after the ascendant (i.e., the first horoscopic place,) is the twelfth horoscopic place (not the second horoscopic place). So if a delay takes place, a planet that was due to be in the ascendant will be seen in the twelfth horoscopic place.

[3]**1–4: I, Abraham, who authored this book ... one who cheats.** The same explicit position—supporting the group that questions the reliability of the doctrine of interrogations but supporting interrogations as reliable on condition that the astrologer takes precautions to make sure that the querent is not cheating—is stated in *She'elot* I (§ 3:1–5, quoted in App. 2, Q. 1, § 3:1–5, 399–400). Ibn Ezra admits there that interrogations are usually reliable, although not reliable as nativities, but also seconds Māshā'allāh's warning that one must not pronounce a judgment on any interrogation for a man who is cheating or mocking.

⟨I 4⟩

[1]**2: To make it easier ... [*lit.* in the beginning of the Book of Wisdom].** Corresponds to *El*, I 7:4

[2]**2: According to the properties of the places which I mentioned in the *Book of the Beginning of Wisdom* [*lit.* in the beginning of the Book of Wisdom], Latin: *cum manieribus domorum quorum mentionem feci in Principio Libri de Sensu*.** Ibn Ezra wrote two versions of his *Book of the Beginning of Wisdom*. Because the treatment of the properties of the twelve horoscopic places is a commonplace in any introduction to astrology, this may be a reference to *Reshit ḥokhmah* § 3.5:1–4, 142–143 through § 3.16:1–2, 146–147, where this topic is advanced, although it cannot be ruled out that the reference is to the second lost version of the same book. Note that Ibn Ezra's ספר ראשית חכמה (Book of the Beginning of Wisdom) is here mistranslated *Principium libri de sensu*, "Beginning of the book of wisdom." In other loci, too, the book's title receives divergent and erroneous translations. See *Int*, II ii 1:3 and II vi 1:3. Here (and elsewhere) the Latin translator of *Interrogationes* must have been confused about the proper translation of the name of Ibn Ezra's book, probably because of an awkward French intermediary.

⟨II i 1⟩

[1]**1: According to what the astrologers ... person who thinks.** Corresponds closely to *Ṭeʿamim* I, § 3.6:1, 66–67 (quoted in App. 5, Q. 16, 469); also corresponds also to *Ṭeʿamim* II, § 3.1:2–4, 202–203.

[2]**2: They said always ... respect to the Sun.** The same statement reappears in *Int*, II i 7:1.

[3]**3: Fixed signs, Latin: *signa veridica*, lit. truthful signs.** The current passage translates מזלות נאמנים, "enduring signs," to denote the fixed signs (Taurus, Leo, Scorpio, Aquarius). This is borne out by the fact that מזלות נאמנים is used for the fixed signs in the Modena fragment of *Sheʾelot* III. See *Sheʾelot* III, II vi 2:2, 492. *Electiones* and *Tractatus particulares* also use *signa veridica* to render the same Hebrew term. However, whereas the current and numerous other passages in *Interrogationes* have *signa veridica*, *Int*, II i 1:3 uses *signa stabilia* to denote this type of signs. Likewise, whereas *Tp*, I iii 1:2 has *signa veridica*, *Tp*, I iv 3:4, and IV 6:4 use *signa fixa*. The same applies to *Mishpeṭei ha-mazzalot*: *Mishpeṭei ha-mazzalot* § 2:3, 488–489 uses נאמנים, *Mishpeṭei ha-mazzalot* § 49:3, 536–537 has מזלות עומדים. The inconsistent terminology for "fixed signs" marks all of Ibn Ezra's astrological oeuvre, although not within a single work (as in *Interrogationes*,

Tractatus particulares, and *Mishpeṭei ha-mazzalot*). In Ibn Ezra's introductions to astrology and in most of his works on nativities, elections, and interrogations, the fixed signs are referred to as מזלות עומדים or עומדים על דרך אחת. See *Reshit ḥokhmah* (§ 2.5:2, 86–87; § 2.8:2, 102–103); *Ṭeʿamim* I (§ 2.13:1, 52–53); *Ṭeʿamim* II (§ 2.3:3, 188–189). *Reshit ḥokhmah* II (2010, 51, 56); *Moladot* (III i 7, 3, 104 et passim); *Mivḥarim* I (§ 1.2:3, 52–53 et passim); *Mivḥarim* II (§ 6:16, 148–149); *She'elot* I (§ 4.7:1, 260–261 et passim); *She'elot* II (§ 2:1, 348–349 et passim). By contrast, נאמנים or מזלות נאמנים occurs in *Tequfah* (§ 18:1, 386) and *Me'orot*, (§ 17:1, 466–467). This terminology links *Mishpeṭei ha-mazzalot* with *Interrogationes*, and connects *Tractatus particulares* and *Electiones* with *Tequfah* and *Me'orot*.

[4]**5: Burning, Latin: *reflammatio*.** This term refers to one of the conditions of the planets with respect to the Sun. See note to *El*, II i 1:5, s.v. "burnt." Note that for the same term, *Int*, II i 2:1 uses *inflammatio* and *Int*, II i 3:5 uses *combustio*. The inconsistent Latin translations, here and elsewhere, may indicate merely that the Latin translator did not remember how he had translated a term earlier, or by divergent French intermediate translations or Hebrew terminology for the same concept.

[5]**5: Planet, Latin: *stella servientis***: This is a literal translation of כוכב משרת, "servant star," used by Ibn Ezra to denote a planet, usually in contrast to the fixed stars. For one example, see *Ṭeʿamim* I, § 1.5:7, 34–35 (quoted in App. 5, Q. 17, 470). Ibn Ezra's most distinctive neologism is משרתים, "servants," frequently used in his scientific and nonscientific writings to denote the seven planets. For a use of משרתים in the Hebrew text of *She'elot* III extant in the Modena fragment, see *She'elot* III, II vi 1:7, 491–492. A similar translation of משרתים occurs in the title of one of the components of *Tractatus particulares*. See *Tp*, II vii 14:1, and note.

[6]**3–5: Know that the fixed ... the cardines do.** Corresponds to a passage in the introduction to the third part, on interrogations, of the *Epitome* (quoted in App. 2, Q. 8, 402). Cf. *Epitome*, ed. Heller (1548), III:1, O3v. The first section of the passage corresponds to *She'elot* II, § 2:1, 348–349.

⟨II i 2⟩

[1]**1: Abraham, the author, Latin: *Abraham Addens*.** For this name, see notes on *El*, I 1:1 and *Int*, I 3:1.

[2]**1: Burning, Latin: *inflammatio*.** This term refers to one of the conditions of the planets with respect to the Sun. See note to *El*, II i 1:5, s.v. "burnt." Note that for the same term, *Int*, II i 1:5 has *reflammatio*, and *Int*, II i 3:5 has *combustio*. See note on *Int*, II i 1:5.

[3]**1–2: I Abraham, the author … will not be full.** For the conditions of the superior planets (Saturn, Jupiter and Mars) with respect to the Sun, see *Reshit ḥokhmah* § 6.6:1–21, 192–195; *Mishpeṭei ha-mazzalot* § 26:1–3, 510–511; and *Ṭeʿamim* I, § 6.2:1–5, 86–87. For the conditions of the inferior planets (Venus and Mercury) with respect to the Sun, see *Reshit ḥokhmah* § 6.7:1–10, 194–195; *Mishpeṭei ha-mazzalot* § 29:1–6, 512–515; and *Ṭeʿamim* I, § 6.3:1–6, 86–87.

⟨II i 3⟩

[1]**2: Cadent from the cardines, which are the third, sixth, ninth, and twelfth.** For this concept, see note on *Interrogationes* II xii 9:4.

[2]**5: Burning, Latin: *combustio*.** This term refers to one of the conditions of the planets with respect to the Sun. See note to *El*, II i 1:5, s.v. "burnt." Note that for the same term, *Int*, II i 1:5 has *reflammatio* and *Int*, II i 2:1 has *inflammatio*. See note on *Int*, II i 1:5.

[3]**1–5: The tropical signs signify … cadent places do.** Corresponds to a passage in the introduction to the third part, on interrogations, of the *Epitome* (quoted in App. 2, Q. 9, 402). Cf. *Epitome*, ed. Heller (1548), III:1, O3v.

⟨II i 4⟩

[1]**1: The bicorporal signs, Latin: *signa que sunt domini duorum corporum*, lit. the signs that are lords of two bodies.** In this Latin expression, *dominus* misconstrues בעל, *lit.* "lord," "master" or "husband," but here with the sense of "having," "owner," or "possessor." The Latin expression *signa que sunt domini duorum corporum* is a calque of בעלי שני גופות, "having two bodies," used in the Hebrew text of *She'elot* III extant in the Modena fragment (see *She'elot* III, II vi 2:2, 492) and in some of Ibn Ezra's works to denote the bicorporal signs. See *She'elot* II, § 2:3, 348–349; § 4:4, 350–351; § 1.4:2, 358–359; *Mivḥarim* I, § 10.3:3, 84–85; *Mishpeṭei ha-mazzalot* § 2:4, 488–489; § 49:3, 536–537.

[2]**3: Stations, Latin: *stationes*.** The stations are those parts of a planet's orbit where the planet appears to stand still briefly before changing its course. The place where the motion of a planet shifts from direct to retrograde motion is called the "first station"; the place where its motion reverses from retrograde to direct is called the "second station."

[3]**1–3: The bicorporal signs … one of their stations.** Corresponds to a passage in the introduction to the third part, on interrogations, of the *Epitome* (quoted in App. 2, Q. 10, 402). Cf. *Epitome*, ed. Heller (1548), III:1, O3v.

⟨II i 5⟩

[1]**1–2: Abraham says … will not take place.** Corresponds to *She'elot* II, § 5:1–2, 350–351 (quoted in App. 5, Q. 18, 470).

⟨II i 6⟩

[1]**1: Bicorporal signs, Latin: domini corporum, lit. lords of bodies.** For this expression, denoting the bicorporal signs, see note on *Int*, II i 4:1.

[2]**1–2: Know that the bicorporal signs … requested matter.** Corresponds closely to *She'elot* I, § 7.9:5, 280–281 (quoted in App. 5, Q. 19, 470), *Mishpeṭei ha-mazzalot* § 49:3, 536–537 (quoted in App. 5, Q. 20, 470), and to *Tp*, IV 6:4, where a similar statement is attributed to Māshā'allāh.

[3]**8–9: Consequently they say … wars and disasters.** *Mivḥarim* I (§ 4.3:1–2, 62–63; quoted in App. 5, Q. 21, 471) assigns this negative opinion about Scorpio to Māshā'allāh. By contrast, *She'elot* I (§ 3:6–7, 242–243; quoted in App. 5, Q. 22, 471) and *She'elot* II (§ 9.2:7, 380–381; quoted in App. 5, Q. 23, 471) focus on the falsehood of Mars, Scorpio's lord, and assign this negative opinion to Abū Maʿshar.

[4]**10: Scezen, Abū Maʿshar's disciple, Latin: *Even Maasar Scezen discipulus*.** This refers to Abū Saʿīd Shādhān ibn Bahr, Abū Maʿshar's disciple. He composed *Mudhākarāt Abī Maʿshar fī asrār ʿilm al-nujūm* (Sayings of Abū Maʿshar on the secrets of astrology), a collection of astrological precepts and anecdotes in the form of a dialogue between the astrologer Abū Maʿshar and his otherwise unknown pupil. Abū Saʿīd Shādhān's *Mud-*

hākarāt contains much valuable information about the practice of astrology in ninth-century Baghdad and is frequently cited by Muslim historians of the period. It was translated into Greek and into Latin. See Pingree 1970. At least fragments of this work were already known to Latin scholars in the twelfth century. See Burnett 2003. A Latin version, probably derived from an abbreviated Greek translation, was available in the thirteenth century. See Thorndike 1954; *Albumasar in Sadan*, ed. Federici Vescovini (1998). Abū Saʿīd Shādhān is mentioned again, as Abū Maʿshar's mouthpiece, in *De nativitatibus*, II ii 3:1 (see note there).

[5]**10: Scezen, Abū Maʿshar's disciple … Mars is ascending.** This paraphrases a passage from Abū Saʿīd Shādhān's *Mudhākarāt* (quoted in App. 5, Q. 27, 473).

[6]**11: But this is not so regarding Aries … divine worship.** That Aries is a "just sign" and that it is "a place of divine worship" is explained in *Ṭeʿamim* II, § 2.4:13, 192–195 (quoted in App. 5, Q. 24, 471–472). See also *Reshit ḥokhmah* § 2.1:18, 58–59, which is explained in *Ṭeʿamim* I, § 2.2:14, 38–39.

[7]**12: House of exaltation, Latin: *domus honoris*.** This is a calque of בית כבוד "house of honor," used everywhere by Ibn Ezra to denote "house of exaltation." Exaltation is traditionally the second of the planets' five essential dignities. To denote this concept, Ibn Ezra coined כבוד, "honor," a loan translation from شرف, used in Arabic astrological literature to denote the concept of exaltation. The Latin works that fall within the ambit of Ibn Ezra's astrological and astronomical oeuvre use the corresponding Latin calque *honor* for exaltation; e.g., *De nativitatibus*, I 21:2, 268–269, et passim; *Nativitates*, I vii 2:1, 92–93, et passim; *Epitome*, ed. Heller (1548), 1–12, B1r–C2r et passim; *De rationibus tabularum*, ed. Millás Vallicrosa (1947), 85. Note, however, that *El*, II vii 5:5, *Int*, II i 3:2, II x 1:6 as well as *Tp*, II v 3:1, all three also use *exaltatio*, the term in vogue in Latin medieval literature for the concept of exaltation. *Mishpeṭei ha-mazzalot* (§ 4:1–9, 490–491; quoted in App. 5, Q. 25, 472) enumerates the signs or degrees where the planets have their exaltation, that is, the signs or degrees where a planet is said to be "lord of the exaltation." Ibn Ezra explains the term in *Ṭeʿamim* I, § 2.16:1–14, pp. 54–57 and *Ṭeʿamim* II, § 2.7:1–14, pp. 199–201.

[8]**12: House of dejection, Latin: *domus vilitatis*.** This is a calque of בית קלון "house of shame," frequently used by Ibn Ezra to denote the concept of "house of dejection." A planet is said to be in its house of dejection (Arabic

هبوط, *lit.* "falling") if it is in the house opposite its exaltation. To denote this concept, Ibn Ezra coined קלון "shame," because it is the antonym of כבוד "honor," which he uses for "exaltation." Latin works that fall within the ambit of Ibn Ezra's astrological oeuvre use the corresponding calque: *De nativitatibus*, II x 8:2, 344–345, et passim (*humiliatio*); *Nativitates*, I vii 1:1, 92–93 et passim (*vilitas*).

[9]**3–13: Know that the lower ... upper ⟨planet⟩.** Corresponds closely to *She'elot* II, § 4:1–4, 350–351 (quoted in App. 5, Q. 26, 472), which reports Enoch's opinion. It turns out that according to Enoch's reasoning, Aquarius is more truthful than the other fixed signs because it is the house of Saturn, the highest and the slowest among the planets. Then comes Leo, because is the house of the Sun, which is higher than Venus, the lord of Taurus, one of the two remaining fixed signs. Scorpio, however, is an exception, because its lord is Mars, which is higher than the Sun. But Mars and Scorpio are considered to be the planet and the sign of falsehood. See *Int*, II i 6:7–9.

⟨II i 7⟩

[1]**1: In every question ... ⟨and⟩ the planets.** The same instruction is given in *Int*, II i 1:2.

[2]**2–3: If there are two ... one testimony ⟨alone⟩.** Corresponds to *She'elot* II, § 7:1, 352–353 (quoted in App. 2, Q. 11, 402–403).

[3]**5: Cadent, Latin: *cadens*.** This term, when referring to a planet (not on a horoscopic place), refers to an inconjunct planet, meaning one that neither forms an aspect nor is in conjunction with another planet. This meaning is conveyed in *Reshit ḥokhmah* § 5.1:4, 182–183, where Ibn Ezra translates the word, ساقط, literally "cadent," found in Abū Ma'shar's *Kitāb al-Mudḫal al-kabīr* (VII:6, [2]:677), while he mentions planets that "do not aspect nor are with another planet." See note on *Reshit ḥokhmah* § 5.1:4 in Sela 2017, 418–419. In his Hebrew oeuvre, Ibn Ezra conveys this meaning with respect to planets by means of נופל, "cadent." See *Mivḥarim* II, § 7.2:1, 164–165; *She'elot* II, § 12.3:5, 388–389. Note, however, that *cadens* in works that do not fall within the ambit of Ibn Ezra's astrological oeuvre may denote a planet in the house of its dejection. See note on *Tp*, I i 1:4.

[4]**4–8: The lord of the ascendant … in the ascendant.** This passage is a close replica of a passage in the third part of the *Epitome*, on interrogations (quoted in App. 2, Q. 12, 403). Cf. *Epitome*, ed. Heller (1548), III:2, O4r.

⟨II i 8⟩

[1]**1–4: If the Moon … signifies the outcome.** This corresponds closely to a passage in the third part of the *Epitome*, on interrogations (quoted in App. 4, P. 5, Q. 3, 437).

⟨II i 9⟩

[1]**1: Lot of Fortune, Latin: *pars gratie*.** This is a calque of מנת החן "lot of grace," used in *Mishpeṭei ha-mazzalot* (§ 45:1, 616–616 et passim) and *Tequfah* (§ 16:3, 384–385). *Pars gratie* to denote the lot of Fortune is also found in *Nativitates*, II i 4:1, 136–137 et passim. This establishes a terminological link among *Interrogationes*, *Mishpeṭei ha-mazzalot*, *Tequfah*, and *Nativitates*. To denote the lot of Fortune, *Tractatus particulares* uses *pars fortune*, which corresponds to גורל הטוב, commonly used by Ibn Ezra in his astrological corpus. See, for example, *Tp*, II i 1:1–5, which is a close replica of *Mishpeṭei ha-mazzalot* § 51:2, 538–5539, and makes the lot of Fortune identical with the lot of the Sun.

[2]**1: Always observe the ruler … lot of Fortune.** This passage refers to the "five places of dominion" or five aphetic places. For this concept, see note on *Int*, II i 15:1. The same statement is repeated in *Int*, II xii 2:4 (see note there), and *Tp*, I i 4:4. A similar statement is found in (1) *She'elot* I, § 7:1, 244–245 (quoted in App. 2, Q. 13, 403), on the authority of Ya'qub Al-Kindī; (2) *She'elot* II, § 9:1–3, 354–355 (quoted in App. 2, Q. 14, 403), on the authority of Māshā'allāh; and (3) *Epitome*, ed. Heller (1548), III:2, O4r (quoted in App. 2, Q. 16, 2, 404), on the authority of Dorotheus.

[3]**1: Abraham, the author … lord of the hour.** The same statement, in a different wording, occurs in *Int*, II xii 2:4 and in *Tp*, I i 4:4.

[4]**3: Know that the power … lord of the house.** This corresponds to *Epitome*, ed. Heller (1548), III:2, O4v (quoted in App. 2, Q. 16, 1, 404), on the authority of the Indian masters.

[5]**5: Benefic or malefic planet.** According to *Ṭeʿamim* II (§ 5.8:2, 232–233; quoted in App. 5, Q. 44, 479), Jupiter and Venus are benefic planets, Saturn and Mars are malefic, and Mercury is mixed. Ptolemy (*Tetrabiblos*, ed. Robbins (1980), I:5, 39; quoted in App. 5, Q. 45, 480), on the authority of the Ancients, includes the Moon among the benefic and says that the Sun is mixed.

⟨II i 10⟩

[1]**2: Because the tenth ⟨place⟩ signifies the mast in the ⟨chapter on the⟩ sixth place of the *Book of nativities*.** No mention of the topic of this cross-reference is found in the extant Hebrew version of *Sefer ha-moladot*. But an explicit reference to the link between the tenth horoscopic place and the mast of a ship occurs in *Nativitates*, II vi 8:5, 136–137 (quoted in App. 5, Q. 28, 473), the Latin translation of the now-lost Hebrew second version of *Sefer ha-moladot*. This proves without a shadow of doubt that the two cross-references from *Interrogationes* to a *Book of nativities* (*Int*, II i 10:2 and II i 15:1) point to *Moladot* II, whose Hebrew original is lost but which survives in a Latin translation. Because this passage refers to *Book of nativities* as a fait accompli, it may be taken as a past-tense cross-reference to *Moladot* II. Given that *Moladot* II was composed in 1158 (see Sela 2019, 43–45), 1158 is the *terminus post quem* of *Interrogationes* and of *She'elot* III.

⟨II i 11⟩

[1]**1: Māshā'allāh says ... [the Moon's] house.** This quotation does not match anything in *She'elot le-Māshā'allāh*, whose Hebrew translation is assigned to Ibn Ezra, nor anything in Māshā'allāh's works that survive in Latin translation.

[2]**2–3: There is a dispute ... to what they signify.** This corresponds to *She'elot* I, § 1.1:1–5, 246–249 (quoted in App. 2, Q. 17, 404).

[3]**3: And likewise for all ... the *Book of the Beginning of Wisdom*.** As in *Int*, I 4:2, this may be a reference to *Reshit ḥokhmah* § 3.5:1–4, 142–143 through § 3.16:1–2, 146–147, where the properties of the twelve horoscopic places are stated, although it cannot be ruled out that it refers to the lost second version of the same book. As in *Int*, I 4:2, Ibn Ezra's ספר ראשית חכמה (Book of the beginning of wisdom) is here mistranslated *Principium libri de sensu*, "Beginning of the book of wisdom."

⟨II i 12⟩

[1]**3: Māshā'allāh says … place for the enemy.** This quotation does not match any place in *She'elot le-Māshā'allāh*, whose Hebrew translation is assigned to Ibn Ezra, nor any place in Māshā'allāh's works that survive in Latin translation.

[2]**4: Expert on astrology, Latin: *dominus signorum*, lit. master of the signs.** This Latin expression is a calque of בעל המזלות, "master of the signs," used by Ibn Ezra throughout his oeuvre. See, for example, *Moladot*, II 8:5, 98–99; *Ṭeʿamim* I, § 2.12:14, 52–53; *Me'orot* § 3:2, 454–455. *Nativitates*, II ii 7:4, 122–123, too, uses *domini signorum* with the same meaning, which means that the lost *Moladot* II also used בעלי המזלות to denote the "masters of the signs."

[3]**1–5: There is a dispute … assigned to his opponent.** This corresponds closely to *She'elot* I, § 7.4:1–5, 272–273 (quoted in App. 2, Q. 18, 404–405), which reports the same opinions as this passage but assigns them to different sources, such as Māshā'allāh, Dorotheus, Abū ʿAlī, and Abū Maʿshar. This passage also corresponds closely, although without disclosing the sources, to *Epitome*, ed. Heller (1548), III:12, Q2r (quoted in App. 2, Q. 19, 405) and to *She'elot* II, § 7.3:1–4, 370–371 (quoted in App. 2, Q. 20, 405), which mentions only Dorotheus.

⟨II i 13⟩

[1]**1: If he poses a question … is the Moon.** This statement is expanded in *Int*, II viii 2:1–3. See notes there.

[2]**2: King Dorotheus says … for the querent.** This corresponds to *She'elot* I, § 1.1:4, 246–247 and *Int*, II i 11:3.

[3]**3: Receiver of power.** For an explanation of the planetary condition of "reception," see note on *Tp*, I iv 2:3.

[4]**3: The thing asked about will come to pass on condition that the receiver of power is not in the sixth or twelfth place.** This corresponds to *Int*, II i 3:3 and II i 9:5.

[5]**6: If you see that the thing … thing asked about.** This corresponds to *She'elot* II, § 12.8:4, 394–395.

⟨II i 14⟩

[1]**1: Do not forget to know the nature of the planets.** The same injunction is given in *She'elot* II, § 6:1, 353–353.

⟨II i 15⟩

[1]**1: Five places of dominion, Latin: *.5. loci principatus*.** These five places are the positions of (1) the Sun, (2) the Moon, (3) the last syzygy before the native's birth, (4) the degree of the ascendant, and (5) the lot of Fortune. For an account of the "five places of dominion," see *Mishpeṭei ha-mazzalot* § 45:1, 530–531 (quoted in App. 5, Q. 29, 473). *Electiones* (II ii 1:3) and *Nativitates* (I v 4:1, 90–91 et passim) also use *loci principatus* to designate these five places. Ibn Ezra introduces these five places in his astrological work under various names, as follows: (a) *Moladot* (III i 3:1–2, 100–101, et passim) presents them as מקומות החיים "places of life;" (b) *Ṭe'amim* II (§ 6.2:1–11, 236–239) terms them המושלים "the rulers;" (c) *Neḥoshet* II (194v–195r) designates them השרים "the rulers;" (d) *Mishpeṭei ha-mazzalot* (§ 45:1, 530–531) names them מקומות השררה "places of dominion." It turns out, then, that *Interrogationes* (II i 15:1; II xi 1:2; II xii 2:4), *Electiones* (II ii 1:3), and (I v 4:1, 90–91 et passim), which use *loci principatus*, are all translating מקומות השררה "places of dominion," used in *Mishpeṭei ha-mazzalot*. This creates a terminological link between *Mishpeṭei ha-mazzalot* and the lost third versions of *Sefer ha-She'elot* and *Sefer ha-Mivḥarim* and the lost second version of *Sefer ha-moladot*.

The "five places of dominion" play two main roles in the prediction of the native's expected lifespan. (a) One of the five, after a complicated process of checking and selection, is chosen to be "directed" (see note to *Int*, I 1:2) along the zodiac to a "place that destroys life" (which signifies threats to the native's life and, ultimately, his death), describing an arc that serves to calculate the native's lifespan. (b) The planet that is considered to be the strongest in the chosen aphetic place, the so-called "ruler of the five places of dominion" (*prepositus .5. locorum principatus*), will ultimately give "its years" (see note to *Tp*, II:8) to gauge the native's lifespan. In Arabic astrology, the "five places of dominion" are usually designated *haylāj*. For a detailed account, Sela 2013, 45–57.

Ibn Ezra's "places of dominion" are similar but not identical to the "prorogative places" of *Tetrabiblos*, ed. Robbins (1980), IV:10, 449; III:10, 273–279, and virtually the same as those presented in Dorotheus's *Carmen astrologicum* (ed. Pingree (1976), III 2, 242), although not in the same order. Similar but not identical lists are found in treatises on nativities or introductions to astrology composed by Arabophone scholars earlier than Ibn Ezra, such as Māshā'allāh (*Liber Mesellae de Nativitatibus*, ed. Kennedy and Pingree (1971), 148), Abū 'Alī al-Khayyāṭ (*Liber Albohali*, el Heller (1549), II, sig. B3r–B4r), 'Umar b. al-Farrukhān al-Ṭabarī (*De nativitatibus*, ed. Hervagius (1533), I, 120), Abū Bakr al-Ḥasan b. al-Khaṣib (*De nativitatibus*, ed. Petreius (1540), XII, sig. E1r–E34), 'Alī ibn abī-l-Rijāl (*Iudizios*, ed. Hilty (2005), IV:3, 164–166), and al-Bīrūnī's *Kitāb al-Tafḥīm* (*Elements*, ed. Ramsay Wright (1934), § 522, 324) and *Introduction* (ed. Burnett et al. (2004), IV:4, 111–113). The main difference between these accounts and Ibn Ezra's is that Ibn Ezra presents the five "places of dominion" as a list of five items, whereas the other texts do not give the five "prerogative places" in a list but integrate them into the instructions for choosing the "ruler of the nativity" among them. The only exception I have found is the *Epitome* (ed. Heller (1548), II:2, H4v), where the five "places of life" are given as a list, as Ibn Ezra does.

[2]**1: If the querent poses a question ... in the *Book of nativities*.** This refers to a section of the lost second version of Ibn Ezra's *Sefer ha-moladot* that addresses the calculation of the native's lifespan. For a Latin translation of this passage, see *Nativitates*, II i 4:1–16, 106–109 (quoted in App. 5, Q. 30, 473–475). That this cross-reference points to the lost second version of Ibn Ezra's *Sefer ha-moladot*, and not to the first version of this work, which is extant in numerous manuscripts, can be inferred from the content of the cross-reference to Ibn Ezra's *Sefer ha-moladot* in *Int*, II i 10:2. See note there.

[3]**2: The great years of a planet ... the middle years.** For these concepts, see note to *Tp*, II:8.

[4]**2: And the root of the directions.** This expression means that the native's lifespan should be calculated using the procedure of "directions," as in the doctrine of nativities, on the basis of the natal horoscope. For this procedure, see note on *Int*, I 1:2.

[5]**1–2: If the querent poses ... root of the directions.** This corresponds closely to *She'elot* I, § 1.2:1–3, 248–249 (quoted in App. 4, P. 1, Q. 1, 431), where

this statement is assigned to Māshā'allāh. This corresponds also to *She'elot* II, § 1.1:1–2, 356–357 (quoted in App. 4, P. 1 Q. 2, 431), where Māshā'allāh is not mentioned.

[6]**3: Ptolemy says in the *Book of the 100 statements* ... like a nativity.** This paraphrases aphorism 17 of Pseudo-Ptolemy's *Centiloquium* (quoted in App. 5, Q. 31, 475).

[7]**3: Revolution of each year.** This refers to a horoscope cast at the anniversary of the native's birth, that is, at the time "when the Sun returns to the degree in the sign where it was at the moment of the birth, and the same minutes." See note to *Int*, II i 1:2.

[8]**4: The same applies ... which he comes.** The link between nativities and interrogations with respect to cities is highlighted in *Moladot*, IV 28:1, 202–203 (quoted in App. 3, P. 14, Q. 3, 428).

⟨II ii 1⟩

[1]**2: Riches will be at his disposition without effort.** Here I have translated according to the logical sense of the passage. The Latin text reads precisely the opposite: *divicie sibi deerunt sine labore* = "riches will be lacking to him without effort." But this is clearly a mistake, because not only is it incompatible with similar loci in Ibn Ezra's astrological corpus (see next note), it is also inconsistent with the general intent of the sentence.

[2]**1–2: If the querent poses ... disposition without effort.** This corresponds to *She'elot* I, § 2.1:2–3, 250–251 (quoted in App. 4, P. 3, Q. 1, 432) and to *Epitome*, ed. Heller (1548), III:5, P1r (quoted in App. 4, P. 3, Q. 2, 433). See also *She'elot* II, § 2.1:1, 360–361, and *Moladot*, III ii 8, 1, 128–129.

[3]**3: According to the nature of the intermediate planet, as is written in the *Book of the Beginning of Wisdom*.** Ibn Ezra wrote two versions of his *Book of the Beginning of Wisdom*. Because the treatment of the "natures" of the planets is commonplace in any introduction to astrology, this may be a reference to chapter four of *Reshit ḥokhmah* (§ 4.1:1–2, 146–147 through § 4.7:1–29, 182–183), where this topic is treated, although it cannot be ruled out that it refers to an analogous chapter in the lost second version of the same book. Note that Ibn Ezra's ספר ראשית חכמה (Book of the beginning

of wisdom) is here translated *Liber capitis sensis*, "Book of the beginning (*lit.* head) of wisdom," in contrast to the names applied to the same book in other parts of *Interrogationes*.

⟨II ii 2⟩

[1]**3: If the planet gives the spark from the first [i.e., the ascendant] to the other [i.e., the seventh place], Latin: *Et si stella dederit scintillationem prima secunde*.** For this terminology ("gives spark" = *dederit scintillationem*) and the corresponding planetary condition, see *Int*, II vii 1:3 and note.

[2]**1–3: ⟨For⟩ one who poses … will not be sold.** An almost exact replica of this passage is found in *She'elot* II, § 11.1:1–2, 384–385 (quoted in App. 4, P. 2, Q. 1, 431–432). A close correspondence and possibly the ultimate source of this passage is found in Sahl's *Book of Interrogations* (quoted in App. 4, P. 2, Q. 2, 432).

[3]**4: Know under the spark of which planet it [the Moon] is, Latin: *scias cuius stelle sua scintillatio fuerit supra*.** The mention in this passage of "being a planet under the spark of another planet" indicates that *scintillatio* (a translation of ניצוץ "spark,") refers to a certain number of degrees in the zodiac, ahead of or behind the planet, where its influence is still felt. This shows that the meaning of *scintillatio* in *Interrogationes*, a translation of ניצוץ, is identical with that of *radiatio* (= "ray") in *El*, II vi 6:4. See note there.

[4]**3–4: If the planet gives the spark … the second the buyer.** This corresponds to *Epitome*, ed. Heller (1548), III:23, R1v (quoted in App. 4, P. 2, Q. 3, 432).

[5]**7: In the cardines … in the first cardo … in the seventh ⟨cardo⟩ … in the tenth ⟨cardo⟩ … in the fourth ⟨cardo⟩, Latin: *in cavillis … in cavilla prima … in .7o. … in .10o. … in .4a*.** This passage refers explicitly to the four cardines (see note on *Int*, II xii 9:4) and to the first cardo, and in the same breath alludes to the third, fourth, and second cardines by employing the ordinal numbers of the seventh, tenth and fourth horoscopic places (i.e., seventh ⟨cardo⟩, tenth ⟨cardo⟩, fourth ⟨cardo⟩). This is typical of Ibn Ezra's style. See, for example, *She'elot* II, § 3:1–2, 348–349 (quoted in App. 5, Q. 32, 475). For other instances of the same case, see *Int*, II iii 2:2; II vii 1:5–6, II vii 2:4.

⟨II ii 3⟩

[1]**4: Likewise, if a planet … located in the ascendant.** For the planetary condition presented in this passage, and the terminology used to convey it, see *Int*, II vii 1:3 and note.

[2]**1–13: Regarding a stolen or lost … lord of the seventh ⟨place⟩.** This corresponds closely to *She'elot* I, § 7.7:1–11, 276–279 (quoted in App. 4, P. 4, Q. 1, 1–11, 432–433) and to *She'elot* II, § 7.7:1–9, 374–375 (quoted in App. 4, P. 4, Q. 2, 1–9, 434-435). In some sentences, *Interrogationes* is virtually a *verbatim* Latin translation of *She'elot* I and *She'elot* II. See particularly *Int*, II ii 3:2–4, *She'elot* I, § 7.7:2–4, 276–279 (quoted in App. 4, P. 4, Q. 1, 2–4, 433–434) and *She'elot* II, § 7.7:1–3, 374–375 (quoted in App. 4, P. 4, Q. 2, 1–3, 434-435). Although a section of Sahl's *Book of Interrogations* (*De latrocinio*, Paris, BnF, MS lat. 16204, 457b–458b) bears some resemblances, the ultimate source of this passage is an unknown work on interrogations by Māshā'allāh, as attested by the first sentence of the account in *She'elot* I (§ 7.7:1, 276–277; quoted in App. 4, P. 4, Q. 1, 1, 433). A comparison shows that this work by Māshā'allāh is not identical with *Sefer ha-She'elot le-Māshā'allāh* or *Liber interpretationum*. The occasional closeness between *She'elot* I, *She'elot* II and *Interrogationes* suggests that Ibn Ezra may have carried a copy of this work by Māshā'allāh with him during his peregrinations in Latin Europe.

⟨II ii 4⟩

[1]**1–2: Judgment on when the thief … capture him [the thief].** This corresponds to *She'elot* I, § 7.7:12, 278–279 (quoted in App. 4, P. 4, Q. 1, 12, 433–434) and to *She'elot* II, § 7.7:11, 374–375 (quoted in App. 4, P. 4, Q. 2, 11, 435).

⟨II ii 5⟩

[1]**1–4: Judgment about when … the thief will escape.** This corresponds to *She'elot* I, § 7.7:13, 278–279 (quoted in App. 4, P. 4, Q. 1, 13, 433–434) and to *She'elot* II, § 7.7:9–10, 374–375 (quoted in App. 4, P. 4, Q. 2, 9–10, 435).

⟨II iii 1⟩

[1]**1–3: If one arranges a journey … is in the ascendant.** This corresponds loosely to *She'elot* II, § 9.1:2, 378–379 (quoted in App. 4, P. 16, Q. 1, 2, 452–453).

⟨II iii 2⟩

[1]**2: Since the Moon's joy is in this place.** This refers to the third horoscopic place, which is considered to be the Moon's "joy" or where the Moon "rejoices." "Joy" and "mourning" are two correlated properties of the seven planets in the horoscopic places. The horoscopic place of the planet's joy, where the planet "rejoices" when located there, is considered to be auspicious, while the horoscopic place of its mourning, which is opposite its place of joy, is considered to be inauspicious. Ibn Ezra lists the planets' places of joy and mourning in *Mishpeṭei ha-mazzalot* § 6:1–7, 492–493 (quoted in App. 5, Q. 33, 476). Ibn Ezra explicates the doctrine of the planets' joys in *Ṭe'amim* I, § 4.9:1, 82–83 (quoted in App. 5, Q. 34, 476). *Ṭe'amim* II (§ 4.12:1–6, 216–217) offers a similar explanation. See also *Great Introduction*, ed. Burnett and Yamamoto (2019), VI:26, [32]:548–550; *Elements*, ed. Ramsay Wright (1934), § 469, 277; *Introduction*, ed. Burnett et al. (2004), I:70, 55; *Abbreviation*, ed. Burnett et al. (1994), I:121, 31.

[2]**2: In the first cardo … in the tenth ⟨cardo⟩ … in the seventh ⟨cardo⟩.** For this confusion of cardines with horoscopic places, typical of Ibn Ezra's style, see note on *Int*, II ii 2:7.2.

[3]**3: Fixed, tropical or bicorporal, Latin: *veridicus vel mobile vel biscorporum*.** This passage refers to a well-known tripartite classification of the twelve zodiacal signs: מתהפכים (منقلبة; *signa mobilia*), עומדים/נאמנים (ثابتة; *signa veridica, signa stabilia, signa fixa*), בעלי שתי גופות (ذوات جسدين; *signa bicorpora, signa communia*). *Ṭe'amim* II (§ 2.3:1–3, 188–189; quoted in App. 5, Q. 35, 476) explains that the rationale behind this classification has to do with the season and prevailing weather when the Sun travels through the signs in its annual path. The ultimate source of this classification is *Tetrabiblos* (ed. Robbins (1980), I:11, 65–69,) which explains it as based on the correspondence between the seasons and the annual motion of the Sun and further divides the tropical signs into equinoctial (Aries, Libra) and solstitial (Cancer, Capricorn). This tripartite classification is found and explained

in Arabic introductions to astrology: *Great Introduction*, ed. Burnett and Yamamoto (2019), II:6 [1–3]:298–313; *Elements*, ed. Ramsay Wright (1934), § 380, 231; *Abbreviation*, ed. Burnett et al. (1994), I:7, 27.

⟨II iv 1⟩

[1]**1: Straight or crooked, Latin:** ***recta vel tortuosa***. These are calques of מזלות ישרים and מזלות מעוותים, which refer to two groups of six signs each—the "straight" signs (from Cancer to Sagittarius) and the "crooked" signs (from Capricorn to Gemini)—which divide the zodiac according to their rising times. They are listed in *Mishpeṭei ha-mazzalot* § 2:6, 490–491 (quoted in App. 5, Q. 36, 477). The rationale behind these terms is explained in *Ṭeʿamim* II § 2.3:21, 190–191 (quoted in App. 5, Q. 37, 477).

[2]**1: ⟨For⟩ one who asks ... judge accordingly**. This corresponds to *She'elot* I, § 4.1:1–5, 256–257 (quoted in App. 4, P. 5, Q. 1, 1–5, 436) and to *She'elot* II, § 4.1:1–5, 362–365 (quoted in App. 4, P. 5, Q. 2, 1–5, 436–437).

⟨II iv 2⟩

[1]**1–4: Know that if the querent ... ⟨places⟩ to the king**. This corresponds to *She'elot* I, § 4.3:1–2, 258–259 (quoted in App. 4, P. 6, Q. 1, 437–438). Cf. *She'elot* II, § 7.5:1–3, 372–373.

⟨II v 1⟩

[1]**3: The sixth, eighth or twelfth ⟨place⟩**. These three are referred to as a distinct group of inauspicious horoscopic places throughout Ibn Ezra's astrological corpus. See note on *El*, II i 1:6.

[2]**5: The fifth, eleventh or ninth ⟨place⟩**. These three are considered to be auspicious, and stand in contrast to the three inauspicious places—the sixth, eighth and twelfth. See *Moladot*, IV 26:1–2, 200–201, quoted in the note on *El*, II i 1:6.

[3]**6: A place of barren root**. This refers to a horoscopic place that coincides with a barren sign. *Ṭeʿamim* II (§ 2.4:15, 194–195) explains that all the signs with a human shape are barren, because human beings produce few chil-

dren. According to *Mishpeṭei ha-mazzalot* § 2:14, 490–491, the signs with a human shape are Gemini, Virgo, Libra, the first half of Sagittarius, and Aquarius.

[4]**1–7: If the querent asks ... in the fifth ⟨place⟩.** This corresponds closely to *She'elot* I, § 5.2:1–6, 262–265 (quoted in App. 4, P. 8, Q. 4, 441). It also corresponds to *She'elot* II, § 5.1:1–5, 364–367, and to *Epitome*, ed. Heller (1548), III:9, P3r–P3v (quoted in App. 4, P. 8, Q. 3, 3, 440–441).

⟨II v 2⟩

[1]**2: If there is no aspect ... fifth ⟨place⟩.** This contrasts with *Int*, II v 1:2.

[2]**3: If the lord of the hour ... lord of the ascendant.** This contrasts with *Int*, II v 1:3.

[3]**4: It is worse ... from the cardines.** This contrasts with *Int*, II v 1:4–5.

[4]**4: Cadent from the cardines.** These are the first words whose Hebrew source text is extant in the Modena fragment of *She'elot* III. See *She'elot* III, II v 2:4, 489.

⟨II v 3⟩

[1]**1–6: If the question ... bicorporal sign.** This corresponds closely to *She'elot* I, § 5.1:1–4, 262–263 (quoted in 4, P. 7, Q. 1, 1–4, 438), which reveals that Dorotheus is one of Ibn Ezra's sources. It also corresponds to *She'elot* II, § 5.2:1, 366–367 (quoted in App. 4, P. 7, Q. 2, 1, 438) and to *Epitome*, ed. Heller (1548), III:9, P3r (quoted in App. 4, P. 8, Q. 3, 1, 440). The Hebrew source text of this whole section is extant in the Modena fragment of *She'elot* III. See *She'elot* III, II v 3:1–5, 490.

⟨II v 4⟩

[1]**4: The woman will have an abortion, Latin: *mulier erit impotens*.** The translation of the present passage is based on the corresponding Hebrew text in the Modena fragment of *She'elot* III: תפיל האשה. See *She'elot* III, II v 4:4, 490.

[2]1–6: **This indicates that ⟨the woman⟩ ... the fifth place.** This corresponds closely to the following loci: (1) *She'elot* I, § 5.1:3, 262–263 (quoted in App. 4, P. 7, Q. 1, 3, 438); (2) *She'elot* II, § 5.2:2, 366–367 (quoted in App. 4, P. 7, Q. 2, 2, 438); and (3) *Epitome*, ed. Heller (1548), III:9, P3r–P3v (quoted in App. 4, P. 8, Q. 3, 2, 440–441). The Hebrew source text of this entire section is extant in the Modena fragment of *She'elot* III. See *She'elot* III, II v 4:1–6, 490.

⟨II v 5⟩

[1]1–4: **If ⟨the astrologer⟩ is asked ... feminine powers.** This corresponds closely to (1) *She'elot* I, § 5.3:1–6, 264–265 (quoted in App. 4, P. 8, Q. 1, 439), which reveals that al-Kindī is Ibn Ezra's source; (2) *She'elot* II, § 5.3:1–4, 366–367 (quoted in App. 4, P. 8, Q. 2, 439–440), which reveals that Dorotheus is one of Ibn Ezra's sources; and (3) *Epitome*, ed. Heller (1548), III:9, P3v (quoted in App. 4, P. 8, Q. 3, 4, 440–441). The Hebrew source text of this entire section is extant in the Modena fragment of *She'elot* III. See *She'elot* III, II v 5:1–4, 490–491.

⟨II vi 1⟩

[1]3: **Under the light of the Sun, Latin: *sub claritate Solis*, Hebrew: תחת אור השמש, *lit.* under the light of the Sun.** The Hebrew of this phrase (see *She'elot* III, II vi 1:2, 491) is Ibn Ezra's calque of تحت شعاع الشمس, which he found in Abū Ma'shar's *Great Introduction* (ed. Burnett and Yamamoto (2019), VII:6, [5]:788–789). Being "under the ray of the Sun" is one of the conditions of the planets with respect to the Sun. According to *Reshit ḥokhmah* (§ 6.6:4, 192–193), Saturn and Jupiter are said to be "under the ray of the Sun" when they are between 6° and 15° from the Sun; Mars, between 10° and 18° (§ 6.6:4–7, 192–193); Venus and Mercury, between 7° and 12° (§ 6.7:2–3); and the Moon, between 6° and 12° (§ 6.8:3–4, 194–195). A comparison of the Latin of this passage with its Hebrew counterpart in the Modena fragment of *She'elot* III shows that here and elsewhere in *Interrogationes* the expression *sub claritate Solis* translates תחת אור השמש "under the light of the Sun." See *She'elot* III, II vi 1:3, 491. Note, however, that *Int*, II vii 3:5; II viii 1:1; II viii 2:1, uses the divergent expression *sub radiis Solis* for the same planetary condition with respect to the Sun. This is because in these loci Ibn Ezra used תחת ניצוץ השמש. Also *El*, II vi 6:4; II vii 2:1; II vii 3:4; II ix 4:2; II x 2:2 uses *sub radiis Solis*.

[2]**3: According to the computation I have mentioned in the *Book of the Beginning of Wisdom*.** This cross-reference may point to the sixth chapter of *Reshit ḥokhmah*, where Ibn Ezra specifies the number of degrees between the seven planets and the Sun when the seven planets are said to be "under the ray of the Sun." See previous note. However, it cannot be ruled out that this is a reference to the lost second version of *Reshit ḥokhmah*. Note that Ibn Ezra's ספר ראשית חכמה (Book of the beginning of wisdom) is here translated *Liber principii sensuum*, "Book of the beginning of wisdoms," a name that stands in stark contrast to the names by which *Reshit ḥokhmah* is referred to in other parts of *Interrogationes*.

[3]**1–3: ⟨A question about a sick person⟩ … malefic planet.** This corresponds to *She'elot* I, § 6.1:1–2, 266–267 (quoted in App. 4, P. 9, Q. 1, 1–2, 442); and *She'elot* II, § 6.1:1–2, 366–367 (quoted in App. 4, P. 9, Q. 2, 1–2, 442–443).

[4]**8: Lord of the first triplicity; Latin: *dominus triplicitatis prime*; Hebrew: בעל השלישות הראשונה.** Here *Interrogationes* designates the first lord of one of the four triplicities as the lord of the first triplicity. This is because *Interrogationes* follows Ibn Ezra, who was in the habit of designating the first, second, or third lord of any of the four triplicities as the lord of the first, second, or third triplicities. For the concept of triplicity and its lords, see note on *Tp*, IV 3:2. An example of this is a passage in *Moladot*, III i 6:3, 104–104 (quoted in App. 5, Q. 38, 447).

[5]**8: Dorotheus says … great power.** This translation follows the Hebrew text that corresponds to this passage. See *She'elot* III, II vi 1:8, 491–492. The Latin translation of this locus is sometimes unclear or meaningless.

[6]**9: Māshā'allāh says … very strong.** This quotation does not match anything in *She'elot le-Māshā'allāh*, whose Hebrew translation is assigned to Ibn Ezra, nor anything in Māshā'allāh's works that survive in Latin translation.

[7]**10: Judge that the person … three places.** This corresponds to *She'elot* I, § 6.1:4, 266–267 (quoted in App. 4, P. 9, Q. 1, 4, 442); *She'elot* II, § 6.1:4, 366–367 (quoted in App. 4, P. 9, Q. 2, 4, 443); and *Epitome*, ed. Heller (1548), III:10, P4v (quoted in App. 4, P. 9, Q. 3, 3, 443)

[8]**1–12: ⟨A question about a sick person⟩ … signifies bad fortune.** The Hebrew source text of this entire section is extant in the Modena fragment of *She'elot* III. See *She'elot* III, II vi 1:1–12, 491–492.

⟨II vi 2⟩

[1]**1: Know that the disease ... slow or retrograde.** This corresponds to *She'e-lot* II, § 6.1:6, 368–369 (quoted in App. 4, P. 9, Q. 2, 6, 443).

[2]**2: The fixed signs ... life or death.** Such a statement is commonplace in sections of Ibn Ezra's works related to astrological medicine. See the following loci: (1) *She'elot* I, § 6.1:5, 266–267 (quoted in App. 4, P. 9, Q. 1, 5, 442); (2) *She'elot* II, § 6.1:6, 368–369 (quoted in App. 4, P. 9, Q. 2, 6, 443); (3) *Me'orot* § 17:1, 478–479 (quoted in App. 4, P. 9, Q. 4, 444); and (4) *Epitome*, ed. Heller (1548), III:10, P4v (quoted in App. 4, P. 9, Q. 3, 1, 443)

[3]**3: If a planet ... will be cured.** This corresponds to *She'elot* II, § 6.1:7, 368–369 (quoted in App. 4, P. 9, Q. 2, 7, 443).

[4]**4: In the degree, Latin: *in gradu*.** Here I have rendered the Latin text. The Hebrew text in the Modena fragment of *She'elot* III that corresponds to this locus is illegible.

[5]**4: If you find the lord ... will recover.** This corresponds to *She'elot* I, § 6.1:4, 266–267 (quoted in App. 4, P. 9, Q. 1, 4, 442).

[6]**5: ⟨You may find⟩ ... eighth place.** This corresponds to *She'elot* I, § 6.1:1, 266–267 (quoted in App. 4, P. 9, Q. 1, 1, 442) and *Epitome*, ed. Heller (1548), III:10, P4v (quoted in App. 4, P. 9, Q. 3, 2, 443).

[7]**7: Critical days; Latin: *dies terminorum*; Hebrew: ימי הגבול, *lit.* "days of the limit."** The Latin here is a calque of the corresponding Hebrew as found in the Modena fragment of *She'elot* III. See *She'elot* III, II vi 2:7, 492–493. This refers to the "crises" or "critical days," that is, days in the development of a disease when it tends to reach a climax, for better or worse. From Antiquity through the Middle Ages, they were considered to be connected to and even caused by the Moon's position and condition with respect to its position at the onset of the disease. To denote this notion, Ibn Ezra coined the term גבול, *lit.* "limit" (pl. גבולים), a calque of the Arabic *al-buḥrān*, which is in turn a transliteration from the Syriac *buḥrānā*. Ibn Ezra eschews בחראנים, the Hebrew transliteration of *al-buḥrān* used by other Jewish medieval authors.

[8]**7: If you know ... critical days.** This refers to the sections of *Sefer ha-Me'orot* (Book of luminaries) that discuss the positions of the Moon at the

outbreak of the disease and on the critical days. See, for example *Meʾorot* §4:1–9, 456–459 et passim. This passage corresponds to *Sheʾelot* I, §6.1:7, 266–267 (quoted in App. 4, P. 9, Q. 1, 7, 442).

[9]**8: The twelfth place is the place of prison and jail.** This corresponds to *Mishpeṭei ha-mazzalot* §18:6, 504–505: הבית השנים עשר: ... בית השביה והסוהר והכבל. = "The twelfth place: the place of captivity, prison, and fetters."

[10]**1–8: Know that the disease ... This is what I found.** The Hebrew source text of this entire section is extant in the Modena fragment of *Sheʾelot* III. See *Sheʾelot* III, II vi 2:1–8, 492.

⟨II vii 1⟩

[1]**1–2: ⟨This place⟩ includes ... opposite will be the case.** This corresponds to *Sheʾelot* II, §12.3:1, 388–389 (quoted in App. 4, P. 10, Q. 1, 444) and to *Epitome*, ed. Heller (1548), III:11, Q1v (quoted in App. 4, P. 10, Q. 2, 2, 444). Note that the Modena fragment of *Sheʾelot* III reads מריבות אשה, "quarrels with a woman," instead of "betrothal of women." See *Sheʾelot* III, II vii 1:2, 493.

[2]**3: If a planet takes the spark and gives it to another, or receives the spark from these two, Latin: *Et si fuerit stella capiens scintillationem et ipsa dederit eam alii, vel receperit scintillationem ab illis duobus*.** A comparison with the Hebrew counterpart of this passage in the Modena fragment (see *Sheʾelot* III, II vii 1:3, 493) demonstrates that here and elsewhere in *Interrogationes* the Latin *scintillatio* is a calque of the Hebrew ניצוץ, "spark." The terminology used here ("giving," "receiving," and "taking" the spark) as well as the planetary condition behind these terms, is used in *Int*, II ii 2:3,4 and II ii 3:4, as well as in *Sheʾelot* II, §11.1:1–2, 384–385 (quoted in App. 4, P. 2, Q. 1, 431–432) and *Sheʾelot* I, §7.7:4, 276–277 (quoted in App. 4, P. 4, Q. 1, 4, 433–434). From these parallel passages, it emerges that *scintillatio* also translates אור "light." The vague cross-reference in *Sheʾelot* I, §7.7:4, 276–277, which sends the reader to *Reshit ḥokhmah* to find an explanation of the planetary condition behind the aforementioned quote, points to the seventh chapter of *Reshit ḥokhmah*, which presents and explains 30 planetary conditions. Two of them, "translation" and "reflecting the light," are relevant to this passage. See *Reshit ḥokhmah* §7.10:1–3, 202–203 (quoted in App. 5, Q. 39, 1, 477–478) and *Reshit ḥokhmah* §7.12:1–3, 202–203 (quoted in App. 5, Q. 39, 2, 477–478). The context and use of *scintillatio* in

Int, II ii 2:4 (see notes there) indicates that "spark" in this passage and elsewhere in *Interrogationes* denotes a certain number of degrees in the zodiac, ahead of or behind the planet, where its influence is still felt. As such, the meaning of *scintillatio* in *Interrogationes* is identical with that of *radiatio* (= "ray") in *El*, II vi 6:4 (see note there).

[3]**3: If a planet [A] takes ... an intermediary**. This corresponds to *Int*, II ii 2:3. See note there. It also corresponds to *Epitome*, ed. Heller (1548), III:11, Qiv (quoted in App. 4, P. 10, Q. 2, 1, 444).

[4]**5–6: In one of the cardines ... the tenth ⟨cardo⟩ ... the seventh ⟨cardo⟩.** For this confusion of cardines with horoscopic places, typical of Ibn Ezra's style, see note on *Int*, II ii 2:7.2.

[5]**4–7: Likewise, ⟨the matter⟩ ... will be realized.** This corresponds to *Epitome*, ed. Heller (1548), III:11, Qiv (quoted in App. 4, P. 10, Q. 2, 3, 444).

[6]**9: Know that Mercury causes quarrels**. This corresponds to *She'elot* I, § 6:1–2, 244–245 (quoted in App. 4, P. 11, Q. 5, 446) and to *Mivḥarim* I, § 3.1:6, 58–59 (quoted in App. 4, P. 11, Q. 6, 446).

[7]**11: Lord of the seventh ⟨hour⟩, Latin: *dominum .7e*.** For this reading, where "seventh" modifies "hour," I have relied on the reading of the Hebrew counterpart of his locus in the Modena fragment: קח בעל השעה לשואל ובעל השעה השביעית שהיא מעוותת לאישה = "take the lord of the hour for the querent and the lord of the seventh crooked hour for the woman." See *She'elot* III, II vii 1:11, 493–494.

[8]**11: Her lord, that is, ⟨her⟩ husband, Latin: *pro domino sua, scilicet marito*, Hebrew: לבעלה.** Here the Latin translator felt obliged to disambiguate the Hebrew term בעל, which means "lord" but also "husband." See *She'elot* III, II vii 1:11, 493–494.

[9]**11: If the querent is the woman ... like Venus.** This corresponds closely to *Epitome*, ed. Heller (1548), III:11, Q1v (quoted in App. 4, P. 10, Q. 2, 4, 445).

[10]**10–12: Enoch says ... forms an aspect.** This corresponds to Enoch's "lot of marriage in the nativity of men," which is given as the second of the 13 lots of the seventh horoscopic place in *Reshit ḥokhmah* § 9.10:3, 244–245 (quoted in App. 5, Q. 41, 479). Ibn Ezra's source for the information about this

lot (as well as for that of all the lots of all the horoscopic places) and for the assignment of this lot to Enoch is Abū Maʿshar's *Great Introduction* (ed. Burnett and Yamamoto (2019), VIII:4 31a–32, I, 875; quoted in App. 5, Q. 42, 479).

[11]**1–12: ⟨This place⟩ includes four questions … forms an aspect.** The Hebrew source text of this section, with the exception of a few lacunae, is extant in the Modena fragment of *She'elot* III. See *She'elot* III, II vii 1:1–12, 493–494.

⟨II vii 2⟩

[1]**2: If the person involved … seeks to quarrel.** This corresponds to *She'elot* I, § 7.3:2, 270–271 (quoted in App. 4, P. 11, Q. 3, 446) and to *Epitome*, ed. Heller (1548), III:12, Q1v–Q2r (quoted in App. 4, P. 11, Q. 4, 446).

[2]**4: In one of the cardines … in the seventh or fourth ⟨cardo⟩.** For this confusion of cardines with horoscopic places, typical of Ibn Ezra's style, see note on *Int*, II ii 2:7.2.

[3]**8: Its house of war, Latin: *domus belli sui*.** This is a calque of בית מלחמתו "its house of war," the counterpart of the current locus in the Modena fragment (see *She'elot* III, II vii 2:8, 494–495), used here for the house of detriment, namely, the opposite of the planetary house or the seventh sign from the planetary house of each planet. In the astrological encyclopedia written in Béziers in 1148, Ibn Ezra uses בית שנאה "house of hate" to denote this astrological concept. See, for example, *Reshit ḥokhmah* § 2.1:40, 62–63. *Ṭeʿamim* II § 2.4:10, 192, employs בית רעה "house of evil." By contrast, three of Ibn Ezra's works use "house of war": *Int*, II vii 2:8; *Mishpeṭei ha-mazzalot* § 4:2, 492–493; and *Nativitates*, II ix 1:2, 96–97. This creates a terminological link between *Interrogationes* (that is, *She'elot* III), *Mishpeṭei ha-mazzalot*, and *Nativitates* (that is, *Moladot* II).

[4]**1–10: The second question … the king.** The Hebrew source text of this section, with the exception of a few lacunae, is extant in the Modena fragment of *She'elot* III. See *She'elot* III, II vii 2:1–10, 404–405.

⟨II vii 3⟩

[1]**5: Under the rays ⟨of the Sun⟩, Latin: *sub radiis* ⟨*Solis*⟩.** For this condition of the planets with respect to the Sun, see note on *Int*, II vi 1:3. The Hebrew counterpart of this phrase in the Modena fragment (see *She'elot* III, II vii 3:5, 495) reads תחת ניצוץ השמש "under the spark of the Sun." This demonstrates that here and elsewhere in *Interrogationes*, *sub radiis Solis* translates תחת ניצוץ השמש "under the spark of the Sun." Note, though, that for the same planetary condition with respect to the Sun, *Int*, II ii 3:3, II ii 4:2, and II vi 1:2 use the *sub claritate Solis*. This is because in these loci *She'elot* III has תחת אור השמש. Compare, for example, *Int*, II vi 1:3 with *She'elot* III, II vi 1:3, 491. Also *El*, II vi 6:4; II vii 2:1; II vii 3:4; II ix 4:2; II x 2:2 uses *sub radiis Solis*.

[2]**1–7: The third question ... seventh place**. This corresponds to *She'elot* I, § 7.3:3–4, 270–271 (quoted in App. 4, P. 11, Q. 2, 3–4, 445) and to *She'elot* II, § 7.1:2–4, 368–369 (quoted in App. 4, P. 11, Q. 1, 2–4, 445). The Hebrew source text of this section, with the exception of a lacuna, is extant in the Modena fragment of *She'elot* III. See *She'elot* III, II vii 3:1–7, 495.

⟨II vii 4⟩

[1]**4: On the "left side" or northern; Latin: *sinistre vel septentrionales*.** Here *sinistre, lit.* "on the left side," is a calque of the Hebrew form שמאליים "left," used throughout Ibn Ezra's oeuvre to denote "northern." Hence, *Interrogationes* adds *septentrionales*, "northern," to disambiguate the nonstandard *sinistre*.

[2]**3–7: If the two lords ... southern is victorious.** For the astrological concept of a planet's being "victorious" over another, see note on *El*, II vii 6:3. This corresponds closely to *She'elot* I, § 7.3:12–13, 270–273 (quoted in App. 4, P. 12, Q. 1, 446–447), *Me'orot* § 30:4, 476–477 (quoted in App. 4, P. 12, Q. 2, 447), and *Ṭe'amim* II, § 4.4:1, 210–211 (quoted in App. 4, P. 12, Q. 3, 447).

[3]**1–7: If the planet is in the ascendant ... southern is victorious**. The Hebrew source text of this section, with the exception of a few short lacunae, is extant in the Modena fragment of *She'elot* III. See *She'elot* III, II vii 4:1–7, 495–496.

⟨II vii 5⟩

[1]**1: Abū Maʿshar says ... malefic ⟨planet⟩**. This corresponds closely to *Mivḥarim* I, § 7.2:4, 70–71 (quoted in App. 4, P. 12, Q. 5, 4, 448). *Mivḥarim* I makes this statement, following the opinions of Māshāʾallāh and Dorotheus, in the context of a great dispute among astrologers: they agree that if the lord of the ascendant sign is in the seventh place the army will be defeated, and that if the lord of the seventh place is in the ascendant sign the enemy will be defeated; but they ask how they should pass judgment if Scorpio is the ascendant sign and Mars is in the seventh place, in Taurus. The same dispute is mentioned repeatedly in Ibn Ezra's works on interrogations and elections. See *Sheʾelot* II, § 7.4:1–3, 370–373 (quoted in App. 4, P. 12, Q. 4, 1–3, 447–448), *Mivḥarim* II, § 7.3:1–2, 166–167 (quoted in App. 4, P. 12, Q. 6, 1–2, 448–449); and *Epitome*, ed. Heller (1548), III:12, Q2r (quoted in App. 4, P. 12, Q. 7, 449). The Hebrew source text of this section is extant in the Modena fragment of *Sheʾelot* III. See *Sheʾelot* III, II vii 5:1, 496.

⟨II vii 6⟩

[1]**1: If ⟨the astrologer⟩ ... of love**. These are the last words whose Hebrew source text is extant in the Modena fragment of *Sheʾelot* III. See *Sheʾelot* III, II vii 6:1, 496.

[2]**1–2: If ⟨the astrologer⟩ ... any of the partners**. This corresponds to *Sheʾelot* II, § 7.8:1–2, 376–377 (quoted in App. 4, P. 13, Q. 1, 449) and *Sheʾelot* I, § 7.2:1–3, 268–269 (quoted in App. 4, P. 13, Q. 2, 449–450).

⟨II viii 1⟩

[1]**1–6: ⟨For⟩ one who is afraid ... will be in water**. This corresponds to *Sheʾelot* I, § 8.1:1–5, 282–283 (quoted in App. 4, P. 14, Q. 1, 450) and *Sheʾelot* II, § 8.3:1–4, 376–379 (quoted in App. 4, P. 14, Q. 2, 450–451).

⟨II viii 2⟩

[1]**1–3: ⟨If⟩ someone asks ... he is alive**. This passage expands on *Int*, II i 13:1. It corresponds closely to *Sheʾelot* II, § 1.2:1–5, 356–359 (quoted in App. 4, P. 15, Q. 1, 451), to *Sheʾelot* I, § 1.3:1–2, 248–249 (quoted in App. 4, P. 15, Q. 2,

451–452), and to a passage in Sahl's *Book of Interrogations* (quoted in App. 4, P. 15, Q. 3, 452)

⟨II ix 1⟩

[1]**1–3: If someone asks … nature of the signs**. This corresponds to *She'elot* II, § 9.1:1–3, 378–379 (quoted in App. 4, P. 16, Q. 1, 452–453) and *Epitome*, ed. Heller (1548), III:17, Q4r (quoted in App. 4, P. 16, Q. 2, 453).

⟨II ix 2⟩

[1]**1–7: If he asks you … go and succeed**. This corresponds to *She'elot* I, § 3.2:1–4, 254–255 (quoted in App. 4, P. 17, Q. 1, 453) and *Epitome*, ed. Heller (1548), III:25, R2r (quoted in App. 4, P. 17, Q. 2, 454), which expands on this passage.

⟨II x 1⟩

[1]**1: Aspect of love, Latin: *aspectus dilectionis*.** This is a calque of מבט אהבה, "aspect of love," and refers to the aspect of trine. See note on *El*, II vii 1:3.

[2]**1–3: If someone asks about wealth … take place completely**. This corresponds to *She'elot* I, § 10.1:1–9, 286–287 (quoted in App. 4, P. 18, Q. 1, 454–455), which expands on this passage. See also *She'elot* II, § 10.1:1–8, 382–383 and *Epitome*, ed. Heller (1548), III:18, Q4v (*Utrum quis habiturus sit dominium vel non* = "Whether someone will acquire dominion or not").

[3]**4: Jupiter, Latin: *stella Iovis*.** Here the Latin *stella Iovis* is a translation of one of Ibn Ezra's typical designations of Jupiter: כוכב צדק "the star Jupiter". See, inter alia: *Moladot*, III v 1:3, 144–145; *Me'orot* § 28:1, 472–473; *Mishpeṭei ha-mazzalot* § 47:9, 434–435; *'Olam* I, § 17:1, 76–77; *Mivḥarim* II, § 3.1:1, 154–155.

[4]**6: In their exaltations, Latin: *in exaltationibus suis*.** Here *Interrogationes* uses *exaltatio*, the term in vogue in Latin medieval literature to denote the concept of exaltation. The same applies to *El*, II vii 5:5, as well as to *Tp*, II v 3:1. This stands in contrast with the use of *honor*, a literal translation of כבוד "honor," in *Interrogationes* (II ii 2:2) and in *Tractatus particulares*

(IV 3:2), and with the use of *altitudo* "highness," in *El*, II ii 2:2, two terms used by Ibn Ezra to denote astrological exaltation.

⟨II x 2⟩

[1]**1: If someone asks ... [Mercury's] power**. The link between Mercury and scholars or wisdom is highlighted throughout Ibn Ezra's oeuvre. See, for example: *El*, II ix 3:6; *She'elot* I, § 11.1:8, 292–293 (quoted in note on *Int*, II xi 1:1–3); *Mivḥarim* I, § 1.1:1, 50–51 and § 9.3:1, 80–81; *Mivḥarim* II, § 10.3:5, 172–173 and § 11.4:2, 174–175; *'Olam* I, § 67:1, 94–95; *Reshit ḥokhmah* § 4.6:5, 174–175; *Ṭe'amim* I, § 4.7:2, 78–79; *Ṭe'amim* II, § 5.7:1, 232–233.

⟨II xi 1⟩

[1]**1–3: If someone asks ... ascendant or retrograde**. This corresponds to *She'elot* I, § 11.1:1–8, 290–293 (quoted in App. 4, P. 19, Q. 1, 455), which expands on the role of the planets that indicate the thing asked about. See also *Epitome*, ed. Heller (1548), III:21, R1v (*De amicitia* "On friendship"), and *El*, II xi 1:1–3 and note.

⟨II xii 1⟩

[1]**1–10: If someone asks ... returned to jail**. This corresponds to *She'elot* I, § 12.1:1–9, 292–295 (quoted in App. 4, P. 20, Q. 1, 456–457), *She'elot* II, § 12.1:1–14, 388–389 (quoted in App. 4, P. 20, Q. 2, 457–458), and *Epitome*, ed. Heller (1548), III:26, R2v (quoted in App. 4., P. 20, Q. 3, 458–459); the last of these inverts the order of the presentation and begins with the cases unfavorable for the prisoner.

⟨II xii 2⟩

[1]**2: Ninth part**. According to this doctrine, each sign is divided into nine ninth-parts (Hebrew תשיעיות, Arabic نوبهرات) of equal size (i.e., 3⅓°); each ninth-part is associated with a sign, and the planet that is the lord of this sign is the lord of the corresponding ninth-part.

[2]**2: Some of them ... ⟨horoscopical⟩ place is**. In this passage, "where its horoscopic place is" means that one should observe the ninth-part from

the ascendant to find the horoscopic place associated with this ninth-part. This corresponds to *She'elot* I, § 9:3–4, 240–243 (quoted in App. 4, P. 21, Q. 1, § 1:3–4, 459–460), which includes an example to show how the ninth-part with respect to the ascendant of the interrogational horoscope is associated with a horoscopic place of this horoscope, and how this association makes it possible to know the subject matter of the question. This corresponds also to *She'elot* II, § 10:3, 356–357 (quoted in App. 4, P. 21, Q. 2, 3, 460), which assigns the instruction to use the ninth-parts to Māshā'allāh.

[3]**1–2: Abraham the author says ... ⟨horoscopic⟩ place is.** This is an alternative Latin translation of a section of the lost *She'elot* III, also translated in *Tp*, I i 4:1–3.

[4]**3: Lot of Fortune.** For this concept, see note on *Int*, II i 9:1.

[5]**3: Others say that they ... lot of Fortune.** This is an alternative Latin translation of a section of the lost *She'elot* III, also translated in *Tp*, I i 4:4. Taking into consideration that *Int*, II i 11:1 states, on the authority of Māshā'allāh, that the significator is identical with the Moon, this passage corresponds to the following loci: (1) *She'elot* I, § 10:1–3, § 11:1, 246–247 (quoted in App. 4, P. 21, Q. 1, § 2:1–3, § 3:1, 459–460), which invokes the authority of Māshā'allāh regarding the Moon, and the authority of certain Razeq regarding the lot of Fortune; (2) *She'elot* II, § 10:1–2, 356–357 (quoted in App. 4, P. 21, Q. 2, 2, 460), which invokes the authority of Māshā'allāh regarding both the Moon and the lot of Fortune. Regarding the lot of Fortune, the current statement is affirmed in Māshā'allāh's *Book of interrogations* (see App. 7, P. 2, 1–2, 499).

[6]**4: Others say ... lord of the day.** This is an alternative Latin translation of a section of the lost *She'elot* III, also translated in *Tp*, I i 4:5. For the concepts of "five places of dominion," "lord of the hour," and "lord of the day," see, respectively, the notes to *Int*, II i 15:1, and *Tp*, I:3. This corresponds closely to *She'elot* I, § 11:2–3, 246–247 (quoted in App. 4, P. 21, Q. 1, § 3:2–3, 459–460), where this statement is affirmed by Ibn Ezra himself, who says that he tested it empirically many times and that it was accepted by Dorotheus and also by Māshā'allāh. The same statement, with a different wording, occurs in *Int*, II i 9:1 and in *Tp*, I i 4:5.

[7]**5: Closer to the truth ... in the *Book Samechem*.** *Liber Samechem* is described as a "noble book" in *Int*, II xii 2:9, and referred to implicitly in

Int, II xii 3:1, where it is said that it instructs the astrologer how he can know what is in the querent's hand. The same *Liber Samechem* is referred to as *Liber Tamedas* in *Tp*, I i 4:6,10 and I ii 8:1, which are Latin translations of the same passages of the lost *She'elot* III that were translated into Latin in *Int*, II xii 2:5,9 and II xii 3:1. For this *Liber Samechem*, or *Liber Tamedas*, see above, pp. 67–68.

[8]7: **Which place aspects ⟨the planet that⟩ is in the ascendant**. For this translation, see *Tp*, I i 4:8.

[9]6–7: **Associate with this ... dignity over it**. This corresponds to *She'elot* II, § 10:4–5, 356–357 (quoted in App. 4, P. 21, Q. 2, 4–5, 460–461).

[10]8–9. **It is proper ... noble book**. This passage refers to the contents of *Liber Samechem*, as specified in *Int*, II xii 2:5. See note there.

[11]5–9: **It is closer to the truth ... noble book**. This passage is an alternative Latin translation of a section of the lost *She'elot* III, also translated in *Tp*, I i 4:6–10.

⟨II xii 3⟩

[1]1: **They said that in this way ... in the ascendant**. The method by which the astrologer may know what is in the querent's hand is mentioned in *Int*, II xii 2; the book referred to in this passage is the *Liber Samechem* or *Liber Tamedas*. For this book, see note to *Int*, II xii 2:5. An alternative Latin translation of the Hebrew source text from *She'elot* III that corresponds to the current section (*Int*, II xii 3:1) is found in *Tp*, I ii 8:1–3. See notes there.

⟨II xii 4⟩

[1]1: **Lord of the hour**. For this concept, see note on *Tp*, I:3.

[2]1: **The lord of the hour ... white but not pure**. This corresponds to *She'elot* I, § 4.10:5, 262–263 (quoted in App. 4, P. 22, Q. 1, 461), *De nativitatibus*, II i 6:7, 276–277 (quoted in App. 4, P. 22, Q. 2, 461), and *Epitome*, ed. Heller (1548), III:8, P2v–P3r (quoted in App. 4, P. 22, Q. 3, 461), where a similar statement is assigned to Māshā'allāh, who, just as in *Int*, I 1:7, is taken to be an Indian

astrologer. An alternative Latin translation of the Hebrew source text from *She'elot* III that corresponds to the current section (*Int*, II xii 4:1) is found in *Tp*, I ii 9:1. See notes there.

⟨II xii 5⟩

[1]**1: Lord of the terms**. For this concept see note to *Tp*, I i 7:1.

[2]**1–2: They say that the lord of the terms ... position of the significator**. An alternative Latin translation of the Hebrew source text from *She'elot* III that corresponds to the entire current section (*Int*, II xii 5:1–2) is found in *Tp*, I ii 10:1. See notes there.

⟨II xii 6⟩

[1]**1–2: They said that in this way ... there nearby**. This corresponds to *Epitome*, ed. Heller (1548), III:8, P2v (quoted in App. 4, P. 23, Q. 1, 1–2, 462), which assigns this statement to the *iuniores huius artis magistri*, that is, the more recent masters of the art of astrology.

[2]**3: To find out the place ... in the roof**. This corresponds to (1) *Epitome*, ed. Heller (1548), III:8, P2v (quoted in App. 4, P. 23, Q. 1, 4, 462); (2) *She'elot* I, § 4.7:1, 260–261 (quoted in App. 4, P. 23, Q. 2, 1, 462), which assigns the statement to Abū ʿAlī; and (3) *She'elot* II, § 12.6:1, 392–393 (quoted in App. 4, P. 23, Q. 3, 1, 463), which assigns the statement to al-Kindī.

[3]**4: They said that the Sun ... bed in the house**. This corresponds to (1) *Epitome*, ed. Heller (1548), III:8, P2v (quoted in App. 4, P. 23, Q. 1, 4, 462); (2) *She'elot* I, § 4.7:1, 260–261 (quoted in App. 4, P. 23, Q. 2, 2–3, 462), which assigns the statement to Abū ʿAlī; and (3) *She'elot* II, § 12.6:1, 392–393 (quoted in App. 4, P. 23, Q. 3, 2, 463), which assigns the statement to al-Kindī.

[4]**1–6: They said that in this way ... into these matters**. An alternative Latin translation of the Hebrew source text from *She'elot* III that corresponds to the entire current section (*Int*, II xii 6:1–6) is found in *Tp*, I iii 1:1–6.

⟨II xii 7⟩

[1]**2: If the lord of the ascendant … on his own.** This corresponds to *She'elot* I, § 7.8:1–2, 278–279 (quoted in App. 4, P. 24, Q. 1, 1–2, 463) and *Epitome*, ed. Heller (1548), III:15, Q3v (quoted in App. 4, P. 24, Q. 2, 1, 464).

[2]**3: If it gives power … find the fugitive.** This corresponds to *Epitome*, ed. Heller (1548), III:15, Q3v (quoted in App. 4, P. 24, Q. 2, 2, 464).

[3]**4: ⟨If⟩ the lord … will find him.** This corresponds to *She'elot* I, § 7.8:3, 278–279 (quoted in App. 4, P. 24, Q. 1, 3, 463).

[4]**6: If the significator … found by messengers.** This corresponds to *She'elot* I, § 7.8:4, 278–281 (quoted in App. 4, P. 24, Q. 1, 4, 463–464).

[5]**9: If the significator gives power … the fugitive will die.** This corresponds to *She'elot* I, § 7.8:3, 278–279 (quoted in App. 4, P. 24, Q. 1, 6, 463–464).

[6]**10: Likewise, if the significator … found but dead.** This corresponds to *Epitome*, ed. Heller (1548), III:15, Q3v (quoted in App. 4, P. 24, Q. 2, 3, 464).

[7]**1–10: In addition, this is what they said … found but dead.** An alternative Latin translation of the Hebrew source text from *She'elot* III that corresponds to the entire current section (*Int*, II xii 7:1–10) is found in *Tp*, I iv 1:1–10.

⟨II xii 8⟩

[1]**1–2: Also observe … place of his escape.** This corresponds to *She'elot* II, § 12.1:5, 386–387 (quoted in App. 4, P. 20, Q. 2, 5, 457–458).

[2]**4: Worthless and frightened people.** This is the either a copyist's error or the translator's mistaking the *dalet* for a *zayin* in Judges 9:4: אנשים ריקים ופחזים "worthless and reckless persons."

[3]**1–4: Also observe … frightened people.** An alternative Latin translation of the Hebrew source text from *She'elot* III that corresponds to the entire current section (*Int*, II xii 8:1–4) is found in *Tp*, I iv 2:1–4.

⟨II xii 9⟩

[1]**2: If it [the Moon] ... to his master.** This corresponds to *She'elot* I, § 7.8:8, 280–281 (quoted in App. 4, P. 24, Q. 1, 8, 463–464).

[2]**3: You can know ... seventh place.** This corresponds to *She'elot* I, § 7.9:1–2, 280–281 (quoted in App. 4, P. 24, Q. 1, 9–10, 463–464).

[3]**4: In the cardines, or in the succedent, or the cadent ⟨places⟩, Latin: *in angulis, vel in succedentibus, vel in cadentibus*.** Following Arabophone astrologers, Ibn Ezra divides the twelve horoscopic places into three subdivisions: (1) the four cardines **יתדות** (*anguli, caville*), which correspond to the first, fourth, seventh, and tenth places; (2) the four succedent places **סמוכים** (*succedentes*), which correspond to the second, fifth, eighth, and eleventh places; and (3) the four cadent places **בתים נופלים** (*domus cadentes*; *domus lapsa*; *cadentes a cavillis*; *domus cadentes ab angulis*), which correspond to the third, sixth, ninth, and twelfth places. *Mishpeṭei ha-mazzalot* § 12:1–7, 498–499 (quoted in App. 5, Q. 40, 478–479) defines the four cardines, succedent, and cadent places, with their mutual relationships and relative power, in the framework of the division of the 12 horoscopic places.

[4]**1–4: The general rule ... with respect to the Sun.** An alternative Latin translation of the Hebrew source text from *She'elot* III that corresponds to the entire current section (*Int*, II xii 9:1–4) is found in *Tp*, I iv 3:1–4.

⟨II xii 10⟩

[1]**3–5: They said that the fugitive's location ... first ⟨place⟩.** This corresponds to *She'elot* I, § 7.8:7, 280–281 (quoted in App. 4, P. 24, Q. 1, 7, 463–464).

[2]**1–5: All I have said ... first ⟨place⟩.** An alternative Latin translation of the Hebrew source text from *She'elot* III that corresponds to the entire current section (*Int*, II xii 10:1–5) is found in *Tp*, I iv 4:1–5.

⟨II xii 11⟩

[1]**2: ⟨Ptolemy says⟩ ... great principle.** This quotes the first aphorism of Pseudo-Ptolemy's *Centiloquium* (quoted in App. 2, Q. 7, 401).

[2]**1–2: Abraham says ... great principle**. An alternative Latin translation of the Hebrew source text from *She'elot* III that corresponds to the entire current section (*Int*, II xii 11:1–2) is found in *Tp*, I iv 5:1–2.

PART FIVE

TRACTATUS PARTICULARES

LATIN TEXT AND ENGLISH TRANSLATION

54va ## Incipiunt quidam tractatus particulares[1]
⟨⟨Liber Abrahe Iudei Avenezre⟩⟩

⟨I⟩

(1) Liber hic .4or. continet capitula. (2) Primum de cogitatione[2] hominis ac eius questione. (3) Secundum ad illud est quod[3] occultat in manu, et de colore ipsius, per dominum hore. (4) Tertium de re absconsa, et loco eius. (5) Quartum in loco fugitivi.[4]

⟨⟨(1) Incipit *Liber Abrahe Evenezre Iudei de ocultis*. (2) Iste liber dividitur in .4. capitula. (3) Primum de cogitatione hominis et eius interrogatione. (4) .2m. quid tenet in manu sua et de colore eius per dominum hore. (5) .3m. super rebus absconsis et de inveniendo loco. (6) .4. super loco fugientis et eius inventione.⟩⟩

⟨I i⟩
Capitulum primum[5]
⟨⟨Capitulum primum, de intentione⟩⟩

54vb **1** (1) | Debes quoque aspicere dominum[6] ascendentis in qua fuerit ex[7] .12. domibus, ut[8] non sit combustus neque retrogradatus neque in domo lapsa. (2) Si enim in aliquo istorum fuerit locorum, nulla per eum detur responsio nisi per aliud, sicut declarabo; ponatur ergo quod dominus sit ascendentis[9] boni esse. (3) Si fuerit in ascendente, querit de semetipso. (4) Et si fuerit in secunda, de substantia. (5) Domus autem .3a.[10] dividitur in duo: si ascendentis dominus fuerit in parte prima .3e. domus, vult ire de loco ad locum; in .2a., de fratribus ad sorores. (6) .4a. dividitur in .3a.: et[11] si fuerit

[1]Incipiunt quidam tractatus particulares] DZNL^{m}; B Incipiunt tractatus de cogitatione hominis ac eius questione; P Incipit liber Abrahe Avenesre Judei de cogitatione hominis, de rebus occultatis per hominem in manu de eorum coloribus, de rebus abscondis in quorumque loco, et de loco fugitivi; V omits title but opens an indent of 6 lines. [2]cogitatione] DZBPN; VL cognitione. [3]ad illud est quod] VN; DL quod illud est quod; BPZ ad quod est illud quod; P est ad illud quod quis. [4]in loco fugitivi] VDZLN; B de loco fugitivi; P in est de loco fugitivi. [5]Capitulum primum*] ZLN^{m}B; P > ad sciendum de cogitatio hominis et eius questione; V omits the title but opens an indent of 4 lines; D omits the title but opens an indent of 3 lines. [6]dominum] P < ad. [7]ex] D om. [8]ut] N si. [9]ascendentis] D; VPN ascendens; B om. [10].3a.] DL; VPNZB .2a. [11]et] D om.

Here Begin Certain Particular Treatises.
⟪Book by Abraham Ibn Ezra, the Jew⟫

⟨I⟩

(1) This book contains four chapters. (2) The first is on a man's thoughts and his question. (3) The second is on what he is hiding in his hand, and on its color, by means of the lord of the hour.[1] (4) The third is on the hidden thing and its location. (5) The fourth is on the location of a fugitive.

⟪(1) Here begins the *Book by Abraham Ibn Ezra on hidden things*. (2) This book is divided into four chapters. (3) The first is on a man's thoughts and his question. (4) The second is on what he is hiding in his hand, and on its color, by means of the lord of the hour. (5) The third is on a hidden thing and finding its location. (6) The fourth is on the location of a fugitive and finding him.⟫

⟨I i⟩
The First Chapter
⟪The First Chapter, on Intention⟫

1 (1) You also need to observe the lord of the ascendant, in whichever of the 12 ⟨horoscopic⟩ places it is located, ⟨to determine that⟩ it is not burnt, retrograde, or in the house of dejection.[1] (2) If it is in any of these places, no answer will be given by it [i.e., the lord of the ascendant] but by another ⟨significator⟩, as I shall indicate;[2] so let us suppose that there is a lord of an auspicious ascendant. (3) If it [the lord of the ascendant] is in the ascendant, he [the querent] will inquire about himself. (4) If it is in the second ⟨place⟩, ⟨the querent will ask⟩ about wealth. (5) The third ⟨place⟩ is divided into two: if the lord of the ascendant is in the first part of the third place, he [i.e., the querent] wants to go from one place to another; ⟨if it is⟩ in the second ⟨part⟩, ⟨he wants to go⟩ from the brothers to the sisters. (6) The fourth ⟨place⟩ is divided into three ⟨parts⟩: if the lord of the

dominus ascendentis in prima parte, cogitat de patre eius qui ipsum genuit; in secunda, navem, aut edificium, aut aliquid subterraneum; in .3a., cogitat de seipso. (7) .5a. dividitur in .4or.: prima, pueros aut discentes,[1] aut servos; secunda, gaudium; .3a., vestimenta; .4a., nuntiorum nova, aut literarum. (8) .6a. dividitur in .2. partes: una,[2] morbos; secunda, servos, et ancillas, et animalia parva. (9) Septima in .3a.: prima, mulieres; secunda, socios; .3a., inimicos, latrones aut litigatores, aut sibi contrarium. (10) .8a. dividitur in .3a.: prima, mortem aut timorem, timet quoque ne sibi aliquid contingat; .2a., suas domos, et campos, suasque terras,[3] et omne eius acquisitum; .3a., debitum. (11) .9a. dividitur in .4or.: prima, fidei et veritatis;[4] .2a., itineris; .3a., honoris et nominis in scientia; .4a., est somnii. (12) .10a. dividitur in .3.: prima, regem aut potentem; .2a. scientiam, ingenium et magisterium; .3a., matres. (13) Undecima dividitur in .3a.: prima mercandariam;[5] .2a., divitem[6] aut opulentiam;[7] .3a., amicum aut amicam. (14) .12a. dividitur in .3a.: prima, eius inimicum; .2a., captivationem et infirmitates[8] et carcerem; .3a., bestias.

2 (1) Si dominus ascendentis fuerit combustus, retrogradus aut cadens, vel in signo feminino, et ipse in ascendente, ipsum relinquere debes ac per Lunam respondere.[9] (2) Et vide in qua est domo, et secundum locum domus in qua fuerit debes respondere, secundum partes quas tibi exposui. (3) Si vero Luna fuerit in signo masculino, aut cadens, vel combusta, non respondeas per eam sed per dominum hore. (4) Et sic est faciendum.

3 (1) Aspice quidem quot gradus dominus[10] signi fuerit[11] in signo suo, quos per .12. multiplica, et divide per .30., et proice ab ascendente. (2) Des .30. ascendenti, et similiter .2e. et .3e., eodem modo donec terminentur[12]

[1]discentes] D > vel discipulos. [2]una] LP prima. [3]terras] V om. [4]veritatis] D utilitatis. [5]mercandariam] VDBN; LP mercanciam. [6]divitem] P divitias. [7]opulentiam] D opulentem. [8]infirmitates] D infirmitas. [9]respondere] D responde. [10]dominus] ZB om. [11]fuerit] P fecerit. [12]terminentur] D > vel finiantur.

ascendant is in the first part, he is thinking about his father, who begot him; in the second ⟨part⟩, about a ship, a building, or something underground; in the third, he is thinking about himself. (7) The fifth ⟨place⟩ is divided into four ⟨parts⟩: ⟨if the lord of the ascendant is⟩ in the first, ⟨the querent is thinking⟩ about children, students, or slaves; in the second, about joy; in the third, about clothes; in the fourth, about news from messengers, or letters. (8) The sixth ⟨place⟩ is divided into two parts: in the first ⟨part, the querent is thinking⟩ about diseases; in the second, about slaves, female slaves, and small livestock. (9) The seventh ⟨place⟩ is divided into three ⟨parts⟩: in the first ⟨part, the querent is thinking⟩ about women; in the second, about partners; in the third, about enemies, thieves, litigants, or those who oppose him. (10) The eighth ⟨place⟩ is divided into three ⟨parts⟩. in the first ⟨part, the querent is thinking⟩ about death or fear, he is also afraid of something that may happen to him; in the second, about his houses, fields, estates, and everything acquired by him; in the third, about ⟨his⟩ debts. (11) The ninth ⟨place⟩ is divided into four ⟨parts⟩: in the first ⟨part, the querent is thinking⟩ about faith and truth; in the second, about travel; in the third, about honor and renown in knowledge; in the fourth, about a dream. (12) The tenth ⟨place⟩ is divided into three ⟨parts⟩: in the first ⟨part, the querent is thinking⟩ about a king or a ruler; in the second, about knowledge, intelligence, and authority; in the third, about mothers. (13) The eleventh ⟨place⟩ is divided into three ⟨parts⟩: in the first ⟨part, the querent is thinking⟩ about merchandise; in the second, about a rich person or wealth; in the third, about a male or female friend. (14) The twelfth ⟨place⟩ is divided into three ⟨parts⟩: ⟨If the lord of the ascendant is⟩ in the first ⟨part, the querent is thinking⟩ about enemies; in the second, about captivity, diseases, and prison, in the third, about beasts.[3]

2 (1) If the lord of the ascendant is burnt, retrograde, or in ⟨its⟩ dejection,[1] or in a feminine sign, and it is itself in the ascendant, you need to set it aside and answer by means of the Moon. (2) Observe which place it [the Moon] is in, and you need to respond according to the place it [the Moon] is in, according to the parts ⟨of the horoscopic place⟩ I have told you about. (3) But if the Moon is in a masculine sign, in ⟨its⟩ dejection, or burnt, do not answer according to it but according to the lord of the hour. (4) You should proceed as follows.[2]

3 (1) Observe how many degrees in its sign is the lord of the sign, multiply them by 12, divide them by 30, and cast ⟨the result⟩ out of the ascendant. (2) Assign 30 ⟨degrees⟩ to the ascendant, likewise to the ⟨cusp of the⟩

gradus ex multiplicatione consurgentes. (3) Et ubi finiuntur, illic est eius cogitatio, secundum participationem iam dictam.[1] (4) Si vero dominus hore fuerit combustus aut retrogradus vel cadens aut masculus, et est[2] in signo femino, respice quot gradus ascenderunt de signo ascendente; desque ascendenti .2. gradus cum dimidio, et[3] .2e. similiter,[4] et .3e. iterum, et ubi hic numerus finietur, illic erit eius cogitatio, secundum divisionem domorum supra dictam.

4 (1) Dicit quoque[5] Abraham:[6] scias quod sapientes interrogationum dixe-
55ra runt unum hominem posse scire quid sit | in corde querentis. (2) Et multum in hoc laboraverunt. (3) Sunt enim aliqui dicentes: nos semper aspicere[7] novenariam gradus ascendentis in qua existit domo. (4) Dicunt et alii semper aspiciendum[8] ad Lunam et ad partem fortune. (5) Nonnulli quidem dicunt esse aspiciendum ad planetam habentem fortitudinem in .5. locis dignitatum, et ad dominum hore aut dominum diei. (6) Et veritati propinquius est si sciverit naturam cuiuslibet gradus zodiaci, sicut scriptum est in *Libro Tamedas*. (7) Et adiungere debet domino gradus ascendentis si respiciat, aut[9] si quis planeta apparet in ascendente. (8) Et debes coniungere semper cum planeta existenti in ascendente,[10] quicumque sit ille qui fuerit in ipso, et scire que eius sit natura, et[11] ex qua domo aspicit, aut in qua habet dignitatem. (9) Et rectum est ut homo non ponat se in dubitatione,[12] neque de cogitatione respondeat nisi sciat illud quod significat gradus quilibet. (10) Et hic est liber nobilis.

5 (1) Dicit quidem Messahalla:[13] Significatores cogitationum sunt .3. (2) Unus dominus ascendentis, et[14] receptor fortitudinis aut significator qui recipit dominum orbis, et cui dominus ascendentis coniungitur. (3) Et non dimittas propter parva, si fuerint in ascendente, quoniam querentis secundum hoc erit cogitatio. (4) Et cuius signi fuerit ascendens attende, et secundum hoc iudica in cogitatione.

[1]dictam] D > in domibus. [2]et est] P om. [3]et] V om. [4]similiter] D > id est domui. [5]quoque] D utique. [6]Abraham] V Habraham. [7]aspicere] P > debere. [8]aspiciendum] VZLN; BP aspiciendum esse; D aspicientes. [9]respiciat aut] D respiciatur. [10]Et debes coniungere semper cum planeta existenti in ascendente] P om. [11]et] V om. [12]dubitatione] VZLPN; D > et confusione; B dubietate. [13]Messahalla] DZBLN; V Mesahalac; P Messahallach. [14]et] V om.

second and the third ⟨place⟩, and proceed in the same manner until the degrees produced by the multiplication are exhausted. (3) His ⟨the querent's⟩ thoughts are where ⟨the degrees⟩ are exhausted, according to the aforementioned division ⟨of the places⟩ into parts. (4) If the lord of the hour is burnt, retrograde, in ⟨its⟩ dejection, or masculine, and it is in a feminine sign, pay attention to how many degrees have risen from the ascendant sign; assign 2½° to the ascendant, likewise to the second ⟨place⟩, and also to the third ⟨place⟩; his ⟨the querent's⟩ thought is where the count is completed, according to the aforementioned division of the places.[1]

4 (1) Abraham also says: know that the experts in interrogations said that a man can know what the querent has in his heart. (2) They were much perplexed about this. (3) Some of them said: we always observe which ⟨horoscopic⟩ place is located the ninth-part[1] of the ascendant degree.[2] (4) Others said that one should always observe the Moon and the lot of Fortune.[3,4] (5) Some said that one should observe the planet that has power in the five places of dignities, and the lord of the hour or the lord of the day.[5,6] (6) It is closer to the truth if ⟨the astrologer⟩ observes the nature of any degree of the zodiac,[7] as is written in the *Book Tamedas*.[8] (7) He should associate ⟨the degree of the zodiac⟩ with the lord of the degree of the ascendant if it forms an aspect,[9] or if some planet appears in the ascendant. (8) You always need to associate ⟨the lord of the degree of the ascendant⟩ with a planet located in the ascendant, whichever it is ⟨this planet⟩ that is in ⟨the ascendant⟩ itself, and ⟨you need to⟩ find out what its nature is, and from which place it aspects, or in which ⟨place⟩ it has a dignity. (9) It is right that a person does not have doubts, and that he should not give an answer regarding thoughts unless he knows what each degree signifies. (10) This is a noble book.[10]

5 (1) Māshā'allāh says: there are three significators for thoughts. (2) One is the lord of the ascendant, and the receiver of power or the significator that receives the lord of the orb, and the one that is conjoined with the lord of the ascendant. (3) Do not reject them on account of a short ⟨distance from the degree of the ascendant,⟩ if they are in the ascendant, because the querent's thought will be according to it. (4) Pay attention to which sign the ascendant belongs, and judge about the ⟨querent's⟩ thought according to it.[1]

6 (1) Secundus,[1] ut videas significatorem[2] signi, in qua est domorum. (2) Si in ascendente, ipsummet significat; in secunda, substantiam; et sic de aliis domibus.

7 (1) Tertius, secundum quod dixerunt sapientes indorum, si queris de occulto, respice almutaz[3,{4}] ascendentis, et dominum termini, et faciei. (2) Et respice cui coniungitur fortior eorum: res enim erit secundum naturam occultati. (3) Eorum fortior est fortitudo .12e.[5]

8 (1) Verbi gratia: .12us.[6] gradus Arietis est ascendens, quando quibuslibet .2. gradibus et dimidio[7] dederimus unam domum; et incipies ab Ariete ascendente; numerus deficiet in Leone, qui est dominus (sic) filiorum[8,{9}] secundum ascendens, et illic non sit alius planeta. (2) Tunc respexi[10] Solem, et ipsum inveni in .7a. domo, dixique quod interrogatio esset mulieris querentis de eius filio, ipse quoque de ea non curat; et si Sol fuisset in 6a,[11] quesisset de filio infirmo.[12]

⟨I ii⟩
Capitulum secundum[13]
⟨⟨Capitulum secundum: de intentione per dominos hore⟩⟩

1 (1) Si quis a te quesiverit de aliquo, si fuerit in principio hore Solis, vult querere pro[14] se, aut pro re sua, et socii;[15] et si interrogaverit quid in manu habeat, dicas rem parvam, crescentem in terra. (2) Si autem in medio hore, querit de dominio,[16] aut guerra, vel lite, unde valde dubitat; de eo autem quod est in manu, dicas esse argentum, aut aurum, vel os, aut terram. (3) In
55rb fine hore, querit de iudice uno, qui sibi timorem | incussit, et est huius iratus iudicio; quid autem in manu habet, lanam, vel rem tortam, vel pannum, vel filum.[17,{18}]

[1]Secundus] D > ait. [2]significatorem] D > scilicet ascendentis. [3]almutaz] VNZB; PL almutaç; D almutam. [4]almutaz] G ad almutem. [5].12e.] L duodecime. [6].12us.] VPNZB; DL .12... [7]et dimidio] VL; P cum dimidio; NZB et semis; D cum dimidio ut dando istorum .12. gradus ... Leoni .4. scilicet. [8]dominus filiorum] VNPLBZ; D dominus puerorum. [9]dominus filiorum] G dominus puerorum. [10]respexi] D; VNPLBZ respice. [11]6a] P gradus 6a domus. [12]infirmo] D > vel fuisset infirmus. [13]Capitulum secundum*] ZNLB; P Capitulum .2m. super intentionem querentis et quid in manu teneat; V omits the title but opens an indent of 4 lines; D omits the title but opens an indent of 3 lines. [14]pro] D per. [15]socii] D > sui de qualis horis. [16]dominio] D > vel re dominii. [17]vel filum*] PBZLN; D aut filum; V om. [18]G vel filum.

6 (1) The second is that you should observe the significator of the sign ⟨of the ascendant⟩ ⟨and find out⟩ in which of the places it is. (2) If ⟨it is⟩ in the ascendant, it signifies ⟨the querent⟩ himself; if ⟨it is⟩ in the second ⟨place⟩, ⟨it signifies⟩ wealth; and so on regarding the other places.[1]

7 (1) The third, according to what the Indian scholars said, if you inquire about something hidden, is that you should pay attention to the *mubtazz*[1] of the ascendant, the lord of the term,[2] and ⟨the lord⟩ of the decan.[3] (2) Observe with which ⟨celestial object⟩ the strongest of them is conjoined: the thing ⟨in the querent's mind⟩ will be according to the nature of the hidden ⟨object⟩. (3) The strongest of them is the power of the dodecatemoria.[4,5]

8 (1) Example: Aries 12° is rising when we assign one sign to each interval of 2½°;[1] you begin from Aries in the ascendant; the count is completed in Leo, which is the lord of sons according to the ascendant, and there is no other planet there. (2) Then I observed the Sun and found it in the seventh place; ⟨hence⟩ I said that the question is about a woman who is asking about her son, even though he does not take care of her; but if the Sun is in the sixth ⟨place⟩, she will ask about a sick son.[2,3]

⟨I ii⟩
The Second Chapter
⟨⟨The Second Chapter: On Intention by Means of the Lords of the Hour⟩⟩

1 (1) If someone asks you about something, if this happens at the beginning of the Sun's hour, he wants to ask you about himself, or about something that belongs to him, or ⟨about something that belongs⟩ to a partner; if he asks what he is holding in ⟨his⟩ hand, tell him ⟨that it is⟩ something small that grows in the earth. (2) If ⟨someone inquires⟩ in the middle of the ⟨Sun's⟩ hour, he is asking about dominion, war, or quarrels, about which he is very uncertain; ⟨if he asks⟩ what he is holding in his hand, tell ⟨him⟩ that it is silver, gold, a bone, or earth. (3) If ⟨someone inquires⟩ at the end of the ⟨Sun's⟩ hour, he is asking about one judge who has made him afraid and is angry about his trial; ⟨as for⟩ what he is holding in ⟨his⟩ hand, ⟨tell him that it is⟩ wool, a twisted thing, a piece of cloth, or a thread.[1]

2 (1) In principio hore Veneris, querit de muliere et concubitu; quid autem habet in manu, rem politam,[1] que adhuc ponetur in ignem. (2) In medio, pro re profunde[2] scientie, aut pro argento; quid in manu,[3] rem tortam et[4] latam, de qua profectum non habebit, (3) In fine, pro mulieribus, aut re aspera[5] sibi et eius socio; quid[6] in manu habet, rem supremam[7] in aqua, aut pannum, aut aliquid germinans ex terra.

3 (1) In principio hore Mercurii, querit pro scientia; in manu, autem habet rem subtilem, latam et siccam, exterius, non autem intra,[8] et illam gerens comedit. (2) In medio, querit de infirmitate, aut[9] de[10] infirmitate[11] quam in manu[12] patitur; in manu, autem[13] habet nigrum crescens in terra, comestibile. (3) In fine, pro[14] homine qui fugit ab eius potestate et alterius;[15] quid in manu, lixatorium, aut lapidem perforatum, vel bonum lapidem.

4 (1) In principio hore Lune, petit pro homine patiente in oculo; quid in[16] manu,[17] herbam odoriferam. (2) In medio,[18] pro homine existente in itinere longo, aut muliere, aut pro re aliqua amissa; in manu autem,[19] pulverem nigrum, aut lapidem, vel cotem, (3) In fine, pro ⟪re amissa⟫;{[20]} quid in manu,[21] rem habentem cornua rubea aut rubeam plantam.

5 (1) In principio hore Saturni, sciendum habere in manu eius unum librum, rem nigram cum alba, et querit a te quod intus est edoceri; quid[22] in manu, viride,[23] aut vitrum. (2) In medio, cogitat de muliere pregnante, utrum fetus qui est in utero sit masculus vel femina; in manu, stagnum, aut aliquid quod ponitur in igne. (3) In fine, infirmitatem, dolorem, aut litem; et si querat de infirmitate, dicas eum iam fore liberatum; quid[24] in manu, uppupam, aut caput avis maculate, igitur sunt macule varie.[25]

[1]politam] D > de patani? per ignem. [2]profunde] D de funde. [3]manu] P tenet. [4]et] V; D aut; ZBNLP om. [5]aspera] D > vel dura. [6]quid] P et. [7]supremam] D > vel excellentem. [8]intra] DPLZB; V inter; N in terra. [9]de infirmitate aut] P om. [10]de] V om. [11]aut de infirmitate] B vel dolore. [12]de infirmitate aut de infirmitate quam in manu] VZDLN; B de infirmitate vel dolore; P de infirmitate quam manu. [13]autem] VP; DZLBN om. [14]pro] P < querit. [15]intravit] VBZLN; DP > potestatem. [16]in] V om. [17]manu] P > habeat. [18]medio] P > querit. [19]autem] P tenet. [20]re amissa] G; VDPALBZN admissione. [21]manu] P > habet. [22]quid] P > habet. [23]viride] D > res participans mendicare. [24]quid] P et tenet in manu. [25]igitur sunt macule varie] ZLBN; D igitur vel cuius sunt macule varie; V cuius sunt macule nigre; P in qua sunt macule varie.

2 (1) At the beginning of Venus's hour, he inquires about a woman and about sexual intercourse; ⟨as for⟩ what he is holding in ⟨his⟩ hand, ⟨it is⟩ something polished, which has been put in fire. (2) At the middle ⟨of Venus's hour⟩, ⟨the question is⟩ about some matter of profound knowledge or about money; ⟨as for⟩ what ⟨he is holding⟩ in ⟨his⟩ hand, ⟨it is⟩ something twisted and wide, from which he will not have profit. (3) At the end ⟨of Venus's hour⟩, ⟨the question is⟩ about women, or about something harsh for him and his partner; ⟨as for⟩ what ⟨he is holding⟩ in ⟨his⟩ hand, ⟨it is⟩ the highest thing in water, a piece of cloth, or something that sprouts from the earth.[1]

3 (1) At the beginning of Mercury's hour, he inquires about knowledge; ⟨as for what he is holding⟩ in ⟨his⟩ hand, he is holding something thin, wide and dry, on the outside but not on the inside, and he carries and eats it. (2) At the middle ⟨of Mercury's hour⟩, he inquires about a disease, or about a disease that he is suffering in the hand; ⟨as for what he is holding⟩ in ⟨his⟩ hand, he is holding something black that grows in the earth ⟨and is⟩ edible. (3) At the end ⟨of Mercury's hour⟩, ⟨the question is⟩ about a man who escaped from his [i.e., master's] authority and entered ⟨the authority⟩ of another ⟨master⟩; ⟨as for⟩ what ⟨he is holding⟩ in ⟨his⟩ hand, ⟨it is⟩ cooked food, a pierced stone, or a precious stone.[1]

4 (1) At the beginning of the Moon's hour, he asks about a man who suffers in his eye; ⟨if he asks about⟩ what ⟨he is holding⟩ in ⟨his⟩ hand, ⟨it is⟩ a fragrant herb. (2) At the middle ⟨of the Moon's hour⟩, he ⟨inquires⟩ about a man who is taking a long journey, a woman, or something lost; ⟨as for what he is holding⟩ in ⟨his⟩ hand, ⟨it is⟩ a black powder, a stone, or a flint. (3) At the end ⟨of the Moon's hour⟩, he ⟨inquires⟩ about something lost; ⟨as for⟩ what ⟨he is holding⟩ in ⟨his⟩ hand, ⟨it is⟩ something with red horns, or a red plant.[1]

5 (1) At the beginning ⟨of Saturn's hour⟩, know ⟨that he⟩ has a book in his hand, something black with white; and he is asking you to show him what is ⟨written⟩ inside [i.e., in the book]; ⟨as for what he is holding⟩ in his hand, ⟨it is⟩ something green, or glass. (2) At the middle ⟨of Saturn's hour⟩, he is thinking about a pregnant woman, and whether the fetus in the womb is male or female; ⟨as for what he is holding⟩ in ⟨his⟩ hand, ⟨it is⟩ tin, or something that is put in the fire. (3) At the end ⟨of Saturn's hour⟩, ⟨the question is about⟩ a disease, a pain, or a quarrel; and if he inquires about a disease, tell him that he has already been cured; ⟨as for⟩ what ⟨he is holding⟩ in ⟨his⟩ hand, ⟨it is⟩ a hoopoe, or the head of a bird marked with spots, and the spots are multicolored.[1]

6 (1) In principio hore Iovis, querit pro salute infirmitatis; et si pro muliere, dicas ipsam[1] liberari; quid[2] in manu,[3] rem ponderosam que in ignem ponitur, et hoc est sigillum. (2) In medio, ut[4] habeat aurum[5] aut substantie rem aliam; in manu autem,[6] res que ponitur in libra coloris albi aut rubei, aut sigillum, vel lapidem preciosum,[7] aut viride[8] mixtum rubeo. (3) In fine, querit si poterit pacificare,[9,{10}] ⟪aut, si inveniet in terra[{11}] repositum, quia credit quod sit census in terra, et vult facere questionem utrum cito poterit illum invenire⟫;[{12}] quid in manu, cathenas[13] ferri, aut anulos, cosrigiam,[14] aut corium.

7 (1) In principio hore Martis, petit pro domino quem timet, aut pro viro qui sibi est odiosus;[15] in manu, rubeum,[16] aut cuprum, aut aurum; (2) In medio, pro latronibus, aut latrocinio, aut pro admisso;[17] in manu,
55va rem parvam | et rubeam, (3) In fine, pro carcere,[18] aut infirmitate, aut eius inimico; in manu, quidem[19] siccum vel lignum.

8 (1) Inquit Abraham:[20] diximus quod sapientes ut[21] sciant quid habeat in manu interrogator, sicut per *Librum Tametas*[22] iam dictum, secundum naturam signi ascendentis et eius domini.[{23}] (2) Quoniam Aries, Leo, Sagitarius, significant vitam; Taurus, Virgo, Capricornius, vestimenta; Gemini, Libra, Aquarius, colores; Cancer, Scorpio, Pisces, res perforatas. (3) Et secundum planetam existentem in ascendente.

9 (1) Dominus quoque hore significat colores:[24] Saturnus, quidem[25] griseum; Jupiter, viridem;[26] Mars, rubeum; Sol, glaucum lucidum; Venus, pulchrum, resplendentem; Mercurius, colorem varium;[27] Luna, albedinem non[28] bene lucidam.

[1]ipsam] BZ eam. [2]quid] P et. [3]manu] P > tenet. [4]ut] P dic quod. [5]aurum] D < velut. [6]autem] P eius est. [7]lapidem preciosum] P lapis preciosus. [8]viride] D viridine. [9]pacificare] VPN; ZDB pacificare duos vel duas gentes; L pacificare duos. [10]pacificare] G inter eos pacem reformare. [11]in terra*] G; VDPLBZN intra es. [12]aut si inveniet in terra repositum quia credit quod sit census in terra et vult facere questionem utrum cito poterit illum invenire*] G; VDPLBZN aut si inveniat aliquid credit enim quod intra es sit, unde querit si cito poterit invenire. [13]quid in manu cathenas] P et si querit quid in manu teneat dic cathenas. [14]cosrigiam] P < aut. [15]odiosus] D > vel qui sibi fecit red?. [16]rubeum] P < tenet. [17]admisso] VZLN; BPD amisso. [18]carcere] VDNP; LBZ creati re. [19]quidem] P tenet. [20]Abraham*] NZPLB; VD Habraham. [21]ut] V om. [22]Tametas] DZBLN; P Tomatas; V Amatas. [23]diximus quod ... eius domini] VDPZBLN; G nos diximus quod scire potest sapiens quod erit in manu querentis per Librum Tamtetas quem memorati sumus, et secundum naturam signi ascendentis et domini eius. [24]colores] D rem coloritam. [25]quidem] B om. [26]viridem] D veritatem. [27]varium] D > vel plures colores. [28]non] L ut.

6 (1) At the beginning ⟨of Jupiter's hour⟩, he inquires about recovering from a disease; if ⟨he inquires⟩ about a woman, say that she has been cured; ⟨as for⟩ what ⟨he is holding⟩ in ⟨his⟩ hand, ⟨it is⟩ something heavy which is put in fire, that is, a signet. (2) At the middle ⟨of Jupiter's hour⟩, ⟨the question is⟩ so that he will have gold or something else valuable; ⟨as for what he is holding⟩ in ⟨his⟩ hand, ⟨it is⟩ something white or red that is put in a balance, a signet, a precious stone, or ⟨something⟩ green mixed with red. (3) At the end ⟨of Jupiter's hour⟩, he inquires whether he can bring peace, ⟨⟨or, if he will find a treasure-chest in the earth, because he believes there is a treasure in the earth, and wants to ask whether he can find it quickly⟩⟩; ⟨as for⟩ what ⟨he is holding⟩ in ⟨his⟩ hand, ⟨it is⟩ chains of iron, rings, a flintstone, or leather.[1]

7 (1) At the beginning ⟨of Mars's hour⟩, he asks about a lord he fears, or about someone he hates; ⟨as for what he is holding⟩ in ⟨his⟩ hand, ⟨it is⟩ something red, copper, or gold. (2) At the middle ⟨of Mars's hour⟩, he ⟨inquires⟩ about thieves, a theft, or something lost; ⟨as for what he is holding⟩ in ⟨his⟩ hand, ⟨it is⟩ something small and red. (3) At the end ⟨of Mars's hour⟩, he ⟨inquires⟩ about prison, a disease, or his enemy; ⟨as for what he is holding⟩ in ⟨his⟩ hand, ⟨it is⟩ ⟨something⟩ dry or wood.[1]

8 (1) Abraham says: we have said that the astrologers know what the querent is holding in his hand on the basis of the aforementioned *Book Tametas*, according to the nature of the ascendant sign and its lord. (2) For Aries, Leo, and Sagittarius signify life; Taurus, Virgo, and Capricorn ⟨signify⟩ clothes; Gemini, Libra, and Aquarius ⟨signify⟩ colors; Cancer, Scorpio, and Pisces ⟨signify⟩ pierced things. (3) And ⟨the astrologers know⟩ according to the planet in the ascendant.[1]

9 (1) The lord of the hour[1] signifies colors: Saturn, grey; Jupiter, green; Mars, red; the Sun, bright yellow; Venus, a beautiful, shining ⟨color⟩; Mercury, multiple colors; the Moon, white but not bright.[2]

10 (1) Dixerunt quoque dominum termini significare si occultum est antiquum aut novum, secundum proportionem ipsius ad Solem. (2) Nonnulli autem dicunt fore semper aspiciendum ad locum Lune.

⟨I iii⟩
Capitulum tertium[1]
⟨⟨Capitulum tertium libri: de re absconsa⟩⟩

1 (1) Sapientes dixerunt taliter[2] posse[3] inveniri. (2) Respice primitus: si malorum aliquis sit in angulo, iudica rem fuisse et quod est accepta; et si fortuna,[4] veraciter adhuc est. (3) Ut autem locus sciatur, dixerunt quod signum veridicum[5] denotat eam sub terra;[6] commune autem in pariete;[7] mobile vero in tecto. (4) Et dixerunt Solem denotare aream[8,{9}] curie vel domus; Lunam, prope portam vel hostium; Mars, locum ubi sit ignis, aut locum furni; Jupiter, nobiliorem locum curie et meliorem domus existentem mundum, sicut locus orationis; Venus, locum denotat mulieris[10,{11}] aut locum concubitus; Mercurius, locum librorum aut picture; Saturnus, privatum aut turpiorem locum domus. (5) Et omnibus insunt rationes, non tamen bono fundamento fundate, et similiter est omne quod de hoc dicit Jacob Alkindi[12] in suo libro.[{13}] (6) Et rectum est ut homo cui inest scientia per ista non iudicet.

2 (1) Et ecce verba Messahalla: aspice ascendens, et dominum eius, et dominum hore; et respice quis melius aspiciat ascendens, facque ipsum significatorem. (2) Videas quoque ubi est: si fuerit in ascendente, erit res occulta in oriente. (3) Et si in via ascendentis,[14] erit[15] in linea[16] orientis et eius .4a. (4) Et si in .10., circa meridiem, versus dextram postquam oriens aspicit. (5) Et si in altera .4a., versus septentrionem erit. Et similiter in aliis. (6) Et si fuerit in .12a.,[17] erit propinquior orienti quam meridiei; si in .11a., erit propinquior meridiei quam orienti.

[1]Capitulum Tertium] BD^{m}; P > sermo sapientum super inventione occulti seu abscondi; V omits the title but opens an indent of 4 lines; N omits the title but opens an indent of 4 lines; ZL om. [2]taliter] P > occultatum. [3]posse] N om. [4]fortuna] BDZ > fuerit. [5]veridicum] D > vel fixum. [6]terra] D terram. [7]pariete] N paritatem. [8]aream*] LP; VDZBN aeream. [9]G aream. [10]mulieris] P mulierum. [11]G mulierum. [12]Alkindi] VBPN; DL Alchindi. [13]Et omnibus insunt rationes ... in suo libro] G Et hec omnia verba sunt que non sunt tenenda cum non habeant fundamentum, et eodem modo est de omnibus que dicit Iacob Alkindi de hac in libris suis. [14]ascendentis] D < non vero. [15]erit] V om. [16]in linea] D in Libra in primus gradus. [17]12] P > gradu.

10 (1) They also said that the lord of the term[1] signifies whether the hidden thing is old or new, according to its configuration with the Sun. (2) Many said that we must always pay attention to the location of the Moon.[2]

⟨I iii⟩
The Third Chapter
⟨⟨The Third Chapter of the Book: On the Hidden Thing⟩⟩

1 (1) The astrologers said that ⟨what has been hidden⟩ can be found in this manner. (2) Observe first: if one of the malefics is in a cardo, judge that the thing was ⟨there⟩ and has already been taken; and if a benefic ⟨planet is in a cardo⟩, ⟨the hidden thing⟩ is in fact there. (3) For the place ⟨of the hidden thing⟩ to be known, they said that a fixed sign[1] indicates that it is under the ground; a bicorporal ⟨sign indicates that it is⟩ in a wall; a tropical ⟨sign indicates that it is⟩ in the roof. (4) They said that the Sun indicates the area of the manor or the house; the Moon ⟨indicates that it is⟩ near the door or the entrance; Mars, the place where the fire is, or the place of the oven; Jupiter, a place on the manor that is more remarkable ⟨than other places⟩, and a place in the house that is clean and better ⟨than other places⟩, as the place for prayer; Venus indicates the place of women or the place for sexual intercourse; Mercury, the place of books or picture⟨s⟩; Saturn, the privy or a place in the house that is filthier ⟨than other places⟩. (5) There are explanations for all ⟨these reckonings⟩, but they are not based on a good foundation, and the same applies to everything Yaʿqub al-Kindī says on this matter in his book. (6) It is right that a knowledgeable man not judge according to them.[2]

2 (1) These are Māshāʾallāh's statements: pay attention to the ascendant, its lord, and the lord of the hour; and find out which ⟨of them⟩ is in better aspect with the ascendant, and make it the significator. (2) Observe also where ⟨the significator⟩ is located: if it is in the ascendant, the hidden thing is in the east. (3) If it is in the degree of the ascendant, ⟨the hidden thing⟩ is at the eastern line of its quadrant. (4) If it is in the tenth ⟨horoscopic place⟩, ⟨the hidden thing⟩ is near the south, to the right after you look east. (5) If it is in the other quadrant, ⟨the hidden thing⟩ is to the north, and the same applies to the other ⟨quadrants⟩. (6) If it is in the 12th ⟨horoscopic place⟩, ⟨the hidden thing⟩ is closer to the east than to the south, and if it is in the 11th ⟨horoscopic place⟩, ⟨the hidden thing⟩ is closer to the south than to the east.[1]

3 (1) Alius modus. Si que res[1,{2}] fuerit alicubi reposita[3] in domo et vis invenire,[4] respice ascendens verum quam melius potes. (2) Et dividas domum
55vb in .4or. partes, post quod[5] respice ubi fuerit dominum ascendentis. (3) | Si[6] orientalis, in .4a. orientali. (4) Deinde hanc .4am. accipe, et eam in .4or. partite; aliasque dimitte .4as., et respice ubi dominum inveneris ascendentis. (5) Si fuerit in signis septentrionalibus, accipe latus septentrionis; si in occidentalibus, latus occidentis, et similiter facias.[7] (6) Et respice dominum signi occidentalis et similiter aliarum .4arum. (7) Et .4am. occurrens[8] in .4or. divide, donec venias ad occultatum.

4 (1) Ptholomei[9] verba: Scias locum domini hore, quot fuerint gradus in signo suo, quos multiplica per .12., dividasque per .30., ⟨⟨et quibuslibet .30. des unum signum⟩⟩.[{10}] (2) Et incipe ab ascendente, et respice ubi hic numerus terminatur. (3) Et si fuerit signum orientale, est in parte orientali hospicii; et si meridionale,[11] in parte meridionali hospicii; et[12] si septentrionale,[13] in parte septentrionis; et si occidentale,[14] in occidentali. (4) Deinde hanc partem in .4or. divide, et locum scias domini signi ubi terminatur numerus. (5) Sciasque[15] quot gradus[16] sint in signo, et da cuilibet .7. gradus cum dimidio signum unum, et incipe[17] computare a loco in quo est. (6) Et si terminus numeri fuerit in signo orientali, est in orientali .4a.; et si in meridie, in meridionali; et sic de aliis. (7) Dividas quoque hanc .4am. itidem in .4or., et respice in quot gradus signi numerus completur, daque cuilibet .7. gradus cum dimidio signum unum. (8) Et si fuerit orientalis, erit in oriente, et ita de aliis .4is. (9) Et hoc modo agas, si amplius indiges divisione. (10) Et .4am. ultimam hanc in qua quesitum cadit quere, et tempta donec illud invenias quoniam veraciter[18] existit. (11) Ut sciatur, rei color quod per dominum scies hore,[19] et natura rei quesite accipitur a natura domini ascendentis.

[1]que res] VPN; DZLB qua res. [2]res] G rem. [3]reposita] D > vel oculta. [4]invenire] P fore ibi. [5]post quod] P post hoc. [6]si] P > sit. [7]facias] VLPNZ; B > in aliis; D > aliis. [8]occurrens] L occidens. [9]Ptholomei] VDBNZ; LP Ptolomei. [10]et quibuslibet .30. des unum signum*] G; VPBLZN et cuilibet ternario da unum numerum; D et cuilibet ternario da unum signum. [11]meridionale] P > est. [12]et] V om. [13]septentrionale] P > est. [14]occidentale] P > est. [15]sciasque] D Scias. [16]gradus] D gradibus. [17]incipe] DBPNZ; V < et respice; L incipere. [18]veraciter] D < illic. [19]hore] D > vel accipies a domino hore.

3 (1) Another method. If something is stored somewhere in the house and you want to find it, pay attention to the ascendant as best you can. (2) Divide the house into four parts, and afterwards pay attention to where the lord of the ascendant is. (3) If it is oriental, ⟨the hidden thing is⟩ in the eastern quadrant. (4) Then take this quadrant and divide it into four parts; leave out the other quadrants, and pay attention to where you find the lord of the ascendant. (5) If it [the lord of the ascendant] is in the northern signs, take the northern side; if it is in the western signs, ⟨take the⟩ western side, and proceed in the same manner ⟨regarding the other signs⟩. (6) Pay attention to the lord of the western sign, and likewise regarding the other quadrants. (7) Divide this quadrant into four ⟨parts⟩ until you come to the hidden thing.[1]

4 (1) ⟨These are⟩ Ptolemy's[1] statements: find out the position of the lord of the hour ⟨and⟩ how many degrees in its sign it is, multiply them by 12, divide them by 30, ⟨⟨and assign one sign to every ⟨segment of⟩ 30⟩⟩. (2) Begin ⟨the count⟩ from the ascendant, and take note of where the number ⟨of degrees⟩ is completed. (3) If ⟨the count is completed⟩ in an eastern sign, ⟨the hidden thing⟩ is in in the eastern part of the house; if in a southern ⟨sign⟩; ⟨the hidden thing is⟩ in the southern part of the house; if in a northern ⟨sign⟩, ⟨the hidden thing is⟩ in the northern part ⟨of the house⟩; if in a western ⟨sign⟩; ⟨the hidden thing is⟩ in the western ⟨part of the house.⟩ (4) Then divide this part ⟨of the house⟩ into four, and find out the position of the lord of the sign where the count is completed. (5) Find out how many degrees in the sign is ⟨the lord of the sign⟩, and assign one sign to each ⟨interval of⟩ 7½° degrees, and begin counting from the place where it is. (6) If the end of the count is in a eastern sign, ⟨the hidden thing is⟩ in the eastern quadrant; if in a southern sign, ⟨the hidden thing is⟩ in the southern ⟨quadrant;⟩ and so on regarding the other ⟨quadrants⟩. (7) Then divide this quadrant into four in the same manner, and determine at what degree in the sign the count is completed, and assign one sign to each ⟨interval of⟩ 7½° degrees. (8) If ⟨the count is completed⟩ in a eastern ⟨sign⟩, ⟨the hidden thing is⟩ in the eastern ⟨quadrant⟩, and likewise regarding the other quadrants. (9) Proceed in this manner, if you need to divide further. (10) Find the last quadrant in which the thing you are interested in falls, and keep trying until you find ⟨it⟩, because it is really there.[2] (11) As is known, the color of the ⟨hidden⟩ thing is known from the lord of the hour,[3] and the nature of the thing asked about is known from the nature of the lord of the ascendant.

⟨I iv⟩
Capitulum quartum[1]
⟪Capitulum quartum: de fugitivo inveniendo⟫

1 (1) Dixerunt: fugientem a suo domino sic posse inveniri. (2) Si dominus ascendentis dederit vim planete malo aut retrogrado, revertetur sponte ad dominum suum. (3) Et si ille coniungitur aut domino .7e. vim, dabit aut domino ascendentis, aut domino .8e.,[2] aut domino .2e., invenietur fugitivus. (4) Si dominus ascendentis coniungitur domino .7e., dominus[3] eius ipsum inveniet. (5) Et respice planetam quem aspicit Luna, et planetam cui Luna vim dederit, coniunctione[4] vel aspectu: si respiciunt[5] Solem invenietur fugitivus. (6) Et si Luna, aut dominus ascendentis, dederit vim domino .7e., significat ipsum per nuncium inveniri. (7) Et si dominus ascendentis dederit vim planete fortune non retrograde, evadit fugitivus. (8) Et similiter si dominus .7e. non aspiciat dominum ascendentis, aut non aspiciat planetam a quo separatur Luna, ab aspectu vel coniunctione planete, cui Luna vim dat aspectu vel coniunctione.[6] (9) Et si Luna dederit vim planete combusto, fugitivus morietur. (10) Et similiter si Luna fuerit combusta a Sole, reperietur mortuus fugitivus.

2 (1) Amplius respice:[7] si inveneris Lunam dantem vim[8] planete qui est in
56ra .4a. femenina,[9] iudica[10] fugitivum | egressum a loco in quo steterit. (2) Et si planeta cui Luna vim dederit est in .4a. masculina, significat fugientem existentem adhuc prope locum ad quem[11] fugit. (3) Et si Luna vim dederit planete malo, sitque ab ipso recepta, estque malus in eius loco receptus, significat fugitivum esse propinquum propinquis suis. (4) Et si malus neque recipit neque recipitur, significat fugitivum esse cum hominibus debilibus et timorosis.

3 (1) Et ecce hic unum generale:[12,{13}] Luna significat locum fugitivi. (2) Si dederit vim planete qui est dominus domus .6e., aut .8e., aut .12e.,[14] scias fugitivum capi et ducetur ad eius dominum. (3) Et poteris scire terminum[15] per gradus qui sunt inter Lunam et locum aspectus et coniunctionis, aut

[1]Capitulum quartum] BD^{m}; P Capitulum quartum, sermo sapientum super fugitivo si munietur et quorsum fugit; V omits the title but opens an indent of 4 lines; ZL om; B omits but opens an indent of 2 lines. [2]aut domino .8e.] N om. [3]dominus] P > ascendentis. [4]coniunctione] V coniunctionem. [5]D respiciat. [6]planete, cui Luna vim dat aspectu vel coniunctione] V om. [7]respice] D om. [8]vim] P > suam. [9]femenina] L om. [10]iudica] L < tunc. [11]ad quem] D in quo. [12]generale] D; VPLZBN grande. [13]Et ecce hic unum generale] G Et ecce quedam generalitas. [14]aut .12e.] P om. [15]terminum] D dominum.

⟨I iv⟩
The Fourth Chapter
⟨⟨The Fourth Chapter: On Finding a Fugitive⟩⟩

1 (1) They said: This is how someone who has escaped from his master may be found. (2) If the lord of the ascendant gives power[1] to a malefic or retrograde planet, ⟨the fugitive⟩ will return to his master of his own will. (3) If it [the malefic or retrograde planet] is conjoined with or gives power to the lord of the seventh ⟨place⟩, or to the lord of the ascendant, or to the lord of the eighth ⟨place⟩, or to the lord of the second ⟨place⟩, the fugitive will be found. (4) If the lord of the ascendant is conjoined with the lord of the seventh ⟨place⟩, his master will find him. (5) Pay attention to the planet which is aspected by the Moon, and at the planet to which the Moon gives power, by conjunction or aspect: if they aspect the Sun, the fugitive will be found. (6) If the Moon, or the lord of the ascendant, gives power to the lord of the seventh ⟨place⟩, it signifies that he [the fugitive] will be found by an informer. (7) If the lord of the ascendant gives power to a benefic planet, which is not retrograde, the fugitive will escape. (8) The same applies if the lord of the seventh ⟨place⟩ does not aspect the lord of the ascendant, or ⟨if the lord of the seventh place⟩ does not aspect a planet from which the Moon has separated, by aspect or conjunction with the planet, ⟨or⟩ to which the Moon gives power by aspect or conjunction. (9) If the Moon gives power to a burnt planet, the fugitive will die. (10) The same applies if the Moon is burnt by the Sun; the fugitive will be found dead.[2]

2 (1) Pay attention further: if you find the Moon giving power to a planet in a feminine quadrant, judge that the fugitive has left the place he was staying in. (2) If the planet to which the Moon gives power is in a masculine quadrant, it signifies that the fugitive is still close to the place he escaped from. (3) If the Moon gives power to a malefic planet, and it [the Moon] is received by it [the malefic planet], and the malefic ⟨planet⟩ is received[1] in its own location, it signifies that the fugitive is close to his kindred. (4) If the malefic ⟨planet⟩ neither receives nor is received, it signifies that the fugitive is with weak and frightened people.[2]

3 (1) This is a general rule: the Moon signifies the fugitive's location. (2) If it [the Moon] gives power to a planet that is the lord of the 6th, 8th, or 12th place, know that the fugitive will be caught and taken to his master. (3) You can know the term [i.e., when the fugitive will be returned to his master] by the ⟨number of⟩ degrees between the Moon and the position of

per locum Lune aut domini ascendentis respectu domini .7e. domus. (4) Et planeta velox cursu[1] denotat velocitatem et secundum signum in quo recipiens vim est planeta—si fixum est aut aliter—et secundum[2] planetam—qui fuerit quidem[3] de superioribus aut inferioribus—et si in angulo, aut in succedenti, aut in cadenti, et secundum proportionem eius ad Solem, sicut dictum est in *Libro coniunctionum*.

4 (1) Et quod dixit omne verum existit, siquis quesiverit de fugiente a suo domino. (2) Si autem dominus ipse querat, da ascendens domino, et dominum .7e., aut planetan qui est in .7o., fugitivo,[4] et iudica secundum illud quod apparebit. (3) Et dixerunt: locum fugitivi esse circa angulum aut dominum ascendentis, nisi[5] fuerit querens eius dominus. (4) Et si suus dominus, accipe locum domini[6] .7e. domus, et hoc totum respectu ascendentis in hora interrogationis. (5) Et ponas a principio ascendentis usque ad .4., oriens; et in[7] principio .4e. usque ad principium .7e., septentrionum; et ab initio[8] .7e. ad principium .10e., occidentis; et ab initio .10e. ad initium ascendentis, meridiem.

5 (1) Inquit Abraham: nobilia sunt valde dicta Ptholomei in *Libro .c. verborum*. (2) Dicit enim signorum[9] scientiam ex te et illis esse, et hec radix est magna.

6 (1) Hic liber terminatur, post quem incipit *Liber significationis .7. planetarum in tredecim generibus vel manieribus*.[10]
⟪(1) Explicit *Liber Abrahe dicti Evenezre de occultis*.⟫

[1]cursu] DBLPZ; V cursus; N om. [2]secundum] D om. [3]qui fuerit quidem] P siquidem fuerit. [4]fugitivo] P qui fugit. [5]nisi] B ubi. [6]domini N om. [7]in] VZNBL; DP a. [8]ab initio] B a principio. [9]signorum] V om. [10]Hic liber terminatur, post quem incipit liber significationis .7. planetarum in .13. generibus vel manieribus.] D; LNZ Hic liber terminatur, post quem incipit liber significationis .7. planetarum in .13. generibus; P finis; VB om.

the aspect or the conjunction ⟨of the Moon with the planet that is the lord of the sixth, eighth, or second place⟩, or by the position of the Moon or of the lord of the ascendant with respect to the lord of the 7th place. (4) A planet of swift motion signifies swiftness according to the sign in which it receives a planet's power—whether it is a fixed ⟨sign⟩ or otherwise—and according to the planet—whether it is one of the lower or upper planets—and whether it is in a cardo or in a succedent or cadent ⟨place⟩, and according to its configuration with the Sun,[1] as said in the *Book of conjunctions*.[2]

4 (1) What he said is all true, if someone ⟨else⟩ asks about a fugitive from his master. (2) But if the master himself asks, assign the ⟨lord of the⟩ ascendant to the master, and the lord of the seventh ⟨place⟩, or the planet located in the seventh ⟨place⟩, to the fugitive, and judge according to what is seen. (3) They said: the location of the fugitive is around the cardo or the lord of the ascendant, unless the querent is his [the fugitive's] master. (4) If ⟨the querent⟩ is his master, take the position of the lord of the seventh place, and all this with respect to the ascendant at the time of the interrogation. (5) Assign the east to ⟨the interval⟩ from the cusp of the ascendant to the ⟨cusp of the⟩ fourth ⟨place⟩; the north to ⟨the interval⟩ from the cusp of the fourth ⟨place⟩ to the cusp of the seventh ⟨place⟩; the west to ⟨the interval⟩ from the cusp of the seventh ⟨place⟩ to the cusp of the tenth ⟨place⟩; and the south to ⟨the interval⟩ from the cusp of the tenth ⟨place⟩ to the cusp of the ascendant.[1]

5 (1) Abraham says: Ptolemy's statements in the *Book of the 100 statements* are very well-known. (2) He says that the science of the signs is from you and from them, and this is a great principle.[1]

6 (1) This book is completed, and afterwards begins the *Book on the significations of the seven planets in 13 categories*.

⟨⟨(1) Here ends the *Book by Abraham, called Ibn Ezra, on hidden things*.⟩⟩

⟨II⟩
Tractatus in tredecim maneriebus planetarum[1]
⟪Incipit *Liber Abrahe Evenezre de significationibus septem planetarum*, quem transtulit Arnulphus⟫

(1) De maneriebus[2] .13. exponam significationem cuiuslibet planetarum 7. (2) Prima, quidem est de parte planetarum et quod significat.[3] (3) Secunda, quam partem tenet[4] in hominibus. (4) Tertia, quod[5] eorum magisterium et scientia. (5) Quarta, eorum factura et forma.[6] (6) Quinta, in quo membro corporis partem tenet. (7) Sexta, quanto servit etati hominis.[7] (8) Septima, quot sunt eius anni magni, parvi et medii. (9) Octava, sui morbi et signa.[8] (10) Nona, eius pars domus. (11) Decima, quam denotat bestiam. (12) Undecima, germinantia et arbores.[9] (13) Duodecima, quod metallum. (14) Tertius decima, quam partem significat mundi.

⟪(1) Ego explanabo tibi significatorem .7. planetarum .13. modis. (2) Primus est de sortibus sive partibus planetarum et de significatoribus earum. (3) Secundus, quam gentem habent de hominibus. (4) Tertius, in magisterio eorum et scientia. (5) Quartus, in forma et figura. (6) Quintus, quod membrum in corpore humano signant. (7) Sextus. quanto tempore regunt hominem in vita. (8) Septimus, quot sunt anni eorum, scilicet, parvi, mediocres et maiores. (9) Octavus, quas infimitates signant et de signabilibus eorum. (10) Nonus, quid de domibus et quas domos signant. (11) Decimus, qualia animalia habent significante. (12) Undecimus, quid signant de germinantibus et arboribus. (13) Duodecimus, quid signant de metallis. (14) Tertius decimus, quam partem mundi signant.⟫

⟨II i⟩
De Sole[10]
⟪Significationes Solis⟫

1 (1) Partem Solis: iam diximus longitudinem vite significare hominis, et si proficient omnia eius opera. (2) Et significat sanitatem corporis et

[1]Tractatus in tredecim maneriebus planetarum*] ZN^mL; B Incipit tractatus de .13. maneriebus planetarum; P Incipit Liber Abrahe Avensre Judei in significatione septem in .12. generibus et .13. maneriebus planetarum; V omits the title but opens an indent of 5 lines; D omits the title but opens an indent of 4 lines. [2]De maneriebus] VDBZL; PN In maneriebus. [3]et quod signant] B om. [4]tenet*] BLP; D > vel possidet vel signat. [5]quod] D ad. [6]forma] D figura. [7]hominis] D > id est qua etas huic maneriei .13. attribuntur. [8]signa] D > vel voce. [9]et arbores] N om. [10]De Sole] DLZBN^m; P > et eius significatis; V om.

⟨II⟩
Treatise on the Thirteen Categories of the Planets
⟪Here Begins the *Book by Abraham Ibn Ezra, on the Significations of the Seven Planets*, Translated by Arnoul⟫

(1) I will expound the signification of each of the seven planets, in 13 categories. (2) The first is the lot of the planets and what it signifies. (3) The second is which part of the human beings ⟨the planet⟩ is in charge of. (4) The third is what is their authority and knowledge. (5) The fourth is their shape and form. (6) The fifth is the bodily member that is in its portion. (7) The sixth is how much of human life it serves. (8) The seventh is how many are its great, least and middle years.[1] (9) The eighth is its diseases and symptoms. (10) The ninth is its part of the house. (11) The tenth is which beast it signifies. (12) The eleventh is ⟨its⟩ plants and trees. (13) The twelfth is what metals ⟨it signfies⟩. (14) The thirteenth is what part of the world it signifies.

⟪(1) I will explain for you the signification of the seven planets in 13 modes. (2) The first is the lots or parts of the planets and their significations. (3) The second is what people among human beings are in their portion. (4) The third is their skills and knowledge. (5) The fourth is their shape and form. (6) The fifth is which member of the body they signify. (7) The sixth is how much time of a man's life they rule. (8) The seventh is how many are their years, that is, the least, middle and great. (9) The eighth is the diseases they signify, and their symptoms. (10) The ninth is ⟨which part of⟩ the houses and which houses they signify. (11) The tenth is which animals they signify. (12) The eleventh is what they signify regarding plants and trees. (13) The twelfth is what they signify regarding metals. (14) The thirteenth is what part of the world they signify.⟫

⟨II i⟩
On the Sun
⟪Significations of the Sun⟫

1 (1) The lot of the Sun: we have already said that it signifies a man's lifespan, and whether he will be successful in all his undertakings. (2) It

dispositiones, secundum planetas partem respicientes. (3) Et totum hoc 56rb verificatur | si unus dominorum loci partis eam aspiciat, quicumque sit aspiciens, et secundum vim iudica aspectus. (4) Et si nullo modo aspicit,[1] non ducetur ad effectum parte denotatum, in malo aut in bono, nisi in cogitatione, verbis et sompniis.[2] (5) Et dicitur Solis pars fortune.[3]

2 (1) Secunda: denotat reges in revolutione mundi; et patrem illi[4] qui natus est in die; et altitudinem,[5,{6}] dominium, et famam. (2) Et prelatus in domo Solis[7] ipsius prelatura[{8}] bonum denotat aut malum venturum nato[9] in medietate prima vite ipsius aut in ultima, secundum naturam planete in eius fortitudine et aspicientem, et in qua domo est eius fortitudo respectu ascendentis, et quam aspicit domum. (3) Et Sol in nativitate mulieris significat maritum.

3 (1) Tertia: querit potestatem; et est custos turris ac repositi,[{10}] miles probus in servitio sui domini, sapiens in scientia signorum, aut depurator auri, aut negocians circa metalla.[{11}]

4 (1) Quarta: pulchre forme et coloris, pilosus, facies lata, oculi magni rubei, os latum, recte ambulans, barba rotunda et spissa,[12] supercilia commixta.

5 (1) Quinta: pars eius[13] est oculus dexter nato in die, in nocte sinister; et similiter partem habet in corde, et ore, et latere dextro. (2) Et in coloribus album valde.

6 (1) Sexta: servit in die natis .10. primis annis, natis autem in nocte .39. annis usque ad terminum 49. (2) Et eius est potestas[14] diurna a mane Dominica, noctis autem Iovis nox. (3) Et Ptholomeus dicit ipsum habere potestatem in omnibus natis in die aut in nocte in[15] .22. annis usque ad .41.[16]

[1]si nullo modo aspicit] D > vel nullus sit aspectus. [2]sompniis] VBDNZ; LP somniis. [3]Et dicitur Solis pars fortune] D Et Solis dicitur pars scilicet pars fortune. Hoc secundum dicitur in Libro Rationum de partibus. [4]illi] B illius. [5]altitudinem] DNBZL; VP ultimum. [6]altitudinem] G nobilitatem. [7]Solis] D > vel principator super Solem domo? Solis?. [8]Et prelatus in domo Solis ipsius prelatura] G Et dominus triplicitatis Solis. [9]nato] D natum. [10]custos turris ac repositi] G custodia castrorum et occultorum. [11]negocians circa metalla] G operarius metallorum. [12]spissa] D pissa. [13]eius] L om. [14]potestas] DB; VLNZ portus; P pars. [15]in] D a. [16].41.] P .42. de annis solis.

signifies the body's health and ⟨its⟩ conditions, depending on the planets that aspect the lot. (3) All this is correct on condition that one of the lords over the position of the lot aspects it, whichever aspect it may be; and judge according to the power of the aspect. (4) But if no ⟨planet⟩ aspects ⟨it⟩, the signification of the lot, whether for good or for evil, will not be realized, except for thought⟨s⟩, ⟨spoken⟩ words, and dreams. (5) The lot of the Sun is said to be ⟨identical with⟩ the lot of Fortune.[1]

2 (1) Second: It signifies kings at the revolution of the world⟨-year⟩;[1,2] the father for one born by day; pride, authority, and reputation.[3] (2) The ruler over the lordship ⟨of the triplicity⟩ of the Sun's house signifies good fortune or misfortune which will come to the native in the first or last half of his life, according to the aspecting planet's nature and its power, ⟨according to⟩ the ⟨horoscopic⟩ place with respect to the ascendant in which it exerts power, and ⟨according to⟩ which ⟨horoscopic⟩ place it [the planet] aspects. (3) In a woman's nativity the Sun signifies her husband.[4]

3 (1) Third: He [i.e., one born under the Sun's power] seeks authority; he is a guardian of a tower and a treasure, an able soldier in the service of his lord; an astrologer, a goldsmith, or one who is busy with metals.[1]

4 (1) Fourth: Of handsome shape and color, hairy, broad face, large and reddish eyes, wide mouth, walks with an upright posture,[1] round and thick beard, joined eyebrows.[2]

5 (1) Fifth: In its [i.e., the Sun's] portion is the right eye for one born by day and the left ⟨eye for one born⟩ by night; likewise, the heart, the mouth and the right side are in the ⟨Sun's⟩ portion.[1] (2) Of the colors, intense white.[2]

6 (1) Sixth: It serves those born by day for the first 10 years ⟨of their lives⟩, and ⟨those born⟩ by night from their 39th to their 49th year.[1] (2) In its portion is the rulership of the day⟨time⟩ from the morning of the Lord's day [i.e., from sunrise to sundown on Sunday], and by night ⟨the rulership of⟩ Jupiter's night [i.e., between sundown on Wednesday and sunrise on Thursday].[2] (3) Ptolemy says that it rules over all, whether born by day or by night, from the 22nd to the 41st year.[3]

7 (1) Septima: parvi anni eius sunt .19.,[1] medii .39. cum dimidio,[2] et magni .120.

8 (1) Octava: morbus eius[3] est febris[4] calida et sicca, corpus ut ignis inflammans, tenens cor,[5] et confrangens ossa, neque est ut apparet.[{6}] (2) Si[7] fuerit autem annorum .8., alienabit.[{8}] (3) Si latro, habebit notam in facie, aut ignis cocturam.[9,{10}]

9 (1) Nona: eius pars est domus.[11]

10 (1) Decima: habet equos.

11 (1) Undecima: eius quidem germinantium sunt arbores magne fructificantes, et racemi.[12]

12 (1) Duodecima: metallorum, aurum.[13]

13 (1) Tertia decima: eius est fortitudo in parte orientali.

⟨II ii⟩
De Luna[14]
⟪Significationes Lune⟫

1 (1) Pars Lune est ut accipias distantiam inter Solem et Lunam,[15] et proveniens proice[16] ab ascendente. (2) Et[17] dicitur pars celati.[{18}] (3) Et significat animam hominis, et desiderium nati, et eius ingenium, et eius ⟪invidiam⟫,[19] et quomodo Deum debes[20] timere. (4) Et denotat omne quod incipit operari homo.

2 (1) Secunda: denotat matrem, sororem et mulierem[21] nati, et ⟪gentem vulgarem⟫.[22]

[1].19.] D .10. [2]cum dimidio] VP; DBNL et semis. [3]eius] V om. [4]febris] N om. [5]cor] D > vel finis. [6]neque est ut apparet] G et non est ut ei apparet. [7]si] D < et. [8]alienabit] G erit insanus. [9]cocturam] D cogcturam. [10]cocturam] F combustione ignis. [11]domus] P > Leonis. [12]racemi] D > et uve. [13]aurum] P < est. [14]De Luna] BLZN^{m}; P > et eius significatis et parte eius; VD om. [15]Lunam] D > in nocte vel? alios. [16]proice] P; V prohice; DNBLZ pro hoc. [17]et] D om. [18]pars celati] G pars futurorum. [19]invidiam*] G; VDPZNL mutationem. [20]debes] D debet. [21]mulierem] D > vel uxorem. [22]gentem vulgarem*] G; VDPZNBL seculares.

7 (1) Seventh: Its least years are 19, the middle ⟨years⟩ are 39½ ⟨years⟩, and the great ⟨years⟩ are 120.[1]

8 (1) Eighth: His disease is a hot and dry fever, burning the body as fire, affecting the heart, breaking the bones, and it is not as it seems ⟨to the sick person⟩. (2) If he is eight years old, he will go mad. (3) If he is a robber, he will have a mark on the face or a burn.[1]

9 (1) Ninth: The house is in its portion.[1]

10 (1) Tenth: Horses are in its ⟨portion⟩.[1]

11 (1) Eleventh: Of plants, large trees bearing fruit and grapes are in its ⟨portion⟩.[1]

12 (1) Twelfth: Of metals, gold ⟨is in its portion⟩.[1]

13 (1) Thirteenth: Its power is on the eastern side.[1]

⟨II ii⟩
On the Moon
⟪Significations of the Moon⟫

1 (1) The lot of the Moon is ⟨found by⟩ taking the distance between the Moon and the Sun and cast out the result from the ascendant. (2) It is called the lot of the hidden [i.e., lot of the absent]. (3) It signifies a man's soul, the native's desire, his intelligence, his ⟪envy⟫, and how you must fear God.[1] (4) It indicates everything that a man begins doing.[2]

2 (1) Second: It signifies the native's mother, sister, and wife, and ⟪common people⟫.[1]

3 (1) Tertia: eius opus erit mari[1] navigare, aut locare bestias et eas sequi, aut currere propter mercari de loco in locum; et debes[2] scire recitationes et nova.[{3}]

4 (1) Quarta: est eius figura rotunda facie, os parvum, alba non multum, cito ambulans. (2) Homo minutus,[4] dentes neque longi neque breves, nasus parvus, altero[5] oculorum maior alteri,[6] aut strabus,[7] aut econtrario, conspiciens, neque contingere potest quin aliquod vitium in oculo patiatur, curvus ambulans, facies[8] viridis.

56va **5** (1) Quinta: pars | eius in cerebro et ossibus pulmone,[9] et in parte sinistra, et in oculo sinistro in die, in nocte autem dextrum.[10]

6 (1) Sexta: significat .4.[11] annos separationis,[12] et .9.[13] annos natis in nocte, in die quidem a .32.[14] usque ad .40. (2) Potestas eius est die Lune, et nocte Veneris.

7 (1) Septima: sui anni minores sunt .25., medii .39., maiores .108.

8 (1) Octava: in eius parte sunt termini[{15}] infirmitatum frigidarum et humidarum, aut sortilegii,[{16}] et doloris in epate; et significat egritudines in facie.

9 (1) Nona: in eius parte est hostium hospicii et[17] porta.

10 (1) Decima: animalium currus, et aquatilium animalium.[18]

11 (1) Undecima: eius fortitudo est in omnibus germinantibus humidis crescunt,[19] cucumeres et cucurbite, et similiter eius fortitudo est in fluviis propinquiis mari grandi; et parve arbores sunt eius.

[1]mari] D < per. [2]debes] D debet. [3]debes scire recitationes et nova] G et debet scire discere multa et res rumorum. [4]minutus] D > fortebrevis vel mediocris. [5]altero] B unus. [6]maior alteri] B maius altero. [7]strabus] P Strabo. [8]facies] B > eius. [9]pulmone] B < et. [10]dextrum] P dextro. [11].4.] V om. [12]separationis] D > a lacte et isti sunt anni sicut nutritionis. [13].9.] L contra. [14]32] VP 30. [15]termini] G dies cretici. [16]sortilegii] G fascinationes. [17]doloris in epate, et significat egritudines in facie Nona: in eius parte est hostium hospicii et] N om. [18]animalium currus et aquatilium animalium] G animalia castrata et animalia aquatica. [19]crescunt] P < ubi.

3 (1) Third: His craft will be sailing the sea, track beasts and follow them, or to run from one place to another to trade; and you need to know accounts and news.[1]

4 (1) Fourth: As for his shape, his face is round, his mouth small, he is not very pale, he walks quickly.[1] (2) A small man, ⟨his⟩ teeth neither long nor short, of short nose, one of the eyes bigger than the other, or squint-eyed, or on the contrary, looking attentively, unable to reach something without suffering damage to the eye, walks hunched, ⟨his⟩ face is greenish.[2]

5 (1) Fifth: In its portion is the brain and the bone marrow, the left ⟨side of the⟩ brain, and the left eye by day and the right one by night.[1]

6 (1) Sixth: ⟨The Moon⟩ signifies the 4 years of weaning,[1] 9 years for those born by night, and from the 32nd year to the end of 40th year ⟨for those born⟩ by day.[2] (2) It has rulership over the day of the Moon [i.e., from sunrise to sundown on Monday], and over the night of Venus [i.e., between sundown on Thursday and sunrise on Friday].[3]

7 (1) Seventh: Its least years are 25, the middle ⟨years⟩ 39⟨½⟩, and the great ⟨years⟩ 108.[1]

8 (1) Eighth: In its portion are the critical days of cold and moist diseases, or of divination, and of pain in the liver; it signifies diseases of the face.[1]

9 (1) Ninth: The door of houses is in its portion, and gates.[1]

10 (1) Tenth: ⟨It is in charge⟩ of draft animals and of aquatic animals.[1]

11 (1) Eleventh: Its power is in all plants that grow in humid ⟨places⟩, in melons and pumpkins, and likewise its power is in rivers that are near the Mediterranean;[1] small trees are in its portion.[2]

12 (1) Duodecima: metallorum argentum ⟪pro mulieribus magnatibus⟫.{1}

13 (1) Tertia decima: habet fortitudinem in parte occidentis. (2) Et participat cum Sole in vita hominis. (3) Et principator in dominio triplicitate domus Lune in nocte significat esse quod continget nato in eius vita, de bono aut malo.

⟨II iii⟩
De Saturno[2]
⟪Significationes Saturni⟫

1 (1) Pars Saturni est ab eo usque ad partem fortune, et hunc numerum proice[3] ab ascendente. (2) Et significat carceres, constructiones, captivitatem, litem, et ictus. (3) Et respice: si fuerit in aliquo angulorum, secundum enim aspicientes ipsam erit eius fortitudo. (4) Omnes quoque planete dant vim Saturno[4] cum sibi coniunguntur[5] aut aspiciunt, quia superior existit.[6] (5) Et[7] est planeta scientie, et ingenii, et plenitudinis{8} cogitationis, et dolositatis,[9] timoris, atque tremoris.

2 (1) Secunda: eius sunt Iudei, monachi nigri, pauperes homines, et antiqui.

3 (1) Tertia: artifex,[10] aut[11] marinarius,[12] vel[13] corii preparator, et in eius parte sunt diabolici[14] et spiritus pravi, scire altas res, preparare stratas et terram arare.[15]

4 (1) Quarta: denotat hominem nigrum, habentem oculus parvos et tenues, frontem magnam. (2) Et est viridis, et masculus, non libenter ridens, et nudis ambulat pedibus libenter, quod[16] sordida induit vestimenta et nigra, et pillus frontis[17] eius est spissus, sicque sua barba, humeri lati, et loquitur multum,[18] et est homo diligens aves.[19]

[1]pro mulieribus magnatibus*] G; VLPN dominarum malarum causa; DBZ dominarum maiorum causa. [2]De Saturno] V om; P > eius significatis. [3]proice] V prohice. [4]Saturno] D > dicutm est in Principio Sapientie. [5]coniunguntur] L consurguntur. [6]existit] BZ (in margin) > Non quod secundum estam viam: omnes planete dantur vim suis superiotibus et non eius. [7]Et] B Saturnus. [8]plenitudinis] G multitudinis. [9]dolositatis] V dolorositatis. [10]artifex] D > ut faciens archas pontes et molendinos et tases que sunt in aqua. [11]aut] VDNLP; Z et; B om. [12]marinarius] N marinarum. [13]vel] B aut. [14]diabolici] VLPZ; NB dyabolici; D dyabolica. [15]arare] D < ut. [16]et nudis ambulat pedibus libenter quod] P om. [17]frontis] > vel nistus. [18]multum] D > unbito unus est qui multum loquatur. [19]aves] P haveris.

12 (1) Twelfth: Of metals, silver for ⟨⟨noblewomen⟩⟩.[1]

13 (1) Thirteenth: It exerts power in the western side.[1] (2) It has a share with the Sun in the life of man.[2] (3) The ruler over the lordship of the triplicity of the Moon's house by night portends what will happen to the native, for good or evil, during his life.[3]

⟨II iii⟩
On Saturn
⟨⟨Significations of Saturn⟩⟩

1 (1) The lot of Saturn runs from it [Saturn] to the lot of Fortune, and cast out this number from the ascendant. (2) It signifies prisons, buildings, captivity, quarrel⟨s⟩, and blow⟨s⟩. (3) Observe: if it [the lot of Saturn] is in one of the cardines, its power is in accordance with those that aspect it.[1] (4) All the planets give power to Saturn when they conjoin it or aspect it, because it is the uppermost ⟨planet⟩.[2] (5) It is the planet of knowledge, intelligence, abundant thought, deceit, fear, and palsy.[3]

2 (1) Second: In its portion are the Jews, black monks, paupers, and the elderly.[1]

3 (1) Third: ⟨In its portion is⟩ the craftsman, the sailor, or the tanner; in its portion are the demons, and a wicked spirit,[1] knowing deep things, preparing paved roads, and plowing the earth.[1]

4 (1) Fourth: It signifies a swarthy man, with small and narrow eyes and a broad forehead.[1] (2) Youthful, virile, does not laugh willingly, goes barefoot willingly, wears dirty and black clothes, the hair on his brow is thick, the same applies to his beard, of wide shoulders, garrulous, and he is a man who loves birds.[2]

5 (1) Quinta: habet splenem, et ex coloribus nigrum, aut[1] aurem dextram.

6 (1) Sexta: servit post Lunam in natis in[2] nocte .11.[3] annis. (2) Secundum vero Ptholomeus servit in senectute. (3) Et ipsius est potestas in die Sabati, et in nocte Mercurii.[4]

7 (1) Septima: anni parvi sunt .30. medii .43. maiores .54. aut .57.

8 (1) Octava: eius morbi sunt ex colera nigra ut febris quartana, et scabies sicca aut frigida. (2) Et si fuerit in opposito augis ecentrici est frigidus et humidus, in auge autem frigidus et siccus. (3) Et denotat signum[5] in timpore.[6]

9 (1) Nona: eius[7] pars in domo sunt loca obscura et turpia.

10 (1) Decima: eius sunt asini propter hominis equitare.

56vb 11 (1) Undecima: | eius sunt omnes arbores fetentes habentes soporem acetosum.

12 (1) Duodecima: metallorum plumbum.

13 (1) Tertiadecima: eius fortitudo est ex parte occidentis. (2) ⟪Et ipse est angelus mortis ad interficiendum per aliquem casum vel lapsum a loco alto aut ad submergendum in aqua⟫.{8}

⟨II iv⟩
De Iove[9]
⟪Significationes Iovis⟫

1 (1) Pars Iovis accipitur ab ipso in parte[10] celati, et proicitur[11] ab ascendente; et significat scientiam nati, et ipsius perfectum, et substantiam. (2) Et

[1]aut] VLPNZ; D ac; G et. [2]in] D om. [3].11.] D .13. [4].11. annis. Secundum vero Ptolomeus servit in senectute. Et ipsius est potestas in die Sabbati, et in nocte Mercurii] N om. [5]signum] D vel notam. [6]timpore] VLPN; DN tempore; B tympore. [7]eius] L cuius. [8]Et ipse est angelus mortis ad inerficiendum per aliquem casum vel lapsum a loco alto aut ad submergendum in aqua*] G; VBN Et est sicut (lacuna) aut casus ab alto aut aut in aqua suffocationem inducere; DP Et est sicut aut magna suffocationem inducere; LZ et est sicut terrores vel pericula mortis aut casus ab alto aut aut in aqua suffocationem inducere. [9]De Iove] DZN^{m}BL; P > et eius significationis; V om. [10]parte] VDL; PNZB partem. [11]proicitur] VN prohicitur.

5 (1) Fifth: In its portion is the spleen; of the colors, black, or ⟨it signifies⟩ the right ear.[3]

6 (1) Sixth: It serves those born by night for 11 years, after the Moon. (2) But according to Ptolemy's opinion, it serves in old age.[1] (3) It has rulership over the day of the Sabbath [i.e., from sunrise to sundown on Saturday], and over the night of Mercury[2] [i.e., between sundown on Tuesday and sunrise on Wednesday].

7 (1) Seventh: ⟨Its⟩ least years are 30, middle ⟨years⟩ 43, and the great ⟨years⟩ 54 or 57.[1]

8 (1) Eighth: Its diseases are those caused by the black bile[1] [melancholy] such as the quartan fever, and dry or cold boils.[2] (2) It is cold and moist if it is opposite the apogee [i.e., at perigee] on the eccentric circle,[3] and cold and dry when at apogee.[4] (3) It signifies a mark on the temple.[5]

9 (1) Ninth: In its portion are the dark and filthy places of the house.[1]

10 (1) Tenth: In its portion are donkeys for men to ride on.[1]

11 (1) Eleventh: In its portion is any foul-smelling tree that has [i.e., its fruit] a sour flavor.[1]

12 (1) Twelfth: Of the metals, lead.[1]

13 (1) Thirteenth: Its power is in the western side.[1] (2) ⟨⟨It is like the angel of death, killing ⟨in an avalanche⟩ or by a fall from a high place or by drowning⟩⟩.[2]

⟨II iv⟩
On Jupiter
⟨⟨Significations of Jupiter⟩⟩

1 (1) The lot of Jupiter is taken from it [Jupiter] to the lot of the hidden, and cast out from the ascendant; it signifies the native's knowledge, and his success, and wealth.[1] (2) Jupiter is larger than any other planet, except for

Iupiter est maior ceteris planetis, Sole remoto. (3) Et denotat vitam, pacem, iustitiam, et liberalitatem cordis et beneficium.[1] (4) Et ipse ⟪solus⟫{2} totaliter coniunctione vel aspectu potest removere operationem Saturni, non autem Martis. (5) Et secundum eius fortitudinem natus dives erit.

2 (1) Secunda: eius sunt iudices, leges docentes, orantes pro communitate, atque thezaurisantes, sicut episcopi et legis nove.{3}

3 (1) Tertia: in eius parte sunt artificia dicendi,[4] et scientia signorum,[5] et est campsor,[6] aut pannarius, aut vestimentorum factor, et sutor acu.

4 (1) Quarta: significat hominem cuius figura est alba, rosea,[7] munda, recte incedens, coloris pulchri; fidelis; verecundus, diligit[8] et querit pacem; barba rotunda, et oculi pulchri et pili; et diligit vestimenta pulchra; duo dentium superiorum pertranseunt alios.

5 (1) Eius est sinistra auris, epar et viride oculi.

6 (1) Sexta: servit post Saturnum in die vel nocte .12. annis, et sunt anni ipsius se propinquia.[9] (2) Et eius est potestas in die Iovis,[10] et in nocte diei Lune.

7 (1) Septima: anni eius parvi sunt .12., mediocres .45., maiores .79.

8 (1) Octava: morbus eius est ex habundantia humorum in corpore. Ideo dicit Ptholomeus non debere sumi medicinam laxativam[11] dum Luna[12] Iovem aspiciat, aut sibi sit coniuncta, quod est[13] expertum. (2) Eius est calida et humida natura, et esse potest multum aut parum, secundum quartas epicicli et ecentrici.

9 (1) Nona: eius est orationum locus, aut ubi preparantur necessaria orationibus.

[1]beneficium] V benefactum. [2]solus*] G; VDLPBZN totaliter. [3]thezaurisantes, sicut episcopi et legis nove] G domini pecunie et ipsi signant novam legem. [4]dicendi] D > qui dicat non operandi manus. [5]et scientia signorum] N om. [6]campsor] VP; DZBLN cansor. [7]rosea] B rubea. [8]diligit] VNP; ZBDL diligens. [9]se propinquia] VPN; LZ secundum termini propinqui; D sicut sno? motu propinqui; B sicut naturam? termini propinqui. [10]die Iovis] DP; LBZV die Iovis noctis; N die noctis. [11]medicinam laxativam] VP; LDNBZ medicamina laxativa. [12]dum Luna] N om. [13]est] P < erat et.

the Sun.[2] (3) It indicates life, peace, justice, generosity and charity.[3] (4) This ⟨planet⟩ ⟨⟨alone⟩⟩ is capable of entirely canceling out the effect of Saturn, by means of ⟨its⟩ [Jupiter's] conjunction and aspect, but not ⟨the effect⟩ of Mars.[4] (5) The native will be rich in accordance with its power.[5]

2 (1) Second: In its portion are judges, teachers of laws, cantors before the community[1] and treasurers,[2] like the bishops of the new religion.[3]

3 (1) Third: In its portion are the art of rhetoric, the science of the signs, the money-changer, the draper or one who makes garments, and the tailor [lit. one who stitches with a needle].[1]

4 (1) Fourth: It signifies a man whose features are white, redy, clean, ⟨who⟩ walks erect, of beautiful colors; he is faithful, modest, industrious and seeks peace; of round beard, beautiful eyes and hair; he loves beautiful garments;[1] two of his top teeth stick out from the others.[2]

5 (1) ⟨Fifth:⟩ The left ear is in its portion, the liver, and green eyes.[1]

6 (1) Sixth: It serves those born by day and night for 12 years, after Saturn, and these are close to its ⟨least⟩ years.[1] (2) It has rulership over the day of Jupiter [i.e. from sunrise to sundown on Thursday], and over the night of the Moon's day [i.e., between sundown on Sunday and sunrise on Monday].[2]

7 (1) Seventh: Its least years are 12, the middle ⟨years⟩ 45, and the great ⟨years⟩ 79.[1]

8 (1) Eighth: The disease in its portion is any excess of the humors in the body; therefore, Ptolemy says that no one should take a laxative when the Moon aspects Jupiter or conjoins it, as has been demonstrated empirically.[1] (2) Its nature is hot and moist, and it can be increased or diminished depending on the quadrant of the epicycle[2] and of the eccentric circle ⟨in which it is located⟩.[3]

9 (1) Ninth: Its portion ⟨of the house⟩ is the place of praying, or where what is necessary for praying is prepared.[1]

10 (1) Decima: sui sunt elefantes propter equitationem hominis.[1]

11 (1) Undecima: eius sunt pomi arborum et granati, et arbores habentes dulcem saporem. Et denotat copiam frugum et ventorum.

12 (1) Duodecima: ipsius est stagnum.

13 (1) Tredecima: eius est fortitudo in septentrione.[{2}] (2) Et est planeta veritatis et equitatis.[3]

⟨II v⟩
De Marte[4]
⟨⟨Significationes Martis⟩⟩

1 (1) Pars Martis accipitur ab ipso in partem fortune, et proicitur[5] numerus proveniens ab ascendente. Et significat nati ⟨⟨probitatem⟩⟩[{6}], et tollerationem laboris, et ingressum in pericula. (2) Et omnino, est hic planeta ictus,[7] et infirmitatis subito interficientis;[8] denotat falsifitatem, et calliditatem, et malam deceptionem. (3) Et est planeta crudelis, iratus,[9] accusator, atque bellator.

2 (1) Secunda: eius sunt fratres, propinqui, sorores, generes. (2) In mulierum autem nativitate,[10] denotat virum. (3) Et significat depredatores et latrones.[11]

3 (1) Tertia: effusor sanguinis sicut speculator, aut miles principans bello, si fuerit in sua exaltatione. (2) In opposito autem ipsius, erit flebotomator[12] aut ventosator, eius quoque sunt medici et barberii. (3) Artificium eius est
57ra ferrum aut rei | transeuntis per ignem, sicut est auri[13] depurator aut cupri, aut faber arma faciens vel fornarius. (4) Et in artificiis multum participat, principantes enim artificiis sunt .3.: unus est Mercurius, qui denotat scientiam et mercimoniari; secundus Venus, ut comptum et pulchrum reddatur

[1]sui sunt elelphantes propter equitationem hominis] B om. [2]eius est fortitudo in septentrione] G fortitudo eius est in parte septentrionali. [3]equitatis] B > hic defecit librum in exitu et in principio. sequitur finem. [4]De marte] DZN[m]; P > et eius significatis; V om. [5]proicitur*] ZP; VN prohicitur; D prohibitur. [6]probitatem*] G VDPLBZ bernagium. [7]ictus] D > vel percussionis. [8]interficientis] P interficientes. [9]iratus] VLZ; D natus; P reatus. [10]Nativitate] VP; L nativitatis. [11]latrones] LP; D > vel exspoliatores vel praedones. [12]flebotomator] L falsificator. [13]auri] ZLP; VDN aurum.

10 (1) Tenth: Of riding animals for men, elephants are in its portion.[1]

11 (1) Eleventh: In its portion are apple and pomegranate trees, and trees ⟨whose fruit has a⟩ sweet taste.[1] It indicates a bumper crop and strong winds.[2]

12 (1) Twelfth: Tin is in its portion.[1]

13 (1) Thirteenth: Its power is in the west⟨ern side⟩. (2) It is a planet of truth and justice.[1]

⟨II v⟩
On Mars
⟨⟨Significations of Mars⟩⟩

1 (1) The lot of Mars is taken from it [Mars] to the lot of Fortune, and the resulting number is cast out from the ascendant. It signifies the native's ⟨⟨courage⟩⟩, endurance of hard work, and entering into dangerous ⟨places⟩.[1] (2) In general, it is the planet of plague⟨s⟩,[2] of disease⟨s⟩ killing suddenly;[3] it signifies falsehood, cunning, and malicious deception.[4] (3) This planet is cruel, furious, an informer, and a warrior.[5]

2 (1) Second: In its portions are brothers, relatives, sisters and sons-in-law.[1] (2) In the nativity of women, it indicates the husband.[2] (3) It signifies plunderers and robbers.[3]

3 (1) Third: ⟨Mars⟩ sheds blood like the executioner, or a soldier who is victorious in battle, if it is in its exaltation.[1] (2) But if opposite to its ⟨house or exaltation⟩, ⟨he (the native)⟩ will be a phlebotomist or a cupper; in its portion are physicians and barber-surgeons.[2] (3) The craft in its portion is that based on iron or on things that pass through fire, like those who smelt gold or copper, the armorer, or a baker.[3] (4) ⟨Mars⟩ has a major share in the crafts, ⟨for⟩ there are three lords of crafts: one is Mercury, which signifies knowledge and commerce; the second is Venus, to restore adornment and

artificium; tertia Mars, propter substinere laborem et velocitatem.[1] (5) Et est planeta fervoris,[2] cuius opera impedit Venus. (6) Si autem Iupiter Marti commisceatur, sitque fortior[3] eo, proeliabitur propter Deum.

4 (1) Quartus: eius est forma rubea,[4] facies longa, oculi varii, corpus longum, roseum commixtum nigredini modice, lineas rubeas in facie, paucorum pilorum in barba, similatur enim eunucho, et collum longus gracile.

5 (1) Quintus: ⟪habet pudibundi⟫,[{5}] caput,[{6}] naris dextra; et colera;[{7}] et colorum, rubeus.[8]

6 (1) Sexta:[9] servit in nativitate cuiuslibet hominis post Iovem .7. annis. (2) Et eius est in nocte potestas, et si sit planeta masculus. (3) Et principatur in die Martis, et in nocte Sabbati.

7 (1) Septima:[10] sunt quidem eius anni minores .15., medii .40. cum dimidio, maiores .66.

8 (1) Octava:[11] morbi eius sunt febris tertiana inflammativa et[12] apostemata cordi propinqua ex quibus emanat sanguis, et habet in eius facie nigredinis notam aut aliquam in collo.

9 (1) Nona: ipsius domus pars est coquina.

10 (1) Decima: eius sunt canes, et equitatarum, muli.

11 (1) Undecima: sue sunt omnes arbores cuius[13] amarus est fructus, et omne amarum, ac mortis potus.

12 (1) Duodecima: metallorum ferrum.

13 (1) Tertiadecima: eius est meridiana fortitudo[{14}] et significat tonitruum, coruscationem et lapides cadentes flumine.[15]

[1]et velocitatem*] PG; VDLZN velocitatis. [2]fervoris] D > cuius festinatus violente. [3]fortior] > Marte. [4]rubea] D < russa. [5]habet pudibundi*] G; VDPLZN eius est anus. [6]caput] G ex capite. [7]colera] G colera rubea. [8]rubeus] LP; D rusus rubeus annus propter scorpio caput preparatum. [9]sexta] VP; DZLN septima. [10]Septima] P[a] > de annis Martis. [11]Octava] P[a] > de morbis Martis. [12]et] D ex. [13]cuius] P quarum. [14]eius est meridiana fortitudo] G fortitudo eius est in parte meridiana. [15]flumine] VNLZ; D fulmine; P fulmina.

beauty to the craft; the third is Mars, to endure hard work and quickness.[4] (5) It is a planet of great heat,[5] whose effect is hindered by Venus.[6] (6) If Jupiter is mixed with Mars, its [Jupiter's] power is greater than Mars's, it will wage war for God.[7]

4 (1) Fourth: His outward appearance is red, the face long, the eyes are of various colors, the body is long,[1] red and black mixed moderately, red lines in the face, little hair in the beard, like that of a eunuch, the neck is long and slender.[2]

5 (1) Fifth: ⟨⟨In its portion are the genitals⟩⟩; the head, the right nostril; the ⟨yellow⟩ bile; of the colors, red.[1]

6 (1) Sixth: It serves in the nativity of any man for 7 years after Jupiter.[1] (2) It has rulership over the night, even though it is a masculine planet.[2] (3) It is powerful over the day of Mars [i.e., from sunrise to sundown on Tuesday], and over the night of the Sabbath [i.e., between sundown on Friday and sunrise on Saturday].[3]

7 (1) Seventh: Its least years are 15, the middle ⟨years⟩ 40½, and the great ⟨years⟩, 66.[1]

8 (1) Eighth: Its diseases are inflammatory tertian fever[1] and abscesses close to the heart from which blood flows; he has a black mark on his face or one on his neck.[2]

9 (1) Ninth: Its portion of the house is the kitchen.[1]

10 (1) Tenth: Dogs are in its portion; of riding animals, mules.[1]

11 (1) Eleventh: All trees with bitter fruit, and anything bitter and deadly poison are in its portion.[1]

12 (1) Twelfth: Of the metals, iron ⟨is in its portion⟩.[1]

13 (1) Thirteenth: Its power is ⟨in the⟩ southern ⟨side⟩; it signifies thunder, lightning, and meteors in a stream.[1]

⟨II vi⟩
De Venere[1]
⟪Significationes Veneris⟫

1 (1) Pars Veneris accipitur a parte fortune in partem celati et prohicitur ab ascendente. Et significat figuram corporis nati, et pulchritudinem eius, gaudium, delicia, pastum, et omne genus concubitus.[2] (2) Et est planeta cantus, ludi ac amoris. (3) Et denotat quietem. (4) Removetque malum Martis.

2 (1) Secunda: eius est mater,[3] soror, uxor, meretrices, tripudiatrices.

3 (1) Tertia: eius artificium est medicinale, specierum mercatio, vendere cantus instrumenta, mulierum ornamenta, robas facere, et ornare et anulos et balteos.

4 (1) Quarta: eius figura colli[4] est pulchra, pulcherrime[5] facta, necque longa nimis necque brevis; oculi pulchri et supercilia. (2) Et ⟪intendit⟫[6] libenter faciem componere. (3) Corpore neque pigrior neque macrior, verba dulcia, cito ambulat, facies munda, gratiosus, minutus, parum aut[7] inferior barba.

5 (1) Quinta: eius est turpitudo,[8] naris sinistra, ren dexter.[9]

6 (1) Sexta: .8. servit annis post Solem[10] nato in die. (2) Eius potestas est in die Veneris ac in nocte Martis.

7 (1) Septima: anni minores sunt .8. medii .48. cum dimidio. maiores .81. (2) Et denotat iuventutem.[11] (3) Et communicat in .5. locis vite, natus est[12] letus semper et sustinebit quod ei occurret.

[1]Venere] ZLD^m^N^m^; P > et eius significationis; V om. [2]concubitus] N om. [3]mater] DG; VLPNZ matris. [4]colli] VP; LDN coli; G om. [5]pulcherrime] D > vel bene. [6]intendit*] G; VDLPZN intenta. [7]aut] V autem. [8]turpitudo] D > post expcnam que sit in sua; P < fortitudo. [9]dexter] D > propter linorem. [10]Solem] VPZ; LDN Solis. [11]iuventutem] D > prima vel principie finem unum acc. minuente smon. locutiones hominum in principio eius sapientie et sn. pocc. principia ult. 13 annos. [12]est] D erit.

⟨II vi⟩
On Venus
⟨⟨Significations of Venus⟩⟩

1 (1) The lot of Venus is calculated from the lot of Fortune to the lot of the hidden, and is cast out from the ascendant. It signifies the features of the native's body, his beauty, joy, pleasures,[1] food, and every sort of sexual intercourse.[2] (2) It is the planet of music, games, and love.[3] (3) It signifies rest.[4] (4) It removes Mars's misfortune.[5]

2 (1) Second: In its portion are the mother, the sister, the wife,[1] prostitutes and dancers.[2]

3 (1) Third: The craft in its portion is concerned with medicine, trade in spices, selling musical instruments, women's ornaments, making garments, and decorating rings and belts.[1]

4 (1) Fourth: The shape of his neck is handsome, beautifully made, neither long nor short;[1] with beautiful eyes and eyebrows. (2) He attempts to make up ⟨his⟩ face willingly. (3) The body is neither slow nor thin, of sweet words, walks quickly, of clean face, kind, small, with a small or short beard.[2]

5 (1) Fifth: In its portion are the genitals, the left nostril, the right kidney.[1]

6 (1) Sixth: It serves one born by day for 8 years after the Sun. (2) It has rulership over the day of Venus [i.e., from sunrise to sundown on Friday], and over the night of Mars [i.e., between sundown on Monday and sunrise on Tuesday].[1]

7 (1) Seventh: ⟨Its⟩ least years are 8, the middle ⟨years⟩ 45½, and the great ⟨years⟩ .82. (2) It signifies the days of youth. (3) ⟨If⟩ it has a share in the five places of life [i.e. if Venus is the lord of the five places of life], the native will be always joyful and will be satisfied with his portion.[1]

8 (1) Octava: infirmitas eius est mixta cum modico frigore. (2) Et significat 57rb omne desiderium. (3) Et eius est infirmitas cordis,[1] febris, | dolor ventris et infirmitas ⟨⟨quae sit per fascinationem⟩⟩;[{2}] in ipsius facie est veruca aut signum.

9 (1) Nona: eius pars domus est lectus.

10 (1) Decima: de equitaturis ipsius est camelus.

11 (1) Undecima: eius est arbor, omnis pinguis et omne genus cervisie.[3]

12 (1) Duodecima: eius[4] est cuprum.

13 (1) Tertiadecima: eius est in occidente potestas,[{5}] et participationem habet in pluvia.

⟨II vii⟩
De Mercurio[6]
⟨⟨Significationes Mercurii⟩⟩

1 (1) Eius pars[7] accipitur a parte celati in partem fortune et proicitur ab ascendente. Et significat defectum substantie et amissionem.[8] (2) Et hic est planeta illuminans omnem scientiam, causans signum[9] in anima hominis sicut Luna in corporis complexione secundum eius locum respectu gradus ascendentis.

2 (1) Secunda: eius sunt servientes et servi.

3 (1) Tertia: ipsius scientia est logice, grammatice, versificandi, ritimandi,[10] et epistolas scribendi. (2) Et est planeta scriptorum regis, et eius sunt numeri et mensure.[{11}] (3) Qui si fuerit in loco malo, significat acuum sutores et testores.[12] (4) Ipsius quoque mutabilis est natura, aliquando enim

[1]cordis] VDNP; corde LZ. [2]que sit per fascinationem*] G; VLPZN propter currus; D propter currus duc. quod vaduit in quadrigis. [3]cervisie] D > et forte per hac. potius utuslic?. [4]eius] < metallorum. [5]eius est in occidente potestas] G fortitudo eius est in parte occidentis. [6]Mercurio] ZL; P > et eius significationis; DV om. [7]Eius pars] P pars Mercurii. [8]amissionem] D > vuals?. notavit eam partem paupertatem et modice ingenium. [9]signum] D > et notas. [10]ritimandi] P rigimandi. [11]et eius sunt numeri et mensure] G et signat numeros et mensuras. [12]testores] P textores.

8 (1) Eighth: Its disease is temperate, with a bit of cold.[1] (2) It signifies any desire.[2] (3) In its portion are heart diseases, fever, abdominal pain, and illness due to ⟪enchantment⟫; there is a wart or a mark on his face.[3]

9 (1) Ninth: Its portion of the house is the bed.[1]

10 (1) Tenth: Of riding animals, the camel.[1]

11 (1) Eleventh: In its portion are ⟨diverse types of⟩ tree⟨s⟩,[1] anything fat and every kind of beer.[2]

12 (1) Twelfth: Copper is in its portion.[1]

13 (1) Thirteenth: Its power is in the west⟨ern side⟩, and it has a share in rain.[1]

⟨II vii⟩
On Mercury
⟪Significations of Mercury⟫

1 (1) Its lot is taken from the lot of the hidden to the lot of Fortune, and is cast from the ascendant. It signifies lack of wealth and lost objects.[1] (2) This planet illuminates every knowledge, leaving a mark on the human soul as the Moon does on the bodily temperament according to its position with respect to the degree of the ascendant.[2]

2 (1) Second: In its portion are servants and slaves.[1]

3 (1) Third: In its portion is the knowledge of logic, grammar, versifying, rhyming, and writing letters. (2) It is the planet of the king's scribes, and in its portion are numbers and measures. (3) If it is in an inauspicious position it signifies tailors and weavers. (4) Its nature is changeable, sometimes cold

est frigidus aliquando calidus, aut siccus vel humidus. et iterum aliquando masculus aliquando femina, aliquando quidem fortuna aliquando malus, secundum naturam planetarum aspicientium ipsum aut coniungentium.[1] (5) Eius sunt monetam operantes et perfecti in scientia signorum; et coriarius est eius.

4 (1) Quarta: ipsius est forma extenuata carne, facies longa, labia tenua,[2] barba pulchra, digiti longi manuum.[3]

5 (1) Quinta: ipsius est lingue extremitas, ren sinister.

6 (1) Sexta: servit cuilibet nato .13. annis post Venerem. (2) Et habet postestatem in die Mercurii et in nocte Dominice.

7 (1) Septima: anni parvi eius sunt .20., mediocres .48., maiores .76.

8 (1) Octava: infirmitates sue ⟨⟨fascinatio⟩⟩,{4} et inflatio[5] in ventre. (2) Et Ptholemeus dicit quod in omni nativitate in qua Mercurius[6] fuerit coniunctus aspectu signo ascendenti aut Lune, non mutabitur[7] propter infirmitatem scientia nati. (3) Et habet in suo corpore signum discoopertum, cicatricem aut lentiginem.[8]

9 (1) Nona: eius pars in domo est locus scribarum aut ubi sit artificium.

10 (1) Decima: sunt ipsius ovile.[9]

11 (1) Undecima: eius est parva arbor omnis.

12 (1) Duodeciam: metallorum argentum vivum.

13 (1) Tredecima: eius fortitudo versus sinistram.{10}

14 (1) Hic finitur *Liber servorum*, id est, .7. planetarum.[11]
⟨⟨Explicit⟩⟩

[1]coniungentium] P qui coniunguntur ei. [2]labia tenua] P om. [3]longi manuum] DL; P manuum longi. [4]fascinatio*] G; VDPLBN currus. [5]inflatio] D conflatio. [6]Mercurius] N om. [7]mutabitur] D > id est non fiet fatuus. [8]lentiginem] VZNL; D lenoginem; P lenniginem. [9]ovile] D > ista alta parva. [10]eius fortitudo versus sinistram] G fortitudo eius in parte sinistra. [11]Hic finitur liber servorum, id est, .7. planetarum] ZNL; D Hic terminatur liber servorum, id est, .7. planetarum; VP om.

and sometimes hot, ⟨sometimes⟩ dry and ⟨sometimes⟩ moist; sometimes masculine and sometimes feminine, sometimes auspicious and sometimes inauspicious, depending on the nature of the planets that aspect or conjoin it.[1] (5) In its portion are minters[2] and experts in the science of the signs; the currier is also in its portion.[3]

4 (1) Fourth: His outward appearance is emaciated, with a long face,[1] thin lips, a handsome beard, and long fingers.[2]

5 (1) Fifth: The tip of the tongue and the left kidney are in its portion.[1]

6 (1) Sixth: It serves any native for 13 years, after Venus. (2) It has rulership over the day of Mercury [i.e., from sunrise to sundown on Wednesday], and over the night⟨time⟩ of the Lord⟨'s day⟩ [i.e., between sundown on Saturday and sunrise on Sunday].[1]

7 (1) Seventh: Its least years are 20, the middle ⟨years⟩ 48, and the great ⟨years⟩ 76.[1]

8 (1) Eighth: The diseases in its portion are ⟪enchantment⟫, and a flatulence in the stomach.[1] (2) Ptolemy says that in any nativity where Mercury is in conjunction or in aspect with the ascendant sign or with the Moon, the native will not go mad on account of his illness.[2] (3) He has an exposed mark on his body, a scar or a lentil-shaped spot.[3]

9 (1) Ninth: Its place in the house is the scriptorium and the craftsman's workroom.[1]

10 (1) Tenth: Sheep are in its portion.[1]

11 (1) Eleventh: Every small tree is in its portion.[1]

12 (1) Twelfth: Of the metals, quicksilver is in its portion.[1]

13 (1) Thirteenth: Its power is in the northern ⟨side⟩.[1]

14 (1) This completes the *Book of the servants*, that is, of the seven planets.[1,2]

⟨III⟩
Tractatus de significationibus planetarum in duodecim domibus Abrahe Avenaris[1]
⟨⟨Incipit *Liber Abrahe Evenezre de significationibus septem planetarum, et capitis et caude, per duodecim domos*⟩⟩

1 (1) Primo de prima domo.[2] (2) Sol in domo ista[3] significat potestatem, regnum, et res magnas et multas. (3) Luna, si fuerit lumine plena, significat rerum profectum, et mutationem de loco in locum, et gaudium matris, et[4] mulieres magnas. (4) Saturnus in hac domo significat planctum rei acquirende et terre.[5] (5) Jupiter significat patientiam, timorem,[6] pulchritudinem, magisterium, iudicium, potestatem. (6) Mars tristiciam, pavorem,[7] tormentum, tremorem,[8] caliditatem,[9] substantie ablationem et iram in lite,[10] non pigritia. (7) Venus gaudium, letitiam, gratiam,[11] comestionem, potum, pannos, vestimenta, et rem ferentem odorem. (8) Mercurius[12] scien-
57va tiam, scripturam,[13] | probationem mensurarum et numerorum. (9) Caput draconis augmentum dignitatis et fortitudinis secundum complexionem[14] eius cum planetis. (10) Cauda recessum, peiorationem, periculum, angustiam, et omnium rerum minorationem.

2 (1) De secunda domo.[15] (2) Sol in domo hac[16] significat pulchritudinem, amorem, oculos ridentes. (3) Luna ablationem substantie, angustiam, planctum.[17] (4) Saturnus amissionem substantie, angustiam[18] amicorum. (5) Jupiter congregationem substantie propter scientiam, manerie bona. (6) Mars[19] ablationem substantie, paupertatem, angustiam artificii. (7) Venus profectum ex parte mulierum, honorem, adiutorium. (8) Mercurius profectum substantie, et honorem ex parte regis. (9) Caput[20] augmentationem substantie et boni multi. (10) Cauda paupertatem, perditionem,[21] et defectum eius in quo confidit.

[1]Tractatus de significationibus planetarum in .12. domibus Abrahe Avenaris] DL; NZ Tractatus de significationibus planetarum in .12. domibus Abrahe; P Incipit tractatus Abrahe Avenaris Judei de significatione septem planetarum per .12. domos V om. [2]Primo de prima domo] D; NL De prima domo; P Et primo in domo prima; Z Et primo de prima; V om. [3]ista] P prima. [4]et] N vel. [5]terre] D > vel fiunt super rem acquisitam; P iter error. [6]timorem] D et morem. [7]pavorem] D pallorem. [8]tremorem*] ZPL; D tremo remorem; N om. [9]caliditatem] VZLN; DP calliditatem. [10]lite] P litem. [11]gratiam] D > vel laudem. [12]Here Z is interrupted until III 2:6. But the interrupted fragment appears very blurred in the upper margin of fol. 91. B also resumes in III 2:6. This proves that Z and B are connected. [13]scripturam] P om. [14]complexionem] VP; LN coniunctionem. [15]De secunda domo] V secunda; N om. [16]domo hac] D > scilicet secunda; P secunda domo. [17]planctum] P om. [18]amissionem substantie angustiam] P om. [19]Mars] here B and Z resume. [20]Caput] L Capricornius. [21]perditionem] D > vel amissionem.

⟨III⟩

Treatise on the Significations of the Planets in the 12 ⟨Horoscopic⟩ Places by Abraham Ibn Ezra ⟨⟨Here Begins the *Book by Abraham Ibn Ezra on the Significations of the Planets, and of the Head and the Tail, in the 12 ⟨Horoscopic⟩ Places*⟩⟩

1 (1) First on the first place. (2) The Sun in this place signifies power, kingship, and many and great things.[1] (3) The Moon, if its light is full, signifies profit from properties, relocation from one place to another, the mother's joy, and great women.[2] (4) Saturn in this place signifies complaint about buying property and land.[3] (5) Jupiter signifies endurance, dread, beauty, authority, judgment, and power.[4] (6) Mars ⟨signifies⟩ sadness, terror, torture, tremor, hotness, theft of wealth, anger in quarrels, not sluggishness.[5] (7) Venus ⟨signifies⟩ joy, delight, grace, eating, drinking, cloth, garments, and smelly thing⟨s⟩.[6] (8) Mercury ⟨signifies⟩ knowledge, writing, proving measures [i.e., geometry] and numbers [i.e., arithmetic].[7] (9) The Head of the Dragon ⟨signifies⟩ an increase of dignity and power according to its mixture with the planets.[8] (10) The Tail[9] ⟨signifies⟩ retreat, deterioration, danger, affliction, and the decrease of everything.[10]

2 (1) On the second place. (2) The Sun in this place signifies beauty, love, and laughing eyes.[1] (3) The Moon ⟨signifies⟩ theft of wealth, affliction, and complaint.[2] (4) Saturn ⟨signifies⟩ loss of wealth, and the affliction of friends.[3] (5) Jupiter ⟨signifies⟩ accumulation of wealth because of scholarship, and good manners.[4] (6) Mars ⟨signifies⟩ the theft of wealth, poverty, and affliction related to the craft.[5] (7) Venus ⟨signifies⟩ profit from women, honor, and assistance.[6] (8) Mercury ⟨signifies⟩ profit from property, and honor from the king.[7] (9) The Head ⟨signifies⟩ increase of wealth and many benefits.[8] (10) The Tail ⟨signifies⟩ poverty, ruin, and desertion by someone who is trusted.[9]

3 (1) De tertia domo.[1] (2) Sol rerum profectum ex parte regis, et mutationem de regno in regnum. (3) Luna gaudium, et letitiam divitum, et altitudinem regum, et profectum viarum fratrum et sociorum, et esse cum magnis, ac augmentum amoris.[2] (4) Saturnus destructionem fratrum, et litem inter eos. (5) Jupiter gaudium magnum ex parte illorum.[3] (6) Mars odium fratrum, et modum litis, unusque alium interficiet. (7) Venus iniquitatem, planctum, et res indecenter perficere.[4] (8) Mercurius multitudinem fratrum et sororum et amicorum. (9) Caput coniunctionem veritatis, ac sompnia[5] vera. (10) Cauda separationem fratrum, litem difficilem inter eos, et credo quod erunt in periculo.{6}

4 (1) De quarta domo.[7] (2) Sol absconditum thesaurum, et significat futuram dignitatem, et nomen inter homines. (3) Luna planctum quaestionis ad nunciacionem si fuerit dies, si nox mortem circa principium rei et in fine, nisi res fuerit reposita aut subterranea; in hoc quidem bona multum: discooperietur enim res illa et scietur locus, si Deus voluerit. (4) Saturnus destructionem domorum, terrarum, seminationum, thesaurorum; periculum[8] aut mortem. (5) Jupiter profectum terrarum hereditatum, thesauri[9] et omnis antiqui; mortis[10] hereditatem,[11] remotionem[12] planctus et male cogitationis; et denotat fiduciam omnis rei contingentis perfecte.[13] (6) Mars occisionem, mortem, effusionem sanguinis, et finis rei elongabitur in planctum et tormentum. (7) Venus planctum, tristitiam circa principium rerum ex parte matris, finis tamen erit cum proficuo. (8) Mercurius planctum cogitationis, despectum, pessima verba. (9) Caput augmentum profectus si fuerit in signo igneo vel aereo aut econtrario[14] si fuerit in signo aquatico vel terreo. (10) Cauda paupertatem, odium, et rei sine valore quesitionem.

5 (1) De quinta domo.[15] (2) Sol mutationem ex parte filii, honorem
57vb magnum in honorando gentes[16] et donando. (3) | ⟨⟨Luna multitudinem filiorum masculorum si sit de nocte, sed si de die significabit filias et boni rumores et bona verba venient ei de filio suo, pro quibus letabitur.⟩⟩{17}

[1]De tertia domo] V .3a. [2]amoris] P honoris. [3]illorum] VZNBL; P suorum fratrum; D > scilicet fratrum. [4]perficere] D > vel facere. [5]sompnia] VDBN; ZPL somnia. [6]credo quod erunt in periculo*] G; VBNZPL et forte erunt in periculo; D > vel timeo. [7]De quarta domo] V .4a. [8]periculum] P < cum. [9]thesauri] B thesaurorum. [10]mortis] N om. [11]hereditatem] VP; hereditatum LZB; DN hereditationem. [12]remotionem] L renovationem. [13]perfecte] D > vel ad punctum. [14]econtrario] L contrario. [15]De quinta domo] V .5a. [16]gentes] VDPLN; ZB < reges. [17]Luna multitudinem filiorum masculorum si sit de nocte, sed si de die significabit filias et boni rumores et bona verba venient ei de filio suo, pro quibus letabitur*] G; VPLZN Luna plenitudinem filiorum masculorum si fuerit in nocte, si autem in die significat filias et remotionem malorum verborum. Et nova occurent sibi loginqua de eius filio quibus gaudebit.

3 (1) On the third place. (2) The Sun ⟨signifies⟩ profit from properties from the king, and relocation from one kingdom to another.[1] (3) The Moon ⟨signifies⟩ joy, delight of rich men, exalted status of kings, profit from journeys, brothers and partners, being with powerful people, and increase in love.[2] (4) Saturn ⟨signifies⟩ ruin of brothers, and a quarrel between them.[3] (5) Jupiter ⟨signifies⟩ great joy from them [i.e., the brothers].[4] (6) Mars ⟨signifies⟩ fraternal hatred, a sort of quarrel, and killing one another.[5] (7) Venus ⟨signifies⟩ wickedness, complaint, and accomplishing something indecently.[6] (8) Mercury ⟨signifies⟩ many brothers, sisters, and friends.[7] (9) The Head ⟨signifies⟩ a sincere relationship, and dreams that come true.[8] (10) The Tail ⟨signifies⟩ separation of brothers, a bitter quarrel between them, and that perhaps they will be in danger.[9]

4 (1) On the fourth place. (2) The Sun ⟨signifies⟩ hidden treasure, and it signifies future dignity and renown among people.[1] (3) The Moon ⟨signifies⟩ complaint about a question related to an announcement if ⟨it is asked⟩ by day, if ⟨asked⟩ by night ⟨it signifies⟩ death around the beginning or the end of the undertaking, except if the thing ⟨asked about⟩ has been hidden or is underground; in this ⟨case it signifies⟩ many fortunate things: the thing ⟨asked about⟩ will be discovered and the place will be known, God willing.[2] (4) Saturn ⟨signifies⟩ the ruin of houses, lands, planted land and wealth; ⟨it also signifies⟩ danger or death.[3] (5) Jupiter ⟨signifies⟩ profit from inherited lands, from wealth, and from any old thing; ⟨it signifies⟩ inheritance from the dead, and removal of lamentation and of bad thought; it indicates confidence that every contingent thing will happen.[4] (6) Mars ⟨signifies⟩ slaughter, death, bloodshed, and that the end of something will be prolonged with lamentation and anguish.[5] (7) Venus ⟨signifies⟩ lamentation, sadness around the beginning of undertakings on behalf of the mother, but the end will be beneficial.[6] (8) Mercury ⟨signifies⟩ lamentation due to thoughts, contempt, and very bad things.[7] (9) The Head ⟨signifies⟩ increase of profit if it is in a fiery or airy sign, or the opposite if in a watery or earthy sign.[8,9] (10) The Tail ⟨signifies⟩ poverty, hate, and searching for something worthless.[10]

5 (1) On the fifth place. (2) The Sun ⟨signifies⟩ change with regard to the son, great honor when conferring honor and gifts on people.[1] (3) ⟨⟨The Moon ⟨signifies⟩ many male sons if ⟨the interrogation is made⟩ by night, and if by day it signifies daughters and good news and good reports that will come to him from his son, on account of which he will rejoice⟩⟩.[2]

(4) Saturnus destructionem filiorum,[1] et litem cum nuntio. (5) Jupiter infantium multitudinem, magnum commodum,[2] utilitatem, nomen magnum et auctoritatem quoniam divitibus coniungetur et magnis. (6) Mars pluralitatem puerorum[3] ex meretricio, et modicum profectus et parvum gaudium de eis, et delectationem in ribaldia.[4] (7) Venus in principio angustiam[5] ex parte filii, et habebit in fine gaudium et letitiam. (8) Mercurius nuntiorum emissionem, et librorum scripturas, nova, gaudium, et denotat planctum, periculum,[6] quod propter eius contingit filium. (9) Caput multitudinem infantium, et amorem inter eos. (10) Cauda remotionem boni, et inmissionem mali in pueris, et pannis veteribus et antiquis et paupertatem in pueris.

6 (1) De domo sexta.[7] (2) Sol infirmitatem ex parte filiorum, et vituperabitur per gentem vilem. (3) Luna prelium, et litem ex parte parentum, et lucrum in quadrupedibus, et sanitatem corporis. (4) Saturnus infirmitatem, et insurget servus in eius dominum. (5) Jupiter modicum infirmitatis, et dignitatem propter servos, et profectum ex bestiis quadrupedibus. (6) Mars pluralitatem infirmitatum, febrem[8] calidam consumentem,[9] et turbationem sanguinis, tedium, et planctumque ex parte servorum. (7) Venus infirmitatem ex parte servorum et ancillarum; et significat viduas. (8) Mercurius utilitatem, accusationem, et deceptionem in servis. (9) Caput magnam infirmitatem, augmentum servorum multorum, mutationem bestiarum. (10) Cauda infirmitatem, et pigritiem[10] servorum et servarum, et debilitatem bestiarum.

7 (1) De septima domo.[11] (2) Sol odium divitum[12] et magnatum[13] atque regum.[14] (3) Luna bonum et profectum pro mulieribus. (4) Saturnus destructionem terrarum et mulierum, malumque profectum in fine. (5) Jupiter gaudium propter mulieres, et sponsalia, et concordiam inimici (6) Mars paupertatem, et preliari propter rem Deo pertinentem, et nubere[15] sine iustitia[16] ex quo debet dampnum, et tedium contingere. (7) Venus nubere, et gaudium ex parte muliere et in omni eo quod queritur, ac iure participationis,[17] et gratis fiet quod queret omne. (8) Mercurius despectum

[1]filiorum] VNPL; ZB om; D infantium vel puerorum. [2]commodum] D > vel ediam. [3]puerorum] VNDL; ZPB filiorum. [4]ribaldia] P ribaldariam. [5]angustiam] V angustias. [6]periculum] VZNBL; D om; P < et. [7]De domo sexta] V .6a. [8]febrem] D om. [9]consumentem] D consumentatem. [10]pigritiem] VBNZ; DL pigritiam. [11]De septima domo] V .7a. [12]divitum] DPG; VLZN diminutum. [13]magnatum] L et magistratum. [14]regum] D > et id ne menu quod istos despicio quantium magnos et de eis non curo. [15]nubere] D nubes. [16]iustitia] V iustitiam. [17]ac iure participationis] G et in rebus societatis.

(4) Saturn ⟨signifies⟩ the loss of sons, and a quarrel with a messenger.[3] (5) Jupiter ⟨signifies⟩ many children, a great opportunity, utility, great renown, and authority because he will meet rich and powerful people.[4] (6) Mars ⟨signifies⟩ many children from prostitution, moderate benefit and little joy from them, and delight in dishonesty.[5] (7) Venus at the beginning ⟨signifies⟩ affliction with regard to sons, but in the end he will have joy and delight.[6] (8) Mercury signifies sending messengers, writing books, rumors, joy, and it indicates lamentation, danger as a result of which the son is affected.[7] (9) The Head ⟨signifies⟩ many children, and love among them.[8] (10) The Tail ⟨signifies⟩ the removal of good things, the introduction of bad things in the children, worn-out and old clothes, and poverty of the children.[9]

6 (1) On the sixth place. (2) The Sun ⟨signifies⟩ a disease of the sons, and that he will be censured by vile people.[1] (3) The Moon ⟨signifies⟩ battle, a quarrel with the parent, profit from quadrupeds, and bodily health.[2] (4) Saturn ⟨signifies⟩ a disease, and that a slave will rebel against his master.[3] (5) Jupiter ⟨signifies⟩ a mild disease, dignity due to slaves, and benefit from quadruped animals.[4] (6) Mars ⟨signifies⟩ many diseases, hot and consumptive fever, a disorder of the blood, fatigue, and lamentation with regard to slaves.[5] (7) Venus ⟨signifies⟩ disease of male and female slaves; and it signifies widows.[6] (8) Mercury ⟨signifies⟩ profit, accusation, and fraud regarding slaves.[7] (9) The Head ⟨signifies⟩ a serious disease, an increase of many slaves, and exchanging animals.[8] (10) The Tail ⟨signifies⟩ disease, laziness of the male slaves and female slaves, and weakness of the animals.[9]

7 (1) On the seventh place. (2) The Sun ⟨signifies⟩ hatred of rich men, magnates, and kings.[1] (3) The Moon ⟨signifies⟩ prosperity and profit for women.[2] (4) Saturn ⟨signifies⟩ the loss of lands and of women, and a bad profit at the end.[3] (5) Jupiter ⟨signifies⟩ joy from women, weddings, and harmony between enemies.[4] (6) Mars ⟨signifies⟩ poverty, battling for things pertaining to God, being illegally married from which harm must come, and the occurrence of fatigue.[5] (7) Venus ⟨signifies⟩ a wedding, joy from a woman and in everything he seeks, also in the legal right of partnership, and that everything he seeks will come about without payment.[6] (8) Mercury ⟨sig-

ex parte mulierum et meretricum. (9) Caput coniunctionem, et augmentum meretricii. (10) Cauda destructionem lecti, litem, et inimicos.

8 (1) De octava domo.¹ (2) Sol perditionem, et mortem, et remotionem dominii principum et regum. (3) Luna mortem, destructionem, et remotionem regni, et rerum deteriorationem, atque testimonium | falsifitatis, litem, fugam, angustiam, et mutationem cordis sicut ille qui infatuatur secundum quantitatem Lune, et iuramenta² fantasmata, et magnas cogitationes. (4) Saturnus quaestum hereditatis mortis in rebus antiquis, et planctum, et lamentationes propter mortem. (5) Jupiter ablationem substantie, angustiam, bonum tamen habebit in fine. (6) Mars occisionem, manuum et pedum confractionem,³ diffamationem,⁴ et questum hereditatem mortuorum multarum, et sustinebit penam propter hoc multam ac⁵ amittet suam substantiam et depauperabitur. (7) Venus mortem sororum magnarum, nutricum, atque ancillarum. (8) Mercurius grande odium vicinorum, et vilitatem propter mendacium. (9) Caput fortitudinem vite,⁶ modicumque planctus. (10) Cauda mortem propter mortem,⁷ et hereditatem que destruetur.

58ra

9 (1) De nona domo.⁸ (2) Sol timorem Dei, et fidem, servitium, commemorationem angelorum.⁹ (3) Luna separationem¹⁰ societatis, et divisionem, et mutationem regni¹¹ in regnum, et amare mulieres. Debetque scire ⟨⟨consilia⟩⟩{12} iudiciorum regnorum et ⟨⟨institutiones⟩⟩.¹³ (4) Saturnus destructionem fidei, ingressumque in pessimam cogitationem sicut ille qui infatuatur secundum Lunam,¹⁴ et subfodere mortuos ut ipsos expolient, et tedium in via,¹⁵ et elongare longius. (5) Jupiter gaudium ex parte regis,¹⁶ fidem veram, et explanationem¹⁷ veri sompnii. (6) Mars requisitionem equorum¹⁸ et belli,¹⁹ et potum vini, et non erit iustus, plenus deceptione, sequestratione²⁰ ac dolositate, sacramenta falsa, et somnia, mendacia. (7) Venus gaudium, et iter regium, amorem divinum, religionem, sompnium verum. (8) Mercurius scientiam, magisterium, scientiam astronomie,²¹

---

¹De octava domo] V .8a.   ²et iuramenta] D coniuramenta.   ³occisionem manuum et pedum confractionem] VP; DLNZB occisionem confractionem manuum et pedum.   ⁴diffamationem] ZLB; D < vel visionem; P < fractionem; N famationes.   ⁵ac] VZNPB; D et; L om.   ⁶vite] D > vel vim.   ⁷propter mortem] D om.   ⁸De nona domo] V .9a.   ⁹angelorum] N angulorum.   ¹⁰separationem] L separationum.   ¹¹mutationem regni] G remotionem de regno.   ¹²consilia*] G; VDLPNZB res.   ¹³institutiones*] G; VDLPNZB stabilitates.   ¹⁴Lunam] G cursum Lune.   ¹⁵via] D > vel itinere.   ¹⁶regis] VP; DLNZB regni; G regum.   ¹⁷explanationem] DBLNZ; VP explorationem.   ¹⁸equorum] D < et.   ¹⁹belli] G bellorum.   ²⁰sequestratione] V sequestrationem.   ²¹astronomiae] D astronomiarum.

nifies⟩ scorn by women and prostitutes.[7] (9) The Head ⟨signifies⟩ marriage and increased prostitution.[8] (10) The Tail ⟨signifies⟩ corruption of sexual intercourse [lit. the bed], quarrels, and enemies.[9]

8 (1) On the eighth place. (2) The Sun ⟨signifies⟩ destruction, death, and the deposition of princes and kings.[1] (3) The Moon ⟨signifies⟩ death, destruction, deposition from royal power, deterioration of properties, perjury, quarrels, escape, affliction, a change of heart as when one is infatuated by the phases of the Moon [lit. the size of the Moon], fantastic oaths, and great thoughts.[2] (4) Saturn ⟨signifies⟩ the inheritance of old things from the dead, complaint, lamentation because of death.[3] (5) Jupiter ⟨signifies⟩ theft of wealth, affliction, but in the end he will have a benefit.[4] (6) Mars ⟨signifies⟩ killing, amputation of hands and feet, slander, an inheritance from many dead persons, as a result of which he will be punished, will lose his wealth and will be impoverished.[5] (7) Venus ⟨signifies⟩ the death of older sisters, wet-nurses, and female slaves.[6] (8) Mercury ⟨signifies⟩ great hatred of neighbors, and baseness because of falsehood.[7] (9) The Head ⟨signifies⟩ power of life and a little lamentation.[8] (10) The Tail ⟨signifies⟩ death as a result of death and a ruined inheritance.[9]

9 (1) On the ninth place. (2) The Sun ⟨signifies⟩ fear of God, faith, worship and commemoration of the angels.[1] (3) The Moon ⟨signifies⟩ separation of a partnership, division, the shift of the royal power ⟨from one king⟩ into another, and love of women. He [the querent] must know the counsels and institutions related to the judgments of the kingdoms.[2] (4) Saturn ⟨signifies⟩ destruction of faith, entering into bad thoughts as one who is infatuated by the ⟨phases of the⟩ Moon, burying the dead to plunder them, fatigue on a journey, and absenting oneself for a long while.[3] (5) Jupiter ⟨signifies⟩ joy on account of the king, true faith, and interpreting prophetic dreams.[4] (6) Mars ⟨signifies⟩ confiscation of warhorses, drinking wine, and he [the querent] will not be just, ⟨being⟩ filled with deceit, confiscation and guile, perjury, dreams, falsehoods.[5] (7) Venus ⟨signifies⟩ joy, a royal journey, divine love, religion, a prophetic dream.[6] (8) Mercury ⟨signifies⟩

et famam magnam a cognitis. (9) Caput fidem, et augmentum credulitatis[1] Dei secundum quod erit cum fortunis aut malis. (10) Cauda vim magnam,[2] parumque legalitatis.[3]

10 (1) De decima domo.[4] (2) Sol regnum, potestatem, altitudinem, honorem. (3) Luna rerum profectum, et petitiones, et in hiis erit regis nuncius si fuerit in die; nocte vero perfectum aliquarum rerum ex parte regis et mulierum; cito;{5} et significatum eius[6] in die aut in nocte stabile est minime, ita quod si rex tunc ponatur in regnum ab ipso removebitur cito, ⟨⟨quoniam⟩⟩[7] hic locus Solis bonus, Lune autem modicum. (4) Saturnus[8] planctum, et angustiam duram, et periculum, longumque carcerem. (5) Jupiter denotat altitudinem regis sui regni,[9] confirmationem regni[10] et omnium rerum regni (6) Mars ferrea ictus, inimicos ex parte regis, tristiciam, carcerem, et imminutionem[11] omnis boni in vita sua,[12] pluralitatem preliorum propter Deum in verbis que non pervenient ad effectum. (7) Venus gaudium ex parte regis.
58rb (8) Mercurius potestatem magnam[13] | scripture, mensurarum, numerorum, et cantus. (9) Caput aliquod quesitum a Deo,[14] aut aliquod bonum invisibile, et denotat fortitudinem et altitudinem in bono magisterio. (10) Cauda remotionem[15] domini, et periculum in itinere.

11 (1) De undecima domo.[16] (2) Sol gaudium propter divites, adiuvantes ac administrantes,[17] et scientiam in omni re fidei. (3) Luna gaudium propter amicos, et profectum in omni eo quod sperat. (4) Saturnus planctum, angustiam propter amicos, et parum prosequi in eo quod[18] sperat, spem in re falsa, et duritiam, et caliditatem in pluribus rebus. (5) Jupiter profectum propter amicos et in eo in quo confidit.[19] (6) Mars modicum proficuum, et odium amicorum, perditionem substantie, et ablationem substantie, et defectum in re sperata in eius corde.[20] (7) Venus gaudium, amorem, et res bonas, fiduciam, et bonum propter amicos. (8) Mercurius plenitudinem amicorum, et societatem sapientum. (9) Caput autem et cauda in hac non operantur domo.

[1]credulitatis] D > vel fidei. [2]magnam] D > vel violentiam. [3]legalitatis] G fidelitatis. [4]De decima domo] V .10a. [5]et in hiis erit regis nuncius si fuerit in die, nocte vero perfectum aliquarum rerum ex parte regis et mulierum, cito] G et in hoc erit nuntius regis si fuerit de die sed si sit de nocte significat proficium ex aliquibus rebus regalibus et muliebribus et hoc cito. [6]significatum eius] G res illa qua significat. [7]quoniam*] G; VDPLZN est enim. [8]Saturnus] N om. [9]regis sui regni] VZNPL; D regnis sui; B regis. [10]confirmationem regni] VDZNPL; G stabilitatem regni; B om. [11]imminutionem] VDPLN; ZB dimminutionem. [12]sua] D > vel sacnuras. [13]magnam] P om. [14]quesitum a Deo] G petitionem ad Deum. [15]remotionem] G ablationem. [16]De undecima domo] V .11a. [17]adiuvantes ac administrantes] N om. [18]quod] N om. [19]confidit] P fidit. [20]corde] P om.

knowledge, teaching, astronomy, great renown by his social acquaintances.[7] (9) The Head ⟨signifies⟩ faith and increased belief in God according to whether it [the Head] is with fortunate or unfortunate ⟨planets⟩.[8] (10) The Tail ⟨signifies⟩ great power and little loyalty.[9]

10 (1) On the tenth place. (2) The Sun ⟨signifies⟩ kingship, power, exalted rank, honor.[1] (3) The Moon ⟨signifies⟩ profit from properties, and petitions, in which he will be the king's representative if ⟨the petition⟩ is by day; by night ⟨it signifies⟩ profit from some properties on account of the king, and women; ⟨this will be done⟩ quickly; its signification by day and night is minimally stable, meaning that if a king is then proclaimed in the kingdom, he will be speedily removed, ⟨⟨because⟩⟩ this position of the Sun is auspicious, but that of the Moon only a little.[2] (4) Saturn ⟨signifies⟩ complaint, bitter affliction, danger, and long captivity.[3] (5) Jupiter indicates the exalted rank of the king and of his kingdom, strengthening of the kingdom and of all the matters of the kingdom.[4] (6) Mars ⟨signifies⟩ a hard blow, enemies of the king, sadness, jail, and the decrease of every good thing in his life, a great number of battles because of God in matters that do not produce any effect.[5] (7) Venus ⟨signifies⟩ joy for the king.[6] (8) Mercury ⟨signifies⟩ great mastery of writing, measurements [i.e., geometry], numbers [i.e., arithmetics], and music.[7] (9) The Head ⟨signifies⟩ some request from God, or something fortunate and invisible, and it indicates power and exalted rank in a good mastership.[8] (10) The Tail ⟨signifies⟩ removal of dominion, and danger in travel.[9]

11 (1) On the eleventh place. (2) The Sun ⟨signifies⟩ joy on account of rich people, assistants, and administrators, and knowledge of everything related to faith [i.e., religion].[1] (3) The Moon ⟨signifies⟩ joy because of friends, and profit in everything he hopes for.[2] (4) Saturn ⟨signifies⟩ complaint, affliction on account of friends, seeking a little of what he hopes for, hope in something false, hardness, and heat in many things.[3] (5) Jupiter ⟨signifies⟩ profit on account of friends and of one whom he trusts.[4] (6) Mars ⟨signifies⟩ moderate advantage, hatred of friends, destruction of property, and loss of wealth, and disappointment from what one is hoping for in his heart.[5] (7) Venus ⟨signifies⟩ joy, love, fortunate things, confidence, and good fortune because of friends.[6] (8) Mercury ⟨signifies⟩ abundance of friends, and association with scholars.[7] (9) The Head and the Tail in this ⟨place⟩ have no effect.[8]

12 (1) De duodecima domo.[1] (2) Sol interfectionem divitum, et remotionem a regno et honore, et deteriorationem servorum, et inimicitiam hominum infirmorum. (3) Luna malum, duritiam, tormentationem rerum, litem, et captivitatem propter inimicos. Et si queratur de aliquo quando erit, sitque Luna in .12a. domo, erit quando Luna ex ipsa egredietur; et hoc remotus in itinire adveniet, et hoc si Luna fuerit in fine mensis sui; si autem[2] fuerit in mala dispositione iudica pavorem et tormentum sine dubio. (4) Saturnus angustiam et grave[3] propter regem, et in hoc fortis erit capietque suos inimicos, et timebitur in omnibus eius[4] operibus. (5) Jupiter significat servitium, paupertatem, et indigebit gentes et similiter damnificabitur in bestiis quadrupedibus. (6) Mars caliditatem, latrocinia, et tarditatem in omnibus eius[5] operibus, ablationem substantie, et multiplicationem inimicorum, et preparationem audiendi nova, timorosa verba diabolica, et dampnum propter bestias. (7) Venus tormentum magnorum; et odiet mulieres. (8) Mercurius fatuitatem, parumque scientie, levem cursum, et petitionem rerum non sibi proficientium. Et si habuerit scientiam, erit in cognoscendo quadrupedia. (9) Caput denotat augmentum mali et minorationem boni. (10) Cauda autem bonum malumque minuit.

Explicit.[6]

⟨⟨Explicit⟩⟩

⟨IV⟩

Dogma universale in iudiciis[7]

1 (1) Sciendum in questione omni .3. esse: querens,[8] scilicet, res quesita,[9] et finis[10] quesiti.

2 (1) Et questio[11] est verior[12] quando querens habuerit eam in corde per diem aut noctem, saltem ante. (2) Et cum inveneris dominum voluerisque scire radicem illius, respice a[13] quo separatur planeta significator, scias enim quod significat secundum illum planetam. (3) Et si volueris scire

[1]De duodecima domo] V .12a. [2]autem] V ante. [3]grave] P gravem. [4]eius] P om. [5]eius] N suis. [6]Explicit*] BG; NZDLP om. [7]Dogma universale in iudiciis] V om. [8]querens] L que res. [9]quesita] D inquisita. [10]finis] D > rei. [11]questio] V > modo. [12]verior] L minor. [13]a] DP; VNZBL in.

12 (1) On the twelfth place. (2) The Sun ⟨signifies⟩ the killing of rich men, deposition from kingship and from honor, injury to slaves, and hostility of sick persons.[1] (3) The Moon ⟨signifies⟩ bad fortune, hardness, torment due to properties, quarrels, and captivity because of enemies. If one is asked when something will happen, and the Moon is in the 12th place, it will happen when the Moon leaves it [the 12th place]; this will occur ⟨when the Moon is⟩ far away in the journey, if the Moon is at the end of its month; but if this happens in an inauspicious configuration, judge ⟨that it indicates⟩ terror and torment without doubt.[2] (4) Saturn ⟨signifies⟩ affliction and displeasure because of the king; in this he will be strong and will capture his enemies; he will be frightened in all his deeds.[3] (5) Jupiter signifies servitude, poverty; he will need people, and likewise will be harmed in relation with quadruped animals.[4] (6) Mars ⟨signifies⟩ heat, theft, slowness in all his works, loss of wealth, an increase in ⟨the number of⟩ enemies, preparedness to hear news, frightening diabolic words, and harm because of beasts.[5] (7) Venus ⟨signifies⟩ torment of the magnates; he will hate women.[6] (8) Mercury ⟨signifies⟩ foolishness, insufficient knowledge, a light journey, request for things that will not give him any profit. If he has any knowledge, it is in the knowledge of quadrupeds.[7] (9) The Head ⟨signifies⟩ increase of bad fortune and decrease of good fortune.[8] (10) The Tail ⟨signifies⟩ that he will decrease good and bad fortune.[9]

Completed.

⟨⟨Completed.⟩⟩

⟨IV⟩
General Doctrine of Judgments

1 (1) Three things must be known in every interrogation: the querent [i.e., what motivates the querent to ask the question], and of course the thing asked about, and the end of the interrogation.[1]

2 (1) The interrogation is more reliable when it is held in the querent's heart for a day or a night, ⟨and⟩ even before that [i.e., even more than a day or a night]. (2) When you find the lord and wish to know its [the interrogation's] root [i.e., the cause of the interrogation], observe what ⟨planet⟩ the planet that functions as the significator is moving away from, and know what it [the "root"] is according to this planet [i.e., the planet that is moving away from the significator]. (3) If you wish to know the end

58va finem questionis, | videas cui coniungitur significator, eius namque erit finis significationis.

3 (1) Exemplum: in una questionum ascendens est .10. gradus Tauri,[1] et Venus .15. gradus eius in domo Lune, et Luna .10. gradus Libre, que domus est Veneris. (2) Luna peregrina existit, non enim est in sua domo, honore aut triplicitate, sed est coniuncta Veneri aspectu quarto et recepta. (3) Et dominus partis fortune Saturnus peregrinus in Leone, non receptus.

4 (1) Respexique omnes planetas, neque inveni aliquem adeo fortem ut Venus in suo loco, est enim domina domus,[2] et in eius triplicitatis. (2) Et respexi Lunam dominam domus.[3] (3) Et postea quesivi Lunam ut scirem singificationem ab ea, quoniam est domina ascendentis Venus, enim est domina[4] domus Lune. (4) Inveni enim ipsam in Libra, in domo .6a. a Tauro, que domus est Veneris, et in loco .4o. a Venere. (5) Tuncque scivi quod interrogatio esset de matre pro infirmitate.

5 (1) Et cum volui scire esse ipsius, aspexi a quo separabatur Luna,[5] separabaturque a Saturno. (2) Tunc scivi quod morbus eius frigidus erat et siccus. (3) Et cum volui scire in quo membro esset, inveni secundum divisionem ipsam debere[6] esse in pectore. (4) Et ideo dixi eam pati in pectore aut stomacho.

6 (1) Et cum respexi[7] propter finem, inveni quod coniungebatur Veneri,[8] dixique ipsum liberari propter bonitatem Veneris. (2) Cum autem volui scire terminum[9] liberationis, aspexi gradus existentes inter Lunam et Venerem, dixique ipsam liberari usque ad tot dies sicut[10] erant gradus. (3) Et ideo dixi dies, quoniam erat Venus in signo mobili. (4) Dicit quoque Messahalla quod si receptor[11] fortitudinis est in signo mobili, dabit dies, et si in communi, menses, in fixo, aut annos. (5) Et si fuerit coniunctus Saturno autem Marti, iudicassem mori ipsam in tali termino.

[1]Tauri] D; VLPNZB Cancri; cf. App. 11, II § 4:2, 526: "interrogatio cuius ascendens fuerit Taurus .x.". [2]domus] VLNZB; PD^{m} (on another hand) > Lune. [3]et in eius triplicitatis. Et respexi Lunam dominam domus*] NZPBL; D quando domina domus ante propter receptionem accipit vel domini Lune. [4]domina] DP; VLNZB om. [5]Luna] D > quod. [6]debere] P omits. [7]respexi] D aspexi. [8]Veneri] D Veneris. [9]terminum] D; VNZBL annum; P diem. [10]sicut] VP; NZDBL sic. [11]receptor] D < a.

of the interrogation, observe which ⟨planet⟩ the significator is conjoined with, because the end will be according to it [i.e., the planet with which the significator is conjoined].[1]

3 (1) Example: in one interrogation, the ascendant is Taurus[1] 10°; Venus is 15° in the Moon's house [i.e., Venus is in Cancer 15°]; the Moon is 10° in Libra, which is Venus's house. (2) The Moon is peregrine, ⟨meaning that⟩ is not in its house, exaltation,[2] or triplicity,[3] but it [the Moon] is conjoined with Venus in quartile and it is received. (3) The lord of the lot of Fortune is Saturn, which is peregrine in Leo, and it is not received.[4]

4 (1) I observed all the planets, and I did not find one as strong as Venus in its position, ⟨since⟩ it [Venus] is the lady of the house ⟨of the ascendant⟩,[1] and it [Venus] is in its [Venus's] triplicity.[2] (2) I observed that the Moon is the lady of the house ⟨of Venus⟩.[3] (3) Afterwards I looked at the Moon, to know the signification from it [the Moon], because Venus is the lady of the ascendant,[4] ⟨and Venus⟩ indeed is the lady of the Moon's house.[5] (4) I found that she [the Moon] is in Libra, in the sixth house from Taurus, which is Venus's house,[6] and in the fourth place [i.e., house] from Venus.[7] (5) Then I knew that the interrogation is about the mother, because of a disease.[8,9]

5 (1) Since I wished to know its [the disease's] nature, I observed which ⟨planet⟩ the Moon wasseparating from, ⟨and I found that⟩ it was separating from Saturn. (2) Then I knew that her [the mother's] disease is cold and dry.[1] (3) When I wished to know which part of the body ⟨the disease⟩ is in, I found, according to that division, that it would be in the breast. (4) Therefore I said that she will suffer in the breast and the stomach.[2]

6 (1) When I examined the end ⟨of the interrogation⟩, I found that it [the Moon] is conjoined with Venus, and I said that she will be cured because of Venus's beneficence. (2) When I wanted to know the period of time of the cure, I observed ⟨how many⟩ degrees there are between the Moon and Venus, and I said that she will be cured in as many days as there are degrees. (3) I therefore said ⟨that the period of time is⟩ days, because Venus was in a tropical sign. (4) Māshā'allāh says that if the receiver of power is in a tropical sign, it will give days, if in a bicorporal ⟨sign⟩, months, and if in a fixed ⟨sign⟩, years.[1] (5) If it [the receiver of power] were conjoined with Saturn or Mars, I would have judged that she would die in such a period ⟨of time⟩.[2]

7 (1) Et similiter respice in omnibus rebus absconsis quare querit interrogans. (2) Et hoc est bonum signum si[1] sapiens potest perpendere per seipsum propter quid[2] querit querens. (3) Et debes miscere significatum planetarum cum significato signorum sicut ostendi.

8 (1) Et sciendum quod si Venus fuisset in loco Lune, dixissem ipsum querere pro patre. (2) Et si in .10a., querere pro magno rege. (3) Si vero in ascendente, quesivisse de[3] magno principe dixissem. (4) In .9a., pro fide. (5) In .3a., pro itinere.

9 (1) Et si Mars fuisset loco[4] eius, dixissem querere pro fugitivo aut latrone. (2) Et si ascendente, pro pavore. (3) In .12.a, latrocinium et ablationem substantie. (4) In .3a., pro fratribus. (5) In .7a., pro litigatibus et adversantibus.

10 (1) Si autem Mercurius fuisset[5] in loco eius, quesivissem pro scriptura aut pro scientia scienda. (2) Et si Iupiter in .9a. fuisset, quesivissem pro sompnis. (3) Et iam dixi tibi[6] quomodo debes miscere iudicium planetarum et signorum.

11 (1) Finis quorumdam tractatuum particularium Abrahe Havenare, quos Petrus Paduanus ordinavit in latinum.[7]

[1]si] P et. [2]quid] P quod. [3]de] P pro. [4]loco] P < in. [5]fuisset] L fuissem. [6]tibi] D om. [7]Finis quorumdam tractatuum particularium Abrahe Havenare quos Petrus Paduanus ordinavit in latinum] D; B Finis quorumdam tractatuum particularium Abrahe Havenare quos Petrus Paduanus transtulit de Gallico in latinum; P Finis quorumdam tractatuum particularium Abrahe Avenezre Judei quos Petrus Paduanus transtulit in latinum; N Finis quorumdam tractatuum particularium Habrahe Hevenare quos Petrus Paduanus ordinavit in latinum. Deo gratiae. Scriptum per manus Iacobi de Almania Bassa 1437 19 dei mens octobri hora .23a. Explicit; Z Finis quorumdam tractatuum particularium Abrahe Avençare quos Petrus Paduanus ordinavit in latinum. finitus in parefesto Sancti Galli per me Joannem Ochderumpinna anno domini m cccc lxxxx°; L Finis quorumdam tractatuum particularium Abrahe Avenare quos Petrus Paduanus ordinavit in latinum. Expliciunt peritissimi astrologi Abrahe Avenaris preclara opuscula cum nonullis particularibus tractatibus egresiis astrorum iudicibus satis conducendibus, arte et ingenio solertis viri Petri Liechtenstein in corpus unum (ad commune divino huic negocio inhiantium commodum) miro indagine accumulata Impensaque propria pulcherrimis his characteribus excusa. Venetiis Anno virginei partus supra millesimum quingentesimum septimo pridie kalendas Junias; V amen.

7 (1) Examine in the same manner, regarding all hidden things, how the querent asks. (2) It is an auspicious sign if the astrologer can assess by himself the reason why the querent asks. (3) You ought to combine the signification of the planets with the signification of the signs, as I showed.[1]

8 (1) Know that if Venus were instead of the Moon, I would have said that he [the querent] will inquire about the father. (2) If it [the significator] is in the tenth ⟨place⟩, he will ask about a great king. (3) If it were in the ascendant, I would say that he [the querent] will ask about a great prince. (4) If in the ninth ⟨place⟩, about belief. (5) If in the third ⟨place⟩, about a journey.[1]

9 (1) If Mars were in its [the Moon's] place, I would have said that he [the querent] will inquire about a fugitive or a thief. (2) If in the ascendant, about dread. (3) ⟨If⟩ in the twelfth ⟨place⟩, about theft and the loss of wealth. (4) ⟨If⟩ in the third ⟨place⟩, about brothers. (5) ⟨If⟩ in the seventh ⟨place⟩, about quarrels and adversaries.[1]

10 (1) If Mercury were in its [the Moon's] place, I would have looked for something written or the acquisition of knowledge. (2) If Jupiter were in the ninth ⟨place⟩, I would have looked for dreams. (3) I have already told you how you should combine the judgments of the planets and signs.[1]

11 (1) This is the end of certain particular treatises by Abraham Ibn Ezra, which Peter of Padua translated into Latin,

PART SIX

NOTES TO *TRACTATUS PARTICULARES*

⟨I⟩

[1]**3: Lord of the hour.** This concept bears on the astrological doctrine that the planets, beginning with the Sun and continuing in the order of their orbs, govern each hour of the daytime (divided into 12 hours from sunrise to sunset) and nighttime (divided into 12 hours from sunset to sunrise) of each day of the week. The planet that governs a particular hour is the "lord of the hour." In addition, the planet that governs the first hour of any daytime is the ruler of the corresponding day, and the planet that governs the first hour of any nighttime is the ruler of the corresponding night; the other planets are partners in the lordship of the other hours of day and night assigned to them. Note that the modern names of the weekdays in European languages, particularly the Romance languages, preserve the memory of this astrological theory. *Reshit ḥokhmah*, in the sections on each of planets in chapter 4, lists the days, nights, and hours over which each planet is lord. For Saturn and Jupiter, for example, see *Reshit ḥokhmah*, § 4.1:33, 154–155, and § 4.2:31, 158–159, respectively. *Mishpeṭei ha-mazzalot* lists only the days over which each planet is ruler. For the Sun and the Moon, for example, see *Mishpeṭei ha-mazzalot* § 38:9, 522–523, and § 39:6, 522–525, respectively. The order of the planets' governance of the days of the week and of the hours of each day in the week is explained in *Ṭeʿamim* I (§ 4.2:10, 72–73; quoted in App. 5, Q. 47, 480). For a similar explanation, see *Elements*, ed. Ramsay Wright (1934), § 390, 237–238.

⟨I i 1⟩

[1]**1: House of dejection, Latin: *domus lapsa*.** For this translation of *domus lapsa*, see App. 8, *Sheʾelot le-Talmai*, § 1:2, 505–506, where the same expression is translated בית נפילה "house of falling" and App. 8, Ptolemy's *Iudicia*, § 1:2, 507–508, where the same expression is translated *in casu vel deiectione*, "in the falling or dejection." For the astrological concept of dejection, see note to *Int*, II i 6:3. The expression used here translates هبوط, *lit.* "falling," used in Arabic astrological literature to denote the astrological concept of dejection. See, for example, *Abbreviation*, ed. Burnett et al. (1994), I:83, 24–25; *Introduction*, ed. Burnett et al. (2004), I:15, 24–25, line 65. By contrast, Abraham Ibn Ezra coined and used throughout his oeuvre קלון "shame" to denote the astrological concept of dejection, and never "falling" or a term derived from "falling." Thus, the use of *domus lapsa* here betrays an Arabic Vorlage for the current section of *Tractatus particulares*.

[2]**1–2: You also need … as I shall indicate.** The current passage, about determining the position and condition of the lord of the ascendant at the time of the interrogation, translates and at times paraphrases a passage from *She'elot le-Talmai* (quoted in App. 8, *She'elot le-Talmai,* § 1:1–2, 505–506) and is an alternative Latin rendering of a passage from Ptolemy's *Iudicia* (quoted in App. 8, Ptolemy's *Iudicia,* § 1:1–2, 507–508).

[3]**3–14: If it [the lord of the ascendant] … about beasts.** The present passage, relating the querent's thoughts to the indications of the horoscopic place in which the lord of the ascendant is located, translates and at times paraphrases a passage from *She'elot le-Talmai* (quoted in App. 8, *She'elot le-Talmai,* § 1:3–14, 506–507), and is an alternative Latin rendering of a passage from Ptolemy's *Iudicia* (quoted in App. 8, Ptolemy's *Iudicia,* § 1:3–14, 507–508).

⟨I i 2⟩

[1]**1: In ⟨its⟩ dejection, Latin: *cadens*.** This translation of *cadens* follows from the fact that *She'elot le-Talmai* (App. 8, *She'elot le-Talmai,* § 2:1, 506–507) renders the current locus as בית נפילתו "house of its falling," and that Ptolemy's *Iudicia* (App. 8, Ptolemy's *Iudicia,* § 2:1, 507–508) renders the current locus as *in deiectione,* "in dejection." The same applies to the use of *cadens* with respect to the Moon a few words later. In this case, *She'elot le-Talmai* (App. 8, *She'elot le-Talmai,* § 2:1, 506–507) has בית נפילתה "house of its falling"; Ptolemy's *Iudicia* (App. 8, Ptolemy's *Iudicia,* § 2:1, 507–508) has *in deiectione,* "in dejection." For this use, see also note to *Tp,* I i 1:4. For the concept of dejection, see note to *Int,* II i 6:3.

[2]**1–4: If the lord of the ascendant … proceed as follows.** The present passage, showing when the Moon is to be taken instead of the lord of the ascendant, translates and at times paraphrases a passage from *She'elot le-Talmai* (quoted in App. 8, *She'elot le-Talmai,* § 2:1, 506–507), and is an alternative Latin rendering of a passage from Ptolemy's *Iudicia* (quoted in App. 8, Ptolemy's *Iudicia,* § 2:1, 507–508).

⟨I i 3⟩

[1]**1–4: Observe how many degrees … division of the places.** This passage, using the position of the lord of the ascendant and applying the power of the dodecatemoria (see note to *Tp,* I i 7:3), translates and at times para-

phrases a passage from Ptolemy's *Iudicia* (quoted in App. 8, Ptolemy's *Iudicia*, § 3:1–4, 507–509). Note that there is no counterpart to this passage in *She'elot le-Talmai,* which demonstrates that the author of the Hebrew Vorlage of *Tractatus particulares* used a version of *She'elot le-Talmai* that is more complete, closer to the Arabic Vorlage, and in all likelihood earlier, than the version extant today.

⟨I i 4⟩

[1]**3: Ninth part**. For this concept, see note on *Int,* II xii 2:2.

[2]**1–3: Abraham also says ... ascendant degree**. This passage is an alternative Latin translation of the Hebrew text of an entire section of the lost *She'elot* III, also translated in *Int,* II xii 2:1–2.

[3]**4: Lot of Fortune, Latin: *pars fortune***. The Latin expression used here and elsewhere in *Tractatus particulares* to denote the lot of Fortune translates of גורל הטוב, commonly used by Ibn Ezra in his astrological corpus. By contrast, *Interrogationes* uses *pars gratie,* a translation of מנת החן, used in Ibn Ezra's *Mishpeṭei ha-mazzalot* and *Tequfah*. For the concept of lot of Fortune, see note on *Int,* II i 9:1.

[4]**4: Others said ... lot of Fortune**. This passage is an alternative Latin translation of the Hebrew text of an entire section of the lost *She'elot* III, also translated in *Int,* II xii 2:3. See note there.

[5]**5: Some said ... lord of the day**. This passage is an alternative Latin translation of the Hebrew text of an entire section of the lost *She'elot* III, also translated in *Int,* II xii 2:4. See note there.

[6]**5: Lord of the day**. See note on *Tp,* I:3, s.v. "lord of the hour."

[7]**6: Zodiac**. The planets do not wander all over the celestial sphere but are confined to a narrow strip, inclined with respect to the celestial equator, that divides the celestial sphere in half. This is the zodiac; the fixed stars in it are traditionally divided into the 12 constellations of the zodiac. Like the planets, the Sun moves around the zodiac, making one complete circuit each year. The ecliptic is the apparent path that the Sun follows through the sky over the course of the year. Planets seen in the sky are always near the

ecliptic, which means that their orbits are never far from the plane of the ecliptic. In this regard, the significance of the ecliptic lies in that it traverses the zodiac and serves to measure the planets' latitudes.

[8]**6: It is closer to the truth ... as written in the *Book Tamedas*.** This passage is an alternative Latin translation of the Hebrew text of an entire section of the lost *She'elot* III, also translated in *Int*, II xii 2:5. See note there for the identity of the *Book Tamedas*.

[9]**7: Forms an aspect.** The aspects (Hebrew מבטים, Arabic مناظرات) are four astrologically significant angular relationships (180°, 90°, 120°, and 60°) between planets, zodiacal signs, and other celestial objects. The aspect of trine (120°) is considered to be harmonious or fortunate; sextile (60°) is also harmonious or fortunate, but to a lesser extent; opposition (180°) is disharmonious or unfortunate; and quartile (90°) is also disharmonious or unfortunate, but to a lesser extent.

[10]**6–10: It is closer to the truth ... noble book.** This passage is an alternative Latin translation of the Hebrew text of an entire section of the lost *She'elot* III, also translated in *Int*, II xii 2:5–9. See notes there.

⟨I i 5⟩

[1]**1–4: Māshā'allāh says ... according to it.** This passage begins what is generally a *verbatim* translation, but at times a paraphrase, expansion, or summary, of a section of *She'elot le-Māshā'allāh* that offers an account of the three significators of the querent's thoughts. In particular, the current passage, by mentioning his name, substantiates first that Māshā'allāh is the ultimate author of the whole section, and then offers an account of the first of the three significators. For the Hebrew source text in *She'elot le-Māshā'allāh* behind the current passage, accompanied by an English translation and the alternative Latin translation in *Liber interpretationum*, see App. 7, P. 1, 1–4, 498.

⟨I i 6⟩

[1]**1–2: The second is that you ... other places.** This passage, offering an account of the second of the three significators of the querent's thoughts, is a paraphrase of a passage in *She'elot le-Māshā'allāh*. For the Hebrew

source text, accompanied by an English translation and the alternative Latin translation in *Liber interpretationum*, see App. 7, P. 2, 1–2, 499. Note that the current passage omits Dorotheus, Ptolemy, and Vetius Valens, who are mentioned in *She'elot le-Māshā'allāh* and *Liber interpretationum* as the originators of the account of the second significator, as well as the lot of Fortune, which plays an important role in the account of the second significator in *She'elot le-Māshā'allāh* and *Liber interpretationum*.

⟨I i 7⟩

[1]**1: The *mubtazz*; Latin *almutaz*.** This term, a transliteration of the Arabic المبتزّ, refers to the strongest planet in a horoscopic chart, usually the one that has most dignities (house, exaltation, triplicity, term and decan) in the ascendant. Ibn Ezra never transliterates *al-mubtazz* in his Hebrew oeuvre. Pietro d'Abano and Arnoul de Quincampoix, however, used this Arabic transliteration here in their Latin translations. See *Tp*, I i 7:1 (Latin text), p. 278, n. 3, 4. We do not have the reading for this locus in Māshā'allāh's Arabic original *Book of Interrogations*, but the Hebrew translation in *She'elot le-Māshā'allāh* reads simply בעל, which is the commonplace term for "lord" in Hebrew medieval astrological literature; the Latin counterpart in *Liber interpretationum* has *dominus dignitatis*, "lord of the dignity," which denotes the planet that has the most dignities and contrasts with *dominus* tout court, the common term for "lord" in Latin medieval astrological literature. See App. 7, P. 3, 1, 499–500. This suggests that here Pietro d'Abano and Arnoul de Quincampoix preferred the common Latin term to a literal rendering of what they found in the French intermediary from which they carried out their translations.

[2]**1: Lord of the term, Latin: *dominus termini*.** The "terms" (גבולים; Arabic حدود) are unequal divisions of the signs; a planet, except for the Sun and the Moon, is associated with each of them as lord of the term. Several systems of lords of the terms in the signs were developed in Antiquity (assigned to the Chaldeans, the Indians, Asṭarāṭūs, and others), but those ascribed to the Egyptians and to Ptolemy were the most common, notably because Ptolemy himself provided a detailed list of them in *Tetrabiblos* (ed. Robbins (1980), I:20–22, 97–107). See *Reshit ḥokhmah* § 2.1:43, 62–63, which mentions the terms ascribed to both the Egyptians and Ptolemy, and *Mishpeṭei ha-mazzalot* § 8:1, 495–496, which has a list of the terms ascribed to the Egyptians, but without acknowledging the source.

[3]**1: ⟨Lord⟩ of the decan, Latin: ⟨*dominus*⟩ *faciei*.** The decan (Hebrew פנים; Arabic وجه) is traditionally the fifth of the planets' five essential dignities. Each of the twelve zodiacal signs is divided into three equal divisions, called decans; each decan covers 10° and is assigned to a planet that functions as its lord.

[4]**3: Power of the dodecatemoria.** The dodecatemoria are divisions of the signs into twelve segments, by one of two methods. The first method divides any sign into twelve equal parts of 2.5° each; the first dodecatemorion is assigned to the whole sign, and the lord of this sign is the lord of the dodecatemorion; the subsequent dodecatemoria are assigned to the following signs, and the lords of these signs are the lords of the corresponding dodecatemoria. The second method, usually ascribed to Enoch (or Hermes), assigns the successive degrees of a certain sign to the 12 signs, in sequence; the lords of these signs, beginning with the ascendant sign, are the lords of these degrees or dodecatemoria. For these two methods, see Abū Maʿshar's *Great Introduction*, ed. Burnett and Yamamoto (2019), V:18 [1–4], 520–523, where the first method is ascribed to the Ancient astrologers and the second method to Hermes. The same two methods are presented in *Ṭeʿamim* I (§ 2.11:1–3, 50–51) although in the opposite order and without mention of their originators. As a rule, introductions to astrology present only the first method of allocation. See *Ṭeʿamim* II, § 2.9:7–8, 202–203; *Liber Aristotilis*, ed. Burnett and Pingree (1997), II 14, 26–27; *Elements*, ed. Ramsay Wright (1934), § 456, 267–269; *Introduction*, ed. Burnett et al. (2004), IV:15, 129; *Abbreviation*, ed. Burnett et al. (1994), IV:32, 59; *Epitome*, ed. Heller (1548), I:9, G4v–H1r.

[5]**1–3: The third … the dodecatemoria.** This passage, offering an account of the third of the three significators of the querent's thoughts, is a *verbatim* translation of a passage in *She'elot le-Māshā'allāh*. For the Hebrew source text of this passage, accompanied by an English translation and the alternative Latin translation in *Liber interpretationum*, see App. 7, P. 3, 1–3, 499–500. Like its Hebrew and Latin counterparts, the current passage mentions the Indians as the originators of the account of the third significator and the preponderant role of the dodecatemoria.

⟨I i 8⟩

[1]**1: We assign one sign to each interval of 2½°**. That here 2½° are assigned to any sign makes it clear that the example in *Tp*, I i 8:1–2 bears on the first of the two methods used to determine the lord of the dodecatemoria. For this method, see note on *Tp*, I i 7:3.

[2]**2: Found it in the seventh place … sick son**. The rationale behind the current statement is that the seventh horoscopic place indicates women and the sixth indicates diseases. See *Reshit ḥokhmah* § 3.10:1, § 3.11:1, 144–145.

[3]**1–2: Example … sick son**. This passage, offering an example of how to use the dodecatemoria to determine the querent's thoughts, is a *verbatim* translation of a passage in *She'elot le-Māshā'allāh*. For the Hebrew source text of this passage, accompanied by an English translation and the alternative Latin rendering in *Liber interpretationum*, see App. 7, P. 4, 1–2, 500.

⟨I ii 1⟩

[1]**1–3: If someone asks … or a thread**. This corresponds closely to three parallel texts found in the *Alchandreana*: (1) *Epistola Argafalau*, 2:3–5, in *Alchandreana*, ed. Juste (2007), 474 (quoted in App. 13, I: The Sun, 531–532); (2) *Proportiones*, 17:5–7, ibid., 525–526; (3) *Benedictum*, 7:1–3, ibid. 614.

⟨I ii 2⟩

[1]**1–3: At the beginning of Venus's hour … from the earth**. This corresponds closely to three parallel texts found in the *Alchandreana*: (1) *Epistola Argafalau*, 2:6–8, in *Alchandreana*, ed. Juste (2007), 474–475 (quoted in App. 13, II: Venus, 532); (2) *Proportiones*, 17:8–10, ibid. 526; (3) *Benedictum*, 7:4–6, ibid., 614–615.

⟨I ii 3⟩

[1]**1–3: At the beginning of Mercury's hourm … precious stone**. This corresponds closely to three parallel texts found in the *Alchandreana*: (1) *Epistola Argafalau*, 2:9–11, in *Alchandreana*, ed. Juste (2007), 475 (quoted in App. 13,

III: Mercury, 532); (2) *Proportiones*, 17:11–13, bid., 526; (3) *Benedictum*, 7:7–9, ibid. 615.

⟨I ii 4⟩

[1]**1–3: At the beginning of the Moon's hour … red plant.** This corresponds closely to three parallel textsfound in the *Alchandreana*: (1) *Epistola Argafalau*, 2:12–14, in *Alchandreana*, ed. Juste (2007), 475 (quoted in App. 13, IV: The Moon, 532–533); (2) *Proportiones*, 17:14–16, ibid. 526; (3) *Benedictum*, 7:10–12, ibid. 615–616.

⟨I ii 5⟩

[1]**1–3: At the beginning ⟨of Saturn's hour⟩ … spots are multicolored.** This corresponds closely to three parallel texts found in the *Alchandreana*: (1) *Epistola Argafalau*, 2:15–17, in *Alchandreana*, ed. Juste (2007), 475 (quoted in App. 13, V: Saturn, 533); (2) *Proportiones*, 17:17–19, ibid., 526–527; (3) *Benedictum*, 7:13–15, ibid. 616.

⟨I ii 6⟩

[1]**1–3: At the beginning ⟨of Jupiter's hour⟩ … or leather.** This corresponds closely to three parallel texts found in the *Alchandreana*: (1) *Epistola Argafalau*, 2:18–20, in *Alchandreana*, ed. Juste (2007), 475–476 (quoted in App. 13, VI: Jupiter, 533); (2) *Proportiones*, 17:20–22, ibid. 527; (3) *Benedictum*, 7:16–18, ibid. 616.

⟨I ii 7⟩

[1]**1–3: At the beginning ⟨of Mars's hour⟩ … dry or wood.** This corresponds closely to three parallel texts found in the *Alchandreana*: (1) *Epistola Argafalau*, 2:21–23, in *Alchandreana*, ed. Juste (2007), 476 (quoted in App. 13, VII: Mars, 533–534); (2) *Proportiones*, 17:23–25, ibid. 527; (3) *Benedictum*, 7:19–21, ibid. 616–617.

⟨I ii 8⟩

[1]**1–3: Abraham says … planet in the ascendant.** This passage is an alternative Latin translation of the Hebrew text of an entire section of the lost *She'elot* III, also translated in *Int*, II xii 3:1. See note to *Int*, II xii 2:5 for the identity of the *Liber Tamedas* referred to in the current passage.

⟨I ii 9⟩

[1]**1: Lord of the hour.** For this concept, see note on *Tp*, I:3.

[2]**1: The lord of the hour … white but not bright.** This corresponds to *She'elot* I, § 4.10:5, 262–263 (quoted in App. 4, P. 22, Q. 1, 461) and *De nativitatibus*, II i 6:7, 276–277 (quoted in App. 4, P. 22, Q. 2, 461). *Int*, II xii 4:1 offers an alternative Latin translation of the current passage.

⟨I ii 10⟩

[1]**1: Lord of the term.** For this concept see note to *Tp*, I i 7:1.

[2]**1: They also said … location of the Moon.** This passage is an alternative Latin translation of the Hebrew text of an entire section of the lost *She'elot* III, also translated in *Int*, II xii 5:1–2.

⟨I iii 1⟩

[1]**3: Fixed sign, Latin: *signum veridicum*.** This translates נאמן, "enduring sign," to denote one of the fixed signs (Taurus, Leo, Scorpio, Aquarius). Note that *Tractatus particulares* I iv 3:4 and IV 6:4 use *signa fixa* in the same sense. This terminology links *Tractatus particulares* with *Mishpeṭei ha-mazzalot* and *Interrogationes*. See note on *Int*, II i 1:3.

[2]**1–6: The astrologers said … according to them.** This passage is an alternative Latin translation of the Hebrew text of an entire section of the lost *She'elot* III, also translated in *Int*, II xii 6:1–6.

⟨I iii 2⟩

[1]**1–6: These are Māshā'allāh's statements ... south than to the east.** This is the start of a section composed of three passages, each of which presents a method for finding a hidden object. This section is a *verbatim* translation of three discontinuous passages taken from the Hebrew text of *She'elot le-Māshā'allāh*. This is corroborated by the mention of Māshā'allāh's name in the first sentence of this section (*Tp*, I iii 2:1). In particular, the current passage, on the first method, translates the account of the same method in *She'elot le-Māshā'allāh*. For the Hebrew text in *She'elot le-Māshā'allāh* behind the current passage, accompanied by an English translation and the alternative Latin version in *Liber interpretationum*, see App. 7, P. 5, 1–6, 500–501.

⟨I iii 3⟩

[1]**1–7: Another method ... hidden thing.** This passage, an account of the second method for finding a hidden object, translates the account of the corresponding method in *She'elot le-Māshā'allāh*. For the Hebrew text in *She'elot le-Māshā'allāh* behind the current passage, accompanied by an English translation and the alternative Latin version in *Liber interpretationum*, see App. 7, P. 6, 1–7, 502–503.

⟨I iii 4⟩

[1]**1: Ptolemy.** See note on *El*, II vi 6:4.

[2]**1–10: (1) ⟨These are⟩ Ptolemy's statements ... it is really there.** The current passage, on the third method for finding a hidden object, translates the account of the corresponding method in *She'elot le-Māshā'allāh*. For the Hebrew text in *She'elot le-Māshā'allāh* behind the current passage, accompanied by an English translation and the alternative Latin version in *Liber interpretationum*, see App. 7, P. 7, 1–10, 503–504. Note that Ptolemy, to whom *Tp* assigns the third method, is not mentioned in the corresponding passages of *She'elot le-Māshā'allāh* or *Liber interpretationum*.

[3]**11: As is known ... lord of the hour.** This passage repeats the contents of *Tp*, I ii 9:1 and *Int*, II xii 4:1. See notes there.

⟨I iv 1⟩

[1]2: **Gives power, Latin: *dederit vim*.** A special feature of *Tractatus particulares* is that it always uses the expression *dare vim* to refer to this planetary condition. *Interrogationes* and *Electiones*, though, always use *dare fortitudinem*. This planetary condition is described in *Reshit ḥokhmah* § 7.13:1, 204–205 (quoted in App. 5, Q. 48, 480–481) and *Mishpeṭei ha-mazzalot* § 47:2–9, 532–535.

[2]1–10: **They said ... will be found dead.** This passage is an alternative Latin translation of the Hebrew text of an entire section of the lost *She'elot* III, also translated in II xii 7:1–10.

⟨I iv 2⟩

[1]3: **Received.** The planetary condition of "reception" is explained in *Reshit ḥokhmah* § 7.29:1–5, 208–209 (quoted in App. 5, Q. 49, 481), which translates Abū Maʿshar's *Great Introduction*, ed. Burnett and Yamamoto (2019), VII:5, [30], 784–785, about the condition of قبول, "reception." "Reception" is also explained in *Mishpeṭei ha-mazzalot* § 47:2–9, 532–535. Explanations of "reception" occur in other Arabic introductions to astrology prior to the twelfth century: Abū Maʿshar's *Abbreviation* (III:52–54, 50–51); Sahl's *Nawādir al-qaḍā* (New Haven, Yale University Library, MS Arabic 532, fols. 28b–30a); al-Qabīṣī's *Introduction* (III:19, 98–99); and al-Bīrūnī's *Kitāb al-Tafḥīm* (*Elements*, ed. Ramsay Wright (1934), § 507, 312–313).

[2]1–4: **Pay attention further ... frightened people.** This passage is an alternative Latin translation of the Hebrew text of an entire section of the lost *She'elot* III, also translated in *Int*, II xii 8:1–4.

⟨I iv 3⟩

[1]1–4: **This is a general rule ... configuration with the Sun.** This passage is an alternative Latin translation of the Hebrew text of an entire section of the lost *She'elot* III, also translated in *Int*, II xii 9:1–4.

[2]4: **As said in the *Book of conjunctions*.** This reference to the *Book of conjunctions* is omitted from *Int*, II xii 9:1–4, the alternative Latin counterpart of *Tp*, I iv 3:1–4. Hence this reference is probably a remnant from the lost

version of *She'elot* III that survives only in *Tractatus particulares*. *Book of Conjunctions* translates ספר המחברות, one of the names Ibn Ezra assigns to his *Sefer ha-'Olam, Book of the world*, dealing with general astrology. See *Ṭe'amim* I, § 2.4:5, 42–43. Three versions of Ibn Ezra's *Sefer ha-'Olam* survive, but I could not found the counterpart of the subject matter of the current reference in any of them.

⟨I iv 4⟩

[1]**1–5: What he said is all true ... cusp of the ascendant.** This passage is an alternative Latin translation of the Hebrew text of an entire section of the lost *She'elot* III, also translated in *Int*, II xii 10:1–5.

⟨I iv 5⟩

[1]**1–2: Abraham says ... great principle.** This passage is an alternative Latin translation of the Hebrew text of a passage of the lost *She'elot* III, also translated in *Int*, II xii 11:1–2. The current passage includes a quotation from the first aphorism of Pseudo-Ptolemy's *Centiloquium* (quoted in App. 2, Q. 7, 401).

⟨II⟩

[1]**8: Great, least and middle years.** These are three types of years that astrologers ascribe to each of the planets and that are applied mainly as part of the doctrine of nativities to predict the native's lifespan. Put briefly: starting from some specific natal chart, the astrologer first establishes the "five places of dominion" (see note to *Int*, II i 15:1) and the corresponding "ruler of the places of dominion," meaning the planet that exerts lordship over all these five places or over most of them; then the native's lifespan is considered to be equivalent to the years of the corresponding "ruler of the places of dominion," with the relevant type of years (least, middle, or great) determined by a series of additional factors. According to al-Bīrūnī (*Elements*, ed. Ramsay Wright (1934), § 394, 239), "astrologers of the present day use only the three former degrees [i.e., least, middle, and great years] for determining the length of life at a nativity, and the numbers which they thus elicit must not be interpreted literally as years, but freely, for sometimes they represent years, but sometimes months, weeks, days, or

hours." According to introductions to astrology, such as Ibn Ezra's *Reshit ḥokhmah* and *Mishpeṭei ha-mazzalot*, the least, middle, and great years of the planets are as follows: Saturn: 30, 43½, 57; Jupiter: 12, 45½, 79, Mars: 15, 40½, 66; the Sun: 19, 39½, 120; Venus: 8, 45, 82; Mercury: 20, 48, 76; the Moon: 25, 39½, 108. For Saturn, see *Reshit ḥokhmah* § 4.1:35, 154–155; *Mishpeṭei ha-mazzalot* § 40:13, 524–525.

⟨II i 1⟩

[1]**1–5: The lot of the Sun ... lot of Fortune.** This passage, an account of the lot of the Sun that makes it identical with the lot of Fortune, is a translation of *Mishpeṭei ha-mazzalot* § 51:2, 538–539 (quoted in App. 10, I: The Sun, 2, 517–518)

⟨II i 2⟩

[1]**1: Revolution of the world⟨-year,⟩ Latin: *revolutio mundi*.** This translates תקופת שנת העולם "revolution of the world-year," an expression used in *Mishpeṭei ha-mazzalot* § 38:7, 522–523. The same Hebrew expression also occurs in *Neḥoshet* II, 194v; an alternative Latin translation is found in *El*, II vii 6:5. The term refers to a special type of horoscope, cast each year when the Sun enters Aries, in order to forecast world affairs during the coming year. This concept is frequently applied in *ʿOlam* I and *ʿOlam* II with the alternative name תקופת השנה "revolution of the year." See Sela 2010, s.v. "revolution of the year," 342–343. Elsewhere Ibn Ezra employs the alternative expression תקופת העולם "revolution of the world" (*Ṭeʿamim* I, § 2.11:3, 50–51; *Moladot*, I 5, 1; 2, 86–87). The time for casting these horoscope—every year when the Sun enters Aries—evokes the creation of the world. According to Indian cosmological theories, which Ibn Ezra recounts in some of his scientific works, the world undergoes long and recurrent cycles of creation and destruction; creation occurs when all the planets meet in conjunction in the head of Aries. See *Ibn al-Muthannā's Commentary on the Astronomical Tables of al-Khwārizmī*, translated by Ibn Ezra into Hebrew (ed. Goldstein (1967), 152, 299; quoted in App. 5, Q. 50, 481) and *De rationibus tabularum* (ed. Millás Vallicrosa (1947), 88).

[2]**1: It signifies kings at the revolution of the world⟨-year⟩.** This translates a passage from *Mishpeṭei ha-mazzalot* § 38:7, 522–523 (quoted in App. 10, I: The Sun, 7, 517–518).

[3]**1: The father for one born by day; pride, authority, and reputation.** This translates a passage from *Mishpeṭei ha-mazzalot* § 38:6, 520–521 (quoted in App. 10, I: The Sun, 6, 517–518).

[4]**2–3: The ruler over the lordship ... her husband.** This translates *Mishpeṭei ha-mazzalot* § 38:14–15, 522–523 (quoted in App. 10, I: The Sun, 14–15, 517–518).

⟨II i 3⟩

[1]**1: He [i.e., one born under the Sun's power] ... busy with metals.** This passage has no counterpart in the section on the Sun in the print edition of *Mishpeṭei ha-mazzalot*. It may be an addition by the author of the Hebrew Vorlage of *Tractatus particulares* or taken from a lost manuscript of *Mishpeṭei ha-mazzalot*.

⟨II i 4⟩

[1]**1: Of handsome shape ... upright posture.** This translates *Mishpeṭei ha-mazzalot* § 38:8, 522–523 (quoted in App. 10, I: The Sun, 8, 517–518).

[2]**1: Round and thick beard, joined eyebrows.** This passage has no counterpart in the section on the Sun in the print edition of *Mishpeṭei ha-mazzalot*. It may be an addition by the author of the Hebrew Vorlage of *Tractatus particulares* or taken from a lost manuscript of *Mishpeṭei ha-mazzalot*.

⟨II i 5⟩

[1]**1: In its [i.e., the Sun's] portion ... the ⟨Sun's⟩ portion.** This translates a passage from *Mishpeṭei ha-mazzalot* § 38:6, 520–521 (quoted in App. 10, I: The Sun, 6, 517–518).

[2]**2: Of the colors, intense white.** This translates a passage from *Mishpeṭei ha-mazzalot* § 38:7, 520–521 (quoted in App. 10, I: The Sun, 7, 517–518).

⟨II i 6⟩

[1]**1: It serves those born ... their 49th year.** This translates *Mishpeṭei ha-mazzalot* § 38:10, 520–521 (quoted in App. 10, I: The Sun, 10, 517–518).

[2]**2: In its portion is the rulership ... [i.e., between sundown on Wednesday and sunrise on Thursday]**. This translates *Mishpeṭei ha-mazzalot* § 38:9, 520–521 (quoted in App. 10, I: The Sun, 9, 517–518).

[3]**3: Ptolemy says that it rules over all ... 41st year**. This translates *Mishpeṭei ha-mazzalot* § 38:11, 520–521 (quoted in App. 10, I: The Sun, 11, 517–518), which includes the mention of Ptolemy as the originator.

⟨II i 7⟩

[1]**1: Its least years are 19 ... ⟨years⟩ are 120**. This translates *Mishpeṭei ha-mazzalot* § 38:12, 520–521 (quoted in App. 10, I: The Sun, 12, 517–518).

⟨II i 8⟩

[1]**1–3: His disease is hot ... face or a burn**. This whole passage has no counterpart in the section on the Sun in the print edition of *Mishpeṭei ha-mazzalot*. It may be an addition by the author of the Hebrew Vorlage of *Tractatus particulares* or taken from a lost manuscript of *Mishpeṭei ha-mazzalot*.

⟨II i 9⟩

[1]**1: The house is in its portion**. This passage has no counterpart in the section on the Sun in the print edition of *Mishpeṭei ha-mazzalot*. It may be an addition by the author of the Hebrew Vorlage of *Tractatus particulares* or taken from a lost manuscript of *Mishpeṭei ha-mazzalot*.

⟨II i 10⟩

[1]**1: Horses are in its ⟨portion⟩**. This translates a passage from *Mishpeṭei ha-mazzalot* § 38:7, 520–521 (quoted in App. 10, I: The Sun, 7, 517–518).

⟨II i 11⟩

[1]**1: Of plants, large trees bearing fruit and grapes are in its ⟨portion⟩**. This translates a passage from *Mishpeṭei ha-mazzalot* § 38:7, 520–521 (quoted in App. 10, I: The Sun, 7, 517–518).

⟨II i 12⟩

[1]**1: Of metals, gold ⟨is in its portion⟩.** This translates a passage from *Mishpeṭei ha-mazzalot* § 38:7, 520–521 (quoted in App. 10, I: The Sun, 7, 517–518).

⟨II i 13⟩

[1]**1: Its power is on the eastern side.** This translates a passage from *Mishpeṭei ha-mazzalot* § 38:7, 520–521 (quoted in App. 10, I: The Sun, 7, 517–518).

⟨II ii 1⟩

[1]**1–3: The lot of the Moon ... fear God.** This translates *Mishpeṭei ha-mazzalot* § 51:3, 538–539 (quoted in App. 10, II: The Moon, 1, 518–519).

[2]**4: It indicates everything that a man begins doing.** This translates a passage from *Mishpeṭei ha-mazzalot* § 39:3, 522–523 (quoted in App. 10, II: The Moon, 3, 518–519).

⟨II ii 2⟩

[1]**1: It signifies the native's mother, sister, and wife, and ⟪common people⟫.** This translates a passage from *Mishpeṭei ha-mazzalot* § 39:9, 524–525 (quoted in App. 10, II: The Moon, 9, 519). The last words of the present passage, though, do not occur in the section on the Moon in the print edition of *Mishpeṭei ha-mazzalot*

⟨II ii 3⟩

[1]**1: His craft will be to sail ... accounts and news.** This passage has no counterpart in the section on the Moon in the print edition of *Mishpeṭei ha-mazzalot.* It may be an addition by the author of the Hebrew Vorlage of *Tractatus particulares* or taken from a lost manuscript of *Mishpeṭei ha-mazzalot.*

⟨II ii 4⟩

[1]**1: As for his shape ... moves quickly.** This translates *Mishpeṭei ha-mazzalot* § 39:5, 522–523 (quoted in App. 10, II: The Moon, 5, 518–519).

[2]**2: A small man ... face is greenish.** This passage has no counterpart in the section on the Moon in the print edition of *Mishpeṭei ha-mazzalot.* It may be an addition by the author of the Hebrew Vorlage of *Tractatus particulares* or taken from a lost manuscript of *Mishpeṭei ha-mazzalot.*

⟨II ii 5⟩

[1]**1: In its portion is the brain ... one by night.** This translates *Mishpeṭei ha-mazzalot* § 39:2, 522–523 (quoted in App. 10, II: The Moon, 2, 518–519).

⟨II ii 6⟩

[1]**1: ⟨The Moon⟩ signifies the 4 years of weaning.** This translates a passage from *Mishpeṭei ha-mazzalot* § 39:3, 522–523 (quoted in App. 10, II: The Moon, 3, 518–519).

[2]**1: 9 years for those born ... 40th year ⟨for those born⟩ by day.** This translates *Mishpeṭei ha-mazzalot* § 39:7, 524–525 (quoted in App. 10, II: The Moon, 7, 519).

[3]**2: It has rulership over the day of the Moon ... [i.e., between sundown on Thursday and sunrise on Friday].** This translates *Mishpeṭei ha-mazzalot* § 39:6, 522–525 (quoted in App. 10, II: The Moon, 6, 519).

⟨II ii 7⟩

[1]**1: Its least years are 25 ... great ⟨years⟩ 108.** This translates *Mishpeṭei ha-mazzalot* § 39:8, 524–525 (quoted in App. 10, II: The Moon, 8, 519).

⟨II ii 8⟩

[1]**1: In its portion are the critical days ... diseases in the face.** This passage has no counterpart in the section on the Moon in the print edition of

Mishpeṭei ha-mazzalot. It may be an addition by the author of the Hebrew Vorlage of *Tractatus particulares* or taken from a lost manuscript of *Mishpeṭei ha-mazzalot*.

⟨II ii 9⟩

[1]**1: The door of houses is in its portion, and gates.** This translates a passage from *Mishpeṭei ha-mazzalot* § 39:9, 524–525 (quoted in App. 10, II: The Moon, 9, 519).

⟨II ii 10⟩

[1]**1: ⟨It is in charge⟩ of the animals … aquatic animals.** This translates a passage from *Mishpeṭei ha-mazzalot* § 39:4, 522–523 (quoted in App. 10, II: The Moon, 4, 518–519). The last words of the present passage, however, have no counterpart in the section on the Moon in the print edition of *Mishpeṭei ha-mazzalot*.

⟨II ii 11⟩

[1]**1: Its power is in all the plants … near the Mediterranean.** This translates a passage from *Mishpeṭei ha-mazzalot* § 39:2, 522–523 (quoted in App. 10, II: The Moon, 2, 518–519).

[2]**1: Small trees are in its portion.** This translates a passage from *Mishpeṭei ha-mazzalot* § 39:4, 522–523 (quoted in App. 10, II: The Moon, 4, 518–519).

⟨II ii 12⟩

[1]**1: Of metals, silver for ⟨⟨noblewomen⟩⟩.** This translates a passage from *Mishpeṭei ha-mazzalot* § 39:4, 522–523 (quoted in App. 10, II: The Moon, 4, 518–519). The last words of the present passage, however, have no counterpart in the section on the Moon in the print edition of *Mishpeṭei ha-mazzalot*.

⟨II ii 13⟩

[1]**1: It exerts power in the western side.** This translates a passage from *Mishpeṭei ha-mazzalot* § 39:4, 522–523 (quoted in App. 10, II: The Moon, 4, 518–519).

[2]**2: It has a share with the Sun in the life of man.** This passage has no counterpart in the section on the Moon in the print edition of *Mishpeṭei ha-mazzalot*.

[3]**3: The ruler over the lordship ... during his life.** This translates *Mishpeṭei ha-mazzalot* § 39:10, 524–525 (quoted in App. 10, II: The Moon, 10, 519).

⟨II iii 1⟩

[1]**1–3: The lot of Saturn ... that aspect it.** This translates *Mishpeṭei ha-mazzalot* § 52:1, 540–541 (quoted in App. 10, III: Saturn, 15, 520).

[2]**4: All the planets ... uppermost ⟨planet⟩.** This paraphrases *Mishpeṭei ha-mazzalot* § 40:1, 524–524 (quoted in App. 10, III: Saturn, 1, 519–520).

[3]**5: It is the planet of knowledge ... fear, and palsy.** This translates *Mishpeṭei ha-mazzalot* § 40:4, 524–524 (quoted in App. 10, III: Saturn, 4, 519–520).

⟨II iii 2⟩

[1]**1: In its portion are the Jews, black monks, paupers, and the elderly.** The first portion of this passage ("In its portion are the Jews, black monks") has no counterpart in the section on Saturn in the print edition of *Mishpeṭei ha-mazzalot*. But the concluding words ("paupers, and the elderly") translate a passage from *Mishpeṭei ha-mazzalot* § 40:6, 524–524 (quoted in App. 10, III: Saturn, 6, 519–520).

⟨II iii 3⟩

[1]**1: ⟨In its portion is⟩ the craftsman ... wicked spirit.** This translates a passage from *Mishpeṭei ha-mazzalot* § 40:6, 524–524 (quoted in App. 10, III: Saturn, 6, 519–520).

[2]**1: Knowing deep things … plowing the earth.** The current passage has no counterpart in the section on Saturn in the print edition of *Mishpeṭei ha-mazzalot*.

⟨II iii 4⟩

[1]**1: It signifies a swarthy man … broad forehead.** This translates a passage from *Mishpeṭei ha-mazzalot* § 40:8, 524–524 (quoted in App. 10, III: Saturn, 8, 519–520).

[2]**2: Youthful, virile … loves birds.** This whole passage has no counterpart in the section on Saturn in the print edition of *Mishpeṭei ha-mazzalot*. It may be an addition by the author of the Hebrew Vorlage of *Tractatus particulares* or taken from a lost manuscript of *Mishpeṭei ha-mazzalot*.

⟨II iii 5⟩

[1]**1: In its portion is the spleen … right ear.** This translates *Mishpeṭei ha-mazzalot* § 40:5, 524–524 (quoted in App. 10, III: Saturn, 5, 519–520).

⟨II iii 6⟩

[1]**1–2: It serves those born … in old age.** This translates *Mishpeṭei ha-mazzalot* § 40:11–12, 524–524 (quoted in App. 10, III: Saturn, 11–12, 519–520).

[2]**3: It has rulership over the day of the Shabbat … night of Mercury.** This translates *Mishpeṭei ha-mazzalot* § 40:10, 524–524 (quoted in App. 10, III: Saturn, 10, 519–520).

⟨II iii 7⟩

[1]**1: ⟨Its⟩ least years are 30 … 54 or 57.** This translates *Mishpeṭei ha-mazzalot* § 40:13, 524–524 (quoted in App. 10, III: Saturn, 13, 519–520).

⟨II iii 8⟩

[1]**1: Its diseases are those caused by the black bile.** This translates a passage from *Mishpeṭei ha-mazzalot* § 40:6, 524–524 (quoted in App. 10, III: Saturn, 6, 519–520).

[2]**1: Quartan fever, and dry or cold boils.** This passage has no counterpart in the section on Saturn in the print edition of *Mishpeṭei ha-mazzalot.*

[3]**2: Eccentric circle.** Hipparchus (ca. 190–120 BCE), the Greek astronomer, geographer, and mathematician, introduced the concept of the eccentric circle—a circle whose center is not the Earth but some point slightly offset from it—to explain some anomalies of the motion of the Sun and the Moon.

[4]**2: It is cold and moist ... when at apogee.** This translates a passage from *Mishpeṭei ha-mazzalot* § 40:3, 524–524 (quoted in App. 10, III: Saturn, 3, 519–520).

[5]**3: It signifies a mark on the temple.** This passage has no counterpart in the section on Saturn in the print edition of *Mishpeṭei ha-mazzalot.*

⟨II iii 9⟩

[1]**1: In its portion are dark and filthy places of the house.** This passage has no counterpart in the section on Saturn in the print edition of *Mishpeṭei ha-mazzalot.*

⟨II iii 10⟩

[1]**1: In its portion are donkeys for men to ride on.** This translates a passage from *Mishpeṭei ha-mazzalot* § 40:14, 524–524 (quoted in App. 10, III: Saturn, 14, 519–520).

⟨II iii 11⟩

[1]**1: In its portion ... sour flavor.** This translates passages from *Mishpeṭei ha-mazzalot* § 40:2–3, 524–524 (quoted in App. 10, III: Saturn, 2–3, 519–520).

⟨II iii 12⟩

[1]**1: Of the metals, lead.** This translates a passage from *Mishpeṭei ha-mazzalot* § 40:2, 524–524 (quoted in App. 10, III: Saturn, 2, 519–520).

⟨II iii 13⟩

[1]**1: Its power is in the western side.** This translates a passage from *Mishpeṭei ha-mazzalot* § 40:14, 524–524 (quoted in App. 10, III: Saturn, 14, 519–520).

[2]**2: ⟨⟨It is like the angel of death ... by drowning⟩⟩.** This translates *Mishpeṭei ha-mazzalot* § 40:7, 524–524 (quoted in App. 10, III: Saturn, 7, 519–520).

⟨II iv 1⟩

[1]**1: The lot of Jupiter ... success, and wealth.** This translates *Mishpeṭei ha-mazzalot* § 52:2, 540–541 (quoted in App. 10, IV: Jupiter, 12, 519–520).

[2]**2: Jupiter is larger ... except for the Sun.** This translates *Mishpeṭei ha-mazzalot* § 41:1, 524–524 (quoted in App. 10, IV: Jupiter, 1, 520–521).

[3]**3: It indicates life ... generosity and charity.** This translates a passage from *Mishpeṭei ha-mazzalot* § 41:2, 524–525 (quoted in App. 10, IV: Jupiter, 2, 520–521).

[4]**4: This ⟨planet⟩ ⟨⟨alone⟩⟩ ... ⟨the effect⟩ of Mars.** This translates a passage from *Mishpeṭei ha-mazzalot* § 41:3, 524–527 (quoted in App. 10, IV: Jupiter, 3, 520–521).

[5]**5: The native will be rich in accordance to its power.** This translates a passage from *Mishpeṭei ha-mazzalot* § 41:4, 526–527 (quoted in App. 10, IV: Jupiter, 4, 520–521).

⟨II iv 2⟩

[1]**1: In its portion ... before the community.** This translates a passage from *Mishpeṭei ha-mazzalot* § 41:2, 524–525 (quoted in App. 10, IV: Jupiter, 2, 520–521).

[2]**1: Treasurers.** This translates a passage from *Mishpeṭei ha-mazzalot* § 41:4, 526–527 (ממונים לשמור ממון; quoted in App. 10, IV: Jupiter, 4, 520–521).

[3]**1: Like the bishops of the new religion.** This passage has no counterpart in the section on Jupiter in the print edition of *Mishpeṭei ha-mazzalot*. It may be an addition by the author of the Hebrew Vorlage of *Tractatus particulares* or taken from a lost manuscript of *Mishpeṭei ha-mazzalot*.

⟨II iv 3⟩

[1]**1: In its portion ... [*lit.* one who stitches with a needle].** This entire passage has no counterpart in the section on Jupiter in the print edition of *Mishpeṭei ha-mazzalot*. It may be an addition by the author of the Hebrew Vorlage of *Tractatus particulares* or taken from a lost manuscript of *Mishpeṭei ha-mazzalot*.

⟨II iv 4⟩

[1]**1: It signifies a man ... beautiful garments.** This translates a passage from *Mishpeṭei ha-mazzalot* § 41:9, 526–527 (quoted in App. 10, IV: Jupiter, 9, 520–521).

[2]**1: Two of his top teeth stick out from the others.** This passage has no counterpart in the section on Jupiter in the print edition of *Mishpeṭei ha-mazzalot*.

⟨II iv 5⟩

[1]**1: The left ear ... green eyes.** This translates a passage from *Mishpeṭei ha-mazzalot* § 41:4, 526–527 (quoted in App. 10, IV: Jupiter, 4, 520–521).

⟨II iv 6⟩

[1]**1: It serves those born ... to its ⟨least⟩ years.** This translates a passage from *Mishpeṭei ha-mazzalot* § 41:7–8, 526–527 (quoted in App. 10, IV: Jupiter, 7–8, 520–521).

[2]**2: It has rulership … [i.e., between sundown on Sunday and sunrise on Monday]**. This translates *Mishpeṭei ha-mazzalot* § 41:6, 526–527 (quoted in App. 10, IV: Jupiter, 6, 520–521).

⟨II iv 7⟩

[1]**1: Its least years … ⟨years⟩ 79.** This translates *Mishpeṭei ha-mazzalot* § 41:7, 526–527 (quoted in App. 10, IV: Jupiter, 7, 520–521).

⟨II iv 8⟩

[1]**1: The disease in its portion … demonstrated empirically.** This translates *Mishpeṭei ha-mazzalot* § 41:10, 526–527 (quoted in App. 10, IV: Jupiter, 10, 520–521).

[2]**2: Epicycle.** In the Ptolemaic system of astronomy, the epicycle (Greek: *on the circle*) was a geometric model used to explain the variable velocity and direction of the apparent motion of the planets. In particular, the epicycle explained retrograde motion and the changes in the planets' apparent distances from Earth. In this system, the planets are assumed to move in a small circle, called an epicycle, which in turn moves along a larger circle called a deferent.

[3]**2: Its nature is hot … ⟨in which it is located⟩.** This translates a passage from *Mishpeṭei ha-mazzalot* § 41:3, 524–527 (quoted in App. 10, IV: Jupiter, 3, 520–521).

⟨II iv 9⟩

[1]**1: Its portion ⟨of the house⟩ … praying is prepared.** This translates *Mishpeṭei ha-mazzalot* § 41:11, 526–527 (quoted in App. 10, IV: Jupiter, 11, 521).

⟨II iv 10⟩

[1]**1: Of riding animals … in its portion.** This translates a passage from *Mishpeṭei ha-mazzalot* § 41:2, 524–525 (quoted in App. 10, IV: Jupiter, 2, 520–521).

⟨II iv 11⟩

[1]**1: In its portion are apple ... sweet taste.** This translates a passage from *Mishpeṭei ha-mazzalot* § 41:2, 524–525 (quoted in App. 10, IV: Jupiter, 2, 520–521).

[2]**1: It indicates a bumper crop and strong winds.** This translates a passage from *Mishpeṭei ha-mazzalot* § 41:4, 526–527 (quoted in App. 10, IV: Jupiter, 4, 520–521).

⟨II iv 12⟩

[1]**1: Tin is in its portion.** This translates a passage from *Mishpeṭei ha-mazzalot* § 41:2, 524–525 (quoted in App. 10, IV: Jupiter, 2, 520–521).

⟨II iv 13⟩

[1]**1: Its power is in the west⟨ern side⟩.** This translates a passage from *Mishpeṭei ha-mazzalot* § 41:4, 526–527 (quoted in App. 10, IV: Jupiter, 4, 520–521).

[2]**1: It is a planet of truth and justice.** This translates a passage from *Mishpeṭei ha-mazzalot* § 41:5, 526–527 (quoted in App. 10, IV: Jupiter, 5, 520–521).

⟨II v 1⟩

[1]**1: The lot of Mars ... dangerous ⟨places⟩.** This translates *Mishpeṭei ha-mazzalot* § 52:3, 540–541 (quoted in App. 10, V: Mars, 16, 522).

[2]**2: Plagues⟨s⟩, Latin: *ictus*.** Here "plagues" translates *ictus*, lit. "blow⟨s⟩" and is a calque of מכות, primarily "blows" but also "plagues." See *Mishpeṭei ha-mazzalot* § 42:3, 526–527 (quoted in App. 10, V: Mars, 3, 521–522)

[3]**2: In general ... killing suddenly.** This translates a passage from *Mishpeṭei ha-mazzalot* § 42:3, 526–527 (quoted in App. 10, V: Mars, 3, 521–522).

[4]**2: It signifies falsehood, cunning, and malicious deception.** This translates a passage from *Mishpeṭei ha-mazzalot* § 42:4, 526–527 (quoted in App. 10, V: Mars, 4, 521–522).

[5]**3: This planet is cruel, furious, an accuser, and a warrior.** This passage has no counterpart in the section on Mars in the print edition of *Mishpeṭei ha-mazzalot*. It may be an addition by the author of the Hebrew Vorlage of *Tractatus particulares* or taken from a lost manuscript of *Mishpeṭei ha-mazzalot*.

⟨II v 2⟩

[1]**1: In its portions are brothers, relatives, sisters and sons-in-law.** This translates a passage from *Mishpeṭei ha-mazzalot* § 42:15, 528–529 (quoted in App. 10, V: Mars, 15, 522).

[2]**2: In the nativity of women, it indicates the husband.** This translates a passage from *Mishpeṭei ha-mazzalot* § 42:7, 526–529 (quoted in App. 10, V: Mars, 7, 522).

[3]**3: It signifies plunderers and robbers.** This translates another passage from *Mishpeṭei ha-mazzalot* § 42:7, 526–529 (quoted in App. 10, V: Mars, 7, 522).

⟨II v 3⟩

[1]**1: ⟨Mars⟩ sheds blood … in its exaltation.** This translates *Mishpeṭei ha-mazzalot* § 42:1, 526–527 (quoted in App. 10, V: Mars, 1, 521–522).

[2]**2: But if opposite … barber–surgeons.** This translates *Mishpeṭei ha-mazzalot* § 42:2, 526–527 (quoted in App. 10, V: Mars, 2, 521–522).

[3]**3: The craft in its portion … armorer, or a baker.** This translates a passage from *Mishpeṭei ha-mazzalot* § 42:6, 526–527 (quoted in App. 10, V: Mars, 6, 521–522).

[4]**4: ⟨Mars⟩ has a major … work and quickness.** This translates *Mishpeṭei ha-mazzalot* § 42:9, 528–527 (quoted in App. 10, V: Mars, 9, 522).

[5]**5: It is a planet of great heat.** This translates a passage from *Mishpeṭei ha-mazzalot* § 42:5, 526–527 (quoted in App. 10, V: Mars, 1, 521–522).

[6]**5: Whose effect is hindered by Venus.** This passage has no counterpart in the section on Mars in the print edition of *Mishpeṭei ha-mazzalot*. Instead, it

translates a passage from the section on Jupiter. See *Mishpeṭei ha-mazzalot* § 41:3, 526–527 (quoted in App. 10, V: Jupiter, 3, 520–521).

[7]**6: If Jupiter is mixed … war for God.** This translates *Mishpeṭei ha-mazzalot* § 42:5, 526–527 (quoted in App. 10, V: Mars, 5, 521–522).

⟨II v 4⟩

[1]**1: His outward appearance … body is long.** This translates a passage from *Mishpeṭei ha-mazzalot* § 42:6, 526–527 (quoted in App. 10, V: Mars, 6, 521–522).

[2]**1: Red and black … long and slender.** This passage has no counterpart in the section on Mars in the print edition of *Mishpeṭei ha-mazzalot.*

⟨II v 5⟩

[1]**1: ⟨⟨In its portion are the genitals⟩⟩ … colors, red.** This translates a passage from *Mishpeṭei ha-mazzalot* § 42:7, 526–529 (quoted in App. 10, V: Mars, 7, 522).

⟨II v 6⟩

[1]**1: It serves in the nativity … after Jupiter.** This translates *Mishpeṭei ha-mazzalot* § 42:10, 528–529 (quoted in App. 10, V: Mars, 10, 522).

[2]**2: It has rulership … masculine planet.** This translates *Mishpeṭei ha-mazzalot* § 42:12, 528–529 (quoted in App. 10, V: Mars, 12, 522).

[3]**3: It is powerful … [i.e., between sundown on Friday and sunrise on Saturday].** This translates *Mishpeṭei ha-mazzalot* § 42:11, 528–529 (quoted in App. 10, V: Mars, 11, 522).

⟨II v 7⟩

[1]**1: Its least years … great ⟨years⟩, 66.** This translates *Mishpeṭei ha-mazzalot* § 42:14, 528–529 (quoted in App. 10, V: Mars, 14, 522).

⟨II v 8⟩

[1]**1: Its diseases are inflammatory tertian fever.** This translates *Mishpeṭei ha-mazzalot* § 42:13, 528–529 (quoted in App. 10, V: Mars, 13, 522).

[2]**1: Abscesses close to the hearth ... in the neck.** This passage has no counterpart in the section on Mars in the print edition of *Mishpeṭei ha-mazzalot.*

⟨II v 9⟩

[1]**1: Its portion of the house is the kitchen.** This translates a passage from *Mishpeṭei ha-mazzalot* § 42:15, 528–529 (quoted in App. 10, V: Mars, 15, 522).

⟨II v 10⟩

[1]**1: Dogs are in its portion; of riding animals, mules.** This translates a passage from *Mishpeṭei ha-mazzalot* § 42:8, 528–529 (quoted in App. 10, V: Mars, 8, 522).

⟨II v 11⟩

[1]**1: All trees ... in its portion.** This translates a passage from *Mishpeṭei ha-mazzalot* § 42:4, 526–527 (quoted in App. 10, V: Mars, 4, 521–522).

⟨II v 12⟩

[1]**1: Of the metals, iron ⟨is in its portion⟩.** This translates a passage from *Mishpeṭei ha-mazzalot* § 42:4, 526–527 (quoted in App. 10, V: Mars, 4, 521–522).

⟨II v 13⟩

[1]**1: Its power ... in a stream.** This translates a passage from *Mishpeṭei ha-mazzalot* § 42:8, 528–529 (quoted in App. 10, V: Mars, 8, 522).

⟨II vi 1⟩

[1]**1: The lot of Venus ... joy, pleasures.** This translates a passage from *Mishpeṭei ha-mazzalot* § 52:4, 540–541 (quoted in App. 10, VI: Venus, 10, 523).

[2]**1: Food, and every sort of sexual intercourse.** This translates a passage from *Mishpeṭei ha-mazzalot* § 43:1, 528–529 (quoted in App. 10, VI: Venus, 1, 523).

[3]**2: It is the planet of music, games, and love.** This translates a passage from *Mishpeṭei ha-mazzalot* § 43:2, 528–529 (quoted in App. 10, VI: Venus, 2, 523).

[4]**3: It signifies rest.** This translates a passage from *Mishpeṭei ha-mazzalot* § 43:3, 528–529 (quoted in App. 10, VI: Venus, 3, 523).

[5]**4: It removes Mars's misfortune.** This passage has no counterpart in the section on Venus in the print edition of *Mishpeṭei ha-mazzalot*. Instead, it translates a passage from the section on Jupiter. See *Mishpeṭei ha-mazzalot* § 41:3, 526–527 (quoted in App. 10, V: Jupiter, 3, 520–521).

⟨II vi 2⟩

[1]**1: In its portion are the mother, the sister, the wife.** This translates a passage from *Mishpeṭei ha-mazzalot* § 43:2, 528–529 (quoted in App. 10, VI: Venus, 2, 523).

[2]**1: Prostitutes and dancers.** This passage has no counterpart in the section on Venus in the print edition of *Mishpeṭei ha-mazzalot*.

⟨II vi 3⟩

[1]**1: The craft in its portion ... rings and belts.** This translates a passage from *Mishpeṭei ha-mazzalot* § 43:3, 528–529 (quoted in App. 10, VI: Venus, 3, 523).

⟨II vi 4⟩

[1]**1: The shape of his neck ... long nor short.** This translates a passage from *Mishpeṭei ha-mazzalot* § 43:2, 528–529 (quoted in App. 10, VI: Venus, 2, 523).

[2]**1–3: Beautiful eyes and eyebrows. ... short beard.** This passage has no counterpart in the section on Venus in the print edition of *Mishpeṭei ha-mazzalot.* It may be an addition by the author of the Hebrew Vorlage of *Tractatus particulares* or taken from a lost manuscript of *Mishpeṭei ha-mazzalot.*

⟨II vi 5⟩

[1]**1: In its portion are the genitals ... right kidney.** This translates a passage from *Mishpeṭei ha-mazzalot* § 43:1, 528–529 (quoted in App. 10, VI: Venus, 1, 523).

⟨II vi 6⟩

[1]**1–2: It serves one born ... [i.e., from sunrise to sundown on Friday], and over the night of Mars [i.e., between sundown on Monday and sunrise on Tuesday].** This translates *Mishpeṭei ha-mazzalot* § 43:5–6, 528–529 (quoted in App. 10, VI: Venus, 5–6, 523).

⟨II vi 7⟩

[1]**1–3: ⟨Its⟩ least years are 8 ... with his portion.** This translates *Mishpeṭei ha-mazzalot* § 43:7–9, 528–529 (quoted in App. 10, VI: Venus, 7–8, 523).

⟨II vi 8⟩

[1]**1: Its disease is temperate, with a bit of cold.** This passage has no counterpart in the section on Venus in the print edition of *Mishpeṭei ha-mazzalot.*

[2]**2: It signifies any desire.** This translates a passage from *Mishpeṭei ha-mazzalot* § 43:4, 528–529 (quoted in App. 10, VI: Venus, 4, 523).

[3]**3: In its portion ... mark on his face**. This passage has no counterpart in the section on Venus in the print edition of *Mishpeṭei ha-mazzalot*.

⟨II vi 9⟩

[1]**1: Its portion of the house is the bed**. This translates a passage from *Mishpeṭei ha-mazzalot* § 43:4, 528–529 (quoted in App. 10, VI: Venus, 4, 523).

⟨II vi 10⟩

[1]**1: Of riding animals, the camel**. This translates a passage from *Mishpeṭei ha-mazzalot* § 43:3, 528–529 (quoted in App. 10, VI: Venus, 3, 523).

⟨II vi 11⟩

[1]**1: In its portion are ⟨diverse types of⟩ tree⟨s⟩**. This translates a passage from *Mishpeṭei ha-mazzalot* § 43:3, 528–529 (quoted in App. 10, VI: Venus, 3, 523).

[2]**1: Anything fat and any kind of beer**. This passage has no counterpart in the section on Venus in the print edition of *Mishpeṭei ha-mazzalot*.

⟨II vi 12⟩

[1]**1: Copper is in its portion**. This translates a passage from *Mishpeṭei ha-mazzalot* § 43:3, 528–529 (quoted in App. 10, VI: Venus, 3, 523).

⟨II vi 13⟩

[1]**1: Its power ... share in rain**. This translates a passage from *Mishpeṭei ha-mazzalot* § 43:4, 528–529 (quoted in App. 10, VI: Venus, 4, 523).

⟨II vii 1⟩

[1]**1: Its lot is taken ... lost objects**. This translates *Mishpeṭei ha-mazzalot* § 52:5, 540–541 (quoted in App. 10, VII: Mercury, 10, 524).

[2]**2: This planet illuminates … degree of the ascendant.** This translates *Mishpeṭei ha-mazzalot* § 44:4, 530–531 (quoted in App. 10, VII: Mercury, 4, 523–524).

⟨II vii 2⟩

[1]**1: In its portion are servants and slaves.** This translates a passage from *Mishpeṭei ha-mazzalot* § 44:6, 530–531 (quoted in App. 10, VII: Mercury, 6, 524).

⟨II vii 3⟩

[1]**1–4: In its portion is the knowledge … aspect or conjoin it.** This translates *Mishpeṭei ha-mazzalot* § 44:1–2, 530–531 (quoted in App. 10, VII: Mercury, 1–2, 523–524).

[2]**5: In its portion are minters.** This translates a passage from *Mishpeṭei ha-mazzalot* § 44:6, 530–531 (quoted in App. 10, VII: Mercury, 6, 524).

[3]**5: Experts in the science of the signs; the currier is also in its portion.** This passage has no counterpart in the section on Mercury in the print edition of *Mishpeṭei ha-mazzalot*.

⟨II vii 4⟩

[1]**1: His outward appearance is emaciated, of long face.** This translates a passage from *Mishpeṭei ha-mazzalot* § 44:6, 530–531 (quoted in App. 10, VII: Mercury, 6, 524).

[2]**1: Thin lips, beautiful beard, and long fingers.** This passage has no counterpart in the section on Mercury in the print edition of *Mishpeṭei ha-mazzalot*.

⟨II vii 5⟩

[1]**1: The tip of the tongue and the left kidney are in its portion.** This translates a passage from *Mishpeṭei ha-mazzalot* § 44:5, 530–531 (quoted in App. 10, VII: Mercury, 5, 524).

⟨II vii 6⟩

[1]**1–2: Sixth: It serves any native ... [i.e., between sundown on Saturday and sunrise on Sunday].** This translates *Mishpeṭei ha-mazzalot* § 44:7–8, 530–531 (quoted in App. 10, VII: Mercury, 7–8, 524).

⟨II vii 7⟩

[1]**1: Its least years are 20 ... great ⟨years⟩ 76.** This translates *Mishpeṭei ha-mazzalot* § 44:9, 530–531 (quoted in App. 10, VII: Mercury, 9, 524).

⟨II vii 8⟩

[1]**1: The diseases ... flatulence in the stomach.** This passage has no counterpart in the section on Mercury in the print edition of *Mishpeṭei ha-mazzalot*.

[2]**2: Ptolemy says ... of his illness.** This translates *Mishpeṭei ha-mazzalot* § 44:3, 530–531 (quoted in App. 10, VII: Mercury, 3, 523–524).

[3]**3: He has an exposed mark on his body, a scar or a lentil-shaped spot.** This passage has no counterpart in the section on Mercury in the print edition of *Mishpeṭei ha-mazzalot*.

⟨II vii 9⟩

[1]**1: Its place in the house is the scriptorium and the craftsman's workroom.** This translates *Mishpeṭei ha-mazzalot* § 44:6, 530–531 (quoted in App. 10, VII: Mercury, 6, 524).

⟨II vii 10⟩

[1]**1: Sheep are in its portion.** This translates *Mishpeṭei ha-mazzalot* § 44:5, 530–531 (quoted in App. 10, VII: Mercury, 5, 524).

⟨II vii 11⟩

[1]**1: Every small tree is in its portion.** This translates *Mishpeṭei ha-mazzalot* § 44:5, 530–531 (quoted in App. 10, VII: Mercury, 5, 524).

⟨II vii 12⟩

[1]**1: Of the metals, quicksilver is in its portion.** This translates *Mishpeṭei ha-mazzalot* § 44:5, 530–531 (quoted in App. 10, VII: Mercury, 5, 524).

⟨II vii 13⟩

[1]**1: Its power is in the northern ⟨side⟩.** This translates *Mishpeṭei ha-mazzalot* § 44:5, 530–531 (quoted in App. 10, VII: Mercury, 5, 524).

⟨II vii 14⟩

[1]**1: *Book of the servants,* that is, the seven planets.** The title of this book includes the curious word *servi*, "servants," which is a literal translation of משרתים, *mesharetim*, servants, a neologism that Ibn Ezra employs frequently in his scientific and nonscientific writings to denote the seven planets. Ibn Ezra found the word in Psalms 103:21 (2003, vol. II, 104), where he glossed it as referring to the seven planets: ברכו, צבאיו—הם צבא השמים העליונים, ומשרתיו הם השבע' שהם בשבע' מעונות. = "*Bless, his hosts*—these are the host of the higher heavens, and his servants are the seven that are in seven orbs." The message conveyed by the primary sense is that the seven planets are not self-sufficient astrological agents but work as *servants* of God to *do his pleasure* (Ps. 103:21). For Ibn Ezra's motives in the coinage of this term, see Sela 2003, 129–130.

[2]**14: This completes the *Book of the servants,* that is, the seven planets.** The use here of "servants" to denote the planets, Ibn Ezra's most distinctive neologism, not only betrays Ibn Ezra's alleged authorship of this book but also indicates that its original Hebrew title was *Sefer ha-mesharetim* (ספר המשרתים = Book of the planets).

⟨III 1⟩

[1]**2: The Sun in this place … great things.** This is a parallel Latin translation of the first paragraph (on the ascendant) of the first section (on the Sun) of Gergis's *De significationibus*. The passage is quoted in App. 9, Sol, § 1:1, 510.

[2]**3: The Moon ... great women.** This is a parallel Latin translation of the first paragraph (on the ascendant) of the fourth section (on the Moon) of Gergis's *De significationibus*. The passage is quoted in App. 9, Luna, § 4:1, 512.

[3]**4: Saturn in this place ... property and land.** This is parallel Latin translation of the first paragraph (on the ascendant) of the fifth section (on Saturn) of Gergis's *De significationibus*. The passage is quoted in App. 9, Saturnus, § 5:1, 513.

[4]**5: Jupiter signifies endurance ... judgment, and power.** This is a parallel Latin translation or paraphrase of part of the first paragraph (on the ascendant) of the sixth section (on Jupiter) of Gergis's *De significationibus*. The passage is quoted in App. 9, Jupiter, § 6:1, 514.

[5]**6: Mars ⟨signifies⟩ sadness ... not sluggishness.** This is a parallel Latin translation of part of the first paragraph (on the ascendant) of the seventh section (on Mars) of Gergis's *De significationibus*. The passage is quoted in App. 9, Mars, § 7:1, 514.

[6]**7: Venus ⟨signifies⟩ joy ... smelly thing⟨s⟩.** This is a parallel Latin translation of part of the first paragraph (on the ascendant) of the second section (on Venus) of Gergis's *De significationibus*. The passage is quoted in App. 9, Venus, § 2:1, 511.

[7]**8: Mercury ⟨signifies⟩ knowledge ... numbers [i.e., arithmetic].** This is a parallel Latin translation of part of the first paragraph (on the ascendant) of the third section (on Mercury) of Gergis's *De significationibus*. The passage is quoted in App. 9, Mercury, § 3:1, 511.

[8]**9: The Head of the Dragon ... with the planets.** This is a parallel Latin translation of the first paragraph (on the ascendant) of the eighth section (on the Head of the Dragon) of Gergis's *De significationibus*. The passage is quoted in App. 9, Caput Draconis, § 8:1, 515.

[9]**9–10: The Head of the Dragon ... the Tail.** The Dragon recalls the fate of the dragon Tiamat in the Babylonian creation myth, slain by the sun god Marduk, who then created the heavens from its head and tail. See Bouché–Leclercq 1899, 40, 97; Tester 1987, 120–121. Later astronomers employed this myth to designate the nodes of the planets, that is, the points where the planets cross the ecliptic from south to north and from south to north, respectively.

[10]**10: The Tail ⟨signifies⟩ retreat ... decrease of everything.** This is a parallel Latin translation of the first paragraph (on the ascendant) of the ninth section (on the Tail of the Dragon) of Gergis's *De significationibus*. The passage is quoted in App. 9, Cauda Draconis, § 9:1, 515.

⟨III 2⟩

[1]**2: The Sun in this place ... laughing eyes.** This is a parallel Latin translation of the second paragraph (on the second place) of the first section (on the Sun) of Gergis's *De significationibus*. The passage is quoted in App. 9, Sol, § 1:2, 510.

[2]**3: The Moon ⟨signifies⟩ theft of wealth, anxiety, and complaint.** This is a parallel Latin translation of the second paragraph (on the second place) of the fourth section (on the Moon) of Gergis's *De significationibus*. The passage is quoted in App. 9, Luna, § 4:2, 512.

[3]**4: Saturn ⟨signifies⟩ loss of wealth, and anxiety of friends.** This is a parallel Latin translation of the second paragraph (on the second place) of the fifth section (on Saturn) of Gergis's *De significationibus*. The passage is quoted in App. 9, Saturnus, § 5:2, 513.

[4]**5: Jupiter ⟨signifies⟩ accumulation of wealth because of scholarship, and good manners.** This is a parallel Latin translation of part of the second paragraph (on the second place) of the sixth section (on Jupiter) of Gergis's *De significationibus*. The passage is quoted in App. 9, Iupiter, § 6:2, 513.

[5]**6: Mars ⟨signifies⟩ the theft of wealth, poverty, and affliction related to the craft.** This is a parallel Latin translation of the second paragraph (on the second place) of the seventh section (on Mars) of Gergis's *De significationibus*. The passage is quoted in App. 9, Mars, § 7:2, 514.

[6]**7: Venus ⟨signifies⟩ profit from women, honor, and assistance.** This is a parallel Latin translation of the second paragraph (on the second place) of the second section (on Venus) of Gergis's *De significationibus*. The passage is quoted in App. 9, Venus, § 2:2, 511.

[7]**8: Mercury ⟨signifies⟩ profit from property, and honor from the king.** This is a parallel Latin translation of part of the second paragraph (on the

second place) of the third section (on Mercury) of Gergis's *De significationibus*. The passage is quoted in App. 9, Mercury, § 3:2, 511.

[8]9: **The Head ⟨signifies⟩ increase of wealth and many benefits.** This is a parallel Latin translation of the second paragraph (on the second place) of the eighth section (on the Head of the Dragon) of Gergis's *De significationibus*. The passage is quoted in App. 9, Caput Draconis, § 8:2, 515.

[9]10: **The Tail ⟨signifies⟩ poverty ... who is trusted.** This is a parallel Latin translation of the second paragraph (on the second place) in the ninth section (on the Tail of the Dragon) of Gergis's *De significationibus*. The passage is quoted in App. 9, Cauda Draconis, § 9:2, 515.

⟨III 3⟩

[1]2: **The Sun ⟨signifies⟩ profit ... kingdom to another.** This is a parallel Latin translation of the third paragraph (on the third place) of the first section (on the Sun) of Gergis's *De significationibus*. The passage is quoted in App. 9, Sol, § 1:3, 510.

[2]3: **The Moon ⟨signifies⟩ joy ... increase in love.** This is a parallel Latin translation of the third paragraph (on the third place) of the fourth section (on the Moon) of Gergis's *De significationibus*. The passage is quoted in App. 9, Luna, § 4:3, 512.

[3]4: **Saturn ⟨signifies⟩ ruin ... quarrel between them.** This is a parallel Latin translation of the third paragraph (on the third place) of the fifth section (on Saturn) of Gergis's *De significationibus*. The passage is quoted in App. 9, Saturnus, § 5:3, 513.

[4]5: **Jupiter ⟨signifies⟩ great joy from their part [i.e., the brothers].** This is a parallel Latin translation of part of the third paragraph (on the third place) of the sixth section (on Jupiter) of Gergis's *De significationibus*. The passage is quoted in App. 9, Iupiter, § 6:3, 513.

[5]6: **Mars ⟨signifies⟩ fraternal hatred, a sort of quarrel, and killing one another.** This is a parallel Latin translation of the third paragraph (on the third place) of the seventh section (on Mars) of Gergis's *De significationibus*. The passage is quoted in App. 9, Mars, § 7:3, 514.

[6]7: **Venus ⟨signifies⟩ wickedness ... something indecently.** This is a parallel Latin translation of part of the third paragraph (on the third place) of the second section (on Venus) of Gergis's *De significationibus*. The passage is quoted in App. 9, Venus, § 2:3, 511.

[7]8: **Mercury ⟨signifies⟩ many brothers, sisters, and friends.** This is a parallel Latin translation of part of the third paragraph (on the third place) of the third section (on Mercury) of Gergis's *De significationibus*. The passage is quoted in App. 9, Mercury, § 3:3, 511.

[8]9: **The Head ⟨signifies⟩ a sincere relationship, and dreams that come true.** This is a parallel Latin translation of part of the third paragraph (on the third place) of the eighth section (on the Head of the Dragon) of Gergis's *De significationibus*. The passage is quoted in App. 9, Caput Draconis, § 8:3, 515.

[9]10: **The Tail ⟨signifies⟩ separation ... be in danger.** This is a parallel Latin translation of the third paragraph (on the third place) of the ninth section (on the Tail of the Dragon) of Gergis's *De significationibus*. The passage is quoted in App. 9, Cauda Draconis, § 9:3, 515.

⟨III 4⟩

[1]2: **The Sun ⟨signifies⟩ hidden ... renown among people.** This is a parallel Latin translation of the fourth paragraph (on the fourth place) of the first section (on the Sun) of Gergis's *De significationibus*. The passage is quoted in App. 9, Sol, § 1:4, 510.

[2]3: **The Moon ⟨signifies⟩ complaint ... God willing.** This is a parallel Latin translation of the fourth paragraph (on the fourth place) of the fourth section (on the Moon) of Gergis's *De significationibus*. The passage is quoted in App. 9, Luna, § 4:4, 512.

[3]4: **Saturn ⟨signifies⟩ the ruin ... danger or death.** This is a parallel Latin translation of the fourth paragraph (on the fourth place) of the fifth section (on Saturn) of Gergis's *De significationibus*. The passage is quoted in App. 9, Saturnus, § 5:4, 513.

[4]5: **Jupiter ⟨signifies⟩ profit ... thing will happen.** This is a parallel Latin translation of part of the fourth paragraph (on the fourth place) of the sixth

section (on Jupiter) of Gergis's *De significationibus*. The passage is quoted in App. 9, Iupiter, § 6:4, 513.

[5]**6: Mars ⟨signifies⟩ slaughter ... lamentation and anguish.** This is a parallel Latin translation of the fourth paragraph (on the fourth place) of the seventh section (on Mars) of Gergis's *De significationibus*. The passage is quoted in App. 9, Mars, § 7:4, 514.

[6]**7: Venus ⟨signifies⟩ lamentation ... will be beneficial.** This is a parallel Latin translation of part of the fourth paragraph (on the fourth place) of the second section (on Venus) of Gergis's *De significationibus*. The passage is quoted in App. 9, Venus, § 2:4, 511.

[7]**8: Mercury ⟨signifies⟩ lamentation due to thoughts, contempt, and very bad things.** This is a parallel Latin translation of part of the fourth paragraph (on the fourth place) of the third section (on Mercury) of Gergis's *De significationibus*. The passage is quoted in App. 9, Mercury, § 3:4, 511.

[8]**9: In a fiery or airy sign ... in a watery or earthy sign, Latin: *in signo igneo vel aereo ... in signo aquatico vel terreo*.** These four categories of signs refer to a quadripartite classification that ascribes one of the four elements of the sublunar domain, which is considered to be their common "nature," to each of the four groups. Their name stems from the perception that they form four equilateral triangles across the zodiac. The first triplicity, formed by Aries, Leo, and Sagittarius, has a fiery nature. The second triplicity, composed of Taurus, Virgo, and Capricorn, is earthy. The third triplicity, Gemini, Libra, and Aquarius, is airy in nature. The fourth triplicity, Cancer, Scorpio, and Pisces, is watery. Ibn Ezra addresses the nature of the zodiacal signs in *Ṭeʿamim* I, § 1.4:1–7, 32–33 and *Ṭeʿamim* II, § 2.1:1–14, 184–187. He accepts that the zodiacal constellations are made of a fifth element, different from the four that compose sublunary matter, but puts forward several theories to explain why astrologers maintain that their nature is like that of sublunary matter. His favorite theory is that the signs are said to be hot/cold/dry/wet because of the shape formed by the stars of the corresponding zodiacal constellations; for example, Aries is hot and dry because the Aries has the shape of a ram, which has a hot and dry nature.

[9]**9: The Head ⟨signifies⟩ increase ... earthy sign.** This is a parallel Latin translation of part of the fourth paragraph (on the fourth place) of the eighth section (on the Head of the Dragon) of Gergis's *De significationibus*. The passage is quoted in App. 9, Caput Draconis, § 8:4, 515.

[10]**10: The Tail ⟨signifies⟩ poverty ... something worthless.** This is a parallel Latin translation of the fourth paragraph (on the fourth place) of the ninth section (on the Tail of the Dragon) of Gergis's *De significationibus*. The passage is quoted in App. 9, Cauda Draconis, § 9:4, 515.

⟨III 5⟩

[1]**2: The Sun ⟨signifies⟩ change ... gifts on people.** This is a parallel Latin translation of the fifth paragraph (on the fifth place) of the first section (on the Sun) of Gergis's *De significationibus*. The passage is quoted in App. 9, Sol, § 1:5, 510.

[2]**3: ⟨⟨The Moon ⟨signifies⟩ many ... he will rejoice⟩⟩.** This is a parallel Latin translation of the fifth paragraph (on the fifth place) of the fourth section (on the Moon) of Gergis's *De significationibus*. The passage is quoted in App. 9, Luna, § 4:5, 512.

[3]**4: Saturn ⟨signifies⟩ the ruin ... with a messenger.** This is a parallel Latin translation of the fifth paragraph (on the fifth place) of the fifth section (on Saturn) of Gergis's *De significationibus*. The passage is quoted in App. 9, Saturnus, § 5:5, 513.

[4]**5: Jupiter ⟨signifies⟩ many ... powerful people.** This is a parallel Latin translation of part of the fifth paragraph (on the fifth place) of the sixth section (on Jupiter) of Gergis's *De significationibus*. The passage is quoted in App. 9, Iupiter, § 6:5, 513–514.

[5]**6: Mars ⟨signifies⟩ many ... delight in dishonesty.** This is a parallel Latin translation of the fifth paragraph (on the fifth place) of the seventh section (on Mars) of Gergis's *De significationibus*. The passage is quoted in App. 9, Mars, § 7:5, 514.

[6]**7: Venus at the beginning ... joy and delight.** This is a parallel Latin translation of part of the fifth paragraph (on the fifth place) of the second section (on Venus) of Gergis's *De significationibus*. The passage is quoted in App. 9, Venus, § 2:5, 511.

[7]**8: Mercury signifies sending ... son is affected.** This is a parallel Latin translation of part of the fifth paragraph (on the fifth place) of the third

section (on Mercury) of Gergis's *De significationibus*. The passage is quoted in App. 9, Mercury, § 3:5, 511.

[8]**9: The Head ⟨signifies⟩ ... love among them.** This is a parallel Latin translation of the fifth paragraph (on the fifth place) of the eighth section (on the Head of the Dragon) of Gergis's *De significationibus*. The passage is quoted in App. 9, Caput Draconis, § 8:5, 515.

[9]**10: The Tail ⟨signifies⟩ ... poverty of the children.** This is a parallel Latin translation of the fifth paragraph (on the fifth place) of the ninth section (on the Tail of the Dragon) of Gergis's *De significationibus*. The passage is quoted in App. 9, Cauda Draconis, § 9:5, 515.

⟨III 6⟩

[1]**2: The Sun ⟨signifies⟩ ... vile people.** This is a parallel Latin translation of the sixth paragraph (on the sixth place) of the first section (on the Sun) of Gergis's *De significationibus*. The passage is quoted in App. 9, Sol, § 1:6, 510.

[2]**3: The Moon ⟨signifies⟩ ... bodily health.** This is a parallel Latin translation of the sixth paragraph (on the sixth place) of the fourth section (on the Moon) of Gergis's *De significationibus*. The passage is quoted in App. 9, Luna, § 4:6, 512.

[3]**4: Saturn ⟨signifies⟩ ... against his master.** This is a parallel Latin translation of the sixth paragraph (on the sixth place) of the fifth section (on Saturn) of Gergis's *De significationibus*. The passage is quoted in App. 9, Saturnus, § 5:6, 513.

[4]**5: Jupiter ⟨signifies⟩ ... quadruped animals.** This is a parallel Latin translation of part of the sixth paragraph (on the sixth place) of the sixth section (on Jupiter) of Gergis's *De significationibus*. The passage is quoted in App. 9, Iupiter, § 6:6, 514.

[5]**6: Mars ⟨signifies⟩ many ... regard to slaves.** This is a parallel Latin translation of the sixth paragraph (on the sixth place) of the seventh section (on Mars) of Gergis's *De significationibus*. The passage is quoted in App. 9, Mars, § 7:6, 514.

[6]**7: Venus ⟨signifies⟩ disease ... signifies widows.** This is a parallel Latin translation of part of the sixth paragraph (on the sixth place) of the second section (on Venus) of Gergis's *De significationibus*. The passage is quoted in App. 9, Venus, § 2:6, 511.

[7]**8: Mercury ⟨signifies⟩ ... regarding slaves.** This is a parallel Latin translation of part of the sixth paragraph (on the sixth place) of the third section (on Mercury) of Gergis's *De significationibus*. The passage is quoted in App. 9, Mercury, § 3:6, 511.

[8]**9: The Head ⟨signifies⟩ ... exchanging animals.** This is a parallel Latin translation of the sixth paragraph (on the sixth place) of the eighth section (on the Head of the Dragon) of Gergis's *De significationibus*. The passage is quoted in App. 9, Caput Draconis, § 8:6, 515.

[9]**10: The Tail ⟨signifies⟩ ... weakness of the animals.** This is a parallel Latin translation of the sixth paragraph (on the sixth place) of the ninth section (on the Tail of the Dragon) of Gergis's *De significationibus*. The passage is quoted in App. 9, Cauda Draconis, § 9:6, 515.

⟨III 7⟩

[1]**2: The Sun ⟨signifies⟩ hatred ... and kings.** This is a parallel Latin translation of the seventh paragraph (on the seventh place) of the first section (on the Sun) of Gergis's *De significationibus*. The passage is quoted in App. 9, Sol, § 1:7, 510.

[2]**3: The Moon ⟨signifies⟩ ... for women.** This is a parallel Latin translation of the seventh paragraph (on the seventh place) of the fourth section (on the Moon) of Gergis's *De significationibus*. The passage is quoted in App. 9, Luna, § 4:7, 512.

[3]**4: Saturn ⟨signifies⟩ ... at the end.** This is a parallel Latin translation of the seventh paragraph (on the seventh place) of the fifth section (on Saturn) of Gergis's *De significationibus*. The passage is quoted in App. 9, Saturnus, § 5:7, 513.

[4]**5: Jupiter ⟨signifies⟩ joy ... between enemies.** This is a parallel Latin translation of the seventh paragraph (on the seventh place) of the sixth

section (on Jupiter) of Gergis's *De significationibus*. The passage is quoted in App. 9, Iupiter, § 6:7, 514.

[5]**6: Mars ⟨signifies⟩ poverty … occurrence of fatigue.** This is a parallel Latin translation of the seventh paragraph (on the seventh place) of the seventh section (on Mars) of Gergis's *De significationibus*. The passage is quoted in App. 9, Mars, § 7:7, 514.

[6]**7: Venus ⟨signifies⟩ a wedding … without payment.** This is a parallel Latin translation of the seventh paragraph (on the seventh place) of the second section (on Venus) of Gergis's *De significationibus*. The passage is quoted in App. 9, Venus, § 2:7, 511.

[7]**8: Mercury ⟨signifies⟩ scorn by women and prostitutes.** This is a parallel Latin translation of the seventh paragraph (on the seventh place) of the third section (on Mercury) of Gergis's *De significationibus*. The passage is quoted in App. 9, Mercury, § 3:7, 511.

[8]**9: The Head ⟨signifies⟩ marriage and increased prostitution.** This is a parallel Latin translation of the seventh paragraph (on the seventh place) of the eighth section (on the Head of the Dragon) of Gergis's *De significationibus*. The passage is quoted in App. 9, Caput Draconis, § 8:7, 515.

[9]**10: The Tail ⟨signifies⟩ … quarrel, and enemies.** This is a parallel Latin translation of the seventh paragraph (on the seventh place) of the ninth section (on the Tail of the Dragon) of Gergis's *De significationibus*. The passage is quoted in App. 9, Cauda Draconis, § 9:7, 515.

⟨III 8⟩

[1]**2: The Sun ⟨signifies⟩ … princes and kings.** This is a parallel Latin translation of the eighth paragraph (on the eighth place) of the first section (on the Sun) of Gergis's *De significationibus*. The passage is quoted in App. 9, Sol, § 1:8, 510.

[2]**3: The Moon ⟨signifies⟩ … great thoughts.** This is a parallel Latin translation of the eighth paragraph (on the eighth place) of the fourth section (on the Moon) of Gergis's *De significationibus*. The passage is quoted in App. 9, Luna, § 4:8, 512.

[3]4: **Saturn ⟨signifies⟩ … because of death.** This is a parallel Latin translation of the eighth paragraph (on the eighth place) of the fifth section (on Saturn) of Gergis's *De significationibus*. The passage is quoted in App. 9, Saturnus, § 5:8, 513.

[4]5: **Jupiter ⟨signifies⟩ … have a benefit.** This is a parallel Latin translation of the eighth paragraph (on the eighth place) of the sixth section (on Jupiter) of Gergis's *De significationibus*. The passage is quoted in App. 9, Iupiter, § 6:8, 514.

[5]6: **Mars ⟨signifies⟩ … will be impoverished.** This is a parallel Latin translation of the eighth paragraph (on the eighth place) of the seventh section (on Mars) of Gergis's *De significationibus*. The passage is quoted in App. 9, Mars, § 7:8, 514.

[6]7: **Venus ⟨signifies⟩ … female slaves.** This is a parallel Latin translation of the eighth paragraph (on the eighth place) of the second section (on Venus) of Gergis's *De significationibus*. The passage is quoted in App. 9, Venus, § 2:8, 511.

[7]8: **Mercury ⟨signifies⟩ … because of falsehood.** This is a parallel Latin translation of part of the eighth paragraph (on the eighth place) of the third section (on Mercury) of Gergis's *De significationibus*. The passage is quoted in App. 9, Mercury, § 3:8, 511.

[8]9: **The Head ⟨signifies⟩ … little lamentation.** This is a parallel Latin translation of the eighth paragraph (on the eighth place) of the eighth section (on the Head of the Dragon) of Gergis's *De significationibus*. The passage is quoted in App. 9, Caput Draconis, § 8:8, 515.

[9]10: **The Tail ⟨signifies⟩ … ruined inheritance.** This is a parallel Latin translation of the eighth paragraph (on the eighth place) of the ninth section (on the Tail of the Dragon) of Gergis's *De significationibus*. The passage is quoted in App. 9, Cauda Draconis, § 9:8, 515.

⟨III 9⟩

[1]2: **The Sun ⟨signifies⟩ … commemoration of the angels.** This is a parallel Latin translation of the ninth paragraph (on the ninth place) of the first

section (on the Sun) of Gergis's *De significationibus*. The passage is quoted in App. 9, Sol, § 1:9, 510.

[2]**3: The Moon ⟨signifies⟩ … the kingdoms.** This is a parallel Latin translation of part of the ninth paragraph (on the ninth place) of the fourth section (on the Moon) of Gergis's *De significationibus*. The passage is quoted in App. 9, Luna, § 4:9, 512.

[3]**4: Saturn ⟨signifies⟩ … long while.** This is a parallel Latin translation of the ninth paragraph (on the ninth place) of the fifth section (on Saturn) of Gergis's *De significationibus*. The passage is quoted in App. 9, Saturnus, § 5:9, 513.

[4]**5: Jupiter ⟨signifies⟩ … prophetic dreams.** This is a parallel Latin translation of the ninth paragraph (on the ninth place) of the sixth section (on Jupiter) of Gergis's *De significationibus*. The passage is quoted in App. 9, Iupiter, § 6:9, 514.

[5]**6: Mars ⟨signifies⟩ … dreams, falsehoods.** This is a parallel Latin translation of the ninth paragraph (on the ninth place) of the seventh section (on Mars) of Gergis's *De significationibus*. The passage is quoted in App. 9, Mars, § 7:9, 515.

[6]**7: Venus ⟨signifies⟩ … prophetic dream.** This is a parallel Latin translation of the ninth paragraph (on the ninth place) of the second section (on Venus) of Gergis's *De significationibus*. The passage is quoted in App. 9, Venus, § 2:9, 511.

[7]**8: Mercury ⟨signifies⟩ … social acquaintances.** This is a parallel Latin translation of the ninth paragraph (on the ninth place) of the third section (on Mercury) of Gergis's *De significationibus*. The passage is quoted in App. 9, Mercury, § 3:9, 511.

[8]**9: The Head ⟨signifies⟩ … ⟨planets⟩.** This is a parallel Latin translation of the ninth paragraph (on the ninth place) of the eighth section (on the Head of the Dragon) of Gergis's *De significationibus*. The passage is quoted in App. 9, Caput Draconis, § 8:9, 515.

[9]**10: The Tail ⟨signifies⟩ … little loyalty.** This is a parallel Latin translation of the ninth paragraph (on the ninth place) of the ninth section (on the

Tail of the Dragon) of Gergis's *De significationibus*. The passage is quoted in App. 9, Cauda Draconis, § 9:9, 515.

⟨III 10⟩

[1]**2: The Sun ⟨signifies⟩ ... rank, honor.** This is a parallel Latin translation of the tenth paragraph (on the tenth place) of the first section (on the Sun) of Gergis's *De significationibus*. The passage is quoted in App. 9, Sol, § 1:10, 510.

[2]**3: The Moon ⟨signifies⟩ ... only a little.** This is a parallel Latin translation of the tenth paragraph (on the tenth place) of the fourth section (on the Moon) of Gergis's *De significationibus*. The passage is quoted in App. 9, Luna, § 4:10, 512.

[3]**4: Saturn ⟨signifies⟩ ... long captivity.** This is a parallel Latin translation of part of the tenth paragraph (on the tenth place) of the fifth section (on Saturn) of Gergis's *De significationibus*. The passage is quoted in App. 9, Saturnus, § 5:10, 513.

[4]**5: Jupiter indicates ... the kingdom.** This is Latin translation of the tenth paragraph (on the tenth place) of the sixth section (on Jupiter) of Gergis's *De significationibus*. The passage is quoted in App. 9, Iupiter, § 6:10, 514.

[5]**6: Mars ⟨signifies⟩ ... any effect.** This is a parallel Latin translation of the tenth paragraph (on the tenth place) of the seventh section (on Mars) of Gergis's *De significationibus*. The passage is quoted in App. 9, Mars, § 7:10, 515.

[6]**7: Venus ⟨signifies⟩ joy for the king.** This is a parallel Latin translation of the tenth paragraph (on the tenth place) of the second section (on Venus) of Gergis's *De significationibus*. The passage is quoted in App. 9, Venus, § 2:10, 511.

[7]**8: Mercury ⟨signifies⟩ ... and music.** This is a parallel Latin translation of the tenth paragraph (on the tenth place) of the third section (on Mercury) of Gergis's *De significationibus*. The passage is quoted in App. 9, Mercury, § 3:10, 511.

[8]**9: The Head ⟨signifies⟩ ... good mastership.** This is a parallel Latin translation of the tenth paragraph (on the tenth place) of the eighth section (on the Head of the Dragon) of Gergis's *De significationibus*. The passage is quoted in App. 9, Caput Draconis, § 8:10, 515.

[9]**10: The Tail ⟨signifies⟩ ... the travel.** This is a parallel Latin translation of the tenth paragraph (on the tenth place) of the ninth section (on the Tail of the Dragon) of Gergis's *De significationibus*. The passage is quoted in App. 9, Cauda Draconis, § 9:10, 515.

⟨III 11⟩

[1]**2: The Sun ⟨signifies⟩ joy ... faith [i.e., religion].** This is a parallel Latin translation of the eleventh paragraph (on the eleventh place) of the first section (on the Sun) of Gergis's *De significationibus*. The passage is quoted in App. 9, Sol, § 1:11, 510.

[2]**3: The Moon ⟨signifies⟩ ... he hopes for.** This is a parallel Latin translation of the eleventh paragraph (on the eleventh place) of the fourth section (on the Moon) of Gergis's *De significationibus*. The passage is quoted in App. 9, Luna, § 4:11, 512.

[3]**4: Saturn ⟨signifies⟩ complaint ... many things.** This is a parallel Latin translation of the eleventh paragraph (on the eleventh place) of the fifth section (on Saturn) of Gergis's *De significationibus*. The passage is quoted in App. 9, Saturnus, § 5:11, 513.

[4]**5: Jupiter ⟨signifies⟩ profit ... he trusts.** This is a parallel Latin translation of the eleventh paragraph (on the eleventh place) of the sixth section (on Jupiter) of Gergis's *De significationibus*. The passage is quoted in App. 9, Iupiter, § 6:11, 514.

[5]**6: Mars ⟨signifies⟩ ... in his heart.** This is a parallel Latin translation of the eleventh paragraph (on the eleventh place) of the seventh section (on Mars) of Gergis's *De significationibus*. The passage is quoted in App. 9, Mars, § 7:11, 515.

[6]**7: Venus ⟨signifies⟩ ... because of friends.** This is a parallel Latin translation of the eleventh paragraph (on the eleventh place) of the second section

(on Venus) of Gergis's *De significationibus*. The passage is quoted in App. 9, Venus, § 2:11, 511.

[7]8: **Mercury ⟨signifies⟩ ... with scholars.** This is a parallel Latin translation of the eleventh paragraph (on the eleventh place) of the third section (on Mercury) of Gergis's *De significationibus*. The passage is quoted in App. 9, Mercury, § 3:11, 511.

[8]9: **The Head and the Tail in this ⟨place⟩ have no effect.** This is a parallel Latin translation of the eleventh paragraph (on the eleventh place) of the eighth section (on the Head of the Dragon) of Gergis's *De significationibus*. The passage is quoted in App. 9, Caput Draconis, § 8:11, 515.

⟨III 12⟩

[1]2: **The Sun ⟨signifies⟩ ... sick persons.** This is a parallel Latin translation of the twelfth paragraph (on the twelfth place) of the first section (on the Sun) of Gergis's *De significationibus*. The passage is quoted in App. 9, Sol, § 1:12, 510.

[2]3: **The Moon ⟨signifies⟩ ... without doubt.** This is a parallel Latin translation of the twelfth paragraph (on the twelfth place) of the fourth section (on the Moon) of Gergis's *De significationibus*. The passage is quoted in App. 9, Luna, § 4:12, 512.

[3]4: **Saturn ⟨signifies⟩ ... his deeds.** This is a parallel Latin translation of the twelfth paragraph (on the twelfth place) of the fifth section (on Saturn) of Gergis's *De significationibus*. The passage is quoted in App. 9, Saturnus, § 5:12, 513.

[4]5: **Jupiter signifies ... quadruped animals.** This is a parallel Latin translation of the twelfth paragraph (on the twelfth place) of the sixth section (on Jupiter) of Gergis's *De significationibus*. The passage is quoted in App. 9, Iupiter, § 6:12, 514.

[5]6: **Mars ⟨signifies⟩ ... because of beasts.** This is a parallel Latin translation of the twelfth paragraph (on the twelfth place) of the seventh section (on Mars) of Gergis's *De significationibus*. The passage is quoted in App. 9, Mars, § 7:12, 515.

[6]**7: Venus ⟨signifies⟩ … hate women.** This is a parallel Latin translation of the twelfth paragraph (on the twelfth place) of the second section (on Venus) of Gergis's *De significationibus*. The passage is quoted in App. 9, Venus, § 2:12, 511.

[7]**8: Mercury ⟨signifies⟩ … knowledge of quadrupeds.** This is a parallel Latin translation of the twelfth paragraph (on the twelfth place) of the third section (on Mercury) of Gergis's *De significationibus*. The passage is quoted in App. 9, Mercury, § 3:12, 511.

[8]**9: The Head ⟨signifies⟩ … good fortune.** This is a parallel Latin translation of the twelfth paragraph (on the twelfth place) of the eighth section (on the Head of the Dragon) of Gergis's *De significationibus*. The passage is quoted in App. 9, Caput Draconis, § 8:12, 515.

[9]**10: The Tail ⟨signifies⟩ … bad fortune.** This is a parallel Latin translation of the twelfth paragraph (on the twelfth place) of the ninth section (on the Tail of the Dragon) of Gergis's *De significationibus*. The passage is quoted in App. 9, Cauda Draconis, § 9:12, 515–516.

⟨IV 1⟩

[1]**1: Three things … end of the interrogation.** The current passage is a Latin translation of part of the extant fragment of the Hebrew translation of a lost Arabic work by Māshā'allāh on reading thoughts, and a parallel Latin translation of part of the complete Latin translation of Māshā'allāh's work. The two passages are quoted, respectively in App. 11, I 1:2–4, 525, and II 1:2–5, 525.

⟨IV 2⟩

[1]**1–3: The interrogation is more … [i.e., the planet with which the significator is conjoined].** This is a parallel Latin translation of a passage of the complete Latin translation of Māshā'allāh's work. The passage is quoted in App. 11, II 3:1–5, 526.

⟨IV 3⟩

[1]**1: The ascendant is Taurus.** Note that six of the seven manuscript used for the edition of *Tractatus particulares* make Cancer the ascendant of the current horoscope. See p. 328, n. 1. Nevertheless, I have preferred Taurus for the following reasons: (1) The single manuscript that reads "Taurus" is Oxford, Bodl., Digby 212, the earliest of the seven manuscripts used for this edition; (2) The parallel Latin translation of the complete Latin translation of Māshā'allāh's work also makes Taurus the ascendant of the current horoscope. See App. 11, II 4:2, 526; (3) *Tp*, IV 4:4 implies that Taurus is the ascendant of the current horoscope.

[2]**2: Exaltation, Latin: *honor*.** The use of *honor* here reveals that *Tractatus particulares* was ultimately translated from a Hebrew source text that used Ibn Ezra's peculiar terminology: *honor* is a Latin calque of כבוד, used everywhere by Ibn Ezra to denote the concept of exaltation. See *Int*, II i 6:12 and note.

[3]**2: Triplicity**. A triplicity (Hebrew: שלישות; Arabic: مثلثة; Latin: *triplicitas*) is one of the four groups of three zodiacal signs, separated from one another by 120°, and all linked to the same one of the four elements; consequently, they are considered to have an identical nature. They are "triplicities" because each group has three members. The first triplicity—Aries, Leo, and Sagittarius—has a fiery nature. The second triplicity—Taurus, Virgo, and Capricorn—is earthy. The third triplicity—Gemini, Libra, and Aquarius—is airy. The fourth triplicity—Cancer, Scorpio, and Pisces—is watery. The triplicity is traditionally the third of the planets' five essential dignities; three planets are assigned lordship over each triplicity by day, and three by night. Lists of lords of the triplicities, without theoretical explanations, are found in *Mishpeṭei ha-mazzalot* § 7:1–4, 494–495 (quoted in App. 5, Q. 51, 481–482). The expression "the planet is in its triplicity" means that the planet in question is one of the three lords of the triplicity in which it is located.

[4]**1–3: Example … is not received.** This is a parallel Latin translation of part of the complete Latin translation of Māshā'allāh's work. The passage is quoted in App. 11, II 4:2–5, 526.

⟨IV 4⟩

[1]**1: It [Venus] is the lady of the house ⟨of the ascendant⟩.** The ascendant in the current horoscope is Taurus 10°. Venus is the lord of Taurus. Therefore Venus is the "lady" of the house of the ascendant.

[2]**1: It [Venus] is in its [Venus's] triplicity.** Venus is the lord by day of the triplicity of the watery signs. One of the watery signs is Cancer. Venus in the present horoscope is located at Cancer 15°. Therefore Venus is in its triplicity.

[3]**2: I observed that the Moon is the lady of the sign ⟨of Venus⟩.** The Moon is the lord of Cancer. Venus, in the current horoscope, is located at Cancer 15°. Therefore, in the current horoscope, the Moon is the "lady" of the sign where Venus is located.

[4]**3: Venus is the lady of the ascendant**: Venus is the lord of Taurus. Taurus, in the current horoscope, is the ascendant. Therefore, in the current horoscope, Venus is the "lady" of the ascendant.

[5]**3: ⟨Venus⟩ indeed is the lady of the Moon's house.** The Moon, in the current horoscope, is located at Libra 10°. Venus is the lord of Libra. Therefore Venus is the "lady" of the Moon's house.

[6]**4: She [the Moon] is in Libra, in the sixth house from Taurus, which is Venus's house.** The Moon, in the current horoscope, is located at Libra 10°. Taurus is the ascendant of the current horoscope as well as one of Venus's houses. There are six signs, counting counterclockwise, between Taurus and Libra. The mention of six signs here alludes to diseases, because disease is one of the indications of the sixth horoscopic place. See *Mishpeṭei ha-mazzalot* § 14:6, 500–501.

[7]**4: In the fourth place [i.e., house] from Venus.** Venus, in the current horoscope, is located at Cancer 15°. The Moon, in the current horoscope, is located at Libra 10°. There are four signs, counting counterclockwise, between Cancer and Libra. The mention of four signs here alludes to the mother, because the mother is one of the indications of the fourth horoscopic place. See *Moladot*, III iv 2:1, 138–139.

[8]**5: Then I knew that the interrogation is about the mother, because of a disease.** That the current horoscope includes a prediction about a

disease of the mother follows from the mention in the previous sentence of four signs between Cancer and Libra and of six signs between Taurus and Libra. The four signs allude to the fourth horoscopic place, which indicates the mother, and the six signs allude to the sixth horoscopic place, which indicates diseases.

[9]**1–5: I observed ... because of a disease.** This is a parallel Latin translation of part of the complete Latin translation of Māshā'allāh's work. The passage is quoted in App. 11, II 5:1–5, 527.

⟨IV 5⟩

[1]**1–2: Since I wished to know ... cold and dry.** This is a parallel Latin translation of part of the complete Latin translation of Māshā'allāh's work. The passage is quoted in App. 11, II 6:1–2, 527. For Saturn's cold and dry nature, see *Reshit ḥokhmah* § 4.3:1, 146–147.

[2]**3–4: When I wished ... breast and the stomach.** This passage is expanded in the parallel Latin translation of part of the complete Latin translation of Māshā'allāh's work. The passage is quoted in App. 11, II 6:3–5, 527. Here is the corresponding English translation of the Latin text: "I wanted to know in which member of the body is the disease. I looked at *zuḥal*, Saturn, in the first decan of *al-'asad*, Leo. Among the bodily organs, *Al-'asad*, Leo, is in charge of the stomach. ⟨Then⟩ I said that she will suffer in the stomach." We learn from the parallel Latin translation, then, that *Tractatus particulares* omits the fundamental detail that if the mother will suffer in the stomach, it is because Saturn is located in Leo in the current horoscope, and Leo indicates the stomach. It turns out, then, that lurking behind the expression "according to that division" in *Tractatus particulares* is the doctrine of melothesia, which distributes the parts of the body among the zodiacal signs. For this theory, see note to *El*, II i 2:8–9. According to *Reshit ḥokhmah* § 2.5:29, 90–91 (quoted in App. 5, Q. 52, 482), the chest and the upper abdomen are in the charge of Leo.

⟨IV 6⟩

[1]**4: Māshā'allāh says ... fixed ⟨sign⟩, years.** This corresponds to *Int*, II i 6:2. See note there.

[2]**1–5: When I examined ... period ⟨of time⟩.** This is a parallel Latin translation of part of the complete Latin translation of Māshā'allāh's work. The passage is quoted in App. 11, II 7:1–5, 527. Note that the parallel Latin translation does not mention Māshā'allāh here.

⟨IV 7⟩

[1]**1–3: Examine in the same manner ... as I showed.** This is a parallel Latin translation of part of the complete Latin translation of Māshā'allāh's work. The passage is quoted in App. 11, II 8:1–2, 527.

⟨IV 8⟩

[1]**1–5: Know that if Venus ... about a journey.** This a parallel Latin translation of part of the complete Latin translation of Māshā'allāh's work. The passage is quoted in App. 11, II 9:3–7, 527. Note that at the beginning of the present passage, the parallel Latin translation has the Sun instead of Venus. The latter eems to be the correct reading.

⟨IV 9⟩

[1]**1–5: If Mars were in its [the Moon's] place ... quarrels and adversaries.** This a parallel Latin translation of part of the complete Latin translation of Māshā'allāh's work. The passage is quoted in App. 11, II 10:1–5, 527.

⟨IV 10⟩

[1]**1–3: If Mercury were in its [the Moon's] place ... planets and signs.** This is a parallel Latin translation of part of the complete Latin translation of Māshā'allāh's work. The passage is quoted in App. 11, II 11:1–3, 527.

PART SEVEN

APPENDICES

APPENDIX 1

THE DEBATE ABOUT THE VALIDITY AND THE GENERAL PRINCIPLES OF THE DOCTRINE OF ELECTIONS

Quotation 1: *Moladot*, I 1:1–2, I 8:1–4, I 9:1–5, 85–89:

1 (1) אמר אברהם הספרדי: כל משכיל בחכמת משפטי המזלות ואיננו יודע מהחכמה העליונה יש פעמים שיהיו דיניו כזבים, בעבור שלא נשמר מהדברים הראוים להשמר מהם. (2) וכלל אומר, כי דיני הכללים יבטלו הפרטים, והנה אזכיר מהם שמנה דרכים.

2 (1) והדרך השיביעית מפאת התולדת. (2) כי אם יכנס אדם בספינה בימי הקור בתוך הים והים הולך וסוער, אע״פ שישים במעלה הצומחת צדק ונגה שהם הכוכבים הטובים, לא ינצל, כי התולדת היא כלל והפרט שבחר לא יועילנו. (3) וככה אלף אנשים בים בספינה אחת, ולא תמצא במולד כל אחד מהם שימות באותה שנה. (4) רק ימצא במולד כל אחד מהם שהגיע אחד מפקידי החיים אל מקום מסוכן, ואילו לא היה בתוך הים, שהוא מקום מסוכן, יארע לו מעט נזק וינצל.

3 (1) והדרך השמינית מפאת כח הנשמה, וכחה היא החכמה. (2) כי אם היה הנולד חכם בחכמת המזלות, וראה בתקופת שנתו כי יקרנו חולי מחום בזמן ידוע בהכנס מאדים אל מעלתו הצומחת. (3) והנה אם ישמר הוא קודם בא החולי מכל מאכל חם וישתה משקיות לקרר גופו, הנה תתישר תולדת גופו בהכנס מאדים במעלת הצומחת. (4) וככה הבוטח בשם בכל לבו, השם יסבב לו סבות ולו נתקנו עלילות להצילנו מכל נזק שיש במולדו. (5) על כן, אין ספק כי הצדיק יותר שמור מהמשכיל בדיני המזלות, כי פעמים ישתבשו עליו הדינין, כדרך שאמר הכתוב וקוסמים יהולל, והנה אשרי מי שלבו תמים עם אלהיו.

1 (1) Abraham the Spaniard said: Anyone who is versed in the science of the judgments of the zodiacal signs but is not acquainted with the supernal science will sometimes make erroneous ⟨astrological⟩ judgments, because he is not wary of matters that require caution. (2) I state it as a general rule that judgments about collectives take precedence over those about individuals, in eight ways, which I now present.

2 (1) The seventh way is concerned with nature. (2) If somebody sails on a ship in the cold season and there is a storm at sea—even though he [the astrologer] put Jupiter and Venus, which are the benefic stars, in the ascendant degree ⟨of the electional horoscope⟩—he [the person sailing on a ship] will not survive, for nature affects collectives, and the individual election will not avail him. (3) The same holds for a thousand people sailing together in one ship—⟨all of them will die if there is a storm at sea⟩ even though not one of them has a nativity that determines that he will die that year. (4) But ⟨the astrologer⟩ may find in the nativity of each that one of the

lords of life reached a dangerous place, so that if he [the native] had not gone to sea, which is a perilous place, he would have met with only lesser harm and would have survived.

3 (1) The eighth way is concerned with the power of the soul, whose power resides in wisdom. (2) Consider the case that the native is an astrologer who observes in his ⟨horoscope of the⟩ revolution of the year that he will come down with fever at a certain time when Mars enters the degree of the ascendant ⟨of the horoscope of the revolution of the year⟩. (3) If he takes precautions before the illness comes, abstaining from hot foods and drinking beverages in order to cool his body, then he will maintain a balance in his bodily temperament when Mars enters the degree of the ascendant. (4) Likewise, he who trusts in God with all his heart, God—"by Him actions are weighed" (1Sam. 2:3)—will effect causes for himself that save him from any harm prognosticated in his nativity. (5) Therefore, there is no doubt that the righteous person is better protected than a scholar versed in astrological judgments, since sometimes the scholar's ⟨astrological⟩ judgments will be faulty, as Scripture says (Isa. 44:25), "and make fools of the augurs"; whereas he whose heart is wholly with his God is fortunate.

Quotation 2: *Nativitates*, I ii 1:1, I vi 2:1, 82–83, 92–93:

1 (1) Oportet te scire cuius gentis est natus eo quod commune vincet singulare.

2 (1) Et nunc appone cor tuum cui planete assimilatur natura sua hoc est via communis omnibus natis, propter hoc debes tu antecedere commune ante singulare.

1 (1) You need to know to which nation the native belongs, because the collective prevails over the particular.

2 (1) Now pay attention that what is similar to the planet's nature is a general method that applies to all the natives; therefore you should give precedence to the general ⟨method⟩ over the ⟨method that applies to the⟩ individual.

Quotation 3: *Me'orot*, § 9:2–4, 460–461:

דע כי משפטי חכמת המזלות על שני דרכים. האחד דרך כלל, כמו שכוכב נגה יורה על הנשים וכוכב חמה על החכמה, והשני דרך פרט, כמו בעל הבית השביעי יורה על הנשים ובעל התשיעי על החכמה. והפרט לא יבטל הכלל.

Know that there are two methods for judgments in astrology. The first is a general method, as when Venus signifies women and Mercury wisdom, and the second is a method that applies to the individual, as when the lord of the seventh place ⟨of the natal horoscope⟩ signifies ⟨the native's⟩ women and the lord of the ninth ⟨place⟩ signifies ⟨the native's⟩ wisdom. But the ⟨method that applies to the⟩ individual does not cancel out the general ⟨method⟩.

Quotation 4: *Tetrabiblos*, ed. Robbins (1980), II:1, 117–119:

> Since prognostication by astronomical means is divided into two great and principal parts, and since the first and more universal is that which relates to whole races, countries and cities, which is called general, and the second and more specific is that which relates to individual men, which is called genethlialogical, we believe it fitting to treat first of the general division, because such matters are naturally swayed by greater and more powerful causes than are particular events.

Quotation 5: Ibn Ezra's commentary on Job, ed. Gomez Aranda, 38:33:

> הידעת חקות שמים׳ ששמתי? והוא שאמר המשורר: ׳חוק נתן ולא יעבור׳. ׳משטרו׳— שב אל ה׳שמים׳, בעבור שיש להם ממשלה על ה׳ארץ׳ מן שוטרים.

> "Knowest thou the ordinances of the heavens" which I have established? Regarding this the poet said: "He hath made a decree which shall not be transgressed" (Ps. 148:6)—"the dominion thereof" refers to "heavens," because they exert rulership over the "Earth" ⟨which comes⟩ from the officers (Deut. 1:15; i.e., the planets).

Quotation 6: *Mivḥarim* II, § 1:1–6, 142–143:

> (1) חכמי התורה מודים כי יש יכולת באדם לעשות טוב גם רע. ומשה אדוננו אמר מפורש: ובחרת בחיים, ולולי זה לא היה אדם נענש. גם אמרו קדמוננו ז״ל: הכל בידי שמים חוץ מיראת שמים. (2) וידענו כי כל אשר יעשה האלהים הוא יהיה לעולם, עליו אין להוסיף וממנו אין לגרוע, והנה שלמה דבר על חקות השמים. והנה מי שנולד במערכת חסרה כנגד הדבר השלם אין יכולת בידו להיות כמו הנברא במערכת שלימה, וזהו טעם מעות לא יוכל לתקון וחסרון לא יוכל להמנות. על כן, מי שבמערכת מולדו להיותו עני בלא הון לא יוכל להעשיר. (3) רק בעבור שנשמת האדם נבראה במקום גבוה על כל הכוכבים, יוכל האדם בדעתו לחסר מעט מרעתו. (4) על כן, מי שמזלו טוב, ויבחר בכל דרכיו ועניניו שעות טובות ויום טוב ומזל עולה טוב, יוסיף טובה על טובתו, או יחסר מעט מרעת בעל המזל הרע. (5) על כן אמר תלמי: השמר שלא תבחר יום שיצא בו בדרך לאדם שיש בכח מולדו שיבא לו נזק רב בדרך, כי כח המזל הטוב שתבחר לו לא יראה כנגד כח מה שיש במולד. רק אם לא יהיה הנזק רב בדרך יועיל המבחר ויראה כחו. (6) המבחרים על שני דרכים.

> (1) The sages of the Torah agree that man has the capacity to do both good and evil. Moses, our lord, said plainly: "choose life" (Deut. 30:19); were it not for this ⟨capacity⟩ no one would be punished. Also our ancient sages, their memory for a blessing, said: "Everything depends on the heavens except for the fear of Heaven" (B *Berakhot* 33b; *Megillah* 25a; *Niddah* 37b). (2) But we know that "whatsoever God doeth, it shall be for ever; nothing can be added to it, nor any thing taken from it" (Eccles. 3:14), and here Solomon mentioned the "ordinances of the heavens." So whoever is born in a defective configuration with respect to perfection is incapable of being like someone who was created in a flawless configuration, which is the meaning of "that which is

crooked cannot be made straight and that which is wanting cannot be numbered" (Eccles. 1:15). Consequently whoever is destined by the configuration of his natal horoscope to be poor and impecunious can never get rich. (3) But since the soul of man has been created in a place that is higher than the stars, a man can employ his intelligence to reduce his misfortune somewhat. (4) Therefore, whoever is blessed by a favorable configuration of the stars and chooses favorable hours and a favorable day and a favorable rising sign for all his journeys and undertakings will add good fortune to his good fortune or will reduce slightly the misfortune of the ill-starred. (5) Therefore Ptolemy said: be careful not to choose a day for a man to embark on a journey ⟨if he⟩ has been destined by his natal horoscope to suffer grievous harm on the road, because the power of the favorable configuration of the stars that you choose for him will not prevail over the power of what is signified by the natal horoscope. But if the harm of the journey is not great the election may be useful and its power may be perceptible. (6) There are two methods for elections.

Quotation 7: Babylonian Talmud, *Mo'ed Qaṭan* 28a:

חיי בני ומזוני לא בזכותא תליא מילתא אלא במזלא תליא מילתא.

⟨Length of⟩ life, children and sustenance depend not on merit but ⟨rather⟩ on *mazzal*.

Quotation 8: Ibn Ezra's long commentary on Exodus 32:32, *Commentary on Exodus*, ed. Weiser (1976), 211:

כבר פירשתי בס׳ דניאל וספרין פתיחו (דניאל ז, י), כי כל הגזרות על הכללים ועל הפרטים הם במערכות השמים. וככה, הודו חכמים בני חיי ומזוני, רק השם יוסיף בעבור יראתו כאשר פירשתיו

I have already commented in the Book of Daniel [7:10], "the books were opened," that all the decrees on collectives and individuals depend on the configurations of the heavens. Hence, wise people said "⟨Length of⟩ life, children and sustenance ..." but God may add to ⟨the decrees⟩ because of the fear ⟨of the Lord⟩, as I have commented.

Quotation 9: Sahl Ibn Bishr's *Book of Elections*, Paris, BnF, lat. 16204, 488b:

Omnes concordati sunt quod electiones sunt debiles, nisi in divitibus. Habent enim isti—licet debilitentur eorum electiones—radicem et nativitates eorum que confortant omnem planetam debilem in intinere. Vilibus vero mercatoribus et hiis que sequntur non eligas aliquid nisi supra nativitates et revolutiones annorum illorum et supra nativitates eorum filiorum.

All agree that the elections are week, except for the wealthy. Although their elections are weak, these people [the rich] have a root and their nativities, which strengthen every weak planet in its course. You should not make any election for people of low rank or merchants and those who follow ⟨them in rank⟩ except ⟨if the elections are⟩ supported by their nativities and revolutions of the years and the nativities of their children.

Quotation 10: *Mivḥarim* II, § 9.1:2, 168–169:

הבית התשיעי. כבר אמרתי לך שתשמור שלא יהיה בעל השעה שבתאי בהליכת הים ... ואם היה במזל מים, יעשה סער גדול.

The ninth place: I have already told you to be careful not to set off on a journey by sea when Saturn is the lord of the hour ... if it [Saturn] is in a watery sign, a great tempest will come up.

Quotation 11: *Olam* I, § 55:1, 86–87:

ואם היה שבתאי באחד ממזלות המים, תהיה רעה גדולה לעוברי הים, ואף כי אם היה במזל סרטן. והכלל שיעשה נזק לכל מי שהולך במים, ושיגברו מימי הנהרות וישחיתו הזרע, או יבא גשם גדול שיזיק.

If Saturn is in one of the watery signs, a great misfortune will befall travelers by sea, particularly if it is in the sign of Cancer. In general, this means that it will cause harm to anyone who travels by water, and that the rivers will overflow their banks and destroy the seeds, or that a great ruinous rain will come.

Quotation 12: *Nativitates*, II vi 8:4, 136–137:

Et si fuerit Saturnus in signo aqueo, ipse ostendet super magnum tormentum in mari.

If Saturn is in a watery sign it signifies a great storm at sea.

Quotation 13: *Yesod mora'*, ed. Simon (2007), VII, 140–145:

על כן יש כח במשכיל לבחור הטוב והרע, כי אין הגזירו׳ אלא כפי המקבל, לא כפי הנותן.

Therefore a man of learning has the power to choose good or evil, because the decrees ⟨of the stars⟩ are according to the ⟨disposition of the⟩ recipient, not according to the giver.

Quotation 14: Aphorism 6 of Pseudo-Ptolemy's *Centiloquium*. *Sefer ha-Peri*, BnF héb. 1055, fol. 53v:

אמר בטלמיוס אמנם יקובל תועלת בבחירה כאשר היה כח העת מוסיף על מותר מה שבין שני העצמויות.

Ptolemy said: A benefit is received from an election when the power of the hour increases the advantage between the two entities [i.e., the natal and the electional horoscopes].

Quotation 15: *Mivḥarim* I, § 1:1–4, 46–47:

(1) טרם שאדבר על המבחרים אומר דרך כלל, כי יש לנשמת האדם העליונה כח לבטל קצת הפרטים, ולהוסיף או לגרוע על כל מה שיורו הכוכבים, רק אין כח לה לבטל הכלל. (2) ודמיון זה, אם היה במולד אדם שיארע לו נזק רב בדרך בשנת עשרים ממולדו, אין כח במבחר לבטל אותו הנזק, רק אם יצא מביתו במבחר טוב יחסר מן הנזק; והפך הדבר אם יצא ברע, שיוסיף. (3) על כן אמר דורוניוס: השמר לך לא תבחר יום ידוע ושעה ידועה לאדם שלא תדע מולדו. אבל אם לא ידעת מולדו קח לו שאלה תחילה; אם הוא נותן הדרך אז תבחר לו שעה. (4) והנה המבחרים על שני דרכים.

(1) Before I discuss elections, I give you a rule: The human supernal soul has the power to annul some details ⟨of the natal horoscope⟩ and to augment or reduce anything signified by the stars, but it does not have power to annul the general import ⟨of the natal horoscope⟩. (2) As an illustration, if a man's natal horoscope signifies that a major injury will befall him during a journey in the twentieth year after his birth, the election will be powerless to annul that injury, but the injury may be reduced if he leaves his house as a result of a fortunate election; or the contrary if he leaves as a result of an unfortunate ⟨election⟩: ⟨the injury⟩ will be increased. (3) Therefore Dorotheus said: be careful not to choose a certain day and a certain hour for a man whose time of birth is not known to you. But if you do not know his time of birth, first make an interrogation on his behalf; if he reveals the route, then choose for him an hour ⟨to depart⟩. (4) Now there are two methods for elections.

Quotation 16: Introduction to Ibn Ezra's commentary on Ecclesiastes, ed. Gomez Aranda (1994), 6*–7*:

הנה ראינו ילבינו הבגדים השטוחים לשמש, ויחשכו פני הכובס. והלא הפועל אחד יוצא מפועל אחד! לכן השתנו הפעלים בעבור השתנות תולדות המקבלים. ומחשבות בני אדם משתנות כפי תולדת גויה וגויה, והשתנות התולדות בעבור השתנות המערכות העליונות ומקום השמש והמקבל כחה והמדינות והדתים והמאכלים.

We have seen that the garments spread out in the Sun are whitened, whereas the launderer's face is blackened, even though the action is performed by the same agent! Therefore the effects of actions change according to the difference in the natures of the receivers ⟨of these actions⟩. Also the thoughts of men change according to the difference in the nature of each body, and the natures ⟨of bodies⟩ change according to the differences in the upper configurations, in the position of the Sun, in the one who receives its power, in the cities, religions, and foods.

Quotation 17: Ibn Ezra's long commentary on Exodus 33:21, ed. Weiser (1976), II, 218, and Sela (2010), 276–277:

ואל יעלה על לבך, כי הארבעה תולדות בשמים, ויש בשמש חום וקור בלבנה ובשבתי; חלילה חלילה. כי הבריות העליונות נכבדות הם ועליהן כתוב: ״כי הוא צוה ונבראו, ויעמידם לעד לעולם״ (תה׳ קמח:ה—ו). רק נקראו ככה בעבור המקבלים.

But do not think that the four elements are in heavens, and that there is heat in the Sun and cold in the Moon and Saturn. God forbid. For the uppermost creatures are noble, and about them it is written: "For he commanded, and they were created" (Ps. 148:6). They were called so [i.e., fiery, earthy, airy and watery signs] only for the receivers ⟨of their influence⟩.

Quotation 18: *Me'orot* § 6:2, 458–459:

דע כי כח העושה ישתנה בעבור השתנות כח המקבל, כי הנה השמש תלבין הבגד ותחשיך פני כובסו.

Know that the power of the active ⟨agent⟩ varies according to the variation in the power of the receiver, for the Sun whitens the garment but blackens the face of the person who launders it.

Quotation 19: Aphorism 5 of Pseudo-Ptolemy's *Centiloquium*. *Sefer ha-Peri*, BnF 1055, fol. 53v:

אמר בטלמיוס כבר יוכל ההובר לדחות הרבה מפעולות הכוכבים כאשר היה יודע בטבע מה שירשמו בו והציע לפועל בטרם נפלו מקבל סבלהו.

Ptolemy said: the astrologer may divert many effects of the stars when he knows their influence in nature, and will prepare himself before he receives pain.

Quotation 20: *Mivḥarim* I, § 5:1–2, 48–49:

והדרך השני שתתקן מקום הכוכב שכנגד חפצי המבקש. כאדם שירצה לקחת אשה, בחר שיהיה נגה במקום טוב כנגד המעלה הצומחת, כי זה יועיל בין מי שתדע מולדו ואשר לא תדענו.

The second method is that you determine the position of the planet that conforms to the querent's wishes. ⟨For example, if⟩ a man wishes to marry a woman, choose ⟨to have him do so⟩ when Venus is in a fortunate position with respect to the ascendant degree ⟨of the electional horoscope⟩, because this will work whether or not you know his time of birth.

Quotation 21: *Mivḥarim* II, § 5:1–3, 146–147:

הדרך השנית למבחרים, דרך כלל, שנבקש לעולם הכוכב שיורה על הדבר המבוקש, ואז נעשה מבחר. והאמת כי אם ידענו המולד ונתקן הכלל והפרט, אז יהיה יותר טוב. כי אם בקשנו דברי נשים, נתקן מקום נגה גם הלבנה, וככה כל המשרתים כפי תולדתם.

The second method for elections, ⟨which is the⟩ general method, is that we always try to find the planet that signifies the requested thing and then make the election. But the truth is that if we know the time of birth and ⟨then⟩ proceed to determine the general import and the details ⟨of the natal horoscope⟩, it [the election] will be better. For example, if we are asked about women, we should determine the position of Venus and the Moon, and likewise all the planets according to their nature.

Quotation 22: Sahl's *Book of Elections*, Paris, BnF, lat. 16204, 488b:

Quorum autem ista ignorant, accipiantur eis interrogationes et sciant effectum rei eorum ex eis secundum hoc.

However, those who do not know these [their nativities], interrogations should be made for them and they will know the effect of their undertaking from them [the interrogations] in this way

APPENDIX 2

THE DEBATE ABOUT THE VALIDITY AND THE GENERAL PRINCIPLES OF THE DOCTRINE OF INTERROGATIONS

Quotation 1: *She'elot* I, §1:2–7, §2:1–3, §3:1–5, 240–243:

1 (1) חכמי המזלות נחלקו בשאלות לשתי תורות גדולות. (2) התורה האחת חנוך ובטלמיוס וקדמונים רבים עמהם. וכולם אומרים כי דיני המזלות הם ברורים ונכונים בדברי העולם ובנולדים, רק השאלות אין בהם ממש. (3) וטעמם: ידוע כי כל מה שיקרה בתחתיים הוא בעבור תנועות העליונים, וישתנו כפי השתנות מערכתם זה אל זה. (4) והנה זה דבר התולדת נכון שיורו העליונים על כל הנבראים כפי תולדתם. (5) ובעבור שנשמת האדם עליונה, יוכל להשמר ולהוסיף גם לגרוע. (6) על כן לא יורו העליונים על כל השאלות שתעלנה על לב האדם. (7) ואלה היו חכמים גדולים בדיעות הגלגלים.

2 (1) והתורה השנית ראשם דורוניאוס וחכמי הודו וחכמי פרס וחכמי מצרים וכל חכמי המזלות שהם קרובים אלינו. (2) וכולם מודים כי דיני השאלות נכונים כדיני המולדות. (3) וזה טעמם: ידוע הוא בחכמת התולדת כי מחשבות הנפש תשתנינה כפי השתנות תולדת הגוף, והנה כח הנשמה יתהפך כפי התהפך כח הגוף. ואחר שהכוכבים יורו על תולדת הגוף והתהפכו, הנה נוכל לדעת המחשבות והשאלות.

3 (1) על כן אמר משאללה: השמר לך שלא תדין בשום שאלה לאדם שבא לרמות או ללעוג. (2) וזה אמת בעבור כי יש כח בנשמת האדם לבטל מעט מהפרטים. (3) ואמר במקום אחר: אם לא ישאל השואל כהוגן לא ידין נכונה חכם המזלות. (4) אמר דורוניאוס: מערכת הכוכבים זה אל זה תוליד במחשבת האדם שאלה דומה למערכת. על כן נוכל לדעת מה שיש במחשבת השואל. (5) ואני אברהם אומר כי השאלות נכונות ברוב, רק אינם ככח המולדות.

1 (1) The astrologers are divided into two great schools of thought regarding interrogations. (2) The first is the school of Enoch, Ptolemy, and many of the Ancients. They all maintain that astral judgments are clear and reliable, both with respect to mundane affairs and with respect to natives, but interrogations are of no substance. (3) ⟨This is⟩ their reasoning: it is known that everything that occurs to the bodies of the lower world is caused by the movements of the upper bodies, and they [the bodies of the lower world] change according to the change in the configuration of ⟨the upper bodies⟩ with respect to one other. (4) This follows from nature; ⟨namely,⟩ that the bodies of the upper world give an indication about all creatures ⟨of the lower world⟩ according to their physical nature. (5) ⟨However⟩, since man's soul is supernal, he can protect himself and add to or subtract ⟨from what is caused by the stars⟩. (6) Therefore the upper bodies do not give an indication about all the interrogations a man may think of. (7) These were outstanding scholars in the science of the orbs.

2 (1) The second school is headed by Dorotheus, the scientists of India, the scientists of Persia, the scientists of Egypt, and all the astrologers who are close to us. (2) They all concur that judgments based on interrogations are as reliable as judgments based on nativities. (3) This is their reasoning: It is known in natural science that the thoughts of the mind change in accordance with the change in the physical nature of the body. Therefore, the power of the soul is altered according to the variation of the power of the body; and since the stars indicate the physical nature of the body and how it is altered, therefore we can know thoughts and interrogations.

3 (1) For this reason Māshā'allāh said: be careful not to pronounce judgment on any interrogation for a man who intends to cheat or mock. (2) This is true because man's soul has the power to annul a small part of the details ⟨of the natal horoscope⟩. (3) He also said in another place: if the querent does not pose the question appropriately, the astrologer will not be able to pronounce judgment correctly. (4) Dorotheus said: the configuration of the planets with respect to one other produces in a man's mind a question that is analogous to the ⟨celestial⟩ configuration. Therefore, we may know the querent's thoughts. (5) I, Abraham, say that in most cases interrogations are reliable, but they are not as powerful as nativities.

Quotation 2: *She'elot* II, § 1:1–4, 348–349:

(1) ראשי חכמי המזלות היו שנים, האחד תלמי והשני דורוניוס, ושניהם היו מלכים. (2) ותלמי מודה משפטי המזלות, ויש לו ספרים שלשה בדברי העולם גם במולדות, ואיננו מודה כי השאלות הם נכונות. (3) והנה דורוניוס אמר שהוא נסה פעמים רבות והם אמת, רק שלא יהא השואל מנסה או לועג, רק יהיה לבו בשאלתו, ובבא סימן ששם לנפשו יקח מיד המעלה הצומחת. (4) ומשאללה היה חכם גדול בשאלות ויש לו ספרים רבים בהם, והנה גם אני רדפתי אחריו ויצאתי בעקבותיו.

(1) There have been two leading astrologers: one of them Ptolemy and the other Dorotheus; both of them were kings. (2) Ptolemy endorses astral judgments; he has three books on mundane affairs as well as nativities, but he does not agree that interrogations are accurate. (3) But Dorotheus said that he had tested ⟨them⟩ by experience many times and found them to be truthful, on condition that the querent is not testing or mocking ⟨the astrologer⟩ but is sincere in his question, and that when the indication that he [the astrologer] has determined comes to his mind, he immediately takes the ascendant degree. (4) Māshā'allāh was a great scholar of interrogations and wrote many books on this topic, and I too have pursued him and followed in his footsteps.

Quotation 3: Ibn abī l-Rijāl's *Kitāb al-Bāriʿ*, *De iudiciis astrorum*, ed. Petri (1551), I:5, 16b:

Discordes sunt etiam in quaestionibus et electionibus, quia Ptolemaeus negat quaestiones et electiones, et dicit quod veritas non est nisi in revolutionibus

> annorum suorum, quia ille qui fortunatus est in sua nativitate et revolutione sui anni et divisor, et locus radiorum suorum sunt locis fortunatis, erit fortunatus in illo anno, at si contrarium habuerit, laboriosus et infortunatus erit illo anno.
>
> ⟨The astrologers⟩ disagree concerning interrogations and elections, for Ptolemy rejects the interrogations and the elections, and says that only the revolutions of their years are true, because one who is fortunate in his nativity and in the revolution of its year, and the divisor and the place of its rays are in fortunate positions, will be fortunate in this year, and if the opposite occurs, he will be suffering and unfortunate in this year.

Quotation 4: *Epitome*, ed. Heller (1548), III:2, O4r :

> In omni quaestione est quaerendus dominus signi ascendentis et Luna, et suspice eum potissimum, qui aspicit ascendentem.
>
> In every question one needs to search for the lord of the sign of the ascendant and the Moon, and look up to the most powerful, the one that aspects the ascendant.

Quotation 5: Sahl's *Book of Interrogations*, Paris, BnF lat. 16204, 446a:

> Et si interrogatus fueris de aliqua re de rebus que fuerint in .xii. signis ... aspice dominum ascendentis et Lunam et fortiorem eorum illlum scilicet qui fuerit in angulo.
>
> If you are asked about some matter of the matters related to the .12. signs ... look at the lord of the ascendant and the Moon, and the strongest of them, that is, the one that is in a cardo.

Quotation 6: Aphorism 50 of Pseudo-Ptolemy's *Centiloquium*. *Sefer ha-Peri*, BnF héb 1055, fol. 59v:

> אמר בטלמיוס לא תתעלם מענין המאה ועשרים מחברות אשר לכוכבים הנבוכים כי בהם ידיעת רוב מה שיפול בעולם ההויה וההפסד.
>
> Ptolemy said: do not ignore the 120 conjunctions of the planets, because from them comes the knowledge of almost everything that occurs in the world of generation and corruption.

Quotation 7: First aphorism of Pseudo-Ptolemy's *Centiloquium*. See *Sefer ha-Peri*, BnF héb 1055, fol. 52r:

> אמר בטלמיוס: חכמת הכוכבים ממך ומהם.
>
> The science of the stars is from you and from them.

Quotation 8: *Epitome*, tertia pars, Venice, BNM, Fondo antico lat. Z. 343, fol. 123v:

> Et est sciendum domus firmas significare in hiis que erunt in actu et temporibus prolatatis; et sic anguli, sed prima et decima brevius, et locus planetarum ex proportione Solis scilicet si ascendat ante ipsum vel sit directus vel sit ei iunctus in gradu uno.
>
> One needs to know that the fixed houses signify things that will actually exist and about prolonged periods; the same applies to the cardines, but the first and tenth ⟨places signify⟩ a shorter ⟨period⟩, and the position of the planets with respect to the Sun if ⟨the planet⟩ rises before it [the Sun] and is direct ⟨in its motion⟩ or is conjoined to it [the Sun] in one degree.

Quotation 9: *Epitome*, tertia pars, Venice, BNM, Fondo antico lat. Z. 344, fol. 21a–b:

> Et signa mobilia significant rem non futuram actu, nisi motionem de loco ad locum, vel privationem a regno, et spem et timorem futuri, quod non erit actu; sic etiam domus lapsae nisi .6a. infirmatibus .12a. inimicis et carcere; sic etiam loci planetarum ex proportione Solis cum sunt cremati et retrogradi vel in oppositione.
>
> The tropical signs signify that the thing will not come to be, except for motion from a location to another location, or deposition from the kingdom, and hope and fear of the future that will not come to be; the same applies to the cadent places except for the sixth ⟨place⟩, about sick persons and the twelfth ⟨place⟩ about enemies and prison; the same applies to the positions of the planets with respect to the Sun, when they are burnt, retrograde or in opposition ⟨to the Sun⟩.

Quotation 10: *Epitome*, tertia pars, Venice, BNM, Fondo antico lat. Z. 344, fol. 21b:

> Sed bicorporum domus, et domus post angulos, significant rem futuram semiplene, vel etiam bis, sed .11. et .9. significant dilationem et secundum imaginem eventum, .5a. et .8a. dilationem et improvisionem futuri, sic et loci planetarum cum sunt occidentales Soli vel stant in sua statione.
>
> But the bicorporal houses, and the succedent places, signify that the thing will come to be incompletely, or twice, but the eleventh and ninth ⟨places⟩ signify delay according to the shape of the event, and the fifth and eighth ⟨places signify⟩ delay and lack of foresight of the future, and the same applies to the positions of the planets when they are occidental of the Sun or in their station.

Quotation 11: *She'elot* II, § 7:1, 352–353:

> ויש לך להסתכל, לכל דבר, אם לך שנים עדים, תדין בהם כאשר פרשתי בספר המולדות, ויש לך להסתכל לכל המבטים והמחברות.

For every question you should observe whether you have two testimonies, and pronounce judgment based on them, as I have explained in the *Book of Nativities*; and observe all the aspects and the conjunctions.

Quotation 12: *Epitome*, Venice, BNM, Fondo antico lat. Z. 344, fol. 21rb:

In omni questione est querendus dominus signi ascendentis et Luna, et suspice eorum aspicientem ascendens. Si ambo aspiciant, suspice habentem plures fortitudines in loco suo, ratione domorum, vel Solis, vel Lune sue potestatis. Si ambo sunt pares, suscipe a Luna, et dominum ascendentis cum ea associa. Si nullus vero aspicit et nullus horum dat vim alii planetae, quovis aspectu, qui aspiciat ascendens, ipsum sumas, quo bonum vel malum comperitur, et melius si ipse habet vim in ascendente.

In any question one must find the lord of the sign of the ascendant and the Moon, and observe which of them aspects the ascendant. If both aspect ⟨the ascendant⟩, observe which of them has more powers in its position, on account of the places, the Sun, the Moon and its dignity. If both are equal ⟨in powers⟩, observe the Moon, and associate the lord of the ascendant with it. If none of them aspects and none of them gives power to another planet, in whatever aspect, take the one that aspects the ascendant, and it is better if it has power in the ascendant.

Quotation 13: *She'elot* I, § 7:1, 244–245:

אמר יעקב אל כנדי: הסתכל אל מקום השמש ביום ואל מקום הלבנה ביום ובלילה, ואל מקום מחברת המאורות או נכחם, אי זה מהם שיהיה קודם השאלה, ואל המעלה הצומחת, ואל הגורל הטוב ביום ובלילה, הוא הנתפש בדרך בטלמיוס ככתוב בספר הטעמים, וראה השליט על אלה המקומות, וממנו תדין על השאלה.

Ya'qub Al-Kindī said: observe the Sun's position by day and the Moon's position by day and by night, the position of the luminaries' conjunction or opposition (whichever ⟨is the last that⟩ occurs before the interrogation), the ascendant degree, and the lot of Fortune by day and by night, as calculated according to Ptolemy's method as explained in the *Book of Reasons*; find out the ruler over these positions and pronounce judgment about the interrogation from it.

Quotation 14: *She'elot* II, § 9:1–3, 354–355:

ויאמר משאלה: לעולם הסתכל, אם רצית לדעת על מה שאל השואל, אל הפקיד על הגלגל, והטעם מי שיש לו יותר ממשלה בחמשת השרים, והטעם במקומותם שהם מקומות החיים.

Māshā'allāh said: if you want to know the object of the querent's interrogation, always observe the lord of the orb, meaning ⟨the planet⟩ that has more lordship over the five rulers, meaning ⟨more lordship⟩ over their positions, which are the places of life

Quotation 15: *Epitome*, ed. Heller (1548), III:2, O4r :

Dorothius vero dominum vigoris, qui plus virtutis habet in locis quinque, cuius verbum est ceteris et verius.

Dorotheus ⟨observes⟩ the lord of strength, the one with most powers in the five places, whose influence is stronger than that of the others.

Quotation 16: *Epitome*, ed. Heller (1548), III:2, O4r :

(1) Magistri aut Indi aspiciunt dominum horae sicut nos dominum ascendentis. (2) Dorothius vero dominum vigoris, qui plus virtutis habet in locis quinque, cuius verbum est ceteris et verius.

(1) The Indian masters look at the lord of the hour as we ⟨look at⟩ the lord of the ascendant. (2) Dorotheus ⟨observes⟩ the lord of strength, the one with most powers in the five places, whose influence is stronger than that of the others.

Quotation 17: *She'elot* I, § 1.1:1–5, 246–249:

דע כי מחלוקת גדולה יש בין החכמים בדברי השאלות ... והאמת מה שאומר לך: אם השואל ישאל על נפשו, כח המזל הצומח לו, ואם בעבור אחד מאחיו, אם יתחבר עמו ומה יהיה לו, קח הבית השלישי ומקום מאדים, ומשם תדין. וכמו כן, אם ישאל על אב, הסתכל אל הבית הרביע׳ ובעליו, ועל זה הדרך מי ששאל על בן או עבד או אשה או מלך או אוהב או שונא.

Know that there is a great disagreement among astrologers about interrogations ... But the truth is what I will tell you ⟨now⟩: if the querent poses a question about himself, take the ascendant sign for him; if on behalf of one of his brothers, whether he will meet him and what will happen to him, take the third place and the position of Mars, and pronounce judgment from there. If he poses a question about the father, observe the fourth place and its lord, and proceed likewise ⟨if he poses a question⟩ about a son, a slave, a woman, a king, a lover, or an enemy.

Quotation 18: *She'elot* I, § 7.4:1–5, 272–273:

רק אם שאל אדם על שנים שלטונים, אי זה מהם ינצח את חבירו, הנה השתבשו בדבר זה חכמי המזלות. אמר משאללה: שים המזל הצומח לקטן מהם בשנים והשוקע לגדול בשנים. אמר דורוניאוס: שים המזל הצומח לאשר החל להלחם והשוקע לאויבו. אמר אבו עלי: שים המזל הצומח לאשר הוא השואל ברשותו או יאהבהו יותר. אמר אבו מעשר: קודם שתשאל, שים המזל הצומח לאי זה מהם שתרצה. ואם השואל אדם אחר, אמור לו שלא ישאל רק על אחד מהם, אם ינצח. ונראו לי דברי זה החכם משאר הדברים.

But if someone posed a question about two rulers, which of them will defeat the other, the astrologers were confused. Māshā'allāh said: assign the ascendant sign to the younger of them and the ⟨sign of the⟩ descendant to the older. Dorotheus said: assign the ascendant sign to the one who began the war and the descendant to his enemy. Abū ʿAlī said: assign the ascendant sign to the one under whose authority is the querent or ⟨to the ruler whom the querent⟩ favors. Abū Maʿshar said: before you make an interrogation [i.e., before you cast the horoscope of the interrogation], assign the ascendant sign to whichever ⟨of the rulers⟩ you wish. If the querent is a third party [i.e., is not one of the combatants], tell him to ask about only one of the parties—whether it will be victorious ⟨over the other⟩. This scholar's statements seem to me more satisfactory than all the other statements.

Quotation 19: *Epitome*, ed. Heller (1548), III:12, Q2r:

In questione autem quis sit victurus, astrologi discordati sunt. Quidam enim dicunt primam domum et eius dominum debere suspici pro habente pauciores annos, septimam vero cum suo domino pro etate maiori. Alii domum primam et eius dominum pro inceptore, septimam autem et eius dominum pro altero ponunt. Alii vero dicunt astrologum ante horam quaestionis eligere in animo, pro quo primam et pro quo septimam debeat suspicere. Hanc vero postremam rationem experimentis caeteris praeponimus.

But regarding the question of who will be victorious, the astrologers disagreed. Some sat that the first place and its lord should be assigned to the younger, but the seventh ⟨place⟩ and its lord to the older. Other ⟨said that⟩ the first ⟨place⟩ and its lord ⟨should be assigned⟩ to the one who begins ⟨the war⟩, and the seventh ⟨place⟩ and its lord to the other. Other say that the astrologer should choose in his mind before the time of the question to whom the first and seventh ⟨place⟩ will be assigned. I have preferred the last opinion over the others as a result of proofs.

Quotation 20: *She'elot* II, § 7.3:1–4, 370–371:

והנה, מחלוקת גדולה יש אם ישאל השואל על שני מלכים, אי זה מהם ינצח. יש אומרים, שישים המזל העולה לאשר הוא קטון בשנים והמזל השביעי לגדול ממנו. ואחרים אמרו לא, כי רק יהיה המזל העולה לאשר יחל המלחמה והשביעי לאחר. ודורוניוס אמר כי הנכון שישים בלבו השואל, אי זה מהם שירצה קודם שישאל, והטעם שיאהב יותר, והנה יהיה שלו המזל העולה.

There is a major disagreement about the querent who asks which of two kings will be victorious. Some say that he [the astrologer] should assign the rising sign to the younger and the sign of the seventh place to the older. Others disagreed ⟨and said⟩ that the rising sign should be assigned to the side that starts the war and the seventh ⟨place⟩ to the other ⟨side⟩. Dorotheus said that the correct approach is for the querent to make up his mind which side he prefers, meaning which side he likes more, before he poses the question, and the rising sign should be assigned to it.

APPENDIX 3

ELECTIONS

Part 1: Taking a Purgative

Quotation 1: *Mivḥarim* I, §1.3:1–4, §1.5:1–3, 52–55:

1 (1) ולשתות רפואה, ראה מה רפואה ירצה לשתות. (2) אם לשלשל או להקיא, ושים הלבנה באחד מזלות המים על מנת שתעבור שלש מעלות מעקרב, ואם היתה מתבודדת שלא יביט אליה שום כוכב אז יותר טוב. (3) והשמר שלא תתן כחה לאחד מן הכוכבים שהם למעלה מן הארץ, כי אז יקיא המשקה. (4) ואם תתן כחה לאחד הכוכבים שהם תחת הארץ כנגד המזל הצומח, לא יזיק על מנת שלא תתן הכח ממבט רע לאחד מן המזיקים ולא לכוכב שהוא שב אחורנית, כי יורה על קיא.

2 (1) אמר בטלמיוס: השמר לא תתן רפואת שלשול לאדם והלבנה עם צדק או נגה, או שתתן כחה להם, כי תולדתם להחזיק תולדת הגוף ולא להוציא ממנו כלום. (2) וחכמי הניסיון הבאים [130ב] אחריו לא הודו לו, על כן אמרתי כי טוב גמור הוא שתהיה הלבנה מתבודדת ולא תביט אל כוכב. (3) ואם רצונך לתת משקה להקיא, שים הלבנה במזל שור, או תתן כחה לכוכב שהוא במזל שור או לכוכב שהוא למעלה מן הארץ או לכוכב שהוא שב אחורנית.

1 (1) For taking a medicine, consider which medicine he wants to take. (2) If ⟨the medicine is⟩ a purgative or a vomitive, put the Moon in one of the watery signs, on condition that it is not more than 3° from ⟨the head of⟩ Scorpio; it is more auspicious if [the Moon] secludes itself in such a way that no planet aspects it. (3) Be careful not to do this when it [the Moon] gives its power to one of the planets that are above the Earth, because then he will vomit the potion. (4) But if it [the Moon] gives its power to one of the planets that are below the Earth with respect to the ascendant sign, it [the Moon] will not cause harm, on condition that it does not give its power from an unfortunate aspect to any of the malefic planets or to a retrograde ⟨planet⟩, because this signifies vomitus.

2 (1) Ptolemy said: Be careful not to administer a purgative to a man when the Moon is with Jupiter or Venus, or when it [the Moon] gives its power to them [Jupiter or Venus], because their nature is to hold on to the natural makeup of the body and not to remove anything from it. (2) But the scholars who rely on experience who followed him did not agree with him; therefore I said that it is totally beneficial if the Moon secludes itself and does not aspect any planet. (3) If you wish to administer a vomitive, put the Moon in Taurus, or ⟨do so when⟩ it gives its power to a planet that is in Taurus or to a planet that is above the Earth or to a retrograde planet.

Quotation 2: *Mivḥarim* II, § 1.1:1–2, § 1.2:1–4, 150–151:

1 (1) הבית הראשון. אם רצית לאכול רפואה או לשתות משקה, שים הלבנה באחד ממזלות המים, ומזל עקרב טוב מכולם ובלבד שתעבור מעלת הקלון שהיא השלישית. (2) והטוב שתהיה הלבנה בכחה, והטעם שלא תתן הכח לכוכבים.

2 (1) אמר תלמי: אם היתה הלבנה על מבט צדק בשתות משקה לשלשל, יזיק; רק נגה יותר טוב, והשמר שלא יביט מאדים ולא שבתאי ולא כוכב חמה אם היה בממסך רע, איזה מבט שיהיה. (2) ואם לא יכולת, כך עשה שיהיה המבט מששית או מהשלישית, ועשה שתעבור מעלת המבט, ואפילו במעלה א׳; רק אם היה ממבט נכח או רביעית, כך עשה שתהיה הלבנה רחוקה ממעלת המבט כמספר אור הכוכב הרע. (3) והשמר שלא תתן הלבנה הכח לכוכב החוזר אחור, כי יקיא השותה המשקה. (4) וככה אם תתן הלבנה הכח לכוכב שהוא למעלה מן הארץ כנגד המעלה הצומחת בשעת השתיה; על כן, יש לך להשמר.

1 (1) The first ⟨horoscopic⟩ place. If you want to take a medicine or drink a potion, put the Moon in any of the watery signs; Scorpio is the most auspicious, on condition that it [the Moon] has passed the degree of dejection, which is the third ⟨of Scorpio⟩. (2) ⟨It is more⟩ auspicious if the Moon is at its full strength, meaning that it does not give power to the planets.

2 (1) Ptolemy said: if the Moon is in some aspect with Jupiter when someone takes a purgative, it will cause harm. Venus is more auspicious, but make sure that Mars, Saturn, and Mercury do not aspect ⟨the Moon⟩ in an unfortunate complexion, whatever aspect it may be. (2) If you cannot do this, set it so that the aspect is sextile or trine and it passes the degree of the aspect, even by one degree; but if the aspect is opposition or quartile, set it so that the Moon's distance from the degree of the aspect is ⟨at least equal⟩ to the number ⟨of degrees⟩ of the malefic planet's ray. (3) Make sure that the Moon does not give power to a retrograde planet, because ⟨the patient⟩ will vomit up the potion. (4) The same applies if the Moon gives power to a planet that is above the Earth with respect to the ascendant degree when he drinks the potion; so be careful about this.

Quotation 3: *Epitome*, ed. Heller (1548), IV:2 (De accipiendis purgationibus), R4r:

(1) Cave ne sit Luna in aspectu vel coniunctione Veneris aut Iovis ... (2) Sed melius tamen nullo planeta eam aspiciente, & melius percurrente Luna tertium gradum Scorpionis, vel si sit in Cancro vel Piscibus.

(1) Be careful that the Moon does not aspect or conjoin Venus or Jupiter ... (2) It is even better if no planet aspects her [the Moon], and better when the Moon runs along the third degree of Scorpio, or she is in Cancer or Pisces.

Quotation 4: Pseudo-Ptolemy's *Centiloquium*, aphorisms 21 and 19, *Sefer ha-Peri*, BNF 1055, fol. 55v:

1 (1) אמר בטלמיוס מי שלקח סם משלשל והירח עם צדק תקצר ותחלש פעולתו.

1 (1) Ptolemy said: one who takes a purgative when the Moon is with Jupiter, shortens and weakens its effect.

2 (1) אמר בטלמיוס מי שלקח סם משלשל והירח עם צדק תקצר ותחלש פעולתו.

2 (1) Ptolemy said: one who takes a purgative when the Moon is with Jupiter, shortens and weakens its effect.

Part 2: Reducing Humors

Quotation 1: *Mivḥarim* I, §1.6:1–2, §1.8:1–3, 54–55:

1 (1) ואם תרצה להקיז, השמר שלא תהיה הלבנה במזל תאומים, שהוא מזל הזרוע, ולא תהיה כמו כן עם שבתי או עם מאדים. (2) ואם היה במבט שלישית או ששית עם מאדים הוא יותר טוב ממבט שלישית וששית של שבתי, ומבט רביעית או נכח עם שבתי או מאדים או כוכב חמה מזיק.

2 (1) אמר בטלמיוס: השמר שלא תגע בברזל כלל באחד מאיבריך בזמן שהלבנה באותו מזל שיורה על אותו פרק האיברים. (2) דמיון כגון להקיז בראש והלבנה בטלה, או בצואר והוא בשור, ובן כלם כי יקיז. (3) והוא דבר מנוסה והודו לו הבאים אחריו.

1 (1) If you wish to perform phlebotomy, make sure that the Moon is not in Gemini, which is the sign ⟨in charge⟩ of the arm, or that it [the Moon] is not with Saturn or Mars. (2) If it [the Moon] is in trine or sextile with Mars, this is more beneficial than if it is in trine or sextile with Saturn; but quartile or opposition with Saturn, Mars, or Mercury is detrimental.

2 (1) Ptolemy said: Be careful that no iron touches any part of your body when the Moon is in a sign signifying that part of the body. (2) As an illustration, suppose that one performs phlebotomy from the head when the Moon is in Aries, or from the neck when ⟨the Moon is in⟩ Taurus, and likewise regarding all ⟨the parts of the body⟩ when he performs phlebotomy ⟨from them⟩. (3) This has been verified by experience, and agreed upon by those who came after him [Ptolemy].

Quotation 2: *Mivḥarim* II, §1.3:2–3, §1.4:1–3, 150–153:

1 (1) ומבט מאדים משלישית או ששית טוב להקיז דם, ושבתאי הוא רע, והטוב שלא יסתכל. (2) וכל הקדמונים הסכימה דעתם, שאין ראוי להקיז דם אם הלבנה בתאומים, והטעם ידוע בעבור שהוא בית הזרועות והידים.

2 (1) כי אמר תלמי: השמר שלא יגע ברזל באבר שהלבנה שם, כנגד מזל טלה שהוא הראש. (2) כאילו היתה הלבנה בסרטן, והוא יורה על החזה, אמר שאין ראוי לשים כויה בחזה כי הכויה היא בברזל. (3) וזה הדבר לפי דעתי, ולפי דעת רבים זה מנוסה.

1 (1) ⟨The Moon in⟩ trine or sextile with Mars is auspicious for bloodletting, but Saturn is unfortunate, ⟨so⟩ it is auspicious if it [Saturn] does not form any aspect. (2) All the Ancients agreed that it is not appropriate to perform blood-

letting when the Moon is in Gemini; the reason is well known: it [Gemini] is the sign of the arms and the hands.

2 (1) Ptolemy said: be careful that iron does not touch any part of the body ⟨when the Moon is⟩ there [in the sign which signifies this part of the body], such as Aries, which corresponds to the head. (2) Suppose that the Moon is in Cancer, which signifies the chest; ⟨in this case⟩ he [Ptolemy] said that is not appropriate to cauterize the chest, because cautery is done by iron. (3) I agree with this opinion, and according to the opinion of many others this has been proven by experience.

Quotation 3: *Epitome*, ed. Heller (1548), IV:3, R3v:

(1) Aspice ne sit Luna in Geminis. (2) Sed fac ut in aspectu trino vel sextili Martis sit. (3) Verum ne sit coniuncta ei quavis praedictarum coniunctione, nec in aspectu eiusdem contrario vel quadrato. (4) Simile est iudicium Saturno, et omni alio aspectu ac coniunctione eius … (5) Ptolomeus vero ait, membrum non esse ferro tangendum Luna existente in signo, quod habet illud membrum, ut est in Isagogis assignatum.

(1) Be careful that the Moon is not in Gemini. (2) But make ⟨the Moon⟩ be in trine or sextile with Mars. (3) Certainly, make ⟨the Moon⟩ not be conjoined in conjunction to any of the aforementioned, nor in opposition or quadrature. (4) The same applies to Saturn's judgement, in any other aspect or its conjunction … (5) Ptolemy said: do not touch any member with an iron when the Moon is in the sign in charge of that member, as it [the member] is assigned ⟨to a sing⟩ in the Introduction.

Quotation 4: Pseudo-Ptolemy's *Centiloquium*, aphorisms 20, *Sefer ha-Peri*, BnF héb 1055, fol. 55v:

אמר בטלמיוס משוש הברזל לאבר והירח במזל האבר ההוא רע

Ptolemy said: The touching of a member by the iron [i.e., to carry out phlebotomy] when the Moon is located in the sign assigned to that member, is inauspicious.

Part 3: Buying to Make a Profit

Quotation 1: *Mivḥarim* II, § 2.1:1–3, 152–155:

(1) אם רצית לקנות דבר שתרויח בו, שים הלבנה בחלק הגלגל הקטן, והיא תוסיף בהלוכה, גם רחבה יוסיף, ותהיה על מבט טוב מאחד הכוכבים הטובים. (2) ואם יכולת לשים המעלה הצומחת כדי שתהיה הלבנה באחר היתדות, או באחד הסמוכים, או בבית השלישי, אז יהיה יותר טוב. (3) ואם לא יכולת, שימנה שתתן כח לאחד הכוכבים שהם במקומות הנזכרים—אם הוא כוכב טוב מאיזה מבט שיהיה, ואם רע יהיה מבט ששית או שלישית.

(1) If you want to buy something to make a profit from it, put the Moon in the smaller domain of the zodiac, its motion increasing, its ⟨ecliptic⟩ latitude increasing, and in a fortunate aspect with any of the benefic planets. (2) It is more auspicious if you can set the ascendant degree so that the Moon is in one of the cardines or in one of the succedent places, or in the third place. (3) If you cannot do this, put it [the Moon] ⟨in a position where⟩ it gives power to one of the planets that are in these positions—in any aspect, for a benefic planet, and in sextile or trine, for a malefic ⟨planet⟩.

Quotation 2: *Mivḥarim* I, § 2.1:1–2, 54–57:

(1) אמר בטלמיוס: הרוצה לקנות דבר שירויח בו, ישים הלבנה בחלקה, שהוא החלק הקטן מן הגלגל, שהוא כתחלת מזל דלי עד סוף סרטן. (2) וזה הדבר הוא מנוסה, על מנת שלא תהיה הלבנה עם אחד המזיקים, ולא במבט רע עמהם, ולא במעלות שוות ממרחק קו הצדק, או סוף צפון ודרום עמהם.

(1) Ptolemy said: One who wishes to buy something and make a profit from it should put the Moon in its domain, which is the smaller domain of the zodiac, that is, from the beginning of Aquarius to the end of Cancer. (2) This has been verified by experience, ⟨and it works⟩ if the Moon is not with one of the malefics, nor in an unfortunate aspect with them, nor in degrees that are equidistant from the equator or from the extreme north or south.

Quotation 3: *Ṭeʿamim* I, § 2.5:1–5, 44–45:

(1) ויאמר חנוך: אחר שידענו כי אלה הבתים הם בתי המאורות, חלקו העשרה בתים הנשארים על המשרתים. (2) והנה היה לכל משרת בית בחלק השמש ובית בחלק הלבנה, רק האחד לפנים והאחר לאחור. (3) על כן אמרו חכמי המזלות כי מתחלת אריה עד סוף גדי הוא חלק השמש, והוא החלק הגדול. (4) ויש לשמש כח בחלקה ככח המשרתים בגבולם, גם ככה הלבנה בחלקה הקטן, שהוא מראש דלי עד סוף סרטן. (5) על כן אמרו חכמי הנסיון כי כל דבר שיקנה אדם והלבנה בחלקה הקטן ימכרנו ביותר מאשר קנהו, והפך זה אם היה בחלק הגדול.

(1) Enoch said: because we know that these houses are the houses of the luminaries, they assigned the remaining ten houses to the planets. (2) Accordingly, each planet was assigned a house in the domain of the Sun and a house in the domain of the Moon, although one forward and the other backward. (3) Therefore the astrologers said that from the beginning of Leo to the end of Capricorn is the domain of the Sun, and this is the larger domain. (4) The Sun has power in its domain like the power of the planets in their terms; the same applies to the Moon in its smaller domain, which is from the beginning of Aquarius to the end of Cancer. (5) Therefore the scholars who rely on experience said that if a person buys something when the Moon is in the smaller domain, he will sell it for more than the purchase price, and the opposite occurs if it [the Moon] was in the larger domain.

Quotation 4: *Epitome*, ed. Heller (1548), IV:4, sig. R4r:

Volens causa lucrandi aliquid emere, emas cum Luna fuerit in parte magna circuli, quae dicitur Solis, & est a capite Cancri ad finem Sagittarii, & melius si sit velox, nec sit iuncta planetae infortunae, vel eius aspectui, & melius ea existente in coniunctione, vel aspectu fortunae planetae, vel in aspectu Solis trino vel sextili.

⟨For⟩ one who wishes to buy something to make a profit, buy when the Moon is in the larger part of the circle, which is said to be in the Sun's portion, which is from the beginning of Cancer to the end of Sagittarius, and it is better if it is quick and does not conjoin an inauspicious planet or is in its aspect, and it is better if it is in conjunction or forms an aspect with an auspicious planet, or is in trine or sextile with the Sun.

Quotation 5: Sahl's *Book of elections*, Paris, BnF lat. 16204, 491b:

Et si volueris vendere, pone Lunam in exaltatione sua vel triplicitate separatam a fortuniis et aspiciente malos, sed non sit eis iuncta.

If you wish to sell, put the Moon in its exaltation, separated from the benefics, forming an aspect of trine with the malefics but not in conjunction with them.

Part 4: Setting Off on a Journey

Quotation 1: *Mivḥarim* II, § 3.2:1–3, 156–157:

(1) וללכת בדרך קרובה, השמר שלא יהיה שבתאי בבית השלישי, ואף כי אם הדרך בים או בנהר. (2) וככה, מאדים לא יהיה בשלישי אם הדרך ביבשה. (3) והשמר לך, כי דבר מנוסה הוא מהקדמונים ואני נסיתיו, שלא תכנס לעולם בים בדרך קרובה או רחוקה ושבתאי בעל השעה.

(1) ⟨To choose a time⟩ to set off on a short journey, make sure that Saturn is not in the third place, particularly if the journey is by sea or by river. (2) Likewise, Mars should not be in the third place if the journey is by land. (3) Be careful, because it has been proven by the Ancients and I have verified it by experience: you should never set off on a long or short journey by sea when Saturn is the lord of the hour.

Quotation 2: *Mivḥarim* I, § 3.5:1–3, 60–61:

(1) וחכמי המזלות הסכימה דעתם כי להכנס בספינה באחד מזלות האש הוא סכנה גדולה. (2) וטעם זה ידוע: בעבור כי יהיה הבית השמיני, שבו הפחד והמות, מזל המים; ואחריהם מזלות העפר, וטעמם ידוע: בעבור היות מזלות המים לנכחם. (3) והטובים שבכולם מזלות המים, ואחריהם בטובה מזלות הרוח.

(1) The scholars of the signs agreed that it is very dangerous to take ship when one of the fiery signs ⟨is in the ascendant⟩. (2) The reason is well known: because then [when a fiery sign is in the ascendant] the eighth place, which signifies fear and death, is a watery sign; after them [the fiery signs] ⟨the most dangerous are⟩ the earthy signs, and the reason is well known: because the watery signs are in opposition to them [to the earthy signs]. (3) Best of all are the watery signs, and next best are the airy signs.

Quotation 3: *Mivḥarim* II, § 9.2:1–2, 168–171:

אמר דורוניוס: השמר שלא תהיה הלבנה בתחלת הנסיעה במזל דגים, כי יורה שתטבע. והאמת, כאשר נסיתי, כי הוא דבר קשה, רק אם יביטו כוכבים טובים אל הלבנה ימלטו.

Dorotheus said: make sure that the Moon is not in Pisces at the beginning of a journey, because it indicates that ⟨the ship⟩ will sink. The truth, as I have tested by experience, is that the outcome will be calamitous and they will escape only if benefic planets aspect the Moon.

Quotation 4: *Mivḥarim* I, § 3.4:1, 60–61:

אמרו חכמי הודו: הזהר שלא תכנס בים והלבנה במזל דגים. וכן האמת, רק אם היה במבטה או במחברתה אחד מן הטובים לא תחוש.

The scientists of India said: Be careful not to begin a journey by sea when the Moon is in Pisces. This is true, but if one of the benefic planets is in aspect or conjunction with it [the Moon] you should not be worried.

Part 5: Finding Something Hidden

Quotation 1: *Mivḥarim* I, § 4.5:1–2, 64–65:

(1) ואם רצית לעשות דבר מכוסה שלא יגלה, שים הלבנה תחת אור השמש ובעל המזל הצומח כך. ואם לא יכולת, שימנו בבית הרביעי על מנת שלא יתן כחו לכוכב שהוא למעלה מן הארץ. (2) ואם רצית לבחור שעה לבקש דבר נסתר תחת הארץ, השמר שלא יהיה שבתי באחת היתדות, כי יתעכב הדבר ולא ימצא.

(1) If you want to do something in secret and not have it revealed, put the Moon and the lord of the ascendant sign under the ray of the Sun. If you cannot do this, put it [the lord of the ascendant sign] in the fourth place, but only if it does not give its power to a planet that is above the Earth. (2) If you wish to choose an hour to find something hidden under ⟨the surface of⟩ the earth, be careful not to do this when Saturn is in one of the cardines, because it will be held back and will not be found.

Part 6: Building a Wall to Protect a City

Quotation 1: *Mivḥarim* II, § 4.2:8, 158–159:

ואם רצה המלך לבנות חומה לשמור מדינה ידועה וידעת מזלה, השמר שלא תשים המזל העולה השביעי ממזל המדינה, כי הוא מזל אויביה.

If the king wishes to build a wall to protect a certain city and you know its [the city's] sign, be careful not to put the seventh sign ⟨counting⟩ from the sign of the city as the rising sign, because it [the seventh sign] is the sign of its [the city's] enemies.

Part 7: Pregnancy

Quotation 1: *Mivḥarim* I, § 5.1:1,2,6, 64–67:

מי שרוצה להתחבר עם אשתו בשעה שיהיה לו בן זכר ... ושים כוכב צדק במקום טוב אם יכולת, כי יש לו כח גדול בבנים, ואם יכולת להיותו במזל זכר או מזרחי מהשמש או ברביעית שהוא בחלק זכר, אז יותר טוב ... ודע כי שמחת נגה בבית החמישי. והנה, אם היה שם והוא מערבי מן השמש והמזל זכר, אין צריך לתקן כל מה שהזכרתי, כי בזה די לך.

A man who wishes to have sexual intercourse with his wife at an hour when he will father a son ... If you can, put Jupiter in a fortunate position, because it has great power for sons; and, if you can, it is more auspicious to put it in a masculine sign, or oriental of the Sun, or in a masculine quadrant ... Know that Venus' joy is in the fifth place. Consequently, if it [Venus] is there [in the fifth place] and it is occidental of the Sun and in a masculine sign, there is no need to calculate everything I have mentioned, because this will be enough for you.

Quotation 2: *Mivḥarim* II, § 5.1:4, 158–159:

ואם יכולת להיות צדק באחת היתדות, ואף כי ברביעית זכרות מפאת השמש או מפאת המעלה הצומחת גם במזל זכר, אז טוב.

It is auspicious if you do this when Jupiter is in one of the cardines, particularly in a masculine quadrant with respect to the Sun or ⟨in a masculine quadrant with respect⟩ to the ascendant degree and also in a masculine sign.

Quotation 3: *Mivḥarim* I, § 5.1:5, 64–65:

והשמר שלא יהיה מאדים או שבתי בבית החמישי, או יביטו אליו מבט רביעית או נכח, כי יורו על נפל.

Be careful that Mars or Saturn is not in the fifth place and that they are not in an aspect of quartile or opposition with it, because they signify a miscarriage.

Part 8: Trutina Hermetis

Quotation 1: *Mishpeṭei ha-mazzalot*, § 15:1–5, § 17:1–4, 500–505:

1 (1) אמר חנוך בספרו כי מקום הלבנה במולד הנולדים קרובים אל ט׳ חדשים הוא הצומח בעת ההריון, והצומח עתה הוא מקום הלבנה בהריון. (2) והנה, אם היתה הלבנה קרובה אל סוף הבית השישי, העמידה בבטן היתה רפ״ז ימים; ואם בתחלה הבית השביעי המעמד היה רנ״ט, וביתד הרום רס״ו, ואם היתה במעלה הצומחת היה המעמד רע״ג ימים, וביתד התהום ר״ף. (3) ואל תסמוך על דברי הנשים כי אינם יודעות רגע ההריון. (4) וכבר נסיתי זה פעמים רבות, והוא אמת על תנאי אם לא יצא הנולד בחדש השביעי, והנולד ככה לא יאריך ימים. (5) גם יש מעט המעט שיהיה הנולד בחדש עשתי עשרה; גם הוא יחיה, רק הוא יהיה משונה במעשיו מכל האדם כפי מערכת הכוכבים.

2 (1) והנה אם רצית לדעת בדרך קרובה כמה היה המעמד הנולד בבטן, ראה אם היתה הלבנה ברגע המולד למעלה מן הארץ, ראה כמה מעלות ישרות בין תחלת הבית השביעי עד מקום הלבנה, וקח לכל י״ג מעלות יום אחד והוסף העולה על רנ״ט ימים. (2) ואם היתה הלבנה למטה מן הארץ, ראה כמה המרחק בין המעלה הצומחת ובין מקום הלבנה, וקח לכל י״ג מעלות יום אחד, והעולה הוסיפנו על רע״ג. (3) והמחובר הם ימי המעמד, ודע כי ישאר שלא יתחלק. (4) ואתה יש לך לתקן השעות, שתשים המעלה הצומחת ברגע ההריון מקום הלבנה ברגע המולד, ואם ידעת רגע ההריון הסתכל מקום הלבנה, והוא יהיה המזל הצומח בעת המולד, וראה המעלה הצומחת ברגע ההריון אנה תהיה ברגע המולד, אם למעלה מן הארץ או למטה, אז תוכל לדעת כמה המעמד.

1 (1) Enoch said in his book that the position of the Moon in the nativity of those born after approximately nine months ⟨of pregnancy⟩ is the ascendant at the time of conception, and the ascendant then [at birth] is the place of the Moon at the time of conception. (2) So if the Moon ⟨at the time of conception⟩ was close to the end of the sixth place, the time in the womb lasts 287 days, and if ⟨the Moon⟩ was at the cusp of the seventh place the pregnancy lasts 259 ⟨days⟩, ⟨if⟩ at the upper cardo 266 ⟨days⟩, and if at the ascendant degree the pregnancy is 273 days, and at the lower cardo 280 ⟨days⟩. (3) Do not trust what women say because they do not know the moment of conception. (4) I have myself tested this empirically many times and found it to be true, on condition that the baby is not born in the seventh month, because such a baby will not live long. (5) There are also a very few cases when a baby is born in the eleventh month; he will live, but his deeds will be unusual in comparison with other people, in accordance with the configuration of the stars.

2 (1) If you wish to know approximately how long the newborn was in the womb, find out whether the Moon at the time of birth was above the earth. Calculate the number of equal degrees between the cusp of the seventh place and the position of the Moon, assign one day to each interval of 13°, and add the result to 259 days. (2) But if the Moon was beneath the earth, find out the distance between the degree of the ascendant and the position of the Moon, assign one day to each interval of 13°, and add the result to 273 ⟨days⟩. (3)

The sum is the days of pregnancy; but know that there is a remainder that cannot be divided ⟨into days⟩. (4) ⟨Now⟩ you should calculate the hours: put the degree of the ascendant at the moment of conception where the Moon was at the moment of birth; if you know the moment of conception find out the place of the Moon ⟨then⟩, which will be the ascendant sign at the time of birth; ⟨then⟩ find out the position at the moment of birth of the degree of the ascendant at the time of conception, whether above or beneath the earth, and you will be able to know the ⟨duration of the⟩ pregnancy.

Quotation 2: *Moladot*, II 1:1; II 4:1–5, II 5:1–10, II 6:1–6, 88–95:

1 (1) מאזני המולד. אמר בטלמיוס כי נוכל לדעת המעלה הצומחת מדרך מאזנים שלו, שיקרא בלשון פרס נימודאר.

2 (1) ואלה המאזנים סמכו עליהם דייני המזלות, והם מאזני שקר, כי אני נסיתיו פעמים רבות בכלי נחושת שלם, שדקדקתי רגע המולד, ולא מצאתי מעלות אחת היתדות כמספר מעלות השליט. (2) וחשבתי בלבי שמא הטעות הוא בדעת השליט, והנה תקנתי שאר המשרתים, ולא מצאתי במאורות גם במשרתים שתהיה מעלתו כמעלת אחת היתדות, רק שיהיה ברגע המולד טעות יותר משלישית שעה. (3) על כן התברר לי כי אלו המאזנים הבל המה. (4) גם הזכיר חכם הודו שלשה מאזנים אחרים, ואת כולם ישא רוח. (5) והאמת הם מאזני חנוך, רק הם צריכים שנים תיקונים, כי ככה נסיתים פעמים רבות.

3 (1) מאזני חנוך. אמר חנוך: לעולם, במולד אדם, מקום הלבנה ברגע המולד היא המעלה הצומחת ברגע רדת הטיפה ברחם, והמעלה הצומחת ברגע המולד שם היתה הלבנה ברגע הטיפה. (2) על כן, אם ידענו רגע הטיפה, נוכל לדעת רגע המולד, ואם ידענו רגע המולד, נוכל לדעת מתי היה רגע הטיפה. (3) וככה נעשה: נסתכל ברגע המולד אם היתה הלבנה למטה מן הארץ או למעלה ממנה. (4) והנה אם מצאנוה במעלה הצומחת, ידענו כי הנולד עמד בבטן אמו המעמד האמצעי, שהם מאתים ושבעים ושלשה ימים, ואם היתה הלבנה במעלה השוקעת, הנה מעמדו מעמד הקצר, שהם מאתים וחמישים ותשעה ימים, ואם היתה תחת הארץ והוא קרוב מהמעלה השוקעת, אפילו מעלה אחת, הנה מעמדו המעמד הארוך, שהוא מאתים ושמונים ושבעה ימים. (5) והנה יש בין יתד ליתד שבעה ימים. (6) על כן, אם היתה הלבנה בתחלת קו חצי השמים, הנה המעמד מאתים וששים ושש, ואם היה בתחלת קו יתד התהום, הנה המעמד מאתים ושמנים יום. (7) ואם לא היתה הלבנה בתחלת אחת היתדות, נקח מרחק מקומה מתחלת היתד שעבר, ונקח לכל שלש עשרה מעלות יום אחד, ומה שיתחבר מימים נוספים על מספר הראוי למעמד אלו היתה הלבנה בתחלת היתד. (8) ואם נשאר מן המעלות שלא יתחלק על שלש עשרה, הסתכל: אם המעלות הם שבע, קח להם יום אחד, ואם פחותים מהם הניחם. (9) ואחר כן התסכל יום הטיפה, וככה תקן השעות שתהיה המעלה הצומחת ברגע הטיפה מקום הלבנה ברגע המולד. (10) והנה המספר הנתון לך הוא בדרך קרובה, כי פעמים שתוסיף שעות או תגרע, כפי מרחק שעות רגע הטיפה משעות רגע המולד.

4 (1) והחכמים הבאים אחרי חנוך הודו לו באלה המאזנים. גם אני נסיתי זה ועלה בידי, רק יש פעמים שהוא צריך לאחד משנים תקונים. (2) וכל זה שאמרנו הוא אמת בנולדים בקרוב מתשעה חודשים, והם רובי האדם, רק יש לפעמים שיולד הנולד בחודש השביעי, גם בחודש עשתי עשר. (3) והנה אזכיר לך התקונים. (4) הסתכל: אם היו הימים קרובים מיציאת הנולד, ויכנס נגה או כוכב חמה, שהם הכוכבים השפלים

ותולדתם קרובה מתולדת הלבנה, במקום שהלבנה עתידה להיותה שם ברגע המולד, ויהיה שלטון במקום לנגה או לכוכב חמה, הסתכל ברגע היות הלבנה על מבט רביעית עם הכוכב ההווה במעלה הנזכרת. אז יצא הנולד קודם שבעה ימים מימי המעמד הראוי, כי בעבור היות נגה וכוכב חמה קלים יעשו מעשה הלבנה, ולא כן שאר המשרתים. (5) ואם היה נגה או כוכב חמה במעלה הנזכרת ואין לו שלטון במעלה, אע״פ שהלבנה תביט אליו מבט רביעית, לא יצא הנולד עד געת הלבנה אל המעלה בהשלמת קצב המעמד. (6) והתקון השני. הסתכל אם יכנס מאדים במקום הלבנה ברגע הטיפה; והו א בביתו או בבית כבודו, והזמן קרוב כמו שבעה ימים מסוף המעמד, והתחברה הלבנה עם מאדים, אז יצא הנולד קודם המעמד.

1 (1) The balance of the nativity. Ptolemy said that we can determine the ascendant degree ⟨at the time of birth⟩ by his method of balance, which is called *Nimudar* in the Persian language.

2 (1) This balance was trusted by the astrologers, but it is ⟨like⟩ a crooked balance; I have tested it many times with a complete astrolabe, carefully calculating the moment of birth, but I did not find that the ⟨number of⟩ degrees of one of the cardines was equal to the number of degrees of the ruler. (2) I thought that perhaps the error results from the determination of the ruler, so I calculated the ⟨position of the⟩ other planets; but I found that neither the degree of the luminaries nor that of the planets is equal to the degree of one of the cardines, unless one allows an error of more than one-third of an hour in the moment of birth. (3) Therefore, I realized that this balance is nonsense. (4) An Indian scholar, too, mentioned three other balances, but all of them are foolishness. (5) ⟨Only⟩ Enoch's balance is true, although it requires two corrections; ⟨I know this⟩ because I have tested it many times.

3 (1) Enoch's balance. Enoch said: In the nativity of human beings, the position of the Moon at the moment of birth is always the ascendant degree at the moment of the descent of the drop ⟨of semen⟩ into the womb, and the ascendant degree at the moment of birth is the position where the Moon was at the moment of the ⟨descent of⟩ the drop ⟨into the womb⟩. (2) Therefore, if we know the moment of the ⟨descent of the⟩ drop we can know the moment of birth, and if we know the moment of birth we can know the moment of the ⟨descent of the⟩ drop. (3) We proceed as follows: We observe whether the Moon was below or above the Earth at the moment of birth. (4) If we find it [the Moon at the moment of birth] at the ascendant degree, we know that the term ⟨of pregnancy⟩ of the native was the intermediate, which is 273 days; if the Moon was at the degree of the descendant, then his term ⟨of pregnancy⟩ was the short one, which is 259 days; if it ⟨the Moon⟩ was below the Earth and was closer to the degree of the descendant, even by one degree, then his term ⟨of pregnancy⟩ was the long one, which is 287 days. (5) There are seven days between ⟨when the Moon passes⟩ one cardo and ⟨when it passes⟩ the next cardo. (6) Therefore, if the Moon was at the cusp of ⟨the cardo that begins at⟩ the line of upper midheaven, the term ⟨of pregnancy⟩ was 266 days, and if it was at the cusp of the cardo that begins at the line of lower midheaven, the term ⟨of pregnancy⟩ was 280 days. (7) But if the Moon was not in the cusp

of any of the cardines, we take the distance between its position and the last cardo where it [the Moon] was, assigning one day to every 13°, and add the total number of days to the number ⟨of days⟩ of the term ⟨of pregnancy⟩ if the Moon was at the cusp of the cardo. (8) If there is a remainder of degrees after division by 13, observe: If there are 7 degrees, set them equal to one day, but if there are fewer ⟨than 7 degrees⟩ ignore them. (9) Then observe the day of the ⟨descent of⟩ the drop ⟨into the womb⟩ and calculate the hours so that the ascendant degree is in the position of the Moon at the moment of birth. (10) Now the number that results is an approximation, to which you should sometimes add or subtract, depending on the interval in hours between the moment of the ⟨descent of⟩ the drop ⟨into the womb⟩ and the moment of birth.

4 (1) The astrologers who came after Enoch concurred with him regarding this balance. I also tested and verified it successfully, but sometimes it needs one of two corrections. (2) Everything we have just said is true regarding natives ⟨born⟩ after roughly nine months ⟨of pregnancy⟩, as most humans are; but sometimes a person is born in the seventh or in the eleventh month. (3) I now present the ⟨two⟩ corrections. (4) ⟨The first correction.⟩ Observe: If, on the days close to the native's delivery, Venus or Mercury (which are lower planets whose nature is akin to the Moon's nature), enters the position where the Moon will be at the moment of birth, and Venus or Mercury exercises lordship over this position, observe the moment when the Moon is in quartile with the planet [Venus or Mercury] that is in the aforementioned degree. In this case the baby will be born seven days before the proper term. This is because (given that Venus and Mercury move rapidly) they behave like the Moon, but this is not the case of the other planets. (5) ⟨However⟩, if Venus or Mercury is in the aforementioned degree but does not exercise lordship over this degree, even though the Moon is in quartile with it [Venus or Mercury], the native will not be born before the Moon enters the degree that corresponds to the completion of the term ⟨of pregnancy⟩. (6) The second correction. Determine whether Mars moves into the position where the Moon was at the moment of the [descent of] the drop; ⟨if⟩ it [Mars] is in its house or in the house of its exaltation, and ⟨if⟩ this happens close to seven days before the end of the term ⟨of pregnancy⟩, and ⟨if⟩ the Moon is in conjunction with Mars, in this case the native will be born before term.

Quotation 3: Abraham Ibn Ezra, long commentary on Ex. 2:2. *Commentary on Exodus*, ed. Weiser (1976), p. 16:

(1) שלשה ירחים. י״א כי בחודש השביעי מתחלת ההריון נולד. גם זה דרש, כי לא יוכלו המצרים לדעת מתי הרתה האשה. (2) ולפי דעתי, כי הכתוב ספר החדשים שיכלה להצפינו, כי אין כח באדם לראות באשה מתי תלד, כי רחוק הוא שהוא נולד בחדש השביעי מתחילת ההריון, כי הנולדים ככה הם קצרי קומה. ויותר חיים ונכבדים הם הנולדים באחד עשר, כי רובי הנולדים הם סמוכים לתשעה חדשים. (3) והיודע עת ההריון יכול לדעת עת הלידה, והיודע עת הלידה יכול לדעת עת ההריון. (4) כי דבר

מנוסה הוא לקדמונים, וחמשה פעמים נסיתיו גם אני, כי מקום מזל הלבנה ומעלתה ברגע ההריון, היא מעלת מזל הצומח ברגע הלידה, גם מעלה הצומחת רגע ההריון, שם תהיה הלבנה רגע המולד. והנה המעמד הקוצב הם רנ״ט ימים ושליש יום, והאמצעי רע״ג, והגדול שהוא הארוך רפ״ז; וחכמי המזלות יודו כן.

(1) Three Months. Some say that he [Moses] was born in the seventh month from the beginning of the pregnancy. This is a homiletical interpretation, ⟨and it is implausible⟩ because the Egyptians could not know when the woman [Moses' mother] became pregnant. (2) In my opinion, Scripture counted the months that she [Moses' mother] could hide him ⟨after he was born⟩, because no man can know when a woman will give birth. It is implausible that he [Moses] was born in the seventh month from the beginning of the pregnancy, because those born in such a condition are of short stature. Those born in the eleventh month live longer and are healthier, and the majority ⟨of the babies⟩ are born at approximately nine months. (3) ⟨Anyone⟩ who knows the time of conception can know the time of birth, and ⟨anyone⟩ who knows the time of birth can know the time of conception. (4) It has been demonstrated empirically by the Ancients, and I myself have proved it empirically five times, that the position of the Moon and its degree at the moment of conception is the ascendant degree at the time of birth and the ascendant degree at the moment of conception is where the Moon will be at the time of birth. So the short term is 259⅓ days, the median ⟨term⟩ is 273 ⟨days⟩, and the most extended, which is the long ⟨term⟩, is 287 ⟨days⟩; the astrologers accept this.

Quotation 4: *Ṭeʿamim* II, § 6.1:1–5, pp. 234–235:

(1) מעלות המולד. אמר החכם הנקרא משאללה כי לעולם יולד הזכר בשעה מפורדת במספר והנקבה בזוגות, וזה אמת ברובי הנולדים והנולדות רק לא בכלם. (2) ואמר כי כפי המרחק מיום המחברת או הנוכח שהיה בתחלתו קודם הלידה יהיה מספר חלקי שעה, ולפעמים יהיה כן ופעמים לא. (3) ותלמי אמר כי כמספר מעלות הממונה על מקום המחברת או הנוכח ככה יהיה מספר אחד היתדות. (4) והנה אנכי נסיתי פעמים רבות, שלקחתי מעלות גבהות השמש בשעת הלידה עם החלקים, ורובי השנים תקנתי מקום הכוכבים בלוחות הודו ולוחות תלמי ולוחות פרס והלוחות שהן אמת למראית העין, ולא מצאתי אחד היתדות ממספר אחד הכוכבים. (5) כלל: רק מה שהזכיר חנוך הוא אמת ומנוסה, והוא דרך התולדת.

(1) Degrees of the nativity. The scholar named Māshāʾallāh said that males are always born in an hour whose number is odd, whereas females ⟨are born⟩ in even ⟨hours⟩, and this is true for most natives, male and female, but not for all of them. (2) He said that the number of minutes in the hour ⟨of birth⟩ depends on the distance from the day of the ⟨last⟩ conjunction or opposition ⟨of the luminaries⟩ that began before the birth; sometimes it happens like that and sometimes it does not. (3) Ptolemy said that the number ⟨of degrees⟩ of one of the cardines is equal to the number of degrees of the planet that rules the place of the conjunction or the opposition ⟨of the luminaries⟩. (4) Now I have tested ⟨this⟩ many times, taking the degrees and minutes of the

Sun's apogee at the time of birth, and for most years I corrected the places of the planets in the Indian ⟨scientists'⟩ tables and Ptolemy's tables and the Persian ⟨scientists'⟩ tables and the tables that seem to be correct, but I did not find any of the cardines ⟨to be equal to⟩ the number ⟨of degrees⟩ of any of the planets. (5) As a general rule, only what Enoch said is true and corroborated by experience, and is compatible with nature.

Quotation 5: *De nativitatibus*, I 2:1–3, I 5:1–2, I 7:1–7, 250–255:

1 (1) Animodar vero quod interpretatur trutina, de qua dixit Ptholemeus quod considerandum est quis planeta potestatem habeat in gradu adunationis vel oppositionis Solis et Lune que nativitatem precessit. (2) Quia quot gradus signi in quo est planeta ille preterierunt, tot sunt gradus orientis vel medii celi. (3) Multis probationibus falsum esse constat.

2 (1) Dixit Hermes quod locus Lune in hora infusionis spermatis in matricem erit gradus oriens in nativitate, gradus vero orientis in conceptione est Lune locus in nativitate. (2) Quod verum esse probatione cognitum est, nisi nativitas in septimo vel undecimo mense fuerit.

3 (1) Nunc autem artem trademus qua scire poterimus, cognita nativitate, quot dies pregnans nascenti hospicium prebuerit. (3) Cognito oriente in nativitate, cognito quoque utrum Luna in superiori emisperio fuerit si ea in principio domus septime vel iuxta, inveneris dies more fuerunt .259. (4) Si vero plurimum a principio domus septime distiterit, vide quot gradibus equalibus ab eo distet, et per singulis gradibus sume horam rectam et .50. minuta hore, horas ergo et minuta hore redige in dies, et quod inde pervenerit, prefate dierum summe adiunge. (5) Quod si Luna in gradu orientis fuerit, dies more fuerunt .273. (6) Si autem Luna in inferiori emisperio fuerit, visa differentia gradus orientis ad ipsum in gradibus equalibus operans ut supra; quod productum fuerit adde modo dicte noticie. (7) Dico autem Hermetem in eo quod prediximus verum esse. (8) Contingit vero si prope nativitatem, scilicet .7. vel .14. diebus ante eam, alius planeta quam Saturnus gradum orientem in conceptione occupavit, ibique potestatem habens Lunam vel ex quadrato vel ex opposito respexerit, citius tempore prefinito partus egredietur.

1 (1) With regard to *Animodar*, whose translation is "balance,"[1] Ptolemy said[2] that it is necessary to take into consideration which planet exerts lordship over the degree of the ⟨last⟩ conjunction or opposition of the Sun and Moon that took place before the birth. (2) ⟨This is so⟩ because the degrees of the sign in which the planet is are as many as the degrees of the ascendant or of midheaven ⟨at the time of birth⟩.[3] (3) But it has been established by many proofs that this is false.

2 (1) Hermes[1] said that the position of the Moon when the sperm flows into the womb is the degree of the ascendant at the ⟨time of⟩ birth, and the degree of the ascendant at the ⟨time of⟩ conception is the position of the

Moon at ⟨the time of⟩ birth.[2] (2) This is true and it is known to have been proved, unless the birth takes place in the seventh or the eleventh month ⟨of pregnancy⟩.

3 (1) I now present a method by which, if the ⟨time of⟩ birth is known, we may have knowledge of how many days the pregnant woman provided accommodation ⟨in the womb⟩ to the newborn. (2) If the ascendant at the ⟨time of⟩ birth is known, and if it is also known that the Moon was ⟨then⟩ in the upper ⟨celestial⟩ hemisphere when it [the Moon] was at the cusp of the seventh ⟨horoscopic⟩ place or close to it [to the cusp], you will ⟨then⟩ find that the term ⟨of pregnancy⟩ was 259 ⟨days⟩. (3) But if ⟨the Moon⟩ moved far from the cusp of the seventh place, observe how many equal degrees ⟨the Moon⟩ moved away from it [the cusp of the seventh place], and assign to each of these degrees one equal hour[1] and 50 minutes of an hour, convert these hours with the minutes into days, and add the result to the aforementioned number of days. (4) If the Moon is in the degree of the ascendant, the term ⟨of pregnancy⟩ was 273 days. (5) But if the Moon is in the lower ⟨celestial⟩ hemisphere, observe the distance between the ascendant and itself [the Moon] in equal degrees, and proceed as ⟨indicated⟩ above; whichever the result may be, add it then to the aforementioned calculation. (6) Indeed, I say that Hermes is right about what we have mentioned above. (7) If close to the birth, for example 7 or 14 days before it [the birth], it happens that a planet other than Saturn reaches the ascendant degree at ⟨the time of⟩ the conception, and there ⟨the planet⟩ exerts lordship over the Moon in quartile or opposition, the fetus will come out sooner than the expected time.

Quotation 6: *Epitome*, ed. Heller (1548), II:1, H3r–H3v:

(1) De mora infantis in utero matris. Nunc de nativitatibus. (2) In hora natali invenias ascendens et loca omnium planetarum. (3) Ait autem Hermes quod locus Lunae in conceptione erit ascendens in nativitate, et gradus Lunae in nativitate fuit ascendens in conceptione. (4) Quod si Luna fuit in nativitate in principio primae domus, a conceptione usque ad nativitatem fuerunt ducenti septuaginta tres dies, quod tempus morae medium dicitur. (5) Quod si fuerit in exordio occidentis gradus, fuerunt dies more ducenti quinquaginta octo, quod tempus breve dicitur. (6) Quod is in gradu sequenti occidentem Luna in natali fuerit, dies morae fuerunt ducenti octuaginta octo, quod tempus magnum dicitur. (7) Quod si in alio fuerit a praedictis locis, videas si est supra terram in nativitate, quod si sic, considera percuot gradus distet ab occidente, quos percute in centrum et octuaginta, et dividas in tercentum viginti octo, sic enim contingent horae, quas in dies reducas, et addas tempori brevi, et tantum fuit a conceptione ad nativitatem. (8) Quod si est sub terra, considera quantum distet ipsa ab orientali gradu, et ducas dividasque, ut tibi praediximus, et dies quos collegeris, adde ducentis septuaginta tribus, et habebis tempus a natali ad conceptionem.

(1) On the intervening period of the baby in the mother's womb. ⟨I⟩ now discuss the nativities. (2) At the hour of birth you should find the ascendant and the position of all the planets. (3) Hermes said that the position of the Moon at conception is the ascendant at birth, and the degree of the Moon at birth is the ascendant at conception. (4) If the Moon at birth is in the cusp of the first place, there are 273 days from conception until birth, a term called intermediate intervening period. (5) If ⟨the Moon at birth⟩ is at the beginning of the descendant degree, the intervening period is of 258 days, which is called the small term. (6) If ⟨the Moon⟩ at birth is in the next degree after the descendant, the days of the intervening period are 288, which is called the great term. (7) If ⟨the Moon⟩ is in a ⟨position⟩ different from the aforementioned places, determine whether at birth it [the Moon] is above the Earth; in this case, find out how many degrees it is distant from the descendant, multiply them by 180, and divide them by 328 (sic!), and the result is hours, which you should reduce to days and add to the small term, which gives you how many ⟨days⟩ there are between conception and birth. (8) If it [the Moon] is below the Earth, find out its distance from the ascendant degree, then multiply and divide as mentioned above, and add the days you obtain to 273 ⟨days⟩, and you obtain the term between birth and conception.

Quotation 7: Pseudo-Ptolemy, *Centiloquium*, *Sefer ha-Peri*, BnF héb 1055, fol. 60a:

(1) דבור נ״א. אמר בטלמיוס: מקום הירח בעת המולד היא המעלה הצומחת מן הגלגל בעת נפילת הטפה, ומקום הירח בעת נפילת הטפה היא החלק הצומח עם המולד. 1

Aphorism 51. Ptolemy said: the position of the Moon at the time of the nativity is the ascendant degree of the orb at the moment of the descent of the semen, and the position of the Moon at the moment of the descent of the semen is the ascendant at the nativity.

Part 9: Elections and Lunar Mansions

Quotation 1: Ibn Abī l-Rijāl, *Kitāb al-Bāriʿ fī aḥkām al-nujūm*, *De iudiciis astrorum*, ed. Petri 1551, 342a–b:

De electionibus secundum motum Lunae per mansiones. Ilnath a principio Arietis usque ad duo decimum gradu, .11. minuta et .26. secundas, est mansio prima. Indi dicunt: si quando Luna fuerit in hac mansione, bonum est bibere medicinas, ponere bestias ad pascendum, iter facere in illa die nisi in .2. hora diei. Dorotheus dixit: non est bonum contrahere coniugium quando Luna est in hac mansione nec etiam in toto Ariete, nec emere servos in illa, quia mali erunt et inobedientes vel fugient. Bonum est tamen bestias emere domatas et cicuratas, et facere iter maxime in navi quia significat quod bene navigabit et bono modo. Non est bonum facere societatem in ea quia non durabit sed recedet iratus quilibet ab altero. Dicit etiamque quod qui capitur in ea, fortem et malum habebit carcerem. Item si a te quaesitum fuerit pro furto, Luna existente in Ariete, dic quod est res solita poni super caput vel faciem, vel laborata manu. Bonum est in ea facere arma, plantare arbores, tondere capillos, incidere ungulas, pannos novos induere, et hoc totum existente Luna ab infortuniis libera.

On the elections according to the motion of the Moon through the mansions. *Al-naṭḥ*, from the beginning of Aries until 12°, 11′, 26″, is the first mansion. The Indians say: when the Moon is in this mansion, it is auspicious to drink medicines, to put animals to pasture, to make a travel in this day except for the second hour of the day. Dorotheus said: it is not auspicious to make a marriage contract when the Moon is in this mansion nor in any part of Aries, nor is it auspicious to buy slaves in it, because they will be bad and disobedient, and they will run away. But it is auspicious to buy domestic and riding animals, and to make a travel particularly on a ship because it signifies that he will sail well and in a good mode. It is not auspicious to form a partnership in it because it will not last but each ⟨partner⟩ will fall out with the other. He also says that one who is captured in it, will find the imprisonment strong and unpleasant. Also if you are asked about a theft when the Moon is in Aries, say that it is something that is usually put on the head or over the face, or has been made by hand. It is auspicious to put armor in it, to plant trees, to cut hair, to pare fingernails, to dress new clothing, and all this when the Moon is free from harm.

Quotation 2: *Epitome*, ed. Heller (1548), IV:18, S3r–S3v:

De electionibus Indorum, Dorothii, secundum mansiones Lunae viginti octo, quando Luna est in aliqua ipsarum. Mansio prima. Prima dicitur cornua Arietis, et dicunt Indi Lunam ibi bonam esse pro medicina bibenda, pro pullis et primo equitandis, pro terrestri itinere ante meridiem. Dorothius ait Lunam malam ibi esse, et in toto Ariete, pro uxore ducenda, et etiam pro servis emendis nam fugient nisi sit ibi coniuncta fortunae planetae. Sed bonam esse dicit pro emenda bestia, et navibus mari immittendis. Malam pro communi, nam solvetur communio. Bonam pro exordio armorum, vel aliarum rerum bello necessarium componendarum. Item pro arbore plantanda, pro novis vestibus induendis et incidendis, nisi fuerit cremata vel proportionalis infortunis.

On the elections of the Indians and Dorotheus according to the 28 lunar mansions, when the Moon is in each of them. The first mansion. The first is called the horns of Aries. The Indians say that when the Moon is there it is auspicious to drink a medicine, to feed the poultry and for horse-riding, for travel by earth before noon. Dorotheus said: when the Moon is there, or in the whole Aries, it is inauspicious to take a wife, also the buy slaves because they will run away unless it is conjoined to a benefic planet. But he says it is auspicious to buy an animal, and to send ships to sea. It is inauspicious for partnership, because it will be dissolved. It is auspicious to begin war or other things necessary to arrange war. Also ⟨auspicious⟩ to plant trees, to dress new clothes and incidents unless it [the Moon] is burnt or stricken by misfortunes.

Quotation 3: *Neḥoshet* II, 193v:

הקדרים חלקו הגלגל על שמונה ועשרים חלקים, יקראו מחנות. בעבור, כי קרוב מהמספר הזה תראה הלבנה על הארץ, בכל חדש. ואלה שמותם בלשון קדר, גם הם מתורגמים בלשון הקודש, גם אכתוב צורתם. והנה עלה לכל מזל שתי מחנות ושלישית מחנה. והנה, אם תחלק הגלגל על שמונה ועשרים, יעלה לכל מחנה, שתים עשרה מעלות וחמשים ואחד חלקים.

The Arabs divided the zodiac into 28 parts, called mansions. ⟨They did so⟩ because close to this number ⟨of days⟩ the Moon is seen above the Earth, every month. Their names in Arabic and their translation into Hebrew follow, and I will also write they shapes. So, each sign includes two mansions and one third mansion. So, if you divide the zodiac into 28, every mansion is allotted 12° 51′.

Quotation 4: *Nativitates*, I i 3:9, 82–83:

Et hoc est necessarium scire maxime in verbis coniunctionum magnorum sicut explanabo in *Verbis Iurium Seculi*.

⟨All⟩ this is necessary to know, particularly regarding affaires related to the great conjunctions, as I will explain in the *Book of the Judgments of the World*.

Quotation 5: Latin translation of *'Olam* III: Vatican, BAV, MS Pal. lat. 1407, fol. 56r:

Prima mansio Alnethath, idest cornua que sunt Arietis, et sunt 3 stelle de magnitudine tertia sic deposite °°°.

The first mansion is *al-naṭḥ*, that is, the ram's horns, consists of three third-magnitude stars, arranged in this way °°°.

Part 10: Marriage

Quotation 1: *Mivḥarim* I, §7.6:9, 76–77:

ואם תרצה לעשות מבחר לאשה שתנשא לבעלה, שים מקום שמש או מאדים במקום טוב, כי הם יורו על הבעלים, ואם יביט נגה אז יותר טוב, רק השמר שלא יהיה השמש או מאדים בבית השביעי כלל, כי הם יורו על פירוד, ושבתי במקום הזה לא יזיק כל כך.

If you want to make an election for a woman to marry her husband, put the Sun and Mars in fortunate positions, because they signify husbands, and it is more auspicious if Venus aspects ⟨them⟩; but be careful not to do this when the Sun or Mars is in the seventh place, because they signify separation, although Saturn in this position does not do so much harm.

Part 11: Wars

Quotation 1: *Mivḥarim* I, § 7.4:1–2, 72–73:

אמר מאשא אללה: שים הלבנה, בכל מבחר למלחמה, מתפרדת מכוכב טוב או מכוכב תקיף במקומו, אי זה מהם שיהיה, אם הוא מקבל הלבנה בין במחברת בין במבט, אי זה מבט שיהיה. ושימנה שתתן הכח לכוכב שהוא תחת השמש או חוזר אחורנית או חלש במקומו או יהיה בבית נופל, וטעם זה בעבור כי הכוכב שנתפרדה הלבנה ממנו יורה על היוצא למלחמר והכוכב שתתן הכח לו יורה על האויב. והשמר שלא תעשה הפך מה שאמרנו.

Māshā'allāh said: in any election about war, put the Moon so that it parts from a benefic planet or from a strong planet in its position, either one, on condition that it receives the Moon either in conjunction or in aspect, in whichever aspect it may be. And put it [the Moon] so that it gives power to a planet that is under ⟨the ray of⟩ the Sun or retrograde or weak in its position or in a cadent place, and the reason is that the planet from which the Moon parts signifies the side that launches the war and the planet to which it [the Moon] gives power signifies the enemy. Be careful not to do the opposite of what we have just mentioned.

Quotation 2: *Mivḥarim* I, § 7.1:2, 70–71:

והנה, אם רצית לבחור לצאת למלחמה או להוציא שר גדוד ביבשה, שים המזל הצומח מאחד מבתי הכוכבים העליונים.

So, if you wish to choose ⟨a time⟩ for waging a war or sending out a commander by land, put the ascendant sign in one of houses of the upper planets.

Quotation 3: *Epitome*, ed. Heller (1548), IV:11, S1v:

Pro itinere ad bellum. Eligas signum cuius dominus est ex superioribus planetis.

On the way to war. Choose a sign whose lord is one of the upper planets.

Quotation 4: Sahl's *Book of Elections*, Paris, BnF lat. 16204, 495b:

Scientia horarum exitus ad bellum oportet ut ponat ascendens aliquam domorum planetarum altiorum, quarum fortior est Martis.

⟨For the⟩ knowledge of the hours to set off to war, it is necessary that you should put ⟨as⟩ the ascendant one of the houses of the upper planets, of which the strongest is Mars.

Quotation 5: *Nativitates*, I x 8:1–2, 102–103:

In omnibus eleccionibus non debetur poni locum Lune in domo prima, et illud temptaverunt antiqui et posteriores Ptholomeus. Et dederunt racionem nam gradus ascendens assimilatur nature Solis, et domus septima est principium anguli occidentalis, et fortitudo Lune maior est in occidente quam in oriente.

In all elections you should not put the Moon in the first place; this has been tested by the Ancients and by those who came after Ptolemy. The reason they gave is that the ascendant degree is similar to the Sun's nature, and that the seventh place is the beginning of the occidental cardo and the power of the Moon is greater in the occident than in the orient.

Quotation 6: *Mivḥarim* I, §8:1–2, 50–51:

וכל החכמים הנזכרים, גם חכמי הודו עמהם, הסכימה דעתם שלא תושם הלבנה במזל הצומח. וכבר הזכרתי הטעם בספר המולדות.

All the aforementioned scholars, and the Indian scientists among them, have agreed that the Moon should not be put in the ascendant sign. I have already mentioned the reason in the *Book of Nativities*.

Quotation 7: *Ṭeʿamim* II, §7.1:2, 242–345:

המעלה הצומחת לשמש ובתולדתו; על כן תכרית הלבנה בהגיעה שמה גם הלבנה עליה, בעבור היות הלבנה קרה, הפך תולדת המעלה הצומחת; על כן, אמרו כי אין ראוי להיות הלבנה במזל העולה.

The degree of the ascendant belongs to the Sun and has its nature; therefore it [i.e. the ascendant] will nullify the Moon when it approaches this place, also when the Moon is at this place, because the Moon is cold, which is the opposite of the nature of the degree of the ascendant; therefore they said that it is not appropriate for the Moon to be in the sign of the ascendant.

Part 12: Plunder

Quotation 1: *Mivḥarim* I, §7.5:1–6, 74–75:

(1) אמר אבו מעשר: אם יביטו כוכבים רבים אל המזל הצומח, יהיה לו עוזרים רבים. (2) ואם בעל הבית השמיני יביט מבט טוב, יברח מגדוד האויב אליו. (3) ואם ללכת למלחמה בדרך הים, אין מזל יותר טוב מעקרב, והשמר שלא תהיה הלבנה במזל שור, בעבור שהוא בית כבודה והוא בית האויב. (4) גם מזל דגים טוב, אם היה צדק או נגה במקום טוב. (5) ואם היה שם ככב חמה, יספיק, או שיהיה נשרף או חוזר אחורנית או במזל אריה, שהוא בית שנים עשר לביתו, והשמר שלא יהיה במזל תאומים, כי הוא עשירי לביתו. (6) ומזל סרטן טוב אם היה צדק מזרחי מהשמש, והוא שם, או במזל

דגים, שיהיה בחלוק הבית העשירי כפי מרחב הארץ, או בטלה. ואם היתה הלבנה בסרטן או בשור או בטלה, גם הוא טוב. וכל זה אם לא היה מאדים במזל גדי, ולא שבתי שם ולא במאזנים.

(1) Abū Ma'shar said: if many planets aspect the ascendant sign, he [the commander] will have many allies. (2) If the lord of the eighth place is in a fortunate aspect, ⟨people⟩ will desert the enemy army and join him. (3) No sign is more auspicious than Scorpio ⟨for sending an army⟩ to war by sea, but be careful not to do this when the Moon is in Taurus, because it is the house of its [the Moon's] exaltation and the enemy's place. (4) Pisces is also auspicious, if Jupiter or Venus is in a fortunate position. (5) It is sufficient if Mercury is there [in Pisces], or burnt or retrograde or in Leo, which is the twelfth sign after its [Mercury's] house [i.e., Virgo], but be careful that it [Mercury] is not in Gemini, because it is the tenth ⟨sign⟩ after its house [i.e., Virgo]. (6) Cancer is auspicious if Jupiter is oriental of the Sun and it [Jupiter] is there [Cancer] or in Pisces, on condition that it [Pisces] is in the tenth place in the division ⟨of the places⟩ according to the latitude of the country, or in Aries. It is also auspicious if the Moon is in Cancer, Taurus, or Aries. All this is true if Mars is not in Capricorn, nor Saturn there [in Capricorn] or in Libra.

Quotation 2: *Mivḥarim* II, §7.1:3–5, 162–163:

(3) ולעשות מלחמה מזל עקרב הוא טוב, ובלבד שיהיה מאדים במקום טוב ולא יהיה נשרף ולא חוזר לאחור, ואם יכולת לשים נגה בעל הבית השביעי, שיתן הכח למאדים מאיזה מבט שיהיה, אז יותר טוב, ואין ספק שינצח היוצא את אויבו ויעשה בו חפצו. (4) ואם העלית מזל דגים ולא יהיה צדק במקום טוב, שים נגה במקום טוב ושים כוכב וחמה בעל הבית השביעי במקום רע או נשרף או חוזר לאחור. (5) והשמר שלא יעלה מזל סרטן בעבור שהוא לכוכב שפל, רק אם היה שם צדק, או יהיה צדק באחד היתדות שהן הראשון או העשירי, כי בשביעי הוא בית קלונו, ולהיות בעל הבית העולה בתחלה או הממונה עליו בבית הרביעי איננו טוב.

(3) Scorpio ⟨in the ascendant⟩ is auspicious for waging war, but only if Mars is in a fortunate position and is neither burnt nor retrograde; but it is more auspicious if you can put Venus as the lord of the seventh place when it gives power to Mars in any aspect whatsoever. ⟨Then⟩ there is no doubt that the one who is going to ⟨war⟩ will be victorious over his enemy and do whatever he wants to him. (4) If you put Pisces [which is one of Jupiter's houses] in the ascendant but Jupiter is not in a fortunate position, then put Venus in a fortunate position and put Mercury as the lord of the seventh place in an unfortunate position or burnt or retrograde. (5) Be careful that Cancer is not the ascendant, because it is ⟨the house⟩ of a lower planet [Cancer is the Moon's house], but ⟨it may be suitable to put Cancer as the ascendant⟩ if Jupiter is there [in the ascendant, since Cancer is Jupiter's exaltation], or if Jupiter is in one of the cardines, namely, the first or tenth ⟨place⟩, ⟨but not in the seventh place⟩ because the seventh ⟨place⟩ [i.e. Capricorn] is the house of its [Jupiter's] dejection, and it is unfortunate if the lord of the rising sign at the beginning ⟨of the election⟩ or the ruler ⟨over the ascendant⟩ is in the fourth place.

Part 13: Study

Quotation 1: *Mivḥarim* I, § 9.3:1, 80–81:

והרוצה ללכת ללמוד, יעשה מזל הצומח מבתי כוכב חמה, והשמר שלא ישוב אחורנית, ואם היה תחת אור השמש אל תחוש לו.

Someone who wants to go on a journey in order to study should place the ascendant sign in one of Mercury's houses [Virgo and Gemini]; be careful that it [Mercury] is not retrograde, but pay it no attention if it is under the Sun's ray.

Part 14: Travel

Quotation 1: *Mivḥarim* I, § 9.2:1–8, 80–81:

ואם ירצה אדם ללכת להקביל פני שר או שלטון, הסתכל: אם הוא אדם זקן ויש לו פקידות, שים שבתי במקום טוב; ואם יביט אל המזל הצומח ואל בעליו מבט טוב, אז יותר טוב; ואם יביט אל הלבנה מבט טוב, גם הוא טוב. ואם לדיין או לחכם בתורות, שים במקום שבתי שהזכרנו צדק. ואם לשר צבא, תקן מקום מאדים, ואם לא יכולת, שים המזל הצומח אחד מבתיו. ואם למלך, תקן מקום השמש. ואם לשרית או לסריס, תקן מקום נגה. ואם לחכם בחכמות חיצונות או סופר מלך, תקן מקום כוכב חמה. ואם שאר כל האדם, תקן מקום הלבנה.

If someone wants to go and welcome a prince or ruler, pay attention ⟨and proceed as follows⟩. If he [the querent] is an old man who holds an official position, put Saturn in a fortunate position; it is more auspicious if it [Saturn] forms a fortunate aspect with the ascendant sign or its lord; it is also auspicious if it [Saturn] forms a fortunate aspect with the Moon. If ⟨he is going to welcome⟩ a judge or a jurist, put Jupiter instead of the aforementioned Saturn. If ⟨he is going to welcome⟩ a military commander, calculate the position of Mars ⟨instead of the position of Jupiter or Saturn⟩, but if you cannot, put the ascendant sign in one of its [Mars'] houses [i.e., Scorpio and Aries]. If ⟨he is going to welcome⟩ a king, calculate the position of the Sun. If ⟨he is going to welcome⟩ a princess or a eunuch, calculate the position of Venus. If ⟨he is going to welcome⟩ a scholar in the secular sciences or a royal scribe, calculate the position of Mercury. (8) If ⟨he is going to welcome⟩ anyone else, calculate the position of the Moon.

Quotation 2: *Mivḥarim* II, § 10.3:1–5, 172–173:

ואם הלכת לאדם זקן, תקן מקום שבתאי כאשר הזכרתי בשמש. ואם לאדם חכם בתורות או שופט, תקן מקום צדק. ואם לשר מלחמה, תקן מקום מאדים. ואם לאשה גדולה, תקן מקום נגה גם מקום הלבנה. ואם אצל רב ללמוד חכמה, תקן מקום כוכב חמה, ושיהיה בעל מבט טוב עם בעל הצומחת, ולא יהיה נכח הצומח ולא נכח בעל הצומחת.

If you want to go ⟨see⟩ an elder [i.e., a councilor], determine the position of Saturn as I mentioned regarding the Sun. If you want to go ⟨see⟩ a jurist or a judge, determine the position of Jupiter. If ⟨you want to go see⟩ a military commander, determine the position of Mars. If ⟨you want to go see⟩ an important woman, determine the position of Venus and also the position of the Moon. If ⟨you want to go see⟩ a rabbi to study wisdom, determine the position of Mercury so that it is in a fortunate aspect with the lord of the ascendant and is neither in opposition to the ascendant nor in opposition to the lord of the ascendant.

Quotation 3: *Moladot*, IV 28:1, 202–203:

המדינות. כל מדינה שהוא מזלה ברגע המולד עם כוכב מזיק, היא קשה על הנולד, ובחר לו שידור במקום הטובים.

The cities. Any city whose sign is with a malefic planet at the moment of birth is very unfortunate for the native; ⟨therefore⟩ choose form him that he live in a location ⟨whose sign at the moment of birth is⟩ with the benefic planets.

Part 15: The King

Quotation 1: *Mivḥarim* II, § 10.2:1–2, 172–173:

ואם רצית ללכת אל מלך או אל שר גדול, שים השמש במקום טוב, ואם היה בצומחת והמזל טלה או אריה או עקרב, גם הוא טוב, ובשאר המזלות אינו כן, בעבור שיאמרו חכמי המזלות שאין כח לכל כוכב שהוא עם השמש, וככה הבית. רק בעבור היות טלה בית כבודו, ואריה ביתו. ועקרב יש לו מבט עם הבית שיורה על המלוכה, על כן הוא טוב.

If you want to go ⟨see⟩ a king or a great prince, put the Sun in a fortunate position. It is also auspicious if it [the Sun] is in the ascendant, in Aries, Leo, or Scorpio; but not in the other signs, because the astrologers say that when a planet is with the Sun it loses its power, and this also applies to the house. ⟨The reason why these [Aries, Leo, and Scorpio] are auspicious is⟩ because Aries is the house of its [the Sun's] exaltation, Leo is its house, and Scorpio is in aspect with the place that signifies kingship, which makes it fortunate.

Part 16: Love

Quotation 1: *Mivḥarim* I, § 11.1:1–3, 86–87:

הרוצה לבקש אהבה, יסתכל תולדת האדם שירצה לבקש אהבתו. כי אם הוא קטן בשנים, יתקן מקום כוכב חמה ונגה; ואם אמצעי, מקום השמש ומאדים; ואם זקן, מקום צדק ושבתי. ושים בעל הבית עשתי עשר במזל הצומח, או יסתכל אל בעל המזל הצומח מבט אהבה, והשמר שלא תשימנו בבית שנים עשר ולא בבית השביעי, ולא יהיה מאדים באחת היתדות ולא עם הלבנה ולא במבט רע עמה.

Someone who seeks love should inspect the nature of the person he wants to love. If he [the beloved] is young, he should determine the position of Mercury and Venus; if middle-aged, the position of the Sun and Mars; if elderly, the position of Jupiter and Saturn. Put the lord of the eleventh place in the ascendant sign, or in an aspect of love with the lord of the ascendant sign, but be careful not to put it [the lord of the eleventh place] in the twelfth or the seventh place, and that Mars is not in one of the cardines or with the Moon or in an unfortunate aspect with it [the Moon].

Quotation 2: *Mivḥarim* II, § 11.2:1–4, 174–175:

ואם רצית לבקש אהבה מאדם הסתכל: אם תבקש אהבת מלך, שים השמש בבית הזה, ולא יהיה נכח בעל הצומחת ולא נשרף ממנה. ואם אהבת זקן, שים שבתאי בבית הזה, ויסתכל ממבט טוב לבעל הצומחת. ואם לבקש אהבת שופט, שים צדק בבית הזה, ולא יהיה נשרף ולא חוזר לאחור, ויהיה מקבל בעל הבית הראשון באי זה מקום שיהיה.

If you want to seek ⟨an election⟩ about the amity of some person, pay heed: If you seek the king's amity, put the Sun in this place [the eleventh place], but not when it [the eleventh place] is in opposition to the lord of the ascendant and ⟨the lord of the ascendant⟩ is burnt by it [the Sun]. If ⟨you seek⟩ the amity of an elder [i.e., a councilor], put Saturn in this place so that it [Saturn] forms a fortunate aspect with the lord of the ascendant. If the amity of a judge, put Jupiter in this place [the eleventh place], but neither burnt nor retrograde, and receiving the lord of the first place in any position whatsoever.

Part 17: Animals

Quotation 1: *Mivḥarim* I, § 12.1:3, 56–57:

ואם הבהמה הוא סוס, תקן מקום השמש, ואם פרד, מקום מאדים, ואם חמור, תקן מקום שבתי. זו דעת מאשא אללה, ודורוניאוס אמר כי הלבנה תורה על החמורים, בעבור שהם מרכבת שפלה, ואבו מעשר אמר כי כוכב יורה עליהם. ואין מחלקת כי נגה יורה על הגמלים וצדק על הפילים.

If the animal ⟨you wish to buy⟩ is a horse, determine the position of the Sun; if a mule, ⟨determine⟩ the position of Mars, and if a donkey, determine the position of Saturn. This is Māshāʾallāh's opinion, but Dorotheus said that the Moon signifies donkeys, because they are the lowest of the animals men ride on; Abū Maʿshar said that Mercury signifies them. There is no disagreement that Venus signifies camels and Jupiter elephants.

Quotation 2: *Mivḥarim* II, § 12.1:3–6, 176–177:

ואם רצית לקנות סוס זכר, שים השמש במקום טוב בבית זכר, ואם לקנות סוסיה, שים השמש במזל נקבה, ואם פרד, תקן מקום מאדים, ואם חמור, תקן מקום שבתאי, ואם

שור, תקן מקום לבנה, ואם צאן, תקן מקום כוכב חמה. ולא יהיה כוכב רע במזל טלה בקנות הצאן, ולא בקשת ודגים בקנות הסוס, ולא בעקרב בקנות הפרד, ולא בגדי בקנות החמור, ולא במזל שור בקנות שור. ולקנות גמל תקן מקום נגה, ולקנות הפיל, תקן מקום צדק. ככה אמרו הקדמונים.

If you wish to buy a stallion, put the Sun in a fortunate position in a masculine sign; if to buy a mare, put the Sun in a feminine sign; if a mule, determine the position of Mars; if a donkey, determine the position of Saturn; if an ox, determine the position of the Moon; and if sheep, determine the position of Mercury. There should not be a malefic planet in Aries when you buy sheep; or in Sagittarius or Pisces when you buy a horse; or in Scorpio when you buy a mule; or in Capricorn when you buy a donkey; or in Taurus when you buy an ox. If ⟨you want⟩ to buy a camel, determine the position of Venus; and to buy an elephant, determine the position of Jupiter. This is what the Ancients said.

Quotation 3: *Epitome*, ed. Heller (1548), IV:17, S3r:

In emptione bruti animalis, si equi, sit Sol in bono loco et planeta fortuna in duodecima, dominus eius sit in ascendente, vel aspiciat ipsum, vel dominum ascendentis aspectu amico; si de muli emptione deliberas, Mars dirigatur; si asini, Saturnus; si bovis, Luna; si pecudum, Mercurius. In nulla emptione sit dominus duodecime in septima, nam labetur ex bestiis emptis.

In the purchase of a brute beast, if a horse, be the Sun in an auspicious place and a benefic planet in the twelfth ⟨place⟩, its lord be in the ascendant, and aspects it [the ascendant] or the lord of the ascendant in an aspect of love; if you deal with the purchase of a mule, put Mars; if a donkey, Saturn; if a bull, the Moon; if a sheep, Mercury. In no purchase should the lord of the twelfth be in the seventh ⟨place⟩, because he will fall from the purchased beasts.

Quotation 4: *Ṭeʿamim* I, § 3.3:16, 68–69:

ובעבור היות מחלקי המזל הצומח בבית שנים עשר, אם לא היתה המעלה הצומחת תחלת המזל, על כן אמרו שיורה על הבהמות שהם למרכבת האדם.

Because parts of the sign of the ascendant may be in the twelfth place, namely, when the degree of the ascendant does not coincide with the beginning of a sign, they said that it indicates animals that men ride on.

APPENDIX 4

INTERROGATIONS

Part 1. Lifespan

Quotation 1: *She'elot* I, § 1.2:1–3, 248–249:

אמר משאללה: אם שאל שואל על מספר חייו הנשארים, הסתכל אל מקומות החיים כאשר אתה עושה לנולד. ואם ראית כי השליט על מקום החיים הוא במקום טוב, שיורה במולד על שנותיו הגדולות, לא תתן ככה בשאלות אם היה השואל זקן, והנה אם היה כפי שנות השליט הקטנות, הוא דבר גדול.

Māshā'allāh said: if the querent poses a question about the number ⟨of years⟩ left for him to live, look at the places of life as you do for a native. But whereas if you find that the ruler of the place of life is in a fortunate position, which in a natal horoscope indicates that he [the native] will live the great years ⟨corresponding to the ruler⟩, do not follow the same procedure in interrogations if the querent is an old person, where it is a great thing if ⟨the years he still has to live⟩ correspond to the least years of the ruler.

Quotation 2: *She'elot* II, § 1.1:1–2, 356–357:

אם ישאל אדם על חייו הנשארים, בקש מקומות החיים, שהם החמישה, על דרך שהזכרתי בספר המולדות. ולעולם תן לכל מעלה ממקום הלבנה שנה אחת במעלות ישרות, והסתכל מתי תגיע אל מקום רע, בין במחברת בין במבט, במעלות ישרות.

If someone asks how many years he has left, find the places of life—there are five of them—according to the method that I mentioned in the *Book of Nativities*. Always assign one year to each degree (in equal degrees) from the position of the Moon and observe when ⟨the direction⟩ reaches an unfortunate position, whether by conjunction or by aspect, in equal degrees.

Part 2. Buying and Selling

Quotation 1: *She'elot* II, § 11.1:1–2, 384–385:

אם ישאל שואל על סחורה, אם יוכל למכרה לאדם ידוע, שים המזל הצומח לבעל הסחורה, שהוא המוכר, והסתכל: אם יש מבט בין בעל הצומח ובין בעל הבית השביעי, שהוא הקונה, תשלם הסחורה. וככה, אם היה כוכב לוקח אור בעל הצומח ונותנו לבעל השביעי תשלם הסחורה על ידי אמצעי. ואם לא יהיה כן לא תמכר הסחורה.

If the querent poses a question about merchandise—whether he will be able to sell it to a certain person—assign the ascendant sign to the owner of the merchandise, who is the seller, and observe: if there is any aspect between the lord of the ascendant and the lord of the seventh place, which ⟨signifies⟩ the buyer, the deal will be completed. Likewise, if a planet takes the light of the lord of the ascendant and gives it to the lord of the seventh place, the deal will be completed through an intermediary. Otherwise the merchandise will not be sold.

Quotation 2: Sahl's *Book of Interrogations*, Paris, BnF lat. 16204, 465b:

Et si interrogatus fueris de emptione vel venditione alicuius rei, aspice dominum .VII. et dominus ascendentis. Si sibi iuncti fuerint, erit conventio inter eos, et levitas erit ex planeta pulsanti qui est levior. Si autem non fuerint iuncti et inveneris inter eos planetam reddentem luminem unius eorum ad alterius, erit conventio per manus alicuius viri qui ingredit intero eos.

If you are inquired about buying or selling something, look at the lord of the seventh ⟨place⟩ and the lord of the ascendant. If they are joined to each other, there will be agreement between them, and there will be an easiness from the part of the pushing planet which is lighter. But if they are not joined and you find between them a planet that gives back the light of one of them to the other, the agreement will be by means of someone who goes between them.

Quotation 3: *Epitome*, ed. Heller (1548), III:23, R1v:

De venditione ... si quis planeta dat vim alteri horum, suspiciens ab altero aliquid per mediatorem vendet. Sic si Luna habet vim ullam in ascendente.

On selling ... if some planet gives power to another of them, he will sell by means of an intermediary something he took from another one. The same applies if the Moon has any power in the ascendant.

Part 3. Riches

Quotation 1: *She'elot* I, § 2.1:2–3, 250–251:

יש מי שישאל על ממון שיקוה, אם יעלה בידו ואם לאו. ואם שאל בעבור זה, הסתכל: אם נתן כחו בעל הבית השני אל בעל הצומח או אל השליט עליו, והשליט מביט אל בעל הצומח, יעלה בידו הממון שיקוה.

Some people pose questions about money they hope for, whether they will get it or not. If someone poses such a question, observe: if the lord of the second place gives its power to the lord of the ascendant or to its [the ascendant's] ruler, and the ruler aspects the lord of the ascendant, he will get the money he expects.

Quotation 2: *Epitome*, ed. Heller (1548), III:5, P1r:

Si quis pro pecunia acquirenda quaerit, aspice dominum secundae domus, qui si est in signo ascendente, habebit absque labore ... Luna vero idem habet testimonium commune cum domino secundae domus.

If someone inquires about acquiring money, look at the lord of the second place; if it is in the ascendant sign, he will have it without effort ... The Moon gives the same testimony as the lord of the second place.

Part 4. A Stolen or Lost Article

Quotation 1: *She'elot* I, § 7.7:1–13, 276–279:

(1) אמר משאללה: הסתכל על דבר הגנב אל הבית השביעי ואל בעל הבית, ואם שם כוכב, אי זה כוכב שיהיה, הנח בעל הבית וקח אותו הכוכב. (2) והנה, אם ראית כי בעל הבית השביעי, או הכוכב שהוא בבית השביעי, יתן הכח לבעל המזל הצומח, ישיב הגנב הגניבה לבעליה. (3) וככה, אם מצאת בעל הבית השביעי תחת אור השמש, והוא מביט אל בעל המזל הצומח, ישיב הגניבה בעבור פחד שלטון. (4) וככה תדין אם היה כוכב לוקח אור השמש או אור בעל הבית השביעי ונותנו אל בעל הצומח, וזה הדבר תוכל להבינו מראשית החכמה. (5) וככה אם היה בעל הבית השני במזל הצומח ויסתכל בעל המזל הצומח אל בעל הבית השביעי, וככה אם היה בעל הבית השמיני נותן הכח לבעל הבית השני והוא מביט אל המזל הצומח. (6) ודע כי אם מצאת בעל הבית השני ובעל השוקע ביתדות, דע כי הגנב והגניבה לא סרו מהמדינה. (7) ושתף מקום המורה, כי אם היה נותן כחו לשמש או לבעל המזל הצומח, יורה כי הגניבה תשוב, ואם מצאת בעל הבית השני נותן הכח לבעל המזל הצומח, והוא איננו באחת היתדות, יורה כי הגנבה לא תשוב. (8) וככה אם היה בעל הבית השמיני בצומח או בעל הבית השני בשמיני, וככה אם היה בעל הבית השמיני נותן הכח לבעל הבית השביעי. (9) ואם היה בעל הבית השני נותן הכח לבעל הבית השלישי, או לבעל הבית התשיעי, או לכוכב שיהיה בבתים האלה, אז תדין כי הגנבה כבר הוצאה מהמדינה. (10) ואם היה בעל הבית השני נותן הכח לבעל הבית העשירי, יורה כי הגנב יתן שוחד לשלטון להסתיר עליו. (11) ואם מצאת המורה נותן הכח לבעל הבית השביעי, לא תמצא הגניבה. (12) ואם מצאת בעל הצומח והשוקע נותנים כחם לכוכב שהוא באחת היתדות, יודע הגנב, וככה אם היה המורה עם אחד המזיקים, וככה אם היה בעל הבית השביעי נשרף. (13) ואם המורה עם הכוכבים הטובים, לא ילקח הגנב, וככה אם יתן כחו בעל השוקע אל בעל הבית השלישי או התשיעי, או לכוכב שיהיה באחת אלו המקומות, יורה כי כבר ברח הגנב מהמדינה.

(1) Māshāʾallāh said: regarding the thief, observe the seventh place and the lord of ⟨this⟩ place, and if some planet is there, whichever planet it may be, ignore the lord of the place and take that planet. (2) Now if you see that the lord of the seventh place or the planet that is in the seventh place gives power to the lord of the ascendant sign, the thief will return the stolen article to the owner. (3) Likewise, if you find that the lord of the seventh place is under the ray of the Sun and it aspects the lord of the ascendant sign, the thief will return the stolen article because he is afraid of the authorities. (4) You should

pass a similar judgment if the planet takes the ray of the Sun or the ray of the lord of the seventh place and gives it to the lord of the ascendant; you can understand this from the ⟨*Book of the*⟩ *Beginning of Wisdom*. (5) The same applies if the lord of the second place is in the ascendant sign and the lord of the ascendant sign aspects the lord of the seventh place, and the same ⟨also⟩ applies if the lord of the eighth place gives power to the lord of the second place and it aspects the ascendant sign. (6) Know that if you find the lord of the second place and the lord of the descendant in the cardines, the thief and the stolen article have not left the city. (7) Also take into account the position of the significator, because if it gives its power to the Sun or to the lord of the ascendant sign, it signifies that the stolen article will be returned; but if you find that the lord of the second place gives power to the lord of the ascendant sign and it is not in any of the cardines, it signifies that the stolen article will not be returned. (8) The same applies if the lord of the eighth place is in the ascendant or the lord of the second place is in the eighth place, and the same ⟨also⟩ applies if the lord of the eighth place gives power to the lord of the seventh place. (9) If the lord of the second place gives power to the lord of the third place, or to the lord of the ninth place, or to a planet that is in any these places, judge that the stolen article has already been taken out of the city. (10) If the lord of the second place gives power to the lord of the tenth place, it signifies that the thief will offer a bribe to the authorities to cover up ⟨his action⟩. (11) If you find that the significator gives power to the lord of the seventh place, the stolen article will not be found. (12) If you find that the lord of the ascendant and the ⟨lord of the⟩ descendant give their power to a planet that is in one of the cardines, the thief will be identified, and the same applies if the significator is with one of the malefic planets, and so too if the lord of the seventh place is burnt. (13) If the significator is with one of the benefic planets, the thief will not be captured; likewise, if the lord of the descendant gives its power to the lord of the third or ninth place, or to a planet that is in any of these places, it signifies that the thief has already escaped from the city.

Quotation 2: *She'elot* II, § 7.7:1–11, 374–375:

(1) ובדבר הגניבה, הסתכל: אם נתן הכח בעל הבית השביעי לבעל המזל העולה ישיב הגנב הגניבה לבעליו. (2) וככה אם היה תחת אור השמש, והשמש במזל הצומח או תתן הכח לבעל הצומח, אז ישיב הגנבה על ידי מלך ופחדו ממנו. (3) וככה אם יתן כוכב כח השמש או כח בעל הבית השביעי אל בעל הצומח. (4) ואם היה בעל הבית השני במזל העולה, ישוב ממונו לבעליו, וככה אם יביט בעל הבית השביעי אל בעל הצומח ויתן בעל הבית השני הכח אל בעל הצומח, וככה אם יתן הכח בעל השמיני לבעל הבית השני ויהיה בעל הבית השני ביתד הראשון או העשירי. (5) ואם מצאת בעל הבית השביעי באחד היתדות, דע כי הגנב לא סר מהמדינה, וככה אם היה בעל הבית השני באחד היתדות: עוד הגניבה שנגנבה שם. (6) ודע כי אם היתה הלבנה נותנת הכח לבעל הצומח, הוא חצי עדות שתשוב הגניבה, וככה אם נתנה הכח לשמש. (7) ואם מצאת בעל הבית השני נותן הכח לבעל הצומח והוא לא יביט אל הצומח, לא תמצא הגניבה, וככה אם היה בעל הבית [139ב] השמיני בצומח או בעל הבית השני בבית השמיני, וככה אם היה בעל הבית השמיני נותן כחו לבעל הבית התשיעי. (8) ואם היה בעל הבית השביעי בבית השלישי או בבית התשיעי, כבר יצא הגנב מהמדינה, ואם

היה באחד מאלה הבתים בעל הבית השני, כבר הוצאה הגניבה מהמדינה. (9) ואם היתה הלבנה נותנת הכח לבעל הבית השביעי, לא ימצא הגנב. (9) ואם היתה הלבנה נותנת הכח לבעל הבית השביעי, לא ימצא הגנב. (10) ואם הלבנה עם כוכב טוב, הוא טוב לגנב ורע לבעל הממון, והפך הדבר אם היה עם כוכב רע. (11) ואם נותן בעל הבית השביעי ובעל הצומח כחם לכוכב שהוא באחד היתדות, ילקח הגנב ותשוב הגניבה על יד אחר כפי תולדת הכוכב שהוא ביתד וכפי משפט היתד: כי אם היה היתד העשירי יהיה על יד מלך, ואם בראשון הגנב יבא על יד בעל הממון, ואם בבית הרביעי על יד אחר ממשפחתו ומאבותיו, ואם בשביעי על ידי שותפין.

(1) As for stolen articles, observe: if the lord of the seventh place gives power to the lord of the rising sign, the thief will return the stolen article to its owner. (2) The same applies if it [the lord of the seventh place] is under the ray of the Sun and the Sun is in ascendant sign or gives power to the lord of the ascendant; in this case ⟨the thief⟩ will return the stolen article through the king because he is afraid of him. (3) The same applies if a planet gives the power of the Sun or the power of the lord of the seventh place to the lord of the ascendant. (4) If the lord of the second place is in the rising sign, ⟨the thief⟩ will return the money to its owner; the same applies if the lord of the seventh place aspects the lord of the ascendant and the lord of the second place gives power to the lord of the ascendant; the same applies if the lord of the eighth place gives power to the lord of the second place and the lord of the second place is in the first cardo or the tenth ⟨cardo⟩ [tenth place]. (5) If you find the lord of the seventh place in one of the cardines, know that the thief has not yet left the city, and the same applies if the lord of the second place is in one of the cardines: the stolen article is still there. (6) Know that if the Moon gives power to the lord of the ascendant, this is half a testimony that the stolen article will be returned, and the same applies if it [the Moon] gives power to the Sun. (7) If you find that the lord of the second place gives power to the lord of the ascendant and it [the lord of the second place] does not aspect the ascendant, the stolen article will not be found; the same applies if the lord of the eighth place is in the ascendant or the lord of the second place is in the eighth place, and the same ⟨also⟩ applies if the lord of the eighth place gives its power to the lord of the ninth place. (8) If the lord of the seventh place is in the third or ninth place the thief has already left the city; and if the lord of the second place is in one of the aforementioned places, the stolen article has already been taken out of the city. (9) If the Moon gives power to the lord of the seventh place, the thief will not be discovered. (10) If the Moon is with a benefic planet, this is fortunate for the thief and unfortunate for the owner of the money, and the opposite applies if it [the Moon] is with a malefic planet. (11) If the lord of the seventh place and the lord of the ascendant give their power to a planet that is in one of the cardines, the thief will be captured and the stolen article will be returned by another person, according to the nature of the planet that is in the cardo and according to the judgment of the cardo: if the tenth cardo [the tenth place] ⟨it will be returned⟩ by the king, if the first cardo the thief will come to the money's owner, if the fourth place by one of his relatives or kinsmen, and if the seventh place by partners.

Part 5. The Outcome

Quotation 1: *She'elot* I, § 4.1:1–5, 256–257:

(1) השואל בעבור דבר שירצה להחל, איך תהיה אחריתו, הסתכל אל הבית הרביעי. (2) אם הוא מן המזלות הישרים גם הלבנה במזל ישר, הנה שנים עדים כשרים כי האחרית תהיה טובה. (3) וככה אם יהיה כוכב טוב בבית הרביעי, וככה אם הלבנה היא בביתה או עם כוכב טוב במחברת או במבט. (4) וגם הסתכל אל בעל בית הלבנה, אם הוא ישר בהליכתו, או תחת השמש, או במקום שיש לו שלטון שם, או באחת היתדות, וככה בעל הבית הרביעי אם בבית טוב ואיננו נשרף ולא שב אחורנית. (5) והפך הדבר אם היה בית הרביעי מהמזלות המעוותים, או הלבנה במזל מעוות עם כוכב מזיק במחברת או במבט, או שיהיה כוכב מזיק בבית הרביעי, או יהיה בעל בית הרביעי נשרף או שב אחורנית או בבית רע.

(1) ⟨If the querent⟩ poses a question about the end of an activity he wishes to begin, observe the fourth place. (2) If it is in one of the straight signs and the Moon too is in a straight sign, these are two fit witnesses that the end will be fortunate. (3) The same applies if a benefic planet is in the fourth place, as well as if the Moon is in its house [Cancer] or in conjunction or aspect with a benefic planet. (4) Observe also the lord of the place where the Moon is, whether it is direct in its motion, or under the ⟨ray of the⟩ Sun, or in a place where it [the lord of the house where the Moon is] exercises lordship, or in one of the cardines; the same applies to the lord of the fourth place if it is in a fortunate place and is neither burnt nor retrograde. (5) But the opposite applies if the fourth place is one of the crooked signs or if the Moon is in a crooked sign together with a malefic planet in conjunction or in aspect, or if a malefic planet is in the fourth place, or if the lord of the fourth place is burnt or retrograde or in an unfortunate ⟨horoscopic⟩ place.

Quotation 2: *She'elot* II, § 4.1:1–5, 362–365:

(1) אם ישאל מה יהיה סוף הדבר שיחל, אם טוב ואם רע, הסתכל הבית הרביעי אם הוא מהמזלות הישרים, הנה אות אחד שיהיה סופו טוב, ואם הוא מהמעוותים הפך הדבר. (2) ואם כוכב טוב בבית הרביעי או מביט אליו, ויותר טוב אם הוא מבט אהבה, ויותר אם היה לו שלטון בבית הרביעי, הנה אות שני שהסוף טוב, והפך הדבר אם היה כוכב רע. (3) והסתכל אל הכוכב שהוא בעל בית הלבנה, אם הוא ישר בהליכתו או תחת השמש, או במכום שיש לו שלטון או באחד היתדות, או הפוך כל אלה, והנה הוא אות שלישי שיורה על סוף הדבר. (4) ואם היתה הלבנה בביתה, הסתכל הכוכבים שיביטו אליה ולמי תתן הכח, וקח הסוף ממנו. ואם לא תתן לאחד, הסתכל מה כחה בעצמה. (5) ורבים אמרו שאם היתה כן, עזוב הלבנה וקח בעל הבית הרביעי.

(1) If ⟨the querent⟩ poses a question about the outcome of something he has begun—whether it will be fortunate or unfortunate—find out whether the fourth place is in one of the straight signs, which is an indication that the outcome will be fortunate, but the opposite applies if ⟨the fourth place is⟩ in ⟨one of⟩ the crooked ⟨signs⟩. (2) If a benefic planet is in the fourth place or aspects it, particularly in an aspect of love, and even more so if it exercises

lordship over the fourth place, this a second indication that the outcome will be fortunate, but the opposite applies if it is a malefic planet. (3) Observe the planet that is the lord of the house of the Moon, whether it is direct in its motion or under the ⟨ray of the⟩ Sun, or in a position where it exercises lordship or in one of the cardines, or the opposite of all the aforementioned cases, and this is a third indication of the outcome of the matter. (4) If the Moon is in its house [Cancer], observe the planets that aspect it and to which ⟨planet⟩ it [the Moon] gives power, and determine the outcome ⟨of the activity⟩ from this. But if it [the Moon] does not give ⟨power⟩ to any planet, find out its [the Moon's] own specific power. (5) Many said that if it [the Moon] is like that, you should ignore the Moon and use the lord of the fourth place.

Quotation 3: *Epitome*, ed. Heller (1548), III:2, O4r:

Sumens autem Lunam ad iudicium, poteris scire rei consummationem ex domino domus suae case, que si est in Cancro sua domo, sumas dominum domus .4. ab ascendente, cum est sumptus dominus ascendentis, sic etiam dominus .4. domus suscipitur. Quod si Luna vel dominus ascendentis, secundum quod sumitur, dat vim multis, ab eo cui vim dat in remotione finis etiam supplementum rei quaeritur.

When the Moon is taken for the judgement, you can know the thing of the outcome from the lord of its [the Moon's] house, which if it is in Cancer, its [the Moon's] house, take the lord of the fourth place from the ascendant. Take the lord of the ascendant as was taken the lord of the fourth place. If the Moon or the lord of the ascendant, as it was taken, gives power to many ⟨planets⟩, the provision of the thing ⟨of the outcome⟩ will be asked from the one to which was given power after the final removal.

Part 6. Will the People Conspire against the King?

Quotation 1: *She'elot* I, § 4.3:1–2, 258–259:

ואם היה השואל שלטון, וירצה לדעת אם יקשרו אנשי ארצו עליו או לא, כי הבית הרביעי שהוא בית הקרקעות הוא בית מדינות המלך, הסתכל אל בעל הבית הרביעי. אם היה במבט נכח עם המזל הצומח או עם בעליו, או יהיה כוכב בבית הרביעי מביט מבט רע אל בעל המזל הצומח, או תהיה הלבנה נכח השמש, הנה אלה עדים כי יקשרו, ואם לא היה ככה לא יקשרו.

If ⟨the querent⟩ is a ruler and wishes to know whether the people of his country will conspire against him, observe the lord of the fourth place—for the fourth place, which is the place of landed estates, is also the place of the king's cities. If it [the lord of the fourth place] is in opposition to the ascendant sign or to its lord, or if a planet in the fourth place is in an unfortunate aspect with the lord of the ascendant sign, or if the Moon is in opposition to the Sun, these are witnesses that they will conspire ⟨against the king⟩; but otherwise they will not conspire ⟨against him⟩.

Part 7. Is the Woman Pregnant?

Quotation 1: *She'elot* I, § 5.1:1–4, 262–263:

(1) הבית החמישי: אם שאל שואל על דבר אשה, אם היא הרה ואם לא, הסתכל אל המורה: אם היה באחת היתדות, ויותר טוב ממזלות בעלי הגוף, יורה על הריון. (2) וככה, אם נותן כחו למשרת שהוא באחת היתדות, או שיהיה המשרת בבית החמישי, או שיתן כחו לבעל המזל הצומח או לבעל הבית החמישי, אם הוא מביט אל המעלה הצומחת, אז יורה על הריון. (3) ואם היה המורה נותן כחו לכוכב שהוא באחד הבתים הנופלים, או יהיה המזל הצומח מתהפך, לאות כי אין שם הריון, ואם מצאת המזל הצומח מהמזלות שיש להם שני גופות, לאות על ההריון. (4) אמר דורוניאוס: לעולם הסתכל אל בעל השעה. אם היה באחת היתדות, והוא במזל עומד או שיש לו שני גופות, אל תבקש עדות אחר עמו, כי יורה על הריון, ואם היה מזל מתהפך, עדותו חצי עדות.

(1) The fifth place. If the querent poses a question about a woman—whether she is pregnant or not—observe the significator. If it is in one of the cardines, and, even better, in one of the bicorporal signs, it signifies pregnancy. (2) Likewise, if it [the significator] gives its power to a planet that is in one of the cardines, or if the planet is in the fifth place, or if it gives its power to the lord of the ascendant sign or to the lord of the fifth place, if it aspects the ascendant degree, then it signifies pregnancy. (3) But if the significator gives its power to a planet that is in one of the cadent places, or if the ascendant sign is a tropical ⟨sign⟩, this is an indication that there is no pregnancy, although if you find that the ascendant sign is in a bicorporal sign, this is an indication of pregnancy. (4) Dorotheus said: always observe the lord of the hour. If it is in one of the cardines, and it is in a fixed or in a bicorporal sign, do not ask for any further testimony because it signifies pregnancy; but if it is in a tropical sign it is ⟨only⟩ half a testimony.

Quotation 2: *She'elot* II, § 5.2:1–2, 366–367:

(1) ואם שאל אם האשה היא הרה אם לאו, והנה, אם היתה הלבנה באחד היתדות, ויותר טוב ממזלות בעלי שני גופים, הנה עדות קיימת, ואם המזל העולה ממזלות שנים גופים, גם היא עדות. (2) ואם היה שבתי או מאדים באחד היתדות, אין שם הריון, וככה אם היה בעל השעה במקום נופל.

(1) If someone asks whether a woman is pregnant or not, now, if the Moon is in one of the cardines, and it is more auspicious in the bicorporal signs, this is a valid testimony ⟨that she is pregnant⟩; if the rising sign is one of the bicorporal signs, this too is a testimony ⟨that she is pregnant⟩. (2) But if Saturn or Mars is in one of the cardines, there is no pregnancy, and the same applies if the lord of the hour is in a cadent place.

Part 8. A Boy or a Girl?

Quotation 1: *She'elot* I, § 5.3:1–6, 264–265:

ואם שאל על אשה הרה, לדעת מה תלד אם זכר אם נקבה, אמר אלכנדי: הסתכל אל בעל השעה, ואל מקום השמש ביום ואל הלבנה בלילה, ואל מקום בעל הבית החמישי, ואל מקום צדק בכל השאלות. וראה אם הם אלה הנזכרים במזלות הזכרים או הנקבות, ואם הם ברביעית שהיא זכר מפאת השמש, וזה יהיה לכוכבים העליונים כשיראו מתחת אור השמש עד המעמד הראשון, וככה הרביעית השנית גם היא זכר, שהיא מתחלת נכח השמש עד המעמד השני. גם הסתכל אל רביעיות הגלגל, שהשתים זכרים והשתים נקבות, והזכרים הרביעית שהיא מקו חצי שמים עד המעלה הצומחת וממזל התהום עד המעלה השוקעת. גם דע תולדת בעל השעה, אם זכר אם נקבה, וככה תולדת בעל הבית החמישי. והכוכבים השפלים עם הלבנה, רביעיותם הם זכרים הפך רביעיות העליונים. ועתה יש לך לספור לכל הנזכרים כמה כח יש להם שיורה על הזכרים וכמה כח שיורה על הנקבות, וכפי המספר הרב ככה תדין.

If ⟨the querent⟩ poses a question about a pregnant woman, to find out whether she will give birth to a boy or a girl, Al-Kindī said: observe the lord of the hour, the position of the Sun by day and of the Moon by night, the position of the lord of the fifth place, and the position of Jupiter in all the interrogations. Find out whether the aforementioned are in masculine or feminine signs and whether they are in the quadrant that is considered to be masculine with respect to the Sun (this applies to the upper planets when they are seen under the ray of the Sun up to the first station [i.e., where a direct planet becomes retrograde]), and likewise ⟨whether they are in⟩ the second quadrant ⟨that is considered to be⟩ masculine ⟨with respect to the Sun⟩, too, (this applies from the beginning of opposition to the Sun up to the second station [i.e., where a retrograde planet becomes direct]). Also observe the quadrants of the zodiac, two of which are masculine and two ⟨of which⟩ are feminine; the masculine are the quadrants from the line of midheaven to the ascendant degree and from lower midheaven to the degree of the descendant. Also find out the nature of the lord of the hour, whether it is masculine or feminine, and likewise ⟨find out⟩ the nature of the lord of the fifth place. As for the lower planets and the Moon, their masculine quadrants are the opposite of the ⟨masculine quadrants of the⟩ upper planets. Now, regarding all the aforementioned, you have to count how many portions of power signify masculine and how many ⟨portions of power signify⟩ feminine, and pass judgment according to the larger number.

Quotation 2: *She'elot* II, § 5.3:1–4, 366–367:

ואם שאל מה תלד ההרה, תסתכל אל בעל השעה, ובעל המזל הצומח, ובעל הבית החמישי, ודע תולדת בעל השעה, ותולדת המזל הצומח ובעליו, ותולדת הבית החמישי ובעליו, וספור כמה זכרים וכמה נקבות. גם תתן כח לרביעית שהיא בחלק זכר או נקבה מפאת המעלה הצומחת גם מפאת השמש, והמספר הרב בכח הוא האמת, אם זכר אם נקבה. ודורוניוס אמר כי תשתף עמהם מקום השמש ביום ומקום הלבנה בלילה. ונכון הדבר, רק העיקר בעל מזל הצומח ובעל הבית החמישי.

If ⟨the querent⟩ asks about ⟨the sex of⟩ the baby the pregnant woman will give birth to, observe the lord of the hour, the lord of the ascendant sign, and the lord of the fifth place, and know the nature of the lord of the hour, the nature of the ascendant sign and its lord, and the nature of the fifth place and its lord, and count how many masculine and feminine ⟨witnesses⟩ there are. Also assign ⟨portions of⟩ power to the quadrant that is considered to be masculine or feminine with respect to the ascendant degree or with respect to the Sun. The truth as to whether ⟨the baby⟩ will be male or female emerges from the larger number of powers ⟨of the masculine or feminine witnesses⟩. Dorotheus said that you should associate them with the position of the Sun by day and the position of the Moon by night. This is correct, but the root is the lord of the ascendant sign and the lord of the fifth place.

Quotation 3: *Epitome*, ed. Heller (1548), III:9, P3r–P3v:

(1) Si scire volueris de aliqua, utrum sit praegnans vel non, considera si Luna dat vim planetae, qui est in angulo, vel si dominus ascendentis aut horae sit in domo quinta, vel si dominus quintae dat vim domino ascendentis, vel si Luna dat vim domino quintae domus, vel si ascendens ipsum est signum bicorpoerum. Haec testimonia significant mulierem esse praegnantem … (2) Si vero Luna dat vim planetae, qui est in domo lapsa, vel signum ascendens est domus mobilis, nec aspiciat dominum ascendentis, nec horae, nec Luna dominum domus quintae, mulier non est praegnans. Si dominus quintae domus dat vim planeta infortunio, qui est in angulo, parturiet foetum abortivum. (3) Si quis an sit habiturus filios nec ne, quaerit, et si sit Iupiter in ascendente, vel dominus horae in quovis angulo, et melius si dominus horae sit dominus quintae domus, nonae vel undecimae, aut si dominus ascendentis aspiciat dominus quintae domus, vel si dominus quintae domus est in signo ascendente … haec testimonia filios significant … (4) Pro sexu autem filiorum, aspice ascendens et eius dominum, an aspiciat ipsum. Qui si non aspicit, sumas dominus honoris vel faciei, secundum quod quisque eorum aspicit ascendens et domum quintam, quae est directa secundum latitudinem terrae, cum suo domino. Et tunc aspice naturam signi ascendentis, an sit masculinum vel femininum, et dominum eius signi in quo est, sic et quintam domum cum suo domino, et signum in quo est, et dominum horae, an sit par vel impar. Vide etiam naturam domini signi, in quo est dominus horae, et in qua quarta orientales vel occidentales ratione Solis vel ascendentis sint singuli significatores, quod si testimonia masculorum superant, erit filius masculus, si foeminarum, erit foemina.

(1) If you wish to know about some woman, whether she is pregnant or not, consider if the Moon gives power to a planet that is in a cardo, or if the lord of the ascendant or of the hour is in the fifth ⟨horoscopic⟩ place, or if the lord of the fifth place gives power to the lord of the ascendant, or if the Moon gives power to the lord of the fifth place, or of the ascendant is a bicorporal sign. These are testimonies signifying that the woman is pregnant … (2) If the Moon gives power to a planet in a cadent place, or ⟨if⟩ the ascendant sign is

tropical and does not aspect the lord of the ascendant, nor the ⟨lord⟩ of the hour, nor the Moon ⟨aspects⟩ the lord of the fifth place, the woman is not pregnant. If the lord of the fifth place gives power to an inauspicious place that is in a cardo, the woman will have a miscarriage. (3) If someone inquires about whether he will have sons. These testimonies signify ⟨that he will have⟩ sons: if Jupiter is in the ascendant, or ⟨if⟩ the lord of the hour is in a cardo, and better if the lord of the hour is the lord of the fifth, ninth or eleventh place, or if the lord of the ascendant aspects the lord of the fifth place, of if the lord of the fifth place is in the ascendant sign … (4) To find out the gender of the children, observe the ascendant and its lord, and find out whether one aspects the other. If it does not aspect, take the lord of the exaltation or of the decan, according to whether one of them aspects the ascendant and the fifth place, calculated according to the latitude of the country, with its lord. Then observe the nature of the ascendant sign, and find out whether it is masculine or feminine, and the lord of the sign in which it is, also the fifth place with its lord and the sign in which it is, and the lord of the hour, and whether it is even-numbered or odd-numbered. Observe also the nature of the lord of the sign in which is the lord of the hour, and in which quadrant, oriental or occidental with respect the Sun, are each one of the significators. If the testimonies of the masculine are more numerous, the child will be masculine, if ⟨the testimonies⟩ of the feminine ⟨are more numerous⟩, the child will be feminine.

Quotation 4: *She'elot* I, § 5.2:1–6, 262–265:

ואם שאל שואל אם יהיה לו בן, הסתכל: אם היה בעל הבית החמישי במזל הצומח ואיננו נשרף ולא חוזר, יורה שיהיה לו בן. וככה אם היה בעל המזל הצומח בבית החמישי ויביט צדק אליו, או שיתן הכח בעל הצומח לצדק וצדק באחת הבתים הטובים, או שיתן הכח בעל המזל הצומח לכוכב שהוא בבית החמישי, על מנת שלא יהיה נשרף ולא שב אחורנית. והסתכל אל בעל השעה אם היה באחת היתדות, יורה שיהיה לו בן, ואם היה בבית הששי או בבית השמיני או שנים העשר, לא יהיה לו בן … והסתכל אל המזלות העקרים, שאם היה שם צדק והמורה ובעל הבית החמישי, לאות כי לא יהיה לו בן.

If the querent asks whether he will have a son, observe: if the lord of the fifth place is in the ascendant sign and it is neither burnt nor retrograde, it signifies that he will have a son. The same applies if the lord of the ascendant sign is in the fifth place and Jupiter aspects it, or the lord of the ascendant gives power to Jupiter and Jupiter is in one of the fortunate places, or if the lord of the ascendant sign gives power to a planet that is in the fifth place, on condition that it is neither burnt nor retrograde. Observe whether the lord of the hour is in one of the cardines, ⟨because⟩ it signifies that he will have a son; but if it is in the sixth, eighth, or twelfth place, he will not have a son … Observe the barren signs: if Jupiter and the significator and the lord of the fifth place are there, this is an indication that he will not have a son.

Part 9. A Sick Person—Will He Live or Die?

Quotation 1: *She'elot* I, § 6.1:1–7, 266–267:

(1) השואל על חולה אם ימות מחליו או ירפא, הסתכל: אם היה בעל המזל הצומח נשרף מהשמש, יורה על מותו, ואף כי אם היה באחת היתדות, וככה אם היה בעל הבית השמיני במזל הצומח או בעל המזל הצומח בבית השמיני. (2) ואם היה בעל המזל הצומח באחד הבתים הטובים, ואיננו נשרף ולא חוזר אחורנית, יורה כי ינצל. (3) גם הסתכל אל המורה, שאם היה במחברת או עם מבט רע עם שבתאי או מאדים, יורה על סכנה, ואם היה במחברת או באי זה מבט שיהיה עם הטובים, יורה שיתרפא. (4) ודע כי אם בעל הצומח עם בעל הבית הששי או בעל בית השנים עשר, או שיהיה בעל הצומח באחד אלו הבתים, יורה על רע, ואם הוא קרוב שיצא מאלה הבתים, יורה כי יתרפא מהרה. (5) ודע כי המזלות העומדים יורו על ארך החלי, והמתהפכים יורו על המהירות, בין לטוב בין לרע, והמזלות שיש להם שתי גופות יורו שיצא מחלי אל חלי. וזה שהזכרתי הוא על דרך דורוניאוס ומשאללה. (6) כבר אמרתי בתחלת הספר כי חנוך ובטלמיוס אינם מודים בשאלות. (7) רק הם שניהם אומרים, וחכמי המזלות עמהם, כי ממקום הלבנה ברגע תחלת החלי יוכל אדם לדעת אם יחיה או ימות ואי זה יום הוא גבולו, וכבר פרשתי בספר המאורות שלי.

(1) ⟨If the querent⟩ poses a question about an ailing person—whether he will die from his illness or recover—observe: if the lord of the ascendant sign is burnt by the Sun, it signifies his death, particularly if it is in one of the cardines; and the same applies if the lord of the eighth place is in the ascendant sign or if the lord of the ascendant sign is in the eighth place. (2) But if the lord of the ascendant sign is in one of the fortunate places, and is neither burnt nor retrograde, it signifies that he will survive. (3) Also observe the significator, for if it is in conjunction or in a malefic aspect with Saturn or Mars it signifies danger, but if it is in conjunction or in any aspect with the benefics it signifies that he will recover. (4) Know that if the lord of the ascendant is with the lord of the sixth place or the lord of the twelfth place, or if the lord of the ascendant is in one of these places, it signifies misfortune; but if it is about to move away from these places, it signifies that he will recover soon. (5) Know that the fixed signs signify that the illness will linger on, and the tropical ⟨signs⟩ signify quick changes, for good or evil, and the bicorporal signs signify that after one illness he will come down with another illness. What I have just mentioned corresponds to the method of Dorotheus and Māshā'allāh. (6) I have already said at the beginning of the book that Enoch and Ptolemy do not acknowledge ⟨the value⟩ of interrogations. (7) But both say, and the astrologers concur, that from the position of the Moon at the moment of the onset of the illness one may know whether he will survive or die and which is his day of crisis; I have already explained ⟨this⟩ in my *Book of the Luminaries*.

Quotation 2: *She'elot* II, § 6.1:1–7, 366–369:

(1) אם ישאל שואל על חולה, אם יתרפא, תסתכל: אם היה בעל מזל הצומח באחד היתדות, ואיננו תחת אור השמש ולא שב לאחור, לא ימות. (2) וככה אם היה בבית

החמישי או בבית העשתי עשר, ואם היה בבית השמיני ימות, או אם היה בעל השמיני במזל העולה כוכב טוב, יחיה, ואם רע, ימות. (3) וככה, הסתכל אל מקום הלבנה, שאם יתן הכח לבעל הבית הששי, יחזק לו החולי, וככה אם נתן הכח בעל הצומח אל בעל הבית הששי או אל כוכב רע. (4) גם בעל הבית השנים עשר רע מאד, קרוב כבעל הבית הששי. (5) והמזלות העומדים יורו על אורך החולי, והמתהפכים יורו על קוצר החולי, ובעלי שני הגופים יורו שישתנה חליו לחלי אחר. (6) ואם היה הכוכב הרע, המזיק למזל הצומח במחברת או במבט, או ככה ללבנה או לבעל המזל הצומח, מתאחר בהליכתו, יורה על איחור, והפך הדבר אם היה מהיר. (7) ואם היה בעל הצומח רץ בהליכתו, ויכנס אל מזל אחר במהרה או יצא מבית לבית, ובלבד שלא יהיה הבית הששי או השנים עשר, מיד יסור חליו.

(1) If the querent poses a question about an ailing person—whether he will recover—observe: if the lord of the ascendant sign is in one of the cardines and is neither under the ray of the Sun nor retrograde, he will not die. (2) The same applies if it [the lord of the ascendant] is in the fifth or eleventh place, but if it is in the eighth place he will die; or, ⟨conversely⟩, if the lord of the eighth place is in the rising sign and is a benefic planet, he will survive, but if ⟨it is⟩ a malefic ⟨planet⟩ he will die. (3) Likewise, observe the position of the Moon: if it gives power to the lord of the sixth place, the illness will be aggravated, and the same applies if the lord of the ascendant gives power to the lord of the sixth place or to a malefic planet. (4) The lord of the twelfth place, too, is very unfortunate, almost as much as the lord of the sixth place. (5) The fixed signs signify a long illness, the tropical ⟨signs⟩ signify a short illness, and the bicorporal ⟨signs⟩ signify that after one illness will come another illness. (6) If the malefic star that afflicts the ascendant sign in conjunction or in aspect, or ⟨that afflicts⟩ the Moon or the lord of the ascendant sign, is moving slowly, it signifies delay, but the opposite applies if it is moving rapidly. (7) If the lord of the ascendant is moving rapidly and will soon enter another sign, or if it leaves one sign and enters another, his illness will recede at once, on condition that it [the other sign that the lord of the ascendant enters] is neither the sixth nor the twelfth place.

Quotation 3: *Epitome*, ed. Heller (1548), III:10, P4v:

(1) Signa duorum corporum significant permutationem in alium morbum. (2) Si dominus ascendentis habet coniunctionem cum domino domus sextae, octavae vel duodecimae, et est quem aspicit infortuna, et dominus est infortunatus ex ea, cum consummabitur aspectus, vel coniunctio, ea hora deficit aeger ... (3) Si dominus ascendentis est sub luce Solis, et peius is est in angulo cum pertingit ad cremationem, deficiet

(1) The bicorporal signs signify the replacement of one disease by another. (2) If the lord of the ascendant is in conjunction with the lord of the sixth, eighth or twelfth place, and it aspects an inauspicious ⟨planet⟩, and the lord is made inauspicious by it, when the aspect is completed, in this hour the ill person will die ... (3) If the lord of the ascendant in under the light of the Sun, and even worse, if it is in a cardo when it reaches burning, ⟨the ill person⟩ will die.

Quotation 4: *Me'orot* § 17:1, 478–479:

אם הלבנה בתחלת חולי במזל מתהפך, יורה על מהירות דברי החולה, בין טוב ובין רע, ואם היה במזל נאמן, יאריך החולי, ואם היה במזל שיש לו שני גופים, יצא מחולי אל חולי.

If at the onset of the disease the Moon is in a tropical sign, it signifies a rapid change in the patient's condition, whether for better or for worse; if it [the Moon] is in a fixed sign, the disease will be protracted, and if in a bicorporal sign, after he recovers from a disease he will contract another disease.

Part 10. Marriage

Quotation 1: *She'elot* II, § 12.3:1, 388–389:

הנשים. הסתכל אם היה בעל הצומח מביט או מתחבר עם בעל הבית השביעי או התשיעי במזל העולה, ואינו חוזר לאחור או תחת השמש, אז יהיה הזיווג טוב.

Women. Observe whether the lord of the ascendant aspects or conjoins the lord of the seventh or ninth place in the rising sign and is not retrograde or under the ⟨ray of the⟩ Sun. ⟨If so⟩, then the match will be fortunate.

Quotation 2: *Epitome*, ed. Heller (1548), III:11, Qiv:

(1) Si autem planeta aliquis levium suspicit vim ab uno, et dat alteri eorum, quasi per internuncium coniungentur. (2) Si dominus ascendentis dat vim domino septimae domus, mulier principatum obtinebit, quae vis si recipitur in aspectu amicitiae, amor erit inter eos, si non recipitur, vel est aspectus inimicitiae erunt discordes ... (3) Venus et Luna vim habent in desponsatione, quod si qua earum dat vim domino ascendentis existens in angulo vel loco unde ascendens aspiciat, tota res consummabitur ... (4) Si autem foemina querat, ponas dominum ascendentis et ascendens pro muliere, et septimam et dominum eius pro viro et Solem et Martem.

(1) If some planet takes a slight power from another, and gives ⟨the power⟩ to another of them, they will be joined ⟨in matrimony⟩ as if by a mediator. (2) If the lord of the ascendant gives power to the lord of the seventh place, the woman will obtain governance; it the power is received by an aspect of friendship, love will reign among them, but if it is not received, or if there is an aspect of hate they will be at variance ... (3) Venus and the Moon have power in matters related to the espousal, for if one of them gives power to the lord of the ascendant when it is in a cardo or in a position from which it aspects the ascendant, everything will be completed ... (4) But if the woman is the querent, assign the lord of the ascendant and the ascendant to the woman, and the seventh ⟨place⟩ and its lord to the husband, as well as the Sun and Mars.

Part 11. Wars

Quotation 1: *She'elot* II, § 7.1:2–4, 368–369:

(2) והנה הסתכל: אם היה בעל הצומח מהכוכבים העליונים ובעל הבית השביעי מהשפלים, ושניהם חזקים, ינצח העליון, ואם היה השפל חזק מאד והעליון אמצעי לא ינצח העליון. (3) וככה משפט כל כוכב שיהיה בבית הראשון או בבית השביעי, אם שפל אם עליון. (4) וכל שפל או עליון, אם היה נשרף תחת השמש, אין לו כח והוא מנוצח, וככה השב לאחור יורה שיחלש, רק אם היה מהעליונים לא תהיה חלישותו שלמה.

(2) Now observe: if the lord of the ascendant is one of the upper planets and the lord of the seventh place is one of the lower planets, and if both are strong, the upper planet is victorious; but if the lower planet is very strong and the upper planet is intermediate ⟨in its power⟩, the upper planet will not be victorious. (3) The same rule applies to any planet that is in the first or seventh place, be it an upper or a lower planet. (4) Any upper or lower planet, if it is burnt under the ⟨ray of the⟩ Sun, has no power and is not victorious; the same applies to a retrograde ⟨planet⟩ and this signifies that it will grow weaker, but if it is one of the upper planets its weakness will be not complete.

Quotation 2: *She'elot* I, § 7.3:2–5, 270–271:

(2) הסתכל: אם היה השואל הוא בעצמו הנלחם, והנה שים המזל הצומח שלו, והמזל השוקע של אויבו. (3) והנה, אם היה בעל המזל הצומח תקיף, אם הוא מהעליונים שיהיה מזרחי מן השמש ואם מהשפלים שיהיה מערבי, ולא יהיה תחת אור השמש ולא שב אחורנית, והוא בבית הראשון או העשירי או בבית עשתי עשר, והוא בבית שלטונו או בגבולו ואין כוכב מזיק מביט אליו, ובעל הבית השביעי הפך כל זה, אז ינצח השואל, בין שיהיה בעל המזל הצומח כוכב עליון או שפל. (4) ואם בעל הבית השביעי יהיה כדרך שהזכרתי לבעל המזל הצומח, ובעל מזל הצומח חלש, בין שיהיה בעל הבית השביעי כוכב עליון או שפל, ינוצח השואל. (5) ואם שניהם תקיפים, הסתכל אי זה מהם בעליו הוא כוכב עליון, והוא ינצח את השפל.

(2) Observe: if the querent himself is a combatant, assign the ascendant sign to him and the sign of the descendant to his enemy. (3) Now if the lord of ascendant sign is the stronger, ⟨that is,⟩ if it is one of upper planets and is oriental of the Sun or if it is one of the lower planets and is occidental ⟨to the Sun⟩, if it is neither under the ray of the Sun nor retrograde, if it is in the first or tenth or eleventh place, and if it is in the house where it holds lordship or it is in its term and no malefic planet aspects it (the opposite applies for the lord of the seventh place), then the querent will be victorious, whether the lord of the ascendant sign is an upper or a lower planet. (4) But if the lord of the seventh place is in the same relation as I have ⟨just⟩ mentioned with the lord of the ascendant sign, and the lord of the ascendant sign is weak, the querent will be defeated, whether the lord of the seventh place is an upper or a lower planet. (5) If both are strong, find out which of them [of the ascendant sign or of the seventh place] has an upper planet as its lord; this one will be victorious over the lower planet.

Quotation 3: *She'elot* I, § 7.3:2, 270–271:

הסתכל: אם היה השואל הוא בעצמו הנלחם, והנה שים המזל הצומח שלו, והמזל השוקע של אויבו.

Observe: if the querent himself is a combatant, assign the ascendant sign to him and the sign of the descendant to his enemy.

Quotation 4: *Epitome*, ed. Heller (1548), III:12, Q1v–Q2r:

Si quaerens facturus sit bellum, pro ipso quaeras dominum ascendentis et ascendens, et septimam domum et dominum eius pro eo, cum quo est conflicturus.

If the querent is the one who will make war, inquire the lord of the ascendant and the ascendant about him, and ⟨inquire⟩ the seventh place and its lord about the one who will be in conflict with him.

Quotation 5: *She'elot* I, § 6:1–2, 244–245:

ואתן לך כלל: אם מצאת השליט בבית השביעי, ... והנה יש לך לערב תולדת הכוכב ... והנה, אם ... כוכב חמה יורה על מריבות בעבור דברים שאין להם עיקר רק להראות הניצוח.

I ⟨now⟩ give you a general rule: if you find the ruler in the seventh place ... you should combine the nature of the planet ... if Mercury, it signifies quarrels about groundless things and merely for love of disputation.

Quotation 6: *Mivḥarim* I, § 3.1:6, 58–59:

גם כוכב חמה יורה על קטטות ומריבות בדברים שאין להם שום עיקר, ואם היה שם אחד מן הכוכבים הטובים, אז יורה על טוב שיקרה לו באותו מקום שילך.

In addition, Mercury indicates groundless quarrels and disputes, but if one of the benefic planets is there, it signifies good fortune that will befall him at his destination.

Part 12. Victorious

Quotation 1: *She'elot* I, § 7.3:12–13, 270–273:

גם הסתכל אם יש להם מרחב, כי ההוה בחשב אפודת הגלגל ינצח את הדרומי, וההוה בצפון ינצח את ההוה בחשב אפודת הגלגל ואת הדרומי. ואם מרחב שניהם צפוני, הסתכל מי שיש לו את המרחב הרב, הוא ינצח את האחר, ואם שניהם דרומיים, הסתכל מי שמרחבו מעט ינצח את האחר, וחשוב זה הכח במספר שנים.

Also observe whether they have latitude ⟨with respect to the ecliptic⟩, for the one that is in the ecliptic is victorious over the one that is southern ⟨with respect to the ecliptic⟩, and the one that is northern is victorious over the one that is in the ecliptic or southern. If both are northern, find out which has the greater latitude [i.e., is more northern], and this one will be victorious over the other; and if both are southern, the one whose latitude is less ⟨southern⟩ will be victorious over the other. Consider this power as equivalent to two ⟨portions of power⟩.

Quotation 2: *Me'orot*, § 30:4, 476–477:

ואם יש לאחד מהם רוחב בפאת שמאל והשני בקו גלגל המזלות או רחבו דרומי, ינצח השמאלי. ואם שניהם שמאליים, ינצח בעל המרחב הרב. ואם האחד בקו המזלות ורוחב השני דרומי, ינצח ההווה בקו. ואם שניהם דרומיים ינצח בעל המרחב המעט.

If one of them has some northern ⟨ecliptic⟩ latitude and the second is in the ecliptic or has some southern ⟨ecliptic⟩ latitude, the northern one is victorious. If both are northern, the one at the higher latitude is victorious. If one is in the ecliptic and the other has some southern ⟨ecliptic⟩ latitude, the one that is in the ecliptic is victorious. If both are southern, the one at the lower latitude is victorious.

Quotation 3: *Ṭeʿamim* II, § 4.4:1, 210–211:

והשמאלי ינצח את ההווה בקו גלגל המזלות, וככה את הדרומי, וההווה ינצח הדרומי, ובעל המרחב הדרומי המעט ינצח בעל המרחב הדרומי הרב, בעבור שהכוכב ההווה בפאת שמאל יש לו כח רב, כי הישוב הוא בפאת שמאל, ובהיות השמש במזלות השמאלים אז יש לו כח גדול לחמם האויר.

A northern ⟨planet⟩ is victorious over one that is in the line of the zodiac, and likewise over one that is southern ⟨to it⟩; one ⟨that is in the line of zodiac⟩ is victorious over a southern ⟨planet⟩; and one in a lower ⟨southern⟩ latitude is victorious over one that has a higher southern latitude, because a planet that is in the north has greater power, inasmuch as the ecumene is in the north [with respect to the equator], and when the Sun is in the northern signs it has a great power to warm the air.

Quotation 4: *She'elot* II, § 7.4:1–3, 370–373:

(1) גם כן השתבשו חכמי המשפטים אם היה המזל העולה עקרב ומאדים בשור, וידוע כי אם היה בעל המזל העולה בבית השביעי הוא מנוצח, והפך זה אם היה בעל הבית השביעי במזל העולה. (2) והנה, זה השבוש הוא בעבור היות מאדים כוכב עליון: יש אומרים שינוצח השואל ואחרים אמרו הפך הדבר. (3) ולפי דעתי שרעה תבוא לשואל ולאויב; והנה תסתכל: אם היה נגה תקיף, אז יהיו שוים ברעה, ואם לא יהיה תקיף, אז ינוצח השואל.

(1) The astrologers were also confused about the case in which Scorpio [i.e., Mars' house] is the rising sign, and Mars [that is, the lord of the ascendant] is in Taurus [Taurus is the seventh place after Mars' house and is Mars' detriment], since it is known that if the lord of the rising sign is in the seventh place, he [the side that begins the war] will be defeated, and the opposite applies if the lord of the seventh place is in the rising sign. (2) Now, this confusion arises because Mars is an upper planet: some said that ⟨consequently⟩ the querent will be defeated, and others said the opposite. (3) In my opinion misfortune will befall the querent and the enemy; now observe: if Venus [i.e., Taurus is Venus' house] is strong, then ⟨both sides⟩ will be equally unfortunate, but if it [Venus] is not strong, then the querent will be defeated.

Quotation 5: *Mivḥarim* I, § 7.2:1–4, 70–71:

(1) מחלוקת גדולה יש בין חכמי המזלות. כי כולם מודים, אם היה בעל מזל הצומח בבית השביעי, כי הוא מנוצח, ואם בעל הבית השביעי יהיה במזל הצומח, ינוצח האויב. והנה אמרו: איך נדין אם היה המזל הצומח עקרב ויהיה מאדים בבית השביעי, במזל שור. (2) והנה דורוניוס דן כי בעל המזל הצומח ישחית על נפשו ויהיה מנוצח. (3) ומאשא אללה אמר: בעבור שהוא כוכב עליון, כי הוא ינצח האויב; כי הוא אמר בספר הנסיונות שלו כי יותר טוב הוא שיהיה המזל הצומח לכוכב עליון ויהיה חצי תקיף מאשר יהיה הצומח לכוכב שפל והוא בתקפו. (4) והנה אבו מעשר אמר כי נסה זה פעמים רבות, כי אם היה המזל העולה עקרב ומאדים בשור, כי יבא נזק לשניהם, ואם היה נגה בעל השביעי בתקפו, ינצח האויב, והפך הדבר אם לא היה בתקפו.

(1) There is a great dispute among the astrologers. All agree that if the lord of the ascendant sign is in the seventh place, he [the commander] will be defeated, and if the lord of the seventh place is in the ascendant sign the enemy will be defeated. But they [the astrologers] asked: how should we pass judgment if Scorpio is the ascendant sign and Mars is in the seventh place, in Taurus? (2) Now Dorotheus judged that ⟨in this case⟩ the lord of the ascendant sign [i.e., Mars] will cause harm to him [the commander] and he will be defeated. (3) But Māshā'allāh said: inasmuch as it [Mars] is an upper planet, he [the commander] will be victorious over the enemy; for he [Māshā'allāh] said in his *Book of Experiences* that it is more auspicious if ⟨the lord of⟩ the ascendant sign is an upper planet in half its strength than if ⟨the lord of the sign of⟩ the ascendant is a lower planet in its full strength. (4) Abū Maʿshar said that he tested this many times ⟨and proved⟩ that if Scorpio is the rising sign and Mars is in Taurus, both armies will be battered; if Venus is the lord of the seventh ⟨place⟩ and is in full strength, the enemy will be victorious, and the opposite holds if it is not in full strength.

Quotation 6: *Mivḥarim* II, § 7.3:1–2, 166–167:

(1) והקדמונים אמרו: אם היה כוכב רע בבית השביעי, ינוצח האויב. (2) ואני אומר כי רעה תבוא לאויב, גם להולך אליו, רק אם היה מאדים בגדי, בעבור שהוא בית כבודו. והנה, אם היה בבית השביעי, יועיל לאויב ויזיק להולך להלחם עמו.

(1) The Ancients said: if a malefic planet is in the seventh place, the enemy will be defeated. (2) But I say that evil will befall both the enemy and also the one who is going out ⟨to war⟩ only if Mars is in Capricorn, because it [Capricorn] is the house of its [Mars'] exaltation. But if it [Mars] is in the seventh place, it will be auspicious for the enemy but unfortunate for the one who makes war against it.

Quotation 7: *Epitome*, ed. Heller (1548), III:12, Q2r:

Magistri quoque astrologiae dicunt: cum est ascendens Taurus, et est in ipsa Mars dominus septimae, eius significatio vincetur, sed secundum veritatem ambo patientur.

The masters of astrology say: when Taurus is the ascendant and Mars is in it [the ascendant] lord of the seventh ⟨place⟩, its signification will be defeated, but according to the truth both ⟨combatants⟩ will be battered

Part 13. Partnership

Quotation 1: *She'elot* II, § 7.8:1–2, 376–377:

והשואל בעבור השותפות, הסתכל: אם היה בעל הבית השביעי במבט טוב עם בעל הצומח, ויש לו ממשלת בבית השני או בגורל הלבנה, אז יהיה טוב והאחרית טובה. ואם היה מאדים או שבתי בבית השביעי, ירמוהו השותפין ויכזבו לו ויאנסוהו.

⟨If⟩ someone poses a question about partnership, observe: if the lord of the seventh place is in a fortunate aspect with the lord of the ascendant and exercises lordship over the second place or over the lot of the Moon, ⟨the partnership⟩ will be fortunate and will have a happy outcome. But if Mars or Saturn is in the seventh place his partners will cheat him, disappoint him, and plunder him.

Quotation 2: *She'elot* I, § 7.2:1–3, 268–269:

אם ישאל שואל על דברי שותפות, הסתכל: אם ראית מאדים בבית השביעי, יורה על שותפות רעה שאחריתה לנזק ולמריבה. גם שבתאי, אם היה כך, יורה שאין תועלת בה, והכוכבים הטובים יורו על ריוח וטוב. ואם היה בעל הבית השביעי במקום טוב והוא מביט אל בעל המזל הצומח מבט טוב, יורה כי טוב יהיה לו בשותפות, והפך הדבר אם היה במקום רע או במבט רע.

If the querent poses a question about a partnership, observe: if you see Mars in the seventh place, it signifies an unfortunate partnership that will end in injury and quarrels. Saturn, too, if it is in such a place, signifies that it [the partnership] will not yield any benefit, but the benefic planets signify good profit. If the lord of the seventh place is in a fortunate position and it aspects the lord of the ascendant sign in a fortunate aspect, it signifies that he will find the partnership fortunate, and the opposite applies if it is in an unfortunate position or in an unfortunate aspect.

Part 14. Fear

Quotation 1: *She'elot* I, § 8.1:1–5, 282–283:

אם שאל שואל על דבר שיפחד ממנו, אם יהיה אם לא, הסתכל אל בעל הצומח והמורה. אם היו מביטים אל הצומח ואין כוכב מזיק מביט אליהם, אמור לו שישב לבטח כי לא ירע לו שום נזק, ואם היה בעל הצומח בבית הששי או בבית השמיני או בבית השנים עשר, יורה על רוב מוראו. ואם היה אחד המזיקים מביט מבט רע אליו או אל הצומח, או יהיו במחברת עמו או עם הצומח, בשרנו כי יקרנו רע יותר מאשר יפחד. ואם היה המזיק בעל הבית השמיני יורה עד שימות, ואם היה בעל הבית השני, יורה כי יארע לו רעה גדולה רק ינצל ממנה באחרונה. ויש לך להסתכל אל המזלות אשר בו הבית השמיני, כי המזל המתהפך יורה כי במהרה יסור אותו הפחד או הרע ממנו, ואם היה מזל עומד יורה כי יעמוד ימים רבים, ואם המזל בעל שתי גופות יורה כי ינצל מהרעה ויקרנו פעם אחרת.

If the querent poses a question about something he is afraid of—whether it will occur or not—observe the lord of the ascendant and the significator. If they aspect the ascendant and no malefic planet aspects them, tell him [the querent] that he may rest assured that nothing unfortunate will befall him; but if the lord of the ascendant is in the sixth or eighth or twelfth place, it indicates that most of what he is afraid of ⟨will come true⟩. If one of the malefics aspects it [the lord of the ascendant] or the ascendant in an unfortunate aspect, or if they [the malefics] are in conjunction with it [the lord of the ascendant] or with the ascendant, inform him that a greater calamity than what he was afraid of will befall him. If the malefic ⟨planet⟩ is the lord of the eighth place, it signifies that he will die, and if it is the lord of the second place it indicates that a great calamity will befall him but he will be saved from it at the end. Observe the signs where the eighth place is, for a tropical sign signifies that that fear or ⟨expected⟩ misfortune will soon disappear; if it is in a fixed sign it signifies that ⟨the fear⟩ will linger for many days; and if it is a bicorporal sign it indicates that he will escape the misfortune but it will happen some other time.

Quotation 2: *She'elot* II, § 8.3:1–4, 376–379:

והשואל על דבר שיפחד ממנו, הסתכל: אם היה בעל המזל הצומח והלבנה במקום טוב בגלגל, ואין כוכב רע באחד היתדות ולא עם בעל המזל או הפקיד, אם לא היה הבעל מביט אל המעלה הצומחת, לא יבוא לו הפחד ולא יהיה. ואם עבר הפקיד או בעל הבית או הלבנה מחברת עם כוכב רע כדי אורו או מעלה אחת במבטים, יהיה לו הפחד בנפש ובמחשבות גם בדברים שידבר ובחלומות, רק לא יבא לעולם לידי מעשה. ואם בעל המזל היה תחת אור השמש, או בבית שנים עשר או בבית הששי או השמיני, יהיה לו הפחד ולא יהיה לו נזק רב. רק אם היה אחד מן הכוכבים הרעים באחד היתדות, או הוא עם בעל הצומח באחת היתדות, אז היא רעה גדולה ולא ימלט מן הרעה.

⟨If the querent⟩ poses a question about something of which he is afraid, observe: if the lord of the ascendant sign and the Moon are in a fortunate position in the zodiac, and ⟨if⟩ no malefic planet is in one of the cardines, or with the lord or the ruler of the sign ⟨of the ascendant⟩, ⟨and⟩ if the lord ⟨of the ascendant⟩ does not aspect the ascendant degree, his fear will not come true. If the ruler or the lord of the sign ⟨of the ascendant⟩ or the Moon passed through conjunction with a malefic planet within ⟨the distance of⟩ the ray of its body or aspects ⟨within⟩ one degree, he will feel fear in his mind and thoughts and in what he says and in his dreams, but it will never come true. If the lord of the sign is under the ray of the Sun, or in the twelfth, sixth, or eighth place, his fear will come true but will not injure him severely. But if one of the malefic planets is in one of the cardines, or if it is with the lord of the ascendant in one of the cardines, then a great misfortune will befell him and he will not be able to escape it.

Part 15. Alive or Dead?

Quotation 1: *She'elot* II, §1.2:1–5, 356–359:

ואם היתה שאלה על אדם אם הוא חי או מת, הסתכל: אם מצאת בעל הבית נשרף מהשמש או הוא תחת אורו ומרחבו דרומי, הנו מת, ואם היה תחת הארץ ואף כי ביתד הרביעי, כבר נקבר, ואם היה בבית שנים עשר או הששי, גם הוא רע. לכן, לא תדין עד שיתחבר כח אחר, והוא שתסתכל לעולם אל מקום הלבנה. והנה, אם היתה במזל הצומח ותתן כחה לכוכב שהוא תחת הארץ, ואף כי בבית הרביעי ממנה, כבר מת ונקבר. והנה, אם היה בעל הבית או הלבנה למעלה מהארץ, הנו חי, ואם בעל הבית הצומח בבית השמיני, הנו מת, וככה אם היה בעל השמיני במעלה הצומחת, אפילו שיהיה כוכב טוב.

If the interrogation is about whether someone is alive or dead, observe ⟨as follows⟩. If you find that the lord of the ⟨first⟩ place is burnt by the Sun, or is under the rays of the Sun and its ⟨ecliptic⟩ latitude is southern, he is dead; if it is under the Earth, notably in the fourth cardo [fourth place], he has already been buried; and if it is in the twelfth or the sixth place it is also unfortunate. Therefore, do not pronounce judgment without adding another power; namely, you should always look at the position of the Moon. Now if it [the Moon] is in the ascendant sign and gives its power to a planet that is under the Earth, particularly if it is in the fourth place after it [the Moon], he is already dead and has been buried. If the lord of the ⟨first⟩ place or the Moon is above the Earth he is alive, but if the lord of the ascendant sign is in the eighth place he is dead; and the same applies when the lord of the eighth ⟨place⟩ is in the ascendant degree, even if it is a benefic planet.

Quotation 2: *She'elot* I, §1.3:1–2, 248–249:

ואם שאל שואל על אדם שאין לו ערך אליו, אם הוא חי או מת, הסתכל אל בעל המזל הצומח או השליט עליו. והנה, אם מצאתו שהוא תחת אור השמש באי זה מקום

> שיהיה, יורה שהוא מת, ואם מצאתו שהוא למעלה מן הארץ, שהוא בבית העשירי או העשתי עשר, דע כי הוא חי והוא יושב במקומו, ואם בשביעי או בתשיעי, גם הוא חי אך הוא מתנועע ממקומו, ואם בשמיני, הוא חי רק הוא עומד בסכנת מות, וככה אם בעל הבית השמיני במעלה הצומחת, אפילו שיהיה כוכב טוב.
>
> If the querent poses a question about someone with whom he has no ties of kinship, whether alive or dead, look at the lord of the ascendant sign or its ruler. Now if you find it to be under the rays of the Sun in any place whatsoever, this indicates that he is dead; if you find it above the Earth, which is the tenth or the eleventh place, know that he is alive and living in his home; if ⟨you find it⟩ in the seventh or ninth ⟨place⟩, he is alive, too, but is roaming away from home; and if ⟨you find it⟩ in the eighth ⟨place⟩, he is alive but facing mortal peril; and the same applies if the lord of the eighth place is in the ascendant degree, even if it is a benefic planet.

Quotation 3: Sahl's *Book of Interrogations*, Paris, BnF lat. 16204, 465b:

> Cum interrogatus fueris de viro absente vel de aliquo alio virorum, utrum vivat an sit mortuus, aspice dominum ascendentis et Lunam si fuerit in .4a. ab ascendente, aut in domo mortis, quod est .8a. ab ascendente, aut fuerint combusti, aut in descensione sua, aut cum domino domus mortis, aut cum domino quarte domus, erit mortus … Et si iungitur Luna planete sub terra, erit mortuus, et si iungitur planete super terram, vivit.
>
> When you are asked about an absent person, or about someone else, whether he lives or is dead, look at the lord of the ascendant and the Moon, if it is in the fourth ⟨place⟩ from the ascendant, or in the house of death, which is the eighth ⟨place⟩ from the ascendant, or is burnt, or in its descension, or with the lord of the house of death, or with the lord of the fourth place, he is dead. …. If the Moon applies to a planet below the Erath, he is dead, and if ⟨the Moon⟩ applies to a planet above the Erath, he is alive.

Part 16. Journeys

Quotation 1: *She'elot* II, § 9.1:1–3, 378–379:

> (1) השואל על דבר הליכה, הסתכל: אם בעל המזל העולה בבית התשיעי, ילך ברצון נפשו, ואם היה בעל הבית התשיעי בבית הראשון, לאות כי יבא לו דבר ויתחדש שילך ממקומו, ואם היה בעל הצומח נותן הכח לבעל הבית התשיעי, או הפך הדבר, ילך. וכל זה שאמרתי הוא בדרכים הארוכים. (2) וככה הסתכל לבעל הבית השלישי בדרכים הקרובים, והסתכל אל מקום הלבנה שיש לה כח רב בהליכת הדרכים, וככה מאדים. (3) ויאמר תלמי: אם היה שבתי בבית התשיעי בהליכה בים, יורה על סערה גדולה בים, ואם היה מאדים בבית התשיעי בהליכה ביבשה, יורה על לסטים שיצאו אליו בדרך.
>
> (1) ⟨If⟩ someone poses a question about journeys, observe: if the lord of the rising sign is in the ninth place, he will set out willingly; if the lord of the

ninth place is in the first place, this indicates that something will happen to him and prompt him to leave home; and if the lord of the ascendant gives power to the lord of the ninth place, or vice versa, he will set out. Everything I just told you refers to long journeys. (2) As for short journeys, observe the lord of the third place; ⟨also⟩ observe the position of the Moon, since it has a great power in journeys, and the same applies to Mars. (3) Ptolemy said: if Saturn is in the ninth place in ⟨an interrogation about⟩ a journey by sea, it signifies a fierce storm at sea; if Mars is in the ninth place in ⟨an interrogation about⟩ a journey by land, it signifies that bandits will assault him en route.

Quotation 2: *Epitome*, ed. Heller (1548), III:17, Q4r:

In quaestione quaerentis de suo itinere, si dominus ascendentis est in domo nona vel tertia, perficiet iter. Sic si dominus nonae est in ascendente aut si dominus ascendentis habet iuncturam vel aspectum cum dominum nonae. Quod si est aspectus amicitiae, iter eius pro ipsius arbitrio erit, si inimicitiae eveniet cum contentione et labore.

Concerning a question of a querent about his journey, if the lord of the ascendant is in the ninth or third place, the journey will be accomplished. The same applies if the lord of the ninth ⟨place⟩ is in the ascendant or if the lord of the ascendant is in conjunction or forms an aspect with the lord of the ninth ⟨place⟩. If there is an aspect of love, the journey will be according to his decision, if there is an aspect of hate, ⟨the journey will be⟩ with struggle and effort.

Part 17. Will Someone Return?

Quotation 1: *She'elot* I, § 3.2:1–4, 254–255:

ואם אדם ישאל על אחר שאיננו ממשפחתו, אם ישוב במהרה אל ביתו, הסתכל: אם מצאת בעל המזל הצומח בבית העשירי או בעל השעה, דע כי במהרה יבוא, ויותר קרוב אם היה המזל מתהפך, שיתכן שלא יתעכב ימים רק שעות. ואם היה בבית הראשון יהיה לו עכוב מעט ויבא, ואם היה בבית השביעי הוא ילך למקום אחר ... ואם היה בעל המזל הצומח באחת היתדות חוזר אחורנית, במהרה יבא, ואם היה בבית התשיעי או השלישי, יורה כי הוא בדרך רק יתאחר לבא.

If someone asks whether someone who is not his kin will return home soon, observe: if you find the lord of the ascendant sign or the lord or the hour in the tenth place, know that he will come soon, and even sooner if it is in a tropical sign, since it is possible that it is only hours away and not days. If it [the lord of the ascendant sign or the lord or the hour] is in the first place he will come after a short delay, but if it is in the seventh place he will go to another place ... If the lord of the ascendant sign is retrograde in one of the cardines, he will come soon, and if it is in the ninth or the third place, it signifies that he is on his way but will be delayed.

Quotation 2: *Epitome*, ed. Heller (1548), III:25, R2r:

De amico absente utrum revertatur … Quod si Lunam quovis angulo inveneris, vel dat Luna vim vel ascendentis dominus planetae qui sit in ascendente vel decima domo, redibit cito. Sic etiam Luna dante vim domino ascendentis, in ipso statim recurret. Signa mobilia significant reditum brevem, firma tardum, bicorporea mediocrem. Vide etiam quot gradus sint inter Lunam et dominum ascendentis, et planetam qui in angulo est, cui dat vim ut praediximus. Si dominus horae est in decima, significat horarum distantiam, si in ascendente dies, si in septima menses, si in quarta annos. Si dominus ascendentis est retrogradus, aut si non aspicit ascendens, tardus erit reditus. Si dominus ascendentis dat vim planetae qui est in nona vel tertia domo, vel si Luna dat vim planetae, qui est dominus septimae, vel si dat vim domino ascendentis in septima existenti, tarde reversurus est.

⟨A question⟩ on an absent friend, whether he will return. If you find the Moon in one cardo, and the Moon or the lord of the ascendant gives power to a planet located in the ascendant or the tenth place, he will return quickly. If the Moon gives power to the lord of the ascendant, he will return immediately. The tropical signs signify a quick return, the fixed a tardy ⟨return⟩, and the bicorporal an intermediate ⟨return⟩. Observe how many degrees are between the Moon and the lord of the ascendant, and the aforementioned planet located in a cardo to which it [the Moon] gives power. If the lord of the hour is in the tenth ⟨place⟩, it signifies the distance in hours, if in the ascendant in days, if in the seventh ⟨place⟩ in months, and if in the fourth ⟨place⟩ in years. If the lord of the ascendant is retrograde, or if it does not aspect the ascendant, the return will be tardy. If the lord of the ascendant gives power to a planet in the ninth or third place, or if the Moon gives power to a planet that is the lord of the seventh ⟨place⟩, or if gives power to the lord of the ascendant located in the seventh ⟨place⟩, he will return tardily.

Part 18. Wealth from a King

Quotation 1: *She'elot* I, § 10.1:1–9, 286–287:

אם ישאל אדם על נפשו, אם יהיה לו שולטנות או ממשלה על מקום, או אי זה דבר שיבקש מאת המלך, הסתכל: אם מצאת בעל הצומח במחברת עם בעל הבית העשירי, או במבט טוב עמו, והם בבתים טובים, יורה כי תהיה שאלתו ויאהבנו המלך ... ואם המורה יביט אל בעל הצומח, הנה יורה כי ישלים חפצו כרצונו. ואם אין בעל הצומח מביט אל בעל הבית העשירי ויביט אל השמש מבט טוב והשמש בבית טוב, יורה כי יהיה הדבר ויטיב לו המלך, ואם השמש בבית רע, יורה כי יהיה הדבר רק בסוף ישנאהו המלך ויענישהו. ואם היה בעל הצומח מתחבר עם השמש במעלה אחת ואין ביניהם רק פחות משׁשה עשר חלקים, שהם חצי אלכסון השמש, והכוכב בחשב האפודה והם בבתים טובים, יורה כי המלך יאהבנו כנפשו תמיד, ואם הם בבית רע בתחלה, יאהבנו ולבסוף ישנאנו. ואם יש לכוכב מרחב, יכנו המלך וישים בכבל רגליו, ואם יביט מאדים או שבתאי, יהרגנו.

If someone poses a question about himself—whether he will rule or govern some place, or what he should request from the king—observe: if you find the lord of the ascendant in conjunction with the lord of the tenth place, or in a fortunate aspect with it, and they are in fortunate places, it signifies that his request will come true and the king will love him ... If the significator aspects the lord of the ascendant, this signifies that he will attain the object of his desire. If the lord of the ascendant does not aspect the lord of the tenth place but aspects the Sun in a fortunate aspect and the Sun is in a fortunate place, it signifies that the thing will come true and the king will favor him; but if the Sun is in an unfortunate place it signifies that the thing will come true but in the end the king will hate him and punish him. If the lord of the ascendant conjoins with the Sun in the same degree and ⟨the distance⟩ between them is less than 16′, which is equal to half the Sun's diameter, and the planet [the lord of the ascendant] is in the ecliptic and they [the lord of the ascendant and the lord of the tenth place] are in fortunate places, it signifies that the king will always love him as he loves himself; but if they are in an unfortunate place, he will love him at first but in the end he will hate him. If the planet has ⟨some ecliptic⟩ latitude, the king will have him flogged and placed in leg-irons; if Mars or Saturn are in aspect, he will have him killed.

Part 19. Love

Quotation 1: *She'elot* I, § 11.1:1–8, 290–293:

אם שאל אדם אם ימצא חן בעיני אדם אחר, הסתכל אל בעל זה הבית ... ויש לך לדעת אהבת מי יבקש, כי אם יבקש אהבת זקנים והיה שבתאי בבית טוב בשאלה, אע״פי שלא יהיה בעל בית עשתי עשר, יורה כי יהיה חפצו כרצונו, רק אם שבתאי יהיה שב אחורנית או בעל בית שנים העשר, יורה כי בסוף תהיה ביניהם מריבה גדולה. ואם הוא יבקש אהבת דיין וכומר ומצאת צדק בבית טוב, יורה כי יהיה חפצו, ואם היה עם אחד המזיקים לא יהיה. ואם הוא יבקש אהבת שר מלחמה או אהבת גבור ומאדים במבט טוב אל הצומח ואל בעליו, יהיה חפצו, ואם במבט רע לא יהיה, א״ע״פ שיהיה בעל בית עשתי עשר בצומח. ואם הוא מבקש אהבת שלטון והשמש במקום טוב, מביט מבט טוב אל הצומח ואל בעליו, יהיה כל חפצו. ואם הוא יבקש אהבת נשים ונגה במקום טוב ויביט מבט טוב אל הצומח ואל בעליו, יהיה חפצו, ואם יביט מאדים מבט רע אל אחד מהם, לא יהיה. ואם הוא יבקש אהבת חכם הסתכל אל כוכב חמה ועשה כמשפט.

If someone asks whether he will find favor with another person, observe the lord of this place [i.e., the eleventh place] ... You need to know whose love he seeks; if he seeks the love of old people and Saturn is in a fortunate place at the time of the interrogation, even though it [Saturn] is not the lord of the eleventh place, it signifies that his wish will come true as he expects; but if Saturn is retrograde or if it is the lord of the twelfth place, it signifies that a bitter quarrel will break out between them in the end. If he seeks the love of a judge or a priest and you find Jupiter in a fortunate place, it signifies that his wish will come true, but if it [Jupiter] is with one of the malefics it will not come true. If he seeks the love of a general or of a warrior and Mars is in a fortunate aspect with the ascendant or with its lord, his wish will come true; but if it is in an unfortunate aspect it will not come true, even though the lord of the eleventh place is in the ascendant. If he seeks the love of the ruler and the Sun is in a fortunate position, and is in a fortunate aspect with the ascendant and its lord, all his wish will come true. If he seeks the love of women and Venus is in a fortunate position and is in a fortunate aspect with the ascendant and its lord, his wish will come true; but if Mars is in an unfortunate aspect with one of them [the ascendant or its lord], it will not come true. If he seeks the love of a scholar observe Mercury and proceed according to the rule.

Part 20. Prison

Quotation 1: *She'elot* I, § 12.1:1–9, 292–295:

(1) אם שאל שואל על חבוש שהוא בבית הסוהר, יש לך להסתכל דברים רבים. האחד, אם יצא במהרה מבית הסהר. והנה, הסתכל כל מה שאומר לך. (2) ראה אם המורה מהיר בהליכתו, ובעל הצומח, ואם הם באחת היתדות ונותנים כחם לכוכב שהוא בבית השלישי והתשיעי, או לבעלי הבתים הזנכרים, על מנת שיהיה בעל הבית התשיעי או השלישי מהיר בהליכתו. והנה, כל אלה יורו כי יצא במהרה. (3) ואם בעל הבית השלישי או התשיעי יתן הכח לבעל הצומח, והוא באחת הרביעיות הנקבות, ואף כי אם היה מהיר בהליכתו, הנה יצא ביומו, ואם הוא כוכב טוב יצא בשעתו. (4) והמזלות המתהפכים יורו על מהירות, אם היה ככה המזל הצומח או בעליו במזל מהתפך או הלבנה שם, והמזלות העומדים יורו על עיכוב, ובעלי שני גופות יורו על זמן בינוני. (5) ודע כי אם היה שבתאי באחת היתדות הוא סימן רע, וככה אם היה בעל הצומח בבית הרביעי, כי הוא יותר רע מכל היתדות, כי היתדות בדבר הזה הם קשים, וככה אם יתן המורה כחו לכוכב שהוא ביתד. (6) ויותר רע אם היה בעל צומח בבית שנים עשר או בבית הששי או בשמיני, כי אז יורה כי ימות בבית הסוהר, וככה אם יביט אליו מבט רע בעל בית שנים העשר או בעל הבית השמיני, ויותר רע כי היה כוכב מזיק. (7) ואם מצאת שבעל הצומח או המורה יתן הכח לכוכב שהוא בבית השלישי או התשיעי, יורה כי יצא במהרה אם היה אותו הכוכב מהיר בהליכתו. (8) והנה, יש לך להסתכל: אם היה אותו הכוכב בעל אחת יתדות המזל הצומח, יורה כי אחר שיצא ישוב אל בית הסוהר, וככה אם היה בעל הצומח נותן הכח לכוכב שהוא בבית השני או השמיני. (9) והסתכל אל בעל הבית השביעי, אל כוכב שיהיה שם: אם היה במבט טוב עם בעל הצומח, יורה כי השליס האוסר אותו אין במחשבתו לעשות רע, ואם היה במבט רע, יורה על הפך הדבר.

If the querent poses a question about a prisoner in jail, you should observe many things. First, whether he will be soon released from jail. Now observe everything I tell you. (2) Observe whether the significator and the lord of the ascendant are moving rapidly, and whether they are in one of the cardines and give their power to a planet that is in the third or ninth place, or to the lords of the aforementioned places, on condition that the lord of the ninth or third place is moving rapidly. So, all these ⟨conditions⟩ signify that he will be released soon. (3) If the lord of the third or ninth place gives power to the lord of the ascendant, and if is in one of the feminine quadrants, particularly if it is moving rapidly, he will be released on its day [i.e., the day under the charge of the lord of the ascendant], and if it is a benefic planet during its hour [i.e., the hour under the charge of the lord of the ascendant]. (4) The tropical signs signify swiftness, if the ascendant sign or its lord are there, that is, in a tropical sign, or the Moon is there [i.e., in a tropical sign]. The fixed signs signify delay; and the bicorporal sign signify an intermediate period of time. (5) Know that it is an unfortunate indication if Saturn is in one of the cardines. The same applies if the lord of the ascendant is in the fourth place, because it is the worst of all the cardines and the cardines are unfortunate in this regard. The same applies if the significator gives its power to a planet that is in a cardo. (6) It is more unfortunate if the lord of the ascendant is in the twelfth, sixth or eighth place, because then it signifies that he will die in jail, and the same applies if the lord of the twelfth or eighth place aspects it [the lord of the ascendant]; and it is even less fortunate if it is a malefic planet. (7) If you find that the lord of the ascendant or the significator give power to a planet that is in the third or ninth place, it signifies that he will soon be released, if this planet is moving rapidly. (8) Now you should observe: if this planet is the lord of one of the cardines of the ascendant sign, it signifies that after he is released he will return to jail; the same applies if the lord of the ascendant gives power to a planet that is in the second or eighth place. (9) Observe the lord of the seventh place ⟨and any⟩ planet that may be there [in the seventh place]: if it is in a fortunate aspect with the lord of the ascendant, it signifies that the ruler who imprisoned him does not intend to harm him; but if it is an unfortunate aspect, it signifies the opposite.

Quotation 2: *She'elot* II, § 12.1:1–14, 388–389:

(1) זה הבית יורה על בית הסוהר, גם יורה כן הבית הששי, ויש אומרים גם הבית השמיני, וחנוך אמר היתד הרביעי. (2) הסתכל: אם מהלך הלבנה במרוצה, יורה על מהירות צאתו, והפך הדבר אם היה מתאחר. (3) ואם היתה ביתד ותתן הכח לכוכב ההוא בבית השלישי או התשיעי, יורה על מהירות צאתו, וככה אם נתנה הכח לבעל הבית התשיעי או השלישי ולא יהיה באחד היתדות. (4) וכאשר דנת על הלבנה ככה תדין על בעל הצומח. (5) ודע כי כח גדול יש לרביעיות הגלגל כנגד הצומח, כי הרביעיות הנקבות יורו על מהירות צאת הנאסר, והפך הדבר הרביעיות האחרות. (6) והמזלות המתהפכים יורו על מהירות, והעומדים הפך הדבר, ומזלות שני גופות אמצעיות, גם יתכן אחר שיצא שיושב. (7) ואם באחד היתדות, לא יצא מבית הסוהר, ויותר רע אם היה בעל הצומח בבית הרביעי, או שיתן הכח בעל שנים העשר לבעל הצומח, או בעל הצומח אליו, והוא עוד יותר רע, או שיתן הכח בעל הצומח לכוכב שהוא באחד היתדות. (8) ואם היה הכוכב ההוה באחד היתדות מהרעים הוא יותר רע, ואם היה בעל הבית השמיני, ימות בבית הסוהר. (9) ודע שאם תתן הלבנה הכח לבעל המזל הצומח, גם הוא סימן רע. (10) ודע שאם היה הכוכב שהוא ביתד מתאחר בהליכתו, הוא יותר רע, ואם אין מתאחר בהליכתו, יחסר מרעתו. (11) ויש לך להסתכל, כי הכוכב החוזר לאחור לא יוציא מהרה, ואם בעל הצומח יהיה נשרף, אין ספק שלא יצא, ואם לא יהיה מקובל מן השמש, שם ימות. (12) ואם רצית לדעת איך לב המשים אותו בבית הסוהר, הסתכל אל בית השביעי, ודע מי הוא בעליו או הממונה, אם לא יביט בעל הבית ויביט הוא הממונה. (13) ודע היאך הם מבטיו עם המזל העולה, ועם בעל הצומח, ועם הלבנה, וכפי המבטים תדין. (14) ודע כי דרך השבוי כמו הנאסר, אין ביניהם הפרש.

This place signifies prison; the sixth place, too, signifies this, and some say the eighth place as well, but Enoch says the fourth cardo [tenth place]. (2) Observe: if the Moon is moving rapidly, it signifies his swift release, and the opposite applies if it is slow. (3) If it [the Moon] is in the cardo and gives power to a planet in the third or ninth place, it signifies his swift release, and the same applies if it gives power to the lord of the ninth or third place and it is not in one of the cardines. (4) Pass judgment on the basis of the lord of the ascendant as you passed judgment on the basis of the Moon. (5) Know that the quadrants of the zodiac exercise great power with respect to the ascendant: the feminine quadrants signify the prisoner's swift release, and the opposite applies to the other quadrants. (6) The tropical signs signify swiftness, the fixed signs the opposite, the bicorporal signs are intermediate, and it is also possible that after his release he will be jailed again. (7) If ⟨the lord of the ascendant⟩ is in one of the cardines, he will not be released from prison. It is more unfortunate if the lord of the ascendant is in the fourth place or if the lord of the twelfth place gives power to the lord of the ascendant, and even more unfortunate if the lord of the ascendant ⟨gives power⟩ to it [to the lord of the twelfth place] or if the lord of the ascendant gives power to a planet that is in one of the cardines. (8) It is very unfortunate if the planet that is in one of the cardines is malefic; if it is the lord of the eighth place ⟨the prisoner⟩ will die in prison. (9) Know that it is also an unfortunate indication if the Moon gives power to the lord of the ascendant sign. (10) Know that if the planet that is in one of the cardines is moving slowly, it is even more unfortunate; but if it is not moving slowly its unfortunate influence is less. (11) You should also take into consideration that a retrograde planet does not cause a swift release ⟨from prison⟩; if the lord of the ascendant is burnt, it is certain that he will not be released; and if it [the lord of the ascendant] is not received by the Sun he will die there. (12) If you wish to know what the person who put him in prison intends, observe the seventh place and determine its lord or ruler (if the lord of the place does not aspect [the ascendant sign], it [the lord of the place] aspects the ruler). (13) Determine how it [the lord of the seventh place] aspects the rising sign, and the lord of the ascendant, and the Moon, and pass judgment according to these aspects. (14) Know that one should proceed with a captive as for a prisoner—there is no difference between them.

Quotation 3: *Epitome*, ed. Heller (1548), III:26, R2v:

De incarceratis. Considera ascendens eiusque dominum, si inveneris in quovis angulo, et peius si in quarta, tardabitur liberatio. Sic etiam Luna existente in quovis angulo, et peius si dominus duodecimae est coniunctus cum ea vel aspicit, vel etiam si sextae domus dominus vel octavae cum domino ascendentis coniunctionem vel aspectum habeat, cum est infortunatus dominus ascendentis, deficiet captivus in carcere. Si Luna dat vim domino ascendentis, tarde liberabitur. Sic si ascendens est de signis firmis. Similiter si Luna tarda est in eundo. Mobilia vero signa significant cito evasurum, et si Luna sit velox in eundo, vel tribuat vim domino tertiae vel nonae, aut iuncta sit domino ascendentis, et sit velox, et melius si habeat aspectum cum domino tertiae vel nonae, et si ipse dominus tertiae vel nonae sit in ipsa domo est melius, vel si dat vim planetae, qui sit in aliqua harum, nona vel tertiae, vel si dominus ascendentis velox est in quarta quae est ab ascendente ad quartam domum, vel in quarta huic contraria, et melius si est infortunatus

On imprisoned people. Consider the ascendant and its lord, if you find ⟨it⟩ in some cardo, and it is worse in the fourth ⟨place⟩, the release will be delayed. Also if the Moon is in any cardo, and it is worse if the lord of the twelfth ⟨place⟩ is in conjunction with it [the Moon] or aspects it, or also if the lord of the sixth of eighth place forms a conjunction or an aspect with the lord of the ascendant when the lord of the ascendant is inauspicious, ⟨then⟩ the captive will die in prison. If the Moon gives power to the lord of the ascendant, his release will be delayed. The same applies if the ascendant is in the fixed signs. Likewise if the Moon is slow in its motion. The tropical signs signify that he will escape quickly, also if the Moon is quick in its motion, or gives power to the lord of the third of ninth ⟨place⟩, or is joined to the lord of the ascendant, or is quick, ant it is better if it forms an aspect with the lord of the third or ninth ⟨place⟩, and it is better if the lord of the third or ninth ⟨place⟩ is in the place ⟨of the Moon⟩, or if it gives power to a planet which is in the third or ninth ⟨place⟩, or if the lord of the ascendant is quick in the quadrant between the ascendant and the fourth place, or in the opposite quadrant, and it is better if it is inauspicious.

Part 21. What the Querent Has in His Heart?

Quotation 1: *She'elot* I, § 9:3–4, § 10:1–3, § 11:1–3, 244–247:

1 (3) ורבים אמרו שנסתכל אל הבית שיצאה שם התשיעית, כאשר הוא מפורש בספר ראשית חכמה. (4) והנה אתן לך דמיון: היתה המעלה הצומחת ארבע עשרה מעלות ממזל שור והנה תבא התשיעית במזל בעצמו. והנה לאות כי ישאל על מספר חייו או בריאות גופו, ואם היתה התשיעית בתאומים, הנה ישאל על ממון.

2 (1) אמר משאללה: לעולם הסתכל אל מקום הלבנה. (2) כי אם נפרדה ממחברת שבתאי או מבטו, אי זה מבט שיהיה, דע כי השואל ישאל לראות מה תהיה אחריתו בדבר פחד שיש לו, ואם היתה נפרדת במחברת או במבט מצדק, הנה השאלה על דבר ממון, ואם ממאדים על דבר מריבה או דבר האחים, ואם מהשמש על דבר שלטון או אב, ואם מנגה על דבר נשים ותענוגים, ואם מכוכב חמה על דבר חכמה ותבונה. (3) ואם לא נפרדה מכוכב תורה כי ישאל על דבר בטל.

3 (1) אמר רזק: לעולם הסתכל בכל שאלה אל הגורל הטוב, וכפי מקומו ומקום בעליו ככה תדין. (2) ואני אברהם אומר כי הנכון שתסתכל לעולם אל השליט ותערב עמו בעל השעה, כי יש לו כח גדול בשאלות. (3) וככה הורה דורוניאוס גם משאללה, וככה נסיתי פעמים רבות, ונשתף עמהם דבר הלבנה.

1 (3) Many said that we should observe the place to which the ninth-part was assigned, as explained in the *Book of the Beginning of Wisdom*. (4) I now

give you an illustration: suppose that the ascendant degree is Taurus 14° and that the ninth-part is assigned to the sign itself [i.e., the ninth part is assigned to the first place, the place of life]. This means that he will pose a question about how many years he will live or about the health of his body, but if the ninth-part is assigned to Gemini [i.e., the ninth part is assigned to the second place] he will pose a question about money.

2 (1) Māshāʾallāh said: always observe the position of the Moon. (2) If it has parted from conjunction with Saturn or an aspect with it, whichever aspect may be, know that the querent will pose a question about his end, because of some anxiety he feels; if it has parted from conjunction or an aspect with Jupiter, the question is about money; if ⟨it has parted from conjunction or an aspect⟩ with Mars, ⟨the interrogation is⟩ about quarrels or brothers; if from the Sun, about the government or the father; if from Venus, about women and pleasures; if from Mercury, about wisdom and intellect. (3) But if it has not parted from ⟨any⟩ planet, it means that he will pose a question about vain things.

3 (1) Razeq said: in any interrogation always observe the lot of Fortune and pronounce judgment according to its position and the position of its lord. (2) I, Abraham, say that the correct method is that you should always observe the ruler and associate with it the lord of the hour, because it has a great power in interrogations. (3) This was taught by Dorotheus and also by Māshāʾallāh, and I have tested it by experience many times; and we should associate with them the Moon as well.

Quotation 2: *Sheʾelot* II, § 10:1–5, 356–357:

(1) ויאמר בספר אחר כי לעולם נסתכל אל הלבנה ואל מקומה ומאי זה כוכב נפרדה במחברת או במבט, כי כח גדול יש לה. (2) גם יש להסתכל אל הגורל הטוב, שהוא גורל הלבנה. (3) גם אמר שנסתכל אל כח התשעה מהמזל העולה, ובאיזה בית יהיה כח התשיעית. (4) גם אלה הדברים שאמר קרובים הם אל האמת, רק יש להסתכל לעולם אם היה כוכב ביתד הראשון, תן הכח לו אפילו שלא יהא לו שלטון במקומו. (5) והסתכל מה תולדתו ומה הבתים יש לו ממשלה עליהם ועשה כדרך שהראתיך בספר המולדות, כי שבתי יורה על כל דבר קדמון ועל הפחד והיראה וקרקע ומות וחליים, וצדק יורה על הממון ועל הבנים ועל שלום, ומאדים על האחים והקרובים והמלחמות והמריבות, והשמש על החיים והמלכים והשררה והאב, ונגה על הנשים והתענוגים ועל האחות הקטנה, וכוכב חמה יורה על כל מיני חכמה וספר ואמנות, והלבנה תורה על הנקבה גם על חיים ומחשבות נהפכות.

He [Māshāʾallāh] said in another book that we should always look at the Moon and at its position and ⟨find out⟩ from which planet it [the Moon] has parted ⟨after being⟩ in conjunction or aspect, because it [the Moon] has great power. (2) ⟨He also said that we⟩ should look at the lot of Fortune, namely, the lot of the Moon. (3) He also said that we should look at the power of the ninth-part from the rising sign and ⟨find out⟩ to which sign the power of the ninth-part is assigned. (4) These things he said, too, are close to the truth; but one should always observe whether a planet is in the first cardo and give it power, even if does not have lordship in its position. (5) Find out its nature and what signs it holds lordship over, and proceed as I showed you in the *Book of Nativities*: Saturn signifies anything ancient, fear, awe, landed estates, death and diseases; Jupiter signifies money, sons and peace; Mars signifies brothers, relatives, wars, and quarrels; the Sun signifies life, kings, authority, and the father; Venus ⟨signifies⟩ women, pleasures, and the younger sister; Mercury signifies all kinds of sciences, books, and art; the Moon signifies the female, life, and confused thoughts.

Part 22. Color

Quotation 1: *She'elot* I, § 4.10:5, 262–263:

ובעל השעה יורה על גוון מראה: ואם שבתאי הוא שחור, ואם צדק ירוק, ואם מאדים אדום, ואם השמש לבן וזך, ואם נגה יפה מעורב, ואם ככב חמה גוונים רבים יש לו, והלבנה תורה על לבן שאינו זך.

The lord of the hour signifies the color: if ⟨the lord of the hour⟩ is Saturn, ⟨the hidden thing is⟩ black; if Jupiter, green; if Mars, red; if the Sun, pure white; if Venus, beautiful and mixed ⟨colors⟩; if Mercury, many colors; the Moon signifies white but not pure.

Quotation 2: *De nativitatibus*, II i 6:7, 276–277

Per dominum hore et per planetam in oriente existentem, vel orientem gradum respicientem, colorem scire poteris.

You can know the ⟨native's⟩ color from the lord of the hour and from the planet in the ascendant or ⟨the planet⟩ aspecting the ascendant degree.

Quotation 3: *Epitome*, ed. Heller (1548), III:8, P2v–P3r:

Messahala autem Indorum in iudiciis solertissimus dicit posse inveniri quale sit quod quaerens celat per dominum horae in colore et significatione, et supra annotavimus colores significatos a quibuslibet planetis in Isagogis.

Māshā'allāh, the cleverest among the Indians in the judgements ⟨of astrology⟩, says that it is possible to find what the querent is hiding through the lord of the hour in its color and signification, and I have noted down above, in the Introduction, the colors signified by any one of the planets.

Part 23. Finding a Hidden Thing

Quotation 1: *Epitome*, ed. Heller (1548), III:8, P2v:

(1) Iuniores huius artis magistri dicunt posse inveniri locum thesauri absconditi, quod veteres discreti omiserunt. Aiunt enim si in quaestione inveneris unum ex planetis fortunis in quoquam angulo, census re ibi latet unde erat quaestio. (2) Quod si in angulis est planeta infortunatus, significat ibi fuisse quidem sed extractum esse … (3) Caeterum signa firma significant res subterraneas, mobilia res in tectis, duorum corporum in pariete. (4) Sol significat in loco sibi patenti; Luna propre ianum; Saturnus in loco faetido et humido, Iupiter in divino et obsequii loco; Mars in lare ignis, Venus in loco thalami, Mercurius in domus clausura.

(1) The more recent masters of this art say that the place of the hidden treasure may be found, which some of the ancient ⟨masters⟩ omitted. They said that if in an interrogation you find one of the benefic planets in any of the cardines, the thing is hidden where the question was made. (2) If there is an inauspicious ⟨planet⟩ in the cardines, this signifies that it [the hidden thing] was there but it has been ⟨already⟩ taken … (3) Otherwise, the fixed signs signify underground things, the tropical ⟨signs signify⟩ things in the roof, the bicorporal ⟨signs signify things⟩ in the wall. (4) The Sun signifies ⟨that the thing is⟩ in an accessible place to him; the Moon, near the door, Saturn, in a stinking and humid place; Jupiter, in a place of divine worship; Mars, in the place of fire; Venus, in the place of wedding; Mercury, in an enclosed house.

Quotation 2: *She'elot* I, § 4.7:1–3, 260–261:

(1) אמר אבו עלי: אם רצית לדעת מקומו הסתכל: אם היה הכוכב שיורה על המטמון במזל עומד, הוא תחת הארץ, ואם היה במתהפך, הוא בתקרת הגג, ואם הוא במזל משני גופות, הוא בקיר. (2) ואם היתה הלבנה עם הכוכב הטוב או תביט אליו, הוא סמוך לפתח הבית, ואם תביט השמש ואין שם מבט הלבנה, יהיה באמצע, ואם הכוכב הטוב יתן כחו לשבתאי, הוא במקום מטונף. (3) וצדק יורה על מקום התפלה, ומאדים על מקום מוקד האש, והשמש על המקום הנכבד שיש בבית, ונגה על המטה, וכוכב חמה על מקום הלמוד והאומנות.

(1) Abū ʿAlī said: if you wish to know its [the buried treasure's] location, observe: if the planet that signifies the treasure is in a fixed sign, it is under the earth; if in a tropical ⟨sign⟩, it is in the rafters; and if in a bicorporal ⟨sign⟩, in the wall. (2) If the Moon is with a benefic planet or aspects it, it is close to the door of the house; if it [the Moon] aspects the Sun but there is no aspect with the Moon [i.e., the planet that signifies the treasure does not aspect the Moon], it is in the center ⟨of the house⟩; and if the benefic planet gives its power to Saturn, it is in a filthy place. (3) Jupiter signifies the place of prayer, Mars the hearth, the Sun the ⟨most⟩ honorable place in the house, Venus the bed, and Mercury the place of learning and crafts.

Quotation 3: *She'elot* II, § 12.6:1–2, 392–393:

(1) וכנדה אמר: הסתכל, אם היה הכוכב הטוב במזל עומד, הוא תחת הארץ, ואם הוא במזל שני גופות, הוא בקיר, ואם הוא במזל מתהפך, הוא בִּמְקָרֶה, והטעם בגג המקרה. (2) ואמר: אם היה הכוכב במבט עם מאדים, הוא במקום שידליקו שם אש או אור הנר, ואם במבט שבתי, הוא קרוב לבית הכסא, ואם במבט נגה, הוא במקום קרוב לערש, ואם במבט לבנה, הוא סמוך אל הפתח, ואם במבט השמש, הוא בחצר מגולה לעיני השמש, ואם במבט כוכב חמה, הוא במקום ששם דבר כתוב או מצויר.

(1) Al-Kindī said: observe, if the benefic planet is in a fixed sign, it [the treasure] is underground; if it is in a bicorporal sign, it is in a wall; and if it is in a tropical sign, it is in the rafters, meaning in the roof. (2) He said: if the planet is in aspect with Mars, it [the treasure] is in a place where one makes a fire or lights a candle; if in aspect with Saturn, it is close to the privy; if in aspect with Venus, it is in a location close to the bed; if it is in aspect with the Moon, it is close to the door; if in aspect with the Sun, it is in an open yard exposed to the Sun; and if in aspect with Mercury, it is in a place where things are written or drawn.

Part 24. A Fugitive Slave

Quotation 1: *She'elot* I, § 7.8:1–8, § 7.9:1–2, 278–281:

(1) ואם אדם ישאל על עבד שברח, הסתכל אל המזל הצומח. (2) ואם מצאת בעל הבית שב אחורנית או יתן כחו לכוכב שהוא שב אחורנית, יורה כי הבורח ישוב מעצמו. (3) ואם הוא יתן הכח לכוכב שהוא בבית הששי או השנים עשר, יאסרוהו, ואם יש מבט בין בעל הצומח והשוקע, יתפש. (4) ואם המורה יתן הכח לבעל הצומח, יורה כי שליח ישגר האדון בעבור העבד וישוב אליו. (5) ואם היה בעל השוקע מתפרד מבעל הצומח, לא ימצאנו, וככה אם לא יביט הכוכב שנפרד ממנו המורה אל הכוכב שיתן הכח לו. (6) ואם המורה יתן הכח לכוכב נשרף, ימות העבד בדרך. (7) ואם רצית לדעת מקומו, הסתכל: אם נתן המורה כחו אל כוכב שהוא בין הבית הרביעי ובין הצומח, או לנכח אלה הבתים, ואלה הם השתי רביעיות הנקבות, דע כי העבד כבר הלך ממקום שתחשוב שהוא שם, ואם ברביעיות האחרות, עודנו שם, והכלל במקום קרוב ממקום אדניו. (8) והסתכל אל הכוכב שיתן המורה הכח לו: אם הוא בעל הבית השמיני או הששי או השנים העשר, יתפש במקום שהוא שם ולא ימלט. (9) ואם רצית לדעת מתי יתפש, הנה אתן לך דרך כלל לדבר הזה, ולכל דבר שישאל אדם על זמנו, מתי יהיה. (10) אמר בטלמיוס: הסתכל כמה מעלות ישרות יש בין השליט על השואל ובין השליט על דבר הנשאל, בין במחברת בין במבט, וטעם המבט שיהיה פחות ממעלות המבט.

(1) If someone poses a question about a slave who has run away, observe the ascendant sign. (2) If you find that the lord of the place [i.e., the lord of the ascendant sign] is retrograde or gives its power to a retrograde planet, it signifies that the fugitive will return on his own. (3) If it gives power to a planet that is in the sixth or twelfth place, he will be imprisoned, and if there is an aspect between the lord of the ascendant and ⟨the lord of⟩ the descendant he will be captured. (4) If the significator gives power to the lord

of the ascendant, it signifies that the master will send a messenger to get the slave and bring him back to him. (5) If the lord of the descendant parts from the lord of the ascendant, he [the messenger] will not find him, and the same applies if the planet that the significator parts from it does not aspect the planet to which it gives its power. (6) If the significator gives power to a burnt planet, the slave will die en route. (7) If you wish to know where he [the slave] is, observe: if the significator gives power to a planet that is between the fourth place and the ascendant, or in opposition to these places, which are the two feminine quadrants, know that the slave has already left the place where you think he is; and if in the other quadrants he is still there, and ⟨this means⟩ generally in a place close to his master's place. (8) Observe the planet to which the significator gives power: if it is the lord of the eighth, sixth or twelfth place, he will be captured in the place where he is and will not escape. (9) If you wish to know when will he be captured, I give you now a general method for this and for everything about which someone may ask: when it will happen? (10) Ptolemy said: find out how many equal degrees there are between the ruler over the querent and the ruler over the object of the interrogation, either in conjunction or in aspect (⟨here⟩ aspect means ⟨several⟩ degrees less than the degrees of the [full] aspect).

Quotation 2: *Epitome*, ed. Heller (1548), III:15, Q3v:

(1) Si quis querit pro servo qui fugerit, aspice dominum ascendentis, qui si est retrogradus vel dat vim retrogrado planetae, redibit sponte sua fugitivus. Si autem planeta infortuna sit, capietur ... (2) Si dominus domus ascendentis dat vim domino septimae domus, redibit sponte. ... (3) Si Luna est sub luce Solis, morietur fugiens brevi, nec capietur.

(1) If someone inquires about a fugitive slave, observe the lord of the ascendant; if it is retrograde of gives power to a retrograde planet, the fugitive will return by his own will. If it is an inauspicious planet, he will be caught ... (2) If the lord of the place of the ascendant gives power to the lord of the seventh place, he will return by ⟨his own⟩ will ... (3) If the Moon is under the light of the Sun, the fugitive will die soon, and will not be captured.

APPENDIX 5

PLANETS, SIGNS AND HOROSCOPIC PLACES

Quotation 1: *Moladot*, IV 26:1–2, 200–201:

המזלות הטובים בתחלת כל דבר: הבית הראשון, והשמר שלא יהיה למעלה מהארץ יותר מחמש מעלות, כי אז יהיה בכח השנים העשר, ואחריו הבית העשירי, ואחריו עשתי עשר, ואחריו הבית החמישי. רק השני והשביעי הם אמצעיים, וככה התשיעי, גם השלישי. רק השמיני, והששי, והשנים העשר, הם רעים.

The fortunate places for the beginning of everything: The first place (but be careful that it is not more than 5° above the Earth, because if so it will be under the power of the twelfth ⟨place⟩), next the tenth ⟨place⟩, next the eleventh ⟨place⟩, and next the fifth ⟨place⟩. The second and seventh places are intermediate, and so are the ninth and third ⟨places⟩. But the eighth, sixth, and twelfth ⟨places⟩ are unfortunate.

Quotation 2: *Mishpeṭei ha-mazzalot*, § 19:1–3, 504–505:

אמר תלמי המלך: חלק המזל הצומח על דרך שחלקו חכמי המזלות. אמר: טלה הראש, שור הצואר, תאומים הזרועות, סרטן החזה, אריה הלב והקרב העליון, בתולה הבטן והשריר, מאזנים המתנים, עקרב הערוה, קשת האחור, גדי הירכים, דלי השוקים, דגים הרגלים. ועל זה הדרך חלק המזל הצומח.

King Ptolemy said: assign to the ascending sign ⟨the corresponding part of the body⟩ according to the method used by the astrologers to assign ⟨the signs to the parts of the body⟩. He said: ⟨assign to⟩ Aries the head, Taurus the neck, Gemini the arms, Cancer the chest, Leo the heart and the upper intestine, Virgo the abdomen and the diaphragm, Libra the hips, Scorpio the genitals, Sagittarius the back, Capricorn the thighs, Aquarius the calves, Pisces the feet. Use this method to assign to the ascendant sign ⟨its corresponding part of the body⟩.

Quotation 3: *Ṭeʿamim* II, § 2.4:20–21, 194–195:

מזל טלה. בעבור היותו תחלת המזלות שמוהו להיות לאות על הראש, כי כל נולד שיהיה הפקיד עליו במזל טלה, ואם הוא עם כוכב מזיק, לא יהיו לו רעות בראש. וחלקו כל מזל על אברי בני האדם עד היות דגים לאות על הרגלים.

The sign of Aries. Since it is the first sign, they made it signify the head; no harm will befall the head of any native whose lord is in the sign of Aries, even though it is together with a malefic planet. All the signs were assigned to the limbs and organs of the human body down to Pisces, which represents the feet.

Quotation 4: *Reshit ḥokhmah*, § 6.6:5–6, 192–193:

ובהיות הכוכב נשרף אין לו כח כלל; ובצאתו מגבול השריפה והוא תחת האור אז תשוב הכח אליו מעט, וכל מה שיהיה רחוק הוא יותר טוב.

When a planet is burnt it has no power. When it moves away from the domain of burning and is under the ray, it recovers some of its power; the further away the better ⟨its condition⟩.

Quotation 5: *De rationibus*, ed. Millás Vallicrosa (1947), 98:

Magistri iuditiorum partiti sunt circulum in duo, maiorem partem attribuentes Soli, que est a capite Leonis ad finem Capricorni, minorem vero partem Lune, que est a fine Capricorni usque ad caput Leonis.

The masters of the judgments divided the zodiac into two parts; they assigned the larger part, which is from the head of Leo to the end of Capricorn, to the Sun, and the smaller part, which is from the end of Capricorn to the head of Leo, to the Moon.

Quotation 6: *'Olam* II, 15:1–25, 164–167:

(1) ודע כי מה שאמרתי מזל מדינה זה פירושו המזל שהוא עולה בעת הוסדה. (2) ויש מדינות ידועות כמו: (3) קורטובה, מזלה עשרים ושבע מעלות ממזל תאומים. (4) גרנטא, סרטן. (5) אלמריאה, מאזנים. (6) ולינסיאה, עקרב. (7) אשביליאה, דגים לפי דעת חכמי ספרד ולפי דעתי מזל דלי. (8) מאליקא, מזל דלי. (9) בטליוס, מזל שור. (10) וורונה, מזל שור. (11) מדינת סלאם, מזל דלי. (12) סרקוסטא, מזל טלה. (13) מרשיליה, מזל אריה. (14) טוליטולה, מזל בתולה. (15) מנטואה, מזל מאזנים. (16) גושקא, מזל שור. (17) בוגיאה, אומרים כי מזלה תאומים עשר מעלות. (18) אפריקיאה, דגים שתי מעלות. (19) אל מדיאה, אריה שש מעלות. (20) זוילא, בתולה. (21) קבאס, דגים עשר מעלות. (22) אטאבלס, שהיא על שם אלבר, עקרב, והם אומרים כי לב עקרב תחלת מזלה. (23) רומא, מזל אריה. (24) פיזא, אומרים דגים, ולפי מה שניסיתי היא למזל דלי שלש מעלות. (25) לוקא, לפי מה שניסיתי פעמים מזלה סרטן, רק בגבול צדק.

(1) Know that when I referred to the sign of a city I meant the sign that was the ascendant when it was founded. (2) There are cities ⟨whose signs⟩ are known: (3) Cordoba's sign is Gemini 27°. (4) Granada, Cancer. (5) Almeria, Libra. (6) Valencia, Scorpio. (7) Seville, Pisces according to the scientists of Spain, but in my opinion it is Aquarius. (8) Malaga's sign is Aquarius. (9) Batelius' (?) sign is Taurus. (10) Verona's sign is Taurus. (11) Madinat Sal'am's sign is Aquarius. (12) Saragossa's sign is Aries. (13) Marseilles' sign is Leo. (14) Toledo's sign is Virgo. (15) Mantua's sign is Libra. (16) Gushqa's (?) sign is Taurus. (17) Boujie, some say that its sign is Gemini 10°. (18) Ifrīqiya, Pisces 2°. (19) Al Mahdiyya, Leo 6°. (20) Zawilā, Virgo. (21) Gabes, Pisces 10°. (22) 'At'ables (?), which is called 'Alber, Scorpio, and they say that the heart of Scorpio is the beginning of its sign. (23) Rome, Leo. (24) Pisa, some say Pisces, but according to what I have

verified by experience its sign is Aquarius 6°. (25) Lucca, according to what I have verified by experience several times its sign is Cancer, but in Jupiter's term.

Quotation 7: *Mishpeṭei ha-mazzalot*, § 24:1, 508–509:

אמרו הקדמונים: ניצוץ השמש ט״ו מעלות לפניה ולאחריה; וניצוץ הלבנה י״ב מעלות לפניה ולאחריה; ניצוץ שבתאי וצדק ט׳ מעלות לפניהם ולאחריהם; ניצוץ מאדים ח׳ מעלות לפניו ואחריו; ניצוץ נגה וכוכב חמה ז׳ מעלות לפניהם ולאחריהם.

The Ancients said: The Sun's ray is 15° before and behind it; the Moon's ray is 12° before and behind it; Saturn's and Jupiter's ray is 9° before and behind them; Mars's ray is 8° before and behind it; Venus's and Mercury's ray is 7° before and behind them.

Quotation 8: *Mivḥarim* I, § 7.3:2, 72–73:

והשמר שלא יהיה השמש במזל הצומח, רק אם היה הצומח אריה או טלה.

Be careful that the Sun is not in the ascendant sign, unless Leo [i.e., the Sun's house] or Aries [i.e., the Sun's exaltation] is the ascendant.

Quotation 9: *She'elot* II, § 7.2:2, 370–371:

ואם היו נחברים בעל הבית הראשון ובעל הבית השביעי או הממונה על כל אחד מהם, אם לא היה מביט בעל הבית, הסתכל מי ינצח כאשר כתבתי בספר ראשית חכמה.

If the lord of the first place and the lord of the seventh place, or the rulers over each of them [the first and seventh place], are in conjunction, as long as the lord of the ⟨first⟩ place does not aspect ⟨them⟩, you can find out which of them is victorious ⟨by the method⟩ I have explained in the *Book of the Beginning of Wisdom*.

Quotation 10: *'Olam* I, § 8:1–2, § 10:1, 56–57:

כי אחר שיתחברו במזל טלה יתחברו אחר עשרים שנה בבית השלישות של טלה, שהוא מזל קשת, והוא התשיעי ממקום מחברתם הראשון. ואחר עשרים שנה אחרות יתחברו בבית השלישות האחר, שהוא מזל אריה, שהוא תשיעי למזל קשת ... והנה מחברתם מעשרים שנה לעשרים שנה בבתי השלישות, באיזו שלישות שיהיו, תקרא המחברת הקטנה.

Twenty years after having conjoined in Aries they [Saturn and Jupiter] conjoin ⟨again⟩ in another place of Aries' triplicity, namely, in Sagittarius, which is the ninth ⟨sign⟩ from the place of their first conjunction. After another twenty years they conjoin in the other place of the triplicity, which is Leo, which is the ninth ⟨sign⟩ after Sagittarius ... Their conjunctions that take place every twenty years in the places of one triplicity, whichever triplicity it may be, are called a "small conjunction."

Quotation 11: *Olam* I, § 39:1–9, 78–79:

הנה יש לך להסתכל בכל מחברת, בין גדולה בין אמצעית בין קטנה, אל מקום מאדים. כי אם היה עם שבתאי או צדק בתקופת השנה, או מבט נכח או מבט רביעית עמהם, אז יתחדשו מלחמות בעולם. ויהיה זה בהגיע מזל המחברת אל מקום מאדים. ואתן לך דמיון: נאמר כי בתקופת השנה היה צדק בעשר מעלות משור, ושבתאי בשלש עשרה, ומאדים בטלה על שש ועשרים מעלות, והמחברת היתה על י״ד משור. ואתן לכל מזל שנה, והנה בשנת י״ב יגיע המזל אל מקום מאדים. וכבר אמרנו כי היה על כ״ו מעלות מטלה, והנה תחלת השנה יחל בי״ד מטלה. ונבקש מה ערך י״ב אל שלשים, והנו שתי חמשיות. והנה בשתי חמשיות שנת י״ב למחברת שבתאי וצדק הקטנה יהיה הרג רב בכל מדינה שמזלה טלה, או אחד יתדותיו. גם יש לנו להסתכל בתקופת השנה לראות מקום הכוכבים ואיך יביטו אל מזל טלה שהוא בית הסוף. וככה נדין אם הם כוכבים טובים או רעים.

So you should observe the place of Mars at any conjunction ⟨of Saturn and Jupiter⟩, whether great, middle, or small. For if it [Mars] is with Saturn or Jupiter at the revolution of the year, or ⟨if it is in⟩ opposition or quartile to them, wars will break out in the world. This will occur when the ⟨terminal⟩ sign of the conjunction ⟨of Saturn and Jupiter⟩ reaches the place of Mars. I ⟨now⟩ give you an illustration. Let us suppose that at the revolution of the year Jupiter is at Taurus 10°, Saturn at ⟨Taurus⟩ 13°, Mars at Aries 26°, and that the conjunction ⟨of Saturn and Jupiter⟩ occurs at Taurus 14°. I assign one year to each sign; hence in the twelfth year the ⟨terminal⟩ sign ⟨of the conjunction of Saturn and Jupiter⟩ reaches the place of Mars. We already said that it was at Aries 26°, hence the beginning of the year occurs at Aries 14°. We calculate the ratio of 12 to 30, which is ⅖. Therefore, at ⅖ of the twelfth year after the small conjunction of Saturn and Jupiter there will be great bloodshed in every city whose sign is Aries, or ⟨in every city where Aries is in⟩ one of its cardines. Also, at the revolution of the year we should observe the place of the planets and their aspects to Aries, which ⟨in the previous illustration⟩ is the terminal house. We should pronounce judgment according to whether they are benefic or malefic planets.

Quotation 12: *Ṭeʿamim* I, 2.4:4, 42–43:

אמר חנוך כי סרטן הוא מזל העולם כי בו היה, והשמש בחצי שמים בתחלת מזל טלה במקום ששם קו היושר, כי הוא העקר. ובעבור זה יסתכלו למחברת שבתאי ומאדים במזל הזה בכל שלשים שנה לדעת ממחברתם דברי העולם.

Enoch said that Cancer is the sign of the world because it [Cancer] was there [i.e., in the ascendant], and the Sun ⟨was⟩ in midheaven at the beginning of Aries in the place of the equator, because it [Cancer] is the root. For this reason they look for the conjunction of Saturn and Mars in this sign [Cancer] every thirty years, so as to know the affairs of the world from their conjunction.

Quotation 13: *Reshit ḥokhmah*, § 9.24:1–3, 264–265:

והנה הגורל על שלשה עניינים, השנים מהם עומדים בעצמם תמיד והשלישי הוא המתהפך. והנה האחד העומד הוא שיוקח ממנו הגורל, והשני שיוקח אליו, והשלישי הוא היוצא כנגד המעלה הצומחת, והוא המתהפך כי בכל רגע ישתנה. והוצרכו להשליך אלה הגורלות מהמעלה הצומחת בעבור כי היא תורה על תחלת המעשים; גם ישליכו אותם מתחלת בית שיורה על הענין.

The lot is ⟨calculated⟩ by means of three elements, two of which are always fixed while the third is variable. One of the fixed ⟨elements⟩ is that from which the lot is taken, the second is that to which ⟨the lot⟩ is taken, and the third is the one that is calculated with respect to the ascendant, and it is variable because it changes every moment. We have to cast out these lots from the ascendant degree because it indicates the beginning of actions; they [the lots] are also cast out from the cusp of the place that indicates the matter.

Quotation 14: *Ibn al-Muthannā's Commentary*, ed. Goldstein (1967), 301–302:

אז הובא זה החכם אל המלך, ושמו כנכה, והוא למד לישמעאל יסוד המספר שהם ט' אותיות. אז העתיק מפי החכם, על יד היהודי מתרגם ישמעאל, חכם ושמו יעקב בן שארה, ספר לוחות המשרתים השבעה, וכל מעשה הארץ והמצעדים והנטיה והמעלה הצומחת, ותקון הבתים וידיעת הכוכבים העליונים, וקדרות המאורות.

Then the scholar, whose name is Kanakah, was brought to the king [i.e., the caliph al-Ṣafāḥ, ca. 750 CE], and he taught the Arabs the basis of numbers, which are nine digits. Then a Jew who was a translator into Arabic, a scholar named Jacob B. Shārah, translated a book by this scholar [Kanakah] ⟨containing⟩ the tables of the seven planets, all the procedures of the earth, the rising times ⟨of the zodiacal signs⟩, the declination and the ascending degree, the correction of the horoscopic places, knowledge of the upper stars [i.e. the fixed stars], and the eclipses of the luminaries.

Quotation 15: *Ṭeʿamim* II, § 7.1:1, 242–243:

תלמי המלך יהתל מן הקדמונים על דברי הגורלות, ואינו מודה רק בגורל הלבנה לבדו.

King Ptolemy mocks the Ancients regarding lots, and acknowledges only the lot of the Moon.

Quotation 16: *Ṭeʿamim* I, § 3.6:1, 66–67:

אמר אברהם: בעבור היות המעלה הצומחת שהיא יוצאה מתחת הארץ דומה לנולד כשיצא מבטן אמו, על כן אמרו כי זה המזל יורה על החיים ועל הגוף, ובשאלות על כל מחשבה שהיא בסתר והיא יוצאה לאור.

Abraham said: because the degree of the ascendant that rises from below the Earth is like the native when he emerges from his mother's womb, they said that this *mazzal* indicates life and the body; in ⟨the doctrine of⟩ interrogations ⟨it indicates⟩ any thought that is hidden and ⟨then⟩ emerges into the light.

Quotation 17: *Ṭeʿamim* I, § 1.5:7, 34–35:

והאמת כי אין כוכב משרת ולא עליון שהוא קר או חם, כי הם מתולדת חמישית, כאשר פירש אריסטוטליס בראיות גמורות.

But the truth is that there is neither a planet (*lit.* servant star) nor an upper star that is either cold or hot, because they are made of a fifth element, as Aristotle explained with incontrovertible proofs.

Quotation 18: *She'elot* II, § 5:1–2, 350–351:

ויש לך להסתכל אל הכוכב העליון או השפל. כי אם היה ישר בהליכתו יורה על כל דבר שישלם ויהיה, ואם הוא שב אחורנית לא יקום הדבר, ואם הוא במעמדו השני יהיה אחר יאוש, ואם במעמדו הראשון ישחת הדבר אחר שיהיה קרוב שיעשה.

⟨You⟩ should observe the upper or the lower planet. For if its motion is direct it signifies, for anything, that it will be fully realized and persist, but if it is retrograde the thing ⟨asked about⟩ will not be realized, and if it is in its second station it will be realized ⟨only⟩ after despair [i.e., after it was despaired of], and if it is in the first station it will be thwarted after being close to realization.

Quotation 19: *She'elot* I, § 7.9:5, 280–281:

ויש לך לשתף כח המזלות, כי המזל העומד יורה על איחור, והמתהפך על מהירות, ובעל שתי גופות בינוני; ובעבור זה אמרו רבים כי המזל העומד יורה על שנים, ובעל שתי גופות על חדשים, והמתהפך על ימים.

You should also take into account the power of the signs, for the fixed signs signify delay, the tropical ⟨signs⟩ swiftness, and the bicorporal ⟨signs⟩ are intermediate. Therefore many said that the fixed signs signify years, the bicorporal ⟨signs⟩ months, and the tropical ⟨signs⟩ days.

Quotation 20: *Mishpeṭei ha-mazzalot*, § 49:3, 536–537:

ודע כי המזלות העומדים יוסיפו להעמיד הדבר, והמתהפכים להפך כי הם דומים לבתים הנופלים, ובעלי שתי גופות דומים לסמוכים אל היתדות. גם העומדים יורו על שנים, והמתהפכים על ימים, והנשארים על חדשים.

Know that the fixed signs keep things stable, the tropical ⟨signs⟩ reverse things because they are like the cadent places, and the bicorporal ⟨signs⟩ are like the succedents to the cardines. The fixed ⟨signs⟩ signify years, the tropical ⟨signs⟩ days, and the other ⟨signs⟩ months.

Quotation 21: *Mivḥarim* I, § 4.3:1–2, 62–63:

אמר מאשא אללה כי להחל בנין במזל עקרב הוא דבר קשה, כי לא תהיה לו אחרית טובה. גם אמר בספר השאלות שלו כי זה המזל הוא כולו כזב, ואם ישאלך אדם על שאלה ויהיה הצומח עקרב, אל תדין, כי כל הדין יהיה כזב.

Māshā'allāh said that it is ill-fated to begin a building in Scorpio [i.e., when Scorpio is in the ascendant], because it will not have a good end. He also said in his *Book of Interrogations* that this sign is false through and through, and that if someone asks you a question for an interrogation and Scorpio is in the ascendant you should not pronounce any judgment, because the whole judgment will be false.

Quotation 22: *She'elot* I, § 3:6–7, 242–243:

אמר אבו מעשר: אם מצאת מאדים באחת היתדות ברגע שישאל השואל, לא תדין, כי מה שתדין לא יהיה אמת. ואני אומר כי דברו אמת, רק אם היתה השאלה בעבור מלחמה או מריבה דון, כי דינך אמת.

Abū Maʿshar said: if you find Mars in one of the cardines when the querent poses a question, do not pronounce judgment, because any judgment you pronounced would be false. I say that his statement is true; but you should pronounce judgment if the interrogation relates to war or a quarrel, because ⟨in this case⟩ your judgment will be true.

Quotation 23: *She'elot* II, § 9.2:7, 380–381:

ויאמר אבו מעשר בספריו: השמר לך אם היה מאדים באחד היתדות, ואף כי ביתד השביעי, אל תדין, כי כל מה שתדין יהיה כזב, וככה אמרו רבים על מזל עקרב.

Abū Maʿshar said in ⟨one of⟩ his books: when Mars is in one of the cardines, and particularly ⟨if Mars is⟩ in the seventh cardo [the seventh place], be careful not to pass judgment, because any judgment you pass will be false; and many said the same thing about Scorpio.

Quotation 24: *Ṭeʿamim* II, § 2.4:13, 192–195:

בתי עבודת השם. בעבור היות טלה ומאזנים מזלות טובים וממוסכים יותר מכל המזלות מפני השתוות בהם היום עם הלילה, על כן יורו על דבר הצדק, ומהצדק בתי עבודת השם; וכל מה שיהיה המזל העולה קרוב אל תחלת המזל אז הוא יותר טוב, הלא תראה כי בעלות ראש טלה בכל מקום יהיה ראש גדי בתחלת הבית העשירי, וככה מאזנים לאחור.

Houses of divine worship. Because Aries and Libra are more benefic and temperate than the other signs, inasmuch as day and night are equal in them, they indicate justice, and the houses of divine worship [i.e., Aries and Libra] begin at the equator; the closer the sign of the ascendant is to the beginning of the sign [i.e. Aries or Libra], the better, which you may surely observe since when the head of Aries rises anywhere the head of Capricorn is at the cusp of the tenth ⟨mundane⟩ house, and in like manner Libra is at the back.

Quotation 25: *Mishpeṭei ha-mazzalot*, § 4:1–9, 490–491:

בתי הכבוד: טלה בית כבוד השמש, כל המזל, והקדמונים אמרו במעלת תשע עשרה ... ועל דעת הקדמונים מעלת י״ט ממזל השביעי לכבודו ... שור בית כבוד הלבנה, והקדמונים אמרו במעלה שלישית ... גם הקדמונים אמרו כי תאומים בית כבוד ראש התלי, וכבוד הזנב במזל קשת, ותלמי מהתל בהם והדין עמו. סרטן בית כבוד צדק, והקדמונים אמרו במעלת ט״ו ... בתולה בית כבוד כוכב חמה, והקדמונים אמרו במעלת ט״ו ... מאזנים בית כבוד שבתאי ... והקדמונים אמרו במעלת כ״א ... מזל גדי בית כבוד מאדים ... והקדמונים אמרו במעלת כ״ח. דגים בית כבוד נגה ... והקדמונים אמרו במעלת כ״ז.

Houses of exaltation: Aries, the whole sign, is the Sun's house of exaltation, but the Ancients said ⟨that it is at Aries⟩ 19° ... Taurus is the Moon's house of exaltation, but the Ancients said ⟨that it is at Taurus⟩ 3° ... The Ancients also said that Gemini is the house of exaltation of the Head of the Dragon, and Sagittarius is the exaltation of the Tail; but Ptolemy mocks them and he is right. Cancer is Jupiter's house of exaltation, but the Ancients said ⟨that it is at Cancer⟩ 15° ... Virgo is Mercury's house of exaltation, but the Ancients said ⟨that it is at Virgo⟩ 15° ... Libra is Saturn's house of exaltation ... but the Ancients said ⟨that it is at Libra⟩ 21° ... Capricorn is Mars' house of exaltation ... but the Ancients said ⟨that it is at Capricorn⟩ 28°. Pisces is Venus' house of exaltation ... but the Ancients said ⟨that it is at Pisces⟩ 27°.

Quotation 26: *She'elot* II, § 4:1–4, 350–351:

וככה, יש לך לדעת כי יש במזלות העומדים שאינם נאמנים כל עת בעבור תולדת בעלי הבתים, כמו עקרב. ועוד כי תולדתו כתולדת המים, על כן אמרו הקדמונים כי שור עומד מחביריו. וחנוך אמר כי דלי חזק מכולם, ויותר עומד בעבור היותו בית שבתי, והוא נכון בעיני, וגם במתהפכים אין גדי כמו טלה כי טלה יותר מתהפך. גם בבעלי הגופות השנים יותר עומדים הם בתי צדק מבתי כוכב חמה בעבור היותו כוכב עליון ובעבור תולדתו.

Likewise, you should know that some of the fixed sign are not always trustworthy, and this is because of the nature of the lords of the signs, like Scorpio. In addition, ⟨this is⟩ because its [Scorpio's] nature is watery; therefore the Ancients said that Taurus is more stable than its companions [the other fixed signs]. But Enoch said that Aquarius is the strongest and is more stable because it is Saturn's house; and this is correct in my opinion. Among the tropical ⟨signs⟩ Capricorn is not the same as Aries, because Aries is more changeable. Among the bicorporal ⟨signs⟩, too, Jupiter's houses are more stable than Mercury's houses, because it [Jupiter] is an upper planet and because of its nature.

Quotation 27: Latin translation of Abū Saʿīd Shādhān's *Mudhākarāt*, *Albumasar* in *Albumasar in Sadan*, ed. Federici Vescovini (1998), 8, 303, lines 13–16:

> Si advocaverit te rex ut servas ei in astronomica scientia, non facies iudicium horoscopo Scorpione neque in angulis entibus ex conversis neque Marte in angulo existente. Falsum enim esset iudicium, nam Scorpio mendacii signum est.
>
> If a king summons you to provide him an astrological service, do not make a judgment in which Scorpio is in the ascendant, nor if it is in the cardines and Mars is in a cardo. ⟨In this case⟩ the judgment will be false, because Scorpio is the sign of falsehood.

Quotation 28: *Nativitates*, II vi 8:5, 136–137:

> Si in quarto, accidet ex parvitate navis timor in mari propter malum le mast, et si in quarta frangetur navis in loco.
>
> If ⟨Saturn is⟩ in the fourth ⟨cardo⟩ [the tenth place], there will be fear at sea because of the small size of the ship and because something wrong with the mast, and if ⟨Saturn is⟩ in the fourth ⟨place⟩ [i.e., the tenth place] the ship will be smashed in this place.

Quotation 29: *Mishpeṭei ha-mazzalot*, § 45:1, 530–531:

> מקומות השררה: האחד מקום השמש. השני מקום הלבנה. והשלישי מקום מחברתם שהיתה לפני שיולד הנולד, אם נולד בחצי החדש לפני היות הלבנה מלאה אור, ואם אחר כן מקום הנכח. ומחלוקת בין הקדמונים, כי יש מהם מי שאמר שתקח מקום המאור שיהיה למעלה על הארץ ברגע הנכח, ויש אומרים שתקח מקום ההוה מהם למעלה ברגע המולד. והמקום הרביעי מעלת המזל הצומח. והחמישי מקום מנת החן.
>
> Places of dominion. [1] The first is the Sun's position. [2] The second is the Moon's position. [3] The third is the position of their ⟨last⟩ conjunction [i.e., the new moon] before the native's birth, if he is born in the half of the month before the Moon is full, but if ⟨the native is born⟩ after ⟨full Moon⟩, ⟨the third place of dominion⟩ is the position of ⟨the luminaries'⟩ opposition [i.e., full moon]. There is a disagreement among the Ancients, for some of them said that you should take the position of the luminary that is above the Earth at the moment of opposition, but others say that you should take the position ⟨of the luminary⟩ that is above ⟨the Earth⟩ at the moment of birth. [4] The fourth place ⟨of dominion⟩ is the degree of the ascendant sign. [5] The fifth is the place of the lot of Fortune.

Quotation 30: *Nativitates*, II i 4:1–16, 106–109:

> Et sapientes Persie vocant locum decentem, per quem scitur locus vite, locum in quo est Sol, vel Luna, vel locum coniunctionis vel oppositionis eorum facte

ante nativitatem, et gradum ascendentis, item partem gratie. Hec quinque sunt loca famosa; si unus eorum fuerit decens vocabitur significator et prepositus qui aspicit. Si non dominus, quere vitam ex alio loco. Postquam vero tu sciveris quis eorum est dominus, duc significatorem in gradus equales usquequo contingat ad locum periculosum, sicut explanabo tibi adhuc. Item ducas eum in gradibus mixtis ad aspectus extrahendos per ascensiones mixtas, sicut scriptum est in *Libro primo de sensu*. Si autem non fuerit Sol in nativitate diurna, scilicet in loco decenti ad accipiendum locum vite aut non aspiciat eum aliquis dominus, quere locum Lune. Si ipsa fuerit in signo ascendentis vel in septima vel in quinta vel in undecima, sive sit signum masculinum sive femininum, quere dominum eius. Et si fuerit Luna in domo decima vel quarta, et signum femininum, quere dominum eius, et si masculinum dimitte eum. Et si non fuerit Luna significator et fuerit natus post coniunctionem, quere locum coniunctionis, et si fuerit in aliquo angulorum et signum masculinum vel femininum in domo undecima vel quinta, quere dominum super locum coniunctionis. Et si non fuerit ei dominus aut non sit in loco decenti, quere gradum ascendentis, et si non inveneris, accipe gradum gratie si sit in aliquo angulorum vel in undecima vel in quinta. Et si fuerit natus de die, vide si fuerit Luna in aliquo dictorum locorum ad querendum loca, et post hoc Sol si fuerit in prima vel quarta vel quinta, et post hoc coniunctionem, et post hoc gradum ascendentis et post ea pars gratie. Et si fuerit natus post oppositionem luminarium, prepone gradum gratie gradui ascendenti in nativitate diurna, item in nativitate nocturna, et vide quot anni vite. Et utrum sint significatores plures item plures domini hoc est signum longe vite. Et radix est super ductibus et debes miscere .5. loca, et quando attingit aliquis eorum ad locum periculosum significabit super infirmitatem, et si fuerit significator erit ponderosa. Et si aliquis illorum .5. fuerit in loco cadente, significabit super infirmitate levi excepta Luna, sive de die sive de nocte, quoniam ipsa significat super corpus. Et similiter gradus ascendentis est multum ponderosus, et si Sol de die in aliquo angulorum, duc eum quamvis non sit ei dominus.

The scientists of Persia use the term the "appropriate place," by which the place of life is known, for the position in which the Sun or the Moon is ⟨located⟩, or the place of the ⟨luminaries'⟩ conjunction or their opposition which took place before the birth, and the ascendant degree, as well as the lot of Fortune. These are the well-known five places; if one of them is appropriate, it is called the significator; the ruler ⟨is the one⟩ which aspects ⟨the significator⟩. If it is not the ruler, inquire about the lifespan from another position. When you know which of them is the ruler, direct the significator in equal degrees until it reaches a dangerous place, as I shall explain to you later. Also direct it in mixed degrees to form aspects by mixed rising times, as is written in the *Book of the Beginning of Wisdom*. But if the Sun is not ⟨the ruler⟩ in a birth by day, meaning that it is ⟨not⟩ in an appropriate position to receive the place of life and no lord [i.e., no planet having a dignity in this position] aspects it [the Sun], look for the position of the Moon. If it [the Moon] is in the ascendant sign or in the seventh, fifth or eleventh ⟨horoscopic place⟩, or if it is in either a masculine or feminine sign, inquire about the ruler from it [the Moon]. If the Moon is in the tenth or fourth ⟨horoscopic⟩ place, and the sign is feminine, look for its ruler, but if ⟨the sign is⟩ masculine, ignore it. If the ⟨position of the⟩ Moon is not the significator and the birth was after the conjunction ⟨of the luminaries⟩, look for the position of the conjunction; if it [the position of the conjunction] is in one of the cardines, in a masculine or feminine sign, or in the eleventh or fifth place, inquire about the ruler from the position of the conjunction. If it [the position of the conjunction] has no ruler or if it [the ruler] is not in an appropriate position, look for the ascendant degree, but if you do not find ⟨the ruler there⟩, take the degree ⟨of the lot⟩ of Fortune if it is in one of the cardines or in the eleventh or in the fifth ⟨horoscopic place⟩. If the birth is by night, find out whether the Moon is in any of the aforementioned positions for finding the place ⟨of life⟩, next ⟨do the same with⟩ the Sun if it is in the first, or fourth, or fifth ⟨horoscopic place⟩, next ⟨do the same with⟩ the conjunction, next ⟨do the same with⟩ the ascendant degree, and next ⟨do the same with⟩ the lot of Fortune. If the birth takes place after the opposition of the luminaries, put the degree of the ⟨lot of⟩ Fortune before the ascendant degree in a birth by day, the same applies to a birth by night, and find out how many are the years of the lifespan. If there are many significators there are many rulers, and this is a sign of long life. The root ⟨of this procedure⟩ is the directions, and you need to combine the five places ⟨of life⟩, and when one of them reaches a dangerous place it signifies an illness, and if it is a significator it is of great importance. If one of these five is in a cadent place, it signifies a mild illness except for the Moon, either by day or by night, because it [the Moon] signifies the body. Likewise, the degree of the ascendant is of great importance, and if the Sun by day is in one of the cardines, direct it even if it is not the ruler.

Quotation 31: Aphorism 17 of Pseudo-Ptolemy's *Centiloquium*. *Sefer ha-Peri*, BnF héb 1055, fol. 59v:

אמר בטלמיוס: תברר טבע בעל המשפט וזמנו ופעולתו והפעולתו קודם שתקדים לשפוט עליו.

Ptolemy said: find out the nature of the subject of the judgments, his lifespan, his actions and occurrences before you make a judgement about him.

Quotation 32: *She'elot* II, § 3:1–2, 348–349:

המשרתים בהיותם באחת היתדות יורו על נכון ואמת. והיתד העשירי הוא מהיר, ואחריו היתד הראשון, ואחריו השביעי, ואחריו הרביעי.

The planets, when they are in one of the cardines, signify correctness and truth. The tenth cardo is fast, after it the first cardo, after it the seventh, and after it the fourth.

Quotation 33: *Mishpeṭei ha-mazzalot*, § 6:1–7, 492–493:

השמחה: כוכב חמה ישמח בבית הראשון שתחלתו המעלה הצומחת בקצה המזרח, והשביעי בית אבלו, אי זה מזל שיהיה. ובית שמחת נגה החמישי, והנה העשתי עשר בית אבלו. ובית שמחת מאדים הששי, ושנים עשר בית אבלו. ובית שמחת הלבנה השלישי, ובית אבלה התשיעי. ובית שמחת השמש התשיעי, ובית אבלו השלישי. ובית שמחת צדק עשתי עשר, ובית אבלו החמישי. ובית שמחת שבתאי השנים עשר, ובית אבלו הששי.

Joy. Mercury rejoices in the first place, whose beginning is the ascendant degree on the eastern horizon; the seventh ⟨place after its joy⟩ is its place of mourning, whatever sign that may be. Venus's place of joy is the fifth ⟨place⟩, hence the eleventh is its place of mourning. Mars's place of joy is the sixth ⟨place⟩ and its place of mourning is the twelfth. The Moon's place of joy is the third ⟨place⟩ and its place of mourning is the ninth. The Sun's place of joy is the ninth⟨place⟩ and its place of mourning is the third. Jupiter's place of joy is the eleventh ⟨place⟩ and its place of mourning is the fifth. Saturn's place of joy is the twelfth ⟨place⟩ and its place of mourning is the sixth.

Quotation 34: *Ṭeʿamim* I, § 4.9:1, 82–83:

מקומות שמחת השבעה: כוכב חמה בבית ראשון כי שניהם יורו על הנפש; הלבנה בשלישי כי שניהם יורו על דרכים קרובים והדתים; נגה בחמישי כי שניהם יורו על התענוגים; מאדים בששי כי שניהם יורו על תחלואים; השמש בתשיעי כי שניהם יורו על דרכים רחוקים והאמונות; צדק בבית י״א כי שניהם יורו על מזל טוב וחן וכבוד; ושבתאי בבית שנים העשר כי שניהם יורו על חרפה ומריבות ובית הסוהר.

The places of joy of the seven ⟨planets⟩. Mercury in the first place, because both indicate the soul; the Moon in the third, because both indicate short journeys and religions; Venus in the fifth, because both indicate pleasures; Mars in the sixth, because both indicate diseases; the Sun in the ninth, because both indicate long journeys and beliefs; Jupiter in the eleventh place, because both indicate good fortune and beauty and honor; and Saturn in the twelfth place, because both indicate shame and quarrels and prison.

Quotation 35: *Ṭeʿamim* II, § 2.3:1–3, 188–189:

המתהפכים. בעבור שישתנה הזמן בהכנס השמש במזל טלה, והנה אחר שהיה האויר קר ולח יהיה חם, נקרא מתהפך. וככה סרטן, שתסור הלחות ותהיה במקומה היבשות, וככה מאזנים, יסור החום ויתהפך אל הקור, וככה בגדי, שתסור היבושת ותתהפך הלחות. ונקראו האחרים עומדים, והם שור אריה עקרב דלי, בעבור שהם אמצעיים ויעמוד האויר בם על תולדת אחת.

Tropical ⟨signs⟩. Because the weather changes when the Sun enters Aries, hence, inasmuch as after the air was cold and moist it turns hot, ⟨Aries⟩ is called tropical. Similarly with Cancer, since moistness departs and is replaced by dryness, and similarly with Libra, since heat departs and is transformed into cold, and similarly with Capricorn, since dryness departs and is transformed into moistness. The other ⟨signs⟩ are called fixed—namely, Taurus, Leo, Scorpio, and Aquarius—because they are intermediate and the air in them remains in one nature.

Quotation 36: *Mishpeṭei ha-mazzalot*, § 2:6, 490–491:

מראש סרטן עד סוף קשת ישרים, שהשמש יורד, מראש גדי עד סוף תאומים אז מעוותים, שהשמש עולה.

From the head of Cancer to the end of Sagittarius ⟨the signs are⟩ straight, when the Sun descends [i.e., moves towards the south], and from the head of Capricorn to the end of Gemini ⟨they are⟩ crooked, when the Sun ascends [moves towards the north].

Quotation 37: *Ṭeʿamim* II, § 2.3:21, 190–191:

המעוותים. נקראו כן בעבור עלותם בכל הישוב פחות משתי שעות ישרות, והפך זה הישרים.

Crooked. They are so named because they rise anywhere in the ecumene in less than two equal hours, and the opposite applies to the straight ⟨signs⟩.

Quotation 38: *Moladot*, III i 6:3, 104–104:

ויאמר אל אנדר זגר בן זאדי אפרג׳ כי בעל השלישות הראשונה במזל הצומח יורה על שלישות הראשונה משנות הגמול, ובבעל השלישות השנית תורה על שלישית שנות הגמול האמצעית, ובעל האחרונה על האחרונה.

Al-Andarzagar ben Sadi Afraj said that the first lord of the triplicity [*lit.* the lord of the first triplicity] in the ascendant sign signifies the first third of the years before the age of weaning, the second lord of the triplicity [*lit.* the lord of the second triplicity] signifies the intermediate third of the years before the age of weaning, and the last lord of the ⟨triplicity⟩ [*lit.* the lord of the last ⟨triplicity⟩] ⟨signifies⟩ the last ⟨third of the years before the age of weaning⟩.

Quotation 39: *Reshit ḥokhmah*, § 7.10:1–3, 7.12:1–3, 202–203:

(1) ׳העתקה׳ על שני דרכים ... והדרך השני שיתחבר כוכב קל עם כוכב אחר כבד ממנו, ואותו הכבד עם כבד ממנו, והנה יעתיק האמצעי אור הקל אל הכבד האחרון ... (2) ׳השבת האור׳ על שני דרכים. האחד שלא יתחבר כוכב עם כוכב, ולא יביט זה אל זה, רק הם מתחברים שניהם או מביטים אל כוכב אחר, ואותו הכוכב יביט אל הבית שיש צורך אליו, או אל הכוכב שהוא המבוקש, אז ישיב האור אל המבוקש. והדרך השני שלא יתחבר בעל המזל הצומח עם בעל דבר המבוקש או לא יביט זה אל זה, או שיהיו מתפרדים זה מזה; והנה אם העתיק האור כוכב אחד ביניהם גם זה יחשב כאילו הוא מחברת.

(1) "Translation" has two types ... The second type is when a light planet [A] applies to another planet that is heavier than it is [B], and that heavy planet [B] ⟨applies⟩ to ⟨another planet⟩ heavier than it is [C]; if so, the intermediate planet [B] transfers the light of the light ⟨planet⟩ [A] to the second heavy planet [C] ... (2) "Reflecting the light" has two types. The first is when one planet [A] does not conjoin another planet [B], nor do they aspect each other, but both ⟨planets⟩ conjoin or aspect another planet [C], and that planet aspects the ⟨lord of the⟩ requested ⟨horoscopic⟩ place [D] or the planet that indicates the requested thing [E]; if so, it [C, i.e., the third planet] reflects the light ⟨of both planets⟩ [A and B] onto the requested ⟨planet⟩ [D or E]. The second type is when the lord of the ascendant sign [D] does not conjoin the lord of the object of the query [E] or they do not aspect each other, or they are separating; if a planet [C] has moved between them it transfers the light of one of the two [D] onto the other [E]; this, too, is considered to be a conjunction.

Quotation 40: *Mishpeṭei ha-mazzalot*, § 12:1–7, 498–499:

מחלקות הבתים: כל רגע ביום או בלילה יתחלק גלגל המזלות על ארבע נקודות. האחד חלק א׳ ממעלה צומחת, אי זו מעלה שתהיה מאי זה מזל שיעלה בקצה המזרח, וזה יקרא היתד הראשון. וכנגדו, בבית השביעי, כמספר החלקים והמעלה, נקודה אחרת והיא נקראת היתד השלישי. ובחצי השמים, למעלה, נקודה אחרת והיא הנקודה הרביעית, וכנגדה בחצי השמים תחת הארץ נקודה והיא הנקראת השנית. והנה נחלק הגלגל לארבעה חלקים. וחכמי משפטי המזלות חלקו כל חלק גם לשלשה, והנה עלו י״ב בתים לעולם. ואלה היתדות הם הבתים החזקים; וארבעה אחרים נקראים סמוכים אל היתדות וכחם אמצעי, והם הבית השני והחמישי והשמיני והעשתי עשר; וארבעה בתים האחרים יקראו הנופלים, והם השלישי והששי והתשיעי והשנים עשר. והטובים מאד מהיתדות הראשון והעשירי, גם השביעי טוב מהרביעי; והטובים מהסמוכים העשתי עשר והחמישי, גם השני טוב מהשמיני; והטובים מהנופלים התשיעי והשלישי, גם השנים עשר טוב מהששי.

Divisions of the places. At any moment of the day or of the night four points divide the circle of the zodiac. The first is the first minute of the degree of the ascendant, whatever degree this may be of whatever sign is rising on the eastern horizon; this is called the first cardo. In the seventh place, diametrically opposed to it [the first point] in the number of minutes and degrees, there is another point that is called the third cardo. In the midheaven, above, there is another point, the fourth point; diametrically opposed to it, in the lower midheaven beneath the Earth, there is another point that is called the second ⟨cardo⟩. Thus the zodiac is divided into four parts, and the astrologers further divided each part into three, so that there are always twelve places. The four cardines are the strong places; the four ⟨that come after them⟩ are called succedent to the cardines and are of intermediate power; these are the second, fifth, eighth, and eleventh places; the remaining four places are called cadent ⟨from the cardines⟩; these are the third, sixth, ninth, and twelfth ⟨places⟩. Of the cardines, the most benefic are the first and the tenth, and the seventh is more benefic than the fourth; of the succedent ⟨places⟩, the most benefic are the eleventh and the fifth, and the second is more benefic than the eighth; of the cadent ⟨places⟩, the most benefic are the ninth and the third, and the twelfth is more benefic than the sixth.

Quotation 41: *Reshit ḥokhmah*, § 9.10:3, 244–245:

והשני גורל הבעילות במולד הזכרים לחנוך, יוקח ביום ובלילה משבתאי אל נגה, ויושלך מהצומחת; ועל דעת ואליס יוקח ביום ובלילה מהשמש אל נגה, ויושלך מהצומחת.

The second is the lot of marriage in the nativity of men, according to Enoch, which is taken ⟨for a native born⟩ by day and by night from Saturn to Venus; it is cast out from the ascendant; but in the opinion of Walis, it is taken by day and by night from the Sun to Venus; it [this distance] is cast out from the ascendant.

Quotation 42: Abū Maʿshar, *Great Introduction*, ed. Burnett and Yamamoto (2019), VIII:4 31a–32, I, 875:

The first of them is the lot of marriage of men according to Hermes. Since the indication of precedence and masculinity belongs to Saturn, and the indication of femininity to Venus, and every male precedes the female by nature of masculinity and action, Hermes calculated the lot of partners of men by day and night from Saturn to Venus, added the degrees of the ascendant to it, and cast it out from the ascendant. … The second is the lot of marriage of men, among what Wālīs mentioned, is taken by day and night from the Sun to Venus, it is added to the degrees of ascendant, and it is cast out from the ascendant. Where it ends, there is this lot.

Quotation 43: *Reshit ḥokhmah*, § 1.12:1, 56–57:

ואני אזכיר לך בספר הזה כל מה שהסכימה עליו דעת הקדמונים, מן הבבליים וחכמי פרס והודו ויוון, שראשם בטלמיוס.

In this book I will tell you everything agreed upon by the Ancients—the Babylonians, the scientists of Persia, India, and Greece, whose chief is Ptolemy.

Quotation 44: *Ṭeʿamim* II, § 5.8:2, 232–233:

ויאמרו הקדמונים שהשם ברא שנים מזיקים, והם שבתאי ומאדים והאחד גדול מחברו, וככה שנים מטיבים, והם צדק ונגה, והאחד גדול מחברו, ושני מאורות, וכוכב ממוסך, פעם טוב ופעם רע, והוא כוכב חמה.

The Ancients said that God created two malefic ⟨planets⟩, Saturn and Mars (the former is bigger than the latter), as well as two benefic ⟨planets⟩, Jupiter and Venus (the former is bigger than the latter), two luminaries, and a mixed planet, sometimes benefic and sometimes malefic, namely, Mercury.

Quotation 45: *Tetrabiblos*, ed. Robbins (1980), I:5, 39:

> The ancients accepted two of the planets, Jupiter and Venus, together with the moon, as beneficent because of their tempered nature and because they abound in the hot and the moist, and Saturn and Mars as producing effects of the opposite nature, one because of his excessive cold and the other for his excessive dryness; the sun and Mercury, however, they thought to have both powers, because they have a common nature, and to join their influences with those of the other planets, with whichever of them they are associated.

Quotation 46: Latin translation of *ʿOlam* III: Vatican, BAV, MS Pal. lat. 1407, fol. 56r:

> Incipiemus ergo nunc loqui de iudiciis annorum mundi. Et primo quidem inhibemus ne sustenteris super divisiones que sunt 2000 annorum secundum gradus circuli neque super 2000 secundum numerationes signorum

> We shall now discuss the judgments of the world-years. First we enjoin you not to rely on the cycles of 2000 years according to the degrees of the zodiac, and not on the ⟨cycles of⟩ 2000 ⟨years⟩ according to the reckoning of the signs

Quotation 47: *Ṭeʿamim* I, § 4.2:10, 72–73:

> ודע כי תחלת הימים מיום ראשון; והנה נסו חכמי המזלות כי ביום זה יש כח לשמש יותר משאר הימים, וכאשר חלקו היום על שתים עשרה שעות תמיד נתנו השעה הראשונה לשמש, בעלת היום, והשעה השנית לנגה, שגלגלו תחת גלגל השמש. ועל כן אמרו כי בעל השנית ביום ראשון הוא נגה, והוא משתתף עם השמש, בעלת היום, כי רוב הכח שלה, וככה שאר הכוכבים. והנה שבה השעה השמינית לשמש, ועל זה הדרך יצא בחלק שבתאי יום שבת, ומהלילות ליל רביעי.

> Know that the days ⟨of the week⟩ begin from Sunday; the astrologers found out by experience that the Sun has more power on this day than on any other day. When they divided the day into twelve hours they always assigned the first hour to the Sun, the lord of the day, and the second hour to Venus, whose orb is beneath the Sun's orb. For this reason they said that the lord of the second ⟨hour⟩ of Sunday is Venus and that it is in partnership with the Sun, the lord of the day, which has most of the power, and similarly with the other planets. Then the eighth hour is again under the charge of the Sun. Proceeding with this method, the diurnal part of Saturday is in the portion of Saturn, and of the nights Wednesday night ⟨is in its portion⟩.

Quotation 48: *Reshit ḥokhmah*, § 7.13:1, 204–205:

> ותת הכח הוא שיהיה הכוכב בביתו או בבית כבודו או בבית שלישותו או בגבולו או בפניו, ויתחבר עם כוכב אחר או יביט אליו, הנה יתן כח עצמו אליו.

“Giving power” is when a planet is in its house, or in the house of its exaltation, or in the house of its triplicity, or in its term, or in its decan, and conjoins or aspects another planet—in which case it gives its own power to it.

Quotation 49: *Reshit ḥokhmah*, §7.29:1–5, 208–209:

והקבול, שיתחבר הכוכב, בין במחברת בין במבט, בכוכב שהוא בעל ביתו, או בעל בית כבודו, או בעל בית שלישותו, או גבולו, או בעל פניו; והנה יקבלנו אותו הכוכב. או שיתחבר כוכב עם כוכב ויהיה הכוכב השני בבית הנותן הכח או בבית כבודו, גם זה קבול; רק אם היה בבית שלישותו או בגבולו או פניו לא יקבלנו קיבול גמור. רק אם יתחברו שתי ממשלות, השלישות עם הגבול או עם הפנים, ומבט שלישית וששית; גם הוא קבול. גם הם אם יהיו במעלות מזלות שהם שוים במצעדיהם. והכוכב הטוב יקבל הטוב בעבור היות תולדתו ישרה, ומאדים ושבתאי יקבל זה את זה אם היו במחברת או במבט ששית או שלישית ולא בשאר המבטים.

“Reception” is when a planet [A] moves towards application, whether in conjunction or in aspect, to a planet [B] which is the lord of its [B’s] house, or the lord of the house of its [B’s] exaltation, or the lord of its [B’s] triplicity, or ⟨the lord of⟩ its [B’s] term, or the lord of its [B’s] decan; then it [B] receives it [A]. Reception is also when a planet [A] applies to a planet [B] and the second planet [B] is in the house of the giver of the power [A] or in the house of its exaltation; but if it [B] is in the house of its [A] triplicity, or in its term, or in its decan, it [B] will not receive it [A] in full reception. If they apply ⟨to one another in⟩ two lordships, as triplicity with term or decan, or if they are in trine and sextile ⟨to one another⟩, this is also reception. There is also ⟨reception⟩ if they are in degrees ⟨of⟩ signs whose rising times are the same. A benefic planet receives a benefic one because its balanced nature, and Mars and Jupiter receive each other if they are in conjunction or in sextile or in trine, but not in the other aspects.

Quotation 50: *Ibn al-Muthannā’s Commentary*, ed. Goldstein (1967), 152, 299:

השם הנכבד ברא השבעה משרתים ומקומות גבהותם ומקומות מחברתם בחלק ראשון ממזל טלה וצוה אותם להקיף ונתן לכל אחד מהם מהלך ידוע עד שיתחברו כלם בחלק שברא השם או בשובם אליו יעשה השם בהם חפצו.

God created the seven planets, their apogees and nodes in the first part of Aries and commanded them to go around, giving each of them a fixed motion until they come together again where God created them. When they return there, God will do what he wishes with them.

Quotation 51: *Mishpeṭei ha-mazzalot*, §7:1–4, 494–495:

פקידי השלישות מזלות האש שלשה: השמש ביום ואחריו צדק, ובלילה צדק ואחריו השמש, והשותף עם שניהם שבתאי.

> The lords of the triplicity of the fiery signs are three: the Sun by day followed by Jupiter, Jupiter by night followed by the Sun, and their partner is Saturn.

Quotation 52: *Reshit ḥokhmah*, § 2.5:29, 90–91:

> ובחלקו מגוף האדם החזה, והלב, והקרב העליון, והעורקים, והגב, והמתנים, והצלעות, והמפרקת.

> Its portion of the human body is the chest, the heart, the upper abdomen, the arteries, the back, the hips, the ribs, and the nape of the neck.

APPENDIX 6

THE MODENA FRAGMENTS OF *MIVḤARIM* III AND *SHE'ELOT* III

Two fragments of the lost *Mivḥarim* III and *She'elot* III have recently been identified in the Archivio di Stato, Modena, in MS 368.2, a parchment bifolium that was reused to bind a notarial register from the Notarile di Pavullo, containing the deeds of notary Giovanni Bartolini for the years 1650–1691.[1] This bifolium is part of the "Italian Geniza," a scattered collection of thousands of parchment folios and bifolia from medieval Hebrew manuscripts that ended up in various archives and libraries in Italy, where they were reused, especially during the sixteenth and seventeenth centuries, to bind books or to cover archival volumes and registers.[2] These two fragments lack the title of the work, but it can be stated with certainty that they are from the lost *Mivḥarim* III and *She'elot* III. In brief, this follows from the following points: (1) both include cross-references to several parts of Ibn Ezra's astrological corpus; (2) in one of them the author refers to himself as "Abraham"; (3) they use Ibn Ezra's typical Hebrew astrological terminology; and (4) both have a perfect Latin replica in two corresponding fragments of *Electiones* and *Interrogationes*.

In 2009, together with Renate Smithuis, I published excerpts from the two fragments, with their counterparts in *Electiones* and *Interrogationes*.[3] Relying on a photo of the bifolium, in volume 3 of this series I published the Hebrew text, accompanied by an English translation, of the parts of the two fragments of *Mivḥarim* III and *She'elot* III copied on the flesh side of the parchment, which is quite legible for the most part; but I was unable to decipher the hair side, which is erased and faded and quite illegible.[4] On a recent visit to Modena, with the assistance of an ultraviolet lamp, I was able not only to read the flesh side of the bifolium more accurately, but also to decipher substantial parts of the hair side, particularly the fragment of *She'elot* III.

This appendix presents the fruits of my efforts. In what follows, I offer, one after the other, the fragments of *Mivḥarim* III and *She'elot* III that I have been able to salvage from the parchment bifolium 368.2. For *Mivḥarim* III, the bulk of the recovered text comes from the two columns on the right side of the flesh side of the bifolium, which include most of the long Seventh Place, the entire short Eighth Place, and the initial sentences of the Ninth Place. The fragment of *Mivḥarim* III also includes two isolated paragraphs at the top of the right and left columns of the left side of the hair side of the bifolium. The first paragraph contains

---

1 On the discovery of this bifolium and the process of identification of its contents, see Sela and Smithuis 2009, 225–229.

2 See http://www.morasha.it/zehut/mp02_ghenizaitaliana.html.

3 Sela and Smithuis 2009, 225–240.

4 Sela 2011, 218–223, 438–443.

the account of the elections related to the 24th lunar mansion in the Sixth Place; the second paragraph is the initial sentences of the Seventh Place of *Mivḥarim* III. The rest of the two columns is unfortunately unreadable. For the fragment of *She'elot* III, I have been able to decipher virtually all the relevant Hebrew text on both sides of the parchment. This includes most of the Hebrew text of the Fifth Place, the entire Sixth Place, and almost all of the Seventh Place of *She'elot* III.

My intention here is to make these fragments available to readers in such a way that they may be easily collated with their Latin translations in *Electiones* and *Interrogationes*. I have accordingly divided the fragments into the same parts, sections, and sentences as their counterparts in the latter. Each section of the two Hebrew fragments is accompanied by an English translation, which is not always identical with that of their Latin counterparts in *Electiones* and *Interrogationes*. The Hebrew text of the fragments of *Mivḥarim* III and *She'elot* III presented here are certainly not identical with the Hebrew Vorlage of *Electiones* and *Interrogationes*. This emerges from the fact that the parallel Latin texts of *Electiones* and *Interrogationes* include sentences that are not found in the Hebrew Modena fragments.

The present edition of the Modena fragments takes account of this phenomenon and includes a restoration of the Hebrew texts that were purportedly used as the source for the Latin translation of *Mivḥarim* III. These sentences are included in the English translation as well. The reconstructed Hebrew texts are demarcated by « ... »; the corresponding English translations are in italics, bracketed by ⟪...⟫. Drawing on the parallel Latin translations in *Electiones* and *Interrogationes*, I have also restored the Hebrew of short lacunae within the legible parts of the Modena fragment, along with their English translation. In these cases, too, the reconstructed Hebrew words are within guillemets, and the corresponding English translations are in italics and bracketed by ⟪...⟫. The beginnings of the four columns on the flesh side of the parchment are marked in the Hebrew text as [1/פ] through [4/פ]; the beginnings of the four columns on the hair side have been marked in the Hebrew text as [1/ה] through [4/ה].

I. The Modena Fragment of *Mivḥarim* III

⟨II vi⟩

24 (1) [ה/3] כג. סעד בלילת. אמרו חכמי הודו: טוב לשתות מקשה, וללבוש חדש, ולזרוע, ולהלוות? ממון, גם להליכה. (2) אמר דורוניוס: רע מאוד לאישות, כי האישה תחשוב רע על בעלה, ולקנות עבד רע מאוד, ולהשתתף טוב, ואסיר יצא מהרה.

The rest of the right column in unreadable.

24 (1) Twenty-third: *sa'd al-bula'*. The scientists of India said: it is auspicious to drink a potion, to wear new ⟨clothes⟩, to sow, to lend money, and to travel. (2) Dorotheus said: it is inauspicious to take a wife, because the woman will think evil against her husband; it is very inauspicious to buy a slave; it is auspicious to form a partnership; one who is imprisoned will get out soon.

⟨II vii⟩
Left column of left page of the hair side

1 (1) [ה/4] הבית השביעי. הרוצה לבקש שעה לקחת אישה, הסתכל: אם לא היה נוגה נשרף, או חוזר אחורנית, או עם מחברת כוכב מזיק, או לנכח או מבט רביעית, יבחר שעה נוגה. (2) ואם נוגה במערכת רעה, ישים בעל השעה הלבנה. (3) אם היה מוסיף אורה, ואם לא מצאת, שים בעל השעה לצדק, ואם יוכל לשים בעל הבית השביעי כנגד המזל הצומח, מביט מבט אהבה אל בעל הצומח או אל הצומח, ואם לא ... יותר טוב. (4) ואם היה בעל השביעי בצומח, לא נשרף ולא חוזר אחורנית, הוא טוב מאוד. (5) ואם בעל הצומח בשביעי והוא מקובל במקומו, הוא טוב. (6) ואם בעל המבחר היא האישה, תקן מקום שמש או מאדים ...

The rest of the left column is unreadable.

1 (1) The Seventh Place. For one who wishes to choose an hour to betroth a woman, observe: if Venus is not burnt, retrograde, or conjoining a malefic planet, or in opposition or quartile, he should choose Venus's hour. (2) If Venus is in an inauspicious configuration, he should put the Moon as the lord of the hour. (3) If its [the Moon's] light is increasing, and you do not find ⟨the lord of the hour⟩, put Jupiter as the lord of the hour; and if you can put the lord of the seventh place in opposition to the ascendant sign, the aspect of love aspects the lord of the ascendant or the ascendant; and, if not ... it is better. (4) If the lord of the seventh ⟨place⟩ is in the ascendant, neither burnt nor retrograde, this is very auspicious. (5) If the lord of the ascendant is in the the seventh ⟨place⟩ and it is received in its position, this is auspicious. (6) If the subject of the election is the woman, calculate the position of the Sun and Mars ....

...

3 (3) «והשמר שהמזל הצומח לא יהיה באחד הבתים של השפלים, כי לעליון יש[5]» [פ/1] לו כח גדול, ולא יוכל השפל לנצח את העליון, רק אם היה השפל ביתד הראשון או העשירי והעליון בבית נופל. (4) יתישר השפל ההוה מפאת השמש, «והפך הדבר העליון בהיותו תחת אור השמש; וככה השפל בהיותו ישר[6]» והעליון[7] חוזר אחורנית. (5) ואם יתחברו לשפל דברים רבים טובים והעליון יהיה אמצעי, לא יוכל השפל לנצח העליון ניצוח גמור.

3 (3) ⟪*Be careful that the ascendant sign is not one of the houses of the lower planets, because an upper planet*⟫ has great power, and a lower ⟨planet⟩ cannot be victorious over an upper ⟨planet⟩ unless the lower is in the first or

---

[5] These words are not in the Modena fragment. The Hebrew has been restored according to *El*, II vii 3:3: Et cave ne signum ascendens sit unum de domibus stellarum inferiorum, nam superiori.

[6] These words are not in the Modena fragment. The Hebrew has been restored according to *El*, II vii 3:4: Et superior econtrario et quod scilicet superior sit sub radiis solis; item quod inferior sit directa

[7] בבית נופל יתישר השפל ההוה מפאת השמש והעליון] in the margin.

the tenth cardo and the upper is in a cadent place. (4) A lower ⟨planet⟩ will be strengthened on the ⟨same⟩ side as the Sun, ⟨⟨*and the opposite applies to the upper ⟨planet⟩ when it is under the ray of the sun; that is, when the lower planet is direct* ⟩⟩ and the upper ⟨planet⟩ is retrograde. (5) ⟨Even⟩ if many fortunate things are assigned to the lower ⟨planet⟩ and the upper ⟨planet⟩ is intermediate ⟨in fortunate things⟩, the lower ⟨planet⟩ cannot be completely victorious over the upper ⟨planet⟩.

4 (1) ודע כי אם היה צדק במערכת טובה עם השמש והוא מביט אל סרטן, שים אותו תחת הלבנה. (2) וידוע כי אם היה בעל המזל הצומח בבית השביעי, ינצחוהו אויביו, והפך הדבר: אם היה בעל השביעי בצומח, ינוצח האויב.[8] אם היה הכוכב עליון, לא ינוצח ניצוח גמור. (3) על כן, השתבשו חכמי משפטי המזלות, אם היה הצומח מזל שור ומאדים בצומח. (4) יש מהם שאמרו שתדין כפי כח נוגה בעל הצומח, ואל תדין בעדות מאדים לבדו. (5) ולפי שניסיתי פעמי׳ רבות, נזק יבא לשניהם הנלחמים וכפי כח מאדים גם נוגה מהשמש; יהיה יותר חזק מי שהוא בעליו.

4 (1) Know that if Jupiter is in a fortunate configuration with the Sun and it aspects Cancer, ⟨you should⟩ put it [Cancer] under the Moon. (2) It is known that if the lord of the ascendant sign is in the seventh place, their enemies will defeat them [the side that begins war], and, vice versa: if the lord of the seventh ⟨place⟩ is in the ascendant, the enemy will be defeated. If it [the lord of the sign of the ascendant] is an upper ⟨planet⟩, he [i.e., the side that begins the war] will not be defeated completely. (3) Therefore, the experts in the judgments of the zodiacal signs were confused if Taurus is the ascendant and Mars is in the ascendant. (4) Some of them said that you should judge according to the power of Venus as the lord of the ascendant, and that you should not judge according to the testimony of Mars alone. (5) According to what I have verified many times by experience, harm will befall both warring sides according to the power of Mars and also of Venus from the Sun; the stronger is the one which is its lord.

5 (1) ודע כי שני המאורות יש להם כח גדול, כי אם היה אחד מהם נותן הכח לבעל הצומח, והוא איננו נשרף ולא חוזר אחורני׳, יורה שהוא ינצח, והפך זה אם יתן הכח לבעל הבית השביעי. (2) ודעת הקדמונים, כי אחד משני המאורות במעלה הצומחת להחל המלחמה איננו טוב. (3) וטעמם כי תולדת הלבנה הפך כתולדתו הצומח, כי הוא כתולדת השמש. (4) על כן אמר׳ כי המעלה הצומח׳ תכרות על ניהוג לבנ׳, רק אם היתה בעלת החיים שהמולד בלילה או ביום אין השמש במקום ראוי לבקש החיים ממקומה. (5) ואמרו: כאשר אין כח בכל משרת שיהיה תחת גבול השרפה, רק אם היתה בצומחת מזקת, רק אם היה המזל הצומח טלה, שהוא כבית כבודה, או אריה, שהוא כביתה. (6) ואני או׳: אם היה כן, לא ינצח המחל במלחמה, רק עד שיהי׳ שבתי[9] נשרף בגבול השרפה או שיהיה חוזר אחורני׳.

---

8 אם היה בעל השביעי בצומח ינוצח האויב] in the margin.

9 שבתי] in the margin.

5 (1) Know that the two luminaries have great power, for if one of them gives power to the lord of the ascendant, and it is neither burned nor retrograde, it signifies that he [the side that begins the war] will be victorious, and the opposite applies if it gives its power to the lord of the seventh place. (2) According to the opinion of the Ancients, it is inauspicious to start a war when one of the luminaries is in the ascendant degree. (3) Their explanation is that the Moon's nature is the opposite of the ascendant's nature, which is like the Sun's nature. (4) Therefore they said that the ascendant degree will cause death in a direction of the Moon only if it [the Moon] is the lord of life in a nocturnal nativity, or ⟨if the Moon is the lord of life⟩ in a diurnal nativity and the Sun is not in a position from which it is appropriate to try to find the ⟨place of⟩ life from its position [the Sun]. (5) They said: planets do not exert power when they are in the domain of burning, but if it [the Sun] is in the ascendant it is detrimental, unless the ascendant sign is Aries, which is the house of its [the Sun's] exaltation, or Leo, which is its [the Sun's] house. (6) But I say: if this is so [i.e., the ascendant sign is Aries], the side that starts a war will not be victorious, unless Saturn is burnt in the domain of burning or is retrograde.

6 (1) ודע כי בעל הבית השני מהצומ׳ יורה על גדוד היוצא, ובעל הבית השמיני יור׳ על גדוד האויב. (2) ואם יביט זה אל זה מבט נכח או מבט רביעית תהיה המלחמה חזקה, וכפי כח בעל הבית יורה על ניצוח. (3) ואם היו שניהם מתחברים תהיה המלחמה קשה מאד, אז הסתכל למי הניצוח כאשר הזכרתי בספר ראשית החכמה. (4) ואם בעל השמיני יתן הכח לבעל הצומח, יברחו [פ/2] מגדוד האויב וישובו אל המחל להלחם. (5) ויש לך להסתכל אל תקופת שנת העולם איך יהיו המאורות מסתכלים אל מאדים, או במחברתו, או שיגיע מזל הסוף ממקום המחברת בראשית השלישות אל מקום מאדים, או מזל הסוף מהעשרים שנה, כאשר פרשתי בספר משפטי העולם.

6 (1) Know that the lord of the second place ⟨counting⟩ from the ascendant signifies the army that goes out ⟨to war⟩, and the lord of the eighth place signifies the enemy's army. (2) If one aspects the other in opposition or quartile the war will be fierce, and it indicates victory according to the power of the lord of the house. (3) But if the two of them are in conjunction the war will be very intense; then find out which of them will be victorious, as I mentioned in the *Book of the Beginning of Wisdom*. (4) If the lord of the eighth ⟨place⟩ gives power to the lord of the ascendant, ⟨soldiers⟩ from the enemy's army will run away and go over to the one that began the war. (5) You need to observe the revolution of the world-year ⟨and find out⟩ in what way the luminaries aspect Mars, or in conjunction with it, or whether the terminal sign reaches the place of Mars from the place of conjunction in the beginning of the triplicity, or ⟨reaches⟩ the terminal sign of twenty years, as I have explained in the *Book of the Judgments of the World*.

7 (1) ואם בקשת לבחור שעה לשלוט בים או ללכת להביא עיר במצור, אם היה מאדים, בחר להולך מזל עקרב, כי הוא יורה טוב ממזלות המים. (2) ואם היה צדק חזק מפאת השמש ומפאת המעלה הצומחת, מזל סרטן, ואם יכולת שתתן הלבנה הכח לצדק, טוב. (3) «והשמר שלא תתן הכח לשבתי או מאדים, ואף כי אם היה אחד

מהם חזק, כי יזיק לבעל המבחר.»[10] (4) «מזל דגים טוב אם צדק או נגה במקום טוב; ואם כוכב חמה נשרף או חוזר אחורנית, אז המבחר טוב.»[11] (5) והשמר שלא יהיה במבחר ההליכה בים שבתי בבית העשירי ולא בבית הרביעי,[12] וככה מאדים. (6) ואם ידעת מזל המקו׳ שירצה הבוחר ללכת אליו ולהביאו במצור או לשלוט, השמר שלא תבחר מזל המקום, ואם היתה השביעי, הוא יותר טוב אם היה בית אחד העליונים. (7) ודע כי כל כוכב שיהיה בבית הראשון, אם לא יהיה נשרף או חוזר אחורנית, והוא בגבולו או הוא בעל השמש או הלבנה, חשוב אותו כבעל הבית, כי כח גדול יש לו,[13] אף כי אם היה בעל השעה. (8) וככה תדין אם היה כוכב בבית השביעי.

7 (1) If you inquire about choosing an hour to dominate the sea to lay siege to a city, if Mars is ⟨in the seventh place⟩, choose Scorpio ⟨for the one who is going to dominate the sea to lay siege⟩, because it is the most auspicious of the watery signs. (2) If Jupiter is strong with respect to the Sun and with respect to the ascendant sign, ⟨choose⟩ Cancer, and it is auspicious if you can put the Moon so that it gives power to Jupiter. (3) ⟨⟨*Be careful that it* [*the Moon*] *does not give power to Saturn or Mars, especially if one of them is strong, because harm will come to the subject of the election.*⟩⟩ (4) ⟨⟨*Pisces is auspicious if Jupiter or Venus is in an auspicious position; if Mercury is burnt or retrograde the election will be auspicious.*⟩⟩ (5) In an election about a sea voyage, be careful that Saturn is not in the tenth place or in the fourth place, and likewise for Mars. (6) If you know the sign of the place that the subject of the election wants to besiege or conquer, be careful not to choose the sign of that place; if it is the seventh ⟨sign⟩, then it is more auspicious if it is in the house of one of the upper ⟨planets⟩. (7) Know that any planet that is in the first place—if it is neither burnt nor retrograde, and if it is in its term or if it is the lord ⟨of the house⟩ of the Sun or the Moon—think of it as if were itself the lord of the place, because it has a great power, especially if it is the lord of the hour. (8) Judge the same way if the planet is in the seventh house.

⟨II viii⟩

1 (1) השמיני. אם רצית לבחור שעה ולבקש דבר שאבד או שנגנב, בקש מזל שיהיה בעל המזל חזק, והשמש או הלבנה נותנים לו כח או מביטים אליו, ושיהיה בעל הבית השמיני נותן הכח לו, או שיהיה באחד היתדות. (2) ואם יכולת להיות בעל השעה בעל השיני, או צדק איננו נשרף או חוזר אחורנית או במבט רע עם אחד המזיקים. (3) ואם יכלת לשום בעל הבית השביעי בצומח או יסתכל לבעל הצומח, אז יהיה יותר טוב. (4) והשמר שלא יהיה בעל השעה בעל הבית השביעי. (5) והמזלות המתהפכים ובעלי שתי גופות טובים בדבר הזה מהנאמנים.

---

[10] These words are not in the Modena fragment. The Hebrew has been restored according to *El*, II vii 7:3: Et cave ne det fortitudinem Saturno vel Marti et precipue si fuerit aliquis eorum fortis, quia dampnum veniret domino electionis.

[11] These words are not in the Modena fragment. The Hebrew has been restored according to *El*, II vii 7:4: Signum Piscuum bonum si Iupiter in loco bono vel Venus; et si fuerit Mercurius combustus vel retrogradus, tunc erit electio bona.

[12] הרביעי] above the line.

[13] לו] above the line.

1 (1) The eighth ⟨place⟩. If you wish to choose an hour to look for something lost or stolen, try to find a sign whose lord is strong ⟨there⟩, and the Sun or the Moon give power to it or aspect it [the planet], and the lord of the eighth ⟨place⟩ gives power ⟨to it⟩ [the planet], or it [the planet] is in one of the cardines. (2) If you can, arrange that the lord of the hour be the lord of the second place, or that Jupiter be neither burnt nor retrograde, nor in an unfortunate aspect with one of the malefics. (3) And if you can put the lord of the seventh place in the ascendant or in an aspect with the lord of the ascendant, then this is even more auspicious. (4) Be careful that the lord of the hour is not the lord of the seventh place. (5) The tropical and the bicorporal signs are more auspicious than the fixed ⟨signs⟩.

⟨II ix⟩

1 (1) התשיעי. המבקש לבחור שעה ללמוד או לכתוב ספר, ישים לעולם הלבנה באחד בתי כוכב ולא יהיה כוכב שב אחורנית. (2) ואם היה במעלה אחת עם השמש, אז טוב. (3) «אם כוכב בבית הראשון או עם בעל הצומחת, או אם כוכב הוא בעל השעה, זה יותר טוב.»[14] (4) להיות בעל השעה שבתי, קשה הוא, כי הוא יורה על עצלה. (4) ואם בעל השעה מאדים ...

1 (1) The ninth ⟨place⟩. One who inquires about choosing an hour to study or to write a book, will always put the Moon in one of Mercury's houses when Mercury is not retrograde. (2) If it is in the same degree with the Sun, this is auspicious. (3) ⟪*If Mercury is in the first place or with the lord of the ascendant, or if the lord of the hour is Mercury, this is more auspicious.*⟫ (4) ⟨But if⟩ Saturn is the lord of the hour, this is harsh because it signifies sluggishness (5) If Mars is the lord of the hour ....

II. The Modena Fragment of *She'elot* III

⟨II v⟩

2 (4) «יותר רע אם בעל השעה או בעל החמישי הוא באחד הבתים» [פ/3] הנופלים מן היתדות.

2 (1) ⟪*It is worse if the lord of the hour or the lord of the fifth ⟨place⟩ is in any of the three places*⟫ cadent from the cardines.

3 (1) ואם השאילה אם יש לאשה הריון, אם המורה יתן הסתכל ואמור שהוא, אם היה המורה נותן כחו לכוכב ביתד. (2) וככה אם בעל השעה ביתד. (3) ואם היה צדק

[14] These words are not in the Modena fragment. The Hebrew has been restored according to *El*, II vii 3:3: Et si fuerit Mercurius in domo prima vel cum domino ascendentis vel dominus hore fuerit tunc Mercurius, tunc melius.

או נוגה. (4) וככה אם היה המורה מקובל במקומו.[15] (5) וככה אם היה הצומח נותן כחו לכוכב בחמישי. (6) וככה אם היה המזל העולה מזל שתי גופות.

3 (1) If the question is whether a woman is pregnant, observe and say that this is so if the significator gives its power to a planet that is in a cardo. (2) Likewise if the lord of the hour is in a cardo. (3) ⟨Also⟩ if Jupiter and Venus are ⟨there⟩. (4) Likewise if the significator is received in its position. (5) Likewise if the ascendant gives power to a planet that is in the fifth ⟨place⟩. (6) Likewise if the sign of the ascendant is a bicorporal sign.

4 (1) ויורה שאין שם הריון:[16] (2) אם המורה יתן הכח לכוכב שהוא בבית נופל. (3) וככה אם הצומח מזל המתהפך. (4) ושיהיה כוכב מזיק באחד היתידות, כי אז יורה כי[17] תפיל האשה. (5) וככה אם נתן בעל החמישי הכח לכוכב רע שאין לו מעלה בצומחת «או בבית החמישי.»[18] (6) וככה תדין אם לא יביט המורה אל בעל הצומח ואל הבית החמישי.

4 (1) This indicates that ⟨the woman⟩ is not pregnant: (2) If the significator gives its power to a planet located in a cadent place. (3) Likewise if the ascendant is a tropical sign. (4) If a harmful planet is in one of the cardines, for then it indicates that the woman will miscarry. (5) Likewise if the lord of the fifth place gives power to a malefic planet that has no dignity in the ascendant ⟪*or in the fifth place*⟫. (6) Judge in the same way if the significator does not aspect the lord of the ascendant or the fifth place.

5 (1) ואם השאלה אם זכר או נקיבה תלד ההרה, ראה בעל הצומח או הפקיד המביט אם זכר או נקיבה בתולדותו, ואם הוא בפאת זכרות כנגד המעלה הצומחת גם כנגד הערך אל השמש. (2) וראה המזל שהוא בו, אם זכר או נקיבה, גם כן הבית החמישי ובעליו, ובעל השעה, ומול הלבנה ומקומו בערך אל השמש ובעל השעה כפי תולדתו. (3) ודע כי השעה שתצא[19] זוג בכח הזכרים ואשר לא זוג בכח הנקיבות. (4) וספור כל אלה הכחות ותדין לפי הרב במספר.

5 (1) If the question is whether the pregnant woman will give birth to a boy or a girl, find out whether the lord of the ascendant or the ruler that aspects ⟨the ascendant⟩ is male or female in its nature, and whether it is in a masculine side with respect to the ascendant degree or with respect to the Sun. (2) Also observe whether the sign where it [the lord of the ascendant] is located is male or female, as well as the fifth place and its lord, and the lord of the hour, and the sign where the Moon is and its position with respect to the Sun and according to its nature. (3) Know that an even-numbered hour

15 וככה אם בעל השעה ביתד ואם היה צדק או נוגה וככה אם היה המורה מקובל במקומו] in the margin.

16 הריון] above the line.

17 כי] above the line.

18 These words are not in the Modena fragment. The Hebrew has been restored according to *Int*, II v 4:5: vel in .5a.

19 שתצא] ג. שאתצה Corrected based on the context.

is under the power of the masculine ⟨signs⟩ and an odd-numbered ⟨hour⟩ is under the power of the feminine ⟨signs⟩. (4) Count all these portions of power and pass judgment in accordance with the larger number.

⟨II vi⟩

1 (1) הששי. שאילה על חולה, אם ימות אם ירפא, ואם בארוכה ואם בקצר׳. (2) ואלה הדברים אשר יורו. (3) שיהיה בעל הצומח נקי ממבט כוכב רע, ושיהיה במקום טוב כנגד הצומח, שלא יהיה נשרף או נכנס תחת אור השמש[20] במספר המעלות שהראתיך בספר ראשית החכמה לך. (4) וככה אם היה בעל הצומח מביט או מתחבר עם כוכב טוב שהוא באחד היתדות.[21] (5) וככה דנו הקדמונים, ואני אברהם ניסיתי פעמי׳, שאם היה בעל הצומח נותן כח או מתחבר עם כוכב בבית הרביעית, ימות החולה כי הוא בית הקבר. (6) «אם המורה בבית הרביעי ומוסיף אורו הלבנה, ירפא מחליו כי הוא מהיר.[22]» (7) אמרו הקדמונים: ראה כח המשרתים, אם הם למעלה עם הכוכב מכוכבי היום, והפך במשרת שהוא כוכב הלילה. גם שתף בדבר המורה, כי יש לו כח גדול בדבר הזה. (8) ואמר דורינוס שתשתפנו לעולם עם בעל הצומח, המורה, ובעל השלישות הראשונה בצומחת, [פ/4] כי כח גדול יש לו. (9) ואמר מאשא אלה: גם שתף עם אלה השלשה מורים, בעל השעה, ואל תדין שימות רק אחר שיתחברו אלה השלשה או השנים, או היו חזקים[23] מאד. (10) ותדין שימות האדם ואם היה בעל הצומחת בשישי או בשמיני או בבית י״ב, או יזיקנו במבט או במחברת אחד מבעלי אלה השלשה בתים. (11) ובעל הבית השמיני בצומחת סימן רע, בין שיהיה כוכב טוב או רע. (12) ומבט המזיק מרביעית הגלגל או במבט נוכח אל הצומחת ואל בעליה או אל המורה, סימן רע.

1 (1) The Sixth Place. A question about a sick person, whether he will die or recover, whether slowly or quickly. (2) These are ⟨the things⟩ that signify ⟨that he will live⟩. (3) The lord of the ascendant has no [*lit.* is clean of] aspect with a malefic planet; it [the lord of the ascendant] is in a fortunate place with respect to the ascendant; it is not burnt or entering under the ray of the Sun by the number of degrees that I told you in the *Book of the Beginning of Wisdom*. (4) The same applies if the lord of the ascendant is in an aspect or in conjunction with a benefic planet in one of the cardines. (5) The Ancients judged in this way and I, Abraham, have tested many times ⟨and found⟩ that if the lord of the ascendant gives power or is in conjunction with a planet in the fourth place, the sick person will die because this is the place of the grave. (6) ⟨⟨*If the significator is in the fourth ⟨place⟩ and the Moon is waxing, he [the sick person] will recover from his ailment because it [the Moon] is moving rapidly.*⟩⟩ (7) The Ancients said: observe the power of the planets, if they are above ⟨the Earth⟩ with a diurnal planet, and conversely ⟨if there is⟩ a nocturnal planet; also associate in this matter the significator, because it has a great

20 השמש] in the margin.
21 היתדות] in the margin.
22 These words are not in the Modena fragment. The Hebrew has been restored according to *Int*, II vi 1:6: Et si significator in quarta et sit accrescens lumine, alleviabitur a malo quia festina est ipsa.
23 היו חזקים] in the margin.

power in this matter. (8) Dorotheus said that, together with the lord of the ascendant, you should always associate the significator and the lord of the first triplicity in the ascendant, because it has great power. (9) Māshā'allāh said: also associate the lord of the hour together with these three significators, and do not judge that ⟨the sick person⟩ will die except when these three, or two ⟨of them⟩, are in conjunction, or if they are very strong. (10) Judge that the ⟨sick⟩ person will die if the lord of the ascendant is in the sixth, eighth, or twelfth ⟨place⟩, or if it [the lord of the ascendant] is harmed either in aspect or in conjunction by the lords of any of these three places. (11) The lord of the eighth place in the ascendant is an unfortunate indication, whether it is a benefic or a malefic planet. (12) It is an unfortunate indication if a malefic ⟨planet⟩ is in the aspect of a quarter of the circle [quartile] or in opposition to the ascendant or to its [the ascendant's] lord or to the significator.

2 (1) ודע כי יאריך חליו אם היה המורה ממתין בהליכתו, וככה בעל הצומח או הפקיד כשיהיה שב אחורנית. (2) והמזלות הנאמנים קשים מאד, ובעלי שתי גופות יורו שישוב החולה [צ״ל חולי] או יתחדש עליו חלי אחר, והמתהפכי׳ יורו על מהירות לחיים או למות. (3) ואם היה הכוכב, המזיק אל הצומחת או אל בעליו, מהיר בהליכתו ויצא במהרה אל המזל האחר, יתרפא. (4) ואם מצאת בעל הצומח «במעלה»[24] בצאתו מן הבית, ירפא אם הביט כוכב טוב אליו או יתחבר עמו או יהיו מעל׳ מרחקה שוה «מסוף דרום[25]» או סוף צפון. (5) ויום המות[26] בהיות בעל הצומחת באחד היתידות, והוא בסוף מבט בעל הבית השמיני, או התחברו עמו, או בהגיעו אל מקום בעל הבית השמיני. (6) ואם היה הכוכב המורה, שהוא בעל הצומח, במקום שאין שם מבט, הסתכל אל מבטי המזל השיני שהוא סמוך לו ותנהגנו. (7) ואם ידעת מקום הלבנה ברגע ששכב החולה על מטתו, אז הוא יותר נכון, ככתו׳ בספר המאורות בימי הגבול. (8) לדעת אם אדם חולה, הסתכל בעל בית הששי. אם הוא בבית י״ב חולה הוא, כי בית י״ב הוא בית הסהר.

2 (1) Know that the disease will be prolonged if the significator is slow in its motion, and the same applies if the lord of the ascendant or the ruler is retrograde. (2) The fixed signs are very harmful, the bicorporal ⟨signs⟩ indicate that the disease will return or that the sick person [*sic* for "the disease"] will return or that he will contract another disease, and the tropical signs signify speed ⟨in the development of the disease⟩ towards life or death. (3) If a planet, which is harming either the ascendant or its lords, is quick in its motion and moves rapidly to another sign, ⟨the sick person⟩ will be cured. (4) If you find the lord of the ascendant ⟨⟨*in the degree*⟩⟩ when it moves away from the place, ⟨the sick person⟩ will recover, if it [the lord of the ascendant] aspects a benefic planet, or ⟨if⟩ it is in conjunction with it [the benefic planet], or ⟨if⟩ they [the lord of the ascendant and the benefic planet]

---

24 The word is blurred in the Modena fragment. The Hebrew has been restored according to *Int*, II vi 2:4: in gradu.

25 The words are blurred in the Modena fragment. The Hebrew has been restored according to *Int*, II vi 2:4: in fine meridiei.

26 המות] in the margin.

are in the same degree of latitude from ⟨⟨*the extreme south*⟩⟩ or the extreme north. (5) ⟨You may find⟩ the day of death when the lord of the ascendant is in one of the cardines and is at the end of an aspect with the lord of the eighth place, or when they conjoin with it, or when it [the lord of the ascendant] reaches the place of the lord of the eighth place. (6) If the planet that is the significator, which is the lord of the ascendant, is in a position where it does not form any aspect, observe ⟨the aspects to⟩ the next sign, and direct it. (7) If you know the position of the Moon at the moment when the sick person took to his bed, this is more correct, as is written in the *Book of the Luminaries* regarding the critical days. (8) To know if someone is ill, observe the lord of the sixth place; if it is in the twelfth place, he is ill, because the twelfth place is the place of prison.

⟨II vii⟩

1 (1) השביעי. יש בו ארבעה שאילות. (2) האחת על דבר מריבות אשה. ראה אם יתן הכח בעל הצומחת, במבט או במחברת, אל בעל השביעי; הבעל «יאהב ויבקש אותה», והפך הדבר יקום ההפך. (3) ואם יש «כוכב לוקח» ניצוץ אחד מהם ויתנו לאחר «או מקבל» ניצוצי שניהם, יהיה שלם «על ידי אמצעי». (4) «וככה יהיה שלם אם» הירח נותן הכח לבעל «הצומח» [ה/1] אם כי יש לירח כח בבית השביעי. (5) וככה אם היה נוגה בדרך הירח, על מנת שיהיה בעל הצומח באחד היתידות, והעשירי טוב מכולם. (6) ואם בעל הצומח בשביעי, ואיננו נשרף או שב אחורנית, ואין כוכב מזיק לו, וככה תדין. (7) אם היה בעל הבית השביעי או נוגה או הירח בצומח נקי מכל נזק, שיקום הדבר.(8) וראה: אם לא היה בעל השביעי במקומו מקובל מבעל הצומח והפך הדבר, לא יקום הדבר באחרונה. (9) ודע כי מאדים עושה מריבות, וראה אם היה באחד היתידות, ולא יקום הדבר באחרונה. (10) אמר חנוך: הסתכל בדבר הנשים שתקח מרחק שבתי ממזל נוגה ותוסיף על המעלה הצומחת כי יש לו כח רב על השביעי. (11) ודורונוס אמר: קח בעל השעה לשואל ובעל השעה השביעית שהיא מעוותת לאישה, ואם היתה האישה היא השואלת, שים הצומח לה והשביעי לבעלה, ושתף השמש כאשר שתפתה הירח. ודורוניוס אמר ששתף גם מאדים כי הוא כמו נוגה. (12) וחנוך אמר ששתף בעל מנת הבעלים. וככה תדענו שתקח מרחק מעלת נוגה ממעלת שבתי, ותוסיפנו אל המעלה הצומחת במעלות ישרות, וכפי כח בעל השעה תדין, אם היה מביט.

1 (1) The Seventh ⟨place⟩. ⟨This place⟩ includes four questions. (2) The first is about quarrels with ⟨his⟩ wife. Observe whether the lord of the ascendant gives power, by aspect or conjunction, to the lord of the seventh place; ⟨in this case⟩ the husband ⟨⟨*will love and court her,*⟩⟩ but otherwise the opposite will be the case. (3) If ⟨⟨*a planet takes*⟩⟩ the spark of one of them and gives it to another ⟨⟨*or receives*⟩⟩ the spark from these two, ⟨the quarrel⟩ will be resolved means of an intermediary. (4) ⟨⟨*Likewise, the quarrel will be resolved if*⟩⟩ the Moon gives power to the lord of ⟨⟨*the ascendant*⟩⟩ although the Moon has power in the seventh place. (5) The same applies if Venus is in the path of the Moon, on condition that the lord of the ascendant is in one of the cardines, and the tenth ⟨cardo⟩ is better than the others. (6) Judge in the same way if the lord of the ascendant is in the seventh ⟨cardo⟩, neither burnt nor retrograde, and no malefic planet is there. (7) If the lord of the seventh ⟨place⟩ or Venus or

the Moon is in the ascendant and is free of all hindrance, ⟨this signifies⟩ that ⟨the quarrel⟩ will be resolved. (8) Observe: if the lord of the seventh ⟨place⟩ is not received in its position by the lord of the ascendant or vice versa, that ⟨the quarrel⟩ will not be resolved in the end. (9) Know that Mars causes quarrels, and observe that if it [Mars] is in one of the cardines, ⟨the quarrel⟩ will not be resolved in the end. (10) Enoch said: for matters related to women, observe and take the distance between Saturn and the sign of Venus and add it to the ascendant degree, because it has power in the seventh place. (11) Dorotheus said: take the lord of the hour for the querent and the lord of the seventh crooked hour for the woman, and if the querent is the woman, assign her the ascendant and the seventh ⟨place⟩ to her husband, and associate the Sun as you have associated the Moon. Dorotheus said that you should associate Mars, too, because it is like Venus. (12) Enoch said that you should associate the lord of the lot of husbands. This is how you can know it: take the distance from the degree of Venus to the degree of Saturn, and add it in equal degrees to the ascendant, and judge according to the power of the lord of the lot, if it forms an aspect.

2 (1) שאל שואל על דבר מריבה או מלחמה. (2) אם בעל הריב הוא השואל, שים הצומח לו והשביעי למבקש לריב. (3) ואם אדם ישאל בעד אחר, שים העולה «למחל מריבה או» לאשר שמת בלבך לפני השאילה, וראה אם היה בעל העולה או המורה באחד היתדות או בבית י״א, ובעל השביעי בנופל או הוא נשרף או שב אחורנית; ינצח «מחל המריבה או השואל או מי ששמת בלבך». (4) והפך זה אם היה בעל השביעי באחד היתדות, ואף כי השביעי או הרביעי או החמישי ובעל העולה במקום רע, «וכל המביט אחד» המאורות יש לו חזקה. (5) וככה «אם אחד מהם מחובר לכוכב טוב אם מביט אליו» מבט נוכח או רביעי או «מחברת עמו.» (6) «ואם היה בעל הצומח מביט» מבט אהבה אל בעל [ה/2] השביעי, יעשו פשרה ביניהם. (7) וככה אם היו שניהם במקום אחד וכל אחד «מקובל» מחבירו, ומי שהיה הכוכב המורה לו יורה מהיר בהליכתו הוא יבקש השלום, וככה אם היה נופל מהיתד או באחד הסמוכים. (8) ואם בין בעל הצומח ובעל השביעי מבט רביעי או נוכח, או שיהיה עם כוכב רע, או שיהיה בית קלונו או בית מלחמתו, או שלא יסתכלו זה אל זה, לא יהיה שלום ביניהם, ולמי שיסתכל בעל העשירי המבט אהבה או השמש, יורה כי המלך יעזור אותו. (9) ואם היה בעל העשירי חוזר אחורנית, יורה כי המלך יעשה חמס. (10) ואם היה דין ממון, שים השופט כמו המלך.

2 (1) The querent inquires about matters related to disputes or war. (2) If the disputant is the querent, assign the ascendant to him and the seventh ⟨place⟩ to the one who wants to dispute ⟨with him⟩. (3) If a person poses a question on behalf of someone else, assign the ascendant ⟪*to the person who started the quarrel or*⟫ to the person you were thinking about before the question, and observe whether the lord of the ascendant or the significator is in one of the cardines or in the eleventh place, and the lord of the seventh is in a cadent ⟨place⟩ or is burnt or retrograde; ⟨in this case⟩ ⟪*the one who started ⟨the quarrel⟩ or the querent or the one you were thinking about*⟫ will win. (4) The opposite will happen if the lord of the seventh ⟨place⟩ is in one of the cardines, and especially ⟨if it is⟩ in the seventh or fourth ⟨cardo⟩, or in the fifth place, and ⟨if⟩ the lord of the ascendant is in an inauspicious position,

⟪*and anyone that aspects*⟫ one of the luminaries is strong. (5) Likewise, ⟪*if one of them is in conjunction with a benefic planet or aspects it*⟫ in an aspect of opposition, quartile, or ⟪*conjoins it.*⟫ (6) ⟪*If the lord of the ascendant aspects*⟫ the lord of the seventh place in an aspect of love, they will make arrive at a compromise. (7) The same applies if both of them are in the same place and each of them ⟪*is received*⟫ by its partner, and the one [litigant] who is signified by the significator that is quick in its motion will seek peace, and the same applies if it [the significator] is cadent from the cardo or in a succedent place. (8) If there is an aspect of quartile or opposition between the lord of the ascendant and the lord of the seventh ⟨place⟩, or if it is with a malefic planet, or in its house of dejection or its the house of war, or ⟨if⟩ they do not aspect each other, there will be no peace between them; and the one which is aspected in an aspect of love by the lord of the tenth ⟨place⟩ or by the Sun signifies that the king will help him. (9) If the lord of the tenth ⟨place⟩ is retrograde, it signifies that the king will act corruptly. (10) If the lawsuit is about money, put the judge as if he were the king.

3 (1) מלחמה. (2) ולדעת דבר הנלחמים, עשה כמו שעשית למריבים זה עם זה. (3) וראה אם היה בעל הצומח שפל ובעל השביעי עליון; לא «יוכל המחל מלחמה לנצח נצחון שלם אף כי אם היה בבית הראשון או» העשירי, רק אם התחברו על בעל השביעי ארבעה דברים. (4) האחד, שיהיה בבית הנופל. (5) השיני, שיהיה נשרף, או תחת ניצוץ השמש, או חוזר אחורנית. (6) והשלישי, שיהיה עם כוכב רע, או במבט כוכב רע. (7) והרביעי, שיהיה כוכב רע בבית השביעי.

3 (1) War. (2) To know matters related to the combatants, proceed in the same way as you did regarding litigants. (3) Observe whether the lord of the ascendant is a lower ⟨planet⟩ and the lord of the seventh ⟨place⟩ is an upper ⟨planet⟩; ⟨in this case⟩ ⟪*the one who starts the war cannot be completely victorious over the other, especially if it is in the first or*⟫ tenth place, unless four ⟨things⟩ coexist for the lord of the seventh ⟨place⟩. (4) The first is that it is in a cadent place. (5) The second is that it is burnt or under the ray ⟨of the Sun⟩ or retrograde. (6) The third is that it is together with a malefic planet or forms an aspect with a malefic planet. (7) The fourth is that a malefic planet is in the seventh place.

4 (1) אם היה כוכב עולה, ראה אם היה שפל או עליון, ותן חצי כח לו וחצי כח לבעל הבית, אם הוא מביט «אותו או אם השליט מביט». (2) ואם היה בעל הצומח בשביעי, «ינוצח» אם היה שפל, ואם היה עליון לא ינוצח נצחון שלם, וככה תדין מבעל הבית השביעי. (3) ואם השנים הבעלים מתחברים, ראה איזה חזק מהם והבט למרחביהם. (4) ואם היה האחד מהם שמאלי והאחר דרומי, ינצח מי שמרחבו קטן, השמאלי. (5) ואם שניהם שמאלים, ינצח מי שמרחבו רב. (6) ואם שניהם דרומיים, ינצח מי שמרחבו קטן. (7) ואם האחד בקו המזלות והאחר שמאלי, ינצח השמאלי, ואם דרומי, ינצח הדרומי.

4 (1) If the planet is in the ascendant, observe whether it is a lower or upper ⟨planet⟩, and assign half of the power to it and half of the power to the lord of the place, if it aspects ⟪*it or if the ruler forms an aspect*⟫. (2) If the lord of

the ascendant is in the seventh ⟨place⟩, he ⟨⟨*will be defeated*⟩⟩ if it is a lower ⟨planet⟩, but if it is an upper ⟨planet⟩ he will not be completely defeated; and judge in the same way regarding the lord of the seventh place. (3) If the two lords are in conjunction, observe which is the stronger and their latitude. (4) If one is northern and the other southern, the one with the smaller latitude will be victorious, ⟨or⟩ the northern. (5) If both are northern, the one with the greater latitude will be victorious. (6) If both are southern, the one with the smaller latitude will be victorious. (7) If one of them is in the line of the signs [i.e., on the ecliptic] and the other is northern, the northern will be victorious, and if ⟨the other⟩ is southern, the southern will be victorious.

5 (1) אמר אבו מעשר: אם היה הצומח עקרב ומאדים בבית השביעי, רעה גדולה תבוא לשני הנלחמים, והסוף למי שהוא ויקבל אם מביט כוכב טוב, והפך הדבר אם יביט כוכב רע.

5 (1) Abū Maʿshar said: if Scorpio is the ascendant and Mars is in the seventh place, a great misfortune will happen to both combatants, and the final outcome ⟨of the war⟩ depends on the one which is received and aspects a benefic planet, and the opposite applies if it aspects a malefic ⟨planet⟩.

6 (1) ואם היה שואל על דבר שותפות, ראה אם היתה מתחברת או במבט אהבה.

6 (1) If he asks about a partnership, observe where it is in conjunction or in an aspect of love.

APPENDIX 7

PASSAGES OF *SHE'ELOT LE-MĀSHĀ'ALLĀH* IN *TRACTATUS PARTICULARES*

This appendix brings seven passages from *She'elot le-Māshā'allāh*, whose Latin counterpart—essentially *verbatim* translations, but at times also paraphrases, expansions, or summaries—may be found in seven passages of *Tractatus particulares*. These seven Hebrew passages are accompanied by an English translation, together with their Latin counterpart in *Liber interpretationum*. For *She'elot le-Māshā'allāh* and *Liber interpretationum*, see above, pp. 68–69. Each passage from *She'elot le-Māshā'allāh* is headed by a reference to the corresponding passage in *Tractatus particulares*. The seven passages are presented here in the order of their appearance in *Tractatus particulares*, but they do not always constitute a continuous section of *She'elot le-Māshā'allāh*. Whereas the first four passages are a continuous account of three significators of the querent's thoughts, the other three come from discrete parts of *She'elot le-Māshā'allāh*, separated by intervals of various length. No doubt, they were selected and inserted into the Hebrew source text of *Tractatus particulares* because of their relevance to its contents. The Hebrew text of the seven passages of *She'elot le-Māshā'allāh* offered here is based on a forthcoming complete critical edition of this text and is based on a collation of the following manuscripts, represented by the following Hebrew letters:

ע = Oxford, Bodleian Library, Add. Qu. 160 [Neubauer 2518] (IMHM: F 22230), 1367, fols. 154r–158r
פ = Paris, BnF, héb. 1055, 14th century, fols. 38r–39v
א = Paris, BnF, héb. 1045 (IMHM: F 33996), 15th century, fols. 178r–180r
ק = Cambridge, University Library, MS Add. 1563 (IMHM: F 17475), 15th century, fols. 82v–85v.

The Latin text of the relevant passages from *Liber interpretationum* is based on Paris, BnF lat. 16204, 13th century, 424a–428a, which in some loci has been collated with Paris, BnF lat. 7316A, 14th century, 85ra–88rb, and Paris, BnF lat. 7214, 14th century, 208ra–209rb.

Passage 1: → *Tractatus particulares*, I i 5:1–4 (§ 4:1–4)

(1) ועתה אלמדך שלא תטעה,[1] אם שאל השואל.[2] (2) על נכון[3] שתתקן[4] למורה[5] בעל הצומחת והכוכב שמקבל את[6] כחו, כי המחשבת היא כנגד[7] בעל הצומח, או כנגד המקבל כחו בגלגל. ומאלה שני המקומות תדין[8] ענין המחשבת, כי המחשבת ימצא במעלה[9] הצומחת, שתביט איזה כוכב הוא בצומחת. (3) ואל תניח לעולם הכוכב שהוא בצומחת[10] אם איננה רחוקה מהצומחת.[11] (4) והבט הכוכב שתמצא בצומח, אי זה בית הוא[12] ביתו, כי המחשבת כפי ענין הבית, שהוא[13] בעל ביתו.

(1) Now I will instruct you so that you will not err, if the querent poses a question. (2) You need to calculate to ⟨find⟩ the significator, the lord of the ascendant, and the planet that receives its power, because the ⟨querent's⟩ thought corresponds to the lord of the ascendant, or corresponds to the receiver of its power in the orb. Judge about the subject of the ⟨querent's⟩ thought from these two places, because the ⟨querent's⟩ thought can be found ⟨by looking⟩ in the ascendant degree, so observe which planet is in the ascendant. (3) Never ignore the planet in the ascendant, if it is not far away from the ascendant. (4) Observe the planet you have located in the ascendant, and ⟨find out⟩ which ⟨horoscopic⟩ place is its house, because the ⟨querent's⟩ thought is like the object indicated by the ⟨horoscopic⟩ place that is the planet's house.

(1) Et nunc narrabo tibi aliquid de intentione, quatinus si bene interrogavit interrogator, non errabit si Deus voluit. Hoc est quod fortius inveni de significatoribus. (2) Nunc constituas primum significatorem dominum ascendentis et planetam qui recipit eius dispositionem, quia erit intentio secundum locum dominus ascendentis ex circulo vel secundum locum receptionis dispositionis ex circulo, id est, ab hiis locis accipe eiusdem intentionis signiticatio. Invenitur quod intentio ex eodem gradu ascendente, hoc est, ut aspicias cui planete iungitur gradus ascendentis, quia intentio erit secundum locum eiusdem planete ex circulo. (3) Nec pretermittas planetam qui fuerit in ascendente si non fuerit remotus a gradu ascendentis, quia intentio vel cogitatio erit secundum substantiam eiusdem planete. (4) Aspice igitur cuius domus sit dominus ascendentis ex circulo quia intentio erit secundum ipsam donus quam aspexit.

1 ועתה אלמדך שלא תטעה] עאפ; ק חסר.
2 אם שאל השואל] א; עפ אם השואל שאל; ק חסר.
3 על נכון] עאפ; ק חסר.
4 שתתקן] עאפ; ק שיתקן.
5 למורה] עאפ; ק המורה.
6 את] עאק; פ חסר.
7 כנגד] עאפ; ק מצד.
8 תדין] עפק; א צריך.
9 במעלה] אפק; ע במעלת.
10 בצומחת] עפ; א רצומחת; במזל הצומח.
11 אם איננה רחוקה מהצומחת] עאפ; ק אם אינינו רחוק ממעלה הצומחת.
12 הוא] אפק; ע היא
13 שהוא] עאק; פ > מבט.

Passage 2: → *Tractatus particulares*, I i 6:1–2 (§ 5:1–2)

(1) והמורה השני, לדעת[14] דורוניאוס[15] ובטלמיוס וגייליין,[16] שתדע המזל באיזה חלק הטוב,[17] כי המחשבת יהיה כפי ענין מן הבית[18] ההיא מן הצומח. (2) וזהו, אם החלק הטוב יהיה בצומח, ישאל בשביל עצמו, ואם יהיה בשני, ישאל על[19] ממון, וגם[20] בשלישי ישאל על אחיו, וכן בשאר הבתים לפי הענין שמורים.

(1) The second significator, according to Dorotheus, Ptolemy, and Vetius Valens, is that you should know which ⟨horoscopic place⟩ the lot of Fortune is in, because the ⟨querent's⟩ thought is like the object indicated by this ⟨horoscopic⟩ place from the ascendant. (2) So, if the lot of Fortune is in the ascendant he will ask about himself; if it is in the second ⟨horoscopic place⟩ he will ask about money; ⟨if it is⟩ in the third ⟨horoscopic place⟩ he will ask about his brothers; and so on regarding the object that they [the horoscopic places] indicate.

(1) Secundus quoque significator est secundum Dorotheum et Antiochum et Ptholomeum ac Velium, hoc est ut aspicias signum in quo fuerit pars fortune, quia intentio erit secundum substantiam eiusdem dominus ab ascendente. (2) Id est, si fuerit in ascendente, erit interrogatio de semet ipso, et si fuerit in .ii°., erit de substantia, et si fuerit in .iii°., eiusdem fratres, et sic de reliquiis signis .xii.

Passage 3: → *Tractatus particulares*, I i 7:1–3 (§ 6:1–3)

(1) והמורה השלישי, לדעת אנשי הודו, שאמרו:[21] כשישאלך אדם מדבר[22] שלא תדע, הבט בעל הצומחת, ובעל הגבול, ושר הפנים. (2) אי זה מהם חזק, וכשתדע התקיף, דע לאי זה מתחבר, כי מאשר לפניו תמצא מה שלא תדע. (3) והחזק מזה, שתדע[23] השנים העשר.[24]

(1) ⟨This is⟩ the third significator according to the Indians. They said: when someone asks you about something that is not known to you, observe the lord of the ascendant, the lord of the term, and the lord of the decan. (2) ⟨Find out⟩ which of them is strong, and when you know the ruler, know which ⟨celestial

14 לדעת] עפ; ק שהוא לעדת; א חסר.
15 דורוניאוס] עא; פ דוריאנוס; ק דורינוס.
16 ובטלמיוס וגייליין] ע; ק ואנטייתו ובטלמיוס ואשטרוג וגייאלו; א ובטלמיוס ואנגויילאו; פ ובטלמיוס וגיילאו.
17 המזל באיזה חלק הטוב] עאפ; ק אשר בו הגורל הטוב.
18 מן הבית] עאק; פ מהבית.
19 על] עאפ; ק בשביל.
20 וגם] עא; פק ואם.
21 שאמרו] עאפ; ק שיאמרו.
22 מדבר] עאפ; ק על דבר.
23 שתדע] עאק; פ < מה.
24 השנים העשר] ע; ק בעל הי״ב; א השנים עשר; פ הי״ב.

object⟩ it conjoins, because from it you will find what you do not know. (3) The strongest is when you know the dodecatemoria.

(1) Tertius significator est secundum Indos, qui dixerunt: cum interrogatus fueris de aliqua re que te latuerit, aspice dominum dignitatis gradus ascendentis, et dominum termini vel faciei ipsius. (2) Qui fuerit fortior, et vide cui iungitur, quia apud ipsum erit illud quod te latebat. (3) Et hiis omnibus fortius est ut aspicias .xii. gradus.

Passage 4: → *Tractatus particulares*, I i 8:1–2 (§ 6:6–8)

(1) והדמיון כשהיה הצומחת[25] י״ב מעלות מטלה. ומן הי״ב מעלות תן לכל מזל ומזל ב׳ מעלות וחצי,[26] ותכלה החשבון באריה, שהוא הבית שמורה על הבנים, שהוא חמישי מן הצומח, ולא מצא שם כוכב. (2) ובעבור כן הבט אל השמש, שהיה[27] במזל השביעי מן הצומח. ואכן דון[28] שישאל בשביל בנו לתת לו אשה,[29] ואם היה בששי, היית דן[30] שישאל על חלי בנו.

(1) Example: Aries 12° is the ascendant; from ⟨Aries⟩ 12° assign to each sign 2½°; the count is completed in Leo, which is the place signifying sons, which is the fifth from the ascendant, and there is no planet there. (2) Hence observe the Sun, which is in the seventh sign from the ascendant. Indeed, judge that he will ask about his son, to give him a wife, and if it [the Sun] is in the sixth sign, you would judge that he will ask about his son's disease.

(1) Exemplar est quod ascendens fuerit .xii. gradus Arietis; quos cum proiecissem unicumque signo duos gradus et dimidium, incipiens ab Ariete, que erat ascendens, finitur est numerus in Leone, qui est domus filiorum ab ascendente, in quo non erat Sol vel altera planeta peregrinus. (2) Aspexi igitur Solem quem inveni in .vii. ab ascendente, dixique quod interrogatus esset de filio que petebat mulierem volens ducere eam uxorem, et si esset Sol in .vi. dixissem quod queret de filio infirmo.

Passage 5: → *Tractatus particulares*, I iii 2:1–6 (§ 9:1–4)

(1) וככה[31] תעשה: דע[32] הצומחת, ובעל השעה, ובעליו,[33] ודע איזה מהם יביט[34] מבט טוב אל הצומח, והוא[35] יהיה המורה. (2) ותדע באיזה מקום הוא, כי אם הוא

25 והדמיון כשהיה הצומחת] עא; פ והדמיון כשיהיה הצומח; ק ודמיון כשהיה הצומח.
26 ב׳ מעלות וחצי] ק; עאפ חסר.
27 שהיה] עפ; א שהוא; ק שיהיה.
28 ואכן דון] עאק; פ ואז תדין.
29 לתת לו אשה] עא; ק להשיאו אשה; פ < שהיה לו אשה.
30 היית דן] ע; אק דון; פ תדין.
31 וככה] עפק; א וכן.
32 דע] אפק; ע חסר.
33 ובעליו] עאק; פ ובעליה.
34 יביט] עאפ; ק מביט.
35 והוא] עפ; אק וזה.

בצומח אותו הדבר טמון[36] יהיה בחצי מהמזרח. (3) ואם במעלה הצומחת יהיה הטמון[37] באותו קו עצמו מזרחי מהריבוע.[38] (4) ואם במעלה ספק[39] אם מזל אם מעלה העשירי[40] מן הצומח,[41] יהיה הטמון נגד[42] חצי היום לצד הימין[43] כשתהיה פונה למזרח. (5) ואם הוא ברביעי,[44] יהיה לצד שמאל[45] השמש[46] כשתפנה למזרח. (6) ואם יהיה בין הצומחת ובין הרביעית,[47] יהיה הטמון בין צד מזרח ובין צד דרומי, אך אם יהיה בשני מהצומח יהיה קרוב למזרח מהדרום.

(1) Proceed as follows: know the ascendant, its lord, and the lord of the hour, and know which of them forms an auspicious aspect with the ascendant; this is the significator. (2) Know where it is, for if it is in the ascendant, this hidden thing is in the middle of the east. (3) If it is in the ascendant degree, the hidden thing is in that same line, east of the quadrant. (4) If in the degree of the tenth sign from the ascendant, the hidden thing is opposite the meridian towards the right ⟨side⟩, when you are facing east. (5) If ⟨it is⟩ in the ⟨other⟩ quadrant, it is on the left of the Sun when you are facing east; (6) If it is between the ascendant and the fourth ⟨sign⟩, the hidden thing is between the eastern and the southern side, but if it is in the second ⟨sign⟩ from the ascendant it is closer to the east than to the south.

(1) Et hoc est regula. Aspicies ascendens et dominum eius ac dominum hore et vide quis eorum melius aspiciat ascendens, et hoc est constitute significatorem. (2) Et aspicies ubi sit, qui si fuerit in ascendente erit illud occultum quod queritur in medio orientis. (3) Id est, si fuerit in gradu ascendentis erit in ipsa linea orientali in quadrante. (4) Et si fuerit in .x°. erit versus meridiem ad dexteram tuam dum aspexeris orientem. (5) Et si fuerit in .iiii. erit versus septentrionem ad sinistram tuam cum aspexeris orientem. (6) Et si fuerit in .vii. erit in occidentem post dorsum tuum, scilicet cum aspexeris orientem. Si autem inveneris significatorem inter ascendens et quartum erit inter orientem et septentrionem, quod si fuerit in .ii°. ab ascendente erit propius orienti quam septentrioni.

36 טמון] עא; פ הטמון.
37 יהיה בחצי מהמזרח. ואם במעלה הצומחת יהיה הטמון] עאפ; ק חסר.
38 מהריבוע] עפ; אק מן הרבוע.
39 במעלה ספק] עפ; אק ספק.
40 אם מזל אם מעלה העשירי] עפ; א אם מעלה אם מזל העשירי; ק אם מעלה או מזל העשירי.
41 מן הצומח] ע; אק מהצומחת; פ מהצומח.
42 נגד] עאפ; ק עד.
43 הימין] ע; אפק ימין.
44 לצד שמאל] עאפ; ק בד׳.
45 לצד שמאל] עאפ; ק בצד.
46 השמש] עק; אפ חסר.
47 הרביעית] עאפ; ק הד׳.

Passage 6: → *Tractatus particulares*, I iii 3:1–7 (§ 7:1–6)

(1) אם חברך יסתיר לך טבעת או שום דבר בבית, ותרצה לדעת אותו,[48] תקן הצומחת. (2) ואחר חלק הבית ששם הטמון לארבעה[49] חלקים, ודע בעל[50] הצומח באיזה מקום הוא. (3) אם הוא במזל[51] מזרחי,[52] בחלק[53] הבית מזרחי יהיה הטמון. (4) וקח אותו חלק מזרחי וחלק אותו לד׳ חלקים, ודע אחרי כן בעל המזל מזרחי שמצאת שם בעל הצומח. (5) אם הוא במזלות הצפוניים, קח מן חלק[54] רביע הבית בחלק צפוני, ודע באיזה מקום הוא בעל אותו מזל.[55] (6) כי הוא יהיה במזל מערבי, קח חלק מערבי והנח השאר, והבט באיזה מקום[56] הוא בעל אותו המזל. כי אם יהיה במזל דרומי, קח חלק דרומי והבט באיזה מקום הוא בעל אותו[57] המזל[58] דרומי. (7) וככה חלק אותו הרביע עד שתבוא לאותו המקום[59] ששם הטמון, ותמצאהו[60] בע״ה.[61]

(1) If your friend hides a ring or something else in the house, and you wish to find it, calculate the ascendant. (2) Then divide the house where the hidden thing is found into four parts, and find out where the lord of the ascendant is. (3) If it is in an eastern sign, the hidden thing is in the eastern part of the house. (4) Take this eastern part and divide it into four parts, and determine then the lord of the eastern sign in which you have found the lord of the ascendant. (5) If it is in the northern signs, take the ⟨corresponding⟩ fourth part of the northern part of the house, and determine where the lord of this sign is. (6) If it is in a western sign, take the western part and leave everything else, and observe the position of the lord of this sign. If it is in a southern sign, take the southern part and observe where the lord of the southern sign is. (7) Keep on dividing the quadrant until you arrive at the place of the hidden thing, which you will find with the assistance of God.

(1) Capitulum de occultatione anuli sive alterius rei secundum Dorotheum. Cum aliquis occultaverit tibi anulum vel aliud quodlibet in aliquo loco in domo et volueris invenire eum, constitute ascendens certissime prout melius quiveris. (2) Deinde divide domum in .iiii. partes, post hoc aspice ubi sit dominus ascendentis. (3) Qui si fuerit in signo orientalis, (4) tunc aspice ipsam et divide istam in .iiii. partes et dimitte reliquas quartas. Post hoc aspice

48 אותו] עאק; פ באיזה מקום הוא.
49 לארבעה] פק; עא ולארבעה.
50 בעל] עאק; פ מזל.
51 במזל] עאק; פ חסר.
52 מזרחי] עאפ; ק < אוריינט.
53 בחלק] עאק; פ בחלקת.
54 חלק] עאק; פ החלק.
55 מזל] עפק; א המזל.
56 מקום] עאפ; ק מזל.
57 אותו] עאפ; ק חסר.
58 כי אם יהיה במזל דרומי קח חלק דרומי והבט באיזה מקום הוא בעל אות המזל] עק; פ כי אם יהיה במזל דרומי קח חלק דרומי והבט באיזה מקום הוא בעל אותו מזל; א חסר.
59 המקום] ע; אק מק״ם; פ הרביע.
60 ותמצאהו] ע; פ ותמצאנו; אק ותמצא.
61 בע״ה] עפ; א בגזירת הצור; ק בג״ה.

dominum predicti signi orientali a quo invenisti dominum ascendentis. (5) Qui si fuerit in signo septentrionali, aspice septentrionalem partem eiusdem divisiones et aspice ubi sit dominus eiusdem signi. (6) Si vero fuerit in signo occidentali, aspice partem occidentalem et dimitte reliquas, et aspice ubi sit dominus eiusdem signi. Qui si fuerit in signo meridiano, aspice ipsam quartam meridiana et dimitte ceteras, et aspice ubi sit dominus eiusdem signi meridiani. (7) Et similiter divides ipsam quartam per .iiii. donec venias ad locum occultationis, et inveneris si Deus voluerit.

Passage 7: → *Tractatus particulares*, I iii 4:1–10 (§ 16:3–10)

(1) ואחר[62] הבט כמה מעלות הלך בעל השעה במזל שהוא שם, וכפול אותם המעלות בשנים עשר, והעולה חלק על המזלות, ותן לכל מזל[63] שלשים מעלות. (2) ותתחיל מן הצומחת עד שתכלה[64] החשבון.[65] (3) ודע באי זה מזל יכלה החשבון, אם הוא מזרחי או מערבי או דרומי או צפוני, ובאותו הרביעית[66] שם הטמון, בגו האל.[67] (4) ואחר[68] חלק פעם אחרת[69] החלק הרביעית לד׳ חלקים, והבט אנה בעל המזל שכלה שם החשבון, וכמה מעלות הלך מאותו המזל. (5) וחלק המעלות במזלות,[70] שתתן לכל מזל ז׳[71] מעלות וחצי, והחל מהמזל[72] ששם[73] הכוכב. (6) והבט המזל[74] שכלה שם החשבון, אם הוא מזרחי או מערבי או דרומי או צפוני, ובאותו החלק יהיה שם.[75] (7) ואחר[76] כמו כן חלק אותו החלק[77] לארבע חלקים, ודע בעל[78] המזל שכלה שם החשבון באי זה בית הוא ובכמה מעלות, וחלק המעלות[79] במזלות,[80] שתתן לכל מזל ז׳[81] מעלות וחצי. (8) והחל מן המזל שהוא שם. (9) והמזל שתכלה שם החשבון, דע אם הוא מזרחי או מערבי או אחד מהם, ובאותו החלק שם יהיה.[82] (10) ככה תעשה עד שיהיה המקום מדת ב׳[83] זרתות ברוחב ובאורך, ושם תמצא האבידה[84] בגו׳ הצור.[85]

62 ואחר] עאק; פ > כד.
63 מזל] עאק; פ מזלות.
64 שתכלה] עאק; פ שתגלה.
65 החשבון] עאפ; ק חסר.
66 הרביעית] עא; פק הרביע.
67 בגו האל] ע; א בגזרת האל; ק בג״ה; פ בע״ה.
68 ואחר] עאק; פ > כן.
69 אחרת] עפק; א > שבו.
70 במזלות] עאק; פ למזלות.
71 ז׳] עפק; א ד׳.
72 מהמזל] עאפ; ק מהמעלה.
73 ששם] עאק; פ אשר שם.
74 המזל] עא; פק < אל.
75 יהיה שם] עא; פ ש; ק יהיה.
76 ואחר] עא; פ > כן.
77 כמו כן חלק אותו החלק] עאק; פ חלק אותו החלק פעם אחרת.
78 ודע בעל] עאק; פ ובעל.
79 המעלות] עפק; א המעלה.
80 במזלות] עאק; פ למזלות.
81 ז׳] עפק; א שבעה.
82 והמזל שתכלה שם החשבון, דע אם הוא מזרחי או מערבי או אחד מהם, ובאותו החלק שם יהיה.] עאק; פ חסר.
83 ב׳] עפק; א שתי.
84 האבידה] פ; עאק חסר.
85 בגו׳ הצור] ע; א בגוזר האל; בע״ה; ק בג״ה.

(1) Next observe how many degrees the lord of the hour advanced in the sign where it is; multiply these degrees by 12, divide the result among the signs, assigning 30° to each sign. (2) Begin from the ascendant until you complete the calculation. (3) Know in which sign the calculation is completed, whether it is eastern, western, southern, or northern. The hidden thing will be in this quarter, if God wills. (4) Next divide again this quarter into four parts, and find the location of the lord of the sign where the calculation was completed, and how many degrees it advanced in this sign. (5) Divide the degrees among the signs, assigning 7½° to each sign, beginning from the sign where the planet is. (6) Observe the sign where the calculation is completed, whether it is eastern, western, southern, or northern, and ⟨the hidden thing⟩ is in this part. (7) Next divide again this part into four parts, find out in which sign the lord of the sign where the calculation was completed is located, and how many degrees ⟨in this sign⟩ is, and divide the degrees among the signs, assigning 7½° to each sign. (8) Begin from the sign where the planet is. (9) Find out whether the sign in which the calculation is completed is eastern or western and so on, and ⟨the hidden thing⟩ is in this part. (10) Proceed likewise until the size of the place is 2 spans in width and height, and there you will find ⟨the hidden thing⟩, if God wills.

(1) Deinde aspice quantum perambulavit dominus hore in signo in quo fuerit ex gradibus et multiplica eos in .xii., et quod collectum fuerit divide per signum, dans unicuique signo .xxx. gradus. (2) Incipiens ab ascendente donec finatus numerus. (3) Post hoc aspice quale sit signum in quo finitus est numerus, et aspice orientalem vel accidentalem, meridianum vel septentrionalem, quia in eadem quarta erit, si Deus voluit. Aries, Leo, Sagitarius, orientales; Gemini, Libra, Aquarius, occidentales; scito igitur in qua parte; Taurus, Virgo, Capricornus, meridiani; Cancrum, Scorpio, Piscis, septentrionales; finitus numerus quem multiplicati in .xii. Et scito quod in eadem parte erit, si Deus voluerit. (4) Post hoc divide iterum ipsam partem per .iiii. partes, et aspice ubi sit dominus signi quo cecidit numerus tuus et quantum ambulavit de signo ex gradibus. (5) Et divide eos per signa, dans unicuique .vii. gradus et dimidium, incipiens a signo in quo est planeta. (6) Et quo finitur numerus fuerit, vide ipsum signum utrum sit orientale vel occidentale et cetera, et scito quod sit in eadem parte. (7) Post hoc divide ipsam partem in .iiii. partes, et aspice dominum signi in quo cecidit numerus tuus, in cuius domo sit, et quantum ambulavit dominus eiusdem domus ex gradibus in quo est, et divide ipsos gradus per signa, dans unicuisque signo .vii. gradus et dimidium. (8) Et incipies a signo in quo est. (9) Et quo finitus fuerit numerus, vide quod signum sit, id est, utrum sit orientale et cetera. (10) Et scito quia in eadem erit hoc modo operare quod volueris, donec reddatur locus in mesura unius cubiti in sua latitudine et longitudine et invenies, si Deus voluerit.

APPENDIX 8

A SECTION OF *SHE'ELOT LE-TALMAI* AND ITS COUNTERPART IN PTOLEMY'S *IUDICIA*

This appendix contains an entire section of *She'elot le-Talmai*, accompanied by an English translation, as well as a complete section of Ptolemy's *Iudicia*, "Ptolemy's judgments," also accompanied by an English translation. These two texts are close Hebrew and Latin replicas of each other. However, *She'elot le-Talmai* and Ptolemy's *Iudicia* are in fact parallel translations of a lost Arabic Vorlage on interrogations. For their contents and correspondence, see above, pp. 64–66. These two parallel sections of *She'elot le-Talmai* and Ptolemy's *Iudicia* were selected because they are virtually identical with each other but also with a whole section of *Tractatus particulares* (I i 1:1–14 through I i 3:1–4), as will be shown in the notes to this text. The text of Ptolemy's *Iudicia* is more complete than that in the extant *She'elot le-Talmai*. In other words, the Hebrew counterpart of *Tp*, I i 3:1–2 is missing from *She'elot le-Talmai*, but Ptolemy's *Iudicia* offers an alternative Latin version of it. To highlight the close links among *Tractatus particulares*, *She'elot le-Talmai*, and Ptolemy's *Iudicia*, the two texts in this appendix and their corresponding translations, have been divided into the same section and sentences as *Tractatus particulares*. The Hebrew text of *She'elot le-Talmai* presented here is based on a collation of the following manuscripts: (1) Oxford, Bodleian Library, MS Opp. 707 (Neubauer 2025) [IMHM F 19310], copied in 1410, fols. 130v–138r; (2) Munich, Bayerische Staatsbibliothek, Cod. Hebr. 202 [IMHM F 1649], fols. 130a–137b. The Latin text of the relevant fragments from *Liber interpretationum* is based on a collation of the following print editions and manuscripts: (1) *Sacratissime astronomie Ptholomei liber diversarum rerum quem scripsit ad Heristhonem filium suum tranctans compendiose de diversis rebus* [...] *Explicit liber diversarum rerum Ptholomei Philudiensis Alexandrini astronomorum principis clarissimi*, ed. Petrus Liechtenstein (Venetia, 1509), sigs. B2va–B3ra; (2) Oxford, MS Harley 5402, before 1160, fol. 1r–15r; and (3) Paris, BnF, MS lat. 16208, fol. 62va lines 9–55.

SHE'ELOT LE-TALMAI

1 (1) וכאשר תרצה לדעת איזה דבר בלב, ראה הצומח והשעה ומושל המזל, באיזה מקום הוא. (2) ואם הוא בבית נפילתו או בבית נפילת אחר, ואם הוא שב אחורנית או מתכסה, לא תדין כפיהו. (3) ואם בעל הצומח בביתו, תדע שהוא שואל על עצמו. (4) ואם הוא בשני, שואל על קנין או על עושר. (5) ואם בשלישי עד חציו, שואל על נסיעתו ממקום למקום; ואם בחציו האחרון, שואל על אחיו או אחותו. (6) ואם בפנים הראשונים מן הבית הרביעי, שואל על אביו; ואם בשניים, מפחד על ספינה, או על כרם, או על שדה או גן, או מדבר שהוא על הארץ או מענין אדמה; ואם בשלישיים, שואל על דבר שהוא נאנח מאד עליו ומפחד ממנו. (7) ואם בפנים הראשונים מהבית החמישי, שואל על בניו; ובשניים, שואל על שמחה; ובשלישיים, שואל על מלבושים, או ספר, או כתב מחדשות. (8) ואם במחצית הבית השישי, שואל על

חולה או על דבר נגע; ובמחציתו האחר, שואל על עבדים או על שפחות, או על בהמות שאינן עשויות לרכוב. (9) ואם בפנים הראשונים מהבית השביעי, שואל על אשתו; ואם השואלת אשה, שואלת על בעלה; ובפנים השניים, שואל על רעיו; ובשלישיים, שואל על רעהו גנב ומבקש להפרד ממנו. (10) ואם בפנים הראשונים מהבית השמיני, שואל על מת; ואם בשניים, שואל על חלק עושרו; ואם בשלישיים, שואל על חובו. (11) ואם בפנים הראשונים מהבית התשיעי, שואל על אמונתו; ואם בשניים, על דרך; ואם בשלישיים, על חכמה או מגדולה או מכבוד אחרים, או על חלום. (12) ואם בפנים הראשונים מהבית העשירי, שואל על חדשות מאדוניו; ובשניים, על עצמו, ובשלישי, על אמו. (13) ואם בפנים הראשונים מהבית האחד עשר, שואל על סחורה; ובשניים, על עשיר; ובשלישיים, על אוהב. (14) ואם בפנים הראשונים מהבית השנים עשר, שואל על שונא; ובשניים, על תפישה ועניות; ובשלישיים, שואל על בהמות מרכב.

2 (1) אבל אם מושל המזל מתכסה או בבית נפילתו או שב אחורנית, ראה הלבנה ועל פיה תדין; אבל אם הלבנה הוא בבית הזכרות או בבית נפילתה, אל תשמע אליה.

3 (1) -----.

English translation

1 (1) When you wish to know what is in the ⟨querent's⟩ mind, observe the ascendant, the hour, and the lord of the sign, and ⟨find out⟩ which place it is in. (2) If it is in the house of its falling [i.e., dejection], or in the house of another's falling, and if it is retrograde or burnt, do not judge according to it. (3) If the lord of the ascendant is in its house [i.e., in the ascendant], know that he will inquire about himself. (4) If it is in the second ⟨place⟩, he will inquire about property or riches. (5) If it is in the third ⟨place⟩, up to its ⟨first⟩ half, he will inquire about his journey from one place to another; if in the second half, he will inquire about his brother or his sister. (6) If it is in the first decan of the fourth place, he will ask about his father, if in the second ⟨decan⟩, he will inquire about fear on a ship, or about a vineyard, or a field, or a garden, or about something on the Earth, or related to soil; if in the third ⟨decan⟩, he will inquire about something he sighs a lot about and is afraid of. (7) If it is in the first decan of the fifth place, he will ask about his sons; if in the second ⟨decan⟩, he will inquire about joy; if in the third ⟨decan⟩, he will inquire about clothes, a book, or a written text with news. (8) If in the ⟨first⟩ half of the sixth place, he will inquire about an ill person or a disease; if in the other half, he will inquire about male and female slaves, or about animals that are not for riding. (9) If it is in the first decan of the seventh place, he will ask about his wife; if the querent is a woman, she will inquire about her husband; if in the second ⟨decan⟩, he will inquire about his friends; if in the third ⟨decan⟩, he will inquire about his companion who is thief and wants to separate from him. (10) If it is in the first decan of the eighth place, he will ask about a dead person; if in the second ⟨decan⟩, he will inquire about dividing up his wealth; if in the third ⟨decan⟩, he will inquire about his debt. (11) If it is in the first decan of the ninth place, he will ask about his belief; if in the second ⟨decan⟩, he will inquire about travel; if in the third ⟨decan⟩, he will inquire about wisdom deriving from high status or from the respect of others, or about a dream. (12) If it is in the first decan of the tenth place, he will ask about news from his master; if in the second ⟨decan⟩, he will inquire about himself; if in the third ⟨decan⟩, he will inquire

about his mother. (13) If it is in the first decan of the eleventh place, he will ask about merchandise; if in the second ⟨decan⟩, he will inquire about a rich man; if in the third ⟨decan⟩, he will inquire about a lover. (14) If it is in the first decan of the twelfth place, he will ask about an enemy; if in the second ⟨decan⟩, he will inquire about capture and poverty; if in the third ⟨decan⟩, he will inquire about riding animals.

2 (1) But if the lord of the sign ⟨of the ascendant⟩ is burnt, in the house of its falling, or retrograde, observe the Moon and judge according to it. But if the Moon is in a masculine house or in the house of its falling, do not take it into consideration.

3 (1) ------.

Ptolemy's *Iudicia*

1 (1) Si nosse desideras quid velit dicere, perspice signum quod oritur atque horam, et dominum signi perspice ubi sit. (2) Si est in casu vel in deiectione, videsque si vadet retro vel combustus sit; si enim sic fuerit, non secundum signi dominum respondebis sed sicut in figuris dicemus. (3) Si igitur dominus signi est in eodem, de sua persona querere vult. (4) In secundo autem si fuerit, de bizantiis sui possessione querit. (5) Quod si in medio tertii fuerit, eius voluntas est moveri de loco ad locum; in ultima medietate si inventus fuerit, de sororibus vel fratribus audire cupit. (6) Cum vero in quarti tertia inventus fuerit, de patre cogitat; in secunda tertia de nave dubitat, sed vinea vel iardino vel aliqua re que est sub terra; cum autem in tertia habitaverit, de magna sua cogitatione querit ut quod faciat nescians, dubitans de omni. (7) Quod in prima quinti permanserit quarta, de filiis querit; in secunda quarta, de gaudio; in tertia quarta de vestimentis; in ultima quarta, querit de carta sive libris et novis. (8) Ipso quidem in secunda prima sexti existente, de infirmo est questio; in alia secunda querit de servis seu ancillis. (9) Si in prima septimi tertia requieverit, de uxore sit; in secunda tertia, de socio querit; in ultima, tertia querit de socio et vult separari ab eo. (10) Cum in prima octavi tertia invenietur, de morte sua querit; in secunda tertia de partitione possessionis; in ultima tertia, de debito sit. (11) Cum autem in prima noni quarta ingressus fuerit, de fide cogitat; si in secunda quarta de itinere cogitat vel interrogat; si in tertia quarta, de sapientia et magistratu vel honorem ex magistratu; in ultima quarta, de sompnio. (12) Dicit quod si in prima decimi tertia inierit, querit de domini novis, in secunda tertia de re sua dicit; in ultima tertia, de matre. (13) Cum undecimi prima tertia inierit, de mercato querit; in secunda tertia querit de divite; in ultima tertia de amico fiet. (14) Quod si in dudodecimi prima tertia repertus fuerit, de inimico querit; in secunda tertia de captione et paupere; in ultima tertia de bestiis questio sit.

2 (1) Si autem dominus signi combustus fuerit sive in deiectione vel retrogradatur, Lunam intuere et similiter iudica. Quod si in mansione est masculini generis vel in combusta vel in deiectione, nichil secundum eam dicas.

3 (1) Tunc perspice dominum hore quot gradibus sit in aliquo signo, et gradus illos per .12. multiplica atque per .30. divide. (2) Et unumquodque .30. signis tribue incipiens ab oriente. (3) Et ubi numerus defecerit de ipso querit. (4) Et si dominus hore combustus fuerit vel revertitur seu cadit, vide quot gradus signi sunt erecti,

et illos divide per .2. et dimidium, et quecumque binarium et dimidium da signis similiter ab oriente incipiens et ubi defecerit numerus de illo querit.

English translation

1 (1) If you wish to know what he wants to say, examine the ascending sign and the hour, and look where the lord of the sign is. (2) If it is in ⟨its⟩ falling or dejection, and you see that it moves backward, or is burnt, if it is so, do not answer according to the lord of the sign but according to the figures that I will describe. (3) Therefore, if the lord of the ascendant is in the same ⟨place⟩ [i.e., in the ascendant], he wishes to ask about himself. (4) If it is in the second ⟨place⟩, he will ask about property or possession. (5) If it is in the ⟨first⟩ half of the third ⟨place⟩, his desire is to move from one place to ⟨another⟩ place; if it is found in the latter half, he wishes to hear about ⟨his⟩ sisters and brothers. (6) When it is found in the ⟨first⟩ third of the fourth place, he is thinking about the father; ⟨if⟩ in the second third, he will have fear about a ship, or about a vineyard, a garden, or about something underground; when it is located in the third ⟨decan⟩, he will inquire about a great thought which he does not know to carry out, and he is doubtful about everything. (7) If it remains is in the first quarter of the fifth ⟨place⟩, he will inquire about sons; ⟨if⟩ in the second ⟨quarter ⟩, about joy; if in the third ⟨quarter ⟩, about clothes; if in the last ⟨quartert⟩ about a letter or books and about news. (8) If it is in the ⟨first⟩ half of the sixth ⟨place⟩, the question will be about an ill person; if in the other half, he will inquire about male and female slaves. (9) If it rests in the first third of the seventh ⟨place⟩, it [the question] is about ⟨his⟩ wife; if in the second third, he will inquire about a partner; if in the last third, he will inquire about a partner, and wants to separate from him. (10) If it is found in the first third of the eighth ⟨place⟩, he will ask about his death; if in the second third, he will inquire about dividing up possessions; if in the last third, it [the question] is about debt. (11) If it enters the first quarter of the ninth ⟨place⟩, he is thinking about faith; if in the second quarter, he is thinking or will ask about a journey; if in the third quarter, about wisdom and magistracy and honor deriving from magistracy; in the last quarter, about a dream. (12) He says that if it is in the first third of the tenth ⟨place⟩, he will ask about news from the master; if in the second ⟨third⟩, he will speak about his affairs; if in the last third, he will inquire about the mother. (13) If it is in the first third of the eleventh ⟨place⟩, he will ask about trade; if in the second ⟨third ⟩, he will inquire about a rich man; if in the last ⟨third ⟩, it will be about a friend. (14) If it is in the first third of the twelfth ⟨place⟩, he will ask about an enemy; if in the second ⟨decan⟩, he will inquire about captivity and a poor person; if in the last ⟨third ⟩, the question will be about animals.

2 (1) But if the lord of the sign is burnt, in dejection, or retrograde, take the Moon and judge likewise. If it [the Moon] is in a masculine house, burnt, or in dejection, say nothing according to it.

3 (1) Then observe how many degrees the lord of the hour is in a certain sign; multiply these degrees by 12 and divide them by 30. (2) To each one ⟨of the degrees⟩ assign 30 signs beginning from the ascendant. (3) He will inquire about ⟨the matter indicated by the place⟩ where the number is completed. (4) If the lord of the hour

is burnt, retrograde, or cadent, observe how many degrees are ascending, divide them by 2½°, and likewise assign 2½° to the signs beginning from the ascendant, and he will inquire about ⟨the matter indicated by the place⟩ where the number is completed.

APPENDIX 9

SIGNIFICATIONES PLANETARUM IN DOMIBUS ASCRIBED TO GERGIS

This appendix presents the complete text of *De significationibus planetarum in domibus*, ascribed to Gergis, Iergis, or Girgith. This Latin text is included in the present volume because the entire third part of *Tractatus particulares* is a reworking of Gergis's treatise. See above, pp. 74–75. The present edition of *Significationes planetarum in domibus* is based on Paris, BnF lat. 16204, s. XIII, pp. 428b–432b, which has been collated with Ghent, UB, 5 (416), 15th c., fols. 103v–105v, and Paris, BnF lat. 16208, 12th c., fols. 50va–51vb. Gergis's treatise is organized in nine sections—one each for the seven planets and for the Head and Tail of the Dragon; each section is divided into twelve paragraphs, corresponding to the twelve horoscopic places. For easy reference, I have numbered each of the nine sections and the paragraphs within them. For an English translation of *Significationes planetarum in domibus*, see *Significations*, trans. Dykes (2008).

Liber quem edidit Iergis: quid significent planete in .12. domibus circuli. Incipiunt significationes planetarum in domibus. ⟨I. Sol⟩

1 (1) Sol cum fuerit in ascendente, significat principatum et sublimitatem et magnitudinem rerum. (2) Et in .ii^{o}., pulchritudinem esse et apparitionem dilectionis et letitiam oculorum. (3) Et in tertio, effectum rerum et ex parte regis et mutationem a regione in regionem. (4) Et in .iiii^{to}., thesaurum et apparitionem rei furate et laudem ac sublimitatem inter homines. (5) Et in .v^{to}., mutationem ex parte filii et multitudinem reverentie a vulgo et gaudium ex donationem. (6) Et in .vi^{to}., infirmitatem et tribulationem ex parte servorum et meroroes et blasphemias ab ignobilibus. (7) Et in .vii^{o}., contrarietates a divitibus et nobilibus sive a regibus et potentibus. (8) Et in .viii^{o}., [429a] perditionem ac mortem et ablationem principum ac nobilium et omnipotentium. (9) Et in .ix^{o}., divinum cultum, fidem ac timorem Dei altisimi et commemorationem angelorum. (10) Et in .x^{o}., regnum magnum et gloriam honorem ac profectum. (11) Et in .xi^{o}., gaudium ex parte amicorum et divitum, ministrorum quoque sive auxiliatorum, et ingenium in omni re in qua est fiducia. (12) Et in .xii^{o}., interfectionem divitum et ablationem regni et honoris et tribulationem a servis et inimicis et ab omnibus ignobilibus.

⟨II. Venus⟩

2 (1) Venus cum fuerit in ascendente significat gaudium, et letitiam, et apparitionem voluntatum, comestionem quoque ac potationem, atque vestium, et ornamenta aurea et argentea, et res odoriferas, honestatem quoque morum, et magnitudinem benedictionis, et voluptatem corporis. (2) Et in .ii°., subtantiam et profectum ex parte mulierum et nobilitatem, profectum et honestatem auxilii ex parte profectus. (3) Et in .iii°., incontinentiam et moerorem ex parte malorum operum, et multitudinem amicorum contra Deum. (4) Et in .iv°., moerorum et tristitiam in initio rerum ex parte matrum, et finis eorum erit utilis et laudabilis. (5) Et in .v°., primam tribulationem ex filio, postea gaudium et letitiam. (6) Et in .vi°., infirmitatem et tribulationem ex parte servorum et ancillarum et matrum, et significat viduas. Sed tamen dominus interrogationis adipiscetur omne quod petierit ex rebus. Et si fuerit interrogatio de infirmo, liberabitur de infirmitate sua, et tempus liberationis erit secundum quod exposui tibi in initio libri. Et scito quod fortuna, cum fuerit in domo infirmitatis, alleviabitur infirmitas patientis; si vero fuerit infortuna, aggravabitur, nutu Dei. (7) Et in .vii°., coniugium et gaudium ex parte mulierum et ex omni re quesita ex participatione, et faciliter efficitur ei omnis res quam voluerit. (8) Et in .viii°., matrum mortem ac nutricium et maiorum suorum. (9) Et in .ix°., peregrinationem et mutationem in domibus religionis, [429b] divinum quoque cultum et religionem ac sompnia vera. (10) Et in .x°., gaudium ex parte regis. (11) Et in .xi°., amicitiam et gaudium et usum bonorum ac letitiam et fiduciam ex parte amicorum et fortunam cum eis. (12) Et in .xii°., tribulationem maximam et inimicitatem ex mulieribus et maxime ignobilibus.

⟨III. Mercurius⟩

3 (1) Mercurius cum fuerit in ascendente significat disciplinam et sapientiam et scripturas et bonam facundiam atque disputationes et geometriam atque arithmeticam. (2) Et in .ii°., profectum substantie et honorem apud regem et bonum esse. (3) Et in .iii°., fratres et sorores, et multitudinem eorum, multitudinem quoque amicorum et notorum. (4) Et in .iv°., moerorem et cogitationem et contentionem quoque et locutionem. (5) Et in .v°., adventum epistolarum et rumorum, et gaudium de moerore precedente, et fortunam ex parte filii. (6) Et in .vi°., contentionem et destructionem, et animi involutionem, et deceptionem ex servis et ignobilibus, et contentiones. (7) Et in .vii°., contentionem ex parte mulierum, et luxurie mulititudinem. (8) Et in .viii°., inimicitiam maximam ex vicinis et contemptionem causam mendacii quod dicitur de eo causa mortuorum, propter substantias a mortuis, relictas aut propter rem antiquam transactam. (9) Et in .ix°., disciplinam, sapientiam, scientiam quoque astrorum, et honestam laudem ab hiis qui noverunt eum. (10) Et in .x°., potestatem magnam ex scriptura et arithmetica et geometria, et a principus. (11) Et in .xi°., multitudinem amicorum, gaudium et societatem sapientium. (12) Et in .xii°., stultitiam et perversitatem et paucitatem sensus et levitatem in eundo et redeundo et interrogando de hiis que carent radice. Si autem scientiam habuerit, erit in quadrupedibus.

⟨IV. Luna⟩

4 (1) Luna cum fuerit in ascendente significat principatum et effectum rerum, et mutationes de loco in locum, et gaudium ex parte matrum et magnarum mulierum. (2) Et in .ii°., ablationem substatie, moerorem ac tristitiam. (3) Et in .iii°., gaudium et letitiam ex divitibus, et sublimitatem ex regibus, et effectum rerum, et causas earum, peregrinationem quoque, et amicorum aceptionem et fratrum, et esse cum nobilibus, et augmentationem [430a] amoris. (4) Et in .iv°., moerorem et tristitiam in initio interrogationis, si fuerit in die et erit finis eius laudabilis, si fuerit in nocte significat interitum, et in initio rei et fine eius, nisi sit interrogatio eius de thesauro occulto aut de re sepulta quia in hoc optimum est apparebit enim illa res et detegetur et Deus melius novit. (5) Et in .v^to^., multitudinem filiorum et quod filii erunt masculinis, si fuerit interrogatio nocturna. Si fuerit diurna significat multitudinem filiarum et repulsionem horribilium et rumores venientes ex longinquo loco cum gaudio de filio. Et si volueris scire qui sunt rumores, aspice a quo separatur Luna, quia rumores qui venient erunt secundum planete a quo separatur Luna. Et si volueris scire utrum sint ipsi rumores qui veniunt in cartula vel proferat eos legatus ore, aspice Lunam et Mercurius si iungitur ei aut separatur ab eo, quod si separata fuerit a domino .vii. et iuncta fuerit gradui ascendentis, refert legatus rumores ore suo. (6) Et in .vi°., rixam et contentionem ex parte patrum, et lucrum ex quadrupedibus, et sanitatem corporis. (7) Et in .vii°., bonum esse ex parte mulierum, et coniugium et profectum causa eorum. (8) Et in .viii°., interitum, et consumationem, et depositionem regis vel mortem eius, et conturbationem in operibus, et falsum testimonium, et rixam, et fugam, et tribulationem, et anxietatem animi ut lunatici patiuntur, et timorem, et incantationem, et instabilitatem animi, et malas cogitationes. (9) Et in .ix°., partitionem et malas cogitationes, et mutationes regni a regione in regionem, et nutus mulierum et scientiam dispositionis regni, ac scientiam rerum. Et si fuerit ipsa domus nona ex domibus Mercurii, significat scientiam astrorum. Et si fuerit ex dominbus Veneris, significat subtilitatem, scientiam et cantilenarum ac letitie. Et si fuerit ex domibus Martis, magistratum instrumentorum, et opus armorum. Et si fuerit ex dominbus Iovis, significabit divinum cultum, et scientiam in lege et principatum [430b] iudicum. Es si fuerit ex domibus Saturni, significabit scientiam alkimie et universa eius magistra. Et si fuerit domus Solis, significabit scientiam ac prudentiam in omnibus quadrupedibus. Et si fuerit in Cancro, significabit scientiam atque prudentiam univerasarum substantiarum quae exeunt de aqua. Et scito quod hac sit proprietas Lune inter planetas. (10) Et in .x°., effectum rerum et interrogationum et erit in hoc mandatum a rege, si fuerit in die, si vero fuerit in nocte significat effectum rerum ex parte regis ac mulierum, et erit hoc cito sed res in verisque temporibus, in die ac nocte, non erit durabilis. Et si mulier inceperit in eo reganre, deponetur rex velociter, quia valens est locus hic in significatione Solis, Luna non si est sufficiens nisi modicum in hac significatione. (11) Et in .xi°., gaudium ex parte amicorum, et acceptionen omnis rei in qua sperabat et in qua habebat fiduciam. (12) Et in .xii°., impedimentum et duritiam, et instabilitatem regis, et rixam ac carceres ex parte inimicorum. Et si interrogatur fuerit de aliqua re que erit, et fuerit Luna signatrix tua, fueritque in .xii., erit hac hora exitus Lune de eodem loco, per hoc enim perficietur res, et erit et veniens absens, et maxime si fuerit hoc in fine mensis lunaris et Luna fuerit

impedita a Saturno, tunc enim iudica esse horribile e malum, et non dubites in hoc si Deus voluerit.

⟨V. Saturnus⟩

5 (1) Saturnus cum fuerit in ascendente significat moerorem causa debiti et terrarium. (2) Et in .ii°., ablationem substantie et conturbationem amicorum. (3) Et in .iii°., destructionem fratrum et proiectionem rixe inter inter eos. (4) Et in .iv°., destructionem edificii, et terrarum ac feminum, et thesaurorum et periculum sive interitum causa eorum. (5) Et in .v°., destructionem filiorum et contentionem cum legato. (6) Et in .vi°., infirmitatem et inobedientiam servorum. (7) Et in .vii°., destructionem uxoris et terrarum, et effectum rei maligne in fine. (8) Et in .viii°., petitionem reliquiarum mortuorum, et rei veteris et antique et moerores ac tristitiam, causam mortis, et lamentationem longam. (9) Et in .ix°., destructionem fidei, et [431a] exitum ad malum consilium et lunaticos, et eos qui effodiunt sepulchra causa exspoliandi mortuos, et moerore atque anxietatem in peregrinatione cum prolixitate in more. (10) Et in .x°., moerorem et tristitiam atque gueram ociositatem et periculum ex parte regis et carcerem prolixum. Quod si fuerit dominus eiusdem .x. domus Sol, interificiet eum rex in carcere suo. Et si fuerit domina decime domus Luna, significabit illud quod significabit Sol, nisi sit Luna iuncta Saturno. Et si fuerit dominus decime Iupiter, interficiet eum rex absque culpa, et faciet sibi iustitiam. Et si fuerit dominus decime Mars, peribit culpa sua. Et si fuerit domina decime Venus, consequetur ex hac tribulatione habebit sublimitatem et profectum ac gaudium. Et si fuerit dominus decime Mercurius, interficietur cum iniuria, dicetur super ipsum mendacium. Et si aspexerit Mercurius Martem, percutietur flagellis. Et si fuerit Mercurius cum Sole, faciet ei rex vim, et aufert ei substantiam, et faciet sibi iniuriam in computationem atque scrutabitur eum. Et scito quod hac proprietas sit Saturno in .x°. domo inter ceteros planetas. (11) Et in .xi., multitudinem meroris atque tristitie ex parte amicorum et paucitatem profectis in hiis que sperabat et in quibus habebat fiduciam ex bono et involutionem in rebus ac duritiam earum, et multitudinem fiducie in rebus falsis cui proficiunt. (12) Et in .xii., impedimenta que accidunt ex parte regum, et erit in hoc fortis et audax et capietur ab inimicis, et erit timidus in omnibus rebus fuis.

⟨VI. Iupiter⟩

6 (1) Iupiter cum fuerit in ascendente significat reverentiam et pulchritudinem et honestatem fidei ac religionis discipline quoque ac rationem et erit finis eorum in quibus est ad salvationem et tribuetur ei in hoc principatus. (2) Et in .ii°., collectionem multarum substantiarum cum ingenio et bona dispositione cum adeptione universorum que fiunt causa substantie. (3) Et in .iii°., fortunam ex parte fratrum et sociorum maiorum et multitudinem gaudii ex parte propinquorum. (4) Et in .iv°., profectum ex reliquiis mortuorum et ex terris atque hereditatiubs sive ex thesauris et ex omni re antiqua et ablationem moeroris et cogitationis male, rixeque ac tristitie ac securitatem ex omni re horribili. (5) Et in .v°., multitudinem [431b] fil-

iorum et bonitatem esse eorum, et multitudinem profectus per eos, et honestatem, laudem, coniunctionem divitum et nobilitatem et profectum omnium in quibus habet fiduciam. (6) Et in .vi., paucitatem infirmitatis et sanitatem corporis et sublimitatem ex parte suorum et profectum ex quadrupedibus. (7) Et in .viiº., gaudium ex parte mulierum et coniugium et adeptionem omnis inimici. (8) Et in .viiiº., ablationem substantie domini interrogantis, et quod cadent in manibus inimicorum suorum, et occurere ei ex hac destructione, sed habebit finem laudabilem. (9) Et in .ixº., gaudium ex peregrinatione et honestatem fidei et expositionem somniorum et veritatem sompnorum, si Deus voluerit. Et si te quis interrogaverit quid viderit in sompnis, aspice planetam a quo separatur Iupiter, vel qui separatur ab eo, et dic secundum naturam eiusdem planete a quo separatus est Iupiter vel qui separatus est ab eo. Et si voluerit scire interpretationem illius sompnii, aspice a quo separatur Iupiter ex planetis vel qui separatur ab eo, quia secundum naturam planete erit interpretatio sompnii, scito hoc. (10) Et in .xº., ditationem et collectionem substantiarum et honestatem laudis, sublimitatem quoque atque honorem in omnibus. (11) Et in .xi., laudem ex parte amicorum et profectum et in hiis que sperat de omni re vel in quibus habet fiduciam. (12) Et in .xii., servitutem et paupertatem atque indigentiam, tristitiam quoque ex parte quadrupedum et moerorem a servis.

⟨VII. Mars⟩

7 (1) Mars cum fuerit in ascendente significat tristitiam et timorem et contentionem et rem horribilem, caliditatem quoque et contrarietatem, et ablationem substantie absque laude et introitum in re que non pertinent ad eum. (2) Et in .iiº., ablationem substantie et paupertatem atque indigentiam et conturbationem ministrorum. (3) Et in .iiiº., inimicitatem fratrum, et proiectionem odii inter eos, et interfectionem eorum ad invicem. Et si tertia domus fuerit ex domibus Veneris, significabit gaudium ex fratribus et sororibus. Et si fuerit ex dominbus Iovis, significabit multitudinem substantiarum et negociorum. Et si fuerit Saturni, significabit effossiones sepulchrorum et parientum, et inquisitionem latronicii. Et si fuerit ex dominbus Mercurii, significabit sublimitatem eius per divinitationes et scripturas et falsum testimonium eo quod loquatur extra dicta sapientium, et patietur pericula et tribulationes. Et si fuerit domus Lune, significabit fractionem parietum, inquisitionem latrocinii et impedimentum [432a] latrocinii in foro. Et si fuerit domus Solis, significabit abscisionem viarum et depredationes villarum. Et scito quod hac proprietas sit Martis inter alios planetas. (4) Et in .iv., interitum et interfectionem et effusionem sanguinis, et erit finis huiuis rei in moerorem, et tribulationem prolixam. (5) Et in .vº., multitudinem filiorum ex fornicatione, et vitia ex eadem, et paucitatem profectus et gaudii, et erit initius cum hoc bonus. (6) Et in .viº., multitudinem infirmitatum, et febres calidas et siccas, et exsiccationem sanguinis, moerorem quoque ac tristitiam ex parte servorum. (7) Et in .viiº., negociationem et contentionem contra et coitum, iniustitiam et dampnum propter hoc, et conturbationem in omni re, et contentionem acque horribile et moerorem causa eorum. (8) Et in .viiiº., interfectionem et abscisionem manuum ac pedum, et vituperationem turpissimam, sed acquiret ex rebus mortuorum, et substantiam

maximam et patietur vim propter eas, et habebit de manu sua et cadet in paupertatem maximam. (9) Et in .ix°., petitionem equorum et bellorum atque exercituum, potationem quoque vini, et incontinentiam atque infidelitatem, et multitudinem visionum et sompniorum inendacium. (10) Et in .x°., tribulationem ex parte regis, et percussionem flagellorum, et angustiam ac carcerem et penuriam in victu, et multitudinem belli et contentionis in hiis que non pertinent ad eum. (11) Et in .xi°., paucitatem profectus, et inimicitatem amicorum et amissionem substantie, et ablationem fiducie in hiis que habet in corde. (12) Et in .xii°., ingenia latronis omnibus modis, et dilationem in omnibus que potest operari, et ablationem substantie, et multitudinem inimicorum, et perpetrationem ad audiendum horribile et moerorem causa bestiarum, si Deus voluerit.

⟨VIII. Caput Draconis⟩

8 (1) Caput in ascendente significat augmentationem et sublimitatem ac fortitudinem, secundum coniunctionem suam cum planetis. (2) Et in .ii°., augmentationem substantiarum et fortunam maximam. (3) Et in .iii°., acquisitionem profectus, et aptationem fidei ac veritatem somniorum. (4) Et in .iv°., augmentationem proficuum si fuerit in signis aeris vel igneis. Si vero fuerit in signis terreis vel aquaticis vertit sententiam, id est, dic econtrario. (5) Et in .v°., augmentationem [432b] filiorum, et liberationem ab hominibus adversis. (6) Et in .vi°., fortitudinem infirmitatum, et augmentationem servorum et mutatioenm bestiarum. (7) Et in .vii°., augmentationem et societatem mulierum. (8) Et in .viii°., fortitudinem vite et paucitatem moeroris. (9) Et in .ix°., fidem et augmentationem religionis secundum quod cum venerit cum eo ex planetis fortunis vel malis. (10) Et in .x°., interrogationem de Deo altissimo, de re bona invisibili, et significat sublimitatem et fortitudinem et venerationem ac reverentiam et fortitudinem fortune in magisteriis. (11) Et in .xi°., nullum opus est in eo, et caudis similiter. (12) Et in .xii°., significat augmentationem malorum et paucitatem fortunarum.

⟨IX. Cauda Draconis⟩

9 (1) Cauda in ascendente significat separationem et detrimentum et eradicationem, pericula quoque ac tribulationes, et rerum diminutiones. (2) Et in .ii°., paupertatem et occupationem et casum a locis ex quibus non suspicatur. (3) Et in .iii°., destructionem fratrum et gravitatem rixe amicorum, aut fortassis peribit aliquis fratrum vel sororum. (4) Et in .iv°., penuriam sive et inimicitatem atque inquisitionem rerum absque profectu. (5) Et in .v°., expulsionem filiorum, et dissensionem horribilem in filios, et vetustatem indumentorum, et indigentiam filiorum. (6) Et in .vi°., infirmitatem et segnitiem servorum et ancillarum, et debilitatem bestiarum. (7) Et in .vii°., destructionem thori et fortitudinem inimicorum et contentiones. (8) Et in .viii°., mortem, et reliquas mortuorum, et timorem mortis ac perditionis. (9) Et in .ix°., fortitudinem mutationis et motus, ac paucitatem fidei. (10) Et in .x°., dispositionem et pericula et peregrinationem sive casum. (11) Et in .xi°., nullum opus est eis in eis sicut superius diximus. (12) Et in .xii°., significat paucitatem malorum, si Deus voluerit. Hec sunt significationes planetarum et capitis et caude, et in .xii.

domibus, cum fuerint in meliori esse dic melius. Si vero in malo esse, verte sententiam et dic econtrario, scilicet, post bonum malum, et loquere audaciter, et noli dubitare nec dimittas hod quod dico tibi et non proferas aliud et invenies, si Deus voluerit.

Explicit.

APPENDIX 10

THE ACCOUNT OF THE SEVEN PLANETS IN *MISHPEṬEI HA-MAZZALOT*

The entire second part of *Tractatus particulares* is a reworking of the account of the seven planets in *Mishpeṭei ha-mazzalot*. More precisely, the originator of the Hebrew source text of *Tractatus particulares* gleaned the building blocks of the account of the seven planets from discontinuous passages in *Mishpeṭei ha-mazzalot* and assembled them according to 13 categories and in the order in which they appear in *Liber servorum*, the second part of *Tractatus particulares*. To show this point, the present appendix brings all the relevant passages of the account of the seven planets in *Mishpeṭei ha-mazzalot* that are quoted or paraphrased in *Tractatus particulares*. Here I use *Mishpeṭei ha-mazzalot*, ed. Sela (2017), accompanied by an English translation, and organize the relevant passages in seven sections, on each of the seven planets. For easy reference, the numbering of the relevant passages in each of these seven sections is not consecutive but repeats the original numbering of the relevant passages in *Mishpeṭei ha-mazzalot*, ed. Sela (2017).

I: The Sun: *Mishpeṭei ha-mazzalot* § 51:2, 538–539; § 38:6–15, 520–523:

(2) מנת השמש היא מנת החן הנזכרת. והיא לאות על אורך חיי האדם, ואם יצליח בכל דרכיו; גם תורה על בריאות הגוף והנשמות כפי המביטים אל המנה. וכל זה היה נכון אם אחד מן המושלים על מקום המנה יביט אליה, אי זה מהם שיהיה, וכפי כח המביט ככה תדין. ואם אין מביט, לא יצא למפעל מה שתורה המנה, בין טוב ובין רע, כי אם במחשבה ובדברים ובחלומות. (6) והשמש תורה על האב לנולד ביום; ועל חיי הנולד ועל גבהות נפשו ועל השררה ועל השם; ועל העין הימנית לנולד ביום ובלילה על העין השמאלית; ובחלק השמש הלב, גם יש לה חלק בפה והצד הימין. (7) ובחלקה מן המתכות, הזהב; ומהצמחים, האילנים הגדולים שהם עושים פרי; ובחלקה הענבים; ומהחיים, המלכים בתקופת שנת העולם; וממרכבת האדם, הסוסים; וכחה מן הפאות, המזרח; וממראה העינים, הלבן מאד. (8) וצורת האדם: שתהיה השמש מושלת על תואר פניו, יפה מראה, פניו רחבות, ועיניו גדולות ופיו רחב, והולך בקומה זקופה. (9) וממשלתו בימי השבוע, יום ראשון, ומן הלילות, ליל חמישי. (10) וממשלתו על הנולדים ביום עשר שנים בראשונה, ועל הנולדים בלילה משנת ל״ט עד מ״ט. (11) ותלמי המלך אומר כי יש לה ממשלה על כל הנולדים בלילה או ביום משנת שתים ועשרים עד מ״א שנה. (12) ושנותיה קטנות י״ט, והאמצעיות ל״ט שנה וחצי שנה, והגדולות ק״כ. (13) ויש בחלק השמש הנוצרים כי באריה היתה מחברת של העליונים; ובחלקה הארמונים והחצרות, ובתי כנסיות והמדרשים. (14) והמושלים על פקידות בית השמש ביום יורו על טוב או רע שיקרה לנולד בחצי ימיו הראשון או האחרון, כפי תולדת הכוכב וכחו, ודרך המביטים אליו, ועל אי זה בית יש לו ממשלה כנגד המזל הצומח, ולאיזה בית יביט. (15) והשמש לאות במולד האשה על הבעל.

(2) The lot of the Sun is ⟨identical with⟩ the aforementioned lot of Fortune. It signifies a man's lifespan and whether he will be successful in all his undertakings; it also signifies physical and mental health, depending on which [planets] aspect the lot. All this is correct on condition that one of the lords over the position of the lot ⟨also⟩ aspects it, whichever aspect it may be; pass judgment according to the power of ⟨the planet⟩ that aspects ⟨it⟩. But if no ⟨planet⟩ aspects it, the signification of the lot, whether for good or for evil, will not be realized, but only in thought, ⟨spoken⟩ words, and dreams. (6) The Sun signifies the father for a person born by day; and the native's life, pride, authority, and reputation; the right eye for a person born by day and the left eye for a person born by night; the heart is in the Sun's portion, as well the mouth and the right side ⟨of the body⟩. (7) Of metals, gold is in its portion; of plants, the large fruit-bearing trees; grapes are in its portion; of living creatures, kings at the revolution of the world-year; of riding animals, horses; of the sides ⟨of the horizon⟩, its power is in the east; of the colors, intense white. (8) The human form: the Sun rules over his [i.e., the native who is under the Sun's sway] physiognomy, ⟨so that he is⟩ handsome, his face broad, his eyes large, and his mouth wide, and he walks with an upright posture. (9) Of the days of the week, it rules over the day⟨time⟩ of the first ⟨day⟩ [i.e., from sunrise to sundown on Sunday], of the nights, the night of the fifth ⟨day⟩ [i.e., between sundown on Wednesday and sunrise on Thursday]. (10) It rules over children born by day during their first 10 years ⟨of their lives⟩, and over those born by night from their 39th to their 49th year. (11) King Ptolemy says that it rules over all, whether born by day or by night, from the 22nd to the 41st year. (12) Its least years are 19, the middle ⟨years⟩ are 39½ years, and the great ⟨years⟩ are 120. (13) The Christians are in the Sun's portion, because the conjunction of the upper ⟨planets⟩ [Saturn and Jupiter] took place in Leo; palaces, courtyards, synagogues, and schools are in its portion. (14) The rulers over the lordship ⟨of the triplicity⟩ of the Sun's house by day signify good fortune or misfortune for the native in the first or last half of his life, according to the planet's nature and its power, depending on the planets that aspect it [the lord the Sun's triplicity], and according to the ⟨horoscopic⟩ place with respect to the ascendant sign over which it has lordship and the place it [the lord the Sun's triplicity] is aspecting. (15) In a woman's nativity the Sun signifies her husband.

II: The Moon: *Mishpeṭei ha-mazzalot* § 51:3, 538–539; § 39:2–10, 522–525:

(1) מנת הלבנה: הסתכל כמה המרחק בין מקום הלבנה אל מקום השמש, וספור המספר הזה מהמעלה הצומחת, זאת תקרא מנת התעלומה. והיא תורה על נשמת האדם, ועל יצרי הנולד, ובינתו וערמתו וקנאתו, ויראתו מהשם. (2) ויראה כחה בכל צמח ובכל לח, בקשואים והקרות, בנהרות הסמוכים אל הים הגדול, ובמוח הראש גם מוח העצמות, ובכח תולדת הגוף והמוח השמאלי; ויש בחלקה העין השמאלי ביום והימני בלילה. (3) והיא תורה על כל דבר שיחל האדם, והיא לאות על הנולד עד ארבע שנים. (4) מהאילנים, הקטנים והתאנים; ומהמתכות הכסף; וממרכבת האדם, העגלה; וכחה מערבי; ומהחיים עמי הארץ. (5) ותאר פניו עגול, ופיו קטן, ואיננו לבן

מאד ומהלכו במהירות. (6) וממשלתה בימי השבוע, יום שני, ומהלילות, ליל ששי. (7) ויש לה ממשלה על הנולדים בלילה תשע שנים, ועל הנולדים ביום מתחלת שנת ל״ב עד סוף ארבעים שנה. (8) ושנותיה הקטנות כ״ה, והאמצעיות ל״ט וחצי, והגדולות ק״ח שנים. (9) והיא לאות על האם ועל האחות ועל אשת הנולד; ובחלקה פתחי הבתים. (10) והמושלים על פקידות שלישות בית הלבנה בלילה יורו על כל מה שיקרה לנולד מטוב או רע בימיו.

(3) The lot of the Moon: Find out the distance between the position of the Moon and the position of the Sun and add this number to the ascendant degree; this ⟨position⟩ is called the lot of the absent. It signifies man's soul, the native's impulses, his intellect, shrewdness, and envy, and his fear of God. (2) Its power is visible in every plant and in everything moist, in melons and pumpkins, in rivers that are near the ocean, in the brain and in the bone marrow, in the power of the body's nature and the left ⟨side of the⟩ brain; the left eye is in its portion by day and the right one by night. (3) It portends everything that a person begins and gives an indication about the native until he is 4 years old. (4) Of trees, the small ones and fig trees; of metals, silver; of riding animals, ⟨the animals that pull⟩ the wagon; its power comes from the west; of living beings, commoners. (5) His [the native who is under the Moon's sway] face is round, his mouth small, he is not very pale and he moves quickly. (6) Of the days of the week, it rules over the day⟨time⟩ of the second ⟨day⟩ [i.e., from sunrise to sundown on Monday], of the nights, the night of the sixth ⟨day⟩ [i.e., between sundown on Thursday and sunrise on Friday]. (7) It rules ⟨the first⟩ 9 years for those born by night and from the beginning of the 32nd year to the end of 40th year for those born by day. (8) Its least years are 25, the middle ⟨years⟩ 39½, and great ⟨years⟩ 108. (9) It signifies the native's mother, sister, and wife; and the doors of houses are in its portion. (10) The rulers over the lordship of the triplicity of the Moon's house by night portend everything that will happen to the native, for good or evil, during his life.

III: Saturn: *Mishpeṭei ha-mazzalot* § 40:1–14, 524–525; § 52:1, 540–541:

(1) שבתאי: זה הכוכב עליון, וכל המשרתים יתנו כח לו בהתחברם עמו או על דרך המבטים. (2) ובחלקו העופרת, ובתי החשך והכבוד, וכל אילן פריו נבאש. (3) ומטעמו חמוץ; והוא קר ולח אם היה בשפלות גלגל המוצק, וקר ויבש אם היה בגבהותו. (4) הוא כוכב המרמה והערמה, ורוב המחשבה והדאגה, והפחד, והמורא. (5) ויש לו הטחול, ומהעינים השחורות, והאוזן הימנית. (6) ובחלקו הזקנים והעניים; ואומנות בנאי או ספן או מעבד עורות. ובחלקו השדים ורוח רעה, והתחלואים הארוכים והמומים. (7) והכלל: הוא כמו מלאך המות להמית תחת מפולת או להשליך ממקום גבוה או להטביע במים. (8) ובחלקו הקדחת הרביעית והשחין היבש; והוא לאות על אדם שחור; עיניו דקות קטנות ומצחו גדול, ובמהלכו מסתכל למטה, בעל מרה שחורה. (9) ובחלקו מהחכמות דעת עליון והעקרים, כי חלק השמש התורות, וחלק הלבנה השיחות וכל קבלה קרובה; וכפי כחו בנולד יוכל לסבול העמל. (10) וממשלתו בימי השבוע יום שבת, ומן הלילות ליל רביעי. (11) והוא ישמש אחר הלבנה בנולדים בלילה י״א שנה. (12) ועל דעת תלמי בימי הזקנה. (13) ושנותיו הקטנות ל׳, והאמצעיות מ״ג, והגדולות נ״ז. (14) ומן הפאות, המערביות; וממרכבת האדם, החמורים; והוא כוכב

זכר. (15) מנת שבתאי: משבתאי עד מנת החן, וכמספר הזה מהצומחת. והיא תורה על האסורים והייסורים והשביה. הסתכל אם היא באחד היתדות וכפי המבטים.

(1) Saturn. This is the uppermost planet and all the ⟨other⟩ planets give their power to it when they conjoin it or aspect it. (2) Lead is in its portion, and tombs and privies, and any tree whose fruit is foul-smelling. (3) Its taste is sour; it is cold and moist when it is at perigee on the eccentric circle, and cold and dry when at apogee. (4) It is the planet of deceit and cunning, of excessive thought and worry, fear, and dread. (5) In its portion is the spleen, the dark part of the eye, and the right ear. (6) The elderly and paupers are in its portion; of crafts, the mason, sailor, and tanner; in its portion are the demons and melancholy, chronic diseases and deformities. (7) In general, it is like the angel of death, killing in an avalanche or by a fall from a high place or by drowning. (8) Quartan fever and dry boils are in its portion; it signifies swarthy men; his [the native under Saturn's sway] eyes are small and narrow and his forehead broad, when he walks he looks down, and he is melancholic. (9) Of the sciences, theology and metaphysics; but religions are the Sun's portion, and rhetoric and local tradition are in the Moon's portion; the native will be able to endure hard work in proportion to its [Saturn's] power in his nativity. (10) Of the days of the week, it rules over the day⟨time⟩ of Shabbat [i.e., from sunrise to sundown on Saturday]; of the nights, the night of the fourth ⟨day⟩ [i.e., between sundown on Tuesday and sunrise on Wednesday]. (11) After the moon, it rules those born by night for 11 years. (12) But according to Ptolemy's opinion, ⟨it rules⟩ in old age. (13) Its least years are 30, middle ⟨years⟩ 43, and great ⟨years⟩ 57. (14) Of the sides ⟨of the horizon⟩, west; of riding animals, donkeys; it is a masculine planet. (15) The lot of Saturn: ⟨Find the distance⟩ between Saturn and the lot of Fortune and ⟨add⟩ this number to the ascendant ⟨degree⟩. It signifies prisoners, pains, and captivity. Find out whether it is in one of the cardines and ⟨pass judgment⟩ in accordance with what aspects ⟨it⟩.

IV: Jupiter: *Mishpeṭei ha-mazzalot* § 41:1–11, 524–527; § 52:2, 540–541:

(1) צדק: כוכב גדול גופו מגופי כל המשרתים לבד מהשמש. (2) והוא יורה על החיים, והטוב, והעושר, והצדק, ונדבת לב, וגמילות חסדים; והוא יורה על השופטים, ומלמדי התורות, והמתפללים לצבור; ומשנות בני האדם הקרובות לזקנה; ובחלקו הבדיל, ואילני התפוחים והרמונים; וממרכבת האדם הפיל; וטעמו מתוק. (3) ותולדתו חם ולח, ויחסר או יוסיף על תולדתו כפי רביעית גלגל הקטון וכפי רביעיות גלגל המוצק; והוא לבדו במבטיו או במחברת יוכל לבטל מעשי שבתאי, ולא יוכל לבטל מעשי מאדים, רק נגה לבדו יבטל מעשיו. (4) והוא יורה על כל ממונים לשמור ממון, וכפי כחו יהיה עושר הנולד; גם הוא לאות על כח הנפש הצומחת; ובחלקו האוזן השמאלית; ובחלקו הכבד; ומהעינים הירוק; וכחו בפיאה הצפונית; גם הוא יורה על הרוחות ורוב התבואות. (5) והכלל: הוא כוכב אמת, על כן נקרא שמו צדק, כי שבתאי נקרא כן בעבור שישמש יום שבת, ועוד כי בתולדת המתגבר על מולדו לשבות תמיד, והוא יהיה בטל. (6) ובחלק צדק מימי השבוע יום חמישי, ומהלילות ליל שני. (7) והוא ישמש אחר שבתאי בין ביום ובין בלילה י״ב שנים. (8) וככה מספר שנותיו הקטנות, י״ב, והאמצעיות מ״ה, והגדולות ע״ט. (9) ויש אומרים כי הוא יורה על אחי האב; וצורתו לבן, זך וקומה זקופה,

יפה מראה עיניו, ובישן, אוהב שלום ורודף שלום. (10) ומהתחלואים, כל דבר שנוסף בגוף; על כן אמר תלמי המלך לא יקח אדם משקה משלשל והלבנה על מבט צדק או מתחברת עמו, וזה מנוסה. (11) וחלקו מהבית מקום התפילה. (12) מנת צדק: מצדק עד מנת התעלומה, וכמספר הזה מהצומחת. והיא תורה על שכל הנולד, והצלחתו וממונו.

(1) Jupiter. The body of this planet is larger than the body of any other planet except for the Sun. (2) It signifies life, good fortune, wealth, justice, generosity and charity; it signifies judges, teachers of religion, and cantors; of the ages of man, the years approaching old age; in its portion are tin, and apple and pomegranate trees; of riding animals, the elephant; its taste is sweet. (3) Its nature is hot and moist, and its natural properties are increased or diminished depending on the quadrant of the epicycle and the quadrant of the eccentric circle ⟨in which it is located⟩; only this ⟨planet⟩ is capable of canceling out the influence of Saturn, by means of its [Jupiter's] aspects and conjunctions, but it is incapable of canceling out the influence of Mars; only Venus can do that. (4) It signifies all those who are charged with guarding property, and the native's wealth is in accordance to its power; it signifies the power of the vegetative soul; the left ear is in its portion; the liver is in its portion; of the colors, green; its power is in the northern side ⟨of the horizon⟩; it signifies winds and a bumper crop. (5) In general, it is a planet of truth, so it was named *ṣedeq* [meaning justice], and Saturn is called so [*shabbetai*] because it is in charge of the Sabbat [Shabbat] and also because its [Saturn's] nature is to be always at rest, and when it takes possession of a nativity, ⟨the native⟩ will be idle. (6) Of the days of the week, the day⟨time⟩ of the fifth ⟨day⟩ [i.e. from sunrise to sundown on Thursday], and of the nights, the night of the second ⟨day⟩ [i.e., between sundown on Sunday and sunrise on Monday]. (7) It rules after Saturn, ⟨for those born both⟩ by day and by night, for 12 years. (8) This is also the number of its least years, 12, the middle ⟨years⟩ 45, and the great ⟨years⟩ 79. (9) Some say that it signifies the paternal uncle; his [the native's] complexion is white and clear, his posture erect, with beautiful eyes, ⟨he is⟩ shy, loves peace, and seeks peace. (10) Of diseases, any growth [i.e., tumor] in the body; therefore, King Ptolemy said that none should take a purgative when the Moon aspects Jupiter or conjoins it, which has been demonstrated empirically. (11) Its portion of the house is the place of worship. (12) The lot of Jupiter: ⟨Find the distance⟩ between Jupiter and the lot of the absent, and ⟨add⟩ this number to the ascendant ⟨degree⟩. It signifies the native's intelligence, success, and wealth.

V: Mars: *Mishpeṭei ha-mazzalot* § 42:1–15, 526–529; § 52:3, 540–541:

(1) מאדים: נקרא כן בעבור שהוא אדום, כי הוא שופך דם כשר הטבחים, או ינצח מלחמה אם היה בכבודו. (2) ואם בבית מלחמתו או בקלונו, יורה על מקיז דם, ומוציא בכלי המשך והספד, והרופאים החבורות. (3) והכלל: הוא כוכב המכות והתחלואים הממהרים למות והיציאות. (4) והוא יורה על שקר וכזב ומרמות רע; ובחלקו הברזל; ומהאילנים כל דבר מר; ובחלקו סם המות. (5) והכלל: הוא כוכב מלחמה, ואם יתערב עמו צדק, יהיה כחו רב מכח מאדים, וילחם מלחמות שמים והוא כוכב אכזריות וחמה. (6) וצורתו אדום, ופניו אדומים, ועיניו ירוקים, גם הוא ארוך. ואומנותו קצב או ברזילאי.

והכלל: כל מי שעסקו באש כשַמש הפורני והדומה לו. (7) ובחלקו הגנבים והלסטים; ויש לו חלק בערוה; והוא יורה במולד האשה על הבעל; וחלקו מהראש, האף הימני; ומהגוף המרה, ומהעיניים האדום. (8) ובחלקו הכלבים; וממרכבת האדם, הפרדים; ומן הפאות, הדרום; והוא יורה על הרעמים ועל הברקים ואבן האש הנופלת; ובחלקו הנפש הכעסנית. (9) ויש לו חלק גדול בכל אומנות, כי שלשה הם בעלי האומנות: האחד כוכב, כי הוא לאות על כל חכמה ודעת ותבונה ואומנות וסחורה; והשני משתתף עמו והוא נגה לתקן וליפות; והשלישי מאדים בעבור המהירות ולסבול העמל. (10) והוא ישרת במולד האדם אחר צדק שבע שנים. (11) ובחלקו מימי השבוע, יום שלישי, ומהלילות ליל שבת. (12) וכחו בלילה אע״פ שהוא כוכב זכר. (13) ויש לו מן התחלואים השחפת וקדחת יום והשלישית. (14) ושנותיו הקטנות ט״ו, והאמצעיות מ׳ שנה וחצי, והגדולות ס״ו. (15) והוא יורה על האחים והקרובים, והגיסים, והחתנים; וחלקו מהבית, מקום התבשיל. (16) מנת מאדים: ממאדים עד מנת החן וכמספר הזה מהצומחת. והיא תורה על גבורת הנולד וסבול העמל, ולהכנס במקום סכנה.

(1) Mars: it is called so [*ma'adim*] because it is red [*adom*], because it sheds blood like the chief executioner or is victorious in battle if it is in its exaltation. (2) If ⟨it is⟩ in the house of its detriment or of its dejection, it signifies the phlebotomist, the weaponsmith, the tower [i.e., one who tows a barge], the keener, and the physicians ⟨who dress⟩ bruises. (3) In general, it is the planet of blows, and diseases, of those who will soon die, and fluxes. (4) It signifies lies, falsehood, and deception of one's fellow; iron is in its portion; of the trees, anything bitter; deadly poison is in its portion. (5) In general, it is the planet of war, and if Jupiter is mixed with it, its [Jupiter's] power is greater than Mars's power, it wages wars in heaven (Judg. 5:20) and is a planet of cruelty and fury. (6) His [the native under Mars's sway] outward appearance is red, his face is red, his eyes are green, and he is tall. His craft is butcher or blacksmith. Or, in general, anyone who works with fire, like one who tends an oven and the like. (7) In its portion are thieves and robbers; the genitals are in its portion; in a woman's nativity it signifies her husband; of the head, its part is the right nostril; of the body, the ⟨yellow⟩ bile; of the colors, red. (8) Dogs are in its portion; of riding animals, mules; of the sides ⟨of the horizon⟩, south; it signifies thunder, lightning, and meteors; the choleric soul is in its portion. (9) It has a major share in any craft, for there are three lords of crafts: the first is Mercury, which signifies all science, knowledge, understanding, craft, and trade; the second is Venus, which is associated with it [Mercury] to repair and amend; the third is Mars, ⟨which is associated with Mercury⟩ to provide speed and ⟨the ability⟩ to endure hard work. (10) It rules in the nativity of a man for 7 years after Jupiter. (11) Of the days of the week, the day⟨time⟩ of the third ⟨day⟩ [i.e., from sunrise to sundown on Tuesday]; of the nights, the night of Shabbat [i.e., between sundown on Friday and sunrise on Saturday]. (12) Its power is by night, even though it is a masculine planet. (13) Of diseases, consumption and tertian fever are in its portion. (14) Its least years are 15, the middle ⟨years⟩, 40½, and the great ⟨years⟩, 66. (15) It signifies brothers, relatives, brothers-in-law, and sons-in-law; its portion of the house is the kitchen. (16) The lot of Mars: ⟨Find the distance⟩ between Mars and the lot of Fortune, and ⟨add⟩ this number to the ascendant ⟨degree⟩. It signifies the native's strength, ⟨his⟩ capacity to endure hard work, and ⟨his inclination⟩ to enter dangerous places.

VI: Venus: *Mishpeṭei ha-mazzalot* § 43:1–8, 528–529; § 52:4, 540–541:

(1) נגה: כוכב מאיר מאד; והוא יורה על כל שמחה, ותענוג, ומשתה, וכל מיני משכב; ובחלקו הערוה; ובראש האף השמאלי; ובגוף, הכוליא הימנית. (2) והוא יורה על האם, ועל האחיות הקטנות, ועל אשת הנולד; והוא כוכב הניגון והחשק והאהבה; וצורתו יפה מראה ויפה תאר, ואיננו ארוך. (3) והוא כוכב הרופאים, וסוחרי הבשמים, ומיני אלנות ותכשיטי נשים; והוא יורה על כל מנוחה; ובחלקו מהמתכות הנחשת; וממרכבת האדם הכר והגמל; ובחלקו כל מאכל שמן ודשן וכל מיני שכר; ובחלקו הזונות והמרקדות. (4) ותולדתו ממוסך עם מעט קור; והוא יורה על כל תאוה; וכחו בפאה מערבית; ויש לו חלק במטר; וחלקו מהבית מקום מטת האדם. (5) והוא ישמש שמונה שנים אחר השמש בנולד ביום. (6) ובחלקו מימי השבוע, יום ששי, ומהלילות, ליל שלישי. (7) ושנותיו הקטנות, שמונה, והאמצעיות, מ"ה שנים וחצי, והגדולות, פ"ב. (8) והוא יורה על ימי הבחרות. (9) והכלל: אם היה נגה פקיד על חמשה מקומות השררה יהיה הנולד שמח בחלקו. (10) מנת נגה: ממנת החן אל מנת התעלומה. והיא תורה על תכונת הגוף, ויופי הצורה, והשמחה והתענוגים.

(1) Venus: A very bright planet; it signifies any joy, pleasure, feasting, and every kind of sexual intercourse; the genitals are in its portion; in the head, the left nostril; in the body, the right kidney. (2) It signifies the native's mother, younger sisters, and wife; it is the planet of music, desire, and love; his [the native under Venus's sway] form and features are handsome, and he is not tall. (3) It is the planet of physicians, and of spice traders, diverse types of trees and women's jewelry; it signifies every form of rest; of the metals, copper is in its portion; of riding animals, dromedaries and camels; in its portion are every fat and rich food and all sorts of intoxicating liquors; prostitutes and dancers are in its portion. (4) Its nature is temperate, with a bit of cold. It signifies any passion; its power is in the western side ⟨of the horizon⟩; it has a share in rain; its portion of the house is the bedroom. (5) It rules for 8 years, after the Sun, over one born by day. (6) Of the days of the week, the day⟨time⟩ of the sixth ⟨day⟩ [i.e., from sunrise to sundown on Friday], of the nights, the night of the third ⟨day⟩ [i.e., between sundown on Monday and sunrise on Tuesday]. (7) Its least years are 8, the middle ⟨years⟩, 45½, and the great ⟨years⟩, 82. (8) It signifies the days of youth. (9) In general: if Venus is the lord of the five places of dominion, the native will be satisfied with his portion. (10) The lot of Venus: ⟨Find the distance⟩ between the lot of Fortune and the lot of the absent. It signifies the ⟨native's⟩ physical features, beauty of form, joy, and pleasures.

VII: Mercury: *Mishpeṭei ha-mazzalot* § 44:1–9, 530–531; § 52:5, 540–541:

(1) כוכב חמה: הוא יורה בכל נולד על החכמים, והתבונה, והחכמה, ודיקות לשון, ולעשות חרוזים, ולכתוב אגרות; והוא כוכב סופרי המלך, והחשבנים ובעלי המידות; ומהאומנות, אם היה במקום רע, על כל חייט ותופר ואורג. (2) ותולדתו מתהפכת, פעם חם פעם קר, פעם לח פעם יבש, פעם זכר פעם נקבה, פעם טוב פעם רע, כפי תולדת המשרתים המביטים אליו או המתחברים עמו. (3) אמר תלמי: כל מולד שיהיה כוכב נקשר במבט עם המזל הצומח, או עם הלבנה, לא תסור דעת הנולד בחליו. (4) והכלל: הוא יורה על נשמת האדם, כמו שהלבנה תורה על ממסך הגוף, כפי ערכו ומקומו, ואיך

הוא כנגד מזל הצומח. (5) ובחלקו מהמתכות, כסף חי; ובחלקו, הצאן וכל אילן קטן; ובחלקו מהראש, הלשון; ובגוף, הכוליא השמאלית, ויש לו חלק במעים; וכחו בפאה השמאלית. (6) וצורתו דק בשר ופניו ארוכים; ומקומו מהבית, מקום כתבים או דרך האומנות; ויש לו ממשלה על העבדים והמשרתים, והוא כוכב העניות; ובחלקו בעלי המטבע. (7) ושנות שירות בכל נולד אחר נגה י״ג שנה. (8) ובחלקו מימי השבוע, יום רביעי, ומהלילות, ליל ראשון. (9) ושנותיו הקטנות כ׳, והאמצעיות מ״ח, והגדולות ע״ו. (10) מנת כוכב חמה: ממנת התעלומה אל מנת החן, וכמספר הזה מהצומחת. והיא תורה על חסרון כיס והשיבוש והאבידות.

(1) Mercury: For every native it signifies scholars, intelligence, wisdom, precision in the use of language, composing rhymes and writing epistles; it is the planet of the king's scribes, arithmeticians, and geometricians; of crafts, if it is in an inauspicious position, ⟨it signifies⟩ tailors, sempsters, and weavers. (2) Its nature is changeable, sometimes hot and sometimes cold, sometimes moist and sometimes dry, sometimes masculine and sometimes feminine, sometimes auspicious and sometimes inauspicious, depending on the nature of the planets that aspect or conjoin it. (3) Ptolemy said: In any nativity where Mercury is in aspect with the ascendant sign or with the Moon, the native will not go mad on account of his illness. (4) In general, it signifies the human soul, just as the Moon signifies the complexion of the body, depending on its [Mercury's] configuration and position, and its position with respect to the ascendant sign. (5) Of the metals, quicksilver is in its portion; in its portion are sheep and every small tree; of the head, the tongue is in its portion; of the body, the left kidney, and it has a share of the intestines; its power is in the northern side ⟨of the horizon⟩. (6) His [the native under Mercury's sway] form is gaunt and his face is long; its [Mercury's] place in the house: the scriptorium and the craftsman's workroom; it rules over slaves and servants, and it is the planet of poverty; minters are in its portion. (7) It governs all natives [i.e., born by day or at night] after Venus for 13 years. (8) Of the days of the week, the day⟨time⟩ of the fourth ⟨day⟩ [i.e., from sunrise to sundown on Wednesday], of the nights, the night of the first ⟨day⟩ [i.e., between sundown on Saturday and sunrise on Sunday]. (9) Its least years are 20, the middle ⟨years⟩, 48, and the great ⟨years⟩, 76. (10) The lot of Mercury: ⟨Find the distance⟩ between the lot of the absent and the lot of Fortune, and ⟨add⟩ this number to the degree of the ascendant ⟨degree⟩. It signifies penury, confusion, and lost objects.

APPENDIX 11

MĀSHĀʾALLĀH'S BOOK ON READING THOUGHTS

The whole fourth part of *Tractatus particulares* is predominantly a Latin translation, but sometimes a paraphrase or abbreviation, of the Hebrew translation of a lost Arabic work by Māshāʾallāh on reading thoughts. Only a fragment of 26 words of this Hebrew translation survives. By contrast, a complete Latin translation of Māshāʾallāh's work, variously designated *De interpretatione cogitationis*, *De intentione*, or *De cogitationibus ab intentione* (henceforth *De interpretatione*), survives in at least 42 manuscripts. The present appendix offers the Hebrew fragment, accompanied by an English translation, as well as the full text of the Latin translation of Māshāʾallāh's book on reading thoughts. For an English translation of this Latin translation, see *Interpretation*, trans. Dykes (2008). The edition of the Hebrew fragment (which appears in all the extant manuscripts just before *She'elot le-Māshāʾallāh*) is based on a collation of the same manuscripts used for the edition in this volume of the seven passages from *She'elot le-Māshāʾallāh*. See App. 7, p. 497. The edition of the Latin translation offered here is based on a collation of the following sources: (1) Paris, BnF lat. 16204, 13th c., fols. 422b–424a; (2) Paris, BnF lat. 16208, 12th c., fols. 51vb–52rb; (3) Joachim Heller, Nuremberg, Johannes Montanus & Ulricus Neuberus, 1549, sig. Lii–Liii. For easy reference, both the Hebrew fragment and the Latin translation of Māshāʾallāh's book on reading thoughts are divided into sections and passages.

⟨I.: The Hebrew Fragment⟩

1 (1) אמר מאשא אללה לתקן השליט במעלותיו ושבריו, ולתקן בתים שנים עשר. (2) ואמר כי השאלות הם בשלשה ענינים. (3) הענין הראשון לדעת מאיזה דבר בא השואל לשאול. (4) השני לדעת ...

1 (1) Māshāʾallāh said: you should calculate the lord ⟨of the ascendant⟩ in degrees and minutes, and calculate the twelve places. (2) He said that interrogations are about three things. (3) The first thing is to know what topic the querent comes to pose a question about. (4) The second is to know ....

⟨II.: The Latin Translation⟩

Incipit Liber Messehalla de interpretatione cogitationis.
1 (1) Recipit Messehallah ut constituas ascendens per gradus suus atque minutum et domos certissime. (2) Et dixit quod interrogationes sunt tribus modis. (3) Primo, qua de causa venit interrogator, ut scias et de quo interrogat. (4) Secundo, ut scias qua fuerit causa eiusdem interrogationis. (5) Tertio ut scias utrum [423a] perficiatur an non et quem finem habebit.

2 (1) Cum ergo volueris scire hoc, scito significatorem primum secundum quod narrabo tibi, cuius scientia est ut aspicias ascendens, et dominum eius, et Lunam, et dominum domus eius, Solem quoque, et dominum domus eius, et dominum hore, ac partem fortune. (2) Et operare per eum qui habuerit plures authoritates et meliori loco fuerit. (3) Quod si non invenieris aliud de hiis quod dixi tibi, aspice dominum ascendentis, vel dominum exaltationis eius, dominum quoque termini, ac triplicitatis, et faciei. (4) Et scito quis ex istis sit fortior in ascendente, per multitudinem suarum dignitatum. (5) Et aspiciat et hunc constitues significatorem si fuerit in bono loco, et bonitas loci est ut sit in aliqua dignitatum suarum, aut in bono loco a Sole, vel in angulis liber a malis. (6) Operare ergo per eum qui fortior est et habuerit plures dignitates, et fuerit in meliori loco. (7) Et scito quod dominus ascendentis, cum fuerit in ascendente, ipse est dignior ascendente illo plus ceteris. (8) Quod si ⟨non⟩ fuerit in ascendente et fuerit in eo dominus exaltationis ascendentis, ipse solus erit significator. (9) Si vero fuerint ambo in ascendente, essent ambo participes. (10) Si autem fuerit unus eorum cum hac alia dignitas, et fortior loco, fuerit ipse significator et dignior erit. (11) Si iungatur uni eorum aliquis planeta qui habeat dignitatem in ascendente, aut fuerit Luna in domo unius eorum et iuncta fuerit ei, quod si fuerit ita, erit ipse significator propter multitudinem dignitatum. (12) Quod ⟨si⟩ non fuerit in ascendente, quere significatorem, vel Lunam, vel planetam qui fuerit in ascendente, vel in ceteris angulis, et fuerit fortior caeteris in figura. (13) Et scito quod unusquodque signum habet dominum et ascendit in duabus horis, possunt quoque interrogari multa in eis. (14) Et si dominus ascendentis esset significator omnium, essent omnia interrogata sub eodem signo omnia bona vel omnia mala, secundum significationem domini ascendentis, sed not est ita. (15) Similiter et Luna iungitur alicui planetae per totam diem, vel per maximam partem diei, et tamen significatorem significationes rerum sunt diverse in eadem die, quia quedam earum efficiunt, quedam non. (16) Qua propter necesse nobis [423b] est semper significatorem querere. (17) Scito igitur quis sit significator, et dicam tibi ex quibus eligas eum ex domino scilicet ascendentis, et Luna ac domino domus eius ⟨in nocte⟩, et a Sole quoque in die, et a domino domus eius, et a domo partis fortune, et a planeta qui fuerit in angulis, et maxime in ascendente vel in medio celi, qui fortior fuerit in signs.

3 (1) Et scito quod veracior intentio est quando habuerit interrogator in corde per unam diem et noctem vel plus. (2) Cum ergo inveneris significatorem et volueris scire causam interrogationis, id est, unde orta est interrogatio, aspice a quo separatur planeta significator intentionis. (3) Et scito quod causa intentionis fuerit secundum naturam planete, a quo significator separatus est. (4) Et si volueris scire finem intentionis, scito cui significator iungitur. (5) Et scito quia finis intentionis erit per significationem planete cui iungitur.

4 (1) Et nunc statuam tibi exemplum per quod universas interrogationes et rerum significationes poteris percipere, si Deus volueris. (2) Exemplar, interrogatio cuius ascendens fuerit Taurus .x., et Venus domina eius in Cancro .xv. gradu in domo sciliter Lune. (3) Et similiter Luna in Libra in domo Veneris, in gradu .x. (4) Eratque Luna peregrina, quia non erat in domo sua, neque in exaltatione sua vel triplicitate sed iungebatur Veneri ex .iiii. aspectu et erat recepta. (5) Dominus quoque partis fortune erat *zoal* [*zuḥal*], id est Saturnus, qui erat in Leone peregrinus, neque erat receptus.

5 (1) Aspexi itaque omnes planetas, sed non inveni in eis fortiorem Venere loco, quia ipsa erat domina Tauri, *athale* [*al-thawr* = Taurus], et erat in triplicitate sua. (2) Aspexi ergo dominum domus in quo erat, eratque in domo Lune. (3) ⟨In⟩cepi ergo querere postea ubi esset *alcamara* [*al-qamar*], Luna [above the line], ut ab eo quererem significatorem, eo quod esset domina domus *azore* [*al-zuhrah* = Venus], qui Venus erat domina *athale* [*al-thawr* = Taurus] quem inveni *almuzene* [*al-miyzān* = Libra], id est .viª. domo ab *athala* [*al-thawr*], et in .iiiiº. loco a significatore qui erat *azora* [*al-zuhrah* = Venus]. (4) Et *alacama* [*al-qamar*], Luna [above the line] significat matres. (5) Novi igitur hoc quod interrogaret de infirmitate matris.
6 (1) Et cum voluerit scire esse eius, aspexi a quo separetur *alcamara* [*al-qamar*], Luna [above the line], que separabatur a *zoal* [*zuḥal*], a Saturno [above the line]. (2) Novique quod pateretur infirmitatem frigidam et siccam. (3) Voluique scire in quo membro esset infirmitas. (4) Et aspexi *zoal* [*zuḥal*], Saturnum [above the line], in prima [424a] facie *alased* [*al-'asad*], Leonis [above the line]. (5) Et *alased* [*al-'asad*], Leo [above the line], habet ex membris corporis stomachum. (6) Dixique quod pateretur in stomacho.
7 (1) Cum autem vellem scire quem finem haberet, aspexi cui iungebatur *alcamara* [*al-qamar*], Luna [above the line], que significabat intentionem, que iungebatur *azoare* [*al-zuhrah*], Venus [above the line]. Dixique quod liberaretur propter *azoram* [*al-zuhrah*], Venerem [above the line], que est fortuna, et recipiebat eam. (2) Et cum voluissem scire tempus liberationis eius, aspexi gradus coniunctionis que erant inter *azoram* [*al-zuhrah*], Venerem [above the line], et *alcamaram* [*al-qamar*], Lunam [above the line]. Dixi quod liberaretur post tot dies quot errant gradus. (3) Et posui dies, quia *alcamara* [*al-qamar*], Luna [above the line], erat in mobile signo. (4) Si enim esset in signo communi, ponerem menses, et si in fixo, annos. (5) Et si *alcamara* [*al-qamar*], Luna [above the line], iungeretur *zoal* [*zuḥal*], Saturno [above the line], vel *almarer* [*al-mirraykh*], Marti [above the line], dicerem quod moretur post tantum temporis.
8 (1) Sic aspice in intentione, et in occultis, et in universis rebus de quibus interrogaris, id est, hoc modo scito, quem finem habebit. (2) Et similiter constitue tempore effectus rerum, secundum hoc exemplar et commisce significationes planetarum significationibus signorum, et patebit tibi res omnis intentionis atque interrogationis, secundum quod exposui tibi, si Deus voluerit.
9 (1) Et scito quod si esset Venus in loco Lune, dicerem quod queret de muliere. (2) Si esset tunc in .viiº., dicerem quod tunc queret de coniugio, et si esset in .vº., de filiis, et si in .xiº, de amicis. (3) Et si esset Sol in loco Lune, dicerem quod interrogabat de patre. (4) Et si esset in .xº. de rege. (5) Et si esset in ascendente, de aliquo principatu. (6) Et in .viiii. de fide. (7) Et in .iii. de peregrinatione.
10 (1) Et si esset Mars in loco Lune, quereret de fugitivo vel de latrone. (2) Et si esset in ascendente significaret timorem. (3) Et in secundo latrocinium et ablationem. (4) Et in .iii. fratrem. (5) Et in .vii. adversarium pugnantem contra eum.
11 (1) Et si esset *attatarit* [*al-'utarid*], Mercurius [above the line], in loco *adgoek*, Lune [above the line], quereret de epistola vel de sapientia. (2) Et si esset Iupiter in .ix., dicetur quod quereret de sompnio. (3) Et iam exposui tibi superius qualiter misceas significationes planetarum significationibus signorum.

Explicit Liber Messehalla de interpretatione cogitationis.

APPENDIX 12

THE SECTION ON ELECTIONS AT THE END OF *NATIVITATES*

Nativitates, the Latin translation of the lost *Moladot* II, follows the twelve chapters on the horoscopic places with an additional section headed "Chapter on Generalities." The last paragraphs of this section, which amount to the bulk of it, are devoted to general principles related to the interpretation of the electional horoscope. Here I offer the Latin text, accompanied by an English translation, of the entire section on elections found at the end of *Nativitates*, II vi 8:5, 136–137, as they were published in *Nativitates*, ed. Sela (2019). I have kept the same division of sentences of this text as in this edition.

Was this section on elections a genuine part of *Moladot* II or a later addition? *El*, I 7:3 reads as follows: "After the discussion of the 12 places in the *Book of Nativities*, I have written for you a chapter on elections; do not forget to look at it." This past tense cross-reference demonstrates that the section of *Nativitates* on elections was an integral part of *Moladot* II and not a later addition. Why was such a section placed at the end of a treatise on nativities? The first sentence of the section reads as follows: "If you need to choose for the native an ascendant degree to begin some undertaking, be careful that the ascendant sign ⟨of the electional chart⟩ should not be the sixth, eighth, or twelfth place ⟨of the natal chart⟩ for any undertaking." This shows that this section was incorporated because it deals with the special case of elections in which the querent knows his nativity, which is not always the case, and addresses general principles on elections in which the interpretation of the electional horoscope depends on the features of the querent's natal horoscope.

Capitulum De communitate

1 (1) Si indigueris eligere gradus ascendentis pro nato ad incipiendum aliqua rem, cave ne sit signum ascendens in omni re domus sexta vel octava vel duodecima. (2) Et si sit pro itinere tunc est bonun eligere tertiam vel nonam. (3) Et debes videre duo. (4) Unum est quod Luna non sit in loco stelle malivole, licet sit illa stella mala in honore suo. (5) Et si eligeris diem et punctum in quo Luna sit in puncto in quo fuit stella bona in nativitate tunc bene eliges. (6) Et secundum est quod non ascendat signum in quo fuerit stella mala. (7) Et si non inveneris bene hoc cave ne sit gradus ascendens in loco stelle male nec in facie in qua erat.

2 (1) Verbi gratia: fuerit Saturnus in .8. gradu signi Tauri cave ne sit ascendens in facie signi Tauri prima. (2) Item non ascendat .13. gradus quia deberet quod distancia sit inter gradus ascendentem et locum stelle male plus .5. gradus, et verum quod non sit gradus ascendentis nisi post .17. gradus eo quod radiacio Saturni est .9. gradus ante et retro. (3) Verbi gratia fuerit Saturnus in .21. gradus Tauri, cave ne ascendat facies ultima, et ascendat totam facies prima, et non tota secunda,

hoc est quod non sit ascendens gradus ultima .12. gradus propter scintillacionem Saturni que est .9. gradus. (4) Et si potes in eleccione ascendere gradus in quo est stella non combusta vel in aspectu malo stelle male aut retrograde, item quod non sit prepositus in domo mala respectu gradu ascendentis tunc erit melius. (5) Et sicut locutus fui tibi super loca stellarum ita facies in verbis aspectuum in gradibus equalibus, secundum hoc quod erunt in nativitate et secundum aspectus bonos vel malos sicut scriptum est in *Libro primo de sensu*. (6) Sunt terminata iudicia nativitatum. (7) Laus nomini illius cuius sunt bonitates. Explicit. Amen. Deo gracias per omnia.

Chapter on generalities

1 (1) If you need to choose for the native an ascendant degree to begin some undertaking, be careful that the ascendant sign ⟨of the electional chart⟩ should not be the sixth, eighth, or twelfth place ⟨of the natal chart⟩ for any undertaking. (2) But if ⟨the election is⟩ for a journey, then it is fortunate to choose ⟨as the ascendant sign of the electional chart⟩ the third or ninth place ⟨of the natal chart⟩. (3) You need to observe two ⟨things⟩. (4) The first is that the Moon should not be in the same position as a malevolent star, even if this malefic star is in its exaltation. (5) If you are choosing a day ⟨to begin some undertaking⟩ and the moment in which the Moon is ⟨in the electional chart⟩ is the same as the moment in which a benefic star is in the nativity, then you are choosing well. (6) The second thing is that the sign rising ⟨in the electional chart⟩ should not be the same as the sign in which there was a malefic star ⟨in the natal chart⟩. (7) But if you do not find a benefic ⟨planet⟩ ⟨in the natal chart⟩, be careful that the ascendant degree ⟨in the electional chart⟩ should not coincide with the position of a malefic star ⟨in the natal chart⟩, or in the decan where it [the malefic planet] was.

2 (1) For example: if Saturn is in Taurus 8° ⟨in the natal chart⟩, be careful that ⟨in the electional chart⟩ the ascendant is not in the first decan of Taurus. (2) Also, be careful that ⟨in the electional chart⟩ the ascendant is not in ⟨Taurus⟩ 13°, because there needs to be a distance of more than 5° between the degree of the ascendant ⟨in the electional chart⟩ and the position of the malefic star ⟨in the natal chart⟩; in truth, the ascendant degree ⟨in the electional chart⟩ should be more than 17° ⟨from the position of Saturn in the natal chart⟩, because Saturn's ray is 9°, ahead or behind. (3) For example: if Saturn is at Taurus 21° ⟨in the natal chart⟩, be careful that ⟨in the electional chart⟩ the ascendant is not in the last decan ⟨of Taurus⟩, but allow that ⟨in the electional chart⟩ the ascendant is in the whole first decan ⟨of Taurus⟩, and ⟨be careful that in the electional chart⟩ the ascendant is not in the whole second decan ⟨of Taurus⟩, meaning that the ascendant is not in ⟨Taurus⟩ 12° [i.e., $12 = 21 - 9$], because Saturn's ray is 9°. (4) It is better if in the election [i.e., in the electional chart] you allow that the ascendant is a degree that coincides with the position of a star that is not burnt ⟨in the natal chart⟩, or ⟨with the position of a planet which is not in⟩ an aspect with a malefic star or retrograde, also ⟨with the position of a planet which is not⟩ the ruler in an inauspicious place with respect to the ascendant degree. (5) Just as I have told you what to do about the positions of the stars, so you should proceed about matters related to the aspects in equal

degrees, according to how they were in the nativity, and according to auspicious and inauspicious aspects, as is written in the *Book of the Beginning of Wisdom*. (6) The judgments of the nativities have been completed. (7) Praise to the name of He to whom all good pertains. Completed, Amen. Thanks to God for everything.

APPENDIX 13

FRAGMENTS OF *EPISTOLA ARGAFALAU AD ALEXANDRUM*

This appendix offers a section of *Epistola Argafalau ad Alexandrum* (henceforth *Epistola Argafalau*), which is one of the components of the so-called *Alchandrena*, an astrological corpus translated and adapted from Arabic in the tenth century, but with Hebrew and Latin sources as well. This section of *Epistola Argafalau* has been selected because it has a close counterpart in the section of *Tractatus particulares* that deals with how the astrologer can know the querent's thoughts and what the querent is hiding in his hand, depending on whether the question was posed at the beginning, in the middle, or at the end of the hours during which each of the seven planets is in charge, every day of the week. Here I use the edition of this text by David Juste, who also discovered the relationship of the *Alchandrena* to the *Tractatus particulares*. See *Alchandreana*, ed. Juste (2007), 168–170, 274–275, 277 n. 230. The section of *Epistola Argafalau* is accompanied here by an English translation (not provided in Juste's edition). It has been divided into seven parts, each dealing with the indications related to one of the seven planets. For easy reference, the parts are numbered, and each is headed by the name of the planet in question as well as by a reference to the relevant page in Juste's edition.

I: The Sun (*Epistola Argafalau* 2:3–5, in *Alchandreana*, ed. Juste, 474)

> Igitur si in prima parte horae cui praeest Sol ad te quaerendi gratia aliquid aut quid sit quod in manu clausum abscondit interrogandi venerit, respondas iuxta naturam ipsius planetae velle illum aliquid aut de semetipso aut socio suo tecum agere; in manu autem quod tenet est aliquid terrae. Si autem in parte secunda horae eiusdem, consilium derogandi, sicilicet bello, obsidione, munitione aut potestate quam se adepturum credit, aut de pavore aliquarum inimicitiarum tecum agere, in manu argentum aut os aut terram tenet. Si in fine horae ipsius venerit, iratus, consilium quaerit, qua arte minas quas sibi potens iudex aliquis incussit declinare possit; in manu, lanam labam habens aut particulam albam aut filum laneum album.
>
> Therefore, if during the first part of the hour over which the Sun presides someone comes to inquire for some favor or to ask about something hidden that he is concealing in his hand, answer, according to the nature of the planet, that he wants to deal with you either about himself or about his partner; ⟨as for what he holds⟩ in his hand: this is something made of earth. If in the second part of its hour, ⟨it is about⟩ modifying a decision, that is, about war, a siege, a fortification, or an office that he believes he is about to obtain, or to deal with you about fear of enemies; in his hand he holds silver, a bone, or earth. If he comes at the end of its hour, in a fury, he will ask for advice

about how he can turn away threats that some powerful judge issued against him; in his hand he holds a piece of white wool or something white or a white woolen thread.

II: Venus (*Epistola Argafalau*, 2:6–8, in *Alchandreana*, ed. Juste, 474–475)

Horae vero Veneris si initio venerit, aget tecum de femina quam habere cupit; in manu, animal exanimatum vel aliquid mittendum in focum. Si parte secunda quaestionem moturus advenit qua te temptatum postmodum reprehendat; in manu, vile aliquid tortum. Si in fine horae ipsius, aget tecum de femina et causa quam habet cum socio suo; in manu, germen terrae aut aliquid quod ablui solet.

If he comes at the beginning of Venus's hour, he will deal with you about a woman whom he desires to have; in his hand ⟨is⟩ a dead animal or something that has to be put in a fireplace. If he comes in the second part ⟨of its hour⟩ to pose a question, you will be tempted but later he will find fault with; in his hand ⟨is something⟩ worthless and twisted. If at the end of its hour, he will deal with you about a woman and about a lawsuit he has with his partner; in his hand ⟨is⟩ something that grows from the earth or something that is usually washed.

III: Mercury (*Epistola Argafalau*, 2:9–11, in *Alchandreana*, ed. Juste, 475)

In initio vero horae Mercurii, quaerit sapientiam; in manu, rem edibilem, brevem set amplam, exterius siccam, interius vero sucosam. Si in parte media, de infirmitate sui aut alterius aget; in manu, germen terrae nigrum, edibile. Si in fine horae ipsius, de re perdita aut fugitivo aliquo inquiret; in manu, onichinum vel gemmam aliquam pertusam.

At the beginning of Mercury's hour, he inquires about wisdom; in his hand: something edible, short and broad, dry on the outside but moist on the inside. If in the middle part ⟨of Mercury's hour⟩, he will treat of his or another's disease; in ⟨his⟩ hand: something black that grows from the earth and is edible. If at the end of its hour, he inquires about something lost or a fugitive; in ⟨his⟩ hand ⟨is⟩ a bead [*lit.* something with a hole pierced through it] ⟨made of⟩ onyx or another precious stone.

IV: The Moon (*Epistola Argafalau*, 2:12–14, in *Alchandreana*, ed. Juste, 475)

Inchoante autem hora Lunae si venerit, de infirmitate oculorum quaeret; in manu, herbam odoriferam. Si in altera parte, de homine peregrinante aut re perdita; in manu, lapidem furvum. Si in fine horae ipsius, de re perdita; in manu, auripigmentum uel aliud rubeum.

If he comes at the beginning of the Moon's hour, he will inquire about a disease of the eyes; in ⟨his⟩ hand ⟨is⟩ a fragrant herb. If ⟨he comes⟩ in the second part ⟨of the Moon's hour⟩, ⟨he will inquire⟩ about a person who is abroad or a lost thing; in ⟨his⟩ hand ⟨is⟩ a dark stone. If ⟨he comes⟩ at the end of its hour, ⟨he will inquire⟩ about a lost thing; in ⟨his⟩ hand ⟨is⟩ orpiment or something red.

V: Saturn (*Epistola Argafalau*, 2:15–17, in *Alchandreana*, ed. Juste 2007, 475)

In initio vero horae Satumi si venerit, librum apportat, in quo aliquid a te quaerit; in manu, vitrum aut viride aliquid. Si in parte altera, de femina utrum gravida sit masculo an femina; si in hora masculi, id est in die, masculum; si in hora feminae, id est in nocte, feminam responde; in manu, ferrum vel aliud quod mitti in focum solet. Si in fine horae ipsius, de infirmitate sui aut amicorum, aut bello ineundo, aut dolore aliquo; in manu, caput avis variae.

If he comes at the beginning of Saturn's hour, he will bring a book, in which he asks you something; in ⟨his⟩ hand ⟨is⟩ glass or something green. If ⟨he comes⟩ in the second part ⟨of Saturn's hour⟩, ⟨he will inquire⟩ about a woman, whether she is pregnant with a boy or a girl; if he comes in a masculine hour, that is, by day, it is a boy; if he comes in a feminine hour, that is, by night, answer that it is a girl. In ⟨his⟩ hand ⟨is⟩ iron or something that is usually put in a fireplace. If at the end of its hour, ⟨he will inquire⟩ about his or his friends' disease, or about going to war, or about some pain; in ⟨his⟩ hand ⟨is⟩ the head of a parti-colored bird.

VI: Jupiter (*Epistola Argafalau*, 2:18–20, in *Alchandreana*, ed. Juste 2007, 475–476)

In initio horae Iouis, medicinam de daemoniaco; in manu, rem tortam quae mitti solet in focum aut sigillum aut ferrum. Si in parte altera eiusdem horae, pro pecunia aliqua adquirenda aget tecum; in manu, rubei aut albi coloris aliquid sive sigillum cum gemma uiridi rubeo permixta. Si in fine horae ipsius, quaeret si pacem inter duos aliquos facere possit, aut si inveniet iuxta quod audivit repositam in terra pecuniam; in manu, stagnum aut corrigiam aut corium.

At the beginning of Jupiter's hour, ⟨he will ask for⟩ a medicine for one possessed by an evil spirit; in ⟨his⟩ hand ⟨is⟩ a twisted thing that is usually put in a fireplace, a statue, or iron. If ⟨he comes⟩ in the second part of its hour, he will deal with you about acquiring some wealth; in ⟨his⟩ hand ⟨is⟩ something red or white, or a seal with a mixed green and red precious stone. If at the end of its hour, he will inquire whether it is possible to make peace between two parts, or whether he will find, just as he heard, a treasure deposited in the earth; in ⟨his⟩ hand ⟨is⟩ tin, a shoelace, or a hide.

VII: Mars (*Epistola Argafalau*, 2:21–23, in *Alchandreana*, ed. Juste 2007, 476)

In initio horae Martis, quaeret qua arte illius potentis minas aut illius cuiuscumque insidias declinare; in manu, rem longam, rubeam, de auro aut aera-mine. Si in altera parte, de re perdita; in manu, aliquid parvulum rubeum. Si in fine horae ipsius, de labore inimicitiarum aut infirmitatis tecum aget; in manu, lignum aut aliquid quod est siccum.

At the beginning of Mars's hour, he will inquire about the way to escape from the threats of some powerful person or from the ambush of someone; in ⟨his⟩ hand ⟨is⟩ something long, red, made of gold or bronze. If ⟨he comes⟩ in the second part ⟨of its hour,⟩ ⟨he will inquire⟩ about something lost; in ⟨his⟩ hand ⟨is⟩ something small and red. If ⟨he comes⟩ at the end of its hour, he will deal with you about trouble related to the enemies or a disease; in ⟨his⟩ hand ⟨is⟩ wood or something dry.

APPENDIX 14

ENGLISH-LATIN GLOSSARY OF TECHNICAL TERMS
(*LIBER ELECTIONUM, LIBER INTERROGATIONUM, TRACTATUS PARTICULARES*)

	English	*Electiones*	References	*Interrogationes*	References	*Tractatus particulares*	References
1*	add	addere augere	II v 2:5,6 I 1:2	addere	II vii 1:10,12		
2	airy sign					signa aerea	III 4:9
3*	Aquarius	Aquarius	II ii 1:1; II iv 1:3; II vi 6:4	Aquarius	II i 6:4	Aquarius	I ii 8:2
4	Arabic language	lingua Arabica	II vi 2:2	lingua sarracenaca	I 1:8		
5*	Aries	Aries	II i 2:9; II vi 2:1; II vii 5:5	Aries	II i 6:11	Aries	I i 8:1; I ii 8:2

	English	*Electiones*	References	*Interrogationes*	References	*Tractatus particulares*	References
6*	ascendant	ascendens	II i 1:6; II iii 3:1,2; II iv 2:1; II v 1:1; II vii 1:4,6; II vii 2:1; II vii 4:2,3,4; II vii 5:2,4; II vii 6:1; II viii 1:3	ascendens	II i 6:8; II i 7:5,6,8; II i 12:3,5; II i 13:2,4; II i 14:2; II ii 1:2; II ii 2:1,4,8; II ii 3:2,4,5,6; II ii 5:5; II iii 1:3; II iv 2:1,2,4; II v 1:6	ascendens	I i 1:2,3; I i 2:1; I i 3:1,2; I i 4:7,8; I i 5:3; I i 6:2; I i 8:1; I ii 8:3; I iii 2:1,2,3; I iii 3:1; I iii 4:2
7*	ascendant degree	gradus ascendentis	II ii 1:3; II iv 1:1; II iv 4:1; II v 2:3,4,5,7; II v 3:2; II vii 5:4	gradus ascendentis	I 1:4,5; I 3:3; II i 1:1,2; II i 1:1,2; II i 9:1,2; II i 12:4; II v 5:1; II vi 2:4; II vii 1:10.12	gradus ascenden-tis	I i 4:3,7,8; II vii 1:2
8*	ascendant sign	signum ascendentis signum ascendens	I 7:2; II i 1:7; II ii 1:2; II vii 1:3; II vii 3:3	signum ascendentis signum ascendens	I 1:2; II i 7:4,7; II i 11:1,3; II i 12:2; II i 13:1; II xii 3:1; II xii 9:4	signum ascenden-tis signum ascendens	I I 3:4; I ii 3:1; II vii 8:2
9*	aspect (noun)	aspectus	II i 1:3,4,5; II i 2:1–5; II ii 2:1; II iii 1:1; II iv 2:1	aspectus	II i 4:2; II i 9:6; II i 13:4,9; II ii 2:2; II ii 5:3	aspectus	I iv 1:5,8; I iv 3:3; II iv 1:4; II vii 6:2
10*	aspect (verb)	aspicere	II i 1:1; II ii 1:3; II iii 2:1; II i 3:1; II iv 3:1	aspicere	II i 7:5,6,8; II i 8:3,4; II i 9:2; II i 13:3,5; II ii 1:1	aspicere respicere	I i 4:8; I iii 2:1; I iv 1:5,8; II i 1:3 I i 4:7; II i 1:2

	English	*Electiones*	References	*Interrogationes*	References	*Tractatus particulares*	References
11	aspect of hate (quartile)	aspectus odii	I 2:2				
12*	aspect of love (trine)	aspectus dilectionis	II vii 1:3; II vii 2:1	aspectus dilectionis	II x 1:1		
				aspectus amicabilis	II ii 3:5; II vii 2:6; II vii 6:1		
13*	associate	associare	II xi 1:2	associare	II i 7:7; II ii 2:4; II iii 2:3,4; II vi 1:7,8,9; II vii 1:11,12; II viii 2:3; II xii 2:6,7	adiungere	I i 4:7
						coniungare	I i 4:8
14*	astrologers	sapientes iudiciorum signorum	I 2:1; II vii 4:3	sapientes iudiciorum signorum	I 1:1		
*		sapientes signorum	I 5:5; II i 2:6; II ix 4:1	sapientes signorum	I 3:2; II i 10:2		
		sapientes in iudiciis	I 6:2				
				sapientes dominus signorum	II xii 3:1 II i 12:4; II i 13:1	sapientes	I ii 8:1; I iii 1:1; IV 7:2

	English	*Electiones*	References	*Interrogationes*	References	*Tractatus particulares*	References
						sapiens in scientia signorum	II i 3:2
15*	auspicious	bonum	I 3:2; I 7:1; II i 1:4,5,7; II i 2:2,4,5,6; II iii 1:1	bonum	II i 13:4; II i 3:9; II iii 1:1; II iii 2:4; II vi 1:2; II x 1:2,7; II xii 1:7	bonum	I 1:3; II vii 3:4; IV 7:2
16*	auspicious aspect	aspectus bonus	II v 4:1; II x 2:1	aspectus bonus	II x 1:2		
17*	auspicious position	locus bonus	II ii 1:3,5; II iii 1:1; II iii 3:1; II iv 3:1; II iv 4:1; II x 1:2; II xi 1:1	locus bonus	II i 13:4; II vi 1:3		
18	auspicious sign			signum bonum	II ii 3:9	signum bonum	IV 7:2
19*	author	additor	I 1:1; I 3:1	additor addens	II i 9:1; II xii 2:1 II i 2:1		
20	barren sign			domus radicis sterilis	II v 1:6		

	English	*Electiones*	References	*Interrogationes*	References	*Tractatus particulares*	References
21*	be in conjunction with	coniungere	II ii 2:2	coniungere	II i 2:2; II i 9:5,6; II i 13:3,5; II ii 1:1,3; II ii 2:5		
22*	be victorious	vincere	II vii 3:3,5; II vii 5:1; II vii 6:3	vincere	II vii 3:3; II vii 4:4–7		
23*	below the Earth [i.e., the horizon]	sub terra	II i 1:7; II iv 1:2; II v 2:5	sub terra	II i 1:1; II viii 2:3; II xu 6:3		
24*	benefic star	stella bona	II i 1:2; II ii 1:3; II iii 1:2; II iv 1:1; II iv 2:1; II iv 3:1; II vii 3:1	stella bona	II i 9:5; II ii 5:2; II vi 1:4,11; II vi 2:4	fortuna	I iii 1:2
						planeta fortune	I iv 1:7
25	beneficence					bonitas	IV 6:1
26*	bicorporal signs	signa bicorpora	II viii 1:5; II x 1:5	signa bicorpora	II iii 2:3; II v 3:6; II vi 2:2; II viii 1:6; II ix 2:3; II x 2:4; II xii 1:5; II xii 6:3	communia	I iii 1:3; IV 6:4
				domini duorum corporum	II i 4:1; II i 6:1,2		

	English	*Electiones*	References	*Interrogationes*	References	*Tractatus particulares*	References
27*	birth	nativitas	II v 2:3,4; II v 3:2	nativitas	I 1:2		
		partus	II v 2:1; II v 3:2				
28	body	corpus	I 5:2,3,4; II i 2:8			corpus	II:6; II i 1:2; II i 8:1; II iv 8:1; II v 4:1; II vi 1:1; II vi 4:3; II vii 8:3
29*	burning	combustio	II iv 1:1,2; II vii 5:5,6; II ix 4:2; II ix 4:2	combustio	II i 3:5		
				inflammatio	II i 2:1		
				reflammatio	II i 1:5		
30*	burnt	combustus	II i 1:5; II ii 1:4,5; II iii 1:1; II iv 1:1,3; II iv 2:1; II vii 1:1,4; II vii 3:2; II vii 5:1,6; II vii 1:2; II ix 4:2; II x 1:4	combustus	II i 13:3; II ii 1:2; II ii 4:2; II v 1:6; II vi 1:3; II vii 1:6; II vii 2:3; II vii 3:5; II xii 7:9,10	combustus	I i 1:1; I i 2:1,3; I i 3:4; I iv 1:9,19
				reflammetur	II i 2:1		
31*	cadent (place)	domus cadentes	II ii 1:2; II iv 2:1; II vii 3:3	domus cadentes	II i 3:5; II ii 3:10; II ii 5:2,3; II v 4:2; II vii 2:3; II vii 3:4; II xii 9:4		
				cadentes a cavillis	II i 3:2		

	English	*Electiones*	References	*Interrogationes*	References	*Tractatus particulares*	References
				domus cadentes ab angulis	II v 2:4; II vii 3:7		
32	cadent (planet)			cadens	II i 7:5,8		
33*	calculate	computare	II v 3:2	computare	II v 5:4	computare	I iii 4:5
		preparare	II v 1:1; II v 2:7; II v 4:2,3; II vii 1:6; II vii 2:1; II ix 3:1–7; II xii 1:1,2				
		equare	I 6:1				
34*	Cancer	Cancer	I 2:2; II ii 1:1; II iii 3:1; II iv 3:2; II vii 4:1; II vii 7:2; II xii 1:3	Cancer	I 1:2; II i 6:4; II i 8:3; II vi 2:4	Cancer	IV 3:1; IV 4:1,2,3
35*	Capricorn					Capri-cornius	I ii 8:2

	English	*Electiones*	References	*Interrogationes*	References	*Tractatus particulares*	References
36*	cardines	anguli	II ii 1:2,5; II ii 2:1; II iii 2:1,2; II iv 1:1; II v 1:1; II v 4:3; II vii 3:3; II viii 1:1; II x 1:3	anguli	II iii 2:2; II v 1:3,4; II v 2:4; II v 3:1,2; II v 4:4; II vi 1:3; II vi 2:5; II vii 1:5,9; II vii 2:3,4,7; II vii 6:1; II viii 1:2,3; II ix 2:1,5; II x 1:1,2,4,6; II xi 1:3; II xii 1:2,3,4,6; II xii 6:2; II xii 9:4; II xii 10:3	anguli	I iii 1:2; I iv 3:4; I iv 4:3; II iii 1:2
				caville	II i 1:4,5; II i 3:2; II i 6:9; II i 9:4,6; II ii 1:2; II ii 2:6,7; II ii 3:8		
37	change	mutare	I 1:1; I 3:1			mutare	II vii 3:4
38*	child	infans puer	I 1:5 II v 2:4	infans	II i 1:1	infans puer	III 5:5; III 5:9 I i 1:7; III 5:10
39	choose	eligere	I 2:3,4; I 3,2; I 4,2; I 5,1; I 6,1; II i 1:1; II i 2:7; II iii 3:3; II iv 4:1; II vii 1:1; II vii 3:1; II vii 7:1,6; II vii 1:1; II ix 2:1; II x 1:1,2; II xii 1:1				

	English	*Electiones*	References	*Interrogationes*	References	*Tractatus particulares*	References
40*	circle	circulus	II i 1:2; II ii 1:1; II vi 1:2,3; II vii 3:5; II xii 1:3	circulus	II i 2:1; II i 6:3; II i 13:6; II i 14:1; II xii 2:5		
41*	city	villa	II iii 3:3; II iv 2:1; II vi 7:1; II vi 12:2; II vi 18:1; II vi 20:1; II vi 26:1; II vii 7:1	villa	II i 15:4,5; II ii 3:8,11; II iv 2:1,3		
42	cold (adjective)					frigidus	II ii 8:1; II iii 8:1,2; II vii 3:4
43	cold (noun)					frigor	II vi 8:1
44	collectives	communes	I 1:2	universales	I 2:2		
45	complexion					complexio	II vii 1:2
46*	computation	computatio	I 1:1	computatio	I 2:2		
47	conception	conceptio	I 1:4; II v 2:1,3; II v 3:2				
48*	configuration	dispositio	II vii 1:2; II vii 4:1	dispositio	I 1:2; II i 1:2,5; II iv 2:1; II v 5:1; II ix 1:5; II xii 5:1; II xii 9:4	dispositio	III 12:3

	English	*Electiones*	References	*Interrogationes*	References	*Tractatus particulares*	References
49*	conjunction	coniunctio	II i 1:3,4; II i 2:3,4,5; II vii 3:1; II vii 6:3,5	coniunctio	I 1:3; II i 1:5; II i 9:1; II i 13:4,6; II ii 2:2	coniunctio	I iv 1:5,8; I iv 3:3,4; II iv 1:4
50	count					numerus	I i 3:4; I i 8:1; I iii 4:4,6,7
51* *	country	patria terra	II iv 2:1 II x 1:7	patria terra	II iv 2:2 II i 8:2		
52	course	cursus	II ii 1:4				
53	critical days			dies terminorum	II vi 2:7	termini infirmita-tum	II ii 8:1
54*	crooked sign	signum tortuosum	II x 1:5	signum tortuosum	II iv 1:1		
55*	cusp (of horoscopic place)	principium	II iv 3:2; II v 1:6	principium	II xii 10:5	principium	I iv 4:4
56*	day	dies	I 3:3; I 6:1; II i 2:1; II v 2:4,5; II v 4:3; II vi 1:3,4; II vi 3:1; II vi 7:2	dies	II i 6:2,11; II i 9:1; II i 13:5; II vi 2:5,6; II ix 2:1,5; II xii 2:4	dies	I i 4:5; II i 2:1; II i 5:1; II i 6:1,2; II ii 5:1; II ii 6:1,2; II iii 6:3; II iv 6:1,2

	English	*Electiones*	References	*Interrogationes*	References	*Tractatus particulares*	References
57*	death	mors	I 4:2; II iii 3:1	mors	II vi 2:2,5	mors	I i 1:10; II iii 13:2; III 4:3,4,6; III 8:2,3,4,7,10
58	decan					facies	I i 7:1
59	decreed	divisum	I 2:3				
60	decrees	divisiones	I 1:4; I 4:3				
61*	degree	gradus	II v 2:4; II vi 1:2,3,4; II vi 9:1	gradus	I i 3:4; II i 1:5; II i 2:2; II i 13:5; II vi 2:4	gradus	I i 3:1,2,4; I i 5:6,9; I i 5:3; II iii 4:1
62	dejection (see house of dejection)			vilitas	II i 6:12	lapsus	I i 1:1
63	delivery	partus	I 1:4				
64	dignity	bonum	II vii 3:5	potestas	II v 1:5; II v 4:5; II xii 2:7	dignitas	I i 4:8
65	direct (verb)			ducere	II vi 2:6		

	English	*Electiones*	References	*Interrogationes*	References	*Tractatus particulares*	References
66*	direct in its course	directus in cursu suo	II ii 1:4; II vii 3:4; II x 2:3	directus in cursu suo	II iv 1:1; II x 2:2		
67	direction			ductus	I 1:3; II i 15:2		
68*	disease	infirmitas	I 5:2	infirmitas	II vi 2:1,2	infirmitas	I i 1:14; I ii 3:2; I ii 5:3; I ii 6:1
						morbus	II i 8:1; II iii 8:1; II iv 8:1; II v 8:1; IV 5:2
69*	distance	distantia	II v 2:5,6; II vi 6:4	distantia	II vii 1:10,12	distantia	II ii 1:1
70	diurnal	de die	II vii 5:4	diurnus	II vi 1:7		
71	diversity	diversitas	I 1:1				
72	division of the rising times	divisio ascensiones	II ix 2:5; II x 1:6				
73	doctrines			iura	I 1:2,3		
74	dodecate-moria					duodecime	I i 7:3

	English	*Electiones*	References	*Interrogationes*	References	*Tractatus particulares*	References
75	domain of burning	terminus combustionis	II iv 1:1,2; II vii 5:5,6; II ix 4:2; II ix 4:2				
76	dry					siccus	I ii 3:1; I ii 7:3; II i 8:1; II iii 8:1,2; II vii 3:4; IV 5:2
77*	Earth	terra	II i 1:7; II iv 1:1,2; II v 2:4,5,6; II vi 1:3	terra	II i 1:1; II i 6:6; II i 14:1; II vi 1:7; II viii 2:3		
78	earthy sign			signum terreum	II i 6:6	signum terreum	III 4:9
79	east			oriens	II i 2:1; II xii 10:5	oriens	I iii 2:2,3,4,6; I iii 3:3; I iv 4:5
80	eastern					orientalis	I iii 4:3,6,8; II i 13:1
81	eastern quadrant					quarta orientalis	I iii 4:6,8
82	eastern signs					signa orientalia	I iii 4:3,6,8

	English	*Electiones*	References	*Interrogationes*	References	*Tractatus particulares*	References
83	eccentric circle					eccentricus	II iii 8:2; II iv 8:2
84	ecliptic	medio circuli	II vii 3:5	linea signorum	II vii 4:7		
85	elections	electiones	I 1:1,2; I 2:1,4,5; I 3:3; I 6:2; I 7:3,4; II vi 1:6; II vii 1:6; II vii 3:2; II vii 7:3,4,5				
86	enter under the light of the Sun	intrare sub radiis Solis	II ix 4:2; II x 2:2	intrare sub claritate Solis	II vi 1:3		
87	epicycle					epiciclus	II iv 8:2
88*	equal degrees	gradus equales	II vi 1:4	gradus equales	II vii 1:12		
89*	exaltation	exaltatio altitudo	II vii 5:5 II ii 2:2	exaltatio honor	II x 1:6 II i 6:12	exaltatio honor	II v 3:1 IV 3:2
90	feminine planet					planeta femininus	II vii 3:4

	English	*Electiones*	References	*Interrogationes*	References	*Tractatus particulares*	References
91	feminine quadrant			quarta feminina	II xii 1:2,6; II xii 8:1	quarta feminina	I iv 2:1
92	feminine ruler			prepositus femininus	II v 5:1		
93	feminine signs			signa feminina	II v 5:2	signa feminina	I i 2:1; I i 3:4
94	fetus					fetus	I ii 5:2
95	fiery sign	signa ignea	II iii 3:1			signa ignea	III 4:9
96*	fixed signs	signa veridica	II viii 1:5; II x 1:5	signa veridica	II i 1:3,4,5; II i 6:2,4; II iii 2:3; II vi 2:2; II ix 2:3; II x 2:4; II xii 1:5; II xii 6:3; II xii 9:4	signa veridica	I iii 1:3
				signa stabilia	II viii 1:6	signa fixa	I iv 3:4; IV 6:4
97	fugitive			fugitivus	II xii 7:3,5,7,9,10; II xii 8:1–4; II xii 9:1,2,3; II xii 10:2,3	fugitivus	I iv 1:1,3,5,7,9,10; I iv 2:1–4; I iv 3:1,2,3; I iv 4:2,3; IV 9:2
98*	Gemini	Gemini	II i 2:8; II vi 6:4			Gemini	I ii 8:2

	English	*Electiones*	References	*Interrogationes*	References	*Tractatus particulares*	References
99*	give power	dare fortitudinem	II i 1:7; II ii 1:3,4; II iii 3:2; II iv 1:1,2; II iv 4:2,3; II vii 5:1; II vii 6:4; II vii 2:3; II viii 1:1	dare fortitudinem	II i 8:3; II i 9:5,6; II i 14:3; II ii 1:3; II ii 2:4; II ii 3:2,3,4,7,8,10; II ii 3:13; II ii 4:2; II ii 5:2,3,4; II iii 2:2; II iv 1:1; II v 1:2,3		
						dare vim	I iv 1:2,3,6,7,8,9; I iv 2:1,2,3; I iv 3:2
100	God	Deus	I 1:2,3,4; I 3:1			Deus	II ii 1:3; II v 3:6; III 4:3; III 9:2,9; III 10:6,9
101*	good fortune	bonum	I 4:2; II i 2:6; II iii 3:1; II vi 2:2,4; II vi 3:1,2; II vi 4:1,2	bonum	II ix 1:4; II x 1:6,7	bonum	II i 2:2; III 11:7; III 12:9
		fortuna	I 6:1				
102	great luminary (Sun)			claritas magna	II i 6:12		
103	great years			anni magni	II i 15:2	anni magni	II:8; II i 7:1; II ii 7:1; II iii 7:1; II iv 7:1; II v 7:1; II vi 7:1; II vii 7:1
104	harm (noun)	dampnum	I 7:1; II vii 4:5; II vii 7:3			dampnum	III 7:6; III 12:6

	English	*Electiones*	References	*Interrogationes*	References	*Tractatus particulares*	References
105	harm (verb)	nocere	I 2:5; II iii 2:2	dampnificare	II vi 1:10	dampnificare	III 12:5
106	harmed			impeditus	II xii 1:4		
107	harmful			dampnificans	II i 9:5; II ii 2:7; II ii 4:2; II v 4:4; II vi 1:11; II vi 2:3		
		durus	II iii 2:1; II vii 6:3; II ix 1:4; II ix 2:3	durus	II vi 2:2; II vii 1:6		
108	Head ⟨of the Dragon⟩					Caput	III; III 1:9; III 2:9; III 3:9; III 4:9; III 5:9; III 6:9; III 7:9; III 8:9; III 9:9; III 10:9; III 11:9; III 12:9
109	health					sanitas	II i 1:2
110*	heart	cor	II ix 1:1	cor	I 1:5; I 3:2; II i 1:1; II i 7:4; II i 12:5; II vii 2:3; II xii 2:1	cor	I i 4:1; II i 5:1; II i 8:1; II v 8:1; II vi 8:3; III 8:3; III 11:6; IV 2:1
111	heat	calor	I 5:2,4			caliditas	III 1:6; III 11:4; III 12:6
112*	hidden thing	abscondium	I 2:5; II iv 1:1; II ix 3:2	absconditum	II i 1:1; II iii 2:2,4; II xii 6:1	absconditum	III 4:2; IV 7:1

	English	*Electiones*	References	*Interrogationes*	References	*Tractatus particulares*	References
						occultum	I i 5:7,8; I ii 10:1; I iii 2:2; I iii 3:7
113*	hide	abscondere	II iv 1:2	abscondere	II i 1:1	occultare	I:3
114	hindered			impeditus	II vii 1:7	impeditus	II v 3:5
115	hot					calidus	II i 8:1; II iv 8:2; II vii 3:4; III 6:6
116	hour	hora	I 6:1; I 7:1; II i 1:1	hora	II i 6:2; II i 7:4; II i 9:1,3	hora	I ii 1:1; I ii 2:1; I ii 3:1
117*	house (planetary)	domus	II vii 3:3; II vii 5:5; II vii 7:6,7	domus	I 2:2; II i 6:13,14; II i 11:1; II iv 1:1	domus	II i 2:2; II ii 13:3; IV 3:1,2; II 4:2.3.4
118	house of dejection			domus vilitatis	II i 6:12	domus lapsa	I i 1:1
119	house of war			domus belli	II vii 2:8		
120	humor					humor	II iv 8:1
121	in the house of dejection					cadens	I i 2:1,3; I i 3:4

	English	*Electiones*	References	*Interrogationes*	References	*Tractatus particulares*	References
122*	inauspicious	malum	I 2:4; II i 1:3; II i 2:1,3,5; II ii 2:1; II iv 2:1	malum	II i 9:5,6; II iii 1:1; II iii 2:4; II vii 2:4,8; II vii 3:6; II viii 1:4; II x 1:7; II x 2:4; II xi 1:3; II xii 1:3,4,5,7	malum	II vii 3:3,4; III 12:3
123	inauspicious quadrant			quarta dura	II xii 1:3		
124	inauspicious sign	signum malum	I 2:4				
125*	indicate	ostendere	II vii 6:2	ostendere	II i 1:4,5; II i 5:3	denotare	I iii 1:3,4; II ii 1:4
126*	individuals	singulares	I 1:1	singulares	I 1:2; I 2:2		
127	interrogations			interrogationes	I 1:4; I 2:3; I 3:2; I 4:1; II i 11:2; II xii 2:1	interroga-tiones	I i 4:1
128*	joy	gaudium	II ii 1:2; II ix 2:4	gaudium	II iii 2:2		
129*	judge (verb)	iudicare	II iv 4:3; II vii 4:4; II vii 7:6	iudicare	II i 6:8,10; II i 7:1,3; II i 10:2; II i 13:5; II i 14:3	iudicare	I i 5:4; I iii 1:2,6; I iv 2:1
130*	judgement	iudicium	I 3:3; II v 2:2	iudicium	II i 6:8; II ii 4:1; II ii 5:1	iudicium	IV, IV 10:3

	English	*Electiones*	References	*Interrogationes*	References	*Tractatus particulares*	References
131*	Jupiter	Iupiter	II i 1:3; II i 2:4; II ii 1:5; II iii 2:1	Iupiter	II i 6:3; II v 1:6; II v 3:2	Iupiter	I ii 9:1; I iii 1:4; II iv 1:1,2
				stella Iovis	II x 1:4		
132	just sign			signum iustum	II i 6:11		
133	knowledge	scientia	I 1:2				
134	land	siccitas	II vi 4:2; II vi 6:1; II vi 8:2; II vi 10:2; II vi 16:1				
		terra	I iii 2:2; II vi 3:1; II vi 4:1; II vi 14:1; II vi 25:2; II ix 2:3				
135	latitude			latitudo	II vii 4:3,4,5,6		
136	law	consuetudo	I 1:2				
137	laxative	potio laxativa	II i 1:1,7; II vi 3:2			medicina laxativa	II iv 8:1
138	least years					anni parvi	II:8; II i 7:1; II ii 7:1; II iii 7:1; II iv 7:1; II v 7:1; II vi 7:1; II vii 7:1

	English	*Electiones*	References	*Interrogationes*	References	*Tractatus particulares*	References
139*	Leo	Leo	II vii 5:5; II ix 1:3	Leo	II i 6:5	Leo	I i 8:1; I ii 8:2; IV 3:3
140	lesser luminary (Moon)			claritas parva	II i 6:12		
141*	Libra	Libra	II vi 6:4			Libra	I ii 8:2; IV 3:1; IV 4:4
142*	life	vita	I 1:5; I 4:2; II vii 5:4	vita	II i 15:1; II vi 2:2	vita	I ii 8:2; II i 1:1; II i 2:2; II ii 13:2,3; II iv 1:3; II vi 7:2; III 8:9; III 10:6
143	light	see "ray"		claritas	II ii 3:3; II ii 4:2; II vi 1:3	lumen	III 1:3
144	light of the Sun	see "ray of the Sun"		claritas Solis	II ii 3:3; II ii 4:2; II vi 1:3		
145	longitude			longitudo	II vi 2:4		
146*	lord	dominus	I 2:2; II ii 1:3,4; II iiii 1:1; II iv 1:2	dominus	II i 6:7; II i 7:4; II i 8:1,2,3; II i 9:1–6; II i 11:1,2,4;	dominus	I i 1:1,2,5,6; I i 2:1,3; I i 3:1,4; I i 4:5; I ii 7:1; I ii 8:1
				princeps	II viii 2:1	principans	II v 3:4

	English	*Electiones*	References	*Interrogationes*	References	*Tractatus particulares*	References
147*	lord of the ascendant	dominus ascendentis	I 2:2; II ii 1:3; II iii 1:1,2; II iv 1:2; II iv 2:1; II v 1:2; II vii 1:3,5; II vii 2:1; II vii 4:2,4; II vii 5:1; II vii 6:4; II viii 1:3; II ix 1:3; II x 1:3; II xii 1:1	dominus ascendentis	II i 7:4; II i 8:3; II i 9:3; II ii 1:1; II ii 2:6,9; II ii 3:2,3,4,6,9,10; II ii 4:2; II ii 5:2,3; II iii 1:2,3; II iv 2:1; II v 1:7; II v 2:3; II v 5:1; II vi 1:2,3,4,7,9; II vi 2:1,5; II vii 1:2,4,6,8	dominus ascenden-tis	I i 1:1,5,6; I i 2:1; I i 5:2; I iii 3:2,4; I iii 4:11; I iv 1:2,6,7; I iv 3:3; I iv 4:3
				princeps ascendentis	II viii 2:1		
148	lord of the city	dominus ville	II iv 2:1				
149	lord of the day			dominus diei	II i 9:1; II xii 2:4	dominus diei	I i 4:5
150	lord of the decan					dominus faciei	I i 7:1
151*	lord of the hour	dominus hore	II iv 4:1; II v 1:2; II vii 1:2,3; II vii 7:7; II viii 1:2,4; II ix 1:3,4,5; II x 1:4,6; II xii 1:2,4	dominus hore	II i 9:1,3; II iii 2:3,4; II v 1:4,5; II v 2:2,3,4; II v 3:2; II v 5:2; II vi 1:9; II vii 1:11; II viii 2:4; II ix 2:5; II xii 2:4; II xii 4:1	dominus hore	I; I i 2:3; I i 3:4; I i 4:5; I ii 9:1; I iii 2:1; I iii 4:1,11

	English	*Electiones*	References	*Interrogationes*	References	*Tractatus particulares*	References
152	lord of the lot			dominus partis	II vii 1:12	dominus partis	IV 3:3
153	lord of the term			dominus termini	II xii 5:1	dominus termini	I i 7:1; II ii 10:1
154	lord of the triplicity			dominus triplicitatis	II vi 1:8		
155	lordship					dominium prelatura	II ii 13:3 II i 2:2
156	lordship of the triplicity					dominium triplicitates	II ii 13:3
157	lot			pars	II vii 1:12	pars	II:2
158	lot of Fortune			pars gratie	II i 9:1; II xii 2:3; II xii 7:3	pars fortune	I i 4:4; II i 1:4; II iii 1:1; II v 1:1; II vi 1:1; II vii 1:1; II iv 3:3
159	lot of husbands			pars dominorum	II vii 1:12		

	English	*Electiones*	References	*Interrogationes*	References	*Tractatus particulares*	References
160	lot of Jupiter					pars Iovis	II iv 1:1
161	lot of Mars					pars Martis	II v 1:1
162	lot of Saturn					pars Saturni	II iii 1:1
164	lot of the hidden thing					pars celati	II ii 1:1; II iv 1:1; II vi 1:1; II vii 1:1
165	lot of the Moon					pars Lune	II ii 1:1
166	lot of the planets					pars planetarum	II:2
167	lot of the Sun					pars Solis	II i 1:1,5
168	lot of Venus					pars Veneris	II vi 1:1
169*	lower planet	stella inferior	II vii 3:3,4,5; II x 1:4	stella inferior planeta inferior	II i 6:3; II vii 3:3; II vii 4:1 II i 2:1; II i 5:3; II vii 4:2; II xii 9:4	planeta inferior	I ii v 3:4

	English	*Electiones*	References	*Interrogationes*	References	*Tractatus particulares*	References
170*	luminaries luminaries	luminaria	II vii 5:1,2	luminaria claritates	II vii 2:4 II i 9:1; II vi 9:1		
171*	malefic planet	stella mala stella malivola	II i 1:1; II ii 2:2; II iii 1:1; II iv 1:1; II iv 4:1; II v 4:3; II vi 6:4; II viii 1:2; II ix 2:2; II xi 1:2 II v 1:1; II vii 1:1; II vii 2:1; II vii 5:5; II x 1:1,2	stella mala stella malivola stella dampnificante	II i 9:5,6; II vi 1:3; II vii 5:1; II viii 2:1; II ix 1:4,5 II vii 1:6; II vii 3:6,7; II vii 6:1; II viii 1:1–5; II xii 1:3,4,8; II xii 6:2; II xii 7:2; II xii 8:3,4 II i 9:3; II v 1:6	planeta malus	I iii 1:2; I iv 1:2; I iv 2:3
172*	Mars	Mars	I 5:2,4; II ii 1:5; II ii 2:1; II iii 2:2; II v 3:1	Mars	II i 6:9,10; II vii 5:1; II vii 6:2; II x 1:6; II xi 1:3	Mars	I ii 9:1; I iii 1:4; III 1:6; III 2:6; III 2:6; III 3:6
173	masculine cardines			anguli masculini	II x 1:6		
174	masculine planet					planeta masculinus	I i 3:4; II v 6:2; II vii 3:4

	English	*Electiones*	References	*Interrogationes*	References	*Tractatus particulares*	References
175	masculine quadrant			quarta masculina	II xii 8:2	quarta masculina	I iv 2:2
176	masculine ruler			prepositus masculinus	II v 5:1		
177	masculine sign			signa masculina	II v 5:2	signa masculina	I i 2:3
178*	Mercury	Mercurius	II i 1:4; II i 2:5; II v 3:1; II v 4:2; II vii 7:4; II ix 1:1,3; II ix 3:7; II xi 1:2; II xii 1:2	Mercurius	II i 2:2; II i 6:3; II vii 1:9; II x 2:1; II xii 4:1; II xii 6:4	Mercurius	I ii 3:1; I ii 9:1; I iii 1:4; I iii 6:2; II v 3:4; II vii 6:2; II vii 8:2; III 1:8; III 2:8; III 3:8
179	method	via	I 3:3; II vi 1:5			modus	I iii 3:1
180	middle years			anni mediocres	II i 15:2	anni medii	II:8; II i 7:1; II ii 7:1; II iii 7:1; II iv 7:1; II v 7:1; II vi 7:1; II vii 7:1
181	minute	pars gradus pars prima	II v 2:4 II vi 1:3				

	English	*Electiones*	References	*Interrogationes*	References	*Tractatus particulares*	References
182*	misfortune	malum	I 7:1	malum	II vi 1:6,11,12; II vii 5:1; II viii 1:2–5; II ix 1:4; II xii 1:3	malum	II i 2:2; II vi 1:4; III 12:3,9
183	mixture	temperamentum,	II i 1:4; II i 2:5				
		mixtione	II xi 1:2				
						complexio	III 1:9
184*	moment	punctum	I 1:1; I 1:4; I 7:2; II i 1:6,7; II v 2:3,4	punctum	I 1:4,5; II i 15:5; II viii 2:3; II ix 1:2		
				hora	II vi 2:7		
185*	month	mensis	II i 2:6; II vi 23:2	mensis	II i 6:2; II i 13:6; II ix 2:1,5; II x 1:4	mensis	III 12:3; IV 6:4
186*	Moon	Luna	I i 7:2; II i 1:1,5,6,7; II i 2:1,8,9; II ii 1:1–5	Luna	I 1:4; I 2:2; II i 6:12,14; II i 7:4,5,7; II i 8:1,2,3	Luna	I i 2:1,3; I i 4:4; I ii 4:1; I ii 9:1
187*	motion	motus	II v 2:6	motus	II i 1:5; II i 13:6; II ix 2:6;		
				cursus	II iv 1:1; II vi 2:1,3; II vii 2:7; II ix 2:2; II x 1:3; II xii 1:1; II xii 9:4	cursus	I iv 3:4

	English	*Electiones*	References	*Interrogationes*	References	*Tractatus particulares*	References
188*	native	natus	I 2:2	natus	II i 7:4	natus	II i 2:2; II ii 1:3; II ii 2:1; II ii 13:3; II iv 1:1,5; II v 1:1; II vi 1:1; II vi 7:2; II vii 6:1; II vii 8:2
189*	nativities	nativitates	I 7:3	nativitates	I 2:3; II i 10:2; II i 15:1		
190*	nativity	nativitas	I 2:3,4; I 5:1,2,4; I 6:1; I 7:1; II v 2:7; II vii 5:4; II x 1:1	nativitas	II i 11:3; II i 15:3	nativitas	II i 2:3; II v 2:2; II v 6:1; II vii 8:2
191*	nature	natura	I 5:3; I 6:1; II ii 1:3; II v 3:2; II vii 5:3	natura	II ix 1:3; II xii 1:3,8; II xii 2:5,7; II xii 3:1; II xii 9:4	natura esse	I i 4:5,7; I i 5:8; I ii 8:1,11; II i 2:2; II iv 8:2; II vii 3:4 IV 5:1
192	ninth-part			.9a.	II xii 2:2	novenaria	I i 4:3
193	nocturnal	de nocte	II vii 5:4	nocturnus	II vi 1:7		
194	north			septentrio	II vi 2:4; II xii 10:5	septentrio	I iii 2:5; I iii 3:5; I iv 4:5
195	northern			sinister septentrionalis	II vii 4:4,5,7 II vii 4:5	sinister septentri-onalis	II vii 13:1 I iii 4:3

	English	*Electiones*	References	*Interrogationes*	References	*Tractatus particulares*	References
196	northern signs					signa septentrionalia	I iii 3:5; I iii 4:3
197	number of the ray	quantitas radiationis	II vi 6:4				
198*	occidental	occidentalis	II x 1:4	occidentalis	II 1 2:1; II i 4:3; II i 5:3		
199*	occidental of the Sun	occidentalis a Sole	II x 1:4	occidentalis a Sole	II 1 5:3		
200*	opposition	oppositus	II i 1:5; II iii 1:1; II vii 1:1; II vii 2:1; II vii 6:2; II x 1:3	oppositus	II i 3:5; II i 10:2; II x 1:7; II i 1:5; II xi 1:3	oppositus	II iii 8:1; II v 3:2
				oppositio	II i 9:1,5; II vi 1:12; II vii 2:5,8		
201*	oriental	orientalis	II ix 4:2; II x 1:4	orientalis	II i 2:1; II i 5:3; II x 5:3	orientalis	I iii 3:3
202*	oriental of the Sun	orientalis a Sole	II ix 4:2; II x 1:4	orientalis a Sole	II i 2:1; II 1 5:3		
203*	outcome	finis	II vi 6:2; II vi 26:2	finis	II i 8:1–4; II i 14:3; II i 15:5; II iv 1:1		

	English	*Electiones*	References	*Interrogationes*	References	*Tractatus particulares*	References
204*	partner	socius	II vi 10:2	socius	II vii 2:7; II vii 6:2	socius	I i 1:9; I ii 1:1; I ii 2:3; III 3:3
205*	partnership	societas	II ii 2:1	societas	II vii 6:1	societas	III 9:3
206	peregrine	vaga	II ii 1:3; II ix 4:1			peregrina	IV 3:2,3
207	person who makes an election	elector	I 4:3; II vii 11:6; II vii 7:6				
208	Pisces	Pisces	I 2:2; II i 2:9; II iii 3:2; II vii 7:4			Pisces	I ii 8:2
209*	place (horoscopic)	domus	I 2:2; I 7:3,4; II i 1:6; II ii 1:2; II iii 1:1; II iii 3:1,3; II iv 2:1; II iv 3:1; II iv 4:1,3; II v 1:2; II v 2:4,5; II v 4:1; II vi 20:2	domus	I 3:3; I 4:2; II i 1:2; II i 3:2,3,4,5; II i 4:1,2; II i 6:3; II i 7:1; II i 8:2; II i 9:5; II i 10:1,2; II i 11:3,4	domus	I i 1:1,5; I i 2:2; I i 3:4; I i 5:6; I i 6:2; I iv 3:2; I iv 4:3; II i 1:2; III 1:1,2,4; III 2:1,2; III 3:1; III 4:1; III 5:1; III 6:1; III 7:1; III 8:1; III 9:1; III 10:1; III 11:1; III 12:1; IV 4:4
210*	places of dominion	loci principatus	II ii 1:3	loci principatus	II i 15:1; II xi 1:2; II xii 2:4		

	English	*Electiones*	References	*Interrogationes*	References	*Tractatus particulares*	References
211*	planet	stella	I 6:1; II i 1:7; II ii 1:3,4; II iii 1:1	stella	I 1:4; I 3:3; II i 1:5		
*		planeta	I 3:3; II vii 5:5; II x 1:4	planeta stella servientis	I 2:2; II i 1:2; II i 2:1; II i 33 II i 1:5	planeta servus	I i 4:5,7,8; I i 8:1; I ii 8:3 II vii 14:1
212*	position	locus	I 3:2; II i 1:4; II iii 3:1; II iv 1:1; II iv 2:1; II iv 4:2; II v 1:1; II v 2:3,7; II v 3:1,2; II v 4:2,3; II vi 1:1	locus	I 1:3; II i 1:5; II i 7:8; II i 9:1; II i 11:4; II i 13:4,6; II i 14:1; II i 15:2; II ii 1:2; II ii 2:7; II iii 1:1	locus	I iii 4:1; I iv 3:3; I iv 4:3; II i 1:3; II v 3:2; II vii 1:2; II vii 1:2; II vii 3:3; IV 4:1
213*	power	fortitudo	I 1:2; I 3:1; I 4:1; I 6:1; II iii 1:2; II iv 2:1; II iv 4:3; II v 1:2; II v 3:1; II v 4:1; II vi 1:1,3; II vii 3:3; II vii 4:4,5; II vii 5:1,5; II vii 7:7	fortitudo	II i 5:3; II i 7:8; II i 9:1,3,6; II iii 1:1; II v 5:3,4; II vi 1:6,7; II vii 1:11,12; II vii 4:1	fortitudo	I i 4:4; I i 5:2,9; II i 13:1; II ii 11:1; II ii 13:1; II iii 1:3,4; II ii 13:1; II iv 1:5
		potestas	I 6:1				
						vis	II i 1:3; III 9:10
214	power of the females			fortitudo feminorum	II v 5:3		
215	power of the males			fortitudo masculinorum	II v 5:3		

	English	*Electiones*	References	*Interrogationes*	References	*Tractatus particulares*	References
216	pregnant woman			mulier pregnans	II v 3:1; II v 4:1	mulier pregnans	I ii 5:2
217	quadrant			quarta	II xii 1:2; II xii 1:3,6; II xii 8:1	quarta	I iii 2:3,4; I iii 3:3,4,5,7; I iii 4:6,7,8,9; I iv 2:1; I iv 8:1
218*	quarrel	lis	II vi 12:2; II vi 16:2; II vii 1:6	lis	II vii 1:9; II vii 2:1,2; II vii 6:2	lis	I ii 1:2; I ii 5:3; II iii 1:2
219*	quartile	aspectus quartus	II i 1:5; II vii 2:1; II vii 6:2	aspectus quartus	II i 9:5; II i 13:6; II vi 1:12; II vii 2:5,8	aspectus quartus	IV 3:2
220	querent			interrogans	I 1:5; II i 3:1; II i 6:8; II i 13:2; II xii 2:1; II xii 3:1	interrogans	IV 7:1
				interrogator	II i 11:3; II i 15:1; II ii 1:1; II iv 2:1; II v 1:1; II vii 1:11,12; II vii 2:2	interro-gator	I ii 8:1
		querens	I 6:1			querens	I i 4:1; I i 5:3; I iv 4:3; IV 1:1; IV 2:1; IV 7:2
221*	question	interrogatio	I 4:1; I 6:2	interrogatio	I 4:1; II i 3:3,4; II i 6:8,10; II i 7:1	interroga-tio	I i 8:2
						questio	III 4:3

	English	*Electiones*	References	*Interrogationes*	References	*Tractatus particulares*	References
222	quick in its motion			velox in cursu suo	II vi 2:3; II ix 2:2; II xii 1:1; II xii 9:4	velox cursu	I iv 3:4
223	quick in its motion			festinus in cursu suo	II vii 2:7		
224*	quickness	festinatio	II v 3:1	festinatio	II i 6:3,7; II vi 2:2; II ix 2:4; II xii 1:1	velocitas	I iv 3:4; II v 3:4
225*	ray	radius radiatio	II vii 2:1; II vii 3:4; II x 2:2 II vi 6:4	radius scintillatio claritas	II vii 3:5; II viii 1:1; II viii 2:1 II ii 2:3,4; II ii 3:4; II vii 1:3 II ii 3:3; II ii 4:2; II vi 1:3		
226	ray of the planet			scintillatio stelle	II ii 2:3,4; II vii 1:3		
227	ray of the Sun	radius Solis	II vii 2:1; II vii 3:4; II x 2:2	scintillatio Solis claritas Solis	II ii 3:4; II vii 1:3 II ii 3:3; II ii 4:2; II vi 1:3		
228	receive			capere recipere	II vii 1:3 II vii 1:3	recipere	I i 5:2; I iv 2:4; I iv 3:4

	English	*Electiones*	References	*Interrogationes*	References	*Tractatus particulares*	References
229	received	receptus	II vii 1:5	receptus	II i 13:4; II i 14:2; II ii 1:2; II v 1:4; II v 3:4; II vii 1:3; II vii 2:7; II vii 5:1; II x 1:1; II xii 8:3,4	receptus	I iv 2:3; IV 3:2,3
						recipitus	I iv 2:4
230*	receiver	recipiens	I 4:3	recipiens	II xii 9:4		
				receptor	II i 13:3	receptor	I i 5:2; IV 6:4
231	reduce a humor	minuere	II i 2:1,6,8				
232	religion					lex nove	II iv 2:1
233	retrogradation			retrogradatio	II i 3:5		
234	retrograde	retrogradus	II ii 1:4; II iii 1:1; II iv 1:1,2; II iv 2:1; II vii 1:1,4; II vii 3:2,4; II vii 5:1,6; II vii 7:4,7; II viii 1:2; II ix 1:2; II ix 1:1	retrogradus	II i 2:2; II i 9:6; II i 13:3; II ii 1:2; II ii 5:3; II v 1:6; II vi 2:1; II vii 1:6; II vii 2:3,9; II vii 3:5; II ix 1:1; II ix 2:1,6; II x 1:3; II x 2:3; II xi 1:3; II xii 1:10; II xii 7:2.7.8	retrogradus	I i 1:1; I i 2:1; I i 3:4; I iv 1:2,7

	English	*Electiones*	References	*Interrogationes*	References	*Tractatus particulares*	References
235	revolution of the wordyear	revolutio anni mundani	II vii 6:5			revolutio mundi	II i 2:1
236	revolutions of the years of the native			revolutiones annorum nati	I 1:3		
				revolutiones nativitatum	I 2:3		
				revolutiones cuilibet anni	II i 15:3		
				revolutiones de anno in anno	II i 15:4		
237*	rising times	ascensiones	II ix 2:5; II x 1:6	ascensiones	II i 8:2		
238	rising times of tables of the country			ascensiones tabule terre	II i 8:2		
239*	ruler	prepositus	I 7:2; II iii 1:1; II x 2:2; II xi 1:1	prepositus	I i 1:4; I i 9:1; II ii 1:1,3; II iii 1:3; II iv 2:4; II v 5:1; II vi 2:1; II vii 4:1; II ix 1:3; II x 1:2,3; II x 2:2		
						principator	II ii 13:3
						prelatus	II i 2:2

	English	*Electiones*	References	*Interrogationes*	References	*Tractatus particulares*	References
						principans	II v 3:4
240	ruler of the native	prepositus super natum	I 2:2				
241*	ruler over the five places of dominion	prepositus .5. locorum principatus	II ii 1:3	prepositus .5. locorum principatus	II xi 1:2; II xii 2:4		
242	rulership			prepositura	II ii 2:4,7	potestas prelatura	II i 2:2; II ii 6:2; II iii 6:3; II iv 6:2; II v 6:2; II vi 6:2; II vii 6:2 II i 2:2
243*	Sagittarius	Sagittarius	II v 3:2; II vi 6:4; II xii 1:3			Sagittarius	I ii 8:2
244*	Saturn	Saturnus	I 2:2; II i 1:2; II i 2:1,2,3; II ii 1:5; II iii 2:1,2	Saturnus	I 1:2; I 2:2; II i 6:4; II vii 1:10,12	Saturnus	I ii 5:1; I ii 9:1; I iii 1:4; II ii 1:1,3,4; II iv 1:4
245*	Scorpio	Scorpio	I 2:2; II vii 7:1	Scorpio	II i 6:6,7,10,12; II vii 5:1	Scorpio	I ii 8:2
246*	sextile	aspectus sextilis	II i 1:2; II i 2:2; II iii 3:2	aspectus sextilis	II i 13:6		

	English	*Electiones*	References	*Interrogationes*	References	*Tractatus particulares*	References
247	sexual intercourse	coniugare	II vi 23:2	concubitus	II xii 6:4	concubitus	I ii 2:1
248*	sign	signum	I 1:5; I 2:4; I 3:2,3; I 5:2,4; II i 2:9; II iv 1:3; II vi 1:2,4; II vii 7:6; II viii 1:1	signum	I 1:1; I 1:2; II i 6:4,7; II i 7:1; II i 13:1; II iii 2:3; II v 5:1; II vi 2:3,6; II vii 1:10; II ix 1:3	signum	I i 3:1; I i 5:4,5; I i 6:1; I iii 4:1,4,5,7; I iv 5:1; II iv 3:1; II vii 3:5; IV 7:3; IV 10:3
249	sign of falsehood			signum falsitatis	II i 6:8		
250	sign of the city	signum patrie	II iv 2:1				
251	sign of the world			signum seculi	I 1:2		
252	sign with a human shape	signum qui est super formam filii hominis	II vi 6:4				

	English	*Electiones*	References	*Interrogationes*	References	*Tractatus particulares*	References
253*	significator	significator	I 5:2	significator	II i 8:1; II i 9:4,5,6; II i 10:1; II i 11:1; II i 13:1,5; II ii 1:3; II iii 1:3; II iv 1:1; II v 3:1,4; II v 4:1,2,6; II vi 1:5,6,7,8,11; II vi 2:1,6; II vii 2:3,7; II viii 1:2; II ix 1:2,3; II ix 1:1,2,3; II x 1:1,2; II xi 1:2; II xii 1:1,3,4,8; II xii 2:3; II xii 5:2; II xii 7:6,8,9; II xii 8:1; II xii 9:3	significator	I i 5:1,3,5; I iii 2:1,2; IV 2:3
				stella signatrix	II vi 2:6		
254*	signify	significare	II iv 4:2; II ix 1:4; II x 1:7	significare	I 1:5; II i 1:3; II i 3:1	significare	I i 4:9; I i 6:2; I ii 8:2
255	slow in its course			tardus in suo cursu	II vi 2:1		
256	slowness					tarditas	III 12:6
257	smaller part of the zodiac	pars parva circuli	II ii 1:1				
258	south			meridies	II vi 2:4; II xii 10:5	meridies	I iii 2:4,6; I iv 4:5

	English	*Electiones*	References	*Interrogationes*	References	*Tractatus particulares*	References
259	southern			meridionalis	II vii 4:4,6,7	meridionalis meridianus	I iii 4:3,6 II v 13:1
260	southern quadrant					quarta meridionalis	I iii 4:6,8
261	southern signs					signa meridionalia	I iii 4:3,6
262	spark	see "ray"		scintillatio	II ii 2:3,4; II ii 3:4; II vii 1:3		
263	spark of the planet	see "ray of the planet"		scintillatio stelle	II ii 2:3,4; II vii 1:3		
264	spark of the Sun	see "ray of the Sun"		scintillatio Solis	II ii 3:4; II vii 1:3		
265	stable	stabilis	I 1:1	firmum	II i 3:1		
266	station			statio	II i 4:3; II i 5:1,2,3; II x 2:3		

	English	*Electiones*	References	*Interrogationes*	References	*Tractatus particulares*	References
267*	straight sign	signum rectum	II iv 3:2; II x 1:5,6	signum rectum	II iv 1:1		
268*	strong	fortis	II vii 7:2,3; II viii 1:1	fortis	II i 7:3,6,7; II vi 1:9	fortis	III 12:4; IV 1:1
269	subject of the election	dominus electionis	II vii 1:6				
270	subtract	minuere	II v 2:6; II vi 1:4				
271*	succedent places	succedentes	II ii 1:2; II v 4:3	succedentes	II i 4:1; II vii 2:7; II x 1:1; II xii 9:4	succe-dentes	I iv 3:4
272*	Sun	Sol	II i 1:5; II i 2:3; II iii 3:2; II v 3:1	Sol	II i 1:2,5; II i 2:1,2; II i 3:5; II i 5:3	Sol	I i 8:2; I ii 1:1; I ii 9:1; I ii 10:1
273	surface of the Earth			superficies terre	II i 1:1		
274	Tail of the Dragon					Cauda	III; III 1:10; III 2:10; III 3:10; III 4:10; III 5:10; III 6:10; III 7:10; III 8:10; III 9:10; III 10:10; III 11:10; III 12:10

	English	*Electiones*	References	*Interrogationes*	References	*Tractatus particulares*	References
275*	Taurus	Taurus	II iv 1:3; II vii 4:3	Taurus	II i 6:6	Taurus	I ii 8:2; IV 4:4
276	term	terminus	II vii 7:7	terminus	II xii 5:1	terminus	I i 7:1; II ii 10:1
277	term (of pregnancy)	terminus	II v 3:1				
278	terminal sign	signum finis	II vii 6:5				
279*	test (verb)	temptare probare	II v 2:2; II vii 4:5 II iii 3:2; II v 3:1	temptare probare	I 3:1,2; II vi 1:5 II i 10:1		
280*	testimony	testimonium	II vii 4:4	testimonium	II i 7:1,2,3		
281	thing asked about			res quesita	II i 7:3; II i 9:2,6; II i 11:1; II i 13:3; II i 13:4,5,6; II i 14:3	res quesita	I iii 4:11; IV 1:1
282	thought			cogitatio	I 3:2; II i 4:2; II i 5:1	cogitatio	I i 3:3,4
283*	trine	aspectus trinus aspectus tertius	II i 2:2; II iii 3:2 II i 1:2; II ii 2:2	aspectus trinus	II i 13:6		

	English	*Electiones*	References	*Interrogationes*	References	*Tractatus particulares*	References
		see "aspect of love"		see "aspect of love"			
284*	triplicity	triplicitas	II vii 6:5	triplicitas	II vi 1:8	triplicitas	II ii 13:3
285*	tropical signs	signa mobilia	II viii 1:5; II x 1:5	signa mobilia	II i 3:1,5; II i 6:1,2,14; II i 10:1; II ii 2:71; II iii 2:3; II v 4:3; II vi 2:2; II viii 1:6; II ix 2:3; II x 2:4; II xii 1:1; II xii 6:2	signa mobilia	I iii 1:3; IV 6:4
286*	under the rays of the Sun	sub radiis Solis	II vi 6:4; II vii 2:1; II vii 3:4; II ix 4:2; II x 2:2	sub radiis Solis	II vii 3:5; II viii 1:1; II viii 2:1		
				sub claritate Solis	II ii 3:3; II ii 4:2; II vi 1:2		
287*	upper planet	stella superior	II vii 3:3,4,5; II vii 7:6; II x 1:4	stella superior	II i 6:3; II vii 3:3; II vii 4:1		
		stella alta	II vii 3:1; II vii 4:2; II ix 4:2	planeta superior	II i 4:3; II i 5:1,3; II vii 4:2	planeta superior	I iv 3:4; II iii 1:4
				planeta altus	II i 6:13; II xii 9:4		
288*	Venus	Venus	II i 1:4; II i 2:4; II iii 3:2; II v 1:1	Venus	II i 2:2; II v 3:3; II vii 1:5,6,10,11,12; II x 1:4	Venus	I ii 2:1,3; I ii 9:1; I iii 1:4; II ii 6:2

	English	*Electiones*	References	*Interrogationes*	References	*Tractatus particulares*	References
289*	Virgo	Virgo	II i 6:4			Virgo	I ii 8:2
290*	watery sign	signa aquea	II i 1:1; II iii 3:1; II vii 7:1	signa aquea	II viii 1:6	signum aquaticum	III 4:9
291	waxes (Moon)	crescens	II vii 1:3	accrescens	II vi 1:6		
292	week			septimana	II i 6:2; II i 13:6		
293	west			occidens	II xii 10:5	occidens	I iii 3:5; I iv 4:5; II ii 13:1; II iii 13:1; II iv 13:1; II vi 13:1
294	western					occiden-talis	I iii 3:5,6; I iii 4:3
295	western signs					signa occi-dentalia	I iii 3:5,6; I iii 4:3
296*	will	voluntas	I 1:2; I 6:2; II ix 1:5; II ix 4:1	voluntas	II x 1:1		
297*	womb	uterus	II v 2:4	uterus	II i 1:1	uterus	I ii 5:2

	English	*Electiones*	References	*Interrogationes*	References	*Tractatus particulares*	References
298	world	seculus	I 1:5	seculus	I 1:3; II i 1:1	mundus	II:14
299*	write	scribere	I 4:2; I 7:3; II 9:1	scribere	II i 11:3; II ii 1:3; II vi 2:7; II xii 2:5	scribere	I i 4:6; II vii 3:1; III 1:8; III 6:8; III 10:8; IV 10:1
				addere	I 1:8; I 3:1		
300*	year	annus	I 5:1; II vii 6:5	annus	I 1:1; I 2:2; II i 6:2; II i 12:2; II i 13:6; II i 15:2,3,4; II ix 2:1,5	annus	II i 6:1,2; II i 7:1; II i 8:2; II ii 6:1; II ii 7:1; II iii 6:1; II iii 7:1; II iv 6:1; II iv 7:1; II v 6:1; II v 7:1; II vi 6:1; II vi 7:1; II vii 6:1; II vii 7:1; IV 6:4
301*	zodiac	circulus	II ii 1:1; II vi 1:2; II vii 3:5	circulus	II xii 2:5	zodiacus	I i 4:6

APPENDIX 15

LATIN-ENGLISH INDEX TO THE ENGLISH-LATIN GLOSSARY

Latin	English	*Electiones*	*Interrogationes*	*Tractatus particulares*
abscondere	hide	113	113	
absconditum	hidden thing	112	112	112
accrescens	waxes (Moon)		291	
addens	author		19	
addere	add	1	1	
addere	write		299	
additor	author	19	19	
adiungere	associate			13
altitudo	exaltation	89		
anguli	cardines	36	36	36
anguli masculini	masculine cardines		173	
anni magni	great years		103	103
anni medii	middle years		180	180
anni parvi	least years			138
annus	year	300	300	300
Aquarius	Aquarius	3	3	3
Aries	Aries	5	5	5
ascendens	ascendant	6	6	6
ascensiones	rising times	237	237	
ascensiones tabule terre	rising times of tables of the country		238	
aspectus	aspect (noun)	9	9	9
aspectus amicabilis	aspect of love (trine)		12	
aspectus bonus	auspicious aspect	16	16	
aspectus dilectionis	aspect of love (trine)	12	12	
aspectus odii	aspect of hate (quartile)	11		
aspectus quartus	quartile	219	219	219
aspectus sextilis	sextile	246	246	
aspectus tertius	trine	285		
aspectus trinus	trine	283	283	
aspicere	aspect (verb)	10	10	10
associare	associate	13	13	
augere	add	1		
bonitas	beneficence			25
bonum	auspicious	15	15	

Latin	English	*Electiones*	*Interrogationes*	*Tractatus particulares*
bonum	dignity	64		
bonum	good fortune	101		
bonum	good fortune		101	101
bonum	auspicious			15
cadens	cadent (planet)		32	
cadens	in the house of dejection			121
cadentes a cavillis	cadent (place)		31	
caliditas	heat			111
calidus	hot			115
calor	heat	111		
Cancer	Cancer	34	34	34
capere	receive		228	
Capricornius	Capricorn			35
Caput	Head ⟨of the Dragon⟩			108
Cauda	Tail of the Dragon			274
caville	cardines		36	
circulus	circle	40	40	
circulus	zodiac	301	301	
claritas	light		143	
claritas	ray		225	
claritas magna	great luminary (Sun)		102	
claritas parva	lesser luminary (Moon)		140	
claritas Solis	light of the Sun		144	
claritas Solis	ray of the Sun		227	
claritates	luminaries		170	
cogitatio	thought		282	282
combustio	burning	29	29	
combustus	burnt	30	30	30
communes	collectives	44		
communia	bicorporal signs			26
complexio	complexion			45
complexio	mixture			183
computare	calculate	33	33	33
computatio	computation	46	46	
conceptio	conception	47		
concubitus	sexual intercourse		247	247
coniugare	sexual intercourse	247		
coniunctio	conjunction	49	49	49
coniungare	associate			13
coniungere	be in conjunction with	21	21	

Latin	English	*Electiones*	*Interrogationes*	*Tractatus particulares*
consuetudo	law	136		
cor	heart	110	110	110
corpus	body	28		28
crescens	waxes (Moon)	291		
cursus	course	52		
cursus	motion		187	187
dampnificans	harmful		107	
dampnificare	harm (verb)		105	105
dampnum	harm (noun)	104		104
dare fortitudinem	give power	99	99	
dare vim	give power			99
de die	diurnal	70		
de nocte	nocturnal	193		
denotare	indicate			125
Deus	God	100		100
dies	day	56	56	56
dies terminorum	critical days		53	
dignitas	dignity			64
directus in cursu suo	direct in its course	66	66	
dispositio	configuration	48	48	48
distantia	distance	69	69	69
diurnus	diurnal		70	
diversitas	diversity	71		
divisio ascensiones	division of the rising times	72		
divisiones	decrees	60		
divisum	decreed	59		
domini duorum corporum	bicorporal signs		26	
dominium	lordship			155
dominium triplicitates	lordship of the triplicity			156
dominus	lord	146	146	146
dominus ascendentis	lord of the ascendant	147	147	147
dominus diei	lord of the day		149	149
dominus electionis	subject of the election	269		
dominus faciei	lord of the decan			150
dominus hore	lord of the hour	151	151	151
dominus partis	lord of the lot		152	152
dominus signorum	astrologers		14	
dominus termini	lord of the term		153	153
dominus triplicitatis	lord of the triplicity		154	

Latin	English	*Electiones*	*Interrogationes*	*Tractatus particulares*
dominus ville	lord of the city	148		
domus	house (planetary)	117		
domus	place (horoscopic)	209	209	
domus	house (planetary)		117	117
domus	place (horoscopic)			209
domus belli	house of war		119	
domus cadentes	cadent (place)	31	31	
domus cadentes ab angulis	cadent (place)		31	
domus lapsa	house of dejection			118
domus radicis sterilis	barren sign		20	
domus vilitatis	house of dejection		118	
ducere	direct (verb)		65	
ductus	direction		67	
duodecime	dodecatemoria			74
durus	harmful	107	107	
eccentricus	eccentric circle			83
electiones	elections	85		
elector	person who makes an election	207		
eligere	choose	39		
epiciclus	epicycle			87
equare	calculate	33		
esse	nature			191
exaltatio	exaltation	89	89	89
facies	decan			58
festinatio	quickness	224	224	
festinus in cursu suo	quick in its motion		223	
fetus	fetus			94
finis	outcome	203	203	
firmum	stable		265	
fortis	strong	268	268	268
fortitudo	power	213	213	213
fortitudo feminorum	power of the females		214	
fortitudo masculinorum	power of the males		215	
fortuna	good fortune	101		
fortuna	benefic star			24
frigidus	cold (adjective)			42
frigor	cold (noun)			43
fugitivus	fugitive		97	97
gaudium	joy	128	128	
Gemini	Gemini	98		98
gradus	degree	61	61	61
gradus ascendentis	ascendant degree	7	7	7

Latin	English	*Electiones*	*Interro-gationes*	*Tractatus particulares*
gradus equales	equal degrees	88	88	
honor	exaltation		89	89
hora	hour	116	116	
hora	moment		184	
hora	hour			116
humor	humor			120
impeditus	harmed		106	
impeditus	hindered		114	114
infans	child	38	38	38
infirmitas	disease	68	68	68
inflammatio	burning		29	
interrogans	querent		220	220
interrogatio	question	221	221	221
interrogationes	interrogations		127	127
interrogator	querent		220	220
intrare sub claritate Solis	enter under the light of the Sun		86	
intrare sub radiis Solis	enter under the light of the Sun	86		
iudicare	judge (verb)	129	129	129
iudicium	judgement	130	130	130
Iupiter	Jupiter	131	131	131
iura	doctrines		73	
lapsus	dejection (see house of dejection)			62
latitudo	latitude		135	
Leo	Leo	139	139	139
lex nove	religion			232
Libra	Libra	141		141
linea signorum	ecliptic		84	
lingua Arabica	Arabic language	4		
lingua sarracenaca	Arabic language		4	
lis	quarrel	218	218	218
loci principatus	places of dominion	210	210	
locus	position	212	212	212
locus bonus	auspicious position	17	17	
longitudo	longitude		145	
lumen	light			143
luminaria	luminaries	170	170	
Luna	Moon	186	186	186
malum	inauspicious	122	122	122
malum	misfortune	182		
malum	misfortune		182	182
Mars	Mars	172	172	172

Latin	English	*Electiones*	*Interrogationes*	*Tractatus particulares*
medicina laxativa	laxative			137
medio circuli	ecliptic	84		
mensis	month	185	185	185
Mercurius	Mercury	178	178	178
meridianus	southern			259
meridies	south		258	258
meridionalis	southern		259	259
minuere	reduce a humor	231		
minuere	subtract	270		
mixtione	mixture	183		
modus	method			179
morbus	disease			68
mors	death	57	57	57
motus	motion	187	187	
mulier pregnans	pregnant woman		216	216
mundus	world			298
mutare	change	37		37
nativitas	birth	27	27	
nativitas	nativity	190	190	190
nativitates	nativities	189	189	
natura	nature	191	191	191
natus	native	188	188	188
nocere	harm (verb)	105		
nocturnus	nocturnal		193	
novenaria	ninth part			192
numerus	count			50
occidens	west		293	293
occidentalis	occidental	198	198	
occidentalis	western			294
occidentalis a Sole	occidental of the Sun	199	199	
occultare	hide			113
occultum	hidden thing			112
oppositio	opposition		200	
oppositus	opposition	200	200	200
oriens	east		79	79
orientalis	oriental	201	201	201
orientalis	eastern			80
orientalis a Sole	oriental of the Sun	202	202	
ostendere	indicate	125	125	
pars	lot		157	157
pars celati	lot of the hidden thing			164
pars dominorum	lot of husbands		159	

Latin	English	*Electiones*	*Interrogationes*	*Tractatus particulares*
pars fortune	lot of Fortune			158
pars gradus	minute	181		
pars gratie	lot of Fortune		158	
pars Iovis	lot of Jupiter			160
pars Lune	lot of the Moon			165
pars Martis	lot of Mars			161
pars parva circuli	smaller part of the zodiac	257		
pars planetarum	lot of the planets			166
pars prima	minute	181		
pars Saturni	lot of Saturn			162
pars Solis	lot of the Sun			167
pars Veneris	lot of Venus			168
partus	birth	27		
partus	delivery	63		
patria	country	51	51	
peregrina	peregrine			206
Pisces	Pisces	208		208
planeta	planet	211	211	211
planeta altus	upper planet		287	
planeta femininus	feminine planet			90
planeta fortune	benefic star			24
planeta inferior	lower planet		169	169
planeta malus	malefic planet			171
planeta masculinus	masculine planet			174
planeta superior	upper planet		287	287
potestas	power	213		
potestas	dignity		64	
potestas	rulership			242
potio laxativa	laxative	137		
prelatura	lordship			155
prelatura	rulership			242
prelatus	ruler			239
preparare	calculate	33		
prepositura	rulership		242	
prepositus	ruler	239	239	
prepositus .5. locorum principatus	ruler over the five places of dominion	241	241	
prepositus femininus	feminine ruler		92	
prepositus masculinus	masculine ruler		176	
prepositus super natum	ruler of the native	240		
princeps	lord		146	
princeps ascendentis	lord of the ascendant		147	

Latin	English	*Electiones*	*Interro-gationes*	*Tractatus particulares*
principans	lord			146
principans	ruler			239
principator	ruler			239
principium	cusp (of horoscopic place)	55	55	55
probare	test (verb)	279	279	
puer	child	38		38
punctum	moment	184	184	
quantitas radiationis	number of the ray	197		
quarta	quadrant		217	217
quarta dura	inauspicious quadrant		123	
quarta feminina	feminine quadrant		91	91
quarta masculina	masculine quadrant		175	175
quarta meridionalis	southern quadrant			260
quarta orientalis	eastern quadrant			81
querens	querent	220		220
questio	question			221
radiatio	ray	225		
radius	ray	225	225	
radius Solis	ray of the Sun	227		
receptor	receiver		230	230
receptus	received	229	229	229
recipere	receive		228	
recipere	receive			228
recipiens	receiver	230	230	
recipitus	received			229
reflammatio	burning		29	
reflammetur	burnt		30	
res quesita	thing asked about		281	281
respicere	aspect (verb)			10
retrogradatio	retrogradation		233	
retrogradus	retrograde	234	234	234
revolutio anni mundani	revolution of the word-year	235		235
revolutio mundi	revolution of the word-year			235
revolutiones annorum nati	revolutions of the years of the native		236	
revolutiones cuilibet anni	revolutions of the years of the native		236	
revolutiones de anno in anno	revolutions of the years of the native		236	

Latin	English	*Electiones*	*Interrogationes*	*Tractatus particulares*
revolutiones nativitatum	revolutions of the years of the native		236	
Sagittarius	Sagittarius	243		243
sanitas	health			109
sapiens in scientia signorum	astrologer			14
sapientes	astrologers		14	14
sapientes in iudiciis	astrologers	14		
sapientes iudiciorum signorum	astrologers	14	14	
sapientes signorum	astrologers	14	14	
Saturnus	Saturn	244	244	244
scientia	knowledge	133		
scintillatio	ray		225	
scintillatio	spark		262	
scintillatio stelle	ray of the planet		226	
scintillatio stelle	spark of the planet		263	
scintillatio Solis	ray of the Sun		227	
scintillatio Solis	spark of the Sun		264	
Scorpio	Scorpio	245	245	245
scribere	write	299	299	299
seculus	world	298	298	
septentrio	north		194	194
septentrionalis	northern		195	195
septimana	week		292	
servus	planet			211
siccitas	land	134		
siccus	dry			76
signa aerea	airy sign			2
signa aquea	watery sign	290	290	
signa bicorpora	bicorporal signs	26	26	
signa feminina	feminine signs		93	93
signa fixa	fixed signs			96
signa ignea	fiery sign	95		95
signa masculina	masculine sign		177	177
signa meridionalia	southern signs			261
signa mobilia	tropical signs	285	285	285
signa occidentalia	western signs			295
signa orientalia	eastern signs			82
signa septentrionalia	northern signs			196
signa stabilia	fixed signs	96	96	96
significare	signify	254	254	254
significator	significator	253	253	253
signum	sign	248	248	248

Latin	English	*Electiones*	*Interrogationes*	*Tractatus particulares*
signum aquaticum	watery sign			290
signum ascendentis	ascendant sign	8	8	8
signum ascendens				
signum bonum	auspicious sign		18	18
signum falsitatis	sign of falsehood		249	
signum finis	terminal sign	278		
signum iustum	just sign		132	
signum malum	inauspicious sign	124		
signum patrie	sign of the city	250		
signum qui est super formam filii hominis	sign with a human shape	252		
signum rectum	straight sign	267	267	
signum seculi	sign of the world		251	
signum terreum	earthy sign		78	78
signum tortuosum	crooked sign	54	54	
singulares	individuals	126	126	
sinister	northern		195	195
societas	partnership	205	205	205
socius	partner	204	204	204
Sol	Sun	272	272	272
stabilis	stable	265		
statio	station		266	
stella	planet	211	211	
stella alta	upper planet	287		
stella bona	benefic star	24	24	
stella dampnificante	malefic planet		171	
stella inferior	lower planet	169	169	
stella Iovis	Jupiter		131	
stella mala	malefic planet	171	171	
stella malivola	malefic planet	171	171	
stella servientis	planet		211	
stella signatrix	significator		253	
stella superior	upper planet	287	287	
sub claritate Solis	under the rays of the Sun		286	
sub radiis Solis	under the rays of the Sun	286	286	
sub terra	below the Earth [i.e., the horizon]	23		
sub terra	below the Earth [i.e., the horizon]		23	
succedentes	succedent places	271	271	271
superficies terre	surface of the Earth		273	
tarditas	slowness			256

Latin	English	*Electiones*	*Interrogationes*	*Tractatus particulares*
tardus in suo cursu	slow in its course		255	
Taurus	Taurus	275	275	275
temperamentum,	mixture	183		
temptare	test (verb)	279	279	
termini infirmitatum	critical days			53
terminus	term	276		
terminus	term (of pregnancy)	277		
terminus	term		276	276
terminus combustionis	domain of burning	75		
terra	country	51		
terra	Earth	77		
terra	land	134		
terra	country		51	
terra	Earth		77	
testimonium	testimony	280	280	
triplicitas	triplicity	284	284	284
universales	collectives		44	
uterus	womb	297	297	297
vaga	peregrine	206		
velocitas	quickness			224
velox cursu	quick in its motion			222
velox in cursu suo	quick in its motion		222	
Venus	Venus	288	288	288
via	method	179		
vilitas	dejection (see house of dejection)		62	
villa	city	41	41	
vincere	be victorious	22	22	
Virgo	Virgo	289		289
vis	power			213
vita	life	142	142	142
voluntas	will	296	296	
zodiacus	zodiac			301

APPENDIX 16

AUTHORITIES AND SOURCES IN *LIBER ELECTIONUM*, *LIBER INTERROGATIONUM* AND *TRACTATUS PARTICULARES*

English	*Electiones*		*Interrogationes*		*Tractatus particulares*	
Abraham	Abraham	II xii 1:5	Abraham	II i 5:1; II i 9:1; II i 10:1,2; II vi 1:4; II xii 2:1; II xii 11:1	Abraham	I i 4:1; I ii 8:1; I iv 5:1
Abraham Ibn Ezra					Abraham Avenare	III; III 10:4
Abraham, the author	Abraham, additor	I 3:2	Abraham addens	II i 2:1		
Abraham, the author			Abraham, qui addo hunc librum	I 3:1		
Abraham, the Jew			Abraham Judeus	II xii 11:3		
Abū ʿAlī Al-Khayyāṭ			Even Aeli Alkahi	I 1:7		

English	Electiones		Interrogationes		Tractatus particulares	
Abū Maʿshar			Even Maasar	I 1:7; II i 6:10; II i 12:2; II vii 5:1		
Abū Maʿshar, the Arab			Even Mahasar Sarracenus	I 1:7		
al-Battānī ibn Jābir the Arab			Albategni Gehii Sarraceni	I 2:1		
Alihi			Alihi	I 2:1		
Ancient ⟨rabbis⟩, their memory for a blessing	Antiqui, quorum rememoratio sit benedicta	I 1:6				
Ancients	Antiqui	II vii 5:2; II xi 1:3	Antiqui	II iii 2:1; II vi 1:5,7		
Book by Abraham Ibn Ezra on hidden things					Liber Abrahe Evenezre Iudei de ocultis	I:1; I iv 6:1

English	*Electiones*		*Interrogationes*		*Tractatus particulares*	
Book by Abraham Ibn Ezra, on the significations of the seven planets					Liber Abrahe Evenezre, de Significationibus Septem Planetarum	II
Book by Abraham Ibn Ezra, the Jew					Liber Abrahe Iudei Avenezre	I
Book by Enoch	Enoc in libro suo	II v 2:2				
Book of conjunctions (Abraham Ibn Ezra)					Liber coniunctionum	I iv 3:4
Book of elections (Abraham Ibn Ezra)	Liber electionum	I 1:1				
Book of elections (Abraham Ibn Ezra)	Liber electionum Abraham	II xii 2:1				
Book of interrogations (Abraham Ibn Ezra)			Liber interrogationum	I 1:1; II xii 12:1		
Book of nativities (Abraham Ibn Ezra)	Liber nativitatum	I 7:3	Liber nativitatum	II i 10:2; II i 15:1		

English	*Electiones*		*Interrogationes*		*Tractatus particulares*	
Book of the 100 statements	Liber .c. verborum	I 5:5	Liber .c. verborum	I 5:5; II xii 11:1	Liber .c. verborum	I iv 5:1
Book of the beginning of wisdom	Libro primus de sensu	II vii 6:3	Liber principii sensuum	II vi 1:3		
Book of the beginning of wisdom			Principium libri de sensu	I 4:2; II i 11:3		
Book of the beginning of wisdom			Liber capitis sensus	II ii 1:3		
Book of the judgments the world (Abraham Ibn Ezra)	Liber iurium seculi	II vi 1:5				
Book of the judgments the world (Abraham Ibn Ezra)	Liber iudiciorum seculi	II vi 2:1				
Book of the judgments the world (Abraham Ibn Ezra)	Liber iudiciorum, id est, revolutio-num mundi	II vii 6:5				

English	*Electiones*		*Interrogationes*		*Tractatus particulares*	
Book of the luminaries			Liber claritatum	II vi 2:7		
Book of the servants					Liber servorum	II vii 14:1
Book on the significations of the seven planets in 13 manners					Liber significationis .7. planetarum in tredecim generibus vel manieribus	I iv 6:1
Book Tamedas			Liber Samechem	II xii 2:5,9; II xii 3:1	Liber Tamedas	I i 4:6,10; I ii 8:1
Buzurjmihr?, the Persian king			Bugam, rex persicus	I 1:7		
Centiloquium (Ptolemy)	Liber .c. verborum	I 5:5	Liber .c. verborum	II i 15:3	Liber .c. verborum	II iv 5:1

English	*Electiones*		*Interrogationes*		*Tractatus particulares*
Dorotheus	Doroneus	I 6:1; II iii 1:2; II iii 3:1; II v 4:1; II vi 2:3; II vi 3:2; II vi 4:2; II vi 5:2; II vi 6:2; II vi 7:2; II vi 8:2; II vi 9:2; II vi 10:2; II vi 11:2; II vi 12:2; II vi 13:2; II vi 14:2; II vi 15:2; II vi 16:2; II vi 17:2; II vi 18:2; II vi 19:2; II vi 20:2; II vi 21:2; II vi 22:2; II vi 23:2; II vi 24:2; II vi 25:2; II vi 26:2; II vi 27:2; II vi 28:2; II vi 29:2	Doroneus	I 1:7; II i 13:2; II vi 1:8; II vii 1:11	
Enoch	Enoc	II v 1:2; II v 2:2,3	Enoch	I 2:1; II vii 1:10,12	
great scholars who wrote many books			sapientes magni qui addiderunt libros multos	I 1:8	
Ḥassān the Jew			Hessen Iudeus	I 2:1	
Kanakah, the Indian			Canba Aliendi	I 1:7	
King Dorotheus			Doroneus, rex	I 1:7; II i 13:2	

English	*Electiones*		*Interrogationes*		*Tractatus particulares*	
King Enoch, the son of Jared			Enoch, filius Ige, rex	I 2:1		
King Ptolemy	Ptholomeus rex	II vi 6:4	Bartholomeus rex	I 2:1		
Māshā'allāh	Mesahala	II ii 1:5; II iii 3:2	Mesehala	I 1:7; I 11:1; I 12:3; II vi 1:9	Messahalla	I i 5:1; I iii 2:1; IV 6:4
Māshā'allāh, the Indian			Mesehalla Halehendi	I 1:7		
Ptolemy	Ptholomeus	I 2:4; I 5:6; II i 2:8,9; II vi 6:4	Ptholomeus	II i 15:2; II xii 11:1	Ptholomeus	I iii 4:1; I iv 5:1; II i 6:3; II iii 6:2; II iv 8:1; II vii 8:2
Sahl	Saal	II ii 2:2				
Sahl the Jew			Sahal Iudeus	I 1:7		
Scezen, Abū Ma'shar's disciple			Even Maasar Scezen discipulus eius	II i 6:10		

English	Electiones		Interrogationes		Tractatus particulares	
Scientists of India	sapientes Indie	II vi 1:1; II vi 2:2; II vi 4:1; II vi 5:1; II vi 6:1; II vi 7:1; II vi 8:1; II vi 9:1; II vi 10:1; II vi 13:1; II vi 14:1; II vi 15:1; II vi 16:1; II vi 17:1; II vi 18:1; II vi 19:1; II vi 20:1; II vi 21:1; II vi 22:1; II vi 23:1; II vi 24:1; II vi 25:1; II vi 26:1; II vi 27:1; II vi 28:1; II vi 29:1				
Scripture	scriptum	I 1:3				
Thābit ibn Qurra al-Ḥarrānī			Thebit, filius Kha Alharani	I 2:1		
Tractatus particulares					Tractatus particulares	I; IV 11:1
Treatise on the significations of the planets in the 12 ⟨horoscopic⟩ places by Abraham Ibn Ezra					Tractatus de significationibus planetarum in duodecim domibus Abrahe Avenaris	III

English	*Electiones*		*Interrogationes*		*Tractatus particulares*	
Treatise on the Thirteen Manners of the Planets					Tractatus in tredecim maneriebus planetarum	II
ʿUmar ⟨b. al-Farrukhān⟩ al-Ṭabarī			Aomar Tiberiadis	I 1:7		
Yaʿqub al-Kindī			Jacob Alkindi	I 1:7; II xii 6:5		
Yaʿqub al-Kindī in his book					Jacob Alkindi in suo libro	I iii 1:5
Yaʿqub al-Kindī in his books			Jacobus Alkindi in libris suis	II xii 6:5		

LITERAL RENDERINGS IN *LIBER ELECTIONUM* OF HEBRAISMS AND HEBREW WORDS/EXPRESSIONS EMPLOYED BY ABRAHAM IBN EZRA

Latin	Ref.	Hebrew	Translation
additor	I 1:1	המחבר	the author; *lit.*, one who adds
divisiones	I 1:5	גזרות	decrees; *lit.*, divisions
divise sunt	I 1:5	נגזרו	were decreed; *lit.*, were divided
aspectus odii	I 2:2	מבט איבה	quartile; *lit.*, aspect of hate
prepositum super natum	I 2:2	שליט על הנולד	ruler of the native
rem communitatis	I 3:3	דבר כלל	general rule; *lit.*, general thing
durus	II iii 2:1	קשה	harmful; *lit.*, hard
utrum fortitudo sit in manibus hominis	I 4:1	האם יש כח בידי אדם	whether human beings have the power; *lit.*, whether there is power in the hands of a man
renovatum renovabitur	I 5:2	חדש יתחדשו	will be afflicted; *lit.*, it has been renewed, they will be renewed
contra	II i 1:7	כנגד	with respect to; *lit.*, against
pars parva circuli	II ii 1:1	החלק הקטן מן הגלגל	the smaller part of the zodiac; *lit.*, the small part of the circle
prepara	II v 1:1	תקן	calculate; *lit.*, prepare

Latin	Ref.	Hebrew	Translation
ius est	II v 1:7	הדין הוא	it is right
in siccitate	II vi 4:2	ביבשה	by land; *lit.*, in dryness
parva animalia	II vi 4:2	בהמה דקה	small livestock, i.e. sheep and goats
filii hominis	II vi 6:4	בני אדם	human beings; *lit.*, sons of a man
domus incarceratorum	II vi 7:2	בית סוהר	prison; *lit.*, house of prisoners
domus carceris	II vi 12:1	בית סוהר	prison; *lit.*, house of jail
altus corde	II vi 13:2	גבה לב	haughty; *lit.*, of high heart
dominus mulieris	II vi 22:2	בעל האישה	husband; *lit.*, lord of the woman
dominus electionis	II vii 1:5	בעל המבחר	subject of the election; *lit.*, lord of the election
sub	II vii 4:1	תחת	instead of; *lit.*, under
sapientes iudiciorum signorum	II vii 4:3	חכמי משפטי המזלות	astrologers; *lit.*, scholars of the judgments of the signs
natura	II vii 5:3	תולדת	nature
ad videndum facies regum	II ix 3:5	להקביל פני המלך	to meet kings; *lit.*, to receive the face of the king
sapientes signorum	II ix 4:1	חכמי המזלות	astrologers; *lit.*, scholars of the signs
signa veridica	II x 1:5	מזלות נאמנים	fixed signs; *lit.*, truthful signs

APPENDIX 18

LITERAL RENDERINGS IN *LIBER INTERROGATIONUM* OF HEBRAISMS AND HEBREW WORDS/EXPRESSIONS EMPLOYED BY ABRAHAM IBN EZRA

Latin	Source	Hebrew	Translation
sapientes iudiciorum signorum	I 1:1	חכמי משפטי המזלות	astrologers; *lit.*, scholars of the judgments of the signs
addiderunt	I 1:8	חברו	wrote; *lit.*, added
signa veridica	II i 1:3	מזלות נאמנים	fixed signs; *lit.*, truthful signs
stella serviens	II i 1:5	כוכב המשרת	planet; *lit.*, servant star
e directo circuli Solis	II i 2:1	מקו גלגל השמש	above the line of the Sun's orb
non erit res et non levabit	II i 3:1	לא יהיה ולא יקום	will not come to be or arise
motionem a suo gradu	II i 3:1	סר ממעלתו	demotion; *lit.*, moves from its degree
domini duorum corporum	II i 4:1	בעלי שני גופות	bicorporal signs; *lit.*, lords of two bodies
domus honoris	II i 6:12	בית כבוד	house of exaltation; *lit.*, house of honor
domus vilitatis	II i 6:12	בית קלון	house of dejection; *lit.*, house of shame
per os	II i 7:13	לפי	according to; *lit.*, by the mouth
dominus signorum	II i 12:14	בעל המזלות	astrologer; *lit.*, lord of the signs

Latin	Source	Hebrew	Translation
per manum mediam vel mediocrem	II ii 1:3	על יד אמצעי	by an intermediary; *lit.*, by a middling or medium hand
levabit	II ii 2:5	יקום	will take place; *lit.*, will raise
sub claritate Solis	II ii 3:3	תחת אור השמש	under the light of the Sun
scintillatio	II ii 3:4	ניצוץ	ray, *lit.* spark
aspectus amicabilis	II ii 3:5	מבט אהבה	trine; *lit.*, aspect of love
dominus litis	II vii 2:2	בעל המריבה	the person involved in the quarrel; *lit.*, lord of the quarrel
domus belli sui	II vii 2:8	בית מלחמתו	its house of detriment; *lit.*, its house of war
domo vilitatis sue	II vii 2:8	בית קלונו	its house of dejection; *lit.*, its house of shame
sinister	II vii 4:5	שמאלי	northern; *lit.*, left
timor anime	II viii 1:2	פחד בנפש	fear in the soul
non veniet ad opus	II ix 2:6	לא יבא לידי מעשה	will not be carried out; *lit.*, will not come to action
aspectus dilectionis	II x 1:1	מבט אהבה	trine; *lit.*, aspect of love
non ... in seculo	II x 1:7	מעולם לא	never; *lit.*, to the world not
oculus	II xii 4:1	עין	color; *lit.*, eye

APPENDIX 19

INDICATIONS OF THE HOROSCOPIC PLACES IN *LIBER ELECTIONUM*, *MIVḤARIM* I, *MIVḤARIM* II, AND *EPITOME*

To provide an idea of the contents of the bulk of *Electiones*, the following table presents the subject matter of all the elections addressed in this work. The items in this table are sorted according to their order of appearance in the twelve chapters of *Electiones*. Each item is accompanied by a reference to the corresponding part, chapter, section, and sentence in our edition of *Electiones*. Next to each item, the table presents a reference to *Mivḥarim* I, *Mivḥarim* II, and the fourth part of *Epitome totius astrologiae*, on elections, if the subject matter of any of the elections dealt with in any of these three works has its match in *Electiones*. Otherwise the corresponding cell is left blank. For close correspondences that involve not only the subject matter but particularly the technical contents themselves of the election, readers are invited to consult the notes to the English translation of our edition of *Electiones*. References to *Mivḥarim* I and *Mivḥarim* II in this table use the chapter, section, and sentence numbering of the edition of these two works in volume 3 of this series. These references also specify the corresponding pages in that volume. References to the fourth part of the *Epitome* use the chapters of the printed edition of this work (Nuremberg, 1548). When the matching items do not occur in the same chapter, the references to them appear in bold.

Topic	*Electiones*	*Mivḥarim* I	*Mivḥarim* II	Epitome
		First place		
Drinking a laxative	II i 1:1–7	§ 1.3:2, 52–53	§ 1.1:1–2, 150–151	IV:2, R4r
Drinking a vomitive	II i 1:8	§ 1.3:2, 52–53 § 1.5:3, 52–55	§ 1.6:1, 152–153	
Reducing some humor	II i 2:1–9	§ 1.6:1–2, 54–55	§ 1.3:2, 150–151	IV:3, R3v
		Second place		
Buying to make a profit	II ii 1:1–5	§ 2.1:1–2, 54–55	§ 2.1:1, 152–155	IV:4, R4r
Lending money	II ii 2:1–2	§ 2.3:1, 56–57	§ 2.3:1–2, 154–155	

Topic	*Electiones*	*Mivḥarim* I	*Mivḥarim* II	Epitome
		Third place		
Setting off on a short overland journey	II iii 1:1–2	§ 3.1:1–7, 58–59	§ 3.2:1, 156–157	IV:5, R4v
Setting off on a journey by river or by land	II iii 2:1–2 II iii 2:1–2	§ 3.3:1–4, 60–61 § 3.4:1–5, 60–61 § 3.5:1–3, 60–61	§ 3.2:2–4, 156–157	
		Fourth place		
Finding something hidden	II iv 1:1–3	§ 4.5:2–3, 64–65		IV:8, S1r
Laying the foundations of a wall and fortifying a city	II iv 2:1	§ 4.2:1–3, 62–63 § 4.3:1–4, 62–65	§ 4.2:1–8, 156–159 § 4.3:1–3, 158–159	IV:6, R4v
Buying a manor-house, a vineyard, or a piece of land	II iv 3:1–2	§ 4.4:1–3, 64–65	§ 4.1:1–4, 156–157	
Moving from one place to another	II iv 4:1–3			
		Fifth place		
Finding an hour for conception	II v 1:1–2 II v 2:1–7 II v 3:1–2	§ 5.1:1–7, 64–67	§ 5.1:1–4, 158–159 § 5.2:1–8, 158–161	IV:9, S1r
Sending messengers	II v 4:1–2	***She'elot* I, § 9.2:1–4, 284–285**	***She'elot* II, § 9.3:1–2, 380–381**	
Drinking and making merry	II v 4:3	§ 5.3:1–2, 66–67	§ 5.3:1, 160–161	
		Sixth place		
Elections and lunar mansions	II vi 1:1–6 through II vi 29:1–2			IV:18, S3r–T3v
		Seventh place		
Betrothing a woman	II vii 1:1–6	§ 7.6:1–7, 74–77	§ 7.4:1–6, 166–167	IV:13, S2r

Topic	*Electiones*	*Mivḥarim* I	*Mivḥarim* II	Epitome
Forming a partnership	II vii 2:1	§ 7.7:1–2, 76–77	§ 7.5:1–2, 166–167	
Choosing an hour for a king or a prince to go to war	II vii 3:1–5 II vii 4:1–5 II vii 5:1–6 II vii 6:1–5	§ 7.1:1–4, 70–71 through § 7.5:1–13, 74–71	§ 7.1:1–6, 162–165 through § 7.4:1–3, 166–167	IV:11, S1v–S2r
Going to sea and plunder or laying siege to a city	II vii 7:1–8	§ 7.5:3, 74–75	§ 7.1:3, 162–163	IV:12, S2r
		Eighth place		
Looking for something stolen or lost	II viii 1:1–5		§ 8.1:1–3, 168–168	
		Ninth place		
Writing, studying, writing a book, opening the heart	II ix 1:1–5	§ 9.3:1, 80–81		
Setting off on a long journey	II ix 2:1–5 II ix 3:1–7 II ix 4:1–2	§ 9.1:1–3, 78–79 § 9.2:1–9, 80–81	§ 9.1:1–4, 168–169 § 9.2:1–3, 168–171 § 9.3:1–5, 170–171	IV:16, S2v
		Tenth place		
Taking possession of a kingdom	II x 1:1–7	§ 10.2:1–3, 82–85		IV:16, S2v–S3r
Being introduced to the king or a great prince	II x 2:1–3	§ 10.1:2–5, 80–83	§ 10.2:1–2, 172–173	
		Eleventh place		
Seeking love	II xi 1:1–3	§ 11.1:1–3, 86–87	§ 11.2:1–4, 174–175	
		Twelfth place		
Buying an animal	II xii 1:1–4	§ 12.1:1–3, 56–57	§ 12.1:1–5, 176–177	IV:17, S34

APPENDIX 20

INDICATIONS OF THE HOROSCOPIC PLACES IN *LIBER INTERROGATIONUM*, *SHE'ELOT* I, *SHE'ELOT* II, AND *EPITOME*

To provide an idea of the contents of the bulk of *Interrogationes*, the following table presents the subject matter of all the questions addressed in this work. The items in this table are sorted according to their order of appearance in the twelve chapters of *Interrogationes*. Each item is accompanied by a reference to the corresponding part, chapter, section, and sentence in our edition of *Interrogationes*. Next to each item, the table presents a reference to *She'elot* I, *She'elot* II, and to the third part of *Epitome totius astrologiae*, on interrogations, if the subject matter of any of the questions dealt with in any of these three works has its match in *Interrogationes*. Otherwise the corresponding cell is left blank. For close correspondences that involve not only the subject matter but particularly the technical contents themselves of the question, readers are invited to consult the notes to the English translation of our edition of *Interrogationes*. References to *She'elot* I and *She'elot* II in this table use the chapter, section, and sentence numbering of the edition of these two works in volume 3 of this series. These references also specify the corresponding pages in that volume. References to the third part of the *Epitome* use the chapters of the printed edition of this work (Nuremberg, 1548). When the matching items do not occur in the same chapter, the references to them appear in bold.

Topic	*Interrogat.*	*She'elot* I	*She'elot* II	*Epitome*
		First place		
General principles for interrogations	**II i 1:1–8 through II i 15:1–5**		**§ 2:1–3, 348–349 through § 8:1–5, 354–355**	**III:1, O3v–O4r III:2, O4r–O4v**
		Second place		
Riches	II ii 1:1–3	§ 2.1:2–12, 250–253	§ 2.1:1, 360–361	III:5, P1r
Buying or selling	II ii 2:1–9	§ 2.4:1–2, 252–253	§ 2.2:1–2, 360–361 § 11.1:1–2, 384–385	III:23, R1v III:24, R2r
A stolen or lost article	II ii 3:1–13	**§ 7.7:1–11, 276–279**	**§ 7.7:11, 374–375**	
When the thief will be captured	II ii 4:1–2 II ii 5:1–5	**§ 7.7:12–13, 278–279**	**§ 7.7:9–10, 374–375**	

Topic	*Interrogat.*	*She'elot* I	*She'elot* II	*Epitome*
		Third place		
Whether it is auspicious or inauspicious to take a journey	II iii 1:1–3	§ 3.4:1–3, 256–257 § 9.3:2–4, 284–287	§ 9.1:1–6, 378–379	III:17, Q4r–Q4v
Joy	II iii 2:1–4	**§ 5.3:1–2, 66–67**	**§ 5.3:1, 160–161**	
		Fourth place		
The outcome of something	II iv 1:1	§ 4.1:1–5, 256–257	§ 4.1:1–5, 362–365	
Whether the king's countries or cities will rebel against him	II iv 2:1–4	§ 4.3:1–2, 258–259	**§ 7.5:1–3, 372–373**	IV:20, R1r
		Fifth place		
Whether the querent will have a son	II v 1:1–7 II v 2:1–4	§ 5.2:1–6, 262–265	§ 5.1:1–5, 364–367	III:9, P3v
Whether a woman is pregnant	II v 3:1–6 II v 4:1–6	§ 5.1:1–4, 262–263 § 5.1:3, 262–263	§ 5.2:1–2, 366–367 § 5.2:2, 366–367	III:9, P3r–P3v
Whether the woman will give birth to a boy or a girl	II v 5:1–4	§ 5.3:1–6, 264–265	§ 5.3:1–4, 366–367	III:9, P3v
		Sixth place		
Whether a sick person will die or recover	II vi 1:1–12 II vi 2:1–8	§ 6.1:1–7, 266–267	§ 6.1:1–10, 366–369	III:10, P44–Q1v
		Seventh place		
Betrothal of women	II vii 1:1–12	§ 7.1:1–6, 268–269	**§ 12.3:1–7, 388–391**	III:11, Q1v
Quarrels and strife	II vii 2:1–10			
Wars	II vii 3:1–7 II vii 4:1–7 II vii 5:1	§ 7.3:1–19, 270–273 § 7.4:1–9, 272–273	§ 7.1:2–4, 368–369 through § 7.4:1–3, 370–373	III:12, Q1v–Q2r

Topic	*Interrogat.*	*She'elot* I	*She'elot* II	*Epitome*
Partnership	II vii 6:1–5	§7.2:1–3, 268–269	§7.8:1–2, 376–377	
		Eighth place		
One who is afraid that something may happen to him	II viii 1:1–6	§8.1:1–5, 282–283	§8.3:1–4, 376–379	
Whether someone is alive or dead	II viii 2:1–4	**§1.2:1–5, 356–359**	**§1.3:1–2, 248–249**	III:3, O4v
		Ninth place		
A journey by land or by sea	II ix 1:1–5	§9.3:1–4, 284–287	§9.1:1–3, 378–379	III:17, Q4r
Whether someone will return and when	II ix 2:1–7	**§3.2:1–4, 254–255**	**§1.4:1–6, 358–359**	III:25, R2r
		Tenth place		
Whether someone will get wealth from a king or a prince	II x 1:1–7	10.1:1–9, 286–287	§10.1:1–8, 382–383	III:18, Q4v
Whether someone will learn from a scholar	II x 2:1–4			
		Eleventh place		
Love	II xi 1:1–3	§11.1:1–8, 290–293		III:21, R1v
		Twelfth place		
A man in jail or held captive	II xii 1:1–10	§12.1:1–9, 292–295	§12.1:1–14, 388–389	III:26, R2v
Reading the querent's thoughts	II xii 2:1–9 through II xii 5:1	**§4:1–5, 242–243 through §11:1–3, 246–247**	**§9:1–3, 354–355 through §10:1–6, 356–357**	
Finding a hidden thing	II xii 6:1–6	**§4.4:1–6, 258–259 through §4.10:1–5, 262–263**	§12.6:1–5, 390–393 through §12.7:1–4, 292–395	III:8, P2v

Topic	*Interrogat.*	*She'elot* I	*She'elot* II	*Epitome*
Someone who escaped from his master	II xii 7:1–10 II xii 8:1–4 II xii 9:1–4 II xii 10:1–5	**§ 7.8:1–8, 278–281** **§ 7.9:1–9, 280–283**	**§ 8.1:1–5, 376–377**	III:13–16, Q2v–Q4r

INDEX OF TECHNICAL TERMS AND BIOGRAPHICAL NOTES

English	Latin	Reference
120 conjunctions of the seven planets	120 modi coniunctionum planetarum	*Int*, I 1:3, 227
Abraham, the author	Abraham additor	*El*, I 1:1, 135
Abū ʿAlī Al-Khayyāṭ	Even Aeli Alkahi	*Int*, I 1:7, 234
Abū Maʿshar	Even Mahasar	*Int*, I 1:7, 233
airy sign	signum aereum	*Tp*, III 4:9, 373
Al-Battānī ibn Jābir the Arab	Albategni Gehii Sarraceni	*Int*, I 2:1, 236
Al-Kindī	Alkindi	*Int*, I 1:7, 233–234
ascendant	ascendens	*El*, I 2:2, 137
aspect	aspectus	*Tp*, I i 4:7, 338
aspect of hate	aspectus odii	*El*, I 2:2, 137
aspect of love	aspectus dilectionis	*El*, II vii 1:3, 163
be victorious	vincere	*El*, II vii 6:3, 166
benefic planets	stelle bone	*Int*, II i 9:5, 245
bicorporal sign	signa bicorpora, signa communia	*Int*, II iii 2:3, 252
burnt	combustus	*El*, II i 1:5, 239
cadent places	cadentes; lapsa; cadentes ab angulis; cadentes a cavillis	*Int*, II xii 9:4, 269

English	Latin	Reference
cadent planet	cadens	*Int*, II i 7:5, 243
Cancer, sign of the world	Cancer, qui est in signo seculi	*Int*, I 1:3, 228–229
cardines	anguli; caville	*Int*, II xii 9:4, 269 *Int*, II ii 2:7, 250
conjunction of Saturn and Jupiter	coniunctio .20. annorum	*El*, II vii 6:5, 167
crooked sign	signum tortuosum	*Int*, II iv 1:1, 253
decan	facies	*Tp*, I i 7:1, 340
dejection	vilitas	*Int*, II i 6:12, 242–243
directions	ductus	*Int*, I 1:3, 229
dodecatemoria	duodecime	*Tp*, I i 7:3, 340
domain of burning	terminus combustionis	*El*, II iv 1:1, 146
Dorotheus	Doroneus	*Int*, I 1:7, 230–231
Dragon	draco	*Tp*, III 1:9–10, 369
earthy sign	signum terreum	*Tp*, III 4:9, 373
eccentric circle	eccentricus	*Tp*, II iii 8:2, 355
ecliptic	linea signourum	*Tp*, I i 4:6, 337–338
Enoch	Enoch	*Int*, I 2:1, 234–235
epicycle	epiciclus	*Tp*, II iv 8:2, 358

English	Latin	Reference
exaltation	honor altitudo exaltatio	*Int*, II i 6:12, 242 *El*, II ii 2:2, 144–145 *Int*, II x 1:6, 262–264
fardār	de .75. annis	*Int*, I 1:3, 228
fiery sign	signum igneum	*Tp*, III 4:9, 373
fixed signs	signa veridica, signa stabilia, signa fixa	*Int*, II iii 2:3, 252 *Int*, II i 1:3, 238–239 *El*, II viii 1:5, 169
giving the spark	dare scintillationem	*Int*, II vii 1:3, 258–259
give power	dare vim/fortitudinem	*Tp*, I iv 1:2, 345
great years	anni magni	*Tp*, II:8, 346–347
Ḥassān the Jew	Hessen Iudeus	*Int*, I 2:1, 236
Head of the Dragon	Caput draconis	*Tp*, III 1:9–10, 369
house of war	domus belli	*Int*, II vii 2:8, 260
joy	gaudium	*Int*, II iii 2:2, 252
Kanakah, the Indian	Canba Aliendi	*Int*, I 1:7, 231
King Ptolemy	Ptholomeus rex	*El*, II vi 6:4, 156–157
least years	anni parvi	*Tp*, II:8, 346–347
lord of the day	dominus diei	*Tp*, I:3, 333
lord of the decan	dominus faciei	*Tp*, I i 7:1, 340

English	Latin	Reference
lord of the hour	dominus hore	*Tp*, I:3, 335
lord of the term	dominus termini	*Tp*, I i 7:1, 339
lot	pars	*Int*, I 1:3, 229
lot of Fortune	pars gratie pars fortune	*Int*, II i 9:1, 244
lunar mansions	.28. mansiones Lune	*El*, II vi 1:1, 152–153
malefic planets	stelle male	*Int*, II i 9:5, 245
Māshā'allāh	Mesehalla	*Int*, I 1:7, 231–232
melothesia	in quo membro est secundum divisio ipsa Geminis habet de partibus membrorum hominis	*El*, II i 2:8–9, 143 *Tp*, IV5:3, 386
middle years	anni medii	*Tp*, II:8, 346–347
mobile signs	signa mobilia	*Int*, II iii 2:3, 252
mubtazz	almutaz	*Tp*, I i 7:1, 339
ninth-part	novena novenaria	*Int*, II xii 2:2, 264
peregrine	peregrinus, vagus	*El*, II ii 1:3, 144 *Tp*, IV 3:2, 328–329
places of dominion	loci principatus	*Int*, II i 15:1, 247–248
planet (משרת)	stella servientis	*Int*, II i 1:5, 239
Ptolemy	Ptholomeus Bartholomeus rex	*El*, II vi 6:4, 156–157 *Int*, I 2:1, 235

English	Latin	Reference
ray	radiatio	*El*, II vi 6:4, 157–158
received	receptus	*Tp*, I iv 2:3, 345
receiving the spark	recipere scintillationem	*Int*, II vii 1:3, 258–259
retrograde	retrogradus	*El*, II ii 1:4, 144
revolution of the world-year	revolucio anni mundi	*Tp*, II i 2:1, 347
revolution of the year of the new-born	revolutio anni nati	*Int*, I 1:3, 229–230
rising times	ascensiones	*El*, II ix 2:5, 169–170
Sahl, the Jew	Sahal Iudeus	*Int*, I 1:7, 232–233
Saturn-Mars conjunctions	coniunciones Saturni cum Marte	*Int*, I 1:3, 228–229
sixth, eighth and twelfth horoscopic places	6a., 8a. vel .12a	*El*, II i 1:6, 142
sign of the country/city	signum patrie/ville	*El*, II iv 2:1, 146–147
sign with a human shape	signum qui est super formam filii hominis	*El*, II vi 6:5, 157
smaller part of the zodiac	pars parva circuli	*El*, II ii 1:1, 143–144
spark	scintillatio	*Int*, II vii 1:3, 258–259 *Int*, II ii 2:4, 250
stations	stationes	*Int*, II i 4:3, 241
straight sign	signum rectum	*Int*, II iv 1:1, 253

English	Latin	Reference
succedent places	succedentes	*Int*, II xii 9:4, 269
Tail of the Dragon	cauda	*Tp*, III 1:9–10, 369
term	terminus	*Tp*, I i 7:1, 339
terminal sign	signum finis	*El*, II vii 6:5, 167
Thābit ibn Qurra al-Ḥarrānī	Thebit, filius Kha Alharani	*Int*, I 2:1, 235
triplicity	triplicitas	*Tp*, IV 3:2, 384
tropical sign	signum mobile	*Int*, II iii 2:2, 252
ʿUmar ⟨b. al-Farrukhān⟩ al-Ṭabarī	Aomar Tiberiadis	*Int*, I 1:7, 232
under the rays of the Sun,	sub radiis solis	*Int*, II vi 1:3, 255
watery sign	signum aquaticum	*Tp*, III 4:9, 373
zodiac	zodiacus circulus	*Tp*, I i 4:6, 337–337

BIBLIOGRAPHY

Works by Abraham Ibn Ezra

Abrahe Avenaris (Peter d'Abano), ed. Liechtenstein (1507): *Abrahe Avenaris Iudei Astrologi peritissimi in re iudiciali opera ab excellentissimo philosopho Petro de Albano post accuratam castigationem in Latinum traducta* (Venice: Petrus Liechtenstein, 1507), IIr–XCIv.

Astrolabio, ed. Millás Vallicrosa (1940): *Tractatus de astrolabio conscriptus dictante authori quodam egregio philosopho Mro. Abraham*, ed. José M. Millás Vallicrosa, in "Un nuevo tratado de astrolabio de R. Abraham ibn Ezra," *Al-Andalus*, 5 (1940): 9–29.

Commentary on Daniel (1525): Abraham Ibn Ezra, *Commentary on Daniel, Miqra'ot Gedolot* (Venice, 1525; repr. Jerusalem 1972).

Commentary on Ecclesiastes, ed. Gomez Aranda (1994): Mariano Gomez Aranda, *El comentario de Abraham Ibn Ezra del Eclesiastés* (Introducción, traducción y edición crítica) (Madrid: CSIC, 1994).

Commentary on Exodus, ed. Weiser (1976): *Abraham Ibn Ezra, Commentary on Exodus*, in *A. Weiser* (ed.), *Ibn Ezra's Commentary on the Torah*, II, Jerusalem, 1976.

Commentary on Genesis, ed. Cohen (1997): M. Cohen, ed., *Miqra'ot Gedolot ha-Keter*, *Genesis* vol. I (Ramat Gan, 1997).

Commentary on Job 2004, ed. Gomez Aranda: M. Gomez Aranda, ed., *El comentario de Abraham Ibn Ezra al libro de Job*, edición crítica, traducción y estudio introductorio (Madrid: CSIC, 2004).

De nativitatibus, ed. Ratdolt (1485): *Abraham Iudei de nativitatibus* (Venice: Erhard Ratdolt, 1485).

De nativitatibus, ed. Sela (2019): *Liber Abraham Iudei de nativitatibus* in: *Abraham Ibn Ezra Latinus on Nativities.* A Parallel Latin-English Critical Edition of *Liber Nativitatum* and *Liber Abraham Iudei de Nativitatibus*, ed., trans., and annot. Shlomo Sela (Leiden: Brill, 2019), pp. 250–351.

De rationibus tabularum, ed. Millás Vallicrosa (1947): José M. Millás Vallicrosa, ed., *El Libro de los Fundamentos de las Tablas Astronómicas de R. Abraham Ibn Ezra* (Madrid–Barcelona, 1947).

'Ibbur, ed. Goodman (2011): *Sefer Ha'ibbur, A Treatise on the Calendar by Rabbi Abraham Ibn Ezra*, translated and annotated by Mordechai S. Goodman (Jerusalem: Ktav, 2011).

'Ibbur, ed. Philipobsky (1851): Abraham Bar Ḥiyya, *Sefer Ha'ibbur*, ed. T. Philipobsky (London, 1851).

Ibn al-Muthannā's Commentary, ed. Goldstein (1967): *Ibn al-Muthannā's Commentary on the Astronomical Tables of al-Khwārizmī*, ed. and trans. B.R. Goldstein (New Haven–London, 1967).

Me'orot, ed. Sela (2011): *Sefer ha-me'orot* in: *Abraham Ibn Ezra on Elections, Interrogations and Medical Astrology*, A Parallel Hebrew English Critical Edition of the Book of Elections (3 Versions), the Book of Interrogations (3 versions) and the Book of the Luminaries, ed., trans., and annot. Shlomo Sela (Leiden: Brill, 2011), pp. 452–483.

Mishpeṭei ha-mazzalot, ed. Sela (2017): *Mishpeṭei ha-mazzalot* in: *Abraham Ibn Ezra's Introductions to Astrology*, A Parallel Hebrew-English Critical Edition of the Book of the Beginning of Wisdom and the Book of the Judgments of the Zodiacal Signs, ed., trans., and annot. Shlomo Sela (Leiden: Brill, 2017), pp. 488–555.

Mispar, ed. Silberberg (1895): *Sefer ha-Mispar, Das Buch der Zahl*, trans. and ed. Moritz Silberberg (Frankfurt a.M., 1895).

Mivḥarim I, ed. Sela (2011): First version of *Sefer ha-mivḥarim* in: *Abraham Ibn Ezra on Elections, Interrogations and Medical Astrology*, A Parallel Hebrew English Critical Edition of the Book of Elections (3 Versions), the Book of Interrogations (3 versions) and the Book of the Luminaries, ed., trans., and annot. Shlomo Sela (Leiden: Brill, 2011), pp. 46–89.

Mivḥarim II, ed. Sela (2011): Second version of *Sefer ha-mivḥarim* in: *Abraham Ibn Ezra on Elections, Interrogations and Medical Astrology*, A Parallel Hebrew English Critical Edition of the Book of Elections (3 Versions), the Book of Interrogations (3 versions) and the Book of the Luminaries, ed., trans., and annot. Shlomo Sela (Leiden: Brill, 2011), pp. 142–177.

Moladot, ed. Sela (2013): First version of *Sefer ha-moladot* in: *Abraham Ibn Ezra on Nativities and Continuous Horoscopy*, A Parallel Hebrew English Critical Edition of the Book of Nativities and the Book of Revolution, ed., trans. and annot. Shlomo Sela (Leiden: Brill, 2013), pp. 84–203.

Nativitates, ed. Sela (2019): *Liber nativitatum* (Latin translation of the second version of *Sefer ha-moladot*) in: *Abraham Ibn Ezra Latinus on Nativities*. A Parallel Latin-English Critical Edition of *Liber Nativitatum* and *Liber Abraham Iudei de Nativitatibus*, ed., trans., and annot. Shlomo Sela (Leiden: Brill, 2019), pp. 80–159.

Neḥoshet I: *Keli ha-neḥoshet* (first version), MS Paris, BnF, héb. 1061 (IMHM: F 14645), fols. 148a–164a.

Neḥoshet II: *Keli ha-neḥoshet* (second version), MS Paris, BnF, héb. 1045 (IMHM: F 33996), fols. 188a–196b.

ʿOlam I, ed. Sela (2010): First version of *Sefer ha-ʿOlam*, in: *The Book of the World, A Parallel Hebrew-English Critical Edition of the Two Versions of the Text*, ed., trans., and annot. Shlomo Sela (Leiden-Boston: Brill Academic Publishers, 2010), pp. 52–97.

ʿOlam II, ed. Sela (2010): Second version of *Sefer ha-ʿOlam*, in: *The Book of the World, A Parallel Hebrew-English Critical Edition of the Two Versions of the Text*, ed., trans., and annot. Shlomo Sela (Leiden-Boston: Brill Academic Publishers, 2010), pp. 156–191.

Reshit ḥokhmah, ed. Sela (2017): *Reshit ḥokhmah* in: *Abraham Ibn Ezra's Introductions to Astrology*, A Parallel Hebrew-English Critical Edition of the Book of the Beginning of Wisdom and the Book of the Judgments of the Zodiacal Signs, ed., trans., and annot. Shlomo Sela (Leiden: Brill, 2017), pp. 48–271.

Reshit ḥokhmah II, ed. Sela (2010): *Reshit ḥokhmah* II in: Shlomo Sela, "A Fragment From an Unknown Redaction of *Reʾšit Ḥokmah* by Abraham Ibn Ezra," *Aleph* 10.1 (2010): 43–66.

Sheʾelot I, ed. Sela (2011): First version of *Sefer ha-mivḥarim* in: *Abraham Ibn Ezra on Elections, Interrogations and Medical Astrology*, A Parallel Hebrew English Critical Edition of the Book of Elections (3 Versions), the Book of Interrogations (3 versions) and the Book of the Luminaries, ed., trans., and annot. Shlomo Sela (Leiden: Brill, 2011), pp. 240–297.

Sheʾelot II, ed. Sela (2011): Second version of *Sefer ha-mivḥarim* in: *Abraham Ibn Ezra on Elections, Interrogations and Medical Astrology*, A Parallel Hebrew English Critical Edition of the Book of Elections (3 Versions), the Book of Interrogations (3 versions) and the Book of the Luminaries, ed., trans., and annot. Shlomo Sela (Leiden: Brill, 2011), pp. 348–397.

Ṭeʿamim I, ed. Sela (2007): First version of *Sefer ha-ṭeʿamim* in: Abraham Ibn Ezra: *The Book of Reasons, A Parallel Hebrew-English Critical Edition of the Two Versions of the Text*, ed., trans., and annot. Shlomo Sela (Leiden-Boston: Brill Academic Publishers, 2007), pp. 28–107.

Ṭeʿamim II, ed. Sela (2007): Second version of *Sefer ha-ṭeʿamim* in: Abraham Ibn Ezra: *The Book of Reasons, A Parallel Hebrew-English Critical Edition of the Two Versions of the Text*, ed., trans., and annot. Shlomo Sela (Leiden-Boston: Brill Academic Publishers, 2007), pp. 182–257.

Tequfah, ed. Sela (2013): *Sefer ha-tequfah* in: *Abraham Ibn Ezra on Nativities and Continuous Horoscopy*, A Parallel Hebrew English Critical Edition of the Book of Nativities and the Book of Revolution, ed., trans. and annot. Shlomo Sela (Leiden: Brill, 2013), pp. 372–389.

Yesod Moraʾ, ed. Simon (2007): *Yesod Mora We-Sod Torah*, An Annotated Critical Edition by Joseph Cohen and Uriel Simon (Ramat Gan: Bar-Ilan University Press, 2007).

Primary Sources

Abbreviation, ed. Burnett et al. (1994): Abū Maʿshar, *The Abbreviation of the Introduction to Astrology*, together with the Medieval Latin translation of Adelard of Bath, ed. and trans. Ch. Burnett, K. Yamamoto, M. Yano (Leiden, 1994).

Albumasar in Sadan, ed. Federici Vescovini (1998): *Albumasar in Sadan* in Graziella Federici Vescovini, 'La versio latina degli *Excerpta de secretis Albumasar di Sadan*', *Archives d'histoire doctrinale et littéraire du Moyen Age*, 65, (1998): 273–330.

Alchandreana, ed. Juste (2007): David Juste, *Les Alchandreana primitifs. Etude sur les plus anciens traités astrologiques latins d'origine arabe* (X^e *siècle*) (Leiden and Boston: Brill, 2007).

Al-Kindī, eds, Bos and Burnett (2000): Gerrit Bos and Charles Burnett, *Scientific Weather Forecasting in the Middle Ages: The Writings of al-Kindī* (London and New York, 2000).

Andarzaghar, ed. Burnett and al-Hamdi (1991): Ch. Burnett and A. Al-Hamdi, "Zādānfarrūkh al-Andarzaghar on Anniversary Horoscopes," Zeitschrift für Geschichte der arabisch-islamischen Wissenschaften, 7 (1991/1992): 294–398.

Anthologiae, ed. Riley (1995): Vettius Valens' *Anthologiae*, English translation by Mark Riley, completed in ca. 1995, and based on Wilhelm 1Kroll's 908 and David Pingree's 1986 editions: http://www.csus.edu/indiv/r/rileymt/Vettius%20Valens%20entire.pdf.

Astronomica, ed. Goold (1977): M. Manilius, *Astronomica*, edited and translated by G.P. Goold (London: Loeb Classical Library, 1977).

Baraita de-Mazzalot, ed. Wertheimer (1998): *Baraita de-Mazzalot*, ed. S.A. Wertheimer, in *Po'al haShem*, vol. I (Bne Braq, 1998),

Book of Religions and Dynasties, ed. Yamamoto and Burnett (2000): *Abū Ma'shar on Historical Astrology, The Book of Religions and Dynasties* (*On the Great Conjunctions*) ed. and trans. Keiji Yamamoto and Charles Burnett (Leiden: Brill, 2000).

Book on Eclipses, ed. Sela (2010): Māshā'allāh, *Book on Eclipses* in: *The Book of the World, A Parallel Hebrew-English Critical Edition of the Two Versions of the Text*, ed., trans., and annot. Shlomo Sela (Leiden-Boston: Brill Academic Publishers, 2010), 235–259.

Carmen astrologicum, ed. Pingree (1976): Dorotheus of Sidon, *Carmen astrologicum*, ed. and trans. D. Pingree (Leipzig, 1976).

De divinatione, ed. Falconer (1923): Marcus T. Cicero, *De divinatione* with an English translation by William Armistead Falconer (London: Heinerman [Loeb Classical Library, No 154], 1923).

De iudiciis astrorum, ed. Petri (1551): *Albohazen Haly filii Abenragel libri de iudiciis astrorum*, ('Alī ibn abī-l-Rijāl, *Kitāb al-bāri*), ed. Henrichus Petri (Basel, 1551).

De mundo (Bate), ed. Liechtenstein (1507): Translation of *'Olam* I by Henry Bate, in: *Abrahe Avenaris Iudei Astrologi peritissimi in re iudiciali opera* (Venice: Petrus Liechtenstein, 1507), sig. LXXVIIv2–LXXXVr1.

De nativitatibus, ed. Hervagius (1533): *De nativitatibus secundum Omar*, ed. Iohannes Hervagius (Basel, 1533).

De nativitatibus, ed. Petreius (1540): *Albubater magni Alchasili de nativitatibus*, ed. Iohannes Petreius (Nürnberg, 1540).

Elements, ed. Ramsay Wright (1934): Al-Bīrūnī, *The Book of Instruction in the Elements of the Art of Astrology*, ed. and trans. R. Ramsay Wright (London: Luzac, 1934).

Epitome, ed. Heller (1548): *Epitome totius astrologiae, conscripta a Ioanne Hispalensi Hispano Astrologo celeberrimo, ante annos quadringentos, ac nunc primum in lucem edita. Cum praefatione Ioachimi Helleri Leucopetraei, contra Astrologiae adversarios*, in officina Ioannis Montani et Ulrici Neuber, (Nuremberg, 1548).

Fihrist, ed. and trans. Dodge (1970): *The Fihrist of al-Nadīm*, ed. and trans. Bayard Dodge (New York & London, 1970).

Great Introduction, ed. Burnett and Yamamoto (2019): *The Great Introduction to Astrology by Abū Ma'šar*, ed. Keiji Yamamoto and Charles Burnett (Leiden: Brill, 2019).

Ḥeshbon, ed. Millás Vallicrosa (1959): José Maria Millás Vallicrosa, ed. and trans., *La obra Séfer hesbón mahlekot ha-kokabim* (Libro del cálculo de los movimientos de los astros) de R. Abraham bar Ḥiyya ha-Bargeloní (Madrid: CSIC, 1959).

Hidden things, trans. Dykes (2008): Māshā'allāh, *On hidden things*, trans. Benjamin N. Dykes, in: Benjamin N. Dykes, *Works of Sahl and Māshā'allāh* (Minneapolis: Cazimi Press, 2008), pp. 425–436.

India, ed. Sachau (1888): *Alberuni's India*, An English edition, with notes and Indices by Edward C. Sachau (London: Trübner, Ludgate Hill, 1888).

Interpretation, trans. Dykes (2008): Māshā'allāh, *On the interpretation of cognition*, trans. Benjamin N. Dykes, in: Benjamin N. Dykes, *Works of Sahl and Māshā'allāh* (Minneapolis: Cazimi Press, 2008), pp. 417–423.

Introduction, ed. Burnett et al. (2004): Al-Qabīṣī (Alcabitius): *The introduction to Astrology*, Editions of the Arabic and Latin texts and an English translation, Charles Burnett, Keiji Yamamoto, M. Yano (London-Turin, 2004).

Iudizios, ed. Hilty (2005): Aly Aben Ragel, *El libro conplido en los iudizios de las estrellas, Partes 6 a 8*, traducción hecha en la corte de Alfonso el Sabio, Introducción y edición por Gerold Hilty (Zaragoza: Instituto de Estudios Islámicos y del Oriente Próximo, 2005).

Kitāb al-ulūf, ed. Pingree (1968): David Pingree, *The Thousands of Abū Maʿshar* (London: Warburg Institute, 1968).

Liber Albohali, ed. Heller (1549): *Albohali Arabis astrologi antiquissimi ac clarissimi de iudiciis nativitatum liber unus antehac non editus*, ed. Joachim Heller (Nuremberg: in officina J. Montani, [et] U. Neuber, 1549).

Liber Aristotilis, ed. Burnett and Pingree (1997): *The* Liber Aristotilis *of Hugo of Santalla*, ed. Charles Burnett and David Pingree (London: School of Advanced Study University of London, 1997).

Liber Astronomicus (1550): Guidonis Bonati Forolviensis Mathematici de Astronomia Tractatus X (Basileae, 1550).

Liber Mesellae de nativitatibus, ed. Kennedy and Pingree (1971): *Māshā'allāh's Kitāb al-mawālīd*, based on *Liber Mesellae De nativitatibus*, MS Paris, BnF, Latin 7324, ff. 73–76, in: E.S. Kennedy and D. Pingree (ed. and trans.), *The Astrological History of Māshā'allāh* (Cambridge: Harvard University Press, 1971), pp. 145–165.

Matheseos, ed. Bram (1975): *Ancient Astrology: Theory and Practice—Matheseos Libri VIII by Firmicus Maternus*, trans. Jean Rhys Bram (Park Ridge, N.J., 1975).

Megillat ha-megalleh, ed. Poznanski (1924): Abraham Bar Ḥiyya, *Sefer Megillat ha-Megalle von Abraham bar Chija*, published by A. Poznanski with introduction and notes by J. Guttman (Berlin, 1924).

Nativitas, ed. Steel et al. (2018): *The Astrological Biography of a Medieval Philosopher: Henry Bate's Nativitas* (1280–1281), Carlos Steel, Steven Vanden Broecke, David Juste, and Shlomo Sela (Leuven: Leuven University Press 2018).

Queries on Astrology, ed. Sela (2004): Shlomo Sela, "Queries on Astrology Sent from Southern France to Maimonides, Critical Edition of the Hebrew Text, Translation and Commentary," *Aleph* 6 (2004): 89–190.

Ṣafenat Paʿneaḥ, ed. Herzog (1911): Joseph Bonfils, *Sophnat Pane'ach*, Ein Beitrag sur Pentateuchexegeses des Mittelalters von D. Herzog (Heidelberg, 1911).

Significations, trans. Dykes (2008): Gergis, *What the planets signify in the twelve domiciles of the circle*, trans. Benjamin N. Dykes, in: Benjamin N. Dykes, *Works of Sahl and Māshā'allāh* (Minneapolis: Cazimi Press, 2008), pp. 499–513.

Speculum astronomiae, ed. Caroti et al. (1992): *Speculum astronomiae*, in: Paola Zambelli, *The* Speculum Astronomiae *and Its Enigma* (Dordrecht: Kluwer Academic Publishers, 1992), pp. 208–273.

Tabaqāt al-'umam, ed. Salem and Kumar (1991): Ṣāʿid al-Andalusī, *Kitāb Tabaqāt al-'Umam* in: *Science in the Medieval World, "Book of the Categories of Nations,"* by Ṣāʿid al-Andalusī, Translated and Edited by Semaʿan I. Salem and Alok Kumar (Austin: University of Texas Press, 1991).

Tetrabiblos, ed. Robbins (1980): C. Ptolemy, *Tetrabiblos*, ed. and trans. F.E. Robbins (Cambridge, Ma: Harvard University Press, 1980).

Tractatus pluviarum ed Burnett (2008), "Weather Forecasting, Lunar Mansions and a Disputed Atribution: the *Tractatus pluviarum et aeris mutationis* and *Epitome totius astrologiae* of 'Iohannes Hispalensis'", in *Islamic Thought in the Middle Ages: Studies in Text, Transmission and Translation, in Honour of Hans Daiber*, eds Anna Akasoy and Wim Raven (Leiden and Boston, 2008), 219–265.

Secondary Literature

Adamson 2007: P. Adamson, *Al-Kindī* (Oxford, 2007)

Baron 1958: S. Baron, *A Social and Religious History of the Jews* (New York, 1958).

Birkenmajer 1919: Aleksander Birkenmajer, "La bibliothèque de Richard de Fournival", Travail présenté par le Sécrétaire à la session de la Faculté le 3 juillet 1919, reprinted in Aleksander Birkenmajer, *Études d'histoire des sciences et de la philosophie du Moyen Age*, Studia Copernicana, 1 (Wrocław, Zakład Narodowy im. Ossolińskich, 1970), pp. 117–215.

Birkenmajer 1950: Aleksander Birkenmajer, "A propos de l'Abrahismus'", *Archives internationales d'histoire des sciences*, 3 (1950):378–390, reprinted in Aleksander Birkenmajer, *Études d'histoire des sciences et de la philosophie du Moyen Age*, Studia Copernicana, 1 (Wrocław, Zakład Narodowy im. Ossolińskich, 1970), pp. 237–249.

Bladel 2009: Kevin van Bladel, *The Arabic Hermes* (Oxford/New York: Oxford University Press, 2009).

Bos and Burnett 2000: Gerrit Bos and Charles Burnett, *Scientific Weather Forecasting in the Middle Ages: The Writings of al-Kindī* (London and New York, 2000).

Bouché-Leclercq 1899: A. Bouché-Leclercq, *L'Astrologie Grecque* (Paris, 1899).

Boudet 2006: Jean-Patrice Boudet, *Entre science et nigromance. Astrologie, divination et magie dans l'Occident médiéval (XIIe–XVe siècle)* (Paris: Publications de la Sorbonne, 2006).

Burnett 1976: Charles Burnett, "The Legend of the Three Hermes and Abū Ma'shar's *Kitāb al-Ulūf* in the Latin Middle Ages". *Journal of the Warburg and Courtauld Institutes* 39 (1976):231–234. Reprinted as article V in Charles Burnett, *Magic and divination in the Middle Ages: texts and techniques in the Islamic and Christian worlds* (Aldershot and Brookfield: Ashgate (Variorum), 1996).

Burnett 1993: Ch. Burnett, "Al-Kindī on Judicial Astrology: 'The Forty Chapters,'" *Arabic Sciences and Philosophy* 3 (1993): 77–117.

Burnett 1998: Charles Burnett, "King Ptolemy and Alchandreus the philosopher: the earliest texts on the astrolabe and Arabic astrology at Fleury, Micy and Chartres," *Annals of Science* 55. London, 1998. Addendum, ibid. 57, 2000, pp. 329–368, reprinted as essay I in Charles Burnett, *Arabic into Latin in the Middle Ages* (Farnham: Ashgate, 2009).

Burnett 2002: Charles Burnett, "John of Seville and John of Spain, a *mise au point*," Bulletin de philosophie médiévale 44. Turnhout, 2002, pp. 59–78, reprinted as essay VI in Charles Burnett, *Arabic into Latin in the Middle Ages* (Farnham: Ashgate, 2009), pp. 75–77.

Burnett 2003: Charles Burnett, "'Albumasar in Sadan' in the Twelfth Century," in *Ratio et Superstitio, Essays in Honor of Graziella Federici Vescovini*, ed. by G. Marchetti, O. Rignani, and V. Sorge (Louvain-le-Neuve: Fédération internationale des instituts d'études médiévales, 2003), pp. 59–67.

Burnett 2004: Charles Burnett, "Lunar Astrology. The Varieties of Texts Using Lunar Mansions With Emphasis on Jafar Indus," *Micrologus* XII (2004): 43–133.

Burnett 2008: Charles Burnett, "Weather Forecasting, Lunar Mansions and a Disputed Atribution: the *Tractatus pluviarum et aeris mutationis* and *Epitome totius astrologiae* of 'Iohannes Hispalensis'", in *Islamic Thought in the Middle Ages: Studies in Text, Transmission and Translation, in Honour of Hans Daiber*, eds Anna Akasoy and Wim Raven (Leiden and Boston, 2008), 219–265.

Burnett 2009: Charles Burnett, "Aristotle as an Authority on Judicial Astrology," in *Florilegium Mediaevale. Etudes offertes à Jacqueline Hamesse à l'occasion de son éméritat*, ed. José Meirinhos and Olga Weijers (Louvain-la-Neuve: Brepols, 2009), pp. 39–62.

Burnett 2010: Charles Burnett, "Hebrew and Latin Astrology in the Twelfth Century: the Example of the Location of Pain," *Studies in History and Philosophy of Science Part C: Studies in History and Philosophy of Biological and Biomedical Sciences* 41 2 (June 2010): 70–75.

Carmody 1956: F.J. Carmody, *Arabic Astronomical and Astrological Sciences in Latin Trans-*

lation. A Critical Bibliography (Berkeley and Los Angeles: University of California Press, 1956)

Chabás and Goldstein 2012: José Chabás and Bernard R. Goldstein, *A Survey of European Astronomical Tables in the Late Middle Ages* (Leiden: Brill, 2012).

Fleischer 1930/2: J.L. Fleischer, "R. Abraham Ibn Ezra in France" (Hebrew), *Mizraḥ u-maʿarav* 4 (5690 [1930]): 352–360; 5 (5692 [1932]): 38–46, 217–224, 289–300; repr. in *R. Abraham Ibn Ezra: A Collection of Articles on his Life and Works* (Tel Aviv, 5730 [1970]), 69–106.

Fleischer 1931: J.L. Fleischer, "R. Abraham Ibn Ezra and his Literary Work in England" (Hebrew), *Oṣar ha-ḥayyim* 7 (5691 [1931]): 69–76, 107–111, 129–133, 160–168, 189–203.

Fleischer 1932/3: J.L. Fleischer, "R. Abraham Ibn Ezra and his Literary Work in Rome" (Hebrew) *Oṣar ha-ḥayyim* 8 (5692 [1932]): 97–100, 129–131, 148–150, 169–171; 9 (5693 [1933]): 134–136, 152–155.

Fleischer 1934: J.L. Fleischer, "R. Abraham Ibn Ezra and his Literary Work in Lucca, Italy" (Hebrew) *Ha-soqer* 2 (5694 [1934]): 77–85; 4 (5696/7 [1936/7]): 186–194; repr. in *R. Abraham Ibn Ezra: A Collection of Articles on his Life and Works* (Tel Aviv 5730 [1970]), 107–124.

Freudenthal 2013: Gad Freudenthal, "Abraham Ibn Ezra and Judah Ibn Tibbon as Cultural Intermediaries," in: Haggai Ben-Shammai et al. (ed.), *Exchange and Transmission Across Cultural Boundaries* (Jerusalem 2013), 52–81.

Friedlander 1894/5: M. Friedlander, "Ibn Ezra in England," in *Transactions of the Jewish Historical Society of England* 2 (1894/5): 47–60.

Golb 1976: N. Golb, *The History and Culture of the Jews of Rouen in the Middle Ages* (Hebrew) (Tel Aviv, 5736 [1976]).

Goldstein 1996: B.R. Goldstein, "Astronomy and Astrology in the Works of Abraham Ibn Ezra," *Arabic Sciences and Philosoph*, 6 (1996): 9–21.

Juste 2007: David Juste, *Les Alchandreana primitifs. Etude sur les plus anciens traités astrologiques latins d'origine arabe (Xe siècle)* (Leiden and Boston: Brill, 2007).

Juste 2013: David Juste, "Les textes astrologiques latins attribués à Aristote," in *The Medieval Legends of Philosophers and Scholars, Micrologus* XXI (Florence, 2013), pp. 145–164.

Juste 2016: David Juste, "The Impact of Arabic Sources on European Astrology: Some Facts and Numbers," *Micrologus* XXIV (2016): 173–194.

Kennedy 1956: Edward S. Kennedy, "A Survey of Islamic Astronomical Tables," *Transactions of the American Philosophical Society* 46.2 (Philadelphia, 1956): 123–177.

Langermann 1993: Y. Tzvi Langermann, "Some Astrological Themes in the Thought of Abraham Ibn Ezra," in I. Twersky and J.M. Harris (ed.), *Rabbi Abraham Ibn Ezra: Studies in the Writings of a Twelfth-Century Jewish Polymath* (Cambridge, Mass., 1993), 28–85.

Langermann 2014: Y. Tzvi Langermann, "Abraham Ibn Ezra," *The Stanford Encyclopedia of Philosophy* (Spring 2014 Edition), Edward N. Zalta (ed.), URL = http://plato.stanford.edu/archives/spr2014/entries/ibn-ezra/.

Leicht 2012: Reimund Leicht, "Towards a History of Hebrew Astrological Literature," in *Science in Medieval Jewish Cultures*, ed. Gad Freudenthal (Cambridge: Cambridge University Press, 2012), pp. 262–281.

Lemay 1962: Richard Lemay, *Abu Maʿshar and Latin Aristotelianism in the twelfth century: The Recovery of Aristotle's Natural Philosophy through Arabic Astrology* (Beirut: Catholic Press, 1962).

Lemay 1987: R. Lemay, "The True Place of Astrology in Medieval Science and Philosophy," in P. Curry (ed.), *Astrology, Science and Society* (Suffolk, 1987), pp. 57–73.

Levey 1971: M. Levey, "Abraham ibn Ezra," in *Dictionary of Scientific Biography*, vol. IV, (New York, 1971), 502–503.

Levy 1927: R. Levy, *The Astrological Works of Abraham Ibn Ezra* (Baltimore, 1927).

Levy 2000: T. Lévy, "Abraham Ibn Ezra et les mathematiques; remarques bibliographiques et historiques" in *Abraham ibn Ezra, savanat universel* (Bruxelles, 2000), 60–75.

Lévy and Burnett 2006: Tony Lévy and C. Burnett, "*Sefer ha-Middot*: A Mid-Twelfth-Century Text on Arithmetic and Geometry Attributed to Abraham ibn Ezra," *Aleph* 6 (2006): 57–238.

Long 1982: A.A. Long, "Astrology: Arguments Pro and Contra," pp. 165–192 in Jonathan Barnes, J. Brunschwig, M. Burnyeat and M. Schofield (ed.), *Science and Speculation: Studies in Hellenistic theory and practice* (Cambridge: Cambridge University Press, 1982).

Millás Vallicrosa 1949: José M. Millás Vallicrosa, "El magisterio astronómico de Abraham Ibn Ezra en la Europa latina," in *Estudios sobre historia de la ciencia española*, Barcelona, 1949, pp. 289–347.

Nothaft 2018: Philipp Nothaft, "Ptolemaic Orbs in Twelfth-Century England: A Study and Edition of the Anonymous Liber de motibus planetarum," *Mediterranea*, 3 (2018): 145–210.

Pingree 1970: David Pingree, "Abū Maʿshar," *Dictionary of Scientific Biography* 1 (New York, 1970), 32–39.

Pingree 1989: David Pingree, "Classical and Byzantine Astrology in Sassanian Persia," in: *Dumbarton Oaks Papers* 43 (1989): 227–239.

Pingree 1990: David Pingree, "Astrology," in: *Religion, Learning and Science in the ʿAbbasid Period* (Cambridge, 1990), 290–300.

Pingree 1997: David Pingree, *From Astral Omens to Astrology from Babylon to Bīkāner* (Roma 1997).

Pingree 2019: David Pingree, "ʿUmar Ibn Al-Farrukhan al-Ṭabarī" in Complete Dictionary of Scientific Biography. *Encyclopedia.com*. 7 Feb. 2019 https://www.encyclopedia.com.

Plessner 1954: M. Plessner, "Hermes Trismegistus and Arab Science," *Studia Islamica*, 2 (1954):45–59.

Plessner 1971: M. Plessner, "Hirmis," *Encyclopedia of Islam*, new edition, 3 (Leiden 1971), 463–465.

Roberts 2013: Alexandre Roberts, "The Crossing Paths of Greek and Persian Knowledge in the 9th-century Arabic 'Book of Degrees'" in: C. Noce, M. Pampaloni, and C. Tavolieri (eds.) *Le vie del sapere*, Orientalia Christiana Analecta, 293 (Rome: Pontificio Instituto Orientale, 2013), pp. 279–303.

Samsó 2012: Julio Samsó, "'Dixit Abraham Iudeus': algunas observaciones sobre los textos astronómicos latinos de Abraham ibn ʿEzra", *Iberia Judaica*, IV, (2012):171–200.

Schirmann 1997: J. Schirmann, *The History of Hebrew Poetry in Christian Spain and Southern France*, Edited, supplemented and annotated by Ezra Fleischer (Hebrew) (Jerusalem, 1997).

Schwartz 1996: Dov Schwartz, "The Philosophical Super-commentary on Abraham Ibn Ezra's Commentaries" (Hebrew), *ʿAlei Sefer* 16 (1996): 92–114.

Sela 1999: Shlomo Sela, *Astrology and Biblical Exegesis in Abraham Ibn Ezra's Thought* (Hebrew) (Ramat Gan, 1999).

Sela 2003: Shlomo Sela, *Abraham Ibn Ezra and the Rise of Medieval Hebrew Science* (Leiden: Brill Academic Publishers, 2003).

Sela 2007: Abraham Ibn Ezra: *The Book of Reasons, A Parallel Hebrew-English Critical Edition of the Two Versions of the Text*, ed., trans., and annot. Shlomo Sela (Leiden-Boston: Brill Academic Publishers, 2007).

Sela 2010: *The Book of the World, A Parallel Hebrew-English Critical Edition of the Two Versions of the Text*, ed., trans., and annot. Shlomo Sela (Leiden-Boston: Brill *Academic Publishers*, 2010).

Sela 2010b: Shlomo Sela, "A Fragment From an Unknown Redaction of *Reʾšit Ḥoḵmah* by Abraham Ibn Ezra," *Aleph* 10.1 (2010): 43–66.

Sela 2011: *Abraham Ibn Ezra on Elections, Interrogations and Medical Astrology*, A Parallel Hebrew English Critical Edition of the Book of Elections (3 Versions), the Book of Interrogations (3 versions) and the Book of the Luminaries, ed., trans., and annot. Shlomo Sela (Leiden: Brill, 2011).

Sela 2012: Shlomo Sela, "Astrology in Medieval Jewish Thought" in: G. Freudenthal, (ed.) *Science in Medieval Jewish Cultures*, (Cambridge: Cambridge University Press, 2012), pp. 292–300.

Sela 2013: *Abraham Ibn Ezra on Nativities and Continuous Horoscopy*, A Parallel Hebrew English Critical Edition of the Book of Nativities and the Book of Revolution, ed., trans. and annot. Shlomo Sela (Leiden: Brill, 2013).

Sela 2014: Shlomo Sela, "The Astrological-Astronomical Encyclopedia in MS Paris 1058," 14(1) *Aleph*, (2014):189–241.

Sela 2017: *Abraham Ibn Ezra's Introductions to Astrology*, A Parallel Hebrew-English Critical Edition of the Book of the Beginning of Wisdom and the Book of the Judgments of the Zodiacal Signs, ed., trans., and annot. Shlomo Sela (Leiden: Brill, 2017).

Sela 2017a: Shlomo Sela, "The Ibn Ezra–Henry Bate Astrological Connection and the Three Abrahams," *Mediterranea*, 2 (2017): 163–186.

Sela 2018: Shlomo Sela, "Origins and Transmission of *Liber Abraham Iudei de Nativitatibus*: A New Appraisal Based on the Scrutiny of the Available Manuscripts and other Sources," *Revue des études juives*, 177, 3–4 (2018): 313–348.

Sela 2019 (b): Shlomo Sela, "The Abraham Ibn Ezra–Peter of Limoges Astrological-Exegetical Connection," *Aleph* 19.1 (2019): 9–57.

Sela 2019 (c): Shlomo Sela, "Calculating Birth: Abraham Ibn Ezra's Role in the Creation and Diffusion of the *Trutina Hermetis*," in C. Dopfel and A. Focati (ed.) *Pregnancy and Childbirth from Late Antiquity to the Renaissance* (Turhnout: Brepols, 2019), pp. 79–106.

Sela 2019 (d): Shlomo Sela, "Pietro d'Abano, Translator of Ibn Ezra's Astrological Writings," *Sefarad*, 79:1 (2019):1–82.

Sela 2019 (e): Shlomo Sela, "What is *Tractatus Particulares*, a Four-Part Work Assigned to Abraham Ibn Ezra? A Study of its Sources and General Features," *Archives d'histoire doctrinale et littéraire du Moyen Âge*, 86 (2019): 141–195.

Sela 2019: *Abraham Ibn Ezra Latinus on Nativities*. A Parallel Latin-English Critical Edition of *Liber Nativitatum* and *Liber Abraham Iudei de Nativitatibus*, ed., trans., and annot. Shlomo Sela (Leiden: Brill, 2019).

Sela and Freudenthal 2006: Shlomo Sela and Gad Freudenthal, "Abraham Ibn Ezra's Scholarly Writings: A Chronological Listing," *Aleph* 6 (2006): 13–55.

Sela and Smithuis 2009: Shlomo Sela and Renate Smithuis, "Two Hebrew Fragments from Unknown Redactions of Abraham Ibn Ezra's *Sefer ha-Mivḥarim* and *Sefer ha-Še'elot*," *Aleph* 9.2 (2009): 225–240.

Sela et al. (2020): Shlomo Sela, Carlos Steel, C. Philipp E. Nothaft, David Juste, Charles Burnett, "A Newly Discovered Treatise by Abraham Ibn Ezra and two Treatises Attributed to Al-Kindī in a Latin Translation by Henry Bate," *Mediterranea*, (2020): 191–303.

Sela forthcoming (a): Shlomo Sela, "The Impact of Hagin Le Juif's French Translations on Subsequent Latin Translations of Abraham Ibn Ezra's Astrological Writings," *Jewish Quarterly Review*, forthcoming.

Simon 1993: Uriel Simon, "Interpreting the Interpreter, Super-commentaries on Ibn Ezra's Commentaries" in: *Rabbi Abraham Ibn Ezra: Studies in the Writings of a Twelfth-Century Jewish Polymath* (Cambridge, Massachusetts and London, 1993), pp. 86–128.

Smithuis 2004: Renate Smithuis, "Abraham ibn Ezra the Astrologer and the Transmission of Arabic Science to the Christian West," doctoral dissertation (University of Manchester, 2004).

Smithuis 2006: Renate Smithuis, "Abraham Ibn Ezra's Astrological Works in Hebrew and Latin—New Discoveries and Exhaustive Listing," *Aleph* 6 (2006): 239–338.

Steel et al. 2018: Carlos Steel, Steven Vanden Broecke, David Juste, and Shlomo Sela, *The Astrological Biography of a Medieval Philosopher: Henry Bate's Nativitas* (1280–1281), (Leuven: Leuven University Press 2018).

Steinschneider 1870: Moritz Steinschneider, "Zur Geschichte der Uebersetzungen aus dem Indischen ins Arabische und ihres Einflusses auf die arabische Literatur," *Zeitschrift der deutschen Morgenländischen Geselschaft* 24 (1870): 325–392.

Steinschneider 1880/1925: Moritz Steinschneider, "Abraham Ibn Esra (Abraham Judaeus, Avenare)," *Supplement zur Zeitschrift für Mathematik und Physik*, 25 (1880): 59–128 (= *Gesammelte Schriften*, [Berlin 1925], 407–498).

Steinschneider 1897: M. Steinschneider, Die Handschriften-Verzeichnisse der Königlichen Bibliothek zu Berlin: Verzeichnis der Hebraeischen Handschriften (Berlin: Buchdruckerei der Königlichen Akademie der Wissenschaften [G. Voigt], 1897).

Steinschneider 1925: Moritz Steinschneider, "Abraham Judaeus—Savasorda und Ibn Esra" in *Gesamelte Schriften* (Berlin, 1925), 327–387.
Tester 1987: S. Tester, *A History of Western Astrology* (Suffolk, 1987).
Thorndike 1923–1958: Lynn Thorndike, *A History of Magic and Experimental Science* (New York: Columbia University Press, 1923–1958).
Thorndike 1944: Lynn Thorndike., "The Latin Translations of the Astrological Tracts of Abraham Avenezra," *Isis* 35 (1944):293–302.
Thorndike 1954: Lynn Thorndike, "Albumasar in Sadan," *Isis* 45 (1954): 22–32
Thorndike 1956: Lynn Thorndike, "The Latin Translations of Astrological Works by Messahala," *Osiris* 12 (1956):49–72.

INDEX

120 conjunctions of the seven planets, 174–175, 227, 401, 608
28 constellations, 152
28 lunar mansions, 34, 38, 39, 40, 152, 153, 154, 422, see lunar mansions

Aben Esra Israelita, 17, 18
Abraham Additor, 17, 20, 22, 92, 135, 138, 182, 218, 508, 608
Abraham Avenezra (Havenare), 2, 17, 20, 49, 50, 60, 75, 330
Abraham Bar Ḥiyya, 24, 26, 80, 230, 336
Abraham Compilator, 135
Abraham Ibn Ezra's astrological writings, 2–9, 12, 13, 14, 15, 16, 20, 21, 24, 25, 33, 37, 42, 48, 49, 50, 52, 56, 61, 52, 69, 79, 81, 82, 83, 149, 151, 158, 230
Abraham Ibn Ezra's neologisms, 10, 12, 41, 73, 239, 367, 368, 599–602
Abraham Judeus, 11, 590
Abraham Princeps, 24, see Abraham Bar Ḥiyya
Abraham the Author, 22, 23, 27, 30, 93, 135, 138, 179, 183, 219, 237, 239, 240, 244, 265, 538, 599, 608
Abraham the Spaniard, 65, 391
Abū ʿAlī al-Khayyāṭ, 33, 74–75, 234, 508, 608
Abū Bakr al-Ḥasan B. al Khaṣib, 150, 248
Abū Maʿshar, 23, 33, 34, 36, 67, 68, 156, 157, 158, 165, 166, 174–175, 180–181, 186–187, 208–209, 228–229, 233, 234, 241, 242, 243, 236, 255, 260, 262, 340, 345, 405, 426, 428, 448, 471, 479, 496, 591, 596, 608
Abū Saʿīd Shādhān ibn Bahr, 241, 242, 473, see Scezen
airy signs, 318–319, 373, 384, 397, 412, 533, 587, 608
al-Andarzagar, 228, 477
al-Battānī ibn Jābir the Arab, 33, 174–175, 236, 591, 608
al-Bīrūnī, 150, 152, 166, 231, 232, 236, 248, 345, 346
Albumasar in Sadan, 242, 473, 618, 620, 624, see Scezen
Alchandreana, 50, 64, 70, 77, 341, 342, 531–534
Alihi, 33, 176, 177, 236, 591
al-Khwārizmī, 231, 235, 347, 616
al-Kindī, 71, 152, 154, 174–175, 220–221, 228, 233–234, 244, 255, 267, 285–285, 403, 439, 463, 598, 608
Almagest (Ptolemy), 157
al-Qabīṣī, 67, 144, 151, 345
Ancients, 23, 30, 33, 34, 67, 121, 129, 152, 195, 201, 234, 235, 591
animodar, 416, 419
anonymous Latin translations, 13, 16–18, 19, 56, 80, 81, 82
Anthologiae (Vettius Valens), 143, 150, 618
aphorisms, 34, 36, 137, 139, 141, 148, 150, 227, 233, 249, 269, 346, 395, 401, 407, 409, 421, 475
apogee, 166, 191, 303, 419, 481, 520
Aquarius, 40, 99, 103, 181, 283, 555, 579
Arab astrologers and scientists, 2, 29, 33, 34, 153, 154, 167, 175, 228, 231, 233, 234, 236, 248, 269, 423, 469
Arabic astrological literature, 2, 8, 12, 32, 33, 64, 67, 68, 157, 158, 228, 231, 232, 233, 242, 247, 248, 335, 339, 345
Arabic astrology, 2, 8, 9, 34, 67, 228, 233, 247
Arabic language and culture, 1, 18, 29, 33, 29, 40, 41, 50, 65, 109, 141, 152, 153, 155, 156, 175, 231, 244, 257, 264, 338, 339, 340, 384, 535, 583
Arabic sources, 12, 32, 33, 50, 64, 65, 66, 68, 69, 70, 76, 77, 79, 87, 152, 228, 230, 231, 335, 337, 383, 505, 525, 531
Arabic to Hebrew translations, 1, 35, 66, 68, 70, 76, 79, 80, 152, 153, 231, 232, 525, 535
Arabic translations, 34, 65, 66, 69, 70, 231, 469
Arabic transliterations, 41, 42, 64, 155, 339
Aries, 19, 40, 99, 100, 181, 279, 282, 535, 579
Arnoul de Quincampoix, 13, 16, 20, 42, 49, 52, 58, 60, 61, 62, 75, 83, 293
ascendant, 5, 24, 37, 66, 69, 71, 137, 536, 579, 582, 608
aspect (astrological), 44, 338, 536, 537, 538, 564, 569, 573, 579, 586, 599, 602, 608
aspect of hate, 93, 137, 444, 453, 536, 579, 599, 608
aspect of love, 44, 119, 163, 191, 207, 209, 213, 263, 429, 430, 436, 453, 485, 495, 496, 537, 573, 579, 602, 608
astral determinism, 25, 26, 27, 28, 36, 37, 135, 136

astrolabe, 10, 69, 416
astrological encyclopedias, 9, 78, 79, 80, 156, 260
astronomical tables, 10, 11, 12, 170, 231, 235, 236
astronomy, 2, 9, 10, 11, 12, 61, 79, 155, 232, 235, 236, 242, 322, 325, 355, 358, 369, 393, 472
Avraham ha-Naśi', 24, see Abraham Bar Ḥiyya

Babylonian Talmud, 26, 36, 136, 394
Babylonians, 18, 34, 479
Baghdad, 231, 232, 235, 242
balance of Enoch/Hermes, 24, 37, 149, 150, 416, see trutina Hermetis
Baṭalmiyūs, 33, 156, see Ptolemy
belief, 325, 331, 476, 506
Benedictum sit nomen domini, 70, 341, 342
benefic planets, 97, 185, 285, 245, 539, 582, 585, 588, 608
betrothing a woman, 119, 203, 485, 604, 607
Béziers, 9, 156, 260
biblical commentaries (Abraham Ibn Ezra), 1, 2, 9, 15, 22, 28, 36, 37, 135, 136, 227
- Daniel 7:10, 394
- Daniel 10:21, 227
- Deut. 30:15, 36
- Eccles. 1:3, 227
- Eccles. introduction, 28, 396
- Eccles. 1:15, 395
- Eccles. 2:21, 136
- Eccles. 3:1, 152
- Eccles. 3:14, 26, 28, 36, 393
- Ex. (long) 2:2, 37, 38, 148, 151, 417–418
- Ex. (long) 3:15, 227
- Ex. (long) 20:14, 15
- Ex. (long) 26:2, 152
- Ex. (long) 33:21, 157
- Ex. (long) 33:28, 396–397
- Ex. (long) 33:32, 136, 394
- Gen. (long) 1:31, 15
- Gen. (long) 1:14, 227
- Job 38:33, 135, 391
- Pentateuch, introduction to short commentary, 152

bicorporal signs, 41, 46, 60, 125, 179, 252, 285, 539, 580, 581, 587, 601, 608
Book of Elections (Sahl Ibn Bishr), 32, 36, 40, 136, 140, 145, 154, 164, 170, 233, 394, 398, 411, 424
Book of Experiences (Māshā'allāh), 448
Book of Māshā'allāh on the Eclipses, 80, 228, 232, 618
Book of Religions and Dynasties (Abū Ma'shar), 229, 618
Book of the 100 statements (Pseudo-Ptolemy), 34, 95, 139, 189, 223, 249, 291, 593, see *Centiloquium*
Book of the Judgments of the World (Abraham Ibn Ezra), 167, 423, 487
burnt, 47, 65, 97, 179, 239, 273, 540, 546, 580, 583, 586, 589, 608, 609
buying, 39, 40, 93, 99, 103, 109, 111, 113, 115, 117, 119, 127, 409–411, 431–432, 603, 604, 605, 606
Buzurjmihr (Burgam, rex persicus), 33, 174, 175, 232, 594

cadent places, 41, 45, 99, 178, 269, 291, 540, 580, 582, 608
cadent planets, 183, 243, 540, 580, 608
calendrics, 2, 236
caliph al-Ma'mūn, 35, 231
caliph al-Manṣūr, 35, 231
caliph al-Ṣafāḥ, 469
Cancer, 93, 99, 175, 181, 283, 329, 541, 580
Cancer, sign of the world, 175, 228–229, 468, 569, 588, 609
Capricorn, 40, 203, 283, 541, 580
captivity, 94–95, 32, 109, 115, 217, 258, 275, 301, 325, 327, 380, 458, 459, 508, 520, 608
cardines, 41, 45, 46, 69, 71, 72, 99, 179, 269, 250, 285, 541, 558, 579, 580, 609
Carmen astrologicum (Dorotheus), 138, 143, 230, 231, 234, 248, 618, see *Pentabiblos*
caville (cardines), 45, 178, 180, 184, 188, 190, 192, 250, 269, 540, 541, 580, 608
Centiloquium (Pseudo-Ptolemy), 34, 95, 137, 139, 141, 143, 150, 189, 227, 249, 269, 346, 395, 397, 401, 407, 409, 421, 475, 594, see *Book of the 100 statements*
children, 26, 36, 93, 150, 157, 253, 275, 321, 374, 394, 395, 441, 518
Christ, 12
Christians, 518
chronic disease, 520
Cicero, 26, 618
clothes, 39, 109, 111, 113, 115, 117, 155, 275, 279, 281, 283, 301, 317, 321
complexion, 312, 316, 407, 521, 524, 542, 580, see temperament
conception, 26, 35, 38, 93, 105, 107, 149, 150, 414, 415, 418, 420, 421, 542, 580, 604
conjunctions of Saturn and Jupiter, 19, 122, 123, 167, 467, 468, 518, 608
contacts with Christian scholars (Abraham Ibn Ezra), 9–18

continuous horoscopy in nativities, 4, 5, 80, 167, 229
crafts, 32, 299, 307, 311, 315, 317, 462, 520, 522, 524
creation of the world, 19, 347
critical days, 8, 25, 203, 257, 258, 299, 351, 493, 543, 581, 589
crooked hours, 259, 494
crooked signs, 43, 127, 197, 253, 436, 477, 543, 588, 609
cross-references to Ibn Ezra's astrological corpus, 8, 9, 11, 23, 141, 153, 154, 155, 168, 245, 248, 255, 258, 483, 528
cycle of 2,000 years, 174, 175, 227, 480

date of composition (*Liber electionum*), 23–24
date of composition (*Liber interrogationum*), 24–25
De cogitatione hominis ac eius questione, 63, 65, 66, 67, 68, 69, 77, 272
De forma astrolabii (Abraham Ibn Ezra), 10, 616
De luminaribus seu de diebus creticis (Henry Bate), 14, see *Me'orot*
De mundo vel seculo (Henry Bate), 14, see *'Olam* I
De re absconsa et loco eius, 57, 71, 72, 77, 272, 284
death, 32, 95, 101, 203, 229, 247, 275, 303, 319, 323, 412, 442, 452, 461, 487, 492, 493, 508, 520, 544, 584
decan, 69, 231, 279, 340, 541, 555, 581, 582, 609, 610
decrees (astrological), 26, 27, 28, 93, 95, 139, 393, 394, 395, 544, 581, 599
dejection, 181, 242–243, 273, 544, 551, 580, 582, 583, 589, 601, 602, 609
demons, 301, 520
diffusion of Hebrew astrological work (Abraham Ibn Ezra), 12, 37, 149
dignities (astrological), 66, 69, 121, 197, 199, 219, 242, 277, 339, 340, 384, 544, 580, 581
digressions, 41
directions, 167, 175, 189, 229, 248, 431, 475, 487, 545, 582, 609
diseases, 8, 14, 32, 40, 95, 203, 275, 281, 283, 297, 299, 303, 305, 307, 309, 313, 315, 321, 329, 545, 583, 584
doctrine of elections, 19, 25, 26, 28, 35, 135, 139, 142, 149, 391–398, 406–430
doctrine of interrogations, 19, 29, 30, 41, 63, 79, 140, 227, 230, 231–237, 399–405, 431–464
doctrine of nativities, 19, 24, 25, 26, 35, 37, 135, 248, 346
dodecatemoria, 67, 68, 69, 279, 340, 341, 500, 545, 582, 609
Dogma universale in iudiciis, 58, 76, 77, 326–331
domain of burning, 103, 121, 123, 127, 129, 141–142, 146, 466, 487, 546, 589, 609
Dorotheus, 23, 29, 30, 33, 34, 35, 39, 40, 95, 175, 230–231, 595, 609
Dragon, 369
dreams, 295, 319, 323, 331, 451, 518
drinking a laxative, 97, 109, 305, 553, 585, 603
drinking a potion, 97, 109, 111, 113, 115, 117, 119

earlier research (*Liber electionum* and *Liber interrogationum*), 20–21
Earth, 97, 103, 105, 177, 181, 539, 546, 572, 568, 589
earthy signs, 181, 319, 373, 384, 397, 412, 546, 588, 609
eccentric circle, 303, 305, 355, 520, 521, 546, 582, 609
eclipses, 7, 65, 80, 228, 232, 469, 618
ecliptic, 152, 164, 166, 169, 170, 337, 338, 369, 547, 583, 584, 609
Egypt, 18, 26, 157, 234, 235
Egyptians, 339, 418
electional horoscope, 27, 28, 41, 95, 127, 138, 140, 141, 391, 396, 397, 528, 529
Electiones Abraham, 56
enemies, 117, 275, 321, 323, 325, 327, 402, 413, 486, 531, 534
England, 1, 25, 27
Enoch, 23, 30, 33, 35, 36, 38, 104, 148, 149, 150, 151, 175, 205, 228, 234–235, 243, 259, 260, 340, 399, 410, 414, 417, 419, 442, 458, 468, 472, 479, 494, 592, 595, 609, see Hermes, King Enoch
epicycle, 166, 305, 358, 521, 547, 582, 609
Epistola Argafalau ad Alexandrum, 70, 87, 341, 342, 531–534
Epitome totius astrologiae, 9, 10, 33, 39, 40
equal degrees, 107, 205, 414, 420, 431, 464, 474, 494, 547, 583
equal hour, 420, 477
equator, 169, 170, 229, 337, 410, 447, 468, 471
escape from the decrees of the stars, 28, 139
exaltation, 23, 45, 46, 76, 79, 86, 99, 123, 181, 242, 307, 547, 579, 582, 583, 601, 609, see honor

fardār, 175, 228
fear, 32, 93, 179, 191, 209, 275, 283, 301, 602
feminine planet, 315, 547, 585
feminine quadrant, 217, 221, 289, 456, 458, 464, 547, 586
feminine ruler, 199, 547, 585
feminine signs, 199, 275, 277, 430, 439, 475, 548, 587
fiery signs, 101, 319, 373, 384, 397, 412, 482, 548, 587, 609
finding something hidden, 60, 62, 71–72, 103, 127, 219, 272, 279, 284–285, 287, 344, 412, 604, 608
five places of dominion, see places of dominion
fixed signs, 23, 41, 46, 125, 169, 177, 252, 285, 548, 587, 600, 601, 610
fixed stars, 18, 80, 152, 239, 337, 469
fortunate places, 436, 441, 442, 455, 465, 491
four elements, 136, 137, 373, 384, 397
France, 1, 11
free will, 27, 28, 36, 138
French intermediary, 21, 61, 62, 65, 136, 169, 238, 239, 339
friends, 275, 317, 319, 325, 444, 454, 506, 508, 533
fugitive, 57, 72, 221, 223, 273, 284–291, 463–464, 548, 582

Gemini, 99, 111, 283, 548, 582
geometry, 12, 235, 317, 325
Gergis, 74, 75, 77, 80, 87, 368–383, 510–516
gives power, 43, 345, 548, 581, 610, see power
giving the spark, 258–259, see spark
God, 27, 28, 93, 136, 297, 309, 319, 321, 323, 325, 368, 392, 393, 394, 397, 479, 461, 502, 504, 519, 530, 549, 581
grammar, 1, 2, 312, 313
Great Introduction (Abū Maʿshar), 36, 37, 143, 156, 157, 158, 166, 228, 233, 252, 255, 260, 340, 345, 479
great years, 189, 293, 297, 299, 303, 305, 309, 311, 315, 346–347, 518–521, 549, 579, 610
Guido Bonatti, 13

Hagin le Juif, 13, 14, 15, 16, 42, 62
Ḥassān the Jew, 33, 177, 236, 595
haylāj, 247, see significator
Head of the Dragon, 58, 74, 75, 228, 317, 319, 321, 323, 325, 327, 369, 472, 510, 550, 580, 610
Hebraisms, 23, 41, 599–602
Hebrew astrological and scientific vocabulary, 1, 23, 69, 78, 239, 483
Hebrew astrological literature, 2, 9, 12, 20, 26, 37, 50, 51, 62, 64, 78, 136, 149, 339
Hebrew into French translations, 13, 42, 46, 61, 62
Hebrew into Latin translations, 4, 6, 7, 8, 9, 13–21, 49, 61, 62
Hebrew language, 1, 2, 18, 37, 44, 47, 65, 86, 135, 136, 149, 152, 169, 237, 255, 256, 257, 258, 259, 599–602
Hebrew manuscripts 21, 64, 68, 164, 168
Hebrew readers, 2, 9, 25
Hebrew source texts, 17, 18, 20, 22, 23, 24, 35, 48, 50, 51, 62, 63, 65, 70, 73, 75, 76, 77, 84, 89, 162, 163, 164, 166, 168, 169, 260, 261, 266, 266–269, 340, 341, 497, 517, 531
Hec est Nativitas quedam ad instruendum te, et est de iudiciis Abraham, 81
Henry Bate, 13, 14, 15 16, 24, 42, 52, 62, 135, 154
Hermann of Carinthia, 64
Hermes Trismegistus, 152, 234
Hermes, 35, 38, 67, 68, 147, 151, 152, 231, 234, 340, 419, 420, 421, 479, see Enoch
Ḥešbon mahalakhot ha-kokhavim (Abraham Bar Ḥiyya), 230
honor (exaltation), 45, 46, 47, 76, 144, 145, 166, 180, 242, 243, 263, 328, 383, 440, 528, 547, 583, 601, 609, see exaltation
horoscope, 3, 5, 6, 7, 18, 24, 27, 28, 29, 31, 37, 41, 42, 63, 64, 71, 72, 80, 137, 140, 157, 339
horoscopic places, 4, 5, 6, 7, 18, 19, 23, 24, 32, 40, 41, 74, 79, 142, 229, 238, 245, 269, 603–609
house (planets), 79, 86, 260
house of detriment, 23, 269, 602
house of war, 23, 207, 260, 495, 551, 582, 602, 619
Hugo of Santalla, 64, 150, 230

Ibn Abī l-Rijāl, 29, 32, 34, 39, 154, 227, 248, 400, 421, see *Kitāb al-bāri*
Ibn al-Muthannā's Commentary (Abraham Ibn Ezra), 69, 231, 235, 347, 469, 481, 616
Indian scientists, 23, 29, 33, 35, 38, 39, 40, 107–119
inheritance, 319, 323, 378
interrogational horoscope, 30, 31, 41, 71, 72, 140, 175, 177, 185, 187, 195, 215, 230, 265
introductions to astrology, 2, 8, 73, 143, 157, 158, 233, 239, 248, 252, 340, 345, 347
Introductorius ad astronomiam (*Reshit ḥokhmah*, Bate), 14
Italian Geniza, 21, 483

Italy, 1, 11, 21, 483
Iudicia (pseudo Aristotelian), 64, 65, 66
Iudicia (pseudo Ptolemaic), 50, 64, 65, 66, 87, 335, 336, 337, 505–509

Jacob B. Shārah, 469
Jews, 2, 12, 29, 301, 353
John of Seville, 68, 76, 233, 620
Joseph Bonfils, 8, 619
journeys, 32, 411–412, 427–428, 453, 476
joy (astrological), 99, 125, 252, 552, 582, 607, 610
joy, 195, 275, 311, 317, 319, 323, 325, 607
judgments (astrological), 25, 50, 58, 66, 68, 69, 93, 135, 327, 392, 399, 400, 475, 480, 505, 539
Jupiter, 46, 75, 97, 99, 189, 196, 303–306

Kanakah, the Indian, 175, 231, 469, 595, 610
Kelal ha-She'elot le-divrei Talmai, see *She'elot le-Talmai*
King Dorotheus, 23, 29, 34, 175, 187, 230, 246, 595, see Dorotheus
King Enoch, 23, 29, 33, 175, 234, 596, see Enoch
King Ptolemy, 23, 29, 33, 39, 109, 156–157, 158, 175, 235, 237, 518, 521, 596, 610, see Ptolemy
King Talmai, 33, 156, see King Ptolemy
kingdom, 127, 319, 323, 325, 605
kings, 185, 191, 193, 197, 207, 213, 275, 317, 319, 323, 325, 327, 331
Kitāb al-bāri (Ibn Abī l-Rijāl), 29, 32, 34, 39, 154, 155, 156, 158, 159, 160, 161, 162, 163, 227, 248, 400, 421
Kitāb al-tafhīm (Al-Bīrūnī), 150, 248, 345

Latin astrological literature, 45, 47, 48, 50, 62, 67, 166, 339
Latin readership, 9, 10
Latin scholars, 9–12, 149
laying siege to a city, 101, 111, 113, 115, 117, 123, 488, 531, 605
laying the foundation of a building, 111, 113, 232
Le livre des elections Abraham (*Mivḥarim* II; Hagin), 13
Le livre des interrogations (*She'elot* II; Hagin), 13
least years, 189, 293, 297, 299, 303, 305, 309, 311, 315, 346–347, 553, 579, 610
lend money, 99, 111, 113, 117, 484
Leo, 123, 129, 181, 279, 283, 553, 583
Li livres du commencement de sapience (*Reshit ḥokhmah*; Hagin), 13, 15
Liber Abraham de iudiciis (Pierre de Limoges), 15
Liber Abraham de iudiciis signorum (*Mishpeṭei ha-mazzalot*), 81
Liber Abraham de terminatione morborum (Pierre de Limoges), 14
Liber Abraham Iudei de Nativitatibus (Abraham Ibn Ezra), 4, 5, 10, 36, 38, 43, 49, 56, 147, 148, 149, 150, 151, 228, 232, 233, 234, 236, 242, 243, 266, 343, 419, 461
Liber Abrahe Evenezre de significationibus septem planetarum, 73, 74, 292, 316
Liber Abrahe Iudei Avenezre, 56, 59, 60, 272, 592
Liber Aristotilis, 150, 228, 230, 340, 619
Liber astronomicus (Bonatti), 12, 13, 619
Liber causarum seu racionum (*Ṭe'amim* I and *Ṭe'amim* II; Bate), 14
Liber de electionibus (*Mivḥarim* II; Pietro d'Abano), 16
Liber de interrogationibus (*She'elot* II; Pietro d'Abano), 16, 17
Liber de inventione occultorum, 16, 60, 61
Liber de rationibus (*Ṭe'amim* II; Pietro d'Abano), 15
Liber de rationibus tabularum (Abraham Ibn Ezra), 11, 12, 15, 235, 236, 242, 466, 616
Liber electionum ab Abraham Evenezre (*Mivḥarim* II), 81
Liber interrogationibus ab alio editus (*She'elot* II), 81
Liber introductionis ad iudicia astrologie (*Mishpeṭei ha-mazzalot*; Bate), 14
Liber luminarium Aben Esra Israelita (*Me'orot*), 18
Liber Mesellae de nativitatibus, 248, 619
Liber nativitatum (Abraham Ibn Ezra), 4, 24, 25, 36, 43, 81, 135, 137, 141, 142, 145, 147, 165, 169, 227, 228, 232, 244, 236, 246, 247, 248, 260, 392, 395, 523, 425, 473, 528–530, 592, see *Moladot* II
Liber novem iudicum, 64
Liber questionum (*She'elot* II), 17, 56, 82
Liber revolucionum (*Sefer ha-tequfah*), 81
Liber Samechem, 67, 218, 219, 265, 266, 594, see *Liber Tamedas*
Liber servorum, 58, 72, 73, 74, 75, 77, 80, 314, 517, 594
Liber Tamedas, 66, 67, 69, 70, 276, 277, 338, 343, 594, see *Liber Samechem*
Libra, 40, 111, 283, 328, 553, 583
lifespan, 41, 189, 247, 248, 293, 346, 431–432, 475, 518

Livre des jugemens des nativités (*Moladot*; Bate), 13
logic, 2, 312, 313
lord of the day, 66, 107, 183, 219, 265, 277, 333, 337, 480, 555, 581, 610
lord of the decan, 69, 279, 340, 499, 555, 581, 610, see decan
lord of the hour, 66, 71, 72, 103, 105, 183, 185, 273, 275, 335, 555, 581, 610
lord of the term, 71, 219, 279, 285, 339, 499, 555, 581, 610, see term
lords of the triplicity, 201, 477, 555, 581, 384, 482, see triplicity
lost Hebrew texts, 45, 66, 75, 80, 285
lost objects, 191, 281, 283, 313, 489, 524, 532, 533, 534, 605, 606
lot of Fortune, 23, 66, 183, 219, 244, 277, 295, 556, 585, 610
lot of husbands, 36, 205, 494, 556, 584
lot of Jupiter, 308, 346, 521, 556, 585
lot of Mars, 307, 359, 522, 556, 585
lot of Saturn, 301, 353, 520, 556, 585
lot of the hidden thing, 297, 303, 313, 556
lot of the Moon, 297, 350, 449, 519, 557, 585
lot of the planets, 291, 557, 585
lot of the Sun, 293, 295, 347, 518, 557, 585
lot of Venus, 311, 363, 523, 557, 585
lots, 80, 175, 177, 229, 236, 293
love, 32, 111, 119, 311, 317, 428–429
Lucca, 11, 12, 467
lunar mansions, 34, 38–41, 106–119, 152–154, 604, 610, see 28 lunar mansions

magnitude (fixed stars), 423
Maimonides, 26, 619
malefic planets, 44, 97, 99, 185, 197, 245, 285, 289, 557, 588, 610
marriage, 113, 115, 321, 323, 397, 422, 423, 444, 479
Mars, 75, 95, 97, 175, 177, 181, 306–309
masculine planet, 277, 309, 315, 558, 585
masculine quadrant, 221, 289, 413, 439, 558, 586
masculine ruler, 199, 558, 585
masculine sign, 199, 275, 413, 430, 558, 587
Māshā'allāh, 23, 31, 35, 58, 69, 71, 72, 76, 77, 78, 80, 87, 99, 101, 175, 185, 231–232, 277, 285, 525–527, 596, 610
mathematics, 2, 79, 227, 235, 355
mazzal, 26, 36, 394, 470
Mechelen (Malines), 13, 42, 154
Megillat ha-megalleh, 26, 80, 619
melothesia, 143, 386, 611
Me'orot (Abraham Ibn Ezra), 8, 9, 14, 15, 16, 18, 21, 23, 25, 53, 54, 55, 82, 83, 84
Mercury, 75, 97, 105, 107, 179, 181, 205, 281, 283, 285, 313–315
messengers, 107, 117, 151, 221, 275, 321, 464, 604
middle years, 293, 297, 299, 303, 305, 309, 311, 315, 346–347, 559, 579, 611
Miqra'ot Gedolot, 1, 616
Mishpeṭei ha-mazzalot (Abraham Ibn Ezra), 3, 14, 18, 23, 24, 25, 37, 38, 73, 74, 75, 77, 80, 81
Mivḥarim I (Abraham Ibn Ezra), 5, 6, 17, 24, 26, 28, 31, 33, 35, 36, 38, 39
Mivḥarim II (Abraham Ibn Ezra), 6, 13, 16, 17, 24, 26, 28, 31, 33, 35, 36, 38, 39, 53, 54, 55, 81, 82, 83, 84
Mivḥarim III (Abraham Ibn Ezra), 6, 17, 19, 21, 22, 24, 42, 45, 46, 48, 81, 84, 89
mobile signs, 184, 190, 194, 198, 252, 284, 527, 611, 612
Modena fragments, 6, 7, 21, 22, 45, 47, 48, 84, 89, 483–496
Moladot (Abraham Ibn Ezra), 3, 4, 5, 10, 13, 14, 15, 16, 24, 36, 53, 54, 55, 61, 82, 83
Moladot II (Abraham Ibn Ezra), 17, 23, 24, 25, 81, see *Liber nativitatum*
Moon, 8, 38, 39, 40, 41, 48, 66, 71, 75, 95, 97, 175, 177, 296–300
mourning (astrological), 252, 476
mubtazz, 42, 69, 279, 339, 611
Mudhākarāt Abī Ma'shar fī asrār 'ilm al-nujūm (Scezen), 241, 242, 473
multiple versions of works (Abraham Ibn Ezra), 9
music, 311, 325, 523
Muslim Spain, 1, 28, 33

natal horoscope, 24, 27, 28, 29, 37, 64, 127, 138, 141, 148, 149, 195, 248, 343, 346, 392, 394, 396, 398, 400, 431, 528, 529
Nativitas (Henry Bate), 13, 24
nature of the ascendant, 71, 121, 219, 283, 440, 441
nature of the body, 30, 95, 396, 400, 519
nature of the degrees of the zodiac, 66, 67, 68, 219, 277
nature of the planets, 99, 93, 99, 107, 121, 165, 187, 189, 199, 211, 215, 217, 219, 247, 249, 277, 287, 295, 305, 446, 472, 480, 481, 482, 490, 518, 521, 523, 524, 531
nature of the soul, 30
nature of the thing asked about, 181, 187, 287, 474
nature, 560, 582, 584, 600

Nawādir al-qaḍā (Sahl), 36, 233, 345
Neḥoshet I (Abraham Ibn Ezra), 135, 152, 153, 156, 617
Neḥoshet II (Abraham Ibn Ezra), 135, 152, 153, 156, 247, 347, 423, 617
ninth-parts, 219, 264, 265, 277, 459, 460, 560, 611
Nuremberg, 9, 236, 525, 603, 606, 618, 619

Obers de Mondidier, 13, 42
ʿOlam I (Abraham Ibn Ezra), 7, 8
ʿOlam II (Abraham Ibn Ezra), 7, 8, 14, 36, 82
ʿOlam III (Abraham Ibn Ezra), 8, 14, 153, 154, 155, 277, 423, 480
order of the orbs, 228, 335
outcome of undertakings, 27, 109, 117, 179, 183, 189, 197, 209, 562, 582, 607

Pahlavī, 231, 232
pain, 25, 217, 281, 299, 313, 397, 520, 533
paranatellonta, 231
Paris, 13, 14, 49
partners, 39, 90, 99, 109, 209, 275, 449–450
Pentabiblos (Dorotheus), 23, 137, 230, 234, see *Carmen astrologicum*
peregrine, 99, 127, 144, 328–329, 562, 585
perigee, 191, 303, 520
periods of human life, 5, 228
Persian astrology, 228
Persian language, 416
Peter d'Abano, 13, 15, 16, 20, 42, 49, 51, 52, 56, 59, 60, 61, 62, 82, 83, 84, 151, 339
Peter of Limoges, 13, 14, 15, 16, 42
philosophy, 2, 15, 79, 83, 233, 234, 235
physicians, 16, 97, 235, 307, 522, 523
Pisa, 11, 12, 486
Pisces, 40, 93, 99, 283, 562, 595
places of dominion, 43, 99, 189, 215, 219, 244, 247–248, 346, 473, 523, 563, 568, 583, 585
plant trees, 109, 113, 115, 422, 423, 519
poetry (Abraham Ibn Ezra), 1, 2
power, 43, 48, 66, 68, 97, 183, 185, 277, 345, 548, 563, 564, 581, 582, 585, 589, 610, see give power
pregnancy, 24, 35, 37, 38, 105, 148, 149, 150, 151, 413–421, 573, 589, see trutina Hermetis, Enoch's balance
prison, 39, 109, 111, 113, 115, 117, 119, 185, 203, 217, 275, 283, 301, 398
profit, 99, 11, 113, 127, 281, 317, 319, 321, 325, 327, 409–411
Proportiones competentes in astrorum industria, 70, 341, 342
prorogation, 167, 229
Ptolemy, 23, 27, 30, 34, 64, 72, 95, 99, 156–157, 189, 223, 243, 594, 596, 611, see King Ptolemy
Ptolomeus et multi sapientum, 11, 12

quadrants, 285, 287, 564, 571, 586
quarrels, 113, 119, 205, 207, 209, 279, 281, 317, 319, 424–425
Quidam tractatus particulares, 56, 59, 272

ray of a planet, 46–47, 111, 119, 157–158, 207, 209, 554, 561, 565, 568, 571, 574, 580, 586, 588, 602, 611
Raymond of Marseilles, 64
reading thoughts, 30, 31, 41, 63, 67, 76, 77, 87, 140, 237, 272–281, 323, 336, 340, 341, 383, 396, 400, 525–527
received, 119, 187, 189, 197, 289, 329, 345, 566, 586, 611
receiving the spark, 258–259, see spark
reception in the Latin West (Abraham Ibn Ezra), 9–18
rectification of the nativity, 4, 37, 149, 150, 151
reducing humors, 97, 99, 408–409, 566, 584, 603
Reshit Ḥokhmah (Abraham Ibn Ezra), 3, 13, 14, 15, 21, 23, 35, 36, 53, 54, 55, 61, 67, 79, 82, 83
Reshit Ḥokhmah, second version (Abraham Ibn Ezra), 3, 166, 239
retrograde, 99, 101, 144, 179, 184, 273, 275, 567, 586, 611
revolution of the world-year, 123, 167, 229–230, 347, 487, 518, 611
revolution of the year of the new-born, 5, 175, 229–230
riches, 189, 249, 432–433, 506, 606, see wealth
riding animals, 32, 307, 309, 313, 422, 507, 518, 519, 520, 521, 522, 523
rising times, 127, 129, 169–170, 183, 545, 567, 579, 581, 611
Rome, 28, 466
Rouen, 25
ruler of the five places of dominion, 99, 129, 568
ruler of the native, 93, 229, 568
ruler, 95, 101, 129, 175, 183, 189, 294, 301, 568
rulership, 191, 299, 303, 305, 568

Sabbath, 303, 309
Ṣafenat Paʿneaḥ, 8, 619
Sagittarius, 103, 111, 283, 568, 587

Sahl, the Jew, 23, 32, 36, 40, 90, 232–233, 596, 611
Saturn, 25, 75, 93, 97, 175, 177, 300–302
Saturn-Mars conjunction, 175, 177, 228–229, 611
Scezen, 33, 180, 181, 241, 596, see Abū Saʿīd Shādhān ibn Bahr
scholars of the judgments of the signs, 175, 227, 600, 601
scholars of the signs, 95, 97, 127, 185, 472, 600
science of the signs, 291, 305, 315, 366
scientists of Egypt, 29, 400
scientists of Persia, 29, 34, 228, 419, 474, 479
scintillatio, see spark
Scorpio, 40, 93, 123, 181, 209, 283, 569, 587
Scorpio, 40, 93, 123, 181, 209, 283, 569, 587
Sefer ha-Kolel, 79, 80
Sefer ha-middot (Abraham Ibn Ezra), 62, 621
Sefer ha-mispar (Abraham Ibn Ezra), 11, 135, 156, 616
Sefer ha-She'elot (ascribed to Abraham Ibn Ezra), 65, 79
Sefer ha-She'elot le-Māshā'allāh, 68, 251, see *She'elot le-Māshā'allāh*
Sefer ha-tequfah (Abraham Ibn Ezra), 5, 18, 23, 25, 81, 156, 157, 169, 228, 229, 239, 337
Sefer Mishpeṭei ha-ʿOlam, 21
selling, 99, 189, 191, 311, 410, 431–432, 606
sexual intercourse, 117, 150, 221, 281, 285, 311, 323, 413, 523, 569, 580
She'elot I (Abraham Ibn Ezra), 6, 7, 9, 17, 29, 30, 31, 33, 41, 63, 71, 77
She'elot II (Abraham Ibn Ezra), 7, 13, 16, 17, 29, 30, 31, 33, 41, 53, 54, 55, 56, 71, 72, 81, 82, 83, 84
She'elot III (Abraham Ibn Ezra), 7, 18, 19, 21, 22, 42, 45, 46, 47, 48, 66, 67, 71, 72, 77, 78, 81, 84, 89, 483, 484, 489–496
She'elot le-Māshā'allāh, 35, 68, 69, 72, 76, 77, 78, 80, 87, 338, 339, 340, 341, 344, 494–504, see *Sefer ha-She'elot le-Māshā'allāh*
She'elot le-Talmai, 64, 65, 66, 70, 77, 78, 79, 87, 335, 336, 337, 505–509
sick person, 201, 203, 297, 327, 442–444, 607
sign of the city/country, 103, 123, 146–147, 509, 588
Significationes planetarum in domibus (Gergis), 74, 75, 80, 510–516, see Gergis
significator, 41, 68, 69, 95, 183, 185, 187, 189, 195, 277, 279, 285, 327, 570, 587, 588, see *haylāj*
signs with a human shape, 111, 157, 253, 569, 612
slaves, 40, 109–119, 221, 275, 313, 321, 323, 327
small conjunction, 167, 468
smaller part of the zodiac, 99, 143–144, 466, 570, 585, 599, 612
social status, 319, 506
soul, 27, 28, 30, 209, 297, 313, 392, 313, 392, 394, 396, 399, 400, 476, 519, 521, 522, 524, 602
Spain, 64, 466
spark (scintillatio), 47, 157, 191, 203, 250, 258–259, 261, 493, 571, 587, 602, 610, 611, 612
Speculum astronomiae, 12, 619
star lists, 24
stations, 181, 215, 241, 571, 588, 612
sterile signs, 157
stolen articles, 125, 191, 193, 433–435, 489, 605, 606
straight signs, 43, 103, 127, 129, 197, 253, 571, 588, 612
study, 109, 125, 215, 427, 428
succedent places, 41, 99, 107, 179, 207, 213, 223, 269, 291, 572, 588, 612
Sun, 5, 19, 41, 47, 48, 65, 75, 97, 101, 177, 179, 293–296
supercommentaries (Abraham Ibn Ezra), 1, 8
supernal soul, 28, 396

Tail of the Dragon, 74, 75, 228, 369, 510, 572, 580, 612
Talmud, 26, 27, 33, 36, 37, 136, 151, 156, 394
Taurus, 40, 103, 121, 181, 283, 329, 572, 589
Ṭeʿamim I (Abraham Ibn Ezra), 3, 14, 35, 80, 155, 142, 143, 144, 146, 157, 166, 171, 228, 231, 233
Ṭeʿamim II (Abraham Ibn Ezra), 3, 14, 15, 53, 54, 55, 82, 83, 143, 144, 148, 150, 156, 157, 158, 165, 166, 171, 228, 233
temperament, 96, 150, 313, 392, 559, 589, see complexion
Tequfot ha-shanim (*Moladot*), 5
term (astrological), 167, see lord of the term
testimonies, 41, 121, 142, 183, 322, 403, 433, 435, 438, 440, 441, 486, 512, 514, 573, 589
Tetrabiblos (Ptolemy), 25, 34, 135, 137, 144, 157, 167, 229, 232, 236, 245, 248, 252, 339, 393, 480
Thābit ibn Qurra al-Ḥarrānī, 33, 175, 235, 597, 612
thieves, 185, 191, 193, 195, 275, 283, 331

titles of Ibn Ezra's astrological treatises, 8, 50, 59, 60, 73, 74, 85
to sow, 111, 113, 115, 117, 119, 484
to trade, 111, 113, 115, 117, 119, 127, 299, 311, 508, 522, 523
Tractatus de significationibus planetarum in duodecim domibus Abrahe Avenaris, 58, 74, 77, 80, 316
Tractatus in tredecim maneriebus planetarum, 73, 292, 598
tripartite soul, 27, 28
triple Enoch, 36, 235
triplicity, 123, 201, 295, 301, 384, 589, 612, see lord of the triplicity
tropical signs, 41, 125, 127, 179, 181, 252, 285, 329, 587, 612
trutina Hermetis, 24, 37, 38, 148, 149, 150, 151, 414–421, see Enoch's balance, pregnancy

'Umar b. al-Farrukhān al-Ṭabarī, 33, 175, 231, 232, 248, 598, 612
under the ray of the Sun, 111, 119, 121, 207, 209, 255, 574, 588, 612
University of Paris, 13, 15

Venice, 10, 49, 51
Venus, 75, 97, 101, 179, 199, 310–312
Verbis iurium seculi, 423
Vettius Valens, 150, 232, 618
victorious (planet), 121, 123, 164, 166, 207, 209, 261, 445, 446–449, 467, 485, 486, 487, 496, 538, 589, 608
Virgo, 111, 283, 373, 384

wars, 115, 121, 123, 279, 309, 424–425, 445–446
watery signs, 97, 101, 123, 209, 319, 574, 587, 588, 612
wealth, 19, 32, 213, 273, 275, 279, 303, 313, 317, 319, 323, 325, 327, 331, 608, see riches
wearing new clothes, 39, 109, 115, 422, 423
weather forecasting, 7, 138, 152, 153, 154, 252, 478
wife, 39, 109, 111, 113, 115, 117, 109, 111, 113, 115, 117, 119, 297, 311
women, 32, 38, 105, 113, 177, 195, 199, 275, 279, 281, 564, 584, 600, 604, 607
world astrology, 7, 8, 19, 30, 147, 154, 228, 229, 233

years of weaning, 299, 351, 477
Yesod mora' (Abraham Ibn Ezra), 27, 28, 133, 395
Ysagoge in astrologiam, 9

zodiac, 5, 18, 19, 38, 44, 64, 67, 68, 99, 107, 121, 211, 219, 337–338, 576, 580, 589, 512
zodiacal constellations, 337, 373

Printed in the United States
By Bookmasters